Praise for Roland Lazenby's

SHOWBOAT

One of *Men's Journal*'s Best Books of the Year
Finalist for the *Sunday Times*' Biography of the Year
in the Cross British Sports Book Awards

"With surgical precision, Roland Lazenby expertly dissects the life of this generation's most fascinating basketball player. What made Kobe Bryant tick so loud for so long? Lazenby shows you with a tour de force in reporting and an intimate inspection of Bryant's trials, accomplishments, and tribulations."
— Jonathan Abrams, author of *Boys Among Men*

"With the publication of *Showboat: The Life of Kobe Bryant*, it is high time we recognized author Roland Lazenby for what he has become: the finest sports biographer of our time. First with the astonishing *Michael Jordan: The Life* and now with his incredibly researched, beautifully written biography of this enigmatic Laker superstar, Lazenby has entered rarified air: one is wowed by what one learns, and at the same time one can't wait to read what comes next."
— Peter Golenbock, *New York Times* bestselling author

"There is more than enough analysis of Bryant's on-court accomplishments to satisfy the hard-core hoops fan, but the meatier material is in the Bryant family dynamics....Insightful look at a complicated and still relatively young man."
— Phil Taylor, *Washington Post*

"Like Lazenby's recent book about Michael Jordan, *Showboat* finds new angles to approach people we've been looking at every day their whole careers. Mr. Lazenby smartly focuses much of the book at the last few years of Mr. Bryant's career."
— Will Leitch, *Wall Street Journal*

SHOWBOAT

The Life of Kobe Bryant

ROLAND LAZENBY

BACK BAY BOOKS

Little, Brown and Company

New York • Boston • London

Back Bay Books / Little, Brown and Company
Hachette Book Group
1290 Avenue of the Americas, New York, NY 10104
littlebrown.com

Originally published in hardcover by Little, Brown and Company, October 2016
First Back Bay Books paperback edition, December 2017

Back Bay Books is an imprint of Little, Brown and Company, a division of Hachette Book Group, Inc. The Back Bay Books name and logo are trademarks of Hachette Book Group, Inc.

Library of Congress Cataloging-in-Publication Data
Names: Lazenby, Roland, author.
Title: Showboat: the life of Kobe Bryant / Roland Lazenby.
Description: New York: Little, Brown and Company, 2016. | Includes bibliographical references and index.
Identifiers: LCCN 2016016821 | ISBN 978-0-316-38724-8 (hardback) / 978-0-316-38714-9 (paperback)
Subjects: LCSH: Bryant, Kobe, 1978– | Basketball players—United States—Biography. | BISAC: BIOGRAPHY & AUTOBIOGRAPHY / Sports. | BIOGRAPHY & AUTOBIOGRAPHY / Rich & Famous. | BIOGRAPHY & AUTOBIOGRAPHY / General.
Classification: LCC GV884.B794 L395 2016 | DDC 796.323092 [B—dc23 LC record available at https://lccn.loc.gov/2016016821

10 9 8 7 6 5 4 3

LSC-C

Printed in the United States of America

Dedicated to black and white and all the wonderful shades in between, to Ella Mae Austin and to Roger Davis, and to Doc Foster and Estella Hampton, to all of those who bless us by teaching giant lessons in a million precious ways, and to my lovely companion of many years, Karen, who is far beyond measure, to my children, Jenna, Henry, and Morgan, and grandsons, Liam and Aiden.

In loving memory of Jeanie Lazenby Masten.

CONTENTS

FOREWORD   ix

INTRODUCTION: Only the Lonely   3

Part I: Gotta Be Jelly 'Cause Jam Don't Shake

CHAPTER 1: The Bust   11

CHAPTER 2: Fatherhood   18

CHAPTER 3: Pimps of Joytime   29

CHAPTER 4: Pam and Jelly   41

CHAPTER 5: The Bomb Squad   51

Part II: Prodigy

CHAPTER 6: Kobe Bean   65

CHAPTER 7: The Funny Guy   74

CHAPTER 8: Italia   81

CHAPTER 9: The Red Bicycle   89

CHAPTER 10: Lower Merion   99

CHAPTER 11: The Vibe   109

Part III: The Chosen One

CHAPTER 12: Summer Love   121

CHAPTER 13: The Rising   133

Chapter 14: The Bad, Bad Boy — 158
Chapter 15: Come Together — 171
Chapter 16: Team Bryant — 192
Chapter 17: Off to the Stars — 217

Part IV: California Stars

Chapter 18: Pacific Palisades — 239
Chapter 19: On with the Fable — 270
Chapter 20: Chaos Theory — 296
Chapter 21: California Stars — 321
Chapter 22: Wedding-Bell and Other Blues — 355
Chapter 23: Broken Ankles, Shattered Hearts — 373

Part V: Mamba

Chapter 24: Rocky Mountains — 401
Chapter 25: The Damage — 435
Chapter 26: Rise Up — 460
Chapter 27: Legacy — 490
Chapter 28: The Man — 529

Acknowledgments — 576
Notes and Sources — 578
Index — 611

FOREWORD

IN THE BEGINNING, he came across as a fun-loving kid. He wasn't, of course. Kobe Bean Bryant had to work hard to show that nothing bothered him.

Especially that troubled rookie season.

I was there the night he scored his first NBA field goal, a three-pointer, at Charlotte Coliseum, in December of 1996.

He bounced into the locker room after the game and hit me with a soul shake, a little skin, the hooked fingertips, and a tug. He had no earthly idea who I was. Just some guy with a notepad and a recorder. But he was eager to greet the world.

Later that season, I sat alone with him in an empty locker room in Cleveland, as he waited to compete in the slam dunk contest at the NBA's fiftieth anniversary All-Star Weekend, passing the empty time before he went on stage.

We discussed his status as the poster child for a generation of new talent coming into the NBA, much of it very young, the youngest group of players that would ever come into the league. He talked of the difficulties, the expectations, the hazards, the many temptations in big, bad Los Angeles for a player who was just eighteen years old.

He talked about how deeply Magic Johnson's HIV announcement in 1991 had affected him at age thirteen, about how he would avoid the temptations that Johnson would later admit led him to sleep with three hundred to five hundred people every year.

"With me, it's simple," Bryant told me, "because there's a lot I want to accomplish in my life."

Indeed, just minutes later he would leave our relaxed, thoughtful discourse in the locker room to put on an energetic performance and win the slam dunk contest, which turned up the flame on his already white hot ambition.

The next year he would be voted a starter in the All-Star Game, despite the fact that he didn't even start for the Lakers. That would be followed by the disastrous 1999 season in which Lakers owner Jerry Buss blew up an extremely talented team that seemed to be headed nowhere.

In the midst of the chaos of his third season, Bryant was a very lost, lonely, frustrated twenty-year-old.

"I just want to be the man," he told me, reaffirming his goal of making himself into the NBA's top player. "I don't know how I'm going to get there. I just have to find a way."

And he would, despite how unlikely such a goal seemed at the time. As he closed in on the end of his career in 2016, Bryant could look back at the numbers he racked up in twenty seasons and declare that he had earned "a seat at the table" with the game's greatest. In 2015, he had passed his idol, Michael Jordan, to sit third on the league's list of all-time scorers, behind only Kareem Abdul-Jabbar and Karl Malone. More important, Bryant had helped lead the Lakers to five NBA titles, made eighteen appearances on the All-Star team, and had won two Olympic gold medals.

Though that night as a rookie in Cleveland he said that he didn't know how he would get to the top, he had settled on an answer he had known all along. He was going to grind his way there — implacably, relentlessly grind away at the challenges of the game, night after night, game after game, until he found a dominance born of his ability to outwork everyone else.

The events of his career — an unprecedented twenty years with a single NBA team — make the case that Bryant, aloof and uncompromising, brilliant and self-confident, has proved himself to be a grand enigma of American professional basketball. He is easily the most driven competitor in the history of the game, one who over the seasons quietly gained a reputation among the insiders of the sport as an absolute master of study and intense preparation, with a singular focus on detail that astonished those around him. In turn, his life also proved to be a machine that churned out immense conflict, just about all of it the by-product of his push to dominate the sport.

Night after game night, day after day, for two decades, through injury and turmoil, through the rupture of one key relationship after another, there would be no price he would not pay to have his greatness.

In the process, he became what would be described again and again as "the most polarizing player in the NBA," alternately loathed and loved by huge portions of the pro basketball fan base.

From the earliest age, his father, former NBA player Joe "Jellybean" Bryant, had sought to establish in his son a supreme confidence. Above all, it remained his trademark.

That impenetrable, unshakable self-belief was the one trait where Bryant clearly outranked his contemporaries, said psychologist George Mumford, who had worked extensively with both Jordan and Bryant. "It puts him in his own category."

The confidence remained in place because Bryant virtually excluded any challenge to it, explained Mumford. "He won't allow himself to deal with any contrary view."

It guided Bryant through his early struggles as a teenager in the NBA, through his battles with teammates and coaches, through rape charges in 2003, through his conflicts with and estrangement from his parents, and later through his battle back from serious injuries. It was the backbone of his 81-point game, of his many game-winning shots, of his MVP performances, of his total lack of a conscience about the high volume of shots he could take on a given night. It was largely the reason that Bryant made a regular practice over his career of playing through the sort of pain that put others on the injured list, Mumford said.

That confidence was also responsible for another major storyline in Bryant's career, his disconnect with teammate Shaquille O'Neal despite their success in leading the Los Angeles Lakers to three straight NBA championships between 2000 and 2002. In so many ways, his relationship with the giant center forged the arc of his competitive journey, one that drew out in Bryant the penchant for conflict that touched just about every phase of his life.

Thus, the title of this book. Showboat was the nickname that O'Neal gave Bryant when he was a rookie eager to show off his dunking skills and ability to get to the rim.

Bryant intensely disliked that nickname. He thought it demeaned him as someone lacking competitive integrity, which was a charge that had been frequently leveled at his father over the years, mostly in whispers around professional basketball. Yet the nickname also represents the prodigious love of the game that Bryant shared with his father and their delight in playing it in a flashy, entertaining manner.

"My father played basketball, and it has kind of been in my blood since I was a kid," Bryant explained. "I loved playing basketball. I played other sports but I never really got that enjoyment that I get playing basketball."

As a child, he spent many hours watching his father show off in the Italian league, where he had retreated after the premature collapse of his pro career in America.

"It was fun for me to see how people responded to his moves and his charisma when he was playing," Bryant once told me. "I kind of wanted to have that same feeling. Then again it was kind of cool when he was playing. He was Jellybean Bryant."

Sam Rines, his primary Amateur Athletic Union coach, saw the same strong passion in the son as a young teen.

"He loved it, he ate it up," Rines said. "Kobe wants to be the center of attention, he wants to be center court, he dressed the part, walked the part, talked the part. He was a showman by the time he hit the summer of his sophomore year. He was an unbelievable showman, as far as entertaining people."

The alter ego to Showboat would be the nickname—Black Mamba—that Bryant created for himself to counter public disapproval in the wake of his sexual assault charges. Bryant had seized upon the killer snake in a Quentin Tarantino film as the perfect embodiment of his supposedly similarly remorseless competitive nature.

Later in his career he came to portray his process as much about embracing and channeling "the villain" in one's competitive nature. He laughed deeply when HBO's *Real Sports* confronted him with former teammate Steve Nash's declaration that Bryant was a "motherfucking asshole."

The description was true, he admitted.

Despite his embracing of that identity as a difficult, demanding competitor, Bryant softened his approach over the course of the immensely difficult 2015–16 season, which the Lakers spent mired in losing while he engaged in a farewell tour during road games in arenas around the league.

If nothing else, Bryant's final NBA game in April 2016 echoed his love of the game along with its "showboat" elements as he fought through exhaustion to punctuate his career by making basket after basket and scoring 60 points while leading his Lakers to an amazing come-from-behind victory over the Utah Jazz.

On the surface, the game marked a meaningless close to a disappointing regular season for two teams that had failed to make the play-offs. But the moment magically transcended that and instead became a celebration of the love that fans in Los Angeles held for Bryant and his ability to conjure up magic on any given game night. For many years he had been the city's leading man in all things basketball. With his great skills now badly diminished, he somehow managed to close the final chapter with the most theatric of flourishes, displaying himself as the ultimate mind-blowing entertainer within a city that values theatric ability above all others.

What follows is *Showboat,* my effort to capture his fascinating story, in many ways a cautionary tale, relayed by many witnesses from over the years.

Just thirty-eight upon this biography's publication, in 2016, Bryant has the expectation of another career after his playing days. He has built several media companies with the hope that after basketball he might turn to a new career in writing and producing. Whatever his chosen path over the coming years, it seems a fair expectation that he will continue to be ambitious, to face big moments fearlessly, to be aggressive with the endeavors he chooses.

If so, I hope he can begin each of them like that night of his first big bucket in Charlotte. With a soul shake and big, bright eyes for the future.

Roland Lazenby
August 2016

SHOWBOAT

ONLY THE LONELY

Philadelphia
June 15, 2001

ALL THE ACCOUTREMENTS of his triumph are right there amid the sticky, sweet spray of expensive champagne.

The glistening, oversized, phallic-styled golden orb of the National Basketball Association's 2001 championship trophy is nestled loosely in his arms. It is a prize that Kobe Bryant covets like no other, the ultimate treasure for the relentlessly obsessive competitors and alpha males who are drawn to the American pro game.

The freshly minted official Los Angeles Lakers ball cap sits cocked atop his head, emblazoned with CHAMPIONS in a bright-yellow gold right above the team logo.

Even though it's June and he's in a steamy locker room, he's wearing a multicolored special-edition leather jacket that has a patch for each and every one of the L.A. franchise's umpteen titles, signifying his place among the many greats of the team at a mere twenty-two years of age.

There is every reason for him to be tossing back his head, baring his gums, and laughing and celebrating a supreme moment, which has been attained in no less than his hometown of Philadelphia. Bryant has just helped the Lakers on an unprecedented 15–1 run through the play-offs to claim back-to-back titles, capped by a 4–1 defeat of the Philadelphia 76ers and his nemesis Allen Iverson in the championship series.

After all, his mentor, former Lakers great Jerry West, the object of so much affection and glorification from basketball fans, won just a single pro championship over his tortured and painful fourteen-year career. And now young Kobe Bryant has won two of them.

He is on the dizzying fast track to his dreams, with each grand success now seemingly whizzing by like highway signs. He has been raised and cultured and coddled by a family that has long deeply immersed itself in basketball, a family that has nourished Bryant along with the immense expectations of his impending greatness.

His mother, Pam Cox Bryant, has doted on him since birth, much as she did with her own basketball-playing brother years before.

As a close family friend will note, Kobe Bryant's young life reminded her of an old episode of the TV show *The Twilight Zone*, about a child so worshiped by his own family that every day is his birthday.

"It's always his birthday," the friend explained, "and all the adults are like, 'Oh, it's your birthday! It's your birthday.' "

Rather than spoil him, his parents' actions have had the opposite effect, serving to spur him onward from a very young age in pursuit of his dream. Since his startling emergence into the public spotlight as a teen in 1996, Bryant has stood before the public as a bright young man, polite and polished in so many ways, yet possessed of an otherworldly confidence that is off-putting to nearly everyone who meets him, leaving some on occasion to doubt even his fundamental sanity.

The formation of that self-belief was due in part to the efforts of his father, Joe "Jellybean" Bryant, who carefully and continually stoked his son's confidence—the father having watched his own promising career break apart in the swirling crosscurrents of the 1970s NBA.

From his teen years, Kobe Bryant has been shockingly bold in his prediction that he's going to make himself the greatest basketball player ever.

At every turn, his declarations of future greatness have been met with head shaking and raised eyebrows because such dreams are ludicrous, impossible to fulfill. "Kobe's crazy," the people around him concluded time and again with a laugh.

Yet now, here he is, well on the path to the wealth and fame that his great-grandmother once prophesied for someone in the clan. There should be friends and family and high school championship teammates all gathered around him in one of those *It's a Wonderful Life* tableaus.

A short time earlier his Lakers teammates began the champagne-spraying revelry by chanting those anthemic DMX lyrics, "Y'all gon' make me lose my mind, / Up in here, up in here, / Y'all gon' make me go all out, / Up in here, Up in here."

The words themselves epitomize Bryant's life. Yet rather than immerse himself in the revelry, he has moved quietly to the side. He sits in an antiseptic locker-room bathroom stall, braced by its chrome railing, the tile around him the color of fog along the Schuylkill River on a Philadelphia morning. His face is in his hand, his gaze cast to the floor, lost in a thousand-yard stare. He is utterly forlorn and alone, preoccupied and torn by the sudden backwash of emotion that has been flooding over his life in recent months.

Since a young age, when he rode on bus trips with his father's second-tier Italian league team and promised the old man and another of his father's teammates that he was going to be far better than either of them, Bryant's existence has been a singular, almost inhuman, pursuit of that greatness.

Millions of schoolboys in his generation have stoked dreams of matching the greatness of Michael Jordan, but only one among the millions has displayed the iron will and drive to pursue the game as Kobe Bryant has. Even as a teen, he was singled out by representatives of Adidas, the athletic-shoe company, and told that they planned to make him the next Michael Jordan. It was a role that lined up perfectly with his own designs, and within a few short months, he had the part down, from the speech patterns to the confident air, even to the shaved, glistening pate, even though he was only seventeen at the time. The transformation was startling, remembered Sonny Vaccaro, then an Adidas representative who served as kingmaker in the basketball industry.

Now Bryant's face in this moment of triumph provides confirmation that there is no price he will not pay, no sacrifice he will not make, to, as he explains it, "be the man," the most dominant player in the game.

Most recently, he has offered up his immediate family on the altar of his quest. It is a family widely admired as a model of achievement and wholesomeness, yet it now lies in tatters around him, the victim of his unflinching desire.

"He was like the Russians with the Romanovs," observed Vaccaro, looking back. "He got rid of everybody."

Soon he will eliminate his agent, his athletic-shoe company, eventually his coach, Phil Jackson, and fellow star, Shaquille O'Neal. But as of now, he has removed his mother, father, and two sisters from his life with an abrupt and almost surgical precision, banishing them from his presence. Family members have told numerous acquaintances tales of credit cards canceled, vehicles towed, jobs eliminated, phone calls left unreturned, a family residence vacated, relationships ended.

"It's a tragedy, what happened," said Gary Charles, a New York AAU coach and family friend, an opinion repeated by family friends and acquaintances time and again.

"It was unbelievable to watch them together," Charles recalled of a teenaged Kobe's relationship with his father, Joe. "You could see the love and respect Kobe had for his dad. As soon as one of his AAU games was over, Kobe would run over and hug his dad and ask, 'Did you see what I did?' Joe would say, 'Yeah, I saw it.' In all the time I was with them, I never once saw him disrespect his father."

Yet the onslaught of success and desire and the eye-popping amounts of money in Bryant's professional life had somehow formed a gulf in the family, one that astounded everyone who had known them before.

On this night in Philadelphia's arena, the Spectrum, his maternal uncle, Chubby Cox, is the main family representative in the building, and when Cox and his wife quietly meet with the young Lakers star afterward, Bryant finally breaks down completely.

"Joe Bryant told me a story about that night," Gary Charles recalled. "When Kobe's aunt and uncle came in to see him, Kobe hugged them and cried and cried."

The quiet sobbing and the pain on his face on that championship night revealed just how deeply he felt the loss of his family, the alienation. Yet this very determined and willful young star had still deemed it absolutely necessary to move forward without his loved ones.

"It's a tough deal being great, tough cake," said Mo Howard, a longtime Bryant family friend.

"It's sad, it's really sad," observed Anthony Gilbert, another family friend from Philadelphia who had followed Bryant's life and career closely. "It's like F. Scott Fitzgerald. Show me a hero, and I'll show you a tragedy."

PART I

GOTTA BE JELLY 'CAUSE JAM DON'T SHAKE

"I always had the impression that nobody took him seriously, that they just thought that Joe Bryant was the funny guy."

—Paul Westhead

Chapter 1

THE BUST

Philadelphia
May 5, 1976

THE WHITE SPORTS car rolled slowly, almost silently, out of the midnight haze, directly toward the officers in the police van. They, too, were moving along with no great sense of urgency, their radio crackling with the odd, discordant traffic of a Wednesday night in Philadelphia.

As the sports car passed, they saw a large black man hunched over the wheel.

It was early May 1976 in the city's sprawling Fairmount Park, and the man in the car was Joe Bryant, a twenty-one-year-old rookie with the Philadelphia 76ers. Known as the fun-loving Jellybean, he was something of a hero to the local basketball scene.

By many accounts, it was a youthful friend of Bryant's, Mo Howard, who was credited with giving him the nickname.

That wasn't true, Howard would say many years later, explaining that the nickname grew out of the fluid, athletic way Bryant played basketball.

"I think the South Philly guys called him Jelly," Howard recalled. "They called him Jelly because of the way he was shakin' people on the court, you know what I mean? You know what they say, 'Gotta be jelly 'cause jam don't shake.' And it doesn't, right? And that was probably a great way to describe Joey's play."

Bryant also had a taste for the colorful beans themselves. "That was his thing, jelly beans," Howard said with a laugh. "Back then you'd only see jelly beans around Easter time. But Joe always had 'em."

Some would later claim that he got the nickname because fans gave him jelly beans on the sideline during a game one night.

Whatever the genesis, the nickname certainly suited Bryant's style. Jellybean was an easygoing sort with an irrepressible gap-toothed grin. It was a face that made him an instant hit with just about everyone he met.

"He's always been that way," Mo Howard recalled. "Always got a smile on his face. Always laughing and joking. I think that's what drew me to Joe."

It didn't hurt that he had a heart to match the grin. Years later, one of his eighth-grade classmates would recall Joe Bryant as someone who would readily come to the aid of a small Jewish kid being bullied in school.

"Joe was a happy-go-lucky guy," Howard explained. "We'd have the most fun when we'd go into parties and dance. You had to see this guy, this six-nine guy, dancing. He was the smoothest guy there. He could dance like hell, and he was a really, really nice guy. I never ever got the impression that B was worried about anything."

In retrospect, that carefree nature perhaps helps to explain why on this temperate night in early May 1976, as the cherry blossoms were just beginning to unfold, Jellybean Bryant found himself caught up in what seemed to be a mission to tempt fate.

In Bryant's defense—and Lord knows he would need a defense for his actions this night—it had been a difficult, emotional day, beginning with the funeral for his close friend Gilbert Saunders's mother. In a way, she had been a second mother to Bryant. He spent so much time in the Saunders household that it was like a second home. He loved being at her table for the big, sumptuous meals she turned out. His own family was of extremely limited means, and Mrs. Saunders was the one who would notice his need for shoes or a jacket and quietly provide them. Bryant had gone to the Saunders home after the funeral that day and pulled out his paycheck from the 76ers to show how well he was doing.

"Damn," Mr. Saunders said, his eyes widening in surprise.

Bryant had gotten a rookie deal worth nearly $1 million with the team—an incredible sum at the time—and for the past few months had been awash in more cash than he could have ever dreamed of.

Gilbert Saunders—who at the time was playing basketball for John Chaney at Cheyney State—figured Bryant had brought out the check "as a gesture to cheer up my family. He was accepted in my family. We embraced him. The sneakers and coats, those were things my mother had helped him with. His gesture was a way of showing my father, 'This is what I do now.'"

And so the events, the emotion of the day, perhaps helped to explain what had led Jellybean to nearby Fairmount Park hours later at midnight on that mission to tempt fate.

He had a taillight out and no driver's license, only a long-expired learner's permit. He had begun driving seriously only the previous fall, when he purchased two glistening new Datsun 280Zs—one for his wife, Pam, and one for him—after signing his rookie contract with the Sixers.

"Those Zs had a punch," Gilbert Saunders remembered. "That's what Joe and his wife settled on. That's what she wanted, so that's what they got. They got his and hers."

Bryant had been raised right there in Southwest Philly in what he liked to tell people was the "ghetto," a noisy world of screeching trolley lines, elevated trains, groaning city buses, and local gangs fighting for turf on every corner. He had gone from having no vehicle at all to driving the Z, a virtual land-bound rocket. Armed with 170 horsepower while weighing just 2,800 pounds, the fuel-injected two-seaters had the potential to alternately exhilarate and terrify anybody who got behind the wheel, especially Jellybean, who was already a little thin in driving experience.

He understandably loved his vehicle, though, loved bringing it back to his old Southwest Philly neighborhood, recalled Vontez Simpson, a friend. "He showed it to everybody. He wanted to show everybody that he'd made it. That was a hot car at the time."

What's more, Bryant was perhaps flying that night even when the car was stopped, as suggested by the two vials of cocaine and the small, stylish spoon in the vehicle with him.

In another complicating factor, he was out and about with Linda Salter, his former girlfriend, the sister of a teammate from his old school, Philly's John Bartram High, despite the fact that he had a beautiful young wife and a month-old daughter at their lovely new home in the city's wealthy suburbs.

From its first moments, his marriage had been ruled by his wife, Pam, a statuesque beauty with a bit of a mean streak. Old friends had noticed that anytime there was a decision to be made, Bryant immediately looked to his wife submissively. Even family members laughed that the mere thought of crossing her seemed to send Jelly into a panic.

But here he was, crossing her big-time and about to be caught red-handed.

If this had been a scene from a period-piece film, the soundtrack might well have been Johnnie Taylor's "Disco Lady," the number one song for much of that spring of '76, which was perfectly smooth, the way Joe loved a song to be.

> *Shake it up, shake it down*
> *Move it in, move it round, disco lady.*

Whatever song was playing in the Z, whatever flight of fancy Bryant had taken that night, they all immediately crashed as soon as he realized the flashing lights were directed at him. Understandably, he quickly sensed a variety of dangers, not the least of which was that he was a black man in a fancy car in a park late at night in a city that was wracked by gang violence and all sorts of ugly racial issues.

The news of his signing with the Sixers months earlier had been front-page news in the *Philadelphia Tribune*, right next to a story about the dozens of African Americans shot by Philadelphia police in past months.

Over the preceding three years, Philadelphia police themselves had shot and killed 73 people and wounded 193 more. In those days, officers routinely fired "warning" shots at fleeing suspects.

Over the previous twelve months, five Philadelphia police officers had been shot to death, including one who was assassinated from the rooftop of a housing project by a fifteen-year-old, who jarred the city when he told authorities, "I just wanted to kill a cop."

Bryant didn't need a newspaper story to remind him of the circumstances. No black resident of the city did.

Perhaps it truly was a run-of-the-mill traffic stop about a taillight, as the officers would later report, but the context of the moment was strange and tense. And it would grow stranger still.

The officers got their first indication of that when long, tall Jellybean—just a shade under six ten—unfolded himself and stepped out of the car. He tried to be cool as the officer put the light on his face. He immediately identified himself and, having to think on the fly, quickly decided that confessing about the license and throwing himself on the mercy of the officers might be his best plan for avoiding a search of the car.

He handed over his registration, but the officer was confused by Bryant's statement about the license. Something about the interaction triggered an intense and overwhelming sense of panic in Joe Bryant. Perhaps, as others would suggest later, it was the sudden realization that his wife would find him out. Perhaps it was the fear of the police themselves, although Bryant had already provided them his registration and his name.

What happened next would astound the officers, indeed the entire Philadelphia community as well as the insular culture of the 1970s National Basketball Association.

Bryant abruptly turned and got back in his car, leaving the officers to assume that he might be attempting to retrieve his license from the glove box. Instead Bryant fired up the ignition, jammed the Z into gear, and sped off, filling their headlight beams with a spray of gravel and dust and disbelief.

The officers needed an instant to comprehend that Joe Bryant had deserted them at high speed. They then piled back in the van and gave chase while calling in an all-points bulletin on the radio. It took them only a few moments to realize that trying to keep up with the Z was too dangerous. Joe Bryant had zoomed off, covering the distance ahead at an insane speed—well over a hundred miles an hour, according to their estimates—like some bizarre vessel knifing through the night.

In an instant, he was out of the park and flying blind down the streets of the city. With his lights off.

It wasn't until twelve minutes later that another police unit spotted Bryant.

Officer Raymond Dunne would report that he was heading west on Cedar Avenue when he looked in his rearview and saw a sports car with no lights on zooming up on his cruiser from behind. The driver was honking his horn furiously for the police unit to get out of his way.

It was quite a moment. There was Jellybean Bryant, on the highway to hell and blowing for a passing lane.

At the last instant, Bryant swerved around the police car, and Officer Dunne immediately gave chase, only to back off when the speeds again grew very high. Dunne later reported that he was going so fast trying to keep up with Jellybean that he feared he might lose control of the patrol car.

Minutes later, Bryant barreled straight on into a busy intersection on Baltimore Avenue, where a vehicle was blocking the way.

As he attempted to veer around the vehicle at high speed, Jellybean lost whatever grip he still had on the car. First the Z struck a stop sign; then it careened across Farragut Street to take out a No Parking sign before ping-ponging back and forth down the block, destroying a parked car on one side, then bouncing to the other to smash into two more vehicles, then back across the roadway before mercifully jumping the curb and slamming into a wall.

With enough wreckage in his wake to qualify as a small tornado, Bryant and his old girlfriend were left sitting dazed in his smashed and ruined car. It was perhaps then he realized that at no time during his speeding escape had he sought to ditch the coke. Officers would later find it upon searching the Z.

In that instant Bryant made his final terrible decision and took off running into the night.

"He just jumped out of the car and left her sitting there," said one of Bryant's old friends. "Joe panicked and jumped out. There was no need to run. If you were a police officer in the community and you saw a guy that big running off, you knew who it was. Everybody knew Joe. There wasn't no reason for him to run."

It is here at this juncture where the strange calculus of the evening finally breaks down completely, where monumentally bad decisions mingle somehow with good fortune on the far edge of temporary insanity.

Mercifully, the police did not fire the proverbial "warning shot" at the fleeing Jellybean.

In addition to being a fine hoopster, Bryant had been a track star in high school. Yet somehow one of the officers, Robert Lombardi, managed to run him down in a matter of a few yards. When he did, Bryant turned to lash out.

"I grabbed him," Lombardi recalled. "He raised his fist, and I struck him. I subdued and handcuffed him."

Bryant suffered a head injury that would require six stitches to close. Decades later, Gene Shue, who was then Bryant's coach with the Sixers, recalled that police apparently issued a pretty severe beating to Bryant, a beating that would mark him with a profound sense of humiliation, one of many things that later troubled him for a long, long time. Immediately, though, there were the handcuffs, jail, and the horrific anxiety of having to face his wife.

In a little less than a half hour, the ample good fortune of Joe Bryant's young existence had morphed into a world of shit. Many in Philadelphia had done far less yet had wound up in a cadaver drawer down at the morgue. For Joe Bryant, over the coming months and years, it would become increasingly apparent that the incident had done him and his career tremendous harm.

Jellybean's anguished time in custody that night brought the slightest inkling of a revelation. Years earlier his grandmother had prophesied that someone in the family was going to be fabulously rich and famous. This night in May 1976 was Joe Bryant's first hint that the person in the prophecy might not be him.

Chapter 2

FATHERHOOD

Throughout his youth, Joe Bryant's basketball career had proved to be another sort of shiny vehicle in his life, one that could transport him places where few other boys in his community could hope to go. Jellybean, however, would come to possess a very different game, with a style all his own, that first caught traction during childhood days spent at his grandmother's place in West Philly just around the corner from the asphalt playground near Forty-Second and Leidy Avenue. She would allow him out of the house to go play every day except Sunday, when she'd roust him out of bed early so that they could leave her place at 6 a.m. to go spend the Sabbath at the New Bethlehem Baptist Church.

"We stayed all day," Bryant once explained.

The singing, worship, and praise provided the basis of his moral training. His hoops work came every other day of the week, all on the playground.

As he neared adolescence, he and his family moved to Southwest Philadelphia, into a drafty, rickety row house on Willows Avenue, not far from the Kingsessing Playground, which became his new basketball lab.

Willows was a rough little avenue, like many in Southwest Philly. Still, it was a tree-lined street, where Jellybean's old man, Big Joe, would sometimes sit on the front porch and smile and wave at the world.

Most of the time, the world smiled back. In another age, Big Joe might have played defensive tackle for the Eagles. He was six foot three and thickly built, broad in the chest. You could search far and wide and find nary a soul in all of Philadelphia who didn't admire Big Joe for his bearish countenance, for his quiet, friendly ways, and for his love of his son.

His high regard in the community was quite an accomplishment for a man who managed to raise three children despite difficult financial circumstances. Decades later, people of every station easily remembered Big Joe, or Pop Bryant, as the neighborhood kids called him. Over the years, the *Philadelphia Tribune,* which quoted him often in its sports pages, came to refer to him fondly as "the Jolly Gentleman of Willows Avenue."

Watching his son play basketball seemed to be the sweet elixir that stirred Big Joe's joy. He had big, meaty hands and a full face that broke easily into a smile. Still, his sense of discipline ran to an Old Testament, spare-the-rod mentality. He once explained to Philadelphia sportswriter Julius Thompson that he often warned his teen son "not to bring daylight into my house" if he went out at night. In other words, not to be staying out late and coming home after dawn. The son tested the rule once, and Big Joe promptly coldcocked him, so hard that it supposedly took Jellybean twenty minutes to come around. When he did, he had gotten the message, Thompson remembered.

Big Joe was a large presence, determined to watch out for his son. "Pop Bryant, everywhere Joe was, he was right there," recalled family friend Vontez Simpson.

"Big Joe was totally involved every step of the way," longtime Philadelphia basketball writer Dick Weiss remembered. "He was enormously proud of his son."

"Big Joe Bryant was just a terrific guy, just a very engaging guy," recalled Paul Westhead, who would coach Jellybean at La Salle University. "People around the city knew Joe's father. He was interested in good things for his son and family. Good things meaning good things that would help them to be good people. He was a delightful man."

As Big Joe aged and his weight and diabetes became factors, he took to walking with a cane. Even then, he drew a spark, first from Jellybean's play, then from his grandson Kobe. How great was his love? Years later, when his diabetes came to consume his lifestyle, Big Joe would haul his oxygen tank around to his grandson's games.

Out of Georgia

Jellybean's father likely had plenty of woeful stories to tell, but he didn't spend much time talking about the past. He came out of Georgia's "Black Belt," which nearly ran the length of the state along Highway 41, as part of the great twentieth-century migration of African Americans out of the South.

Philadelphia was a common destination. Southwest Philly, in particular, had evolved from farms, country estates, and botanical gardens in the nineteenth century, to become a magnet first for European immigrants and then eventually for African Americans to work as the area blossomed into an industrial landscape featuring soap and locomotive factories, tank farms, oil refineries, and, in 1927, an airport.

At the turn of the twentieth century, the so-called City of Brotherly Love's population was overwhelmingly Caucasian, but that had begun to change in the 1920s, '30s, and '40s as millions of blacks headed north.

Many of them arrived each day on the trains that made stops throughout the South, collecting African Americans — or Negroes, as they were called in that era — explained Julius Thompson, one of the first black sportswriters hired at a major newspaper on the East Coast when he went to work for the old *Philadelphia Bulletin*, in 1970.

Having been failed by the collapse of the farm economy in the 1930s, they packed up their destitute lives and headed north to fill the country's cities, looking for jobs and a new way to live. The migration was driven by desperation caused by the collapse of agricultural prices during the Depression, which put an end to the failed economic systems of sharecropping and tenant farming, still the only work available to many African Americans in a country that had long barred them from educational opportunity.

The migration was also hastened along by the violence of white lynch mobs that for decades had targeted black people in one ugly incident after another, documented, often in graphic detail, by newspapers in the South.

The lure of the North grew in the 1940s with the promise of wartime jobs in Philadelphia shipyards and other locations. The opportunity only increased after the war as the economy surged back to life.

In Georgia, Big Joe Bryant had worked in agriculture alongside his father—the first of a succession of three Joe Bryants—putting in sixty-hour weeks for pennies a day. Census records indicate that Big Joe's grandfather was born into slavery in the 1840s and spent his life, as his son would after him, working in the South's harsh, unforgiving fields.

Like so many others, Big Joe Bryant was a refugee when he arrived in Philadelphia as a young man. Still, the life he left behind had provided him with certain assets, including resilience and a strong spirit. Fatherhood was apparently long prized in the Bryant clan. In his early years, Big Joe made the transition from the country to the city and started a family. He and his wife produced three children, and he adored all three, especially his oldest child, his namesake.

"I'll tell you what, man, in Mr. B's eyes, Joe could do no wrong," family friend Mo Howard recalled.

Jellybean's basketball journey began when he was an adolescent, spending hours at a hoop put up on a utility pole right there on Willows Avenue. From there, he'd venture across Cobbs Creek Parkway to the park there, where the courts brought more competition. Beyond that, it was on to other courts around Southwest Philly, mainly down at Forty-Eighth and Woodland Avenue, and to the big playground on Kingsessing Avenue.

Jellybean was painfully thin, but his height meant the older players who dominated the playgrounds allowed him into their games. For that he would remain forever grateful. Because he was thin, he learned the game from the perimeter. Those hours on the asphalt going against older boys gave him an identity: he came to see himself as a player. Years later, his son, Kobe, would do the same. It was a gift they would share—their early understanding of their destiny, their love for the game.

"He loved the game. He just wanted to play, to get that feel,"

Julius Thompson said of Jellybean, though he could have said the same about Kobe.

One of Jellybean's early heroes was Earl "the Pearl" Monroe, who had played at John Bartram High in the early sixties. Monroe had a fancy handle with the ball and was magical in leading Bartram to the Philly Public League title in 1963, when little Joe Bryant was a wide-eyed nine-year-old. The Public League teams were so tough, so physical, that the rest of Pennsylvania's high schools wouldn't even allow them to play in the state tournament. "If they had, the Public League teams would have won it every year," said Vontez Simpson, repeating a commonly held belief.

"There were so many great players in the Public League back then," Dick Weiss explained.

"I've never seen so much talent come through a city," said Julius Thompson, who covered the Public League for the *Bulletin*. "It was just churning on and on and on from the sixties to the seventies."

Soon enough, Earl Monroe was off to Winston-Salem State and then the old Baltimore Bullets and finally the New York Knicks. He was like a meteor across the sky for young Joe Bryant and others in the generation that followed. So were the stars on the 76ers roster—players such as Wali Jones, Chet Walker, Hal Greer, Luke Jackson, and Wilt the Stilt—in 1966–67, when they won the NBA title and Joe Bryant was twelve. Shortly after that, he became a fan of Kenny Durrett, who starred at La Salle.

Joe especially loved the flashy style and spent hours working on dribbling the ball between his legs, behind his back, no look here, no look there, things that most big men wouldn't even consider attempting in that era.

Pretty soon, people noticed that there wasn't anything that JB, as he was called at Shaw Junior High and later at Bartram, couldn't do with a basketball. He was already showing a natural flair, a borderline genius, for the showtime elements of the game that only a select few could master, a mix of flavors that included Earl the Pearl, Bob Cousy, the Globetrotters, and Pistol Pete Maravich. Wherever JB played, people would marvel. Tall guys just weren't supposed to be able to handle the ball like that.

Trouble Everywhere

By ninth grade, Jelly was approaching six foot seven and possessed a long running stride. When he wanted to go somewhere, he would just take off jogging and be there soon, a trait that would endear him to the city's track coaches as well as its basketball scouts.

At face value, Philadelphia basketball in the late sixties and early seventies would seem to have been a sweet, nostalgic story except for one big factor. The city was trapped in a dark place where gangs guaranteed there was plenty of trouble for boys growing up on the angry streets. The *Philadelphia Daily News* would later report that there were 106 different gangs strangling the city, each with a very specific territory, their members usually armed with homemade zip guns. Scores of young men died in gang violence during the period as turf wars extended to the hallways of the city's schools.

How tight was the hold on Philadelphia's young males? Many days, you couldn't even get to school—let alone survive once there—if you didn't throw in with a gang. There was strength in numbers and hell to pay for everybody else.

"In my hometown, Philadelphia, Pennsylvania, vicious black street gangs seemingly ruled every inch of the black community, and it was a dangerous time to be a young black teenager living in the treacherous terrain of the urban wilds," wrote Reginald S. Lewis, himself a former gang member.

In 1969 alone, Joe Bryant's freshman year at Bartram High, the city recorded forty-five gang-related deaths. Tensions were felt in every high school in the city. The gangs began early, pulling boys from elementary schools to become associates.

Jellybean Bryant somehow managed to be one of the lucky ones. "If you weren't an athlete, you were in trouble," Julius Thompson said. "The people who made it through had strong support at home."

"As I look back on it," observed Gilbert Saunders, "it was about direction. Like a lot of kids, Joe had a lack of direction. It took the proverbial village to raise Joe Bryant."

Basketball provided that "village," or at least became the force that pulled it all together. In addition to the watchful eye of Big Joe, the kindness of Saunders's parents, and the public school coaches, easily the biggest factor in Bryant's life would be Philadelphia legend Sonny Hill and his basketball leagues. Hill would be there at virtually every juncture to right mishaps and turn disaster into opportunity.

He played a similar role in the lives of many young players from Philadelphia.

As Gilbert Saunders pointed out, "Sonny Hill literally saved my life. And the lives of lots of others, too."

At the time, Philadelphia was a city teeming with all sorts of basketball leagues, Julius Thompson said. "Everywhere you looked kids were playing basketball sunup to sundown."

Still, most of the elite leagues were suburban until Hill came along.

"He ran a labor union," Thompson explained. "I call him the old-line basketball figure of Philadelphia. Sonny had good political skills. He got everybody involved."

A short, wiry guard who played in the old Eastern League in the days when the NBA had only ten teams and a scant few blacks on its rosters, Sonny Hill would later become a sports broadcaster of note as well as a union boss and community organizer. Hill had come off the streets of the city himself and had a keen understanding of the challenges young players faced in their lives and in the sport itself.

In the early 1960s, Hill founded the Baker League, a summer competition for professional players. It soon gained widespread notice for helping the New York Knicks' Bill Bradley improve his game after he returned from a sabbatical to study overseas.

"When Sonny started his league, he played it at Great Hope Baptist Church," recalled Dick Weiss, the famed Philly basketball writer. "I still remember going up there to watch Earl Monroe play against Bill Bradley right after he got back from his Rhodes Scholar studies. Bradley used the Baker League to help get ready to play for the Knicks in order to give himself a feel for the best league that simulated the NBA. He came down to Philadelphia from Princeton to play in the Baker League."

The Baker League games in the summer were often far better than the NBA's own regular-season games in that era, Weiss allowed.

Soon Hill's league caught the attention of other players, everybody from Wilt Chamberlain to Walt Frazier, and was recognized as a treasure of summertime play in the age before the NBA formed its own official summer leagues.

His success with the Baker League helped prompt Hill to found another program in 1968, just as Joe Bryant was emerging from eighth grade. The Sonny Hill League provided a structured playing format for the region's top high school players and would become the hallmark of Hill's influence.

The amateur league was staged as preliminary games before the Baker League contests. "The place would be packed," Dick Weiss recalled. "It became a gathering place for all of the black community."

"It was like the big picnic," agreed Mo Howard, who played in the Hill League and later starred as a guard for coach Lefty Driesell at the University of Maryland. "My earliest recollection of basketball was going to the Baker League games. I remember going into the church basement, where they had this beautiful gym, and watching Bill Bradley, Cazzie Russell, Wali Jones, Hal Greer. Watching these guys come in and play in a summer environment and playing hard."

By the time Howard reached high school, the Hill League had begun play, and suddenly he found himself participating in games right before the pros played in the Baker League.

"You talk about inspiring the young people," Howard recalled, "to play before a Baker League game, there were going to be x amount of people at the Baker League game, you knew that. It was a given. Now you got all these great high school players on each team. There might have been ten or fifteen boys, and they were from every geographical part of Philadelphia, which had many high schools. So you talk about the very best high school players."

With high school players competing before the pro games, it wasn't long before informal relationships formed, Howard said. "It was nothing for Wali Jones to grab me and say, 'Young fella, you need to work on your left hand,' or for Earl Monroe to say, 'You got to practice your bank shot.' I mean, we had full access to these guys. And oftentimes—I don't know why it happened this way—but they would approach us. It was unbelievable."

There were a variety of leagues for the area's top high school players in that era, and until the Hill League came along, the tops was the Narberth League, played in the suburbs of Philadelphia on outdoor courts. What set the Hill League apart was that it was a city league and was played indoors.

"After a while, the Sonny Hill League became the elite league," Julius Thompson remembered.

The Hill League and the Baker League helped build tremendous pride in Philadelphia basketball during troubled times, especially during the years that Frank Rizzo was the police commissioner, then later mayor, of Philadelphia, Weiss explained. "Obviously in the sixties there was a lot of anger. There was a riot back in the post–Martin Luther King days. I mean, it was dangerous to be out during the Rizzo administration. There were a lot of tensions between blacks and whites. But basketball was the one sport that seemed to bring everyone together."

Hill founded the Sonny Hill League in part to battle the gangs that engulfed the city. With so many local gangs so protective of their territories, it was difficult for boys to cross over from one neighborhood to the next on the city's public transportation. If they tried, they often found trouble awaiting them in a turf showdown. However, if a player was carrying one of the distinctive gym bags of the Sonny Hill League, gang members usually allowed them to pass without trouble, which meant players could travel to league games around the city. Hill had smartly filled the coaching corps and adult cadre of his league with a number of parole officers and public-safety figures, so gangs quickly learned that they shouldn't mess with Hill League players.

The Sonny Hill League was also rock-ribbed in its discipline. "There was no arguing with officials, no outbursts of any kind," recalled Gilbert Saunders, who played in the league. "They did not care how talented you were. They held you accountable for your grades and your behavior."

"Sonny was a big one for discipline," agreed Dick Weiss. "You had to have your shirt tucked in to play in his league. And you could never argue with officials. He would step right in. He was a big believer that there should be personal pride in your game, personal pride in your approach, in doing things the right way."

The Hill League's longevity and success were made possible only because of the unique talent and power of Hill himself, Weiss explained. "He was able to organize an entire city with that league.... He had enormous political clout within the community, and he used it to start that league."

Hill's league may have brought a new focus to basketball in the inner city, but not everyone was pleased. Some accused Hill of using his influence to channel the best players to certain high schools, then to certain colleges. Hill denied it flatly and spent plenty of time offering proof to the contrary.

"A lot of people just saw him as a carpetbagger taking kids away from another league," Weiss explained. "But his critics didn't realize that he was building pride in Philadelphia and how important it was for Philadelphia to have a sense of pride in something that was theirs."

Sonny Hill recalled that Jellybean joined the Hill League as an eighth or ninth grader, but he didn't stick. While he was tall and athletic, he lacked the maturity to compete, Hill remembered. "He came back about a year later to the league, and he had matured. I think a lot of that was because of his father."

Big Joe loved the discipline and structure of the league, to the point that long after both of his sons had graduated from the Hill League, he continued to volunteer.

It was in these summer leagues that Jellybean first met Mo Howard and became fast friends with him.

"Joey and I played together in the Narberth League as well as the Sonny Hill League, and we played on another team in another league," Howard recalled. "It made for a very busy summer. And that's not including the rec leagues and the neighborhood summer leagues. So we got a lot of ball in. There were always places to play, always games going on."

As high school juniors, Jellybean and Mo Howard won the Sonny Hill League on a team that also included Andre McCarter, who was headed to UCLA to play for John Wooden.

Soon Mo Howard's father, Edward, met Big Joe Bryant, and the two fathers realized they were both from Georgia. A kinship formed almost instantly.

"They were two fathers who were really influential," Julius Thompson said of Howard and Bryant. "Both of them would give you the shirt off their back."

"There were no two men whose chests stuck out farther than Mr. B and my dad," Howard recalled with a laugh, adding that whether he and Jellybean were on the same team or opposite teams, "Mr. B and my dad would sit together and talk shit. That's what they did, they sort of kind of fell into each other's laps. Mr. B was a big guy. He was tall and he was big. Now, my dad was a short, big guy. My dad was a truck driver, and the first person he would look for when he walked into the gym was Joe Bryant, Mr. Big. We called him Mr. Big. It was just a dynamic relationship for Joey and myself and our dads."

The previous generation of African Americans never had the opportunities with sports that their sons had, Howard said, looking back. "To them, it was like, 'Whatever's going on with you guys, whatever fame and glory you're getting, you got to share that with us.' What it did was, it sort of validated who these men were. They were our fathers, and it gave them a sense of pride that maybe they had never felt in their lives. Here they had two sons who were great basketball players.

"That was Mr. B's thing and Dad's thing. They loved each other, my dad and Mr. B. I would be remiss if I didn't say when you talk about kids who have a certain amount of success in sports, especially black boys, then the father comes on the scene after the kid makes the money. Our dads were there from the beginning. Our dads were buying the shoes, our dads were buying the socks, they were giving us money to buy hot dogs after the game. Those guys were in our lives. These guys would go everywhere with us. You talking about support, they believed that we don't show up, somebody's going to think that we don't care about our sons. And I will tell you to my dying day, my dad and Mr. Bryant, everybody knew them, everybody respected them."

Chapter 3

PIMPS OF JOYTIME

Whatever the trouble permeating the city, whatever the pitfalls of his early years, Jellybean had been able to move through them, pulled along by his basketball talent and the various people who were willing to nurture it. His personal charm was ever present, but more important to his basketball mentors was the way he played.

There was little question that the colorful Jellybean was a product of the playgrounds. He loved the free-flowing nature of the outdoor games, and the playground loved him back. That was where he learned to shine in both pickup games and city recreation leagues. Big Joe would show up to the playground just to watch what his son would do next. But he wasn't alone.

"When Joe had a game, it was jam-packed," Vontez Simpson explained. "You couldn't even get in the playground sometimes. Everybody loved to watch Joe."

"He was always kind of smiling," explained Paul Westhead, who later coached Jellybean. "You would hear people say, 'We'll go out and play basketball and have fun.' That's such a truism that it's kind of absurd, but Joe was one of those few guys who really did have fun playing. Because of his size and skill set, he just had a certain way of how to play the game."

"Joe brought people a lot of joy with the way he played," agreed Dick Weiss.

Jellybean's skills remained unique as he developed them through pickup games and the Baker League. His blend of size, athleticism, and ball-handling ability helped him stand out among the city's elite.

"The thing that floored everybody was, here was a six-nine guy, and all the six-nine guys we played with were post players," Mo Howard explained. "Everybody would run down to the block and turn and face out to the ball. Well, Joey would make the plays. You give him the ball, and he'd be running like a point guard. He would pull up for a twenty-footer, or he'd put it on the floor and throw you a no-look pass. Nobody in Philadelphia was playing like Joey at that time."

One of the memorable games of the era featured Jellybean in a showdown with Jimmie Baker of Olney High, who would later play at UNLV and the University of Hawaii before a stint in the ABA.

"Jimmie Baker was an unbelievable talent, maybe even better than Joe," Julius Thompson said, "but he ended up an addict. The drugs got to him."

"He was about six eight, and he was a great jump shooter," Mo Howard recalled. "He was another athletic tall guy, even though he was more one-dimensional than Joey, because Joey could do it all. He could dribble, he could pass, he could shoot. I can remember Joey and Jimmie Baker having a shoot-out, man, in one of the Sonny Hill games, man. It was crazy. I think Jimmy had, like, 32 and Bean had 28, but they were all jump shots. The two biggest guys on the floor shooting jump shots, nobody down on the box. It was untraditional, it was unconventional. That was not how you were supposed to play basketball back then."

Mostly what set Jellybean apart was how well he handled the ball. "I've seen people fall on the ground from Joe shaking them down and breaking them down," Gilbert Saunders recalled with a laugh.

It would be easy to assume that Jellybean's style would mean trouble once he got to a team with a more traditional high school coaching staff in the Public League. Especially at Bartram High, where he played for basketball coach and strict disciplinarian Jack Farrell, who also taught English and was the dean of boys at the school, charged with trying to keep the influence of the gangs at bay. He was assisted by a man named Jack Gallagher, a big, tough Irishman who made a point of trying to help as many young athletes as he could.

Farrell knew talent when he saw it. "He had a great affinity for black kids," remembered Julius Thompson, who covered Farrell's teams. "He was a character. Unique. He understood people. A lot of coaches back then didn't understand the players they were dealing with. Jack Farrell understood. He was dealing with tough kids, not choirboys."

"He listened to Joe about a lot of things," recalled Vontez Simpson, who served as a team manager at Bartram and later played on the varsity team. "He listened to Joe's ideas. Mr. Farrell gave him a lot of freelance with the ball."

Most important, the coach readily accepted the idea of using Jellybean's full range of talents, which meant using the center's dribbling and passing skills to help the guards bring the ball up the floor against the many full-court presses the team encountered.

"The first time I ever saw Joey play in the Public League, he was breaking a press," Mo Howard recalled with a laugh. "You didn't see other big men doing that. Coaches wouldn't allow it."

"JB, he gave Coach Farrell a lot of flexibility when it came to breaking the press," agreed Gilbert Saunders, who also played at Bartram. "Joe got people involved because Jack Farrell basically let him play point guard."

Farrell also gave Jellybean the proverbial green light to shoot freely.

"He never took a shot he didn't like," Simpson recalled, laughing. "He always took the deep shot from the corner. You always knew that if he had that shot, he was gonna take it."

Just about anywhere else in America, a big man jacking up shots from the corner would have found himself on the bench getting a lecture immediately. Such a shot would become a staple of basketball in the twenty-first century, but in 1972, it was considered a sign of an outrageous lack of discipline.

"Joe found in Jack Farrell someone who could contain him to get the best out of him but would give him leeway to do his thing," offered Paul Westhead, who would later do the same.

The freedom created something to behold, Mo Howard said with admiration. "Now he's unguardable for ninety-four feet, and he was unguardable at twenty-five feet. Coach Farrell knew how good Joey was. He allowed him to do whatever he needed to do to let his team win. Think about it. Every other high school team that had a six-nine guy, he was on that damn block. So now Bartram has a six-nine guy that's hardly ever on the block. And Joey, even as a young guy, he had tremendous basketball IQ. Here's a guy that could have been just stuck on himself, man. If he was just stuck on himself, he would have got 40 a game, but he wasn't. He was a team guy, he liked winning."

Even though he wasn't a selfish player, Bryant still would have his share of very big-scoring nights.

"Bartram was not a real strong team," Howard added, "but having a guy like Joey, who could do the things that he did and had the freedom to do it, made them an exceptional team. You talk about dribbling and passing the ball and having the flair to do it. He was unbelievable, man."

Bryant was a strong competitor, but with his stylish game, there were also times when it appeared he might have been a bit more interested in style points than making the simple play. It would be a perception that followed him later, into college and professional basketball.

There was some truth to the perception, said Vontez Simpson. "That's where Kobe gets it from."

The Debate

Years later, a favorite debate among the old hands of Philadelphia basketball was whether Kobe or Joe Bryant was the better high school basketball player.

More often than not, the old-timers would side with Joe, citing his size and unique skills to make the case that he was better than Kobe as a teen. Looking back on Jelly's career, Julius Thompson said that he was a twenty-first-century player.

"I love Kobe and everything, but I saw Joe in his prime," said

Thompson, who spent years writing about the game and coaching it. "Joe was six ten and could do everything Kobe could do at six six."

Plus, Joe Bryant could claim an accomplishment that his son never achieved—leading a team to the Philadelphia Public League title.

Wearing number 23, Jellybean did that in 1972, his senior year, as fans packed the school's gym to cheer him and his teammates on. Down the stretch of the season, he scored 57 points (on a school-record 26 field goals) in one game and 40 points in another. He was named the MVP of the Public League tournament after leading Bartram to victories over Gratz High (coached by a young John Chaney, right before he entered college coaching) and Germantown, led by future NBA player Mike Sojourner.

At six nine, 240 pounds, Sojourner played in a frontcourt alongside a seven-footer, making Germantown a big, strong high school team—even for the Public League—but Joe rose to the challenge, Julius Thompson recalled. "Joe just went crazy against them. He just took over, scored about 30 points that day."

Jellybean scored 30 points with 12 rebounds in the championship game, but it was the inspired play of teammate Joe "Mad Dog" Pride that boosted the late comeback for the victory.

Afterward, Joe and his father stood arm in arm, smiling for a *Tribune* photographer, their arms draped around each other's shoulders, their fingers pointing skyward, number one. Big Joe's face absolutely beamed.

High school success brought Jellybean to the full attention of the entire city, and he was ready for it, Dick Weiss recalled. "Joe had enormous personality as a high school kid. Enormous personality. He was always laughing, was always fun to be around. He was quiet, he was a gentleman, he was always happy to see you, I think a terrific ambassador for not just the Sonny Hill League but for the entire city because you couldn't help but smile when you saw him play. Everybody knew him, and everybody liked him."

"That all went back to Big Joe, who was the same way," Julius Thompson offered. "Joe could talk. People loved the nickname Jellybean. He was effervescent, lively. Very friendly."

Next up was the city-championship game that pitted the Public

League champs against the top team of the Catholic League. The Public League almost always defeated the Catholic team for the title. That year, St. Thomas More had nearly beaten Bartram in a close contest the very first game of the season. Still, many reasoned that Bartram remained an overwhelming favorite to win the trophy, due to Joe's strong play.

Most of the Catholic League teams tried to slow the game to take away the athleticism of the Public League. But the St. Thomas More team had athleticism that could play with Bartram.

"[Bartram] went in there overconfident," Vontez Simpson recalled. "They thought they were gonna roll over St. Tommy More. Oh, man, that was a heartbreaker."

Jellybean was despondent after the loss, Simpson recalled. But the MVP award in the Public League was just one of several for Bryant that season, and they came with an abundance of interest from college coaches across the country. There were so many calls to his house, Big Joe had to change his phone number.

In those days, Sonny Vaccaro, who would later gain fame as an athletic-shoe executive, was a bushy-haired middle school special-ed teacher from Pittsburgh who ran the country's elite high school all-star game each season. Called the Dapper Dan Roundball Classic, the event drew all of America's top college coaches, who came to Pennsylvania each spring get a look at the country's best high school talent.

Both Mo Howard and Jellybean were invited to play in the game. Their fathers couldn't wait to make the trip to the event. "I had a Pinto," Howard recalled of the small Ford he drove, "and I still don't know how they got their fat asses in and drove up to Pittsburgh just so they would be there for Joey and I. You're talking about two guys from down south. I know my dad didn't know who his dad was. We came from humble beginnings, man, and our dads were working stiffs, man. Us having achieved a certain amount of notoriety as young guys, that was more than the biggest paycheck our dads could get."

The profile got bigger for Big Joe Bryant that weekend. His son was named the all-star game's most valuable player, which brought Jellybean to the attention of even more colleges, much to Big Joe's consternation. The family wanted Joey to play college ball in Philly so that they could be close for his rise to fame.

The award was added to Bryant's collection of trophies at the house over on Willows Avenue, a truly impressive display, recalled Gilbert Saunders. Saunders would be selected to play in Vaccaro's game the following season. Part of the introduction for the 1973 Dapper Dan was the viewing of the film of the 1972 game in which Jellybean dominated the nation's best high school players. "That's the first time I got an idea of just how talented Joe was," Saunders said.

"Joe could literally do anything you want on the floor," Dick Weiss recalled, "and he had the ability to play all five positions. He could handle the ball, he could play inside, he had all the offensive skills. He had some Magic Johnson to his game. I'm not saying he was Magic, but he mastered all five positions. So, prior to Magic (who would come on the scene in the late seventies), Joe Bryant played the same style, where he was very good with the ball in the open floor, making plays for others but creating situations where he could really excite the crowd with the things he did."

From the writers to the coaches to opposing players, just about everybody had the opinion that Jellybean was headed for the very big time. He could have gone almost anywhere, but Jellybean also wanted to stay close to home. He understood that he was a hometown hero in Philly, he loved soaking in his local celebrity status, and he wanted to play in the city's Big Five. It came down to Temple and La Salle, and Jellybean chose La Salle because that was where one of his heroes, Kenny Durrett, had played. La Salle coach Paul Westhead deployed an open-court, up-tempo approach that looked like a lot of fun.

"La Salle had a huge reputation for producing great individual players," Dick Weiss explained. "That went all the way back back to Tom Gola in the late forties early fifties. Joe was supposed to be the next great player. In fact, 1972 was a really special year in Philadelphia high school basketball because Joe Bryant and Mike Sojourner— who ended up going to Utah—and Mo Howard were all in the same class, and they were the big three. They were the three players everybody wanted."

Paul Westhead confirmed that Joe was supposed to be their next great player. In those days, coaches really didn't find out about players until toward the end of their high school careers, Westhead explained. "I really didn't track him as a young boy at age twelve, thirteen, or fourteen. Nowadays he'd be on the radar of college coaches at an early age, like, twelve. They'd say, 'There's this kid in West Philly that can really play.' When I first got involved with Joe, he was a senior in high school. He had a marvelous natural gift. And he liked the game, so he worked at it. It wasn't like Joe was a lazy player. Not at all. 'Cause he loved the game. Basketball seemed to be who he was. He could do that. That was never a problem."

While Joe was deciding on La Salle, Mo Howard had agreed to play at the "UCLA of the East," as coach Lefty Driesell called his Maryland program.

Their decisions now made, the two basketball friends spent the spring and summer attacking the city's courts, Howard recalled with a laugh. "As high school seniors, Joe Bryant and I did almost everything together. I would pick him up after he got out of school. I would drive from my school to his school and pick him up. We'd get in the car, we'd go looking for basketball games. Man, all over the city, different rec centers, playgrounds. There were a couple of leagues out in the suburbs. We were high school seniors playing against men, and we would thrash those dudes, man. We thrashed 'em."

Explorers

What Mo and Joe could not thrash was the National Collegiate Athletic Association. The governing body of college athletics changed its academic eligibility rules yet again, this time in an effort to "predict" the academic success of incoming athletes. The new formula meant that neither Bryant nor his friend Howard would be eligible as freshmen.

Howard went off to Maryland anyway, and Joe Bryant spent a lot of time at Gilbert Saunders's house in what became a lost year. He played intramural games at La Salle and kept a heavy presence at his old haunts, the playgrounds.

Still impossibly thin as a college sophomore (he weighed less than two hundred pounds), he first played for the La Salle Explorers during the 1973–74 season and brought an immediate upgrade to the school's talent pool. Westhead, who had already gained a reputation as something of an expert on Shakespeare, presided over games with a scholarly demeanor, clothed in turtlenecks and sports jackets.

Jellybean did his part by playing the game in what amounted to a basketball version of iambic pentameter. A La Salle student publication described him as a "flamboyant genius."

"It was not just his size," Westhead remembered. "He was just a fluid player. He could flow in and out. Static he did not know. That word didn't mean anything to him. He was always moving right, left, up, down. He had a lot of bounce to his game. That would be true defensively, too. He was always looking to make a steal."

As a young coach, Westhead loved the open-court game, which meant that his team did a lot of pressing in order to do a lot of running. First off, Bryant could grab a rebound off the defensive board, and, due to his ball-handling skills, he didn't have to pass to the point guard.

"He's the kind of guy who could get a defensive rebound and go wire to wire with the ball on the dribble," Westhead explained. "In the seventies and years later, you didn't see much of that taking it the whole way."

Five years later, a six-foot-nine Magic Johnson would gain fame for that kind of skill while leading Michigan State to a national championship and then, later, driving the Lakers to five NBA titles.

In 2015, Draymond Green would help push the Golden State Warriors to win the NBA title by being a particularly strong play-making power forward who could run the fast break. But a big man with guard skills was practically unprecedented in 1974.

"Joe Bryant did that before the world knew you could do that or before you were permitted to do that," Westhead said.

Jellybean's presence helped create that quick tempo that Westhead desired. "He believed that you should totally outrun people," Julius Thompson said. "If he didn't score 50 by halftime, he'd be upset."

"Westhead was a run-and-gun coach," Gilbert Saunders offered.

Westhead phrased it another way: "I think I was able to recognize his talent, recognize how good he could be, and let him do his thing. I didn't play him as a point guard. But during the game he would evolve into doing everything. It wasn't like Joe was all over the place doing whatever he felt like. Joe was the kind of guy who could find a way to do his thing, especially when he got the ball in his hands. I tried to minimize how much half-court offense we had. I was trying to push the envelope. We always played at a pretty fast pace."

La Salle got off to a good start in November of 1973, and Mo Howard felt the urge to go see them play (in those days, before cable and widespread broadcasting, La Salle games weren't often on TV). Howard discovered that Westhead didn't seem to know where the brakes were and had almost no inclination to use them anyway. His teams were all out, the perfect style for Jellybean.

"It was B. That's how B played," Howard recalled. "For it to be a great team, Joey had to do what he does. Westhead never tried to put the cuffs on. La Salle would press up on you, full court, three-quarter court. They played very fast 'cause Joey could run with the guards. Often time he'd be the guy in the middle with the fast break."

Philadelphia's Big Five was a virtual training ground that season for NBA coaches, with Chuck Daly at Penn, Jack McKinney at St. Joe's, Don Casey at Temple, and Westhead at La Salle. The only Big Five coach who didn't move up to the NBA was Rollie Massimino at Villanova, who would reign for decades as one of the top coaches in college basketball. Bryant did his best to put on a show for all of them.

He averaged 18.7 points and led the Big Five in rebounds at 10.8 a game that first season. Big Joe was there for every home game. The next season, Jellybean upped those numbers to better than 20 points and 11 rebounds a game.

"The quest for the new season involves controlling the agile giant's immense talents," said a preview in one of La Salle's student publications.

Bryant's second college season brought lots of highlights—a

win over Atlantic Coast Conference power Clemson; an upset of sixth-ranked Alabama to win the Sugar Bowl Classic holiday tournament, which was sealed on Bryant's late tip-in; his 34 points versus Memphis State; and his game-winning shot against Chuck Daly's Penn team.

At one point, La Salle rose as high as eleventh in the national polls that season. Bryant and teammates Bill Taylor and Charlie Wise would make the All–Big Five First Team in 1975 after leading the Explorers to a 22–7 record and a regular-season league championship. But in those days, the NCAA tournament gave almost no at-large bids. The only way to make the big event was to win your conference tournament.

It was there that Jellybean left Westhead with a searing memory.

"The league championship games were at Lafayette College," Westhead remembered. "We're in the final game, and if you win you're going to go to the NCAA. We're in the final game with Lafayette College. And there's inside two minutes to go, and we're up, I want to say, seven points. Joe Bryant steals the ball and is going down for an uncontested layup to put us up nine. He goes in and jumps up as high as he could, and he slam-dunks the ball and turns with this big grin on his face. During that time, dunking was not allowed in college basketball. It was illegal."

The officials blew an immediate technical foul, wiping out the basket while awarding Lafayette two free throws and the ball. Still grinning broadly, Bryant walked over to the bench and told Westhead, "Coach, I just had to do it."

"So a seven-point game goes to a four-point game," Westhead recalled forty years later, still with the trace of disbelief in his voice. "I was stunned. I can't say that I jumped up and patted him on the back and said, 'Joe, you're my man.' I didn't yell at him. I was in shock. He knew exactly what he was doing. And I can say he probably calculated, 'I've been waiting all year to do this, and we're going to win this game, so, so what?'"

The moment encapsulated Jellybean's career for Westhead. "In that game he probably had 20-some points, a lot of rebounds," the coach said. "I still remember him stealing the ball and driving the length, because nobody was in thirty feet of him."

La Salle held on for the win and took on highly regarded Syracuse in a first-round game at the Palestra, in Philadelphia. Joe Bryant had an outstanding game, but he missed a game-winning shot with three seconds to go, and the Explorers lost in overtime. Syracuse went on to reach the Final Four of the tournament.

After the season, Jellybean announced he was declaring hardship and entering the NBA draft that spring. Westhead knew the timing was right.

"In retrospect Joe Bryant was the first six-foot-nine point guard in America," the coach said. "But at that time no one thought of players of that size as point guards or ball handlers and people that had those kinds of skills. In fact, many people who saw Joe play thought that he had too much juice, that he did too many things, that he should have toned down his game befitting a forward and not act like he was a point guard."

Westhead heard the criticism from scouts and other coaches, but he didn't agree. To Westhead, the string-bean Jelly was a force to be deployed. And the coach agreed that his best player was ready for pro basketball.

With the love of those Philly crowds ringing in his ears, Joe Bryant was sure he was headed for the big time. That there might be another outcome was a thought that hardly crossed his mind.

Chapter 4

PAM AND JELLY

It was during his years at La Salle that Joe Bryant fell under the sway of a striking, statuesque young woman named Pam Cox, much to her father's dismay.

"Pam Cox could have been a lawyer or something," remarked John Smallwood, the longtime *Philadelphia Daily News* sports columnist. "Instead, she wound up with crazy Joe Bryant."

That pretty much summed up the viewpoint of her father, John Cox II. He apparently couldn't stand the thought of his daughter taking up with Jellybean. Family members recall him asking how that guy would be able to support her and the lifestyle she was used to.

"She could have done anything she wanted," agreed Dick Weiss. "She had the look of a runway model, a beautiful girl. I'm sure [her father] expected her to marry a doctor or a lawyer," Weiss said. "He never expected her to marry a pro basketball player from Southwest Philadelphia."

Yet their pairing would merge two deep basketball gene pools. Pam's brother, John Arthur Cox III, nicknamed Chubby, was a high school All-American guard who later played college ball at Villanova and the University of San Francisco. And Joe was already making his way to the NBA.

Yet neither Joe nor Chubby could provide the key personality element that would make Kobe Bryant one of the game's all-time great competitors.

"That killer, that killer, is Pam Cox, man," explained Mo Howard with a laugh, an opinion repeated time and again among the couple's friends. "She's a beautiful woman, but there's a side to her that's cold-blooded killer."

Pam Cox also had uncommon personal discipline, another key trait she would instill in her son.

"She's the one who made Joe walk the straight and narrow," said Vontez Simpson. "Joe's like a big kid. You couldn't do nothing but like him."

Some friends said it was no coincidence that once Pam and Joe got together, Bryant's coach found him to be more focused and under control as a junior. Westhead laughed at the notion. "Because they started dating did he stop putting the ball behind his back?" the coach asked. "No, I didn't notice that. I'm only kidding. I knew, in meeting her, you could tell she was a good person and therefore she was going to be helpful to Joe."

To some observers, the pairing seemed improbable. First of all, the families were very different. Whereas the Bryants were relatively late arrivals in the city, refugees from Georgia who found themselves immediately locked into financial straits, the Coxes were an older Philadelphia family, the kind whose weddings and social events could be found in the pages of the *Philadelphia Tribune*, one of the oldest African American newspapers in the country.

The original John Cox, who was married in 1933, was a pillar of the St. Ignatius Parish, an old-line institution in West Philadelphia that had served German immigrants since its founding in the 1890s. Cox had been involved in the Holy Savior Parish, which was founded in 1924 as a Catholic worship community for African Americans in West Philly. But the area's German-speaking population had experienced a marked decline, and by 1928, the white St. Ignatius congregation had approached Holy Savior about a merger.

From that union, St. Ignatius soon grew into a strong parish with an ambitious community agenda, with a school and a nursing home among its initiatives. John Cox Sr. stepped into the role as manager of the St. Ignatius thrift store, the profits from which provided major funding for the nursing home and other programs. By

the 1950s, the thrift store was so strong—and so well run by Cox—
that the parish required no extra funding from the Philadelphia
Archdiocese, the *Tribune* reported.

The influx of African American migrants created an array of
social and racial tensions across the city over the decades, but St.
Ignatius would serve as an integrating factor in the face of conflict.
A sign of that perhaps came in 1956 when, after years of being
left out, John Arthur Cox Sr. was finally selected as one of the first
blacks admitted to the Knights of Columbus, a charitable and social
fraternity of the faith. The lack of integration in the local lodge had
long been an item of contention in the congregation, although Cox
seemed to downplay that while professing a fundamental optimism in an interview with the *Tribune*.

"There is nothing hard about joining the organization or staying
in it," he said of the Knights of Columbus. "We know there is some
animosity in some people's hearts, but it is being beaten down
every day."

His son, John Arthur Cox Jr., would gain notice in the late forties
and early fifties for his prowess as a boxer and for playing basketball on community teams, but it remained very much an era of limited opportunity for young blacks. Instead of going to college, the
junior Cox went into the service.

By 1953, he was a twenty-year-old U.S. Army private who had
returned home from training for a quick wedding to Mildred Williams, a seventeen-year-old beauty, in a 7:30 a.m. Mass at St. Ignatius that was reported in the *Tribune*. The wedding was so hasty
that there was no time for a reception. The couple said vows at the
breakfast ceremony, and Private Cox then hustled off to Alaska to
serve in the military police.

John Arthur "Chubby" Cox III would be their first child, soon
followed by sister Pam.

Once his military duty was completed, John Cox II returned to
Philadelphia and began a career in the city's fire department as it
struggled through the first years of a difficult, often ugly attempt to
integrate. He would rise through the harsh years of the Rizzo
administration to become one of the early black fire lieutenants in
the department, no small feat in itself.

He exuded that certain Philly toughness. "Mr. Cox, he was a city guy," Mo Howard explained. "He grew up in West Philly. He never had a silver spoon in his mouth or anything like that. Between him and his wife, they afforded quite a lifestyle for Pam and Chub. When I first met Chubby and Pam, they lived in Fairmount Park, which is the largest urban park in the world. So to have a house near Fairmount Park, that's an accomplishment, especially for black people."

The area, loosely known as Parkside, marked a profound difference from the section of West Philly where John Cox had grown up, Howard said. "It was better than down in the bottom. For Mr. and Mrs. Cox, I guess, growing up that way gave them the drive and motivation to have the success they did."

There have been depictions of John Cox II as a difficult, often condescending man, divisive even within his own family. Gail Williams, a close relative of Mildred Williams Cox, wrote a fictional account of the family of a basketball star that painted an unflattering portrait of characters that represented both Pam Cox and her father. Family friends in interviews confirmed some difficult elements of the personalities of father and daughter, yet many acquaintances also talked of the redeeming qualities as well.

One curiosity of their circumstances was that Big Joe Bryant, a man of very limited means, was quoted and photographed with great frequency in the local papers, while John Arthur Cox II—a man of accomplishment and rank in the city fire department—was seemingly never quoted or photographed, despite the fact that he was the parent of a noteworthy son, son-in-law, and grandson. It was almost as if he studiously avoided public notice.

Basketball Love

John Cox may have disliked his daughter's taking up with Jellybean, but it would be a union that lasted for decades and produced three high-achieving children. The Pam and Jelly story itself would become a central and defining element in the life of their famous son, from his upbringing to the intense conflict that later marked all of their lives.

Pam would recall that she first became aware of Joe as a child because their grandparents lived close to one another. At that time, Jellybean was certainly not someone she was interested in, she once told a reporter.

"Joe always knew Pam through Chubby," Gilbert Saunders explained. Her brother and Joe Bryant both had easygoing personalities and immense talent. Jelly and Chubby liked each other and saw the world in much the same way as young players.

Chubby was a year behind Jellybean and Mo Howard in school, and they often competed against him and with him, too, Howard recalled. "Chubby's whole thing was, 'I want to be good like you guys. Whatever you guys are doing, that's what I want to do.' To do that, you gotta get buckets, man. Joey had one of the highest averages in the Public League; Chubby was one of those guys right below him in scoring. Chubby was a class behind us. Chubby was a very, very good player."

He played with a noticeable air of confidence. Years later, Howard would watch a young Kobe Bryant and be reminded of Pam's brother. "Early in Kobe's career, that swag was Chubby Cox," Howard said.

One unusual factor that seemed to catch everyone's attention was how much Pam Cox doted on her brother. "In her eyes, Chubby could do no wrong," Vontez Simpson recalled.

In time, it became clear that Chubby Cox was spoiled by doting parents and a doting sister, to the point that his father sought out Sonny Hill for help in dealing with the issue.

"The Cox family turned him over to me," Sonny Hill recalled. "Chubby came from an upper-class family. He was sort of spoiled to a large degree, and his family turned him over to me in my league. I became a huge part of Chubby's life in terms of structure, discipline, and basketball."

It wasn't just swag and style that Chubby Cox shared with his nephew Kobe. It was also that both were the favorites, constantly fawned upon by family members.

Chubby and Pam started out in Philadelphia, attending Overbrook High School, but the family purchased a home off the Main Line in the city's Parkside suburbs, which meant that Pam and

Chubby switched to Roxborough High, a school with an uneven basketball tradition, where Chubby could readily ascend as a star.

The Coxes purchased a suburban home that had been owned by Muhammad Ali. It included a pool and a pool house and was quite exclusive, a property the family could afford with John Cox's rank in the fire department and his wife Mildred's employment with the federal government.

"The Coxes were hardworking people who were able to afford their children a great lifestyle," Mo Howard observed. "They didn't think they were better than anybody. They treated everybody the same. When I met them, they were doing quite well."

Some thought that Chubby's family home and his attractive sister provided a draw for Jellybean, to the point that he found time to visit the Cox household frequently. Yet Mo Howard disagreed. "I don't think any of the attractions of material success swayed Joey. Joey was the same guy when he didn't have it and when he did have it. Their house had all the amenities. And Joey just went with it, you know? That stuff didn't define what Joey was."

Meanwhile, Mr. Cox gained a reputation as someone who disliked having people hanging around, swimming in his pool.

It wasn't just the pool that John Cox was guarding. "Mr. Cox didn't want just anybody coming up in the house to eat dinner with the family and date his daughter," Gilbert Saunders said.

Pam Cox herself once recalled that her feelings for Jellybean surfaced one night when her brother's Villanova team played La Salle. The families were on opposite sides of the court, and when she got up to go over and greet Big Joe Bryant, she discovered that Jellybean was headed in the opposite direction to say hello to her parents. It was one of those moments, she explained later.

Pam had been attending college in Pittsburgh and doing well when she abruptly transferred to Villanova before the start of her junior year. She later said Joe wasn't the reason she returned to Philadelphia, but the very fact that she had to explain that only seemed to raise more questions, not to mention her father's concerns.

By then, Jellybean was doing well at La Salle, but to outsiders he still seemed to lack direction. "Joe was a diamond in the rough," Gilbert Saunders explained. "Pam polished him up. JB wasn't the first choice of her father. But he was open to being polished. Pam polished him up. Pam made a statement by becoming his wife."

At some point, Jelly and Pam decided to move in together into an apartment, Saunders recalled. "They lived in a tiny little apartment in Germantown when she could have stayed home in luxury with her parents in that comfortable house on City Line Avenue. She loved him enough to accept him for what he was, regardless of her father."

It helped ease the tension a little when Jellybean was drafted by Golden State, the fourteenth overall selection of the first round of the NBA draft that June. The Warriors had just won the NBA championship and were coached by Al Attles, a tough-minded guard who had played pro ball for the old Philadelphia Warriors with Wilt Chamberlain. It seemed like a perfect spot for Jellybean to begin his career.

The Bryant family was excited, and Attles would later recall that he was quite eager to coach Joe Bryant. But apparently, the team's early discussions with agent Richie Phillips didn't go well. The Warriors were thinking in the neighborhood of $100,000 per year. Phillips wasn't going to have that.

As the summer moved along, the Warriors were strangely silent about the contract. During that period of uncertainty, Pam and Joe got married. Soon enough, friends learned she was pregnant.

"It seemed they had been together for just a minute," Vontez Simpson recalled. "Things happen."

For decades, weddings in the Cox family had been formal affairs, all detailed later in the society pages of the *Tribune*. But Pam and Jellybean were married quietly at the home of Virgil Davis, a friend who lived in West Philly. It was a very small affair that wasn't accompanied by paid notice in the *Tribune*.

The Contract

In those days, teams were required to submit a contract offer to their draft picks by early September. If teams failed to do that, they lost the rights to the pick, and the player was allowed to become a free agent.

"If you didn't send that contract, you lost rights to him," recalled Pat Williams, who was the general manager of the Philadelphia 76ers at the time. "You lost the player. And so one day I get a call from Richie Phillips, a former assistant district attorney in Philadelphia who represented some athletes and also the Major League Baseball umpire's union. Richie and I were friends. He was Jellybean's agent."

Phillips asked Williams about the contract rule and told him that they hadn't heard anything from the Warriors.

Williams was stunned. To lose the rights to a first-round draft pick was a major blunder. Franklin Mieuli, the owner of the Warriors — which moved to California from Philadelphia in 1962 — had a close relationship with the ownership of the Sixers. Williams knew the Sixers would not want to embarrass Mieuli, so he suggested that they wait a few days to see if the contract arrived.

A few days later, Phillips phoned again and told Williams that they still didn't have a contract. Phillips had also approached the New York Knicks, who also quickly expressed interest.

Williams went to Sixers owner Irv Kosloff and apprised him of the situation: no offer had come from Warriors executive Dick Vertlieb.

"Ohhh, I hate to do this to Franklin," Kosloff told Williams, who replied, "Well, somebody's going to get him, Kos, somebody's going to end up getting Joe Bryant. A pretty good young player, and you know he wants to sign with us and stay in Philadelphia."

Meanwhile, Sixers assistant coach Jack McMahon had just seen Jellybean perform brilliantly during his time in the Baker League. The coaching staff was in favor of signing him.

The Sixers were just two years removed from their disastrous 1973 season, when they went 9–73, the NBA's all-time worst record. Under coach Gene Shue they had steadily rebuilt themselves, but they needed all the young players they could get.

"So we started negotiating," Williams said.

As a free agent, Jellybean Bryant now had leverage. "We thought he was going to be a star," Williams explained. "We were after talent. Joe was a young hero in Philly. He had the advantage of a tough negotiator in Richie Phillips. Richie had an absolute bonanza fall right in his lap."

The 76ers already had two fascinating draft picks of their own that season, eighteen-year-old Darryl Dawkins and twenty-one-year-old Lloyd Free (soon to become World B. Free). Dawkins, the number five pick in the draft, had signed a seven-year deal for $1.4 million that paid him a little more than $100,000 a year on the front end.

Joe Bryant, the fourteenth pick in the draft, was given a three-year deal worth $900,000, paying him $300,000 each season.

Just two years earlier the Chicago Bulls were paying veteran Tom Boerwinkle $45,000 per year and struggling with the thought of paying fan favorite Jerry Sloan $60,000, recalled Williams, who had come to Philadelphia after serving as the Bulls GM.

"At the time, it was a big bite," Williams said. "We began to work the deal out and got it resolved, and the next thing you know, we signed him and had a press conference. This was a big deal in Philly. The local college phenom was suddenly a member of the Philadelphia 76ers."

At his home on Willows Avenue, Big Joe got the family together. All his support of his son's basketball had paid off in ways he'd never imagined. "That night he signed with the 76ers we all cried and prayed together," the father later recalled.

Thereafter, Jellybean would declare that his play in Sonny Hill's Baker League had earned him an extra $800,000, a declaration that Sonny Hill would repeat many times over the ensuing decades.

The loss of a first-round draft pick presented the Warriors with a huge blow. NBA teams live by their ability to develop young talent. Though the folding of the American Basketball Association the following season would create an abundance of available players, the loss of a first-round pick in an administrative oversight was a blunder the team was not eager to disclose. Thus, for years the circumstances would be misrepresented as a trade.

"I don't even know what the Sixers gave us for Joe Bryant," Al Attles would later say obliquely. "Dick Vertlieb handled it. I wanted Joe."

Despite Joe's big contract, the times would prove quite precarious for pro basketball players. On top of the loss of the ABA teams, the NBA further trimmed its team rosters by one player, making the elimination of jobs even worse for players.

The timing and circumstances had seemed almost perfect for Joe Bryant, coming out of La Salle. If he didn't already have huge expectations, the giant contract told him he was expected to be an instant star.

"We had fallen upon an arsenal of young talent," Pat Williams said, looking back.

"It was an embarrassment of riches," Dick Weiss said of the Philly roster.

Basketball fans in Philadelphia held Jellybean as their favorite son, and they celebrated knowing that one of their own was now a Sixer.

"Everybody was thrilled, man," Mo Howard recalled. "Joey's going to be in Philly, he's going to be a Sixer. We just knew there was somebody on that team that he was going to put on the bench. There was somebody who was going to have to sit because of Joey."

The situation immediately raised a question. Just whom might Jelly replace?

Chapter 5

THE BOMB SQUAD

In the minds of both Paul Westhead and Mo Howard, Joe Bryant was top-notch talent for the NBA. But adding Jellybean to the mix made for a strange roster for the Sixers, with a starting lineup of hard-nosed veterans with a brace of very young reserves.

Playing in front of Bryant were excellent veteran forwards Billy Cunningham, Steve Mix, and George McGinnis. The rookies were all young, inexperienced, and wildly inconsistent. Consequently, they saw limited action at first.

The young talent off the bench—Free, Dawkins, and Bryant— would come to be known as the Bomb Squad, for their predilection for firing away from anywhere on the court. Having been a local favorite for years, Bryant clearly had stars in his eyes, and his first NBA season brought a rude awakening.

"Joe got his minutes here and there," Pat Williams remembered. "It was hard for him to get the playing time he wanted. He was colorful as a ball handler. He was a showman, and he had that great nickname. I remember many a night he would be out there, having the crowd roaring. I'm not sure the coaches appreciated it, but he was absolutely a showman. That was always the sense with him."

The coach was Gene Shue. "He was a veteran who had been through the mill," Williams said. "We had suddenly presented him with this arsenal of young players."

Like most coaches in that era, Shue was not known as a teacher.

It was not part of the job description, as it would be in the twenty-first century, when NBA teams routinely began taking on younger players. In 1975, pro basketball remained the domain of grown men.

"Gene was a veteran basketball guy, expected his players to know what they were doing," Pat Williams said. "He was an old pro himself. He'd been coaching for years. Coaching those great Bullets teams. Gene was Gene. His approach was, 'Here's how the game should be played.' He expected them to do it."

The Sixers had discovered Darryl Dawkins at a Florida high school, stashed him away before the draft, then paid him to turn pro, one of the first cases of a player going directly from high school into the NBA (though a year earlier Moses Malone had gone from high school into the ABA).

"Shue had a stable full of young players, all of whom wanted the ball, wanted minutes," Williams said, "and it was hard to get them minutes. We've got Joe, we've got Darryl, we've got World B. Free, all trying to get to play enough. It was quite a scene, the '75 to '76 76ers. It was definitely an adventure."

With Bryant playing inconsistent minutes, the writers for the *Tribune*, the paper serving the African American community, seemed furious that Shue didn't use him more.

"We were perplexed," Mo Howard said of Bryant's collection of friends and basketball buddies, "because we couldn't see how come nobody else could figure out who Joey was as a basketball player. People would go to games just to see Joey, you know what I'm sayin'? I used to go watch Joey play, man. Understand that I've always seen him play the way that he played. He'd be on the perimeter; you'd see a behind-the-back pass. He'd get the hook from the coach. He's running the break, he'd catch the ball, like, fifteen or twenty feet from the basket, and he'd pull up and shoot the jump shot. If he missed it, he got the hook. You know, we weren't used to seeing that happen in Philly."

Suddenly Jellybean's local following became something of a burden. Everywhere he went, Bryant would have to try to explain why he wasn't playing, which was hard because he didn't understand it himself. For the first time in his life, he found himself on the outside looking in on the game he loved. He wore his frustrations on his sleeve.

"We would just go to see Joey play, and not being able to see him, as we say, 'get off' the way we knew he could—it was frustrating for us, too," Mo Howard explained. "Especially with him being a Philly guy, especially at home. He was a six-nine perimeter player who could make plays and shoot the basketball. He was a constant team player. He didn't do any of this stuff selfishly; he did everything he had to do to help his team win. That's who Joey was. Now, granted, he did it with a little more flair than some of the guards."

Both Shue's fondness for Bryant and his frustration with the circumstances were still evident in an interview forty years later.

"Joe played some minutes, but all these players were young kids at the time," Shue recalled. "They wanted to play more, and the minutes just weren't there for them. I always liked Joe Bryant. I liked World B. Free, but again, they were just very, very young kids. I think Darryl might have been eighteen and Joe was probably twenty and World B. Free was probably nineteen. There just weren't the minutes available for Joe to really excel, so he got limited minutes coming off the bench."

Soon the Sixers found themselves with a media problem, then a community-relations problem, all while trying to rebuild after 1973, the disastrous season that transformed the atmosphere for pro basketball in the city's arena, the Spectrum, into a mausoleum. Shue was brought in to turn the team around on the court, but the fans wanted to see Bryant in action.

"In '73 there were no writers," the coach recalled. "There was no coverage, there were no fans. We played for, like, a handful of fans. It was the worst team in the history of the game."

Shue boosted the win total to twenty-five in his first season, thirty-four in his second, and was in the process of coaching the team to forty-six wins and a play-off berth in Bryant's rookie year. With the success, the media had returned to covering the games, he said. "Now all of a sudden these writers started crawling back. All of a sudden now we're a team. And they're crawling back."

Beat writers covering the team later recalled Dawkins, Free, and Bryant all pushing for stories to be written about their lack of playing time.

"I don't blame the players at all," Shue recalled, still with strong feelings forty years later. "I blame the writers because they were looking for negative stories every day about why you're not playing. They'd get with Darryl, get with Joe, and they'd get with World B. Free. And these players were showing their frustration because they weren't playing. They wrote some things about the team, some dissension things. The players, all they wanted was more time."

There was hope Jellybean's presence might help to ease an age-old problem for pro basketball in the city, one that began when the Philadelphia Warriors won the title in the NBA's first season with a white jump shooter out of Kentucky named Jumpin' Joe Fulks. They won the title again in 1956, again with white stars, in particular Paul Arizin, Neil Johnston, and Tom Gola, who was one of several players on the team from Philadelphia. "They never really were able to connect with the North Philly crowd, with the black community, and they had these fabulous players," Dick Weiss explained.

They later added Wilt Chamberlain, in the early sixties, which helped them fill seats, Weiss added. "And those old Philly Warriors with Wilt, Arizin, and Gola, they were bigger than life. People in Philadelphia today will still say Wilt was the best ever to play in the league."

Even though they had success on the court, the Warriors were sold off to the West Coast after the 1962 season, in which Chamberlain had averaged an ungodly 50.4 points and 25.7 rebounds. That March, Wilt the Stilt, the ultimate favorite son of Philadelphia, scored 100 points in a game, and the team reached the conference finals in the play-offs.

To move the Warriors after such a great season, wrote *Philadelphia Inquirer* columnist Frank Fitzpatrick, was "a sting as sharp as death's. And while healing came with time, wisdom did not. I didn't understand the move then, and, fifty-three years later, I still don't."

Longtime Philadelphia Warriors owner Eddie Gottlieb took his rationale for the move with him to his grave in 1979. At the time they were sold, the Warriors had the fifth-best attendance in what was then just a nine-team league, about 5,500 people per game (which indicates how different a presence the NBA had in that era).

In the wake of the Warriors' departure, the Syracuse Nationals moved to Philadelphia and became the 76ers, who reacquired Chamberlain and won the NBA title with him in 1967, only to trade him to the Lakers a year later.

To say the least, being a pro basketball fan in the city was a torturous, up-and-down experience, and the Sixers hoped to shore up the fan base by showcasing some native Philly talent. But since he didn't play much, Jellybean's tenure with the team frustrated fans even more, Weiss explained. "That's why Philadelphia really shied away for the longest time from drafting Philadelphia-born players. Because they figured that if the Philly guys didn't play, you couldn't win with the fans. Because all of the fan base would come and wonder why the Philly guy wasn't playing. And that's what happened with Joe."

Much of the team's trouble on the court that first season stemmed, as Shue said, from the youth, lack of experience, and inconsistency of all three talented rookies. Rookies are often given time to adjust to the speed of the NBA, but the organization was under pressure from fans and the media to get Joe in the game.

The *Philadelphia Tribune*—a key media outlet in the team's hopes of pulling fans from the community—let it be known that it wasn't happy with how Joe Bryant was being received just weeks into his rookie season.

SHUE PLAYING POLITICS WITH JOE BRYANT'S FUTURE, the paper declared on December 13, 1975.

What complicated the situation even further were common opinions about "showboat" players in that age of basketball. When the NBA was all white in the 1940s, the league struggled to sell tickets, but then it found some success by pairing NBA games with Harlem Globetrotter games. That alone has long been credited with allowing the league to survive its lean early seasons.

As the NBA became a bit more established, the all-white Minneapolis Lakers and the all-black Globetrotters battled in a series of straight-up basketball games in the 1940s and '50s, games that were sometimes contentious. Given the racial climate in America at the time, it's understandable that the situation fostered both understanding and animosity between the races.

Even the act of dunking was disputed within the ethos of that era. Jim Pollard, the athletic star of the Minneapolis Lakers, once explained that white players who could dunk were loath to do so because it was considered "showboating," or showing up the opposition.

And, while the Globetrotters offered plenty of showtime entertainment with fancy ball handling and comedy routines that thrilled fans, they, too, did little dunking in the era just after World War II. It simply wasn't part of the game.

Over time, the debate about showboating would prove far more complicated than mere race, however. One of the the greatest showboat players in the history of the game, Pistol Pete Maravich, came to the Atlanta Hawks as a rookie in 1970, signed to a $2-million contract even as the team was refusing to give veteran stars such as Lenny Wilkens and Joe Caldwell modest raises on their salaries, which were less than $100,000 a year.

Richie Guerin, the coach of the Hawks, had a reputation for years as one of the NBA's hard-nosed competitors, and he built the Hawks into a winning team with gritty play. "Pete's style of play offended me as a coach and our players," Guerin said in 1992, looking back on the two seasons he coached Maravich for the Hawks.

Those attitudes remained prevalent in 1976, which played into how Jellybean's flashy style was received. But before he could even get a chance to showboat, Bryant had to get on the court.

In January, team star Billy Cunningham suffered a knee injury, which opened up playing time for Bryant. In keeping with his showboat antics, Bryant had shown a penchant for attacking the baskets with soaring dunks that embarrassed opposing centers. He did that in early January over Milwaukee Bucks seven-footer Elmore Smith, pumping his fist in celebration.

His energy was palpable. "I just want to play so bad," he told the *Delaware County Times.* "That's the thing that's keepin' me in there. Every chance I get I'm in there playin' my heart out."

"Joe Bryant is a real pro player," Shue told reporters that night. "His biggest development has been his overall confidence. In the earlier part of the year he was struggling because he couldn't get his game together. That was partly because I had him on a string, running in and out of games."

By February, Bryant told incredulous reporters that he was still holding out hope for Rookie of the Year honors.

"I have set that honor as my goal." He wouldn't achieve it. Alvan Adams would claim the award by averaging better than 19 points and 9 rebounds while helping the Phoenix Suns to an NBA championship-series appearance that spring. Over the regular season, Jellybean appeared in seventy-five games, averaging sixteen minutes, 7.4 points, and 3.7 rebounds, solid enough numbers for a rookie but not enough to match Bryant's and the community's expectations. Bryant would not even make the All-Rookie Team, although the *Tribune* would declare him its Rookie of the Year and Best Freshman Forward in an April story, another indication of the community's affection for its favorite son.

The Sixers finished the regular season with forty-six wins and took on the Buffalo Braves in a best-of-three-games first-round series. Bryant played little in the first game, a loss, then scored 12 points in a Game 2 victory that evened the series.

On the eve of Game 3, the *Tribune* ran a story about Pam, MRS. J. B., A LADY AT 20. That the newspaper did a story on the wife of a player who didn't have much influence on the Sixers' play-off hopes indicated the level of celebrity that the Bryants enjoyed in the community.

"Joey and I talk an awful lot about ball," she told the paper, adding that she understood it was her job to encourage him and help keep him mentally ready, despite his frustrations.

Pam told the *Tribune* that she and her husband didn't have much time for dealing with family. Her parents lived nearby. She and Joe had lived with them for a time, until the newlyweds purchased a nice home not far away, in Lower Merion, in the city's rich suburbs. They didn't get back to Southwest Philly often, she said, adding that Big Joe still would phone often to check on her, first during her pregnancy, then to hear about new granddaughter Sharia after she was born, in March.

Despite the frustrations of the season, the Bryants' house had quickly become quite a haven, recalled Mo Howard. "It was a beautiful house. That's where we'd go after the games. Sit around and watch TV. Play music and eat and stuff. And in the off-season, we'd go over there. We'd work out in the daytime, go over there and hang out, because, you know, they were one of the few people that we knew that had central air in those days."

The day after the story ran, the Sixers lost the deciding game to the Braves, 124–123. Jellybean fouled out after scoring 9 points.

The Trial

Three weeks after the season, Jellybean's life was upended by his flight from the police and the subsequent wreck and arrest. It was an astounding and devastating development for many people, from Big Joe to Sonny Hill to Bryant's many friends and fans. Most devastated of all was Jellybean himself.

"He was absolutely just frantic," former Sixers GM Pat Williams recalled. "He saw the worst. His career was over, and he was going to be disgraced in his hometown. It was just a nightmare for him."

It wasn't uncommon in that era for drug offenders to go right into prison on a first offense, often for lengthy sentences. Beyond that was the public safety issue. Joe Bryant had sped around the city with his lights out, fleeing police, and caused substantial property damage. Add that to the cocaine, and a judge could throw the book at him, make an example.

His wife, Pam, immediately spoke to a *Trib* reporter and vowed that she would stand by her husband "to the end."

Some thought the situation would send John Cox into apoplexy, but the Cox family had already encountered legal troubles in August of 1974, when Chubby had been charged in a very public purse-snatching incident that left him facing a variety of felony charges. He had been driving around with a group of friends in his car when he suggested that one of them jump out and snatch a woman's purse. Chubby would later swear that he was joking, but the incident quickly blew up into reporters knocking at the door of the family's house to write nightmarish news stories in all the Philadelphia papers.

Richie Phillips, the former prosecutor who would become Joe's agent a year later, had represented Chubby Cox on those charges and eventually got them all cleared. The young guard was able to transfer to the University of San Francisco and become a star there, playing alongside Bill Cartwright.

With Joe's legal disaster, Phillips emerged as quite comfortable in the dual roles of agent and defense attorney. The lawyer confidently announced to reporters that his client would be exonerated on all charges, which was somewhat astounding, considering the mountain of evidence against him.

The preliminary hearing was scheduled for early June, which generally meant that the prosecution would air its evidence to send the case to a grand jury for indictment. At this stage in the process, the defense never put on evidence.

But, as a former prosecutor, Phillips wanted to speed up the process. He planned to provide evidence for the defense at the preliminary hearing, a public-relations move that was highly unusual.

Despite the harsh sentences being handed down routinely for drug charges, cocaine wasn't considered a particularly serious drug in 1976. Although the drug had been around for ages, the South American drug cartels had been able to gain access to the American markets during the decade and began flooding the country with the powder, which was hip and instantly popular among the well-to-do in the age of disco.

The American Psychological Association had yet to declare that the drug was addictive, and it seemed to turn up everywhere in the culture, especially in an NBA in which the changing salary structure provided the players with plenty of disposable cash.

By 1976, a number of players were putting that disposable cash "up their noses," according to the vernacular of the times. Soon, the NBA would gain a reputation for drug abuse.

"Everybody was using," recalled Sonny Vaccaro, the shoe executive. "And I mean everybody. The whole culture in the NBA was drugs in those years."

Pete Newell, then the GM of the Lakers, recalled in a 1992 interview that the seventies were a low, low time for the league, with the distinctive odor of pot smoke thick in the hallways of team hotels, and cadres of women stalking the players and creating an atmosphere of sexual frivolity. Cocaine was considered an aphrodisiac, if the atmosphere wasn't already enough of one.

Many players became sex addicts, former Laker Lou Hudson explained in 1992. "They were eaten up with it."

Newell said that team executives just didn't know what to do about the situation in a time when the league itself had no real drug policy. With Los Angeles serving as something of a ground zero for the counterculture, the Lakers took to employing off-duty vice detectives from the LAPD to track the movements of players.

That tactic hardly slowed the cocaine train. Ron Carter, a rookie out of the Virginia Military Institute, came to the Lakers in 1978 and recalled an eye-opening party at an L.A. club thrown for Kareem Abdul-Jabbar by two well-known actors who were super-fans, in which bowls of coke mysteriously appeared on the tables.

"Keep in mind that we knew nothing about this stuff," explained Pat Williams. "I remember, we would hear these reports, these rumors, and none of us in the front office had a clue. I mean, we had no idea what was going on. So I remember picking up the paper one day and reading that Joe Bryant had been arrested in Fairmount Park."

Philadelphia was one of many teams finding themselves caught up in the rapidly changing popular culture. The Jellybean case would be among the first that would bring the problem into the public spotlight.

"There were a lot of people in Philly who were worried about him, because they liked him and they didn't want to see him go south," explained Dick Weiss, who was covering the 76ers during that era. "The NBA was filled with it. I was always amazed no one was stopped on plane trips into these cities to play games. They used to carry it right with them.

"Players were never open to talking with the writers about it, he said. "It never occurred to us to make a big deal out of it. Now if this happened, it would probably be all over the media. Then, it was part of the culture."

Even so, Bryant's arrest had made the newswires. The incident had left him nearly inconsolable, but, in addition to having Richie Phillips as his lawyer, he had another huge force working for him—his relationship with Sonny Hill, whose league was populated with parole officers and other officials of the courts.

Gilbert Saunders explained that Hill wasn't about to lose one of the players he had rescued from Philadelphia's streets. The strange nature of Bryant's preliminary hearing confirmed that.

Jellybean arrived in courtroom 285 at city hall wearing a solemn look and a fine suit with a loosely knotted tie. He was toting his darling, wide-eyed baby daughter, Sharia, in a frilly hat. Pam, her hair now in a short, pixie style, strode in to his right in a sleek pantsuit, hardly looking as if she was two months removed from pregnancy. Their representatives flanked the couple down the courtroom aisle. Richie Phillips wore a three-piece and sunglasses.

Phillips had lined up twenty character witnesses to speak on Bryant's behalf, an unheard-of tactic in a preliminary hearing. The list included Bryant's coach and the team's GM. The team had just been sold, but longtime owner Irv Kosloff had immense affection for Jellybean and showed up to speak on his behalf, as did his track coach, the Reverend Eugene Festus, a former member of the famed Harlem Hellfighters of World War I and a Philadelphia legend in his own right.

The prosecution had an abundance of evidence, but in the hearing of the *Commonwealth v. Joseph Washington Bryant III*, Judge J. Earl Simmons quickly ruled that there was no probable cause for police to have searched Bryant's vehicle. It was an astounding ruling, considering Bryant's actions that night a month earlier.

The judge told Bryant: "I expect you to live a straight life from here on. You hold a high position in the community and I expect you to live up to it.... You are an idol among Philadelphia's youngsters. I would hope you continue to earn that idolatry."

"The ball club stood by him," Pat Williams recalled. "He was broken, very relieved and grateful. I think that scared the wits out of him."

BRYANT GOT OFF EASY, the *Delaware County Times* declared the next day in a headline, a sentiment shared by local media.

Jellybean should have at least been given a slap on the wrist, they said. As it was, he "got off with little more than a scolding," said the *Times*.

There would be no punishment, not officially, but the specter of the incident would follow Bryant throughout his career. Jellybean would come to believe he was faced with the worst sort of punishment, one from which there was almost no parole.

Still, over time it would become apparent that the courtroom decision had preserved the family. If not for a lenient judge, Joe Bryant could easily have gone to prison, and there likely would be no Kobe Bean Bryant. Los Angeles Lakers fans would likely never have had the megawatt presence of the one who would name himself the Black Mamba.

PART II

PRODIGY

Chapter 6

KOBE BEAN

The 76ers ran off to a 14–1 winning streak in November of 1977. They blasted the Celtics in Boston, 121–112, the Friday before Thanksgiving, then caught a flight back to Philly for two games over three days and notched another pair of wins, on Saturday against Milwaukee and on Tuesday against Houston, before loading up early Wednesday to make a game that night in Detroit, followed by another flight on Turkey Day itself.

Somewhere in the midst of that hectic schedule, Joe and Pam Bryant found the time to conceive their third child. Sharia was born in 1976, and their second daughter, Shaya, in 1977. And then, exactly nine months after that Sixers pre-Thanksgiving home stand, their first and only male child made his appearance on the planet, on August 23, 1978, right after Joe had concluded another successful summer in the Baker League.

The Bryant family line ran back through three Josephs. The Coxes likewise had a succession of three Johns. But Pam and Joe elected to name their son Kobe, supposedly because during Pam's pregnancy they had a scrumptious meal at a Japanese steak house in nearby King of Prussia, Pennsylvania. Actually, they would both explain later, they liked the sound of the name and pronounced it *Ko-bee*, not *Ko-bay*, as it is in Japanese.

Not wanting to dispense with father-son connections entirely, they made his middle name a link to his father's nickname. Bean. As in Kobe Bean Bryant.

As if the world needed more proof of the couple's wackiness, some observers would say later. But it was the seventies, a decade when a new generation was reaching beyond the traditions of the past. After all, Dr. Patch Adams, the famous doctor-clown, would name one of his own sons Atomic Zagnut.

So Joe and Pam Bryant were perfectly within the spirit of the times to name their son Kobe Bean. After all, they did like the beef very much. And time itself would prove their choice ideal for uniqueness and marketing allure.

It would soon enough make their son a one-name star.

Early on, the Philly papers addressed any stories about the Bryants' new young son by using both names, as in "young Kobe Bean shows promise as a player."

The name made sense, others would point out later, because Kobe beef is precious, produced by a special process, bred and raised and cured to become a most prized and exotic brand, as would be Kobe Bean Bryant himself.

What mattered far more than the name was the gene pool, Paul Westhead observed. "Pam came from an athletic family. Chubby had game. He was no slouch. He was skilled. He didn't have the size of Joe, but he was a skilled player. Projecting ahead the ultimate child that comes from that union, you would say there's a lot of talent there."

Beyond the DNA, the process for great competitors often seems to begin with perfectionist mothers. Pam Cox Bryant has remained a bit of a mystery, because, unlike Michael Jordan's mother, Deloris Jordan, Pam Bryant never wrote a book, never graced magazine covers, never toured the world in support of family health. Instead, she maintained a low-key life.

In her son's formative years, it was her special talent for behind-the-scenes manipulation that brought her both the admiration and ire of family and friends. By all accounts, she was quite bright, attractive, charming, refined, a lover of sophistication and the fine things in life, yet, like her father, she preferred to elude the bright spotlight that would fall on her son.

The greatest evidence of her perfectionist bent came with her family itself. Her brood of three were well groomed and dressed and raised, the two daughters and the son exemplary in manners, speech, behavior, bearing, countenance, from an early age.

"If other people raised their children the way the Bryants raised their three, we would have a lot of productive people in this world," observed Leon Douglas, Joe's teammate from the Italian league who had witnessed Pam at work.

Still, family and friends point out that it was Kobe who received the full force of her affection and attention, and there was a close bond between mother and son.

"When Pam finally had a male child, she was just ecstatic," explained a family friend. "And she loved the girls, don't get me wrong, but the center of their universe was Kobe. Maybe that's because that's what Joe wanted, and she wanted to keep Joe. He was the son they could pour everything into."

Pam's doting on Chubby during their adolescence would prove to be mere practice for the main event of raising her son.

"When Kobe came, Pam just lit up," Mo Howard recalled. "She had a son, and probably after that, the love of her life was Chubby. She just doted on Chubby unreal. Now she had her own son."

Pam was relentless in cultivating her family's perfect image. "Whatever was going on with her family, it was always portrayed to us as being perfect," explained the family friend. "I mean, whenever she spoke of anybody, it was always perfect. She tried to portray one thing, that everything was perfect. Kobe. Her daughters. Everything."

That perfection encompassed Pam's own demeanor as well, explained the friend. "She was always very attractive, very sweet, very approachable, very, very nice, and both of her daughters were the same thing."

Her approach extended to the notion of achievement. The presence of their individual athletic gifts was never allowed as any sort of excuse for her children. They were expected to do their schoolwork and to be dutiful and responsible.

From his very first moments, Kobe Bean was raised in a family admired by others, and not just in the Philadelphia papers, but wherever they went.

Pat Williams remembered the Bryants proudly bringing their new son to the Spectrum, the Sixers arena: "People would say to me, 'What do you remember about Kobe Bryant?' And I would say I remember his grandparents, they're rocking him, or carrying him in a baby cart to the games. Let's just say he grew up in the Spectrum. The first year of his life was involved with the 76ers."

Gilbert Saunders recalled running into Joe with his toddler son in tow, coming off an elevator after a summer basketball game. Young Kobe Bean was riding a toy motorcar.

"It was a Mercedes," Saunders remembered with a chuckle.

Jellybean was the picture of a proud papa—whenever he was around.

Kobe Bryant would later be known for the basketball bond with his father. But, with the father's celebrity and the frequent travel of a professional athlete during the son's formative years, it was understandable that Kobe Bean's earliest and closest bond would form with Pam Bryant. His sisters would brand Kobe as an incurable mama's boy.

Thus, her son mirrored much of Pam's personality, far from the happy-go-lucky countenance of his father.

"From the enthusiasm aspect, his love to play, I'm more like my father," Bryant said in 1999. "But on the court, I'm more like my mother. She's more like a pit bull.

"Her temper is like that," he said, smacking his hands together to make a sharp crack. "Very competitive. So I got the best of both worlds."

Mother and son shared pleasant personalities for the most part, right down to demeanors that could turn surprisingly cold in a flash. That coldness could be startlingly off-putting to those who encountered it. And, combined with their capacity for sudden, sharp anger, both mother and son would use it to define the parameters of their lives.

The primary driving element, however, was the perfectionism. Tex Winter, the veteran coach who worked so closely with both Jordan and Bryant, would often say it was chief among the many fundamental traits the two superstars shared—their intense perfectionism. In terms of Bryant's achievement, it's fair to say in so many ways, the mother made the man.

Championship Blues

Joe Bryant's growing family may have brought him joy, but his career itself stirred different emotions. In the 1977 off-season, the team had worked a multimillion-dollar deal to bring in Julius Erving, the great "Dr. J" from the New York Nets, just as the ABA was collapsing. Suddenly, Joe Bryant was buried even deeper in Gene Shue's rotation. The lean playing time that Jellybean had complained about as a rookie was cut almost in half.

"He had his moments," Pat Williams said. "There was no question in any of our minds that Joe Bryant was a talent, and we all felt very good about our future with these young players. However, we now had a veteran group who were ahead of them. McGinnis, Julius, Steve Mix, Harvey Catchings, and we're trying to bring Darryl along. I mean, we were overloaded with talent."

When he did play, Jellybean remained a member of the infamous Bomb Squad, which didn't help his development, Mo Howard said. "Those guys that played in that second unit, they didn't give a shit. They didn't really give a shit, you know. They had to play behind Julius and those guys. It was like, 'When we get to the game, we're just going to do our shit.' I think that's where Joe's bad rap may have come from."

The entire team was a loose group.

"That locker room was filled with great interviews," remembered Dick Weiss, who covered the club. "There wasn't a bad talker. Julius set the tone for that because he was the ultimate professional. They had a bunch of gregarious and outgoing guys, and funny guys like Steve Mix and Caldwell Jones."

A huge, young physical specimen, Dawkins was known as Chocolate Thunder, a poet who talked of coming from the planet Lovetron. Lloyd Free would change his name to World B. Free.

"Darryl was hilarious," Weiss said. "Lloyd Free and Joe would say anything. You could open up your notebook, and those guys would just fill it up."

McGinnis would conduct interviews while smoking cigarettes. Jellybean sometimes seized on that practice, talking to reporters while strumming an air guitar and smoking.

"I asked Joe about the Sixers," Vontez Simpson recalled, "because they were really talented. He said they did not have a role model to keep them in check. They had a lot of young guys with money partying hard after games." He told Simpson that Erving didn't get into a lot of partying himself, but he also wasn't inclined to tell other players how to live their lives.

On the court, all the Sixers had to adjust to a talent like Erving. "Everybody got along," Dick Weiss said. "Julius set the tone for everything else. It wasn't like the ABA, where he was superhuman, but he was still was pretty damn good."

McGinnis, who had been the leader of the team, struggled but eventually came to terms with the reality that the hierarchy had changed. It was solidified when the Sixers played their way into the 1977 league-championship series versus the Portland Trail Blazers, led by Bill Walton.

"I don't think Joey had any idea that they were going to contend for a championship," Mo Howard recalled.

It wasn't the kind of elevated thinking that usually occurred to a second-year player, especially a deeply frustrated one.

McGinnis began struggling during the play-offs, which suddenly meant more playing time for Jellybean. Oddly, it was his defense that impressed coaches and fans alike during the championship series. The Sixers went to Portland and won the first two games, but things started to change when, toward the end of Game 2, Dawkins and Portland power forward Maurice Lucas got into a tussle.

"Up to that moment it looked like we were going to sweep those Trail Blazers," Pat Williams recalled. "It was a real fight."

Dawkins was furious afterward that none of his teammates had come to his aid in the melee (Doug Collins apparently tried but got whacked inadvertently by Dawkins). The young center went on a tirade in the locker room, attacking the toilets, which caused a flood.

"He knocked the sink down, kicked the commode over, just destroyed the locker room," Williams remembered. "He was a six-eleven, 270-pound twenty-year-old in a fury. It just turned into a mess, a total mess."

Much later, some would laughingly remember the expensive shoes and clothes of teammates floating around, but at the time no one was laughing. The entire incident seemed to shatter the team's mind-set and chemistry, World B. Free would later observe. Despite their 2–0 lead, the Sixers didn't win another game. They promptly lost three at home.

Contrite, Dawkins, ever the poet, wrote an "Ode to Game 6" to prepare for the close-out game. The Sixers played well but lost a tight one.

Their troubles extended into the first half dozen games of the next season. The team's new owner, F. Eugene Dixon, had grown angry over contract negotiations with Shue because the coach was one of the first to employ an agent, the ever-present Richie Phillips.

"Fitz Dixon was not happy," Williams recalled. "He thought that Shue had held him up for more money just because he was a new owner."

Dixon sat behind the team's bench, and one night, after a poor showing the first week of the season, he waved for Williams to come down to the floor from the press box, where he ordered his GM to fire Shue and hire former Sixer Billy Cunningham as coach.

"Nothing was going to change his mind," Williams said.

Shue and the entire league were understandably stunned by the move, but Cunningham, a crowd favorite, came in and directed the team to the 14–1 record for November that served as a prelude to Kobe Bean's conception.

Cunningham brought a no-nonsense approach to the job. Joe Bryant played well enough during the play-offs to earn a contract extension with the team. He stayed in Philadelphia two more seasons, a time when Cunningham, with assistant coaches Chuck Daly and Jack McMahon, made a point of eliminating the Bomb Squad atmosphere.

After the team lost to the Bullets in the 1978 play-offs, the coaches told Williams to trade World B. Free.

"We had drafted Mo Cheeks at this point," Williams recalled, "and we've traded George McGinnis for Bobby Jones with Denver. The coaches come to me and say we have to move Lloyd Free. I loved Lloyd. He was a show and a half, and he was a great offensive producer and fearless.

"I just had the hardest time with that," Williams remembered. "They were adamant that we were not going to get where we needed to get. I said he was going to go somewhere and average 35 points a night, and so I shopped him. That was my responsibility. I went all around the league and got nary a nibble. And finally Gene Shue, who was coaching San Diego by then, showed some interest — not great, but some. And I was finally able to make a deal where we sent them Lloyd Free, and we got the Clippers' first-round pick in 1984, which by the way turned out to be Charles Barkley."

With the Bomb Squad defused, the team made the play-offs again in 1979. During a critical series with San Antonio, Cunningham put Joe Bryant in the game only to see him immediately launch a deep shot that missed and led to a run-out basket by the Spurs.

Cunningham quickly pulled Jellybean out of the game, which the Sixers went on to lose.

"Billy was always holding his breath with Joe," Pat Williams explained. "The coaches said, 'We just can't corral him, we just can't harness him.'"

"I remember that shot," Mo Howard said. "And he didn't play anymore. He didn't play at all. I remember clearly the shot you're talking about. Maybe it was only because he had just gotten into the game. Those were the shots that he took."

For four years in Philadelphia, Bryant had been complaining to reporters that he wanted to be traded. Suddenly that became a possibility.

"We're getting ready for the next season when Billy and Chuck and the staff say we need to move Joe Bryant," Williams recalled.

The GM phoned every team in the league, trying to trade Jellybean. "I didn't get a nibble," he said.

Finally, in October, as the new season was ready to begin, Gene Shue again offered his team's first-round draft pick in 1986 for Joe

Bryant. That draft pick would later be traded to Cleveland and used to select North Carolina center Brad Daugherty.

"I remember informing Joe what we had done," Williams recalled. "I think he was relieved. He wanted to play. He knew his time had come. He was eager to get somewhere where he could have an opportunity and do the things that he wanted to do."

To Bryant's many fans and friends in the city, his time as a Sixer felt like wasted opportunity.

"He was special," Mo Howard observed. "The Philadelphia people really, really respected Joey's play. I often thought they would put him in the game just to pacify all the Philly people, and he would play a little bit, and then they'd take him out of the game and he'd never play again. Given the opportunity to play through his mistakes or what were perceived as mistakes, he would have been a superman. Philadelphia had a lot of really good basketball players, but Joey was special. He was doing stuff the other guys weren't doing, man. He would have been like George Gervin."

During his first four years, Jellybean had managed to play minutes at all five positions for the Sixers and had performed well as a guard and a forward and even at center.

In looking back years later, Pat Williams would offer that Bryant was versatile but was never quite good enough to excel at any position. He wasn't quite quick enough to be a great guard, not quite athletic enough to be an exceptional forward, not strong enough to work regularly at center.

Added to that, he proved to be maddeningly inconsistent, brilliant in one game, a borderline disaster in another.

Elements of the party atmosphere in Philadelphia hadn't been good for a young family with three children under age four. The move to San Diego brought weather more to Pam's liking, and the climate on the court proved better as well.

Chapter 7

THE FUNNY GUY

GENE SHUE HAD promised to bring an exciting, up-tempo style of play to the San Diego Clippers, who were owned by film producer Irv Levin and New York lawyer Harold Lipton. Shue had brought forty-three wins and a fifth-place finish in the West in the franchise's first year in San Diego, so hopes soared with the September 1979 acquisition of center Bill Walton, followed by the addition of Jellybean a month later.

Walton, however, would soon sustain yet another foot injury, beginning a round of frustrations with his career. Reunited with Shue, Joe Bryant found regular playing time and an important new identity — role player. No longer under the pressure to be a star that he felt in his hometown, he settled in with the Clippers and became a double-figures scorer.

The change brought Jellybean a revelation about the "peer pressure" he had been under in Philadelphia. His mind had become "clearer," he said.

"It seemed like I had to play the role of a superstar," he would say of the expectations in his hometown. "Playing the role of a superstar is not my bag."

Even out of the limelight, he could still deliver highlights, such as the time in his first moments with San Diego when he brought down a towering slam dunk against the Lakers that sent the great

Kareem Abdul-Jabbar running for cover, or the evening he clearly outplayed Boston's Larry Bird.

But with Walton playing just seventeen games that season, the Clippers fell to thirty-five wins, and their average attendance in the San Diego Sports Arena slipped to fewer than six thousand people a night. The owners let Shue go after the season and brought in Paul Silas, a first-time head coach who had earned a reputation as a tough, smart pro after winning two titles alongside Dave Cowens in the Boston Celtics' frontcourt.

That spring of 1980, Joe Bryant watched Magic Johnson, a six-foot-nine point guard, lead the Lakers to a six-game win over Philadelphia in the league-championship series. Johnson had played guard, center, and forward during the showdown. He was the perfect realization of the player Jellybean wanted to be, and this would spark both his frustration and a debate over what might have been.

"I think Joe was a little ahead of his time," Sonny Hill said in a 2015 interview. "That was before you had players of his size that were playing in the league. That's why he always thought of himself as an early edition of a guy like Magic Johnson. Because the tall guys were thrust right into a situation that they had to play the big man's role."

"When you speak of Magic Johnson, you're speaking of one of the greatest players who ever played, and Joe was nowhere near that," Gene Shue offered, looking back. "Joe did have some of those similarities in his game. He was more of an outside player: he could handle the ball, he could pass the ball. But Joe in his pro career was never the man, never the guy, where you would say, 'OK, Joe, we want you doing this all the time.'"

"Never the man." It was a phrase that would haunt Joe Bryant's career and an idea that would fuel his son to do the opposite.

"I just want to be the man," Kobe Bryant would say over and over again during the early years of his career.

The coach of the Lakers during Magic's rise was none other than Paul Westhead, who still deployed his up-tempo style. Even so, Westhead recalled the team having absolutely no discussion about attempting to acquire Bryant, the star of his old teams at La Salle. Westhead explained that he was just the coach, with little input on personnel management, a job handled quite well by Lakers GM Bill Sharman and his assistant, Jerry West.

Although Jellybean played for the Clippers, some recall that his young son was outfitted in a tiny Lakers jacket. Major change was in the air of the game, and Joe Bryant had quickly come to idealize the Lakers and Magic Johnson, as would his son over the coming years.

Jellybean could only watch from afar and keep to his role. "Every day I'm on the road during the season, I call home and talk to Pam and each of the children," he said at the time.

"And I still call my parents, win or lose."

His wife soldiered on with the challenge of the young household, despite his schedule, he admitted. "You have to stay on top of the kids so they don't form bad habits. My wife is the strong hand as far as discipline."

It took a particularly strong-willed woman to manage finances and keep an NBA husband headed in the right direction, Pat Williams recalled. "Pam had to run the family. Joe was a hail fellow well met. He was a loose cannon in a lot of ways."

The Bryant family montage in the early 1980s included memories of little Kobe dunking on a tiny plastic goal while his father played for the Clippers on TV. By the start of Joe's third season in San Diego, his son had grown, and so had the goal, so much so that Kobe drew the first newspaper headline of his career, in the *Philadelphia Tribune*.

BRYANT'S SON — DUNKING AT THREE? the newspaper asked.

"Kobe is three, but he loves basketball already," Big Joe told veteran Philadelphia sportswriter Herm L. Rogul. "He runs down the hallway, hops on his little trampoline, and slams his mini-basketball through an eight-foot-high hoop."

Apparently, he had hijacked the trampoline from his sisters. Years later, both girls maintained that their brother was already working on his left hand at that same age.

"He would run around the house dribbling the basketball. I wanted him to be a doctor," Big Joe remembered. "He told me, 'Pop-Pop, I want to be a basketball player.' I would say to him, 'You'll get all tired and sweaty playing basketball.' Then he would say, 'Pop-Pop, that's what basketball players are supposed to do, get tired and sweaty.'"

As Good as It Got

No longer a bench player left hoping for a little garbage time, Jellybean was getting full runs each game night for the first time in his career. Silas, like Cunningham in Philadelphia, took a no-nonsense approach, but the twenty-six-year-old Jellybean had his best season under the first-year coach, averaging 11.6 points, 2.3 assists, and 5.4 rebounds in 28.8 minutes a night, though it was a constant battle for Silas to keep him in line.

The team improved its record to thirty-six wins, and Bryant still brought a flair that pleased the crowds, or so he reported in his regular phone calls to Big Joe.

"Joe is as popular as ever," Big Joe told Herm Rogul. "In San Antonio, the Baseline Bums gave him one of their shirts with his name on it. Kids run up to him at Disneyland and SeaWorld. One said, 'We like the way you play.' "

Whatever good times there were would vanish that off-season as real estate magnate Donald Sterling bought the team. Though he bought the team while boasting about his personal wealth, Sterling would soon become known for his penny-pinching and odd moves that began the long, painful process of driving the franchise into the ground.

After unloading some of their players to save salary, the Clippers suffered through a 17–65 campaign in 1981–82. During that season, Jellybean had complained that the team wasn't flying first-class, as stipulated by the union's agreement with the league. When his complaints brought no response, he threatened to lead the team in a boycott of an upcoming game. Silas finally talked him out of the boycott, but the damage was done with the front office. It was almost as if Joe was on a personal mission to destroy his career. Now he was adding "clubhouse lawyer" to the list of the other negative traits in his profile.

Some of the only relief in that miserable year would come from the sight of little Kobe working the ball at Clippers' practices. "I used to see him playing in the arena," Silas told writer Jonathan Abrams. "He was just a little bitty guy."

Jellybean's therapy for all the losing came on his days off, when he took Kobe to Lakers games. "Kobe is nearly four and he's all boy," Jellybean said at the time. "I've taken Kobe to Lakers games and introduced him to players. He's a Magic Johnson fan."

The translation, of course, was that Joe Bryant himself was a Magic fan. The big Lakers guard represented something that Bryant himself badly wanted to be, something clearly now beyond his reach.

After the season, Joe was shipped with a second-round draft pick to the Houston Rockets for a second-round pick.

Asked in 1999 about his time with Joe Bryant in San Diego, Bill Walton replied, with a laugh, "He was a good player, but let's put it this way. NBA coaches didn't stay up all night devising defenses for Jellybean Bryant."

The move meant that he was going from one tanking team to another, although Bryant didn't realize that at first. He thought he would be playing on the Moses Malone "gravy train." The Rockets were coached by Del Harris and had been to the league-championship series in 1981, but for the 1982–83 season, they planned to lose games in order to get University of Virginia star Ralph Sampson with a top pick. Moses Malone departed for the Sixers, and Houston settled in for a long year.

The Rockets spiraled into a 14–68 season, and Jellybean spiraled with them. He averaged 10 points and 25.4 minutes a game, playing in eighty-one games. The one game he missed made headlines when he went bust in an all-night poker game and didn't have money for a cab to make the team bus. The solution for that was said to be Pam giving him just a little more money in his weekly allowance, a five dollar bill to be stuffed in a sock for just such emergencies.

After that season, his eighth as a pro player, it became clear that absolutely no one in the NBA wanted the Jellybean anymore, even though he was just twenty-eight and in his prime years as a player.

Looking back much later, Jerry West would observe: "He threw away his career."

Paul Westhead would always wonder why the star of his college team wasn't a respected NBA player. He suspected that the reason began with the nickname and was reinforced by his drug bust.

"I don't know how he got that name," Westhead said in 2015. "It's kind of interesting, and, to be honest, as his career developed, more after he left La Salle and went to the pro game, the nickname Jellybean, depending on who you were, could have been a positive or a negative."

Bob Ryan, who covered the league during that era for the *Boston Globe*, would agree with Jerry West and in one of his columns would describe Joe Bryant as "an utter goofball."

It was an opinion many shared.

"When I think of Joe Bryant, and people say Jellybean, I see the smiling, happy, very mobile, behind-the-back passer," Westhead said. "Some of the NBA people said that's his problem. It wasn't from me, but I think, in a way, it impacted what the public and pro general managers thought of him as being too fancy."

"It got ugly there," his friend Mo Howard recalled. "He had all this gift, and the industry wouldn't let him use it."

"Just from a distance, keeping my eyes on how he was doing, I'd hear what people would say," Westhead recalled. "Anybody who'd want to listen, I'd say, 'This guy has a lot of skill and talent. He can do almost anything he wants on the basketball court.' I always had the impression that nobody took him seriously. That they just thought that Joe was the funny guy."

After the 1983 season, he wound up out of the game, selling cars for Rockets owner Charlie Thomas. At first, after a life of nothing but basketball, Jellybean decided he liked the business experience, the time talking to people, selling vans, trucks, and cars. But the country was in another tough recession; interest rates were high, sales were slow. Joe Bryant had no college degree, no true identity other than as a basketball player.

It clearly was not a happy time for the Bryants as they retreated to Philadelphia.

The one thing Joe had—besides the family that his wife had held together—was his relationship with Sonny Hill. He had continued to play in Baker League games, where he could trot out his full showtime talents, where the crowds still showered him with love. Plus, he had begun coaching in the Sonny Hill League and discovered that he loved it.

Hill, in turn, prized Joe Bryant as one of his biggest success stories. But the connection was about more than that. So many of the players from his leagues were still young and thoughtless. As they aged, they would come to realize just how much Hill had meant to their lives, and they would cherish the experience of playing in the Hill league.

But Jellybean was one of those few who understood it early, who reveled in his time spent in Hill's leagues. His presence each summer added strength to the league, but it also helped sustain Hill himself through the very challenging effort to keep things going.

Hill knew Bryant had a lot of basketball in him and began encouraging him to think about playing in Europe. The money was good there, he told Joe.

In many ways, it was the last thing Pam Bryant wanted to hear. She had dragged her young brood from Philly to San Diego to Houston, holding the relationship together with a far-flung NBA husband, and now he was talking about taking things across the sea to Europe?

It took months for that idea to settle in. Meanwhile, they lived in Houston, with Joe trying to sell cars. Asked later what she liked about Houston, Pam would reply obliquely, "The horses." She who tried to put a perfect face on everything had little to offer about the experience in Texas.

Now Joe was pushing for a move to Italy. Her kids were already talking about the difficulties of making friends and having to change them with each move.

Joe sold it by saying it would be a quick year, a chance to see someplace very different. Plus, they needed the money. Pam's tastes ran to the expensive. She was eager to stay in her nice home in the Philadelphia suburbs. "She hated the idea of leaving Philadelphia again," Joe recalled. But she reluctantly agreed to give it a try.

That summer of 1984, before they departed for Italy, Kobe watched on TV the U.S. Olympic team getting ready for the Games in Los Angeles. Their preparation was a series of games against pro players. It was the first time he had ever noticed Michael Jordan. "It was a collegiate team," he remembered. "They were getting ready for the Olympics. They were playing against a pro team. This guy dribbles on the fast break and took off—I think it was over Magic—and dunked and flew past Magic. That's not supposed to happen. Who was this kid? I don't like this kid 'cause Magic was my guy. I think that's the first time I saw him."

Chapter 8

ITALIA

The dark face appears amused, caught in a half smirk amid a backdrop of Caucasian players at a basketball camp in Italy. He stands alone at the lower right corner of the photo, in front of two rows of beaming Italian faces. They're older than he is, but, as the look on his face seems to show, a young Kobe Bryant knows he's already a far better player than any of them will ever be. Above them all, standing tall, is the smiling hero Joe Bryant, the celebrity guest of the camp, his face awash in its own light.

Though Jellybean was always smiling, friends from that era would remember that Kobe was already just the opposite, especially anytime he took to the court.

"His face was always serious, always serious, when he played," recalled Michella Rotella, who was an older boy who often played against the young Bryant on a mountainside court in the Tuscan village of Ciriglio. "No smiles. Very determined."

"He was always so serious about everything he did as far as sports, always so intense," remembered Sharia, his sister.

"The mentality of Kobe was very concentrated to win, win, win," said Jacomo Vittori, another childhood friend from Italy.

"When he was eight and I was eleven, we were in the same basketball league," Sharia recalled in 1999. "The rest of the kids just wanted to play, and he was like, 'I want to win.' One time there was only thirty seconds left, and we're down by two, and he was like, 'Give me the ball.' I mean, he was into it. He was always that way."

He said he first realized that he could take over games by himself "when I was very young, nine or ten, playing little leagues. When the game is on the line and you're put in that situation and your back's against the wall, I come out fighting. It's that fight-or-flight mentality, and I've always been a fighter."

Years later, in the eyes of his Los Angeles Lakers coaches, Italy would loom as the place where he learned to discount his less-experienced and less-talented teammates, to trust only his own powers. When he would play selfishly as a member of the Lakers, some of his coaches would quietly comment that Kobe Bryant had "gone back to Italy."

"He was really selfish," recalled Jacomo Vittori, adding that the selfishness came from the fact that Kobe was so much better than all the other players. "Everybody noticed. He was the only black kid here. Everybody noticed. He was very skilled."

It was during these formative years that the pointed personality traits he shared with his mother first emerged. He was her doll baby, and she seemed to love dressing him nattily as a little man in sweaters and other gentlemanly clothing, suggesting not so much a child as a miniature adult.

Pam Bryant had a certain carriage to her person, and even as a little child there was something similarly distinctive in Kobe's manner. Italy and an upbringing steeped mostly in European culture would forever cast him as a very different cat, especially when he reached American professional basketball.

Asked about how formative his experience in Italy was when he first entered the NBA, Bryant would reply, "I jump high. Everything else is groomed Italian-style."

Italian-style treated the whole family well. Joe's flashy bag of tricks and passes, the ones that had left Philly crowds howling, went over well in Italy. It took only one game for Joe to realize that he could make a living and have again that love from the fans that he craved so much.

Amazed by his ability with the ball, the Italians would settle again and again on a word to describe Joe's play—"beauty."

Indeed, Italy would prove to be a wondrous place for the young family of Joe Bryant, a force that pulled them closer together. At the same time, it seeded and reinforced other things, things they would not see at the time, things that would prove difficult to understand among all the great passions they found in Italy, things that drove into their lives a certain chill, things that young Kobe Bean would wrap into his life and make his own.

Just as in America, the Bryant family would move several times in Italy, which further served to establish alienation as a norm that would last his entire life. As a child, he would always struggle to make friends; then, as soon as he did, it seemed it was time to tell them ciao.

The Bryants' first Italian home was in Rieti, where the family moved and Kobe started school just weeks after his sixth birthday. Sharia was eight, Shaya seven. It was a small, ancient city a short distance northeast of Rome, known as the home of the Sabines, the tribe that surrendered their women to build the population of Rome. Bordered by the Velino River and a scenic lake, the mountain region had become something of a residential retreat favored by the popes.

The Bryants found an easy adjustment there. The team provided them with housing and a car. They didn't know the language, but the children spent afternoons teaching each other through word games. Within months they had found a comfort level in a world vastly different from the one they had left behind. It would be an important bonding experience for the clan.

"We were very comfortable there," Kobe would remember. "We fell right in. That's the kind of attitude we developed in Italy. The backbone is the family. Once you have that, then everything else is cool. Whether you score 50 points or 0, your family is going to be there. The Italians have the same thing. They're very warmhearted people."

Thus, his family became the bedrock of the confidence that his father kept emphasizing. Joe Bryant would later explain that he had always rued his own lack of confidence and partly blamed it for his failings. He seemed determined that his son would have none of that weakness.

Also boosting Kobe's confidence was his full exposure to the game at a young age, including traveling to games on the team bus with the old man. Each pro team also had its own youth team, and playing on the youth team and going to practices with his father rapidly built the base of his understanding of the game.

In retrospect, his time in Italy became the most comprehensive basketball school one could imagine. "I started playing basketball over there," he said, "which was great, because I learned fundamentals first. I think most kids who grow up here in America learn all the fancy dribbling. In Italy, they teach you true fundamentals and leave out all the nonsense."

Again, at every turn, there seemed an acute awareness of the "nonsense" that had undone his father.

Certain coaches would later disagree, arguing that the experience had given Bryant his own brand of disconnection that made him a suspect teammate. Yet even his detractors could not deny the polish to so many aspects of his game. "I think, basically, Italy was the foundation for his game," observed Leon Douglas, Joe's Italian-league teammate. "He was able to play the all-around game over there and learn every aspect."

Throughout his career, if he was deficient in something, Bryant would display the work ethic to build every element of his competitive portfolio with an almost manic insistence, another product of his Italian experience.

In fact, he never seemed to stop working at the game, even at that very young age. If he wasn't playing the game, then he was watching videotape of NBA stars, remembered Vittorio, who spent many hours with him as a child. "Kobe always wanted to play basketball. Always."

Over the next several years, he would show that he had already grasped the powers of concentration and developed what he would later call "the code." He knew from that early age that he wanted to be a professional basketball player, which would mean scant little inefficiency in his curriculum vitae. And Italy would prove essential to making him into the player he wanted to be. Despite the genial people and laid-back atmosphere, there was passion everywhere, from Italy's many Renaissance-era cathedrals and chapels to its basketball arenas, jammed with singing, dancing fans.

It was both the experience and Joe's insistence that drove his unshakable self-belief. As it grew, the confidence, in turn, led to his disregarding his teammates even more. In the years since, some teammates in Italy have recalled the low feelings brought by his treatment of them. They complained to the point that his Italian coaches began removing him from games to allow the other players to have room to find their own games.

"I used to get in a lot of trouble when I was younger, running my mouth, talk, talk, talk, which gets the older guys even more upset," he recalled.

It was in those first years in Italy that the Bryants saw their son's future and helped him toward it. "They have mini baskets for seven-year-olds," Joe explained at the time. "One game, Kobe's team scored 22 points, and he had 16. They moved him up to play with ten-year-olds, and he dominated there too. He has a yellow belt in karate and he took ballet lessons too."

Family Time

As strangers in a strange land, the Bryant children and their parents learned what it meant to depend on one another. "We were adapting to another culture," Kobe remembered. "My family and I really had to bind to one another. It's like going into another world. Didn't know anybody else out there, so all you have is one another, so you really have to stay together."

The cultural change also brought a shift in Joe Bryant's basketball life. Although soccer was a much bigger spectator sport in southern Europe, Italians still displayed a remarkable passion for their local basketball teams. In Italy, each team was allowed just two American players. The hoops imports usually found the money to their liking and a schedule that actually allowed for a family life, as opposed to the NBA grind of three to five games per week and constant travel.

In Italy, the focus was on practices, usually held twice a day, which would have been unthinkable in American professional basketball. Games, on the other hand, were usually played only once per week—most often on Sundays—in a season that often lasted from October to May.

"I'm able to take the kids to school and pick them up in the afternoon," Joe told the *Philadelphia Tribune*.

While Jellybean had felt constrained by the NBA, he quickly took to the competition in Italy and found stardom, averaging 30 points per game (many of the Italians he played against were only around eighteen years old). If he felt like trotting out his flamboyant game, no problem. The fans sang songs in praise of his skills. "You know the player who's better than Magic or Jabbar?" went one set of lyrics that Kobe committed to memory in Italian. "It's Joseph, Joseph Bryant!"

Joe averaged 37.8 points per game in Rieti over the winter of 1986. His biggest fan was the little boy who followed him to practice many afternoons. "He just played with so much charisma," Kobe later recalled of his father's time in Europe. "He taught me to enjoy the game."

In addition to allowing Joe to spend more time with his kids, the move also allowed his relationship with Pam to heal from his NBA life.

"Pam and I spend much more time together than when I was in the NBA," Joe would confide to a reporter in 1986. "We are best friends now. We're friends and lovers. We work out and jog together. We jog five or six miles. Pam runs eight to ten miles. We may enter some races next year.

"Pam hated having to leave Philadelphia, but she's fared well," he added.

In addition to playing basketball, Kobe and his sisters took ballet, and Shaya found that she liked karate almost as much as her brother. The schools were Catholic, run by no-nonsense nuns, and the children received outstanding educations.

"The kids speak so well they've been interviewed on national television," Joe said. "My father has to remind them to speak English. Pam and I learned Italian this season. I can read the sports pages. They're really brutal to soccer players who have had a bad game."

Soccer dominated the Italian landscape, so much so that the few public basketball courts also doubled as small soccer fields. His time in a foreign land had already begun to reinforce the isolationist nature that Kobe shared with his mother, spurred along by his desire to shoot alone and work on his game. When a few Italian children would show up to play, Bryant would share the goal with them until larger numbers collected to force a soccer quorum, at which point he would finally have to agree to play soccer, his tall, thin frame lending itself well to playing in goal. Others would later recall that he also showed great promise as a striker, which reflected both his footwork and dribbling.

The game was fun, and the experience would make him a life-long fan, but it had nothing of the grip that basketball held on him.

It was Pam, not Joe, who finally made the effort to put up a hoop at their residence, which hastened both his singular pursuit of the game as well as his tendency to isolate himself from other children.

His grandparents in Philadelphia kept the family's connections with American culture alive by sending a steady flow of videotapes of sporting events, mostly basketball games, and TV programs, with a heavy helping of *The Cosby Show*. Kobe was said to be so impressed by what he saw on the tapes that he took up break dancing for a time. But by far the most important thing he saw was the basketball games, which came at a rate of about forty per season.

"They used to send us all types of TV shows, movies," he remembered, "but what I looked most forward to getting was the basketball games. I wanted to see basketball because over there I had to stay up to three in the morning to see these games, and I had school the next day. That wasn't happening. I had to wait for the tapes. I used to wait for the mail guy to drop them off all the time."

Soon Joe was subscribing to a service that delivered video of games directly. Joe and Kobe would pore over them together, taking note of all the key subtleties, the footwork, a primer of drop steps and jab steps and V-cuts, the various offensive and defensive styles of NBA teams and their stars.

"I used to watch everybody from Magic to Bird to Michael to Dominique Wilkins," Bryant recalled. "I used to watch their moves and add them to my game."

It was the beginning of a career-long focus on studying game recordings, normally the domain of the Xs and Os wonks who serve as assistant coaches. By the time he was an NBA player, he would invest long hours each day in breaking down his own performances and those of opponents, far more than what any other NBA player would ever contemplate undertaking.

In Italy, he took to using freeze-frames and slowed tracking to review sequence after sequence, with his father often pointing out key elements. When Joe was away, Kobe pursued his studies alone, virtually memorizing entire sequences, especially those that revealed player tendencies. By age nine, he had put together his first scouting tape, a look at relatively obscure Hawks guard John Battle. Michael Jordan, too, had begun his mesmerizing assault on the NBA in those years, but the unquestioned star of the Bryant household during Kobe's young life was Magic Johnson.

"I wanted to see Magic," he recalled. "Just the enthusiasm he had for playing the game. He just loved playing, you could tell. Plus, his forward passes used to drive me nuts."

The Lakers were in the midst of their Showtime heyday, their run of championships in the 1980s highlighted by Johnson's dazzling ball handling, which in turn made the L.A. franchise a network darling. Dominated by a huge poster of the Lakers point guard, Kobe's room was a shrine to Johnson, who by no small coincidence was his father's frequent example of what a great player should be.

On the family's TV screen, he would play and replay the Magic highlights, which some critics later found surprising, since there was so little evidence of the great ball distributor's game in Bryant's own approach as a pro.

Though Joe offered Kobe videos of his own younger days, Kobe didn't need them. He had the real thing to measure himself against. Joe would play one-on-one with him when available, but with so many hours a day in Italy dedicated to professional practice, it wasn't humanly possible for his father to play enough to slake Kobe's thirst.

So he played alone, in imaginary games against himself. "Shadow basketball," he called it. "I play against my shadow."

That, of course, involved intense visualization of the NBA stars he had stored in his imagination from the video screen. His pursuits were strikingly similar to those of Jerry West four decades earlier, as a skinny kid in the West Virginia hills spending hours alone at an outdoor hoop.

Chapter 9

THE RED BICYCLE

Each summer, the Bryants would load up and head back to Philly, where Joe reveled in his own Baker League play and the opportunity to coach in the Sonny Hill League. After two seasons in Rieti, the Bryants would move to Reggio Calabria, a coastal town with a climate similar to San Diego's, for the 1986–87 season. After the off-season in Philadelphia, the family returned to Italy to live in yet another new city, just as their son was really getting to an age when he could do things on the court.

The new team was in Pistoia, a small but ancient city in Tuscany that was gearing up to play in the A2, the second tier of Italian-league teams. Acting on a tip from his son, Piero Becciani, the team president of Olimpia Pistoia, had purchased Joe's contract from Reggio Calabria for the unheard-of sum of 150 million lire (roughly $115,000 at the time). The Pistoia team had ambitions of moving up in the basketball world and wanted an offensive attraction in hopes of building momentum for the construction of a new arena.

Leon Douglas, the other American signed by the team for the 1987–88 season, recalled that Pistoia's addition of Joe Bryant and him was a last grasp at survival by the team, which couldn't even play its games at home their first year. Instead, the team traveled for each home game to Florence, more than twenty-five miles away.

Bryant was the big offensive entertainment needed to enthuse fans, Douglas said, adding that he had played for years against Joe in Italy and had once seen him score 70 points in a single game.

He was still the same Joe who in high school loved taking shots, except now he was no longer a reed-thin two-hundred-pounder, and there were no more constraints on his conscience—if there had ever been any. "I remember the Bryant family had this saying when he started scoring: 'Bust 'em up, Joe. Bust 'em up,'" Douglas said with a laugh. "Joe was a shooter. A lot of Kobe's game reminds me a lot of Joe's game. A lot of the things Kobe does are the things his father used to do. His dad was a prolific scorer."

Joe delighted in discovering that he could thrill Italian fans by launching jumper after jumper.

"He had a large set of weapons," Alessandro Conti, a marketing and communications employee of the Pistoia team, explained. "Joe Bryant was quite famous in Italian basketball. Pistoia had to pay a huge buyout to have him here."

The gamble worked. Wherever Pistoia played, the team was met by enthusiastic crowds cheering for Joseph Bryant.

"He was like God," Jacomo Vittori, Kobe's childhood friend, remembered. "Everything he did, everything he said, was like a bible. Kobe had that same confidence."

Vittori met Kobe that first year, when both were "mop boys" for the team, mopping up sweat and sweeping up debris from the floor during pauses in the action at the "Palace of Florence."

"He was one of those kids who got the sweat off the floor," Leon Douglas recalled.

"Being a ball boy got me close to the game," Kobe remembered. "I was able to get a feel for the speed and how physical the game was."

Those who saw him remembered Kobe as a kid who loved the spotlight, so much so that he might take to mopping the floor even when it wasn't necessary because he liked performing before the crowd.

At halftime, Kobe would take to the empty court to conduct his shadow games and shooting and dribbling routines, often to the applause and wonderment of the enthusiastic crowds, who were waving flags, singing songs, doing anything to urge on father and son.

"And during the time-outs the ref would toss me the ball," Kobe recalled, "and I would dribble around a little bit, go out on the court, do a lay-up, take a free throw until the players came back on the court."

"At every one of our games at halftime, it was the Kobe show," Leon Douglas remembered with a laugh. "He'd get out there and get his shots up. We'd come out of the locker room after halftime and have to chase him off the court."

Vittori, the team's other mop boy, who would sometimes join Kobe's shooting display, recalled that his friend was clearly showing off "because in his mind, he was concentrating on the future. Nothing else."

Roberto Maltinti, one of the owners of the Pistoia team, said fans enjoyed the skinny little boy with the huge feet working the ball at halftime. "They used to say he was talented, but not as much as his father," Maltinti recalled. "Kobe in his movements copied Joe."

Years later, former Lakers teammate Metta World Peace would play his very first Italian-league game before the lively and passionate crowd in Pistoia and immediately afterward would phone Kobe and tell him, "OK, I know now why you play like you do."

"Fans in America are not even close to their passion for the game," Leon Douglas said of Pistoia.

Alessandro Conti's girlfriend confirmed it. She traveled to America and took in a game at the supposed basketball mecca Madison Square Garden but was stunned to find that the fans there didn't really even seem to watch the game.

"The passion here made an imprint on Kobe at a young age," Conti said.

"He grew up here in Pistoia and saw our fans," Jacomo Vittori explained. "Here he learned to fight with this intensity."

What particularly lit up the fans was the team's rivalry with Montecatini, another small mountain city in Tuscany, just three miles away, whose team featured a high-scoring Italian star. Kobe was fascinated by the Italian star, as well as with Mike D'Antoni, another American who led Olimpia Milano's great teams during the era.

Kobe made a habit of riding along on the team's bus to road games, leaving an impression on many of his father's teammates.

"A lot of kids, when they're young, they don't communicate or talk with people," Leon Douglas observed. "They're withdrawn. Kobe was not withdrawn at all. He'd communicate. He knew how to deal with grown people. He was just a kid, but he knew how to switch back and forth between adults and people his own age."

Douglas saw that on the team's bus rides. Kobe watched so much tape of NBA games, he was more than aware that his father was playing on a lower-ranked Italian team, which paled in comparison to the glamour of the NBA.

"Kobe made a statement to us that was very profound one time," Douglas recalled. "He said, 'When I get older, I'm gonna show you guys how to play.' He made the statement he was going to be a great player. It was instilled in his head at an early age."

Leon Douglas said he and Joe Bryant became quite close on those bus rides and with the time their families spent together, that they indeed were like family. "Joe made a comment once that his grandmother was a preacher," Douglas remembered. "He said she had told him that there would be greatness in the family, that someone would come along and do incredible things that would change the entire family. She prophesied, and her prophecy was Kobe. Joe didn't think that he himself was that person. He did not say it was himself."

"I remember about Kobe as a kid as well as his beautiful and bonded family," said Eugenio Capone, a player for Pistoia in that era. "I always remember that at the end of practice or after the game, Joe used to play with him and had him do ball-handling exercises and shooting practice. They were having fun, but at the same time that was also very serious training. We said: 'Don't bother him, Joe! He's just a kid.' And now that Kobe has become the player we all know, the first thing that comes to my mind is that of a father playing with his son and teaching him all that stuff."

Throughout the entire experience, Joe was his companion and guide. The disappointment of his own career had committed Joe to making sure that his son avoided the same fate. Yet, as much as Joe wanted a son who would be great, it was Kobe's internal motivation that drove the machine.

"My father never really came to me and said, 'OK, son, you have to do this and that,'" Kobe explained. "I came to him and asked him when I needed help."

He clearly had his own hoop dreams, and they were stoked far beyond any influence provided by his father.

Ciriglio

With the move to Pistoia, Joe and Pam had wanted something away from the hustle and bustle of the city, and they found it in large villa in the hamlet of Ciriglio, high up a winding road in the mountains outside the city.

It was an idyllic spot. The residents there still openly talk of when the basketball giant Joe Bryant first arrived, driving up hunched oddly over the wheel of his white Volvo station wagon and stopping in a local bar for a cup of cappuccino, which he insisted on drinking out of a huge mug.

Soon, Roberto Maltinti said with a laugh, "Joe Bryant was like the mayor of Ciriglio." His easy smile, his presence in the local cafés, his beautiful family, his larger-than-life presence, all served to capture hearts.

Years later, the people of the village as well as the team owner himself clung to their memories of the Bryants.

Maltinti recalled Kobe striking his first endorsement deal at age nine. The league held its all-star game in Rome, and Kobe offered to work it as a mop boy. Maltinti liked his offer but wanted Kobe to wear a sweater advertising a Maltinti business. Kobe agreed to do it, but he drove a hard bargain—he wanted a new bicycle.

Kobe phoned early the morning after the event. "I want the bike in red," he said.

He now had transportation. He could ride the bike the short distance down the mountainside in Ciriglio to the court at the local school to play hoops with the older boys in the village. If they weren't there, he would play by himself. "He could come home, get his homework done, then go outside and play and pretend he was Dr. J," Leon Douglas said with a laugh.

Maltinti recalled that mother and son were quite alike. The

owner counted himself among the many fans of Mrs. Joe Bryant. Even many years later, he spoke of her wistfully and pronounced her name with great romance: *Pah-mell-ah.*

"Pamela was like an army sergeant," Maltinti said, laughing, in a 2015 interview. "She was the head of the family, the chief of the family. She was beautiful, sweet, fierce…"

Joe obviously feared her. Maltinti learned not to cross her as well. One time Joe's paycheck was late, and she immediately let him know about it. The check was never late again.

The Bryant villa was so large that in the years since they left, it has been divided into two houses. Pam decorated the place beautifully, Maltinti recalled, especially at Christmas, when she created a setting of absolute serenity. Years later, when he would hear of the Bryant family's great heartache and division, he would offer that if they could only return to Ciriglio for Pam's Christmas, they would find a means to peace and healing.

Vittori spent a lot of time with the Bryant family in Ciriglio—he was so close that Shaya Bryant was his first sweetheart—and recalled how many meals Kobe ate at the Vittori home. "He liked pasta," Vittori recalled. Kobe always impressed Vittori's parents with his manners—though they didn't extend to the basketball court.

"You could never get him to pass," Vittori recalled with a laugh. "But he always wanted to play basketball. Always. He wanted to have shooting contests."

The shooting contests were Kobe's fantasies come to life. He was always far away, in the NBA, counting down the final seconds when he would score against Jordan or Magic or Dr. J or his own father, whoever happened into his mind on a given day. In addition to Magic, Dr. J was often prominent on Kobe's personal Mount Olympus of stars because Joe talked often of the greatness of his former teammate, Maltinti said.

Kobe had worked so hard at copying the moves of the stars, he would later say that they didn't impress him all that much because he could do their moves. And he could.

The Bryant children spent many afternoons at the Vittori household, and sometimes when he picked them up, Joe Bryant would show up with flowers for Vittori's mother. Likewise, Vittori stayed often up in Ciriglio with the Bryants.

Things weren't exactly perfect with the team in Pistoia, but Joe Bryant and Leon Douglas had helped the club achieve its goals. When they arrived for their second season with the team, a brand-new five-thousand-seat arena was waiting for them. It was a squat building, almost like a Quonset hut, but the locals loved it.

"It was always sold out," explained Alessandro Conti, the Pistoia team official.

During the first warm-up of the grand-opening game, both glass backboards shattered, keeping the mop boys busy sweeping up the glass. Joe Bryant had another very good year, christening the building with two 50-point games and leaving Roberto Maltinti hopeful that Jellybean would return for a third season.

But Maltinti never got a chance to offer Joe a new contract. He signed with another team, Reggio Emilia, and the Bryants were off on the next phase of their Italian experience.

There, as in other locations, the pro team also had a youth team, and Kobe fell into his old pattern: he trained hard but remained aloof in the locker room. On the floor, he insisted on trying to do everything himself, which left teammates feeling useless.

He was so much better than those around him, so determined, that it was impossible for him to relate to lesser players on the floor, it seemed. Ultimately, they would come to resent him for not passing the ball.

Later, Kobe recalled that they would tell him, "You're good over here, but once you get back to America, you won't be so good. It's a different game over there."

They weren't wrong, at least at first. Back for the summer in Philadelphia and competing in the Sonny Hill League at age eleven, Kobe went the entire schedule without scoring a single basket. Yes, he was playing "up"—against older players—but he was crushed.

"Kobe actually grew up in this league," Tee Shields, who had coached Joe in the Sonny Hill League, would tell reporters years later.

In one of his early seasons in the league, a counselor who was scanning the player applications, looking for problems, noticed that under *Career Plans,* Kobe had listed "NBA."

The answer represented just the kind of unrealistic attitude the league wanted to guard against. For the Hill League, basketball was the carrot used to lure boys away from the treacherous pitfalls of Philadelphia's streets. The game itself was certainly prized, but the emphasis was on a realistic future.

The counselor had seen answers like this before. In fact, they were just about all like this. Many players believed they were headed for the NBA's huge glory and even huger paychecks. This was where the best young talent in Greater Philadelphia went at each other, and the swagger ran deep. It was a game of confidence, and playing it well could bring huge surges of self-assurance that could also be blinding. It was the mission of the league to build that confidence in young players while at the same time forcing them to see the light.

So the counselor made it a point to admonish Kobe. "Only one in a million make it to the NBA," the counselor said, "so you have to plan on a future other than basketball."

"I'm going to be that one in a million," Kobe allegedly replied. After all, he explained, Magic Johnson had done it, Michael Jordan had done it. Why not him?

It was just the level of confidence and expectation that his father had encouraged in him. Some would later label Bryant's attitude pure arrogance. Many would find it hard to stomach. Others were simply awed by seeing someone so young with such a sense of purpose, not to mention an elevated skill level, regardless of how many points he scored at age eleven.

Yet in Kobe's insular experience, the answer was merely routine and logical. He had been raised not to see himself as an average young player. He was well aware of his bloodlines.

"My dad and uncle Chubby spent a lot of time with me," Bryant once explained of his youth. "They worked on my shooting, rebounding, and defense. In addition, they encouraged me to play hard all the time."

In the early stages, it had confirmed his worst fears, what his Italian teammates had been telling him in anger. But he kept at it.

"I believe Kobe is out here most summers, not because I started a trend or anything, but he really wanted to play this game at a young age," Joe Bryant would later tell the *Philadelphia Tribune* in 1994. "We see it as educational."

In all, Joe Bryant spent eight pro seasons in Europe, playing and coaching in Italy, Spain, and France. The experience meant that young Kobe Bean traveled extensively, viewing a range of wonders from the Alps to the Vatican to the ruins of Rome to the romantic wonders of the Venetian canals. Only later when they looked back would the Americans who played in Italy come to grasp how relaxed the place was, wherever they played. Joe Bryant would recall strolling the local streets in the evenings with his family, eating ice cream—the kind of memories they could return to again and again much later, after things had turned so bad.

In August of 1991, Joe planned to play at least one more season and maybe more. By then, Pam seemed content with living abroad. She had become an excellent Italian cook and had adapted many European influences to her lifestyle and eye for design. "It's wonderful in Italy," she said at that time. "The people are so pleasant, and everybody knows everybody. For Joe to play there has been a blessing in disguise."

"I have to say my wife has been there with me till the end," Joe confessed to the *Tribune*. "I love her for keeping me and our family together."

The death knell for the Bryants' time in Italy came with a late-night phone call in the fall of 1991. Kobe's grandparents shared the stunning news that Magic Johnson had announced he had contracted the HIV virus and was retiring from basketball. The next morning, Pam and Joe broke the news to Kobe without going into the details of the disease that was forcing the Lakers star from the game. It didn't matter. The thirteen-year-old was crushed. He cried, he struggled to eat, a mourning that lasted more than a week.

"I was just trying to understand," he remembered. He didn't know what HIV was, but he researched it, trying to find out. "I cried. I didn't know what it was about. I read some books, rented a movie on it. To see. As a kid you just don't know what to do. Hoping I could help him out in some type of way. It was very difficult."

Joe had begun that season with a fragile little team in France, while his kids attended a Swiss school just across the border. He could have played on in Europe forever, or at least for two more seasons, he figured, heaving up jump shots for one team or another. But, despite her comfort in Europe, Pam was understandably road weary and homesick, and the kids needed to get back to America to complete their lives.

With no college degree, Joe was again anxious about his life after his playing career. Maybe he could coach. After sixteen seasons playing pro ball, he called it quits just days after Johnson's announcement. Jellybean's basketball journey had taken him as far as he could go. It was becoming Kobe's turn, and the pace would quicken to a blur.

Kobe would return to Ciriglio in the summer of 2013, toting a floral backpack and wearing pastel shirts. He would pose beside the Welcome sign outside the village, and he would go down to the little mountainside court in the stand of trees to find it in disrepair, with even the soccer field right below it now seemingly abandoned.

The world had changed.

In Pistoia, he and a bodyguard went to the arena that was brand-new when he was ten. He went right to the upper level and knew how to find the door that used to always allow him access, even without a key. He walked around the upper level of the arena, looking down on the floor where as a mop boy he staged his half-time shows. He paused to reflect, then exited quickly.

In 2015, he returned again to Pistoia, appearing suddenly early one morning at the city's center and surprising people coming and going. "Is that really Kobe?" they asked.

Alessandro Conti, the team's communications employee, heard that Kobe was in town and ran over from his residence to greet him. But the world's great superstar had vanished, pushing on to yet another location to stalk his many childhood ghosts.

Chapter 10

LOWER MERION

THE BRYANTS RETURNED to Philadelphia in November 1991 to find the world astir. There were bombings in Belfast, civil war in Croatia, and a presidential election under way in the United States. A relatively unknown Arkansas politician named Bill Clinton was seeking to gain traction in his bid for the Democratic Party's nomination. Clarence Thomas, who was up for a Supreme Court seat, faced accusations that he had sexually harassed Anita Hill.

The album of the year was Quincy Jones's *Back on the Block,* and the Bryants were certainly that as they moved back into their old suburban home in Wynnewood. Soon Joe and Kobe were duking it out in titanic one-on-one matches in the driveway. Each day, Kobe was growing as a player, which meant that Joe became increasingly physical in trying to hold on to his dominance. The resulting busted lips and shouting matches would draw an irate Pam out into the yard to break up the pushing and shoving, with a dirty eye cast Joe's way.

Just before Thanksgiving—a few weeks after Magic Johnson's HIV announcement—Freddie Mercury, the front man of the rock band Queen, died of AIDS, which served to amp up emotions for the Lakers and their fans, who believed that Johnson might suffer a similar fate. An atmosphere of mourning engulfed the franchise, and without Johnson's leadership, the team's fortunes plummeted.

Meanwhile, Kobe Bean was intent on jumping headlong into his

American high school career. An eighth grader, he encountered some difficulty blending into the urban African American experience. The eight years abroad had left him with a unique identity. His schoolmates in the Philadelphia suburbs would marvel at the new brother in class with the strange accent.

As usual, he threw himself into basketball. He recruited a neighborhood kid, Robby Schwartz, who was scrawnier and shorter but in many ways just as driven, to join him for shooting and playing drills. Mostly, Schwartz rebounded and wound up on the losing end of 100–10 games of full-court one-on-one.

Bryant had shot up to well over six feet and was startlingly thin, with long arms that snaked out from his slim shoulders.

But his coaches found him to be a harsh, impatient young customer who glowered anytime a move was made to substitute for him in a game, so much so that Joe took to speaking to him in Italian to calm him down. It was his willfulness that struck people time and again. Bryant's obvious task was to prove himself, over and over and over again.

The first opportunity for that didn't take long.

He was eating lunch in the cafeteria of Bala Cynwyd Junior High on his first day in eighth grade that November when another boy walked up and stood over him.

"I hear you're a pretty good basketball player," the boy said. "Well, to be the man, you have to beat the man."

"So I played him after school," Bryant would recount later. "I shut him out. And I got my respect there.

"That's what I had been looking for all my years in Italy. My adrenaline was running so much. He had no idea."

The "man" of Bala Cynwyd Junior High wouldn't be the only one to be humbled by thirteen-year-old Kobe. Now much older, Mo Howard still fancied his game solid and played pickup with a group of old friends that included Joe at a health club in Philadelphia. "If we only had eight or nine guys, we'd ask one of our sons to fill in," Howard remembered. "And, man, the first time Kobe filled in, I'm going to tell you something, I was guarding him, and that kid busted my ass. He had to be thirteen years old. You know how later, as a Laker, when he scored, he'd give them that look? I saw that at thirteen. This kid just fucked my ego up, totally destroyed it."

Word soon enough leaked out about the new kid on the team at Bala Cynwyd, the son of an NBA player. Gregg Downer, the thirty-three-year-old coach at nearby Lower Merion High, dropped by to take a peek at an eighth-grade game.

"When I went to that ballgame, it wasn't like the Kobe Bryant Show," Downer recalled in a 2015 interview. "I went there and he was kind of being yanked in and out of the game and I couldn't really get a feel for how good he was. He was thin, a little more than six feet and about 135 pounds. It looked like he wanted to play point guard. I mean he wanted the ball in his hands."

Downer was in his second season as the coach at Lower Merion, a program in suburban Montgomery County that had last won the state championship in 1943. He wasn't quite sure how he was going to revive the program, but watching that first time, the coach got the idea that the skinny kid on the floor was part of the answer.

"When I took the job in 1990, it was pretty much of a complete rebuild," Downer recalled. "When I interviewed for the job, they told stories of ending games with four players on the court due to academic ineligibility. One game they lost 54 to 13 and didn't score any points in the second half."

So Downer invited the new eighth grader to visit varsity practice at Lower Merion High.

"That's when I got a real sense as to what he was," the coach said.

For starters, the prospect walked in with his six-foot-nine father.

"When I worked Kobe out initially, Joe was standing in the corner," Downer said. "And I began to put two and two together as to who this was genetically."

Downer had played point guard at Lynchburg College, a Division III school in Virginia, in the 1980s. But in the 1970s, he had been a serious Sixers fan, with seats in the Spectrum. He idolized Doug Collins, but his memories of Jellybean began to come back to him. He even remembered that Jellybean had a father who sat near his seats in the Spectrum.

Joe Bryant didn't come on strong that day at Lower Merion's

practice, preferring instead to stay in the background to allow Kobe the moment, an approach that would become a trend. It was just a few minutes into the scrimmage when Downer realized he was watching someone with pro-level skills, a mere kid who was cutting up his varsity players with ease.

The older players at Lower Merion saw the same and were struck with the first inkling that a rising freshman might soon be dominating their lives.

"Once you saw his initial skill set," the coach recalled, "once you understood the genetic piece of this, and once you began to really think about it, once you saw his work ethic and kind of that alpha mentality, you just began to know that you were dealing with something very special, very unique."

As he watched, he remarked to an assistant that he was confident this was the type of player who would allow them to keep their jobs.

His college days were long over, but Downer still played competitive recreation-league games. So something prompted him that day to take on the eighth grader himself in a little one-on-one. The coach suffered the same fate as his players, the same fate as Mo Howard, the same fate as Joe Bryant's European teammates—embarrassment at the hands of a thirteen-year-old.

That summer, a player about the same age named Donnie Carr encountered Kobe Bean in a Sonny Hill developmental league. They were both coming out of eighth grade, but both were playing "all the way up the ladder" in Hill's league for eleventh and twelfth graders.

Carr had heard so much about this son of an NBA player with supposedly unlimited potential. "But the first time I saw him," Carr recalled, "it was this skinny, long kid that had two knee pads on. It wasn't what I was expecting. He was still growing, and, with his knees always hurting, he had a problem bending down, stuff like that. He was really long. Long arms, long frame. He was a pretty big young kid. He had grown to almost six four."

The knee issues were Osgood-Schlatter disease, which brings intense knee pain in athletically inclined adolescents. The condition slowed Bryant and left him looking awkward. At that time, to get off a shot, he had to get his defenders to a spot on the floor, then start using a series of pump fakes to get his shot off. Once he got liftoff, he could usually elevate enough to get his shot over the top of defenders, Carr recalled. "But, to be completely honest, back then we saw potential, but it wasn't like it was nothing special because, again, he wasn't as fast or as explosive as he would later become. He was kind of like a lanky kid that was kind of moving in slow motion.

"We were all like, 'He's good, but is he that good?' No one said it to his face, obviously, but we would all speak amongst ourselves and say, 'I don't see nothing special.'"

Their great high school rivalry would begin that summer, right there in the Sonny Hill League, Carr recalled, laughing. "That's how our rivalry started, because we would trash-talk to each other. I would talk smack to him; he would talk smack back. Even though Kobe was from the suburbs, I would tell people this all the time: he never acted like a suburban kid. He always acted like an inner-city kid, and it wasn't synched, or faked. He always had Philadelphia toughness and this mentality like he would never back down. He loved challenges. Like, if you started talking to him, he would really get locked in and focused, and you could just see that determination in his face, and he would just start playing even harder."

As Carr got to know Kobe Bean, he realized this kid in the knee pads spent a lot of time creating challenges for himself. "He would just look for anything that would motivate and challenge him," the rival said. "He had the same mentality when he was a young guy that people would talk about later. He was always just trying to find something that would fuel that fire and have him playing with that edge. He had a lot of that in his game back then, when he was heading into ninth grade."

Among those to get an early view of Kobe in the Hill League was Eddie Jones, then a six-foot-six forward at Temple University. "Even back then, when he was thirteen, he could play," Jones recalled. "Even back then he could bust people."

"It was great competition, great fun," Bryant remembered of the Sonny Hill League. "The guys from Temple University used to come down and watch us play because we would play in their gym. Eddie Jones used to come down there, and Aaron McKie, and Rick

Brunson. These were the guys that would play after we would. So I would stay and check them out a little bit. Eddie used to select me to play on his team for pickup games. He thought I had a little game, so he would pick me up, and I would hoop with them."

Early Aces

That fall at Lower Merion, Downer discovered that Bryant had a startling work ethic. He pushed himself through a grueling self-improvement schedule that included road work, weights, and seemingly nonstop basketball. In team practices, he was determined to never lose a team drill or contest. For almost four years he would maintain a perfect record in that regard.

"When I started to figure out how good this character named Kobe Bryant was, I hired people on my coaching staff based on playing ability," he said. "My sole intention was, 'I've got to find people that can guard this kid, that can compete with this kid, that can challenge this kid.'"

He picked up a former college player, an athletic guard named Jimmy Kieserman. Then he talked his own brother Drew, who had size and strength, into leaving the corporate world to work as a coach.

The inside joke of the Lower Merion program became, "Holy shit, I'll jump on a plane. I'll come guard this fourteen-year-old. This isn't going to be a problem." The punch line, of course, was that they all would be beaten by the ferocious freshman.

Downer's other hire was his young star's father. In the back of the coach's mind was another concern, that a suburban program like Lower Merion's could lose its new addition to one of Philadelphia's established powerhouse programs, such as Roman Catholic, where Carr himself was on the roster. Having Kobe's father as a coach would help cement the relationship; plus, the family's two daughters were already at Lower Merion, adjusting well and playing volleyball.

It would be an issue that hovered silently over the program for the next few seasons. But it would become increasingly clear that Bryant liked having a program he could dominate, one in which he could find all the playing time he needed to develop, one that fed his attitude.

"The first couple times we played inner-city schools, there'd be a buzz about me," he once explained. "Half of 'em would say 'Oh, he's soft, from the suburbs.'"

Part of the negative vibe came from Lower Merion's record in Bryant's freshman year. A season earlier, Downer had coached the team to a twenty-win season. Expectations had been high, but graduation and injury had depleted the roster. The 1992–93 Lower Merion Aces, featuring a freshman Kobe Bryant as a starter, would go 4–20.

"It was not pretty," Downer said.

The coach and his future star would discover that they shared an absolute hatred for defeat. "Losing that many times was probably earth-shattering for him," Downer said, and the losing made it harder to get him out of games. "He did it all for us as time went on, you know, played spot five through one, but he was a hard guy to bench, I'll tell you that."

Like his father, Kobe Bean was prone to taking some bad shots. Downer would pull him out of the game to try to discourage that.

"I mean, we tried that a few times, and that didn't go over too well," Downer recalled. "He'd scowl at you and bark at you. He didn't like that."

When things got bad, Joe would again speak Italian to calm his son. Downer never knew what his assistant was saying, but it seemed to work.

"I think Joe was a good buffer," the coach explained. "You know, Kobe didn't bark at me a lot, but if he did, I think he would have his dad to answer to."

It didn't hurt that the young coach began reconsidering the idea of taking him out of games. The coaching staff adjusted to a new philosophy: "A bad shot by Kobe is better than a fumbled pass by a teammate."

"He had the basketball IQ, obviously," the coach explained. "He was a very good passer, even as a freshman. He could make his teammates better, but I think when we were struggling, when our talent base wasn't that good, he just said, 'You know what? I've got to do a lot of this on my own.'"

The circumstances were a perfect recipe for problems between young Bryant and his older teammates—the same problems that he'd faced in Italy, that he would later face in the NBA.

"As time went on, the alpha kicked in," Downer admitted of Bryant's dominating personality.

But the obvious point for any coach in such circumstances was that Bryant's presence also made many things easier. "The easy stuff was the work ethic and his spongelike mentality to be the best that he could be and absorb information," Downer said. "I always thought his brain was a sponge, and obviously if you've coached, you know that you can't say this about all your players. You tell Kobe something once, you don't have to say it again. Like, it's in there. Kobe changed things in the sense that we now had a centerpiece, but it wasn't like he was surrounded with a lot of great talent.

"The easy stuff," Downer added, "was just him winning all the sprints, him being the hardest worker on the team, him getting up in the faces of his teammates, holding them accountable."

Such an approach brought inevitable friction, especially with the losses of that first year, but the other players found it hard to deny Bryant's dedication, the coach said. "In terms of the seniors and some of the older guys that hadn't had a lot of success, I mean, once they saw how hard he worked and how passionate he was about the game, I think it was hard for them to second-guess us or not somewhat get on board with what we were trying to do."

Evan Monsky, one of the older players on that club, said that in looking back at Bryant, it's also important to understand that his push to be great wasn't a constant, unrelenting component of his personality in the locker room. "He was a happy, normal kid, laughing and joking with everybody else," Monsky said.

Still, the coaches found it hard at times to digest young Kobe Bean's overwhelming presumption. "I found him to be a little stubborn," Downer admitted. "I found him to be a little arrogant, but these were qualities that make you great."

Downer liked his players to "front the post," or defend post players by playing in front of them to deny them the ball. "We were barking at Kobe one day in practice to front the post, and he said,

'Well, that's not what I'm going to do in the NBA.' We barked back, 'Well, this isn't the NBA.'"

Some would argue that the dominating personality of Kobe Bryant, aided by the presence of his father on the coaching staff, totally took over the Lower Merion program. There were perhaps elements of truth to that, but, Downer pointed out, Joe Bryant made a point of never crossing the line of impropriety, of always attempting to be a normal parent, never pushing or campaigning for any advantage.

Joe was diligent in his coaching duties and became a solid junior-varsity coach and an excellent assistant on the varsity team.

"Back then, they had this thing called the seat-belt rule, where coaches had to sit down," Downer remembered. "Dumb rule, a really dumb rule, but, literally, you could not stand up when you were coaching. I spent, like, probably ten years of my coaching career with this rule where you had to sit down."

One game that first year, Joe stood on the bench to argue a call and drew a technical foul. The next game, he was nowhere to be found, gone from the bench. One of the coaches looked up during the first half and spied Jellybean sitting high up in the arena. Downer sent an assistant up at halftime to find out what was wrong. Joe said he didn't want to be a negative influence on the team and had quietly decided to remove himself from the cauldron of games.

Downer and the other coaches laughed and insisted that Joe return to the bench, that his presence was too valuable to lose. Besides, none of the others spoke Italian.

Although Downer was a young coach at the time, he would go on to become a dean of Pennsylvania high school basketball, with three state championship teams on his résumé. The experience of coaching Kobe Bryant was formative, he said. "You know, when you put the whole puzzle together now and you look at his age and you know, kind of, the journey he's made, just his singularity, the focus, was just incredible. I don't know if 'crazy' is the right word, but he was certainly unique."

The losses of the first season certainly made life difficult for both the young coach and the star freshman, but rather than drive them apart, they served as a bonding element, Downer said. "We didn't like to lose. We were not very good. I mean, after every loss, we just couldn't wait to get in the gym the next day to get back to work."

"My first year was very difficult," Bryant remembered. "I think we were 4 and 20. It was a very hard year. But I gained some experience. My high school coach was a great coach, and he stayed with me late after practice and came early to help me before practice. We would talk about the game, and he really helped me grow and mature as a player."

Despite his frustration with his team's heavy losses that first season, Bryant still produced some spellbinding displays of athleticism, a development that raised eyebrows in Philadelphia high school basketball circles.

His talent and drive were attractive to many coaches across the city. Sam Rines, an Amateur Athletic Union coach in Philadelphia and thus a guy always on the lookout for talent, recalled the first time he saw Bryant.

"He wasn't that established," Rines recalled. "I mean, you could tell he was good, and he was the kind of guy you would look at and say, 'Holy shit, he's only in ninth grade.'"

Shortly after that, young Bryant injured his knee and missed the final few games of his freshman season. "He was fourteen years old and about six foot two," Jeremy Treatman, a local basketball writer and broadcaster, recalled. "He wasn't dunking or anything then. He was really thin. In fact, he broke his kneecap because somebody just bumped knees with him. That's how thin he was."

The situation provided Downer with an opportunity to see how bleak things would have been without Bryant's presence on the team. "I always thought we were one Kobe Bryant ankle sprain away from being an average high school team," he said, "and we probably were."

Even after that first season, Downer recognized the immense pressure Bryant had brought to the team. He realized that the pressure was only going to grow dramatically over the coming years. Kobe Bryant had a clear destination in mind, and if you weren't on board, he had clearly conveyed the idea that he was the sort who wouldn't hesitate to grab you by the collar and throw you right off the train.

Chapter 11

THE VIBE

THE SCENE KEPT shifting for Kobe Bryant, but each location seemed to riff on a familiar dynamic. His sophomore season at Lower Merion abruptly featured two black faces in a fluffy soft field of whiteness. That was how he and Jermaine Griffin met, one a refugee from a life of privilege in Europe, the other escaping Far Rockaway in Queens, New York.

Griffin had come to Lower Merion as a sophomore, fresh from the hard streets of "Far Rock," as part of a youth program called ABC, or A Better Chance. He was one of eight youths who lived in a house with a counselor. The experience provided them with an opportunity to change the direction of their lives.

"They take a lot of kids from the inner city," Griffin explained in a 2015 interview. "I felt it was the best decision for me to make at the time."

Coach Gregg Downer said that Griffin's giving his life over to a program such as ABC required tremendous character from the young man who showed up at Lower Merion in late summer, 1993. He encountered a very different world from the one he had inhabited in "Far Rock," a seaside community that features acres of public housing and thousands of aging bungalows left over from an earlier age, when Far Rockaway was a resort, unmarked by urban blight.

"This area was very bad," Carmela George told the *New York*

Times. "There was shooting, and drugs, and prostitution, and gang wars, and the bungalows were burning."

That atmosphere clashed with growing gentrification in the seaside community as yuppies moved in to claim available real estate. Griffin had seen much in his young life, but A Better Chance had offered him an opportunity to experience different things.

"Where I came from was predominately black," he explained. "The school I went to at Lower Merion was predominately white. So it was definitely, like, a culture shock to me."

The move wasn't about basketball, but that quickly became part of the equation. One of the first people he met during his initial tour of the school was Downer, who immediately noted that Griffin was six three. The coach didn't take long to spell out the circumstances, and the sophomore from Queens liked what he heard, "just seeing his vision of what he wanted to accomplish as a team and hearing about the heartaches and pain, about the season prior to when I got there."

He soon got to know Kobe Bean, and the two found a mutual admiration. "When I first met him, he was a cool kid," remembered Griffin. "We just, you know, locked eyes. He was working on his game. I was working on my game."

"The basketball thing was a piece of it," Downer observed, "but I think he and Kobe just connected. We had other pretty good players on that team, but he and Jermaine became very close. Jermaine kind of became the second fiddle on that ball club. Jermaine was an important piece, and I think that he became Kobe's partner in crime."

"You know Kobe was our most confident," Griffin said. "I think that's the reason why Kobe and I was so close in school. I'm a confident guy myself. Being that I came from New York, I was a little different, had a little different talk, a little different slang, a little different style, but that was much needed."

As such, Griffin was able to provide a decidedly different perspective on the events and decisions that his new friend faced. Bryant was going through his own sort of culture shock at Lower Merion. He seemed quite comfortable at the suburban high school, yet he also clearly hungered to experience all things African American, to gain some sense of his cultural roots, to stop feeling like a stranger in a strange land. "Kobe would say, 'This is the way it goes.' I'd say, 'Kobe, I think we should go this way,'" Griffin recalled. "That's the reason why we were able to click so well, because we both were confident. He didn't have to hold my hand. I didn't have to hold his hand. He could lead in his way, and I could lead in my way."

Griffin had met a select few on the streets of Far Rock who were, by necessity, extremely confident people. However, Bryant's confidence even as a sophomore was clearly over the top. Griffin looked beyond that and soon learned about other facets of his new friend's personality. Beneath the air of superiority lurked a sensitivity leavened by a take-care-of-business approach. "I definitely witnessed another side that some other people might not have seen or heard or been around before," he said.

In many ways, Bryant was "just like everybody else," Griffin observed, except that he was clearly an alpha male, on his way to becoming a world-class basketball player.

Looking back on the period, another Bryant teammate, Evan Monsky, agreed that Kobe was just another adolescent trying to find his place in the sometimes complex world of high school, where he was the smiling, dark face in the hallways, tall, standing above the mostly white throng moving between classes.

Soon enough, celebrity would come crashing in on that experience, and Bryant would embrace it hungrily like any teen, smirking all the while. In many ways his sophomore year would provide his last hours of innocent youth and amateur freedom before the life he wanted so badly took hold and carried him away—like a childhood star, several acquaintances would observe—to a place where he could only look back later and wonder at what treasures he had failed to collect.

"In high school we were definitely jokesters and pranksters and things like that," remembered Griffin, who came to revel in his experience at Lower Merion and his friendship with Bryant. "When it came to school, you have days you don't want to be there. You have your days you want to skip out for a second. We enjoyed school, but it was also a time when you barked out or you just wanted to go out and get something to eat or you wanted to go out and take a little break, get away for a second just to listen to some music or whatever."

They shared those escapes, slipping off from school, just as they shared the discovery they found in the sophomore English classes of Jeanne Mastriano, a bespectacled young woman with a hint of countercultural flair. "She was just one of my favorite teachers," Griffin said. "There was just something about her. She always gave me great critiques, you know, on all my writings and things like that. We always had in-depth conversations just out of the normal realm of things. Being in her class just changed me, just gave me an outlook as far as writing, as far as life, just talking, and a lot of books that we read. It just took me to a whole other level."

"We did a lot of writing in tenth grade," Mastriano recalled in 2015. "A lot of freewrites, a lot of writer's notebook freewrites, just getting the words out—the good words and the bad words, too."

The writing work meant much to Griffin in terms of assessing his early experiences in Far Rock, just as it helped Bryant examine his own young life—so much so that in 2015 he would look back and describe Mastriano as his "muse," which in turn brought a laugh from his former teacher for being labeled a demigoddess.

"A muse, one of the nine sister goddesses of inspiration, right?" she told a radio interviewer. "Yeah, he wasn't even calling me a muse when he was in high school, but we had a good relationship."

Bryant always seemed to be gone from class, taken away by the long weekends playing on one elite team or another, but he always returned to school with his assignments done, which earned Mastriano's hard-won respect. "He was remarkably disciplined in high school," she recalled.

The discipline was Pam Bryant's work, family friends said. She insisted on it as part of her effort to control her son's rapidly changing environment.

Even though Bryant's focus on his schoolwork didn't approach the mental effort he directed toward basketball, Mastriano also sensed his sizable hunger for gaining all sorts of knowledge. "He sees learning as empowering. He listens very intently," she offered in 2014. "Could you imagine what the world would look like if everybody lived that way?"

Mastriano would grade the pieces by Griffin and Bryant and push them to ask what they wanted out of the writing, to infuse it with purpose.

"He would always write about basketball," she said. "He'd always talk about being a pro ballplayer."

Bryant had long shown an affinity for writing, for poetry, that delighted Big Joe, who had been amazed over the years by the things his grandson would present to him. Big Joe had long raised the issue that Kobe was so talented in other pursuits, he might want to think about being something other than a basketball player, but Jellybean and his son were so locked in on the world of basketball, there seemed little chance of that.

The Rapper

His writing life as a teen would help Bryant find sustenance beyond the narrow confines of the game. Part of his effort to deal with his own identity crisis had brought an exploration of the African American culture around him, the one his parents had come from. He had already begun that interface by the time he met Griffin, first with the Sonny Hill League and in the many pickup games he sought out in the gyms and on the playgrounds of North Philly.

Strangely, one of his strongest connections to the black experience had come at the Jewish Community Center on City Avenue, right there in suburban Wynnewood. Joe had started working there as the fitness director, a position that was part of a patchwork of part-time jobs he kept up to stop the intense drain on the family's cash reserves now that he was no longer playing professionally. In addition to working at the JCC and being on the payroll at Lower Merion, he coached the girls' varsity team at a private Jewish school, Akiba, in Wynnewood, where he had been a huge hit with his players.

"He was phenomenal," recalled Jeremy Treatman, then the Akiba boys junior-varsity coach. "He was so involved and he was so fun. He made it fun for the girls. I mean, he really taught. They weren't very good, but he really taught them. He was enthusiastic as hell."

Treatman and Joe Bryant soon became fast friends as the boys coach watched Jellybean launch his enthusiasm into showing the girls all the various fundamentals, right down to ball fakes and footwork. Bryant seemed to enjoy the coaching so much, Treatman figured he might have stayed at the school for a long time if the job had paid better.

Treatman remembered Kobe, in that early teen period, tagging along to Akiba practices, where he would run through stunning displays at a side basket. His game wasn't the game of a kid.

Treatman asked Joe if he had been as good as his son at a similar age.

"Hell, no," the father replied with his ever-present laugh.

"Really?" Treatman asked.

"Trust me," Joe said. "He's so much better than I was at this age. Just watch him."

Beyond basketball, the huge impact on the teenaged Kobe's life would come at the Jewish Community Center. Father and son would shoot around in the JCC's gym, which is where young Kobe got to know Anthony Bannister, a custodian at the center who was about sixteen at the time. Bannister was a blossoming expert on all things rap, from the golden oldies of the genre to the next exploding phase of black music—hip-hop, R&B, the swirling strands of expression based in anger, machismo, and bling that for more than a decade had captured the imaginations of every cultural stripe of global youth. The rapid-fire delivery of the spoken language of rap resonated with the young poet in Kobe Bryant.

Bannister presented an intriguing figure with his sizable talents as a writer and ambitions as a record producer, all hatched right there in the janitor's side room at the Jewish Community Center. It was tucked just off a dimly lit hallway beside the gym, and it would become the classroom where Bryant learned all the nuances of hip-hop that he had missed growing up in Europe. They'd shoot hoops together, then retreat to the office to bang out lyrics, rhymes, beats, and other pieces of expression.

As Griffin's friendship with Bryant grew, he too was drawn into the Jewish Community Center and the Bannister experience, which included other figures aspiring to make a name in the Philly rap scene.

"He was definitely an influence," Griffin remembered of Bannister. "He was a cool, laid-back guy who loved music, loved writing, loved to entertain. He had a few years on us. We'd go over there and, you know, do music, write music. We'd listen to them free-style, listen to them rap. Kobe and I played basketball. You know, that definitely was, like, a hangout. Like, he was one of the reasons why we kind of got even deeper and deeper into music and started writing and things like that, because we was listening to him."

"This kid is amazing," Kobe told Griffin.

"He could rap," Griffin remembered of Bannister. "He had a way with words."

Bannister showed Bryant much of the process of the genre, sampling beats and slices of songs, then laying your words and ideas over them, using things in new ways, juxtaposing something from one song with something from another.

"Kobe was fourteen, skinny, wiry but passionate and determined," Bannister once explained to writer Thomas Golianopoulos.

Bryant would repay Bannister for his help by visiting a sort of basketball terror upon him in the JCC gym.

"He was definitely that kind of guy," Griffin said of Bryant with a laugh. "You know, he definitely pushed the envelope. I'm quite sure Anthony got pissed off plenty of days, you know."

It helped that Bannister had a sense of humor and could actually hold his own on occasion.

"Kobe would work out, test out his new moves on Anthony," Griffin remembered, explaining that Bryant would always try his most "hot dog" creations in the JCC gym before daring to trot them out on Philly's playgrounds. In that regard, Bannister became something of a basketball lab rat for Bryant.

The next stop for this new interest in music was a collection of similar figures in the Lower Merion lunchroom who passed the time by freestyling, throwing out lyrics and beats, sparring with other rappers. It was there that Bryant met another influence, Kevin "Sandman" Sanchez. Bryant impressed him by writing a rhyme about being a cyborg who battled MCs. If you were a child of influence bent on entering the world of hip-hop, a genre that thrives on street authenticity, it was probably best that your first efforts came in the cafeteria of your suburban high school. It allowed for a low-impact landing for Bryant that helped him to get his bearings in a genre of the music industry driven by the muscular funk of the streets.

"A lot of times," Griffin said, "people would tell him, 'Oh, you're privileged, you've got this kind of lifestyle. You can't rap this way. You can't talk about this. You're not supposed to rap, or if you do rap, you've got to rap like this.' But for him, music was more an escape, more of another way of communicating, another way of telling a story, just like basketball was a way to escape."

Some observers would see Bryant's effort to be a rapper as a naked attempt to gain street cred in his new environment. Many had already begun to dismiss Bryant as a player because he toiled for Lower Merion against what was seen as second-rate, suburban talent, nothing like the hard-nosed Philly game laid down in the Public League.

But if Bryant was after credibility, he came at it obliquely, Griffin explained. Any street cred that happened to come along was usually associated with the beats he created or from their a capella approach. It wasn't like Bryant was trying to pose as a creature of the streets, he said.

Rap music evolved in many different ways in American cities. In Philadelphia, so much of it was based on the battles, the sharp-tongued public exchanges, that seemed custom-made for a competitive spirit like Kobe Bryant. Street cred also came from winning rap battles where participants were spitting slick rhymes at each other laced with sly insults and professions of ultimate machismo.

"You put on your best rap, and whoever wins is the champ," Griffin said. "That's what street cred was to us."

In many ways, Bryant was merely learning to articulate his athletic intentions in a way that his new contemporaries, like Donnie Carr, could understand. The rap game quickly allowed him to gain a means of relating. Even better, it would become the foundation of his style as a trash talker on the floor, essential for playing confidence games with opponents.

The rap battles were raw, in-the-moment confrontations, and Bryant quickly displayed a talent there. It didn't hurt that he was on his way to being an imposing six foot six, with every ounce of confidence that Joe Bryant could pack into his lanky frame.

Indeed, the competitive elements of rap, plus the free-styling, its loose format, struck Bryant and Griffin as being much like basketball.

"Basketball is thinking about the next move, whether you've got to counter a move or whether you're making a move," Griffin said. "The same thing with rap. You want to keep your opponents off balance. You don't want them to get too accustomed to your moves, which way you're going with it."

Bryant, the rapper, would soon venture out further to cut his teeth on the Philly hip-hop scene. "He got into battles with guys who had been writing for years and years and years," Griffin said, "and we had just picked it up. We'd be like, 'Look, we're going to take you guys on.' We were going to get into this battle or fight, what they call it, and we're going to show them that we can hang with some of the best of them."

The basketball influenced the battles, which influenced the writing, which in turn led Bryant and Griffin to look around for things they could sample and pull together into the effort. They were especially influenced by Bannister, Griffin said. "When you're starting out, you're hearing different people, you're trying to develop your sound or develop your theme, you take a little bit here, you take a bit there. So we definitely took some things from him, from a lot of his other guys, his friends that used to come by and rap. We'd get his instrumentals from the latest hip-hop artists. We would just record and free-style. We would write. Kobe had talent musically, a lot of talent. We had fun doing that. He was telling stories, rapping. He was putting words together. You know, sometimes you put words together and you're telling a story, sometimes you're just making a joke, sometimes, you know, we were just playing, listening to a beat, and whatever comes to you is what you would kick in, you would relay, you would spin. They call it spin. We didn't always go in there with a plan. You don't go in there with a plan and say, 'I'm going to talk about this.' "

At first they would write down notes ahead of time, but Bryant quickly learned to go with it. It came down to hearing a beat, feeling a rhythm, and pulling something right out of your heart to go along.

"We didn't have to write stuff down anymore," Griffin explained. "You just go off the top of the dome and kick rhymes, kick raps."

In this atmosphere, the seed of Kobe Bryant the legit rapper was planted, and the project he would form with Bannister and other artists would eventually grow into a major recording deal with Sony Music, bringing with it a whole new round of influence that would change the lives of the Bryants forever.

They named the group CHEIZAW, an acronym for Canon *Homo sapiens* Eclectic Iconic Zaibatsu Abstract Words, something they pulled from the Chi Sah gang in a martial arts movie by Shaw Brothers, *The Kid with the Golden Arm*.

They added members and fought rap battles all over Philly, at South Street, Parkside, Temple University, and Belmont Plateau, at clubs and malls and wherever.

Bryant called himself the Eighth Man and would often avoid the group's public sessions, choosing instead to go at it when they brought things out raw right at one another and showing an affinity for catching his opponents off guard. When Bryant did appear publicly with the group, Griffin was struck by how much the assemblies resembled rowdy basketball games, some of the fans on your side, some on the other, some in between, all waiting to be swayed.

CHEIZAW became the toast of the city's rap-battle scene. "Kobe was nice, man. He was lyrical. I wouldn't have put him in the group if he wasn't," Bannister explained to *Grantland*.

It wasn't long before Gregg Downer could look in the back of the team bus and see Bryant, his face animated, his teammates and Griffin gathered round, leading the group in wild bouts of free-style, with the laughter and looseness ringing out loud. They were all his age, and young Kobe Bryant was very much engaged in closeness with his teammates. At the time, no one realized how special and rare those moments would be, how impossible to find they would become as time and events rolled on.

"If you're with friends, you might touch a soul," Jermaine Griffin said, looking back. "So that's how it is with music. That's how it is with basketball."

PART III

THE CHOSEN ONE

Chapter 12

SUMMER LOVE

For years, Joe Bryant had held a fascination with, almost an envy of, Julius Erving. His experience as a teammate of the famed Doctor J had left him with a revelation that was confirmed again by the quick rise of Magic Johnson. Joe Bryant came away from his NBA experience understanding that if you really wanted to reign supreme in pro basketball, you had to be the man—you had to possess that combination of skill and confidence, that air of assumption to be a team's most dominant player. Jellybean had seen it. The man commanded a different treatment than everybody else.

Jellybean certainly had had the skill. Like many good athletic performers, Joe also had a really hungry ego. But the very best, the elite sports stars like Erving and Johnson, had somewhere along the line found a way to bend a team to their will and individual talent. Just about everything was built around them.

Jellybean had never been quite talented enough, or determined enough, to be the man on an NBA team. Yet it became part of the instructional mantra the father offered for his son. Never, if Joe had anything to do with it, would his son fall short of confidence as he himself had. Beyond even Joe's instruction, time would reveal Kobe Bean's own instinctive drive to dominate that surfaced at every stage of his competitive life, from basketball to the combat of rap.

Thus, at every level, on every team, Kobe Bean cleared a path to dominate, to "be the man," as he himself would say time and again. If he found himself in a situation where he wasn't dominant, then he and his family would seek another situation.

Gregg Downer had begun watching it happen in his high school program. The coach admitted his early concern that Bryant would go to another, bigger school, but it would become clear that such a move would never happen because Bryant had already found his place to dominate at Lower Merion.

Secure in that, Bryant at the end of his freshman season began talking about leading the suburban high school to the unthinkable, a state championship. The Aces then made a big step that year by winning sixteen games and losing just six, with Bryant averaging 22 points and 10 rebounds, sizable numbers for a thirty-two-minute high school game.

Despite such success, it could be argued that Kobe Bryant's main development happened elsewhere, away from Lower Merion and public high school basketball. The rise of full-time, off-season basketball, mostly through what is known as Amateur Athletic Union basketball, had become a huge factor in the development and identifying of elite talent in the early 1990s, and that role would grow even larger over the ensuing years.

It wasn't strictly AAU so much as it was a collection of elite tournaments that brought the best talent face to face in events around the country. As Sam Rines, the coach of Bryant's AAU team, the Sam Rines All-Stars, explained in a 2015 interview, he coached Joe Bryant's son from March to October each year, while Gregg Downer had him for a relatively short few months, from late October to early March.

Despite the role that Sam Rines played in Bryant's formative years, he was mystified over the decades that he was never interviewed by any of the writers or media figures attempting to understand the global phenomenon of Kobe Bryant.

Bryant could have played with many better-known, more powerful AAU teams, Rines explained, but he preferred Rines's lesser-known, less-ambitious team because he could dominate the roster and be its featured player.

When the Bryants began shopping for AAU teams, Sam Rines

was a young coach, just beginning to run the team that had been set up and founded in 1992 by his father, also named Sam Rines. The elder Rines had won a state championship as a Pennsylvania high school coach in the 1970s, then spent a dozen years as an assistant coach at La Salle University, until he stepped down in 1992.

Before Kobe could begin with Rines's team, Joe had to make sure that Kobe would be the man. In one sense, that status could be measured simply by the number of shots he could take in an hour-long AAU game. The more shots, the better the opportunity.

"A conversation came up between Joe and my father originally to make sure Kobe had a good situation," the younger Rines explained. "There's a difference between you shooting twenty shots and you shooting five shots."

Kobe had to have the fifteen extra shots to develop. The coaches and other players would have to understand that Kobe was the top of the team's hierarchy.

Rines quickly learned that Bryant hated coming off the floor, just as he did in games for Lower Merion. The AAU coach recalled that Bryant reacted so negatively to substitution that the team elected to carry just nine players to avoid the conflict. Even then, there remained substantial confrontation.

"We normally carried nine because we tried to leave Kobe in," Rines admitted in a 2015 interview. "He loved his playing time, and we knew that. We knew we couldn't sub five and five like we normally do when Kobe was playing because he didn't want to come out. Kobe was Kobe. I mean Kobe was a showman. Kobe on stage was probably the most focused kid I've ever seen on the court. No bullshit, no taking it easy. He's not going to smile at you. He's going to kill you from bell to bell, no mercy. He didn't give a fuck.

"He was a straight alpha male," Rines continued. "If there was ever a definition for a basketball player as an alpha, he was the total alpha male every time he stepped on the court. He was that way at thirteen and fourteen and fifteen and right down the pike."

If anything, Bryant's demands to stay on the floor were even more severe, irrational even, with his AAU team because those teams were a collection of the best players from many schools, not from a single school, like suburban Lower Merion. But adding a player like Kobe Bryant helped the Rines program grow. It had actually started out as a weekend clinic to help players improve their games and had expanded from there.

"We picked up one kid here, one kid there to make the team better," Rines explained, "and then once we made the team better, we were able to get other guys because guys like Kobe came in. Kobe was an addition. At that time we were a new group to the big-time level because we never had those kinds of players. Back then we were considered a second-tier AAU team because we only had maybe two or three lower-level Division I guys. There was a lot of opportunity, when Kobe came out. AAU was starting to become really big. People were starting to host tournaments. Kobe used to beg for us to go to more tournaments."

AAU competition was already gaining a reputation as a playing environment with little stress on teaching or fundamentals, but the elder Rines wanted to develop young talent by focusing on basics and playing mostly regional tournaments. The format also allowed his son to gain experience as a head coach while the father influenced things as an older, trusted assistant.

Kobe clearly respected the older Rines and soon clashed with the younger head coach.

"We're up 25 points," the younger Rines recalled of one of his first games coaching Kobe. "He didn't think he played well enough to rest. He wanted back in. We argued about it."

"Put me back in," Kobe told him.

"No," Rines said. "You're not going back in because you talked to me the way you did."

"We had our disagreements," Rines recalled. "We had a couple of bad situations, a few debates."

And Jellybean was right there in support of Kobe's demands.

"Joe and I bumped heads," Rines recalled. "He had the mannerisms of a parent."

The parents of AAU players were known for becoming aggressive with coaches over playing time. AAU ball in those days was a place for elite talent to be seen by college coaches. To be seen, players had to play. Plus, there was a financial cost to play on such teams. Parents wanted their money's worth for their sons. "When me and him would argue, Joe would talk to him in Italian," Rines said of his debates with Kobe. "So nobody understood, nobody knew what he was saying, and Kobe would snap out of it. But you know, Kobe was something else with anger problems."

A good portion of the anger remained mysterious, but another part of it stemmed from Bryant's inability to handle the ball at an elite level. Even so, there was so much about his game that resonated with coaches from the very first time they watched him play. Rines recalled first seeing Bryant in an elite tournament.

"It was down in Delaware," the coach said. "I watched him close, I didn't know who he was. I was standing there watching him...I see this tall six-four, six-five lanky kid hitting jump shots. He was phenomenal, especially being in ninth grade playing with twelfth graders. Obviously he didn't have the strength at the time to battle inside, but he had the athleticism, the shot."

Rines didn't see anything that day that made him think he was looking at an NBA player. "You could see he was one of the better freshmen because of his size and athleticism," he said.

His conclusion at the time was that Bryant could be a very good high school player.

"Kobe was so young and so good young," Rines explained. "He wasn't a ball handler. But where he lacked in certain areas, he was able to work hard and push his game up. I watched him work out."

The more time he spent coaching Bryant, the more he came to see a teenager who was spending just about every available minute on basketball. "His morning," Rines said, "would be at the Bellevue Hotel working out with the pros, afternoons would be St. Joe's University on the track with the parachute with the ball handling. Then at night he would go and work out by himself at the Jewish Y."

And the summertime games became his lab for testing everything. As the money came into the sport, AAU coaches were beginning to recruit top players for their teams, which then attracted other top players and the interest of shoe companies and other support. It was quickly understood that Kobe would be the priority for Rines's team.

"If Kobe took a bad shot," Rines said, "that was part of the learning process of getting Kobe to the next level. We had to accept who he was and what he was. We knew his goal was to get to the next level, we knew what his goals were.

"So he went through a stage of being totally, totally selfish," Rines added. "Then he went through a stage of learning how to dribble and crossing over to the point where he would kick the ball out of bounds eight times, seven times, in a row, just trying to pick up a move. How can you coach that? If he's trying to pick something up and that's what he wanted to do then he would do it. Finally I was like, 'What the fuck? Can we win the game? Let's win the game, and you can work on whatever move you want.' Because the next thing you know, we're down 12, 14, 16 points, with him trying to work on a crossover move in an AAU game."

Bryant's extreme focus on his own development obviously hurt the team many times and disrupted the nature of AAU ball, because the games were basically a showcase for players to be seen by college scouts.

"People depended on the game for scouts," Rines explained. "But if you're a teammate waiting for that jump shot, and Kobe doesn't see it or loses the ball out of bounds, then that teammate's not able to hit as many shots as he should because somebody didn't swing the ball or we weren't playing the right way. This affects the teammate. This affects the guy with the ball, and it affects the shooter, because scouts are saying, 'He's good, but he's lacking something.'"

Bryant's ball-handling deficiencies required an adjustment in elite play, Rines explained. "We had to surround him with other guards for him to look good. He got his lumps and bumps from a couple of guys, especially guys who could play."

A player like elite point guard Shaheen Holloway could expose Bryant's weaknesses, which in turn only drove his determination to eliminate them.

"The best part about it," Rines said, "is that there were good players everywhere. Every team you played, nothing was watered down. The most watered-down team back then might have been a team with seven Division I players."

In the process of the competition, the coaches would identify a problem that would plague Bryant at every stage of his basketball life. "A lot of Kobe's issues, he over-thinks," Rines said. "He over-thinks, over-analyzes. Me and Joe talked about this before. Joe has this mannerism that is unbelievably laid-back. He's telling Kobe, 'Don't think about it, just play. Fuck this, fuck winning, you know what I mean? Just play. You're here to get better. We didn't drive up here for you to have a hissy fit. You're worried about one play when we're going to play three more games today.'"

Obviously, Joe was ever-present, much as his own father had been for his games, except that Joe was using his extensive experience to guide his son through the vagaries of each level of the game, all the while being careful to maintain Kobe's elevated sense of self. Usually such a parental effort can create intense debate around teams, but Joe Bryant knew how to move discreetly. And Pam Bryant, who had such a strong will herself, seemed to avoid the AAU scene almost completely. Even around the Lower Merion team she stayed almost exclusively in the background, focusing her efforts instead on the day-to-day traffic in Kobe's personal life.

Rines was such a young, inexperienced coach, he found himself caught up in the fundamental confrontation with the headstrong young teen, hearing him ask, "Why is this guy yelling at me? Why is he pushing me?"

It took a while for Rines to get Bryant to buy into the concept that the game wasn't about beating everybody by himself off the dribble, as he had learned in Italy. He reluctantly began to embrace some elements of team play, the coach said. "My show had to be more of a psychologist to him, saying, 'Kobe, you know you're going to get the ball back. Why are you trying to dribble into three, four, people when we're going to swing the ball back to you anyway?' It took him maybe three tournaments to understand he was the go-to guy."

"Come on, man," Rines would tell him. "You're better than this. The ball's coming to you."

Once they got a few of the basic team principles established, Rines witnessed another development. Opposing teams began defending Bryant with a box and one defense, playing zone on his teammates and isolating a good defender on Bryant. It wasn't ideal for teams to do that in an AAU game, but opposing coaches cared about winning, Rines said. "Once we were able to get the ball to him, then opponents started playing the box and one. They tried not to, but it was kind of hard when you're trying to win because everything's about winning. I'll give Kobe credit. He didn't give a fuck about winning. He cared only about his own personal progress, his own personal accomplishments. Not that he was counting points, but he was definitely aware of how he played. He tested everybody, and that was him. He finally bought into the passing and cutting, playing without the ball, because he knew he was going to get the ball back."

Bryant's selfishness, frankly, was something to behold, Rines recalled. "It was at another level, but I had to respect him because he produced."

Staying with the process took an effort on the part of the Bryants, but Joe seemed aware that his son had much to learn, that bending his will to the needs of an elite team would bring benefit.

"The crazy thing is," Rines said, "his sophomore year, he started responding. So when I seen a player that was slipping, not getting as good as he should be, reaching that great potential that I thought he had, I pushed them. I didn't care. Fuck 'em."

At the time, Rines still didn't see Bryant becoming a pro player. But as he worked more with Bryant, he came to view him as someone who could be a top college prospect, someone who might actually get signed by a top program, such as the University of North Carolina. The young coach started to sense a bit of mutual respect developing between him and his high-maintenance player.

"I think I raised the bar on him where he had to respect me," Rines said. "He worked harder than any other kid I've seen ever. Pro, college, high school, whatever. He was probably the hardest-working basketball player ever. He wanted it, he wanted it more than anybody."

Which in turn raised more issues. The people around Joe Bryant, including his own wife, had always thought he was too locked in on basketball, that he talked of it incessantly. The son's focus eclipsed the father's, easily.

"When we talked about basketball, we had a good relationship," Rines said of any personal connection he developed with Kobe. "But how much can you talk about basketball? His whole life was driven by the ball. So if it's driven by the ball, me being a young coach, I can only talk to you for so long, and I'm going to have to move on because there's only so much interest we can have."

Most who dealt with Bryant in basketball knew almost nothing about his interest in rap music. The descriptions of his basketball work habits raise questions as to how he could have had any sort of time to even contemplate music. A reporter would ask about Bryant's life outside basketball in his early years with the Lakers, and he would reply, "Basketball, there is nothing else."

To others not driven to find perfection in a pursuit, such an answer would seem ludicrous, and such an approach would seem a wasteland for trying to live a life. Some close observers would look at Bryant's youthful pursuit and think that in many ways he had no life.

Rines wondered about both that and Bryant's levels of seemingly inexplicable anger.

"The source of it," the coach concluded, "was him trying to be great and him having a vision versus somebody else seeing something that could help him. Kobe always had a problem being coached because he wouldn't allow people to help him. He had his own way of doing things, his own style, his own philosophy."

In that regard, his constant video study of basketball greats had put up a wall of sorts, the coach concluded. If you're breaking down tape of Magic Johnson and Michael Jordan and so many other greats and you come to consider them your teachers, along with your father, a former pro, what could a mere high school or AAU coach have to say of real value? Others would look back and conclude that, considering the challenge, Joe Bryant was doing an outstanding job channeling a son possessed of an immensely strong will.

"We should have had a lot better experience than what we had," Rines said of those early summers together, trying to contend with the rising star, "but we had to ride Kobe out."

The Family

Jermaine Griffin laughed years later, hearing tales about Kobe Bryant's adjustment to elite basketball. Having watched his new friend in both rap and high school basketball, Griffin had come to appreciate what a fine experimental mind he possessed. He experimented with everything, not just crossover moves and rhymes and beats.

"That's what greatness is about, experimenting," Griffin offered. "If we all did everything the same exact way and came to the same exact answer, the same exact way, then there is no greatness. What makes greatness is, everyone is doing it this way, and I come and show people, 'Look, you don't have to do it that way.' Now, there is trial and error with anything. There's trial and error in order for you to perfect it, but to reach greatness, you have to do those things. You can't take everything at face value. You have to be able to manipulate things. You have to be able to change things, or all we'll ever be is robots."

Experimenting, of course, required testing. In his father, Bryant had the source of his first major test, one that had lasted for years, in their increasingly physical one-on-one battles.

"Joe talked about these backyard battles," Gregg Downer recalled, "and, you know, the elbows were flying, and Kobe was getting better and better, and they're popping each other in the mouth. This thing is starting to get pretty intense, and Joe's record is undefeated, and Kobe's closing in on the age of fourteen, closing in on the age of fifteen, and all of a sudden, Kobe beats him. It was almost like a coming-out party. And Joe just said, 'That was it. I didn't play him anymore, because I knew I couldn't beat him.'"

"That's how you know he's arrived, when he beat his dad one-on-one," recalled Jermaine Griffin, who had witnessed the battles between father and son, the constant trash talking between the two and the very real physicality. He came away with what he considered a near-perfect role model for how deeply a father should care. "His dad played in Italy, his dad played in the NBA, so I know Kobe idolized him, looked up to him," Griffin explained. "But just to climb that mountain and say, 'I finally did it,' was it. You know, his dad was competitive. His dad wasn't giving Kobe anything. He was like, 'No, I'm not letting you win.' You get to the point when you win, then that's what you get."

Griffin also saw the Joe who drove Kobe to practice, who taught him so much about the game.

The ABC program that had transplanted Griffin from Queens to Lower Merion aimed to help him change the way he once viewed the world, including family relationships, and the Bryants showed him the dynamic of a life well lived. "Mr. Bryant was another guy that helped me with my transition," Griffin explained. "He was definitely like a great leader, somebody I looked up to."

Joe presented the type of role model that Griffin would use later when he too became a father. "I use a lot of what he did as far as with Kobe, as far as Kobe's development, as far as the people he put Kobe around," Griffin said, "the way he worked Kobe, pushed Kobe at the game, you know, talking to Kobe in Italian, you know, telling him certain things to do. He was definitely one of those guys that I look up to, basketball-wise, and also as a family man and just as a person in general."

Griffin had a box-seat view of the love between a father and his son, imperfect in so many ways yet so essential, clearly a gift passed down along the Bryant line of men, from one Joe to another, finally to this teen prodigy.

"He was a great guy for me," Griffin said of Joe. "So then you can imagine how Kobe felt about his dad."

Griffin was invited into the Bryant household on a regular basis in those years, which gave him a further opportunity to witness family love in full force. "I saw it in high school, coming over and spending the night and things like that," he said. "You know, he had a lot of love for his father, respected his father in every way. From what I seen, his father was everything, his mom was everything. Like, they were just everything. I have a lot of memories. His family, they were like my second family. I had my guys at the ABC house and, you know, the house parents that I had at the ABC house. Outside of the ABC program, that was my other family that I had in Pennsylvania. I was definitely one of the people who, you know, his family accepted in their life. You know, I was around them a lot in high school, those high school years."

In addition to having a strong relationship with Joe, it was clear that, despite the everyday things that happen between teens in a household, Bryant loved his sisters very much. And cousin John Cox IV, a few years younger, was like a brother to Kobe, Griffin recalled.

Pam Bryant was a mix of sweet and stern and vigilant. It was obvious that she was manipulative in a variety of ways. She remained low-key but ever watchful.

Some were confused by Pam Bryant's efforts, but Griffin felt like he understood. "What happened is, you have to be a hard-ass to survive. You have to be in this world. You don't have to be that all the time. So you have your moments where it calls for you to be sweet and kind and smile. Then there comes a time, sometimes there are moments in life where you can't be sweet, you can't put on a smile. You have to have a little harder edge in your voice, you have to have a little more volume. A lot of times, when those situations occur, some people know how to take that. Sometimes, people, they get upset that they can't push you over because you're not letting them do whatever they want to you."

Pam Bryant could be a master coddler, but she was no pushover. She constantly scanned her son's environment for bad influences and she pushed him in terms of schoolwork. As another family friend, Jeremy Treatman, pointed out, the Bryants' world was changing rapidly with Kobe's rise in basketball. Pam Bryant had little choice but to be watchful, Treatman said.

"You know what?" Griffin said. "Mothers have to protect their sons. If you look at any species, the mother protects their sons. They've got to protect their kids, and that's what she did. She protected her kid the best way she could. She was a great woman. You know, she could cook. Weekends I came over in the morning, and we'd wake up, we had breakfast. The kitchen was just all about her. You know, you got eggs and bacon and biscuits, things like that."

The whole experience showed him family life, one that he continued to cherish many years later.

"You know," he said, "it's like being at home."

Chapter 13

THE RISING

As the game consumed a bigger and bigger part of Kobe Bryant's life, so did its trappings—and for stars like him, that meant shoes. As with many things Bryant, the timeline dated back to Jordan. A basketball shoe revolution began in 1984 with Nike's explosively popular Air Jordan product line, and by the early 1990s, three characters at the heart of that revolution had left Nike and were running Adidas America and hoping to recreate that old magic by finding a charismatic young athlete to be the face of a new product line. The three men—former Nike VP Rob Strasser, longtime Nike designer Peter Moore, and basketball guru Sonny Vaccaro—would watch as their efforts ignited the shoe war of the 1990s between Nike and Adidas, a war that would turn ugly and personal.

Much of it was spurred by Vaccaro's strategy of invading American youth basketball in an effort to give Adidas a firm grip on the next generation of talent. Some would see Vaccaro's strategy as brilliant. Others would identify it as a further pollution of the sport by moneyed interests, one that would shift the focus to very young players and flood elite Amateur Athletic Union teams with cash from the shoe industry.

Whatever the long-term damage to the sport, Nike founder Phil Knight would soon recognize the competition as an immense threat to the stranglehold his company wanted on the global basketball shoe market.

As former Nike employees, Vaccaro, Moore, and Strasser were quite eager to compete with Knight and their old company. Their dreams were stoked by memories of working with the iconic Jordan as a young wonder, the kid who could both fly and sell shoes like no other.

The launch of Air Jordan in the fall of 1984 proved to have been a wild ride, a moment upon which they looked back with tremendous nostalgia. And with good reason. It made lots of money, and it would be the crowning achievement of their lives, one that imbued their careers with the sparkle of Jordan's magic.

Hell, even David Stern wanted an autograph. That's what Peter Moore would remember with a laugh, looking back thirty years later.

In 1984 both Nike and Adidas were struggling athletic shoe companies, muddling along in search of markets and identity. Nike's stock in particular could be had for about seven dollars a share.

Then came Sonny Vaccaro's big idea—launch an entire product line around Michael Jordan, this young kid out of North Carolina. CBS broadcaster Billy Packer and Vaccaro had dinner with Phil Knight during the 1984 Olympics in Los Angeles, where Packer listened as Vaccaro made an impassioned plea for Nike to sign Jordan to a major deal. He told Knight that Jordan would be the next big thing. Packer remembered that Knight seemed almost indifferent to Vaccaro's pitch.

However, Rob Strasser had already watched Vaccaro work his magic in college basketball. Nike had first hired Vaccaro in the late '70s, based on his idea of paying coaches under the table to have their amateur players wear Nike shoes. That strategy had allowed the company to surge to the lead in the field. So Strasser, an animated hulk of a man, was willing to listen again to Vaccaro on Jordan, despite Knight's indifference.

The Jordan magic with Nike had begun at the very first meetings with the young star's representative, David Falk, who came up with the name Air Jordan, recalled Peter Moore, who was then a top designer for Nike. "David named it—not me. It was perfect sense. We had this thing called Air, this guy could jump out of the gym. We had a flyer, a guy who could fly."

Within minutes, Moore sketched up the product line's first logo, with wings.

Then came Nike's presentation to the petulant young star and his mother in Portland later that year, Moore's first great moment with Jordan, where he explained the company's vision for what Air Jordan could be. Jordan was going to be the first team athlete with his own product line, before he had even played an NBA game. Then just twenty-one, Jordan went into the meeting with a dismissive attitude about Nike.

"At North Carolina, Jordan wore Adidas shoes in practice and all over the place," Moore explained. "Dean Smith told him for games, you wear Converse. And he did, in all these pictures he's wearing Converse shoes. He wanted to sign with Adidas."

Neither Adidas nor Converse could come close to matching the Nike deal, which offered an unprecedented royalty on shoes sold. No endorser had ever gotten a percentage of profits, as Strasser and Nike had offered Jordan.

"We presented to his family and we lit them up," Moore said, especially Jordan's mother, Deloris. "We impressed the shit out of them— that somebody would care that much for her kid. He was not going to be impressed, and he lit up, which was even more satisfying."

As Jordan warmed to the idea during the meeting, Moore gained the first sense of his magnetism.

"This kid, he walks into a room," the designer recalled. "Michael Jordan's the only black man I know who could walk into a Lion's Club meeting in Jackson, Mississippi, and in five minutes, nobody would care if he's black, white, green. They'd just want to get to know him. He had that kind of charisma."

It was Strasser, the Nike VP, who formed the first real bond between Jordan and the company. Known as the "fat guy" at Nike in the shoe industry, Strasser was a large, bearded man, a Berkeley-trained lawyer with immense charisma of his own, so much so that he would quickly charm Jordan. "Michael was like butter in his hands," Moore remembered. "He loved Rob."

Nike was set to promote Jordan and his product line like no athlete had ever been promoted. "Jordan was the first guy on a team to be a marketing icon," Moore offered, "and that was the whole idea of him. We were going to take a team sport guy and make him bigger than anything else. Make him like Arnold Palmer."

For his first exhibition games that October of 1984, Nike dressed Jordan in red and black Nike Air Ships, which prompted a phone call from the office of NBA commissioner David Stern, telling Strasser that Jordan would be banned from wearing the shoe because only white shoes were allowed in the league.

Moore remembered the exchange clearly: "David Stern calls Rob and says, 'Hey, I'm going to ban your shoe.' Rob says, 'Wait, wait, let me come back East and talk.' Rob gets on a plane, flies to New York, goes in front of David and says, 'Look, this shoe is perfectly legal.' Stern says, 'No, it's not. You can't wear all the colors at one time.'

"He bans the shoe," Moore recalled. "So on the way out the door, Stern says, 'Rob, I have a favor to ask of you and I'm embarrassed to ask it.' Rob says, 'You've already ruined my day, go ahead.' Stern says, 'My son thinks I'm a jerk. Can you get me a pair of the shoes autographed for him?' That's a true story."

Strasser would have laughed out loud if he hadn't been sick to his stomach.

He was told Jordan would be fined five thousand dollars a night for every game he wore the shoe. Both Moore and Vaccaro recalled the VP's immediate response when he got back to Portland. "He said, 'Fuck it, we'll pay the fines,'" Vaccaro recalled.

Just when and how the NBA would begin the fines remained unclear. The league wouldn't actually follow up with a letter until late February. By then Strasser had seized the day.

Nike's "fat guy" had received a marketing ploy gift-wrapped by Stern, and he told Moore, his balding, bespectacled sidekick, to run with it.

"Rob says, 'Fuck! Okay, I've got fifty thousand pairs coming. They're on a boat.' He was beside himself. He said, 'We got to do something.' So that's when we did the 'Clank, Clank' commercial," Moore recalled.

Thanksgiving 1984 was upon them. They hastily arranged to shoot an ad during a Bulls road trip at Golden State that November 27. The Bulls' arrival the day before the game provided just enough of a window to shoot if they rushed. "So we get him to the studio, dress him up in the 'banned' shoes, socks, not in a Bulls uniform, but still black and red shit," Moore remembered. "The camera starts at his head and it pans all the way down to his shoes."

As Jordan flips a ball around and begins dribbling, a voiceover says, "On September 15, Nike created a revolutionary new basketball shoe. On October 18, the NBA threw them out of the game. Fortunately, the NBA can't stop you from wearing them. Air Jordans. From Nike."

"We were going to say that David Stern banned them," Moore recalled, "but Rob decided we better just say the NBA. And so the camera comes down to the shoes and two black bars go clank, clank across his shoes...

"Fifty thousand pairs sold out like that," Moore said, snapping his fingers.

Nike quickly followed with another ad, shot in New Orleans during another Bulls road trip, the designer recalled. "He's got the ball, he starts running towards the basket. You don't see anything else, just him coming towards the basket and he goes up and dunks it. That's all it is. He's wearing his red and black shorts, you know, Air Jordan shit, and the sound track is this voice saying, 'You're cleared for take-off.' And you hear this roaring jet that takes off as he jumps. The voice comes on and says, 'Who says man was not meant to fly?' Well, fuck, every kid in the world starts jumping around saying, 'Who says man was not meant to fly?' That was all basketball, all about him flying."

It wasn't until February that Stern's deputy, Russ Granik, finally got around to sending a letter almost halfheartedly reminding Strasser that the shoes were not in line with NBA regulations. Shoe aficionados later studied video footage and photographs of Jordan's performances that season and couldn't find any evidence of him actually wearing the red and black Air Jordan 1 shoes in a game.

Strasser and Moore had simply seized on the NBA's lightweight attempt at enforcement and run with it as one of the all-time great marketing coups, one that soon drove better than $150 million in sales.

Yet the Jordan revolution wasn't just shoes. His persona quickly showed he could drive fashion as well. That began with the basic NBA uniform. Jordan hated the "Daisy Duke" basketball shorts worn by teams at the time.

"Michael was always on me about the shorts," Moore said.

"I want the shorts longer," Jordan told Moore.

"Fuck 'em," Moore remembered saying finally. "We're breaking the rules as it is. What do you want me to do? What is it with these long shorts? You look like you're wearing your father's pants."

Jordan then made an admission.

"He says, 'I got skinny legs.' That was his deal," the designer recalled.

"Michael, your calf muscles are what allow you to jump as high as you jump," Moore told him. "What do you mean? Those legs allow you to jump this high above the rim. I wouldn't worry about those legs. They look just fine.' He was unbelievably self-conscious about it."

Even Moore had to admit Jordan was right, however.

"They looked like poles, like little sticks coming out of those short shorts," he said.

Two years later, Jordan would make his first appearance in the longer shorts. Soon his Chicago Bulls teammate Scottie Pippen picked them up, then players across the NBA wanted the new pants.

"Michael Jordan, to my knowledge, is responsible for the long shorts," Moore said. "He's the guy, and that's why it came about. He probably didn't want to tell this story, but that's the truth."

"It's just something that seemed more natural, more comfortable to me," Jordan explained at the time. "They felt great."

The foundation for what Moore wanted to do with Jordan's new image had actually come during the 1984 Olympics when photographer Jacobus Rentmeester shot Jordan in a warmup suit for *Life* magazine. Moore paid $150 for temporary use of the photo, which Rentmeester had posed in a unique way.

Rentmeester would later file suit with Nike, claiming that the company had used his shot to stage the famous shot of Jordan stretching and jumping across the Chicago skyline, the one Moore wanted to use for Jordan's second logo.

The sense of a Russian dancer was part of what Moore sought in Jordan's new image. The creation of the Jumpman logo was Moore's second-proudest moment in terms of his work with Jordan and Nike, after the success of the initial proposal. The logo would first appear on the third version of Air Jordan in 1987, designed by Moore's one-time assistant, Tinker Hatfield.

Thus, the Jumpman logo concept took root, which would eventually become the signature of Jordan's own immensely successful product line with Nike.

Central to the entire revolution were Jordan's own instincts, his ambitions related to style—something that would find its echo in Bryant years down the line. "Michael wanted it," Moore said. "He wanted to be what he is."

It wasn't much later that the designer saw a photo of Jordan's Jumpman poster hanging on the wall of a hut in the Philippines, bringing him to realize the "it" factor for Jordan appealed to people across the world.

In 1986, a largely unknown young movie director named Spike Lee issued the indie film *She's Gotta Have It,* which quickly caught the attention of key people in the ad industry. "I was in a film editing session for Nike," Peter Moore recalled, "and a guy named Larry Bridges was the editor. He said to me, 'Have you seen *She's Gotta Have It?*' I said 'No, doesn't sound like the kind of film I normally go see.'

"He said, 'It's a black cult film. It's about this guy Mars Blackmon, and he's boffin' this gal and above the bed is your poster with Michael flying across the air.' I went, 'Really? The guy's got his Air Jordans on while he's boffin' this girl? Oh, Jesus, that's great.' So he said, 'I think you guys should do a TV commercial with this Spike Lee guy as Mars Blackmon.'"

Moore turned to Jim Riswold, the art director for Wieden and Kennedy, Nike's ad agency, and told him, "Why don't you work something up, and we'll see what we can do."

It would take a couple of years for the company to implement its plan to include Spike Lee, which would bring a dramatic addition to Jordan's image. Moore had once designed a hip-hop-style campaign for Jordan as an inside joke that was never intended to reach the public. The glaring contrast between Jordan and hip-hop culture was laughable in 1986.

"He was not street in any way," Moore remembered. In fact, Jordan routinely described himself as a country boy.

The ads directed by and starring Lee would change that.

"Spike Lee made him street," Moore explained. "Spike Lee made him attractive to the street kid. Just by association."

The Spike Lee success, however, would be achieved without either Strasser or Moore, a development which almost caused Jordan to leave Nike.

Just when it was gaining tremendous momentum, the whole Air Jordan revolution almost came crashing down, due to internal crosscurrents within Nike. The company had missed out on the aerobics workout shoe craze of the early 1980s, which resulted in a drag in its stock prices. The explosion of the Air Jordan line had helped counter that, but it had brought media coverage that depicted Rob Strasser as "the man who saved Nike."

A longtime friend of Phil Knight's, Strasser would suddenly find himself in a cooling relationship with the company boss.

It seemed to some observers that Knight was intent on driving away anybody who might get credit for Nike's success. Strasser first took a leave of absence from Nike, then departed for good in June 1987. A week later, Moore followed him out the door.

Asked by a reporter about the departures of two of the key people who made his signing with Nike happen, Jordan replied, "It's very big and very deep. It clearly involves things that I can't even begin to understand."

Jordan was not happy. He did not like Knight, Moore explained. "Phil Knight doesn't think Nike needs to be dependent on a given athlete. Athletes, yes, given athlete, no. But remember, Michael Jordan is a basketball player, Phil Knight was a track athlete, a track and field athlete, ran the mile. Lonely runner. Totally different minds, you know."

But Jordan and Knight certainly shared a competitive nature that bordered on insanity, Moore added. "If you think Jordan and Kobe are competitive, go meet Phil Knight. He's a no bullshit competitor. It's, 'You play for me or I can't stand you, I will kill you.' That's Phil Knight, full stop. And he's not shy about it."

When Strasser and Moore quickly formed a new marketing company, Jordan wanted to get involved in a major way and leave Nike.

"When Rob and I left we started a company called Sports Incorporated," Moore explained. "He wanted to become a part of Sports Incorporated. Michael wanted to come and be with us. Michael approached us about doing this."

After considering the incredible deal that Nike had given Jordan, which included the unprecedented royalty on shoe sales, Strasser and Moore told him it would be foolish to give up his Nike shoe endorsement contract. It simply paid him too much.

Jordan agreed it was smart to stay with Nike for the shoes, but Nike wasn't pursuing the idea of casual wear and a broader Jordan brand.

Jordan wanted Strasser and Moore to help him create a new company, Michael Jordan Inc., that could build and promote a Jordan clothing and equipment brand.

That could be a good venture for all three of them, Jordan reasoned, and they might get Nike to kick in to finance some of it. After all, Jordan's original deal was coming up for renewal in 1989. Jordan, Strasser, and Moore decided to schedule a meeting with Knight to discuss their amended idea.

"It went bad," Moore recalled.

Dressed in a three-piece suit and toting a briefcase, Jordan led the way into the meeting. "It was going to be a transition," Moore remembered, "and eventually we would build him into his own brand. It was an ill-conceived idea, but to be honest, we did it at Michael's request because he was pissed."

If he was angry before the meeting, he was doubly so afterward. "That's not possible," Knight supposedly replied after Jordan laid out the plan. "We're not going to do that."

The meeting did help Jordan get his own brand eventually. And Strasser and Moore headed off on another path to take over Adidas America, a subsidiary of the German shoe company that had struggled to challenge Nike in the United States.

After going through a succession of executives, Adidas hired Strasser to run its American company in early 1993 and brought in Moore as the number-two man in its operations. They were immediately charged with the task of growing the company dramatically and snatching market share away from Nike, which had almost 40 percent of the industry at that point. In other words, their mission was to find the next Air Jordan.

The two quickly met with Sonny Vaccaro in a New York pub. "Very few people get to climb the same mountain twice," Strasser told Vaccaro. Was he ready to find the next big young talent?

Vaccaro, a chubby character with the droopy eyes, literally leaped at the opportunity. He disliked Phil Knight intensely.

Despite using Vaccaro's basketball relationships to drive billions in shoe sales over a dozen years, Knight had dismissed the sport's guru in 1990 without a penny of severance pay. Just why Vaccaro was dismissed has never been disclosed.

Vaccaro's other sworn enemy, the National Collegiate Athletic Association, had attempted to strong-arm him in an attempt to get at his friend, UNLV coach Jerry Tarkanian, going so far as to hire a former FBI agent to rummage through Vaccaro's banking transactions. Vaccaro was eager to repay both Nike and the NCAA.

To do that he hatched a plan—to find the game's next great talent and sign him to an Adidas contract right out of high school.

Such a strategy for Adidas would help him to strike at both nemeses, Vaccaro admitted in a 2015 interview. He could beat Nike by signing that next great player, like Jordan, who had both the skills to be great and the charm to sell shoes. In so doing, Vaccaro could deliver a blow to the NCAA by helping the next great talent bypass college basketball and go straight to the NBA from high school.

His battle with the NCAA was largely philosophical, Vaccaro explained. Young athletes had long made their way into professional baseball and tennis without going to college. Vaccaro saw basketball players as no different. He considered the NCAA a cynical enterprise that made billions off of young athletes without paying them. College sports presented fine opportunities for many athletes, he conceded, but elite athletes were on a different level. Their services as professionals were highly sought after, and nothing should prevent them from playing professionally at a young age.

Many critics considered Vaccaro, who had a history with the gambling industry in Las Vegas, to be a corrupting influence in basketball. But Moore had come to see him as something quite different, a figure who was far more interested in his ideas than in making money from them. Vaccaro was mostly interested in making sure athletes got paid, sometimes to his own detriment, Moore concluded.

A decade later, Chris Dennis, an adviser to high school phenomenon LeBron James in Ohio, offered a similar, unsolicited view of

Vaccaro. "Sonny's always about getting the money for the players," Dennis observed. "That's what he cared about most."

Charged with finding the next great player for Adidas in 1993, Vaccaro had at first set his sights on New York high school star Felipe López. He had soon hired one of López's relatives and set about the business of getting to know the player and grooming him for professional life and a shoe contract.

López had great charisma, and indeed, time would reveal him to be a first-rate person. But many scouts, including Vaccaro himself, had wildly overestimated López's abilities. Plus López himself was reluctant about the idea of becoming a professional out of high school. The game in that era was very much the domain of men, and while a handful of tall players had gone directly from high school to professional life over the years, it was considered a foolish proposition for a guard or a wing.

In fact, Vaccaro would encounter that difficulty often in his work for Adidas. There weren't that many supremely talented players, and the ones who were talented showed little interest in skipping college.

Plus Adidas America was struggling to find its footing in the marketplace. "We had no money at that time," Vaccaro explained, looking back.

In hopes of making a deal, Vaccaro had arranged for Lopez to receive a $500,000 contract to play professionally in Europe, but the young star still declined the offer and enrolled at St. John's to play college basketball.

Vaccaro's efforts with López had not gone unobserved. Word soon leaked out in the shoe industry that Phil Knight was fearful of Vaccaro putting his Rolodex of basketball contacts to work for Adidas. The Nike boss had sharp questions for his underlings as to how Vaccaro had gotten ahead of them on López.

The potential conflict might have escalated then, but just ten months into the Adidas revival, Rob Strasser died suddenly at age forty-seven while attending a company meeting in Germany in October 1993.

It was yet another blow for the athletic shoe industry in 1993. In August, the body of James Jordan, Michael's father, had been found in South Carolina, and two men were charged with his murder.

That October, within days of Rob Strasser's death, Jordan abruptly announced he was done with pro basketball. As the shoe industry recoiled from the news, the personal value of Phil Knight's Nike stock was said to plummet by more than $15 million.

Upon learning of Strasser's death, Peter Moore phoned Phil Knight with the news.

"He was very gracious," Moore recalled. "We had a memorial for Rob. A lot of people were invited, Nike people and Adidas people. A lot of Nike people came, but a lot of Nike people didn't come."

Although the Jordans were still grieving, Michael's mother reportedly flew to Portland to attend the service, only to be persuaded not to attend by someone at Nike, Moore said. "She actually flew out here, but they convinced her that wouldn't be the best thing for her."

"I certainly didn't see anyone from Nike there," Vaccaro recalled. "Maybe some people sitting at the back."

The basketball guru made a fiery speech at Strasser's service.

"We're gonna turn that Swoosh upside down and make it a question mark," Vaccaro promised the gathered mourners.

In the wake of his friend's death, Vaccaro again turned his busy mind to the search. Out of the many talented young players in high school, who would be the next big guy? Was there a kid out there who was bold enough to dare to be Jordan?

Intro

The competition between Nike and Adidas geared up in July 1994, as they both prepared to open their elite camps for high school players the very same week, Nike in the Chicago suburbs and Adidas at Fairleigh Dickinson University, in New Jersey. Sonny Vaccaro, who used to run his ABCD Camp for Nike, now was doing the same for Adidas. Just to add a little spice to the mix, he had made sure his camp was scheduled for the same week as Nike's. He wanted the top players to have to choose between the two. There were other top camps, but they all charged participants for the opportunity to be seen by college coaches. Nike and Adidas were the elite, invitation-only camps, and they were basically free, complete with many goodies for players who participated.

"This was the start of the first real battle between Adidas and Nike," Vaccaro recalled.

The day before camp opened that July, Vaccaro looked up to find Joe Bryant standing before him, in need of a favor. Vaccaro hadn't seen Jellybean since he was the MVP of his Dapper Dan high school all-star tournament in 1972, at least not in person.

Joe quickly explained that he was now an assistant coach at La Salle and that he had a son who had just finished an excellent high school sophomore season but that no one would let him into one of the elite camps.

"When I was in high school nobody would take a chance on me to come to a camp, to come to an all-American camp," Kobe would recall later.

The translation, of course, was that Nike had not allowed Bryant into its camp.

Sonny Hill was a top representative of Nike in Philadelphia, and there was even a teacher at Lower Merion who represented the company to amateur basketball players. Neither of them had seen fit — or been able — to have Kobe included in the lineup of top hot prospects at the Nike camp. "I think the problem with Sonny Hill and those guys, they couldn't see beyond what they were looking at," Vaccaro said, looking back. "If you didn't go to Overbrook or West Philly or one of those main Philadelphia high schools, you weren't a top player. Kobe went to Lower Merion. That was hard for them to overlook. He wasn't accepted in Philadelphia."

Mostly, the people involved with the Sonny Hill League at the time had a view of Kobe Bryant that was similar to the view held by Donnie Carr — Kobe was good but no big deal as a player.

At the time, Vaccaro had never heard of Kobe Bryant. "I didn't know anything about him," he said. "I had never seen him play."

Just about all the players invited to Vaccaro's camp were highly touted rising seniors. There were three rising juniors, however.

So Joe Bryant literally begged Vaccaro, on the eve of the invitation-only camp, to allow his son in. Just being included would change Bryant's prospects dramatically by putting his name in front of every college coach in America.

"I let him in," Vaccaro said, "because Joe had played in my game in 1972 and been the MVP."

"Sonny V.!" Kobe said in 2001, upon being asked about Vaccaro. "Sonny V. gave me my first opportunity. Sonny V. gave me my first opportunity to go to a camp to show my skills as a basketball player. I love that guy. He's so open, loves the game. More important, loves the kids. He loves giving them the opportunity to showcase their skills. He's great. He's a wonderful man."

That year's camp is recalled in basketball lore because Stephon Marbury, a point guard from Brooklyn, was named ABCD's MVP after unleashing a legendary dunk, then promptly strutting out of the gym.

But Vaccaro recalled it for another reason. He watched Bryant the first day, saw that he was very good, and followed his progress that week, saw that he was a good-looking kid and found out that he had been raised in Italy and spoke multiple languages. But the real impression came once the camp was over, when Kobe walked up to Vaccaro, thanked him, and gave him a hug.

It was a very Italian thing in some ways for Vaccaro, who was known for giving players a kiss on both cheeks.

"I wasn't the best player at your camp this week," Bryant told Vaccaro. "But next year I will be."

Vaccaro recalled the moment giving him chills. In an instant, he sensed that the game's next great player had just made himself known. Bryant's gesture represented the blend of chutzpah and charm that only the great ones seemed to have. Combining this with all the other things Vaccaro had learned about the fifteen-year-old, he suspected that Bryant was in possession of the "it" factor needed to sell shoes. He wasn't entirely sure, but he had a strong hunch.

Vaccaro mostly kept his impressions to himself about his discovery, except that he talked to Sam Rines. He revealed his thoughts to Bryant's AAU coach after the camp had ended.

"Sonny was a very, very smart guy," Rines recalled. "I'll never forget the summer after Kobe's tenth-grade year, that first time meeting him. We're talking, and I'm trying to figure out what's going on, and he was like, 'This is the one. This is the guy that we think is going to be the next superstar.' This was at ABCD. It was my first time seeing a camp like that. We were up at Fairleigh Dickinson. And he was explaining the blueprint of Kobe. I probably talked to him during the whole process ten to fifteen times. But every time I talked to him, I learned something new every time because Sonny was basically able to explain the blueprint of what he wanted Kobe to be."

Without doubt, Vaccaro's talk with Rines also shaped the young AAU coach's view of his own player. This elite kid who was such a pain in the ass was not only on the radar of the game's kingmaker, but he had been moved to the fast track.

"I enjoy playing against great competition," Bryant told reporters at the time. "That's how you get better. I knew that, playing for Lower Merion, I would be facing the best players from the suburban area. I knew that the Sonny Hill League would give me a chance to face the top players from the city. The ABCD All-America Camp put me up against the best players in the country."

In the wake of his camp, Vaccaro attempted to place Bryant with coach Jimmy Salmon's elite AAU team out of Paterson, New Jersey, which featured Tim Thomas and other top players. At the time, Thomas was thought to be the best college prospect in Bryant's class.

"What happened was, he played a tournament with them, and, not that he didn't like it—it just wasn't for him," Rines explained. "Kobe had to be in control. He had to have the ball, and he had to know the ball was coming to him. He tried to play with a couple teams. There were two teams he tried to play for, and even the Sonny Hill All-Stars. He did it out of respect for Sonny Hill, but the first thing he said was, 'I wish I had played with y'all.' What happened was, the guys in Philly respected Kobe, but they didn't think he was that good."

That summer and early fall, Bryant marched through impressive off-season work, with more fine showings in the Sonny Hill League and in elite tournaments. During days that stretched from early mornings to nine at night and beyond, he played in six different leagues and attended two summer camps.

There has long been an urban myth that Bryant won the AAU

national championship playing for Paterson with Thomas and Vince Carter. Bryant did play with Paterson a few weekends in both 1994 and 1995, Rines said, but there's no evidence that they ever won the AAU national championship. What they likely won were national elite tournaments, Rines said. After all, Carter was from Florida, Bryant from Pennsylvania, and Thomas from New Jersey. The AAU rules of the period for teams in the national-championship field were based on players with eligibility by state, Rines pointed out.

"In my opinion, that was the best AAU team ever," Bryant later said of the New Jersey team, looking back in 2001. "I put that AAU team against anybody."

The roster included Bryant, Thomas, and Carter, plus top players Edmund Saunders and Kevin Freeman, Bryant recalled. "We were beating people by 45 or 50 points every night. One tournament we had at Florida State University, we just creamed everybody. It was an experience because I had heard a lot about Vince Carter because he was a year older than I was. He was in that great senior class, and Tim Thomas, he was the number one junior in the nation at that time. They put me at point guard, and I had a field day throwing lobs and no-looks, and it was fun."

Both Rines and Vaccaro said independently in 2015 that they had noticed Bryant's penchant for tall tales over the years. Yet there is no question that Bryant did play on occasion with the Paterson team, and to great effect.

"Obviously once they saw Kobe, Sonny wanted to make sure that he picked Kobe to be his guy," Rines said of Vaccaro. But that wouldn't include taking him away from Rines's team.

In the wake of Bryant's big impression at the 1994 ABCD Camp, Rines made further efforts to bolster the lineup. The biggest addition was Richard "Rip" Hamilton, a shooting guard from Coatesville, west of Philadelphia, who seemed to have no trouble with Bryant's demands for playing time.

"Rip accepted his beta role unbelievably in that regard," Rines said. "Actually, I have to respect him for it because he never said a word about anything. Rip didn't care because we were able to sub around both of them. Let's say we took Rip out; we would take Kobe out after three minutes extra and put Rip back in."

Hamilton, who would have an outstanding NBA career, was perfectly capable of earning MVP honors in tournaments playing with Bryant, Rines recalled. "He wasn't a better player, but he played just as well as Kobe at times. They were like peanut butter and jelly. They were the perfect backcourt. And when people talk about a tandem, it's a shame they never played together in the NBA, because they were unbelievable together. You talk about unbelievable chemistry. We knew once we got Rip to play with us, that was it."

In their time together, Hamilton and Bryant would even take on the Paterson AAU team with Tim Thomas and Vince Carter in a tournament at the University of Maryland. "We played them on court 1 in Cole Field House, and there're games going on alongside of us," Rines remembered. "They had to stop one game on the next court, get the spectators off the court, because there were about three hundred people surrounding our court, trying to watch Kobe play. People couldn't watch the other game, and they couldn't play the other game. Paterson had Tim Thomas; they had Vince Carter, Edmund Saunders, but Kobe was the show. It was an unbelievable game to watch, to coach, and just be a part of the whole show.

"Kobe loved it, he ate it up. Kobe wants to be the center of attention, he wants to be center court, he dressed the part, walked the part, talked the part. He was a showman by the time he hit the summer of his sophomore year. He was an unbelievable showman, as far as entertaining people."

For all his growth that summer as a player, there were still times he and Rines clashed. "We had our moments, me and him," the coach said, "because my thing with Kobe was, 'It can't be just about you. Don't be selfish. These are you teammates. They need to get to college. You got to help them out. You got to be a team player.' So we still bumped heads a couple of times."

But by the end of the long 1994 elite-tournament season, their relationship began to improve.

"Kobe, I just want you to be the best ever," the coach told him.

It was just the message Bryant wanted to hear.

"He had to go through that stage in the game where he wanted to prove himself," Rines said. "It was still pretty positive. I don't want you to think it was just negative, negative, negative."

Donnie Carr finally saw what people were talking about with the kid from Lower Merion. "Honestly," Carr said, "Kobe's summer going into his eleventh-grade year, everything came together. That's when he started doing special things on the basketball court. It was like, 'Wow, this is the guy.'

"When he was younger, he had the mentality, he had the will. He was the most determined person I'd ever seen, but everything hadn't come full circle yet."

For two years Carr had felt that he had not just bested Bryant but dominated him whenever they met on the floor. Now things had changed. Heading into that junior year, Carr saw Bryant's physical development. Plus, Kobe had spent lots of time in West Philadelphia, where Joe had hatched his own game—on the playgrounds.

"By the eleventh grade he was, you know, almost a finished product," Carr observed. "He had become much more explosive, much more athletic. You could see his bones had started getting stronger, so you could see his explosiveness, his athleticism. He already had the mentality. Even though he lived in the suburbs, he played a lot of ball in West Philly. The Sonny Hill League, that team he played for, was in West Philly, and he would spend a lot of time in the inner city. He always had an inner-city mentality, a guy that wanted to rip your heart out."

Bryant's status had changed as well. No longer was he the skinny son of Joe Bryant. With his hard work, Bryant's transformation had caught people off guard, which perhaps helps to explain why Nike had not selected him for its camp. After that point, Kobe Bryant had become very good very quickly.

"Now he was the most feared," Carr explained. "For the eleventh- and twelfth-grade years, he was the most feared player in the city, in the state, and the surrounding areas. No one wanted to get out there on the floor against Kobe Bryant."

The Junior

During Kobe's junior year at Lower Merion, the hard work began to pay off. In the 1994–95 season, Bryant averaged 31.1 points, 10.4

rebounds, 5.2 assists, 3.8 blocks, and 2.3 steals. He was no longer an unknown. His teammates delighted in seeing big-name coaches from Kentucky and Duke in attendance at Lower Merion games.

"The kids look at the Kobe Bryant equation as a positive," Downer told a reporter. "They play in front of bigger crowds. They see the Pitinos and the Krzyzewskis in our gym. They cherish that."

Bryant particularly took a liking to Coach K.

Rapidly approaching six foot six, Bryant pushed his team to an elite level while playing mostly in the post on defense and as a guard at the other end. The Aces finished 26–5 and managed to unseat rival Ridley, the six-time defending champions of the Central League. In the game that clinched the league title, Bryant scored 42 points in a 76–70 Lower Merion victory.

Bryant and Lower Merion also faced Rip Hamilton and Coatesville twice that junior year, once claiming an overtime victory in the regular season, then winning in an early district play-off game. By then, the two players knew each other well. "They went at each other with their high school teams. It was a clash," Rines said with a laugh.

From there, Lower Merion went to the AAAA state quarterfinals, where their play-off run ended after a late Bryant turnover. He scored 33 points in the game, including 10 points in the fourth quarter, fighting through a defense that collapsed on him constantly, to lead Lower Merion back from seven down—but with ten seconds to go, the game tied at 59–59 and the ball in Bryant's hands, he was stripped by a defender. The game went to overtime, and Lower Merion did not score again.

Even in 1999, five years after the close of that junior-year season, Bryant said he considered that loss one of the most painful experiences of his life. Afterward, emotion washed over him as he apologized, in tears, to his teammates in the locker room. "He blamed himself for the play-off loss," Jeremy Treatman recalled, even though he scored 33 points and added 15 rebounds. "The only reason we were even there was because of him."

Gregg Downer has a slightly different memory of Bryant's reaction to the loss.

"It was a horrific loss," the coach recalled in 2015. "We were playing Hazleton, with, like, three thousand Hazleton fans in the building and about a hundred Lower Merion fans. We don't score one point in overtime. I think Kobe may have actually maybe fouled out, and we have kind of this epic moment in the locker room where it's time for everyone to say good-bye to the seniors. I'm waiting for Kobe to say something kind of poetic, and he says, 'For you guys that are leaving, thanks for everything.' And he immediately, like, turns to the guys that are coming back, and he says, 'Whoever is coming back, this can't happen again. You have to do everything that you need to do. This will never happen again under my watch.'"

There was a certain coldness to the moment, Downer recalled. "I found it to be kind of, like, this shallow send-off to the current seniors, but maybe a little bit of this leadership out of him where he's just saying, 'Look, OK, it happened, but it's never going to happen again.'"

Treatman considered Bryant a clear choice to be the Philadelphia-area high school player of the year for the 1994–95 season, but the writer learned that the *Inquirer*'s preps editor was about to designate Howard Brown, another good player, as the recipient. To avert what he considered a mistake, Treatman said he intervened with the *Inquirer*'s sports editor to make sure Bryant got the award.

In addition to carrying out his duties as a correspondent for the *Inquirer*, Treatman had begun working on a local TV show covering high school sports. In that capacity, Treatman said, he produced the first TV feature on Bryant and was impressed by the player's media skills. "He was perfect, just a natural," Treatman recalled. "He knows what to say and how to say it. He listens to the question. A lot of people don't do that. He listens."

Despite the loss, Downer had been pleased by the team's progress and how well Bryant had followed the path laid out for him to become the national player of the year as a senior.

"As a freshman you're amongst a pool of a hundred," the coach had said in a frank discussion with the young player. "You know, fifty of those won't work hard, or fifty of those won't be coachable, or fifty of those will discover drugs, or fifty of those will discover girls."

The pool of potential great players would halve itself every year, Downer explained. "If we can follow this pattern, a hundred is fifty, fifty is twenty-five, twenty-five is ten, ten is five."

For three seasons, Bryant had worked maniacally and avoided those pitfalls.

"From that junior to senior year, he kind of made that jump from, like, twenty to, like, five," the coach recalled. "He used to get furious at me when I would needle him that somebody was better than him. I told him, 'You know, that Tim Thomas has a bigger reputation than you. Vince Carter has a bigger reputation than you.' I knew how to get under Kobe's skin to get him to work harder, and I knew that, the alpha dog that he was, the only acceptable outcome for Kobe would be to be considered the National Player of the Year."

In the wake of the play-off loss, Downer saw Bryant grow yet again as a player. Donnie Carr witnessed the same thing. Late that spring, many of the area's high school teams participated in an off-season league that featured both Carr's Roman Catholic High teammates and Bryant's Lower Merion group.

Late that spring, Carr was on the phone with his girlfriend a few days before Carr's team was set to face Bryant's. A call-waiting buzz interrupted his conversation, and Carr clicked over to take it.

The voice on the line said, "Don, what's up?"

"Who's this?" Carr inquired.

"It's Kobe. What's up, man? I was just thinking, I'm looking forward to the game."

Bryant had heard a rumor that Catholic was losing Arthur Davis, a top-fifty player who partnered with Carr in a very good Catholic backcourt.

"Me and Arthur Davis was like a tandem on the wings," Carr recalled in 2015. "We probably were the most feared guys together on the wing because everybody knew we were a load."

Bryant wanted to know if Davis would still be playing with Catholic in the upcoming game. Carr already knew that Davis was leaving the school but replied that he didn't know.

"I just wanted to see if he was going to be at the game," Bryant told him, "because if it's just you, I don't even know if it's worth me coming. But if it's you and him, then you know I'm saying we can probably get it on."

Carr was stunned. Years later, when reports emerged that Bryant had phoned Ray Allen to play mind games with his opponent, it gave Carr a flashback to Kobe juicing up the proceedings in the late spring of 1995.

"All the way back then, he called," Carr remembered. "I'll never forget it. I hung up the phone. I started calling my brother, my family."

"I can't believe what he just did," Carr told them.

"He was basically, like, you know, creating a challenge," Carr said. "He was letting me know, 'I'm coming to kill you, I'm coming to rip your heart out when you get on court with me.'"

On game day, Bryant quickly resumed his trash talk.

"You know you in for a long night, man," Bryant told Carr.

The woofing grew in volume when Bryant blocked one of Carr's shots.

"I mean, it was constant," Carr said. "It was all game long."

"I don't give a fuck about you," Carr told him at one point.

"It was all ear game," Carr recalled. "It was like cold fingers, like, I knew whenever I was playing against Kobe, I had to get my rest, you know what I mean? I had to really focus because he was coming to dominate you. He was coming to embarrass you, and I just wanted to be on my A game because I knew he's going to be on his."

It may have backfired on Bryant in the first half of that summer-league game. "I had 25 points in the first half; Kobe had 4," Carr recalled.

As he came off the court at halftime, he walked past Joe Bryant, who told him, "Calm down, Don. You're doing too much. Giving them too much. Slow down a little bit."

As if Kobe himself wasn't talking enough trash.

Sure enough, the numbers flipped in the second half, Carr recalled. "He ended the game with 36, 10 rebounds, and 7 assists. I ended the game with 30 points, 7 rebounds, and 7 assists."

Bryant held him to 5 points in the second half while scoring 32. Lower Merion won by a point. Devastated, Carr collapsed on the court.

"I'll never forget that," he said. "I was in the middle of the floor, covering my eyes, and he came and picked me up, man."

"Man, get up, man," Bryant said as he lifted Carr off the floor. "Don't worry about it. We'll see ya again."

"He hugs me," Carr recalled, "and he said, 'Man, thanks for bringing out the best in me. Man, I love just to be playing against you.'"

Carr said Bryant told him that day he'd love to have him as a teammate on the college level. Carr himself would go on to play at La Salle, although major injury would limit his career. Kobe Bryant was headed off in a different direction, as the events of that summer would reveal.

That June, Carr and Bryant attended an elite camp in Preston, New Jersey. They ran into each other during check-in. The camp's lineup included Lamar Odom, Jermaine O'Neal, Tim Thomas, Loren Woods, and Lester Earl, all top prospects in high school basketball.

"At check-in, they gave us window fans and a key," Carr remembered. "We didn't have TVs because they wanted everyone to interact with each other and get a chance to network and meet friends."

Bryant and Carr walked to their dorm rooms together.

"Don," Bryant told him, "you and me have known each other for years, and, uh, don't take this personally, man, but don't come to my room. I'm not coming to your room. I'm not even going outside of my room."

Carr was taken aback, so Bryant explained, "I'm leaving this camp as the number one player in the country."

Bryant had already risen dramatically in the player rankings. In a couple of them, he hovered in the top five. Carr said Bryant's team beat Lamar Odom's team for the championship of that camp, and Bryant was named MVP.

July brought round two of Sonny Vaccaro's camp. Nike had made a big push to get Bryant in its camp, but he was true to his promise. "It was never in doubt," Vaccaro said. "He was the one who made the declaration about returning to my camp and being the best. By the next year, he was somebody, and Sonny Hill was embarrassed that he missed him."

"He's the most advanced player at the high school level I've seen in a while," basketball recruiting analyst Bob Gibbons told a reporter in advance of the Adidas camp. "He is the closest thing to Grant Hill you will ever see at the high school level."

His performance at the 1995 Adidas camp didn't disappoint.

Bryant was named the MVP, and Rip Hamilton was selected as one of the camp's top ten. The lineup of Bryant's team featured Jermaine O'Neal of Eau Claire High (in Columbia, South Carolina), Tim Thomas of Paterson Catholic (in Paterson, New Jersey), and Lester Earl of Glen Oaks High (in Baton Rouge, Louisiana).

"I think these four big kids will go one, two, three, four in the NBA draft some year," Vaccaro told a reporter.

"The big thing for him that summer was the Adidas camp," Downer recalled. "I saw him explode."

In the wake of the Adidas camp, Sonny Vaccaro was finally and completely convinced that Bryant was the player he needed to sign to give Adidas the "next Jordan." He quietly began plotting how he was going to make that happen.

As the summer was winding down, Carr found himself facing Bryant yet again, this time with the Sonny Hill All-Stars in yet another tournament.

"He kind of dominated me that game," Carr admitted. "I had sprained my ankle. I was good enough to play, but I wasn't myself."

"You shouldn't be out here," Bryant told him. "I don't care if you got a sprained ankle. All I see is you in front of me, and I'm ready to eat. I don't feel sorry for you. I'm telling you now, I'm coming after you."

"All game long he was just on me, I mean, just on me," Carr recalled.

They ended up splitting the MVP award for the tournament. Carr knew he would have one final shot at Bryant during the upcoming high school season, and the dream of being college teammates seemed less and less likely. There were already rumors flying about Bryant going to the NBA out of high school.

"If he's a pro, I'm a pro," Carr said testily when a reporter asked him about the situation.

In one of the final events of the biggest year of Kobe Bryant's life to that point, the Sam Rines All-Stars finally relented to their marquee player's demands and agreed to play a national tournament in Las Vegas.

"That's the best I've ever seen him play," Sam Rines said. "That's what made Kobe great to me, because he was just able to turn that corner. People say he would have made out better playing with a better AAU team. He made out better with us because he made himself a star. He took on other teams that maybe had four or five Division I players, and he just controlled the whole game."

Most important, Bryant always knew he was going to get his volume of shots with the Rines All-Stars, the AAU coach observed. The team didn't win the Vegas tournament because Rip Hamilton couldn't make the trip, but Bryant still led them deep into the field.

"My father didn't even want to do Vegas," Rines said. "Kobe forced us to do it. Vegas was an AAU elite national team event where they took all the elite Adidas teams."

Even as they played, the teams had the sense they were pawns in a bigger battle.

"People still talk about the sneaker war; that's where it started," Rines said. "Nike did a tournament at UNLV at the same time. Both Nike and Adidas came to Vegas that year. I guess Sonny did it on purpose. That was a great time. Just imagine for the kids, all the college coaches being able to talk to you, hang out with you, spend time with you. It was crazy."

Sonny Vaccaro sat courtside during the tournament and watched Bryant play, trying to contain his glee. He was going to figure out just how he was going to snatch this prize player from college basketball and deliver him to the NBA as an Adidas star. If anyone in all of basketball knew how to make it happen, Vaccaro was sure to be the man.

Chapter 14

THE BAD, BAD BOY

KOBE BRYANT CERTAINLY craved the attention, even if he had little thought for returning the love. His performance in the ABCD Camp meant a barrage of calls and recruiting efforts from many college basketball coaches as he headed into his senior year. Bryant didn't connect with a lot of them.

High school teammate Robby Schwartz remembered Kobe collecting his recruiting letters from the main office at the school and treating them dismissively. "He's like, 'Here, look at this.' He throws down all these letters on the table, and it was, like, Duke, North Carolina, Georgetown. I remember picking them up. There were, like, fifty of them, all recruitment letters."

He had a scheduled visit with coach Rick Pitino at Kentucky. "I visited Kentucky by myself," his high school coach, Gregg Downer, recalled. "He didn't go. Because I had so much respect for Pitino, I went down there. Obviously he was hoping that I could be the hook that could help with a guy like Kobe, but he had to think it was a little bit strange that Kobe wasn't there."

The biggest hit continued to be Duke's Mike Krzyzewski, who had won back-to-back national titles in 1991 and 1992. Bryant had admired his work with Grant Hill for the Blue Devils. Plus, each time Coach K called, they talked little about basketball and much about everything else, especially Italy. Krzyzewski knew that Jellybean would be trying to get Kobe to go to La Salle, so he kept it light and fun, but he obviously understood the pressures Bryant faced. Already given to visualization, Bryant allowed himself to explore in his mind what life would be like playing at Duke's Cameron Indoor Stadium, with its crazy student fan base.

Villanova intrigued him as well. Kerry Kittles and Eric Eberz would be on their way out, which meant that Bryant could step in and have the program much to himself. Plus, he had a good relationship with Villanova assistant coach Paul Hewitt. Tim Thomas was considering going there, and that would have made a nice combo.

Another assistant coach who really impressed him was Scott Perry from Michigan, who had followed his summer progress closely. Kevin Garnett, who had raised eyebrows that spring by going from high school to the NBA because he feared he might not qualify academically for college, had said that Michigan was his favorite, and Bryant could see why.

Bryant also fancied the University of Arizona because he had gotten close with Stephen Jackson at the McDonald's All American Game, and Jackson was headed there. So was Mike Bibby, and Bryant mentioned that he might like being a Wildcat.

"Yeah, right," Bibby replied.

But the real recruiting pressure came when Bryant got home each day, even though it involved hardly a word. His father had been hired at La Salle to help coach Speedy Morris rebuild the talent base. Morris had enjoyed a strong run of conference-championship seasons and NCAA tournament appearances in his early years at the school but had seen his progress slowed in recent seasons.

Joe was recruiting Roman Catholic High big man Lari Ketner during Kobe's junior year at Lower Merion. Joe would stage pickup games with Ketner and Kobe and the La Salle players. Bryant had fun throwing lobs to Ketner and running up wins against the school's varsity. The La Salle players seemed genuinely excited about the prospect of adding Kobe and Ketner.

However, he had seen a number of La Salle games in recent seasons, and he had developed a distaste for the coaching of Speedy Morris, who was viewed as Philly's version of Bobby Knight. Bryant thought he yelled too much.

Bryant finally told his father, "It's not on you. I just don't like the way Speedy Morris coaches."

His father said he had no problem with that. But in response, he hatched a plan to become the head coach at the school, assuming that Morris would be fired for a poor season. He would admit this frankly to both Sonny Vaccaro and old friend Vontez Simpson.

From the start, any good adviser would have pointed out to Joe that Morris had won more than six hundred college games, including a strong record of 177–95 at La Salle. His previous three teams had hovered around .500, but prior to that Morris had averaged better than twenty wins for six straight seasons.

With Joe recruiting him hard, Ketner had made an oral commitment to the Explorers and said he would sign as soon as Kobe committed as well.

Joe's vision was that once he was the head coach, Kobe's presence would allow him to add Tim Thomas, Jermaine O'Neal, Lester Earl, Richard Hamilton, Shaheen Holloway, and Donnie Carr, all players with whom the Bryant family had warm relationships. It certainly would have made La Salle a top college program. Kobe thought they might be better than Michigan's famed Fab Five. The school apparently would ponder Joe's idea over in the 1995–96 season as Morris's team lost lots of games.

The situation's first hurdle was set for November 1995, an early deadline for Kobe to declare his intentions. But he still had doubts. Kevin Garnett's move to the NBA in 1995 had him thinking that he, too, just might be able to make the jump straight to the league. So he hesitated to commit either way that November, which left everyone in limbo as the high school season got started.

The Secret Mission

Gary Charles and Sonny Vaccaro didn't seem like the ideal pair to carry out a secret mission. Charles wore loud suits, and Vaccaro had a big-time rep and loved talking to people. He was known for carrying on conversations with a dozen different coaches at a time in the hotel lobbies during his days running his high school all-star game in Pittsburgh.

But the fall of 1995 found them trying to sign Kobe Bryant to Adidas on the down low. Vaccaro had been accused over the years of doing many secretive deals, but nothing was like the Bryant deal, he would say twenty years later, looking back. "In my world, that was my most clandestine thing."

In truth, Vaccaro admitted years later, nobody in the industry in 1994 or 1995 seriously considered the likelihood that Bryant would turn pro out of high school. Thus, no one had devised a strategy for using a major shoe contract to lure such a young player into turning pro without going to college. It just hadn't been done.

Sure, there were rumors that Bryant was thinking about it, but they were largely considered to be based on the brash utterances of a cocky young player.

"This was the first time something of this magnitude ever happened with a high school player," Vaccaro said.

Garnett's going pro out of high school that June of 1995 seemed an iffy thing that had created minimal interest among sports marketing minds and resulted in only a minor shoe deal. Still, Garnett's move had spurred Vaccaro to become more serious about scouting high school players to be his next major star. Then Bryant had played so well in the Adidas camp that July.

"I am the best this year," Bryant had boasted to Vaccaro after he was named MVP of the camp. "And I'm going to be the best pro, too."

The comment had finally cemented the notion in the shoe guru's mind. Bryant would actually do it, Vaccaro thought. He would actually turn pro.

What Bryant said gave him a reason to step up his efforts at signing him, Vaccaro recalled. "I had to have something that gave me encouragement."

Plus the "it" factor just glared at him every time he looked at Bryant, Vaccaro explained. "Everything followed this child. He lived under this halo. It was unbelievable."

The shoe executive knew that if he moved to Philadelphia and began attending Bryant's games at Lower Merion, it would create a firestorm and also alert Nike to his plans. Yet Vaccaro needed a way to get in close. So he talked Adidas into spending $75,000 to move him from the West Coast into a stylish uptown New York apartment.

Vaccaro would then deploy Gary Charles, the one-time coach of the Long Island Panthers AAU club, as his go-between with the Bryants. "Gary was my conduit to personal contact with the family," Vaccaro explained. "Gary gave me access."

Vaccaro couldn't attend Kobe's high school games, but Gary Charles could because he was Joe Bryant's friend. They had met when Joe, in his job as an assistant coach at La Salle, was scouting one of Charles's AAU players. "We developed a rapport," Charles explained. "He'd be watching us play, and then he would ask me to come see his son play, and so I'd leave my court after my game and I'd see Kobe play. The more and more I watched Kobe, the more fascinated I got. Plus, I liked Joe's personality — he joked a lot, smiled a lot, said the right things. Easy to get along with, easy to like."

It wasn't just Kobe's play but his überconfidence that struck a note. "I told people that Kobe was probably the first loud assassin I ever met," Charles recalled. "You know, assassins are usually quiet. But he told you he was coming at you, and you still couldn't do anything about it.

"A lot of guys his age didn't really believe in themselves yet. It's not enough to be good; you've got to know you are good. Kobe, he believed it. Kobe was not shy about any of that. He'd tell you, 'I'm going to be that guy.'"

Charles had worked with Vaccaro in the courting of Felipe Lopez, but he noticed that Lopez seemed not to care whether his team won or lost. "I started to have doubts," Charles recalled. "His fire burned differently."

But another train of thought had emerged among many who met Bryant. He was so cocky, it was over-the-top, said Michael Harris, the owner of Best Sports Consultants, a sports marketing firm. Harris, who had played college basketball himself, saw all the work Bryant was doing and the nonstop focus. "I didn't take him seriously," he admitted. "I thought he was a bit overzealous."

Taken with his emerging talent, Bryant's chutzpah, however, had begun to impress the right people. Over two summers, he had erased lots of doubt. That, in turn, led to more conversations between Gary Charles and Joe.

"Joe obviously knew I was a consultant for Adidas," Charles recalled.

One day Joe mentioned to Charles that Kobe was thinking about turning pro right after high school.

"What!?!" Charles replied.

"Yeah," Joe said.

"You don't want to take any chances," Charles warned him, mentioning that such a move was very risky. Bryant could turn pro too early, run into trouble, and quickly destroy a promising future in the game, especially in the NBA of the 1990s. It was a game for the manliest of men. The conversation gave Charles the opportunity to toss Vaccaro's plan out there.

"What about a shoe deal to guarantee the money will be there?" Charles suggested.

Joe jumped immediately. His belief in Kobe was every bit as big as Kobe's belief in himself. In fact, it could be argued that Joe's lifelong effort to build that confidence had made the moment possible. It didn't hurt that the men who did the Air Jordan deal for Nike were the same men who were now offering a similar opportunity from Adidas.

"Let's talk about that," Joe replied.

"That's when I broke it down about Adidas and everything else," Charles recalled. "It wasn't like I was pushing one way or the other. I didn't think it would happen, but then he made a statement."

"I love it," Joe told Charles. "Let me go talk to Kobe and my wife."

"That's what started the process," Charles remembered.

On the surface, Bryant's senior year in high school was all about winning a Pennsylvania state championship. But behind the scenes, it hinged on negotiations for a shoe contract that would allow the young star go right from high school to the NBA.

The situation held considerable risk for Vaccaro, who had once encouraged a fledgling Nike to bet its entire budget on a twenty-one-year-old Jordan as an endorsement star. He was now set to advocate that Adidas America take a flyer on a mere seventeen-year-old, and a guard at that.

"The world knew who Michael was when we recruited him,"

Vaccaro said. "The world did not know who Kobe was when we worked this deal for Adidas. This was a much bigger gamble."

When Nike went for Jordan in 1984, Vaccaro had already worked college basketball coaches and had made millions for the company, which helped soften the gamble. In 1994 and 1995, he was beginning to grow the Adidas portfolio, but there had been no time to build a base of profit similar to that at Nike.

"Adidas America was much smaller than Nike," Vaccaro said. "We bomb on Kobe, and we may not have been open for business by '99."

Vaccaro, who had been fired by Nike, was again risking his own job, but the upside of the gamble was just as substantial. A bright young talent like Kobe Bryant could be a huge score and help Adidas gain on Nike in terms of market share. The industry needed a young star to court the next generation of players and fans, and Vaccaro desperately wanted to deliver that star to Adidas.

Peter Moore had also gone to Adidas after Nike and was now the chairman of the company. When Vaccaro had first told him about Bryant, in the summer of 1995, he had responded, "We're going after a seventeen-year-old kid?"

But in the wake of Jordan's success, the athletic-shoe and equipment industries now treated basketball as they did tennis and golf, in which top individual stars were used in marketing and could be identified at a much younger age than in the past. If they targeted young players who offered the potential to be truly legit stars, the players could be encouraged to turn professional at younger ages. That process had long been in place in European basketball. Vaccaro's plan was to drive that trend in American hoops as well. After all, it allowed the very best players to begin earning money earlier in relatively short athletic careers.

And, of course, it would allow Adidas to sell tons of shoes.

The strategy also had the side benefit of allowing Vaccaro to score points against his two main foils, Nike and the NCAA. Vaccaro, like a growing number of critics, felt the governing body of major college athletics had an exploitative edge, earning hundreds of millions of dollars from the labors of highly talented young amateurs who were paid nothing in return other than scholarships.

The key to pulling it all off, Vaccaro astutely figured, was to keep the negotiations with the Bryants quiet and to come up with a sweet side deal for Kobe's cash-strapped family.

"They had major money issues," he recalled. "There wasn't a lot left over from Joe's career."

The Pickup

Shaun Powell, a veteran sportswriter covering pro basketball, was a columnist for *Newsday* in New York in the fall of 1995. At training camp that October, Powell was chatting with Rick Mahorn, a forward with the New Jersey Nets, when the player began talking about a teenager he had seen over the summer. The NBA was locked out briefly in yet another labor dispute, and Mahorn had worked out with a variety of pro players in Philadelphia, including several from his former team, the 76ers. They would play pickup games, then lift weights so that they could prepare for the season, despite the lockout. The teen had played really well—so well, in fact, that each time the pros picked sides for their pickup games, the teen wasn't the last player picked.

Mahorn told him it was Jellybean's kid. Powell had to think a minute before he remembered Joe Bryant. The story sounded intriguing, so he stored it away as an idea to pitch to his editors.

Even as they talked, the legend of Kobe Bryant's summer workouts was taking off and morphing in the mouth-to-mouth of Philadelphia's basketball grapevine. Much of the talk was coming from Bryant himself and father Joe.

Donnie Carr's ears perked up when he heard it. "He was working out with Derrick Coleman and all those guys like Vernon Maxwell," Carr recalled. "You would just hear the stories of, like, 'Yo, man, Kobe's up there giving them dudes work.'"

Carr asked Kobe about it.

"Don," Bryant said, "I'm just telling you, man, whenever you get a chance to play against them guys, don't be afraid, man. Just play your game. You'll be surprised. They go for all the moves that the high school guys go for."

"Yeah," Carr said. "For real?"

"Man," Kobe boasted. "They go for all the same moves, man. Just play your game. That's what you do."

Bryant had returned from the Adidas tournament in Las Vegas to find an invitation from Sixers coach John Lucas to work out with the team. Kobe arrived at the gym and discovered that Lucas had special plans.

"He came up to me," Bryant recalled later, "and said, 'Kobe, I've got a surprise for you.' I turned around, and Jerry Stackhouse walked in the door. We went head-to-head. It was great, a lot of fun."

In short time, word would spread that Bryant had humbled Stackhouse in a game of one-on-one, until John Lucas stepped in to stop it. The story would take on a life of its own, and Stackhouse would deny it vehemently over the years. As similar stories grew, they tended to make it sound as though Bryant had dominated a number of pros. That didn't happen. Nobody was "killed" that summer in the gym at St. Joseph's. But Bryant's play put more than enough pressure on the pros there. He was a thin high school kid, but he held his own.

One witness to the events was Mo Howard, who had been hired by Lucas, his old teammate at Maryland, to monitor the sessions because no one from the team itself could be involved, under league rules. Lucas, who had a daughter going to Lower Merion and knew the Bryant family, told Howard that Kobe would be joining the workouts. Emory Dabney, a rising sophomore point guard at Lower Merion, joined a few of the sessions, too. He would recall a Bryant eager to have a shot at the pros.

"Man, let me tell you something, that's where I first saw it," Howard recalled of that summer. "God's honest truth. We worked out twice a day. We'd start at ten in the morning; Kobe was there at eight. We'd get done at ten of twelve; Kobe would stay till two. We'd start again at seven at night; Kobe'd be there at five. We'd finish at nine, he'd stay to eleven, every day. None of those pros were doing that."

Howard didn't hear a word of trash talk from Bryant the entire time.

Mahorn, who had been the heart of the Detroit Piston Bad Boys' first title run, came over to Howard and asked, "Who is that kid?"

Maurice Cheeks, a coach who wasn't officially supposed to be there, asked the same question.

"Where's he from?" Cheeks asked.

"Lower Merion," Howard said.

"What college did he go to?" Cheeks asked.

"He plays at Lower Marion," Howard said. "He's going into his senior year of high school."

"His jaw just dropped, ya know what I'm sayin'?" Howard recalled with a chuckle.

Eddie Jones of the Lakers took the time to work with Bryant after those summer sessions. "Kobe," Howard said, "was like a sponge. If he wanted to know something, he'd come and ask you. He'd go to Eddie and say, 'Show me how to do this, show me how to do that.' Eddie's tutoring him, he's mentoring him."

Jones had known Bryant for more than a year at that point. Later, after Bryant arrived in the NBA and wound up taking Jones's job, Howard would often think back to the lack of selfishness Jones displayed in working with the teen.

Even at the time, it was obvious that the teenaged Bryant posed a subtle threat to all the pros around him.

"Shit, whoever was guarding him was aware of it," Howard recalled. "I tell you, who was getting the most frustrated was Jerry Stackhouse. Kobe tuned him up every day. If Jerry Stackhouse was the number two pick in the draft, Kobe had to be two A."

"I felt real comfortable all summer with the guys," Bryant would explain to *Newsday* that fall. "I had no butterflies, no nothing. I never felt intimidated. I could get to the hole, I could hit the jumper, I could score, although not at will, but I could get some shots. I was able to create for my teammates and rebound. Plus, the guys respected me, and when they respect you, that must mean something."

Tony DiLeo, a scout and basketball personnel executive with the Sixers, also saw several of the sessions. He had first met Kobe the previous NBA season, when Joe brought him to the Spectrum to meet Michael Jordan for the first time at a Sixers–Bulls game. "He was a quiet kid," DiLeo recalled of that night.

Kobe's summer session with the NBA players brought mixed results, as would be expected, DiLeo said. "But he held his own. I mean, for a kid who was going to be a high school senior at that time, he did really well. He was athletic and skilled. After one of the games, Stackhouse and Kobe started playing one-on-one, and, you know, Kobe was really playing well, and John Lucas had to go and stop the game."

Sam Rines also showed up several times to watch. "I was down there," the AAU coach recalled, "and Vern Maxwell played against Kobe. Let me tell you something, Maxwell killed Kobe and was talking shit. He was saying everything, like, 'You can't stop me, young boy.' Anything you can imagine. And the crazy part, I know Vernon was out that night before. I'd seen him out at a nightclub, and this is well past two or three in the morning. Then he turned around and got up in the morning and just absolutely killed Kobe."

Bryant was obviously unhappy at getting bested by Maxwell, Rines said. "He didn't take it well, but you had to respect him because he was playing harder than I'd ever seen him play. That's when you knew Kobe was going to be a pro. The next day he turned around and killed Eddie Jones, who was playing for the Lakers. This was in five-on-five. Destroyed Eddie Jones, gave Stackhouse problems."

In one game Bryant faced journeyman pro Willie Burton, who had managed to score 53 points in one game during the previous NBA season. According to various accounts, Burton scored over Kobe and followed it up with a little trash talk. The teen answered with a ten-basket scoring spree while allowing Burton just one more basket. The veteran stormed out of the gym in anger and never returned. He wound up playing in Europe the next season.

Howard couldn't recall Joe Bryant coming to see his son play once the entire summer. Howard had actually been eager to see his old friend. He finally ran into him in November, going into a Sixers game at the Spectrum.

"Has anybody said anything to you about Kobe going to the pros?" Howard asked him.

Joe replied that some people had mentioned it to him.

"Joey," Howard told him, "if he can go, send him. Send him."

"Really, Mo?" Joe asked.

"Bean," Howard said, "this kid, he'll kill them pros, he'll kill those guys."

With so much talk swirling around the sessions and various witnesses remembering things differently, it remained difficult to draw too many conclusions from Bryant's experience working out with the pros that summer except for the one impression that really mattered—Bryant's own. He came away thinking that he could do it, he could play against NBA players right away.

Bryant wasn't the only one. Sam Rines now saw him differently, too. Just in those late-summer months, the coach could see that the player had outgrown him—not just the coaching, but the entire playing format. He had heard the rumors about Bryant's thoughts about pro basketball, but the coach no longer considered them absurd.

"I didn't look at him being different until going into his senior year, when I knew he was great," Rines remembered. "It was kind of like, 'OK, sit back and relax and watch the show.' This dude was, like, throwing the ball to himself off the backboard. It wasn't just the athleticism. The midrange game just became unbelievable, his off-the-dribble, pull-up game. He was shooting over people now. He was stronger, more athletic. So he went from this lanky kid that could only shoot and dunk the ball to, now, a kid that can score against anybody."

Watching Bryant at that time made Rines think back to when he watched Joe playing summers in the Baker League. "Joe's game and Kobe's game were a little bit different," he said. "When I watched Joe I was like, 'Oh, man, he goes out there and just kind of glides around and scores the ball.' He did his thing. Kobe was more cerebral than Joe. Joe was more natural, bouncy, smooth. They show some resemblance, but I don't know if you could ever say he modeled his game after his father's."

Both Kobe and Joe told Jeremy Treatman that summer that Kobe was thinking about skipping college altogether. Joe had gone to Kobe one morning that August in the family kitchen and told him, "You may be ready for the NBA."

"John Lucas was telling everybody, 'He's a bad, bad boy,'" Treatman recalled. Later, Eddie Jones used the same language, telling Treatman, "That's a very bad, bad boy."

Despite Kobe's showing in the pickup games, the Philadelphia basketball community still didn't see all the work he was putting in outside the games and practices, the many hours of watching basketball videotape over and over again. No one could have imagined such an extraordinary effort from someone so young and so advantaged. Joe Bryant was seen as a rich man in Philadelphia, and there was the common assumption that rich men's sons didn't work all that hard. They waited for things to be given to them.

Despite the rumors about his developing game, local fans and coaches and other players still disdained Kobe Bryant as a kid from the suburbs, thus someone not authentic but a creation of his connected father.

"I don't think Joe spoiled him," Rines said. "I just think Joe made it easy for him. Joe made life easy because Joe believed that if you do what you're supposed to do, everything's going to fall in your lap. And when he wasn't happy, Joe immediately switched the situation. Kobe didn't want to play Sonny Hill Future Stars with the Sonny Hill team, and Joe made him play. After every game, he'd say, 'Ah, man, this sucks.'

"Without Joe, Kobe wouldn't be Kobe," Rines concluded. Still, he added, the work itself was all Kobe's. Watching everything unfold, Rines came to a conclusion then.

"Kobe's a genius in basketball," the AAU coach explained. "I think he worked to perfection. I think he studied the game harder than anyone has ever studied the game."

Donnie Carr knew it, too, although he didn't want to admit it at the time. "You might as well say he was homeless because that's how hungry he played and how much heart and determination he played with," Carr said, looking back. "He was always trying to get better, to the point that he cut everything and everyone off. It was just, he had a vision. He had a goal in mind, and that was it, that was the end-all, be-all. He played like every game was his last, every workout was going to be his last. He would outwill people, man. His will was just unmatched."

Late in the summer, after getting used to working out with pros, Bryant led a team from Delaware Valley to a surprise championship in the scholastic division of the Keystone State Games, averaging 38 points a game. Gregg Downer served as the coach for the Philadelphia team, which Kobe bested in the title game with 47 points, earning another MVP award.

His confidence was growing yet again, which barely seemed possible. The kid who had come up in Italy watching his father and riding the bus with the pros, who was close enough to the pro game to mop the sweat off the floor, was now nearing his own big moment.

Chapter 15

COME TOGETHER

THE SLIGHTLY STOOPED, very tall, very thin boy slid behind the wheel of the SUV shortly after 4:30, hit the ignition and the lights, and rolled out of the driveway on Reservation Road into a dark morning marked by sleepy streetlights, a hint of mist, and the thinnest trace of dawn, just showing along the horizon. He would have just enough time to pick up his two younger companions and get to Lower Merion High right as the custodian was unlocking the gym for them at five.

They would warm up a bit, then launch into a few drills. Mostly, he shot while they rebounded.

"It was just nuts," said Robby Schwartz, one of the two companions, looking back twenty years later. Schwartz was a mere five foot four and a junior, a year behind Kobe Bryant. His motivation for aiding and abetting the morning madness was that he was hoping to make the Lower Merion varsity, despite a lack of basketball ability. Due to several players' graduating after Bryant's disappointing junior season, coach Gregg Downer needed a host of new faces on the roster for the 1995–96 season.

"All will and no skill," Schwartz would say of his game with a laugh. "I knew how special that year was going to be, and, you know, not having that much talent and also being short, you are limited in what you can do. I mean, I'd run through a wall if someone asked me to. That was sort of my way to get onto the team."

He admired Bryant because he seemed to know what he wanted, something that almost none of the kids around them had a clue about. Schwartz wasn't able to articulate that at the time, but he thought of those early-morning sessions often as he made his way in adult life through a career as a personal trainer, competitive bodybuilder, and CrossFit practitioner.

"You're fifteen, sixteen years old," Schwartz explained. "You're dying for acceptance. You just want to have friends. He didn't care, just didn't care. It wasn't important to him."

He recalled a seventeen-year-old Bryant who moved with the sort of ferocity that left the new members of the team a bit wide-eyed. The task of explaining their mission for the upcoming season fell to another rising senior, Jermaine Griffin, who had also played in the depressing close to the 1995 play-offs. Afterward, Bryant had vowed to him, "The next time we walk off the floor at the end of a season, it will be as state champions."

Griffin had conveyed the message about the solemnity of the mission to any and all who were hopeful about joining on for the 1995–96 season. They all knew Bryant. Sort of. He was the smiling, scowling, rhyme-spouting figure hovering over the Lower Merion hallways and lunchroom. He had returned for the start of the school year with a new buzz around him to go along with his new SUV. Word had spread quickly that he was now considered the number one high school player in America.

Just the thought of playing for the Aces meant pressure for younger players. "Being ranked so high and having the best player in the country on this team, you know, the expectation was, we were going to win," Schwartz recalled.

The early-morning sessions brought raised eyebrows from Schwartz's parents, who reminded him of the busy schedule, with school and more basketball in the afternoons. But sometimes even five days a week wasn't enough.

"We used to go on Sundays to the Haverford School and play pickup ball," Schwartz explained.

"I think that's what turns a lot of people off about him, because they don't understand that to be the very best, you have to do things that are not going to make you a likable person. You know, you have to sacrifice tons of things. People might think you're arrogant, but you're just focused, like there's that line between him and everyone else. Like people always ask, 'What was he like in high school? Was he an asshole? Was he this?' No, he was just…he knew what he wanted to do at age, like, eight."

Bryant wasn't a type A personality, Schwartz said. "It was more like type AAA."

Big Rick's Tip

Shaun Powell got around to following up on Rick Mahorn's tip just as the high school basketball season was getting under way. He phoned Joe Bryant and asked if it would be OK for him to come down from New York and take in one of Lower Merion's games.

Joe loved the idea and met Powell at the gym on game night. They found seats together.

"The game was, like, thirty, forty seconds old, and Joe got, like, crazy over the referees," the *Newsday* columnist recalled. "He was cursing and everything. I didn't think anything of it. But five minutes later, somebody else makes a call against Kobe, and Joe's out of his seat again, going crazy."

This is miserable, Powell told himself. Bryant had maybe two baskets the entire first half, and the columnist decided that Mahorn's big tip was no good, that he was wasting precious time.

"He wasn't even the best player on the floor," he recalled. "He's being outplayed by whoever the other guard was."

Before the second half, Powell got up and moved to the other side of the gym to put plenty of distance between himself and crazy Joe Bryant. And the scene changed.

"The second half, Kobe went crazy," Powell remembered. "He had spent the first half passing the ball. I know that's crazy for people to believe now. But he did. He spent the first half passing the ball. The second half, he was shooting fadeaways, everything. It was unbelievable."

His faith renewed, Powell made his way down to the locker room after the game and told Bryant that he was doing a story on him and that he wanted to drive back down from New York the next day and interview him.

"Just meet me at school," Bryant told him.

Powell appeared at the Lower Merion front office the next day and asked for Kobe.

"He might be in the gym shooting baskets," someone offered.

Powell made his way through the halls and down a long staircase to the gym, and there was Bryant, in street clothes and dress shoes, very casually putting up shots, with another student rebounding.

Bryant motioned him over, but classes had changed, and a class was moving into the gym. The columnist and Bryant retreated to the hallway, where they sat on the floor and talked.

"I was just mesmerized by his intelligence about the game," Powell admitted. "First of all, you're talking about a kid. I know his father had played, but Kobe broke down the game, what he did the previous night, why he chose not to shoot that much in the first half. He wanted to get his teammates involved, get their confidence up. But in the second half, when he felt they were failing, he kind of took over. He also still looked for opportunity to get the ball to his teammates for layups, easy shots, so they wouldn't feel all the pressure. He took all the tough shots himself. He talked about his upbringing in Italy, spoke some Italian. I was just blown away."

The bell rang, and suddenly the hallway filled with students changing classes, stepping over the columnist and star player, sitting on the tile. Powell didn't care. He was determined not to break the spell of what he considered a magical interview.

"Kobe thanked me," Powell said. "He was stunned that a New York writer would come down and interview him. He had this innocence about him."

On the drive back up the turnpike to New York, Powell pondered how he was going to sell his tough *Newsday* editors on a story about a Philadelphia high school kid.

"He might be the next big thing," he told them when he got back to New York.

The editors responded with a double-truck Sunday special spread across their pages, the first national story on Kobe Bryant.

In the locker room after a Nets game, Powell thanked Mahorn for the tip.

"Man, I told you," the jolly brute of the NBA replied. "He wasn't the last one picked. And we had some good players out there. He blended with the rest of us, and if you can blend with us as a high school player, that says something right there. That says you belong. Dude even tried to 'poster' me. He tried to dunk on me."

The Last Shot

Donnie Carr was a nervous wreck before the second game that season. His Roman Catholic High team was going to play Bryant's Aces. It would be Carr's last chance to best his rival.

"That was the last time we played against each other," he recalled. "I'll never forget how much anxiety I had before the game because I knew Kobe had become the number one player in the country. I knew the game would be sold out. It was at Drexel University, standing room only. I knew NBA scouts were there, a lot of college scouts. All the people that mattered, as far as sportswriters and guys that covered high school sports. We had had some classic battles. I was six three; he was about six six by then.

"It was a lot of nervous energy at the time. Even my friends coming to the game were expecting Kobe to dominate me and dominate the game."

In the days leading up to the event, Carr told his grandmother and brother and mother just how badly he wanted to do well in this final game.

"This is the one that counts," he kept telling them. "Everyone is going to be here. This is the one."

In many ways, the game was even more than that. For longtime Philly hoopheads, it was the best of the "city" versus this kid from the suburbs who was trying to act like he was genuine Philly.

Perhaps the tension explains the disaster. Carr missed his first 4 shots. He knew he was trying too hard. "Relax," he kept telling himself as he eyed Bryant, confident in his Lower Merion maroon and white number 33.

Finally, Catholic's legendary coach, Dennis Seddon, called a time-out.

"Just get one down and you'll be fine," he told Carr. "Relax and let the game come to you."

On the next possession, Carr caught the ball on the left wing, ripped it through, and headed straight into the middle for a runner that fell. It was like a starting bell.

"From there, I had an unbelievable first half, where I scored, like, 19 of my 34," he said.

Emory Dabney, now the Aces' point guard, missed the first several games, so Bryant was left to control the team alone, relying on his power to draw defenses to him, to get his teammates a variety of open shots. But by the second half, Roman Catholic's overall talent edge had the Aces down by six. Bryant answered by shaking off double and triple teams to score on eight consecutive possessions. Out of necessity he had finally taken on the opponent single-handedly. He wound up scoring 30 points.

"He played unbelievably," Carr said. "But that was the thing—I had the better supporting cast. He brought his team back."

"He had to do too much," recalled Jeremy Treatman, who had joined the Lower Merion staff that season as an assistant coach.

Catholic won by a half dozen.

Bryant walked directly toward his rival after the buzzer.

"He was pissed off," Carr recalled. "But when we got to each other, he gave me a big hug."

"Man, I love playing against you," Bryant told him.

Then he said that he would love playing with Carr at the next level, that it would be special.

"He was a class act," Carr said.

"Donnie played just as well as Kobe," Sam Rines said. "But Kobe was so smooth and so talented that you just saw the greatness in him because he made everything seem so easy. And he was able to do it by himself."

As the high school season unfolded late that fall, Powell's story in *Newsday* would catapult the whole basketball community into speculating on Bryant's future, especially in Philadelphia. Prior to that, Treatman had tried to get the *Inquirer* to do a story about it and was met with indifference, but in the wake of Powell's story, local reporters feverishly wanted to discuss the rumors swirling around Bryant.

"Kobe has choices," Joe offered. "He can do whatever he wants. Our family will support Kobe with whatever he decides to do."

Asked if he would attempt to change his son's mind, Joe replied, "Why would I do a thing like that? If Kobe feels he's ready, then he goes with my blessing."

Kevin Garnett had gotten off to a good start in his first month of pro basketball, and reporters asked if that was influencing the decision.

"I'm not studying Kevin Garnett," Kobe said. "I wish him the best and hope he exceeds expectations, but what he does really doesn't have any effect on me."

They asked if he would really attempt to turn pro.

"I can't give an answer now," he said. "It's been my goal ever since I started high school. I always wanted the option of going to the NBA. My father played, but that's not the reason. My decision has nothing to do with him."

The media, fans, coaches, all remained hugely skeptical that Bryant, at a shade under six foot six, was ready to meet the physical and emotional demands of pro competition. He had added about fifteen pounds over the busy summer, to boost his weight to two hundred. Still, he looked thin.

"I've heard a lot of people say I don't have the maturity yet for the NBA," Bryant had told Shaun Powell. "Well, I've seen things in my lifetime that ordinary kids haven't seen or experienced. I've been all through Europe, to France, Germany, lived in Italy, been around professional players my whole life. Growing up the way I have, I think I've matured faster than an ordinary person my age."

He was asked when he would decide.

"Maybe later on this year," he replied. "Then I'll look back to see what I've learned as a player. That's when I'll decide. And if I make the decision I'm going, I'm not going to change my mind."

Cancer

The loss to Roman Catholic was followed by a blowout defeat at the hands of the famous St. Anthony High, out of New Jersey, notable only in that Bryant scored his two thousandth high school point that night.

From there, the Aces headed to Myrtle Beach, South Carolina, to play in a high-profile holiday tournament, the Beach Ball Classic, against teams with stars such as Lamar Odom, Lester Earl, Mike Bibby, and Jermaine O'Neal.

Downer had assigned another assistant coach to room with Bryant for the trip, but the player requested that Treatman share the two-room suite with him instead. Soon it became clear why. One bedroom was larger, more comfortable. Treatman put his gear in there, only to have Bryant suggest that they switch.

"I'm the coach," Treatman said. "I should have this room."

"Well," Bryant said. "Why don't we just take this stuff, put it over here, and then you can come in here and you can hang with the Bean?"

Bryant knew the other coach would have never surrendered the room, Treatman realized. "He was charming about it."

They made the switch and soon the assistant coach discovered the second reason Kobe had requested him. Pam Bryant phoned early and often that week, trying to monitor her son's activities from back home in Philadelphia.

Between Pam's calls, girls phoned the room, looking for Bryant, who was making good use of his time running around at night in the beach community, giving out his room number to seemingly every pretty female he encountered.

"Your mom called," Treatman told Bryant when he did manage to make it back to their suite. "I told her you were asleep."

"OK, good," Bryant said. "Thanks."

"I actually lied," the coach remembered. "I didn't know what to do."

Bryant was well aware of his mother's manipulative nature, Treatman observed, and rolled his eyes about it as any other teen would.

"She was overly protective of Kobe," Treatman said of Pam Bryant. "She was worried. Academics. Sex. Absolutely, she had reason to be. Her son was the top high school basketball player in America. I thought she was controlling, and the sisters were overprotective. She really was hard on him with the homework and going out. They tried to keep him home."

For his senior year, Bryant's sisters and female cousins reportedly conspired to be "cock blockers," trying to prevent him from hooking up indiscriminately with young females. Bryant had a girlfriend, Jocelyn, said to be beautiful and almost as driven academically as he was athletically. In an interview with *Newsweek* eight years later, Jocelyn observed that being Kobe Bryant's girlfriend at that age meant lots of evenings at the Bryants' watching basketball videos.

For such a dominant athlete, his tastes ran decidedly nerdy, from an infatuation with *Star Wars* to the teen comedy *Moesha* (he swooned over the female lead, recording artist Brandy Norwood), which was all the rage in its debut that season.

Even so, he certainly had the typical cockiness of a young star. Treatman explained, "I thought that was understandable, based on the way people were treating him, putting him on a pedestal."

Treatman was on edge about more than just calls from Pam while he was rooming in Myrtle Beach with the rising star. "When I take a shower, the floor is always wet," Treatman explained. "I throw towels everywhere. I was so nervous that he was going to slip, and I would say to myself, 'Make sure that bathroom is not wet. If Kobe Bryant slips, breaks his neck, and I caused the next Michael Jordan to ruin his career, I'll never forgive myself. I'll be hated.'"

In retrospect, the highlight of that week would be the dunk contest, which Bryant competed in with a bandaged-up sore wrist, despite the protests of his sisters.

"His wrist was sore, like, really sore," Gregg Downer recalled, "and he says, 'Oh, yeah, it's from signing too many autographs.'"

Coaches, family, they were all saying, "Do not do this," but he insisted on competing, even jumping over a couple of teammates to complete one dunk, landing and winking at Treatman, seated nearby, as the crowd roared.

"He jumped over a couple of us," Robby Schwartz remembered. No one on the team had ever seen Bryant perform such highlight material. The coaches were stunned.

"He dunked all the time in games and dunked all the time in practice, but never, you know, with showboat-type moves," Schwartz explained.

Obviously Bryant had been practicing those moves away from prying eyes.

"That was something you'll never forget," Downer recalled. "I mean, just the creativity and the electricity of some of those dunks. This guy loves the bright lights. I don't know if you'll find an athlete that likes the bright lights as much as him."

He easily beat Lester Earl, another high school phenom, for the dunk title.

The team events were another matter. The Aces won their first game, beating a team that featured prep star Jason Collier. In the second game, against a team from Jenks, Oklahoma, Lower Merion blew an 18-point lead, and Bryant fouled out late. He sat and watched his teammates get outscored 21–2 in overtime.

"He kept saying, 'No goddamned independence, no goddamned independence,'" Treatman recalled. "I took it to mean, 'These guys can't do anything without me.'"

It was one of the rare times that the assistant coach had seen Bryant on the bench. "He didn't sit out much," he quipped.

In the wake of the loss, with the team's record at 3–3, Downer gathered his players in a hotel room to talk about the "cancer of me."

"He went around the room and defined everybody's role," Treatman recalled, "and he told everybody how they needed to improve."

"Kobe," Downer said, looking at his star, "you've got to be a better teammate, and you've got to lead these guys."

Then the coach turned to the team and said, "You guys have no idea what it's like to be Kobe Bryant, to have this pressure on him, what he's going through, what he means to us and what he's doing for us and how hard he works. If you guys aren't taking his example, every day, then I don't want you around anymore."

Every good basketball team has a critical moment when it establishes its "hierarchy," as Phil Jackson would later describe it. The meeting was Lower Merion's critical moment. Downer was becoming a coach who would later take Lower Merion to multiple state championships.

"He talked about how we played selfish and didn't play as a team," Treatman recalled. "We didn't lose again. We did not lose again. We won twenty-seven straight games."

Woolly Bully

The chemistry on the team was much improved coming out of South Carolina, but the drama was far from over. The public began to sense that something special was happening, because the crowds seemed to grow with each victory. Then Bryant scored 50 in a January blowout of Marple Newtown. A snippet of video from that game would be used years later in a Bryant shoe commercial.

"You know, it wasn't the Internet era yet," Downer recalled. "It wasn't the email era, it wasn't really even the camcorder era, but journalists started stalking us and walking the hallways and shining cameras in our locker room. That took some getting used to, from my perspective, but Kobe was always very accommodating. He became a one-man rock band, quite honestly, towards the end. I mean, autographing his sneakers and, like, throwing them out of the window of the bus to a little kid."

The entire team fed off such fun, Schwartz remembered. "These were guys that were confident in their abilities but not combative. They were the perfect mix. For example, Brendan Pettit was our center. Couldn't shoot, just rebounded and played defense. He was, like, six five. He was the big white guy on the team. He never wanted the ball, was happy rebounding and playing defense. Perfect fit. Jermaine Griffin, who was the power forward, six three, terrible hands, great rebounder, hustled his ass off. Perfect fit. Dan Pangrazio, a great shooter, stood on the three-point line, waited for Kobe to get double-teamed, then kick it to him to make a three. Again, perfect fit. The pieces we had on that year's team, it was never like, 'I need more shots.' It was like, 'I'll get my shots,' you know, because so much attention was drawn to Kobe. It was the perfect formula for a winning team."

Downer was "like a Krzyzewski sort of clone," Schwartz said. "I think he had a good understanding of what he was dealing with in Kobe, and his approach with him clearly worked. There wasn't a lot of, 'Here's what you're going to do.' I mean, it really was a lot of managing the personality."

They had all seen Bryant's trigger-quick temper. As the star himself admitted, he could snap, just like his mother. When that happened, get out of the way.

One day just before practice, the team was informed that it couldn't have the gym, due to a water problem and flooding in another gym. Boys' basketball would have to defer to other teams.

"Gregg had to call off practice," Treatman recalled. "Fourteen guys just sprinted out there, high-fiving, excited, no practice, maybe not in front of the coaches, but they were in the hallway. Nobody was upset."

Except Bryant.

"This is bullshit!" he screamed, slamming a ball off the floor. "This is bullshit! We got practice, I want to practice. This is ridiculous!"

"He was so angry," Treatman said. "And, you know, it's, like...wow!"

"He was just a kid," Schwartz explained, "but I think that when things weren't up to his standard is when you got that sort of bully mentality. I don't even like that word, but I guess it does fit. Like, he just wanted the best out of everyone, and nothing short of that would do. He didn't like losing anything, and you get that 'I'm not only going to beat you, but I'm going to beat you until you just don't ever forget this.'"

No one would forget when Bryant lost a drill in practice, the first time in his four years that he had ever lost to any of his teammates in a drill, the coaches would recall.

"We're doing some drill," Treatman remembered. "It was, like, a three-on-three, full-court drill. And it was a tied game."

Schwartz and Bryant were on the same team, and Bryant was open for the last shot, the only problem being that Schwartz had the ball. Schwartz was often Bryant's teammate in drills and always deferred to the star except for this once.

"He fakes the pass to Kobe, takes one hard dribble, puts up a shot," Treatman said. "Schwartz is literally the last man on the team, number fifteen."

"They're going to think he's getting the ball," Schwartz remembered. "So I faked the pass to him, and my defender went towards him. I drove to the basket and missed the layup. Of course, the other team gets the ball, scores. Kobe lost his mind, like, legitimately lost his mind, screaming, yelling, 'Who do you think you are?' I mean, really, like, I am a sixteen-year-old. I'm short, skinny. I am terrified at this moment, and he just won't let up. 'Why did you take the shot?' And I don't know what to do. I don't know whether to just keep my mouth shut. I did for a while, but then it just went on and on."

"Kobe just lasered his eyes on him," Treatman said, "for the next hour and a half. He followed him into the bathroom, to the water fountain. I thought he was going to kill him. I was like, 'What is he doing? He's the biggest asshole. He's the biggest dick. What's the big deal?'"

None of the coaches made a move to calm Bryant or even to say anything to him.

Finally, Schwartz muttered something under his breath, "Enough already" or "Shut up."

"I don't even remember exactly what it was," he recalled, "but it was was like, 'I get it. We lost. I messed up.' He kind of heard me, and he, like, looked at me."

Suddenly Bryant started for his teammate.

"He didn't say anything when he was running at me," Schwartz said, "but he definitely, like, lunged at me. Now, I wasn't willing to stick around and find out what he was going to do. I turned around and hightailed it. I was really fast."

Schwartz ran out of the gym with Bryant on his tail. "I didn't look back," he said. "The next thing I knew, I was up at the nurse's office, which was a good two hundred yards away, and I turned around. He had stopped chasing me at that point."

After a while, Schwartz returned to the gym. "The rest of the practice definitely had a tone of like, 'Nobody say anything about it,'" he said, "because when I walked back in the gym, it was so uncomfortable. I'm the last man on the totem pole."

The coaches still did not say anything about the incident or try to stop it. Schwartz said if they had, he believed Bryant would have eased off.

Treatman, however, was badly shaken afterward.

"I remember driving home, and I come to a light," the assistant said. "I'm like, 'What a dick. I've known Kobe for three years. I thought he was the nicest kid in the world. What an asshole.' Then, sitting at the light, I go, 'Wait a minute! This is what makes him great! This is what makes him different! This is why he's going to be the next Michael Jordan. This is what makes him different and special.'"

Different and special or not, Schwartz didn't let the incident rest. A few weeks later, he and Bryant were playing against each other in another drill. "I'm on defense with another guy, and Kobe and two other guys are coming down on offense. He pulls up, shoots a three, makes it. We get the ball out of the net, and we're coming down two-on-one against him. I knew he didn't think I'm going to take this. He thinks I'm going to pass it off. So I went down, faked the pass, and he stood there and tried to take the charge."

Instead, Schwartz drove for a layup over Bryant.

"He flops, falls to the ground," Schwartz recalled. "The layup goes in. Nobody calls anything. So I took the ball out of the net, and I kind of threw it at him while he was on the ground. I threw the ball at him. I turned around, and I am on cloud nine at this point, and I am running back down the floor."

Schwartz ran with his arms in the air, celebrating. His teammates looked at him and tried to motion a warning. "I think they're like, 'Yeah, you got him back!' They were pointing. So I swear, divine intervention, I turned around, and a basketball is coming at my head at, like, thirty miles an hour, and I ducked out of the way. I mean, another instant, it would have hit me in the back of the head. He tried to hit me in the head with it. The ball was coming, it was like *The Matrix*. When I turned around, I, like, did, like, one of those moves, and the ball went whizzing by my head. If that thing would have hit me, I would have been knocked out cold.

"That's the only time I remember him launching a ball at someone, because no one was dumb enough to disrespect him," Schwartz said with a laugh, "but I was sour from the other incident. And I felt great about it."

The incidents with Schwartz indicated the pressure that Bryant had heaped on himself for the senior season. In other, more relaxed settings, he found the failings of teammates more tolerable, especially if others were watching, Sam Rines said, recalling that once, at the end of a close AAU game, Bryant had a clear final shot but chose to pass to a less talented teammate who was open. "Coaches still talk about this, which is the crazy part. Kobe has a wide-open, pull-up jump shot. At the last minute he dumps it down to a kid who misses a wide-open layup. Wide open. So Kobe could have easily jumped up and down and went crazy and all that other stuff, but he stayed calm, cool, collected, hugged the kid, and told him, 'Good try.' I had a new respect for Kobe then."

"There was so much going on that we were always together," Schwartz said. "We all liked him. I mean, most times. Sometimes I wanted to kill him, but, like, that was just because of the competitiveness of his personality."

Fans of opposing teams tried to take advantage of his hauteur. During one midseason showdown with a Central rival, the crowd chanted, "Overrated! Overrated!" at Bryant. But it simply wasn't true. He was on his way to breaking Wilt Chamberlain's southeastern Pennsylvania high school scoring record and leading Lower Merion to its first state championship appearance in more than a half century, all done with a team described by everyone involved as significantly less talented than its competition.

Their winning streak stood at seventeen games when they headed into the play-offs on February 17. The postseason would be a drawn-out process that stretched over six weeks, deep into March. First came the District I play-offs. Bryant scored 50 points in the second game, against Academy Park, another blowout.

"Kobe just toyed with them," Gregg Downer recalled. "They didn't guard him in any special way, and this is the kind of stuff that used to, like, keep me awake at night. You know, he's playing as if he could score 50 points left-handed, and at the end of the game, he's going between the legs, the whole nine yards. My whole thing on a night like that was, 'When do I got to get him out of the game?' I didn't want to be unsportsmanlike, and there were a couple of times when he was exploding and having these performances where, if I was a jerk of a coach, he could have gone for 70."

"He hit six three-pointers in the first half alone," Treatman recalled.

It was the last game Bryant would play on Lower Merion's court.

"My career started in this locker room, in this gym," Bryant said afterward. "The fans have shown their support. It's sad, but time goes on."

Three years later, Bryant would say that his two 50-point games in that senior year were almost addictive, an experience he longed to repeat again and again, that feeling of domination. It would become the measure by which a volume scorer established value for his dominance. If it kept Downer awake at night with concern about poor sportsmanship, it also left Bryant lying there in the darkness, basking in the sense of being the man.

Donnie Carr raised his eyebrows at the second 50-point game and would think of it often over the years. It would become a talking point in his conversations about Bryant. "Kobe became a master in the NBA," Carr said, "but the same Kobe Bryant who would be feared for putting 50 on you in the NBA, he was that in his eleventh- and twelfth-grade years in high school. He would come to dominate, and it wasn't just like, 'Oh, well, me and you, we getting it on.' No, he was coming to dominate you. He became a master of that when he got to the NBA, but that was his mind in the twelfth grade. He was coming to get 50."

Carr had always wondered why Bryant practiced the most difficult shots over and over and over again. In games, with the double and triple teams around him, he would pass to open teammates, only to see them often miss shots. At some point, if his team was going to win, Bryant knew he would have to make those shots against multiple defenders. "He knew there would be times in the game, even though he saw guys open, where he had to create a shot for himself," Carr said. "The way he practiced, he was being innovative and creative and just had the mentality that he could get it done."

The Aces charged on through the field to meet Coatesville and his old AAU pal Richard Hamilton in the district semifinals. Jermaine Griffin would prove surprisingly effective in guarding Hamilton, the future pro. The venue for the meeting was Philly's grand old arena, the Palestra, Jeremy Treatman recalled, where the crowd was a sellout, with rumors of ticket scalping. "With just a second to go before the half, Kobe caught the ball in front of the basket and executed a reverse dunk over his head. It was sensational. I'd been in the Palestra for twenty years. I don't think I'd ever heard it louder than that moment. There was a standing ovation from both sides of the stands as we were walking off the floor for halftime. It was just so loud that you had to look up at the crowd. It was, like, this Kobe hysteria."

With a close win, Lower Merion moved on to face Chester, which starred another AAU teammate, superquick guard John Linehan, for the district championship.

The Aces had lost to Chester by 27 points the season before, so each player had written the number 27 on his jersey to keep the memory of that embarrassment fresh. Down by eight at the half, Lower Merion charged back, energized by a Bryant dunk, and won, 70–63.

Both teams advanced to the Class AAAA state championship play-offs. The Aces got three more wins and found themselves again facing Chester and Linehan in the state semifinals, another showdown in the Palestra with the team that had owned them. Linehan, who would later become the NCAA's all-time steals leader, was the weapon deployed against them one final time.

"Chester was so good that year," Robby Schwartz recalled. "I mean, top to bottom, one through five, they were way better than we were."

The intensity went beyond the game itself. Practice that week was infused with it. "We're going to practice hard," Downer recalled, "but, of course, heading into a ballgame like that, the last thing you want is an injury."

"There was another really short guy, a black guy, on our team named Leo Stacy, who was a senior," Schwartz remembered. "We were like twins. He was black, I was white. We were in practice one day, and we used to play seven-on-five, so there'd be two people covering Kobe. It was usually me and Leo who would cover Kobe, just to really get him used to, like, swarming defense. Kobe went to cross over, and Leo went for a steal and went in with his head and busted Kobe's nose. You know, he head butted him right in the nose."

"Leo Stacy is five foot eight at best," Downer said. "Kobe breaks his nose, literally shatters his nose, seventy-two hours before the state semifinal."

"He's bleeding," Schwartz said. "He's got this ice pack on his nose."

The staff saw that he needed immediate medical treatment and led him out of the gym, his face buried in the ice pack in a big towel.

"As he's walking out of the gym, he calls for the ball," Schwartz said. "Somebody threw him the ball. It's at the three-point line. He was about two or three feet behind it on the left-hand side. He grabs the ball, shoots it left-handed, and swishes it as he's walking out of practice with a broken nose. I remember sitting there and being like, 'Are you freaking kidding me?' Like, 'What just happened?' Like, 'That's not possible.' It was like, 'Yeah, OK, my nose is broken. Yeah, I'm bleeding. Just give me the ball.'"

Years later, Schwartz would be reminded of the moment while watching Bryant's documentary, *Kobe Bryant's Muse*, in which Bryant said of his many injuries in pro basketball, "The moment is bigger than the injury. You don't feel the pain."

"We had to find a mask for him quickly," Gregg Downer recalled.

He hated the mask, and in the locker room, before tip-off, he hurled it against the wall while uttering an epithet, which electrified the team.

Linehan, Bryant's teammate on the Sam Rines All-Stars, feasted on Lower Merion's ball handlers that March night in a packed Palestra, with people sitting in the aisles and jostling for seats and a clear view of the clash.

"Kobe had 8 turnovers in the semifinal game against Chester," Jeremy Treatman recalled. "He was turning the ball over left and right."

Bryant fought through the troubles and helped establish a slim lead for the Aces until Linehan drove a fourth-quarter comeback for Chester with a series of steals.

"Our point guard, Emory Dabney, in the fourth quarter turned the ball over, like, three or four times," Schwartz recalled, "and he was, like, crying."

Bryant, who had also been humiliated by Linehan's quickness, wanted nothing to do with the tears, Schwartz recalled. "I mean, Kobe was on Emory's shit, even though he was crying."

"Get it together," Bryant told him during a time-out. "What are you doing?"

"Emory was a sophomore," Schwartz recalled. "He was playing against John Linehan, one of the quickest people I've ever seen in my life. Chester made a comeback and ended up tying the game."

It was the key moment of the entire season in so many ways. "Kobe stayed on top of Emory," Schwartz said, "and Emory ended up blocking Linehan's shot as time expired to send the game into overtime. I always thought that, as down as Emory was in those last moments, Kobe staying on top of him allowed him to come back and block his shot at the end."

It was almost as if the tough talk from Bryant had kept Dabney's competitive fire alive in the worst moment, Schwartz said. "Otherwise, it might have gone out."

"Kobe did have 39 points and the best dunk of his high school career," Treatman remembered.

"In overtime he went coast to coast, dribbled through everybody and dunked and got fouled," Downer said of the moment that clinched the victory.

Never mind that Bryant had so forcefully driven his team through twenty-six straight wins, through a badly broken nose, to the eve of a Class AAAA state championship. The city's airwaves were alive with talk of the boy who shouldn't turn pro, Treatman recalled. "Sports talk radio was killing him. 'This guy is trying to go to the NBA. He can't even dribble the ball against Chester!' I was telling people, 'John Linehan is the quickest guard in the country!'"

In fighting through his adjustment to the broken nose in the first half, Bryant played poorly, taking bad threes, looking very much like he needed about four years of college seasoning. Through the first three quarters, he had taken a whopping 25 shots and made only 8 of them. In the fourth, however he had scored a dozen to help hold off Chester's rally.

The tension on the team was thick on the bus ride up to the championship game against Erie's Cathedral Prep at Hersheypark Arena, in Hershey.

"I used to love those moments before," Schwartz said of the Aces' bus rides, "the tension that's building before a game. Kobe would sit in the back. The back of the bus was, like, where the best guys used to sit. We used to do these rap battles where guys would get up and just free-style for ten, twenty seconds. We used just to go around in a circle. It would just be like, 'You go, you go, you go,' and that was a lot of fun. Guys were taking shots at each other."

At least some of the tension would melt away only to rise again in the long minutes before tip-off. In the championship, Erie immediately seized control of the tempo, and held Bryant scoreless in the first quarter. He scored 8 points in the second, but Erie held a 21–15 lead at the half. The Aces seized a 6-point lead in the third, but Erie again gained control of the tempo and managed to move up, 41–39, late in the game. With a flurry of fouls, Erie sent Bryant and his teammates to the line, which provided just enough edge to give the willful young star the state championship he had talked about since his first days at the suburban school, its first title in more than a half century.

He and Griffin and Downer hoisted the large trophy high for the fans to see there in Hershey.

"I remember the bus ride home was just, like, it was the greatest bus ride ever," Schwartz said. "It was so happy."

There would be a parade with fire trucks and dalmatians riding high with the team. But before all that, they arrived home that first night as champions and gathered at a cheerleader's house. As they had throughout the play-offs, they listened to the Fugees album *The Score*, which was big that winter. They sat up all night, sensing that after sharing so much, they were facing the final moments together. "There's one song that talked about being number one," Schwartz said, "and I just remember being in her living room, in a setting like this, where we were all sitting around, the cheerleaders and the whole team, when that song came on, and it took on this different meaning because now we had just won the state title."

Bryant had told reporters after the game that he was finally going to party a bit.

So he did, hanging out all night with friends his age, soaking up every second, no alcohol or anything heavy except for maybe the Fugees themselves. After all, one of the prime cuts from that record rang through the moment.

"Ready or Not." Here I come.

Chapter 16

TEAM BRYANT

IT WASN'T CLEAR at the time, but Pam Bryant was the dark star, the hidden planet, in son Kobe's universe. Sam Rines had coached Bryant in the AAU for nearly two years and still hadn't met his mother. Sure, he and Pam Bryant talked often on the phone and enjoyed many pleasant moments, but he'd never actually seen her, which indicated just how reclusive she was in terms of her son's basketball life.

Gary Charles never once saw her at an elite or AAU event except very late in the process, when she showed up at a tournament only to be preoccupied playing putt-putt golf with her daughters.

If anything, volleyball games were often bigger family events than basketball games, at least early on. Sharia had gained notice as one of *Sports Illustrated*'s Faces in the Crowd for her play at Temple, and Shaya suited up for La Salle, so the two competed against each other in the old Mid-Atlantic Conference. The entire family, grandparents and cousins included, showed up for volleyball games, recalled Anthony Gilbert, then a student at Temple who had befriended Sharia.

"The sisters had to play against each other," Gilbert recalled. "Kobe's there, the whole family's there, the grandparents, and it was a big deal."

It was only during the late stages of his high school career that Kobe's basketball games were bigger in his family's eyes than his sisters' volleyball games. Early in his senior season, one of his high school games was a sellout at the Palestra, which seated about nine thousand or so. The suburbanite Kobe Bryant may not have been a Philly guy in the eyes of the city's hard-nosed fans, but he could sure sell a ticket or two.

Sam Rines correctly figured that he needed to get to the arena early for that big game, and he staked out a few front-row seats by covering them with coats. Then he watched a woman come along and set aside his coat to take the seats.

"You see my coat there?" Rines asked in disbelief. "Why would you move my coat?"

He had just experienced his first run-in with Pam Bryant. The conflicts were actually few and far between, the coach admitted with a laugh, looking back.

Maybe the incident shouldn't have come as a surprise. Pam was slowly, persistently gaining a reputation among close observers for rearranging things in her son's life. That would become obvious during the state-championship run late that winter of 1996, when Kobe was rumored to have had a budding relationship with Kristen "Ace" Clement, then the junior hoops phenom at Cardinal O'Hara High, in Philadelphia. Clement would later gain notoriety as one of Pat Summitt's point guards for the Tennessee Lady Vols and as a Hawaiian Tropic model. Like Bryant, she was on her way to eclipsing Wilt Chamberlain's Philly preps scoring record.

The rumors of her relationship with Bryant were confirmed when she began attending Lower Merion's games that February and March.

"She was around," Robby Schwartz remembered. "She was a looker, man. She started showing up at games, I want to say it was during the district run. You couldn't miss her. She was, like, six one."

She was there in Hershey, too, near the bus. Later there were rumors that Bryant even managed to sneak her into the team locker room for the championship celebration. It was all innocent stuff, but when the relationship ended quickly, some blamed Pam.

"The ratio for black to white in Lower Merion is, like, five percent," Sam Rines observed. Bryant may have been exploring his

African American heritage during his adolescence, "but how black are you going to be at a school that's basically all white?" Rines observed. "I'm sure he had dated white girls before. He grew up in a culture where that was acceptable, to date a white girl. I know he went out with Kristen Clement and maybe one or two other girls that were Caucasian. There was nothing black you had to be other than on the court. And even on the court, it wasn't about being black."

Sister Sharia explained as much to Anthony Gilbert. "She was like, 'He had all this pent-up aggression of, like, not really knowing if he belonged here and not really knowing who he was as a black man in this city,'" Gilbert offered. "He was like, 'OK, you know what? I don't know what's going on. I don't know what you guys are saying. I don't understand this slang, but when we get between these lines on the court, I'm killing you.'"

Rines's team and Bryant's family had found themselves increasingly involved with merging interests over their months together in the effort to monetize Bryant's talents.

"We really started to bond with Kobe and the family," Rines recalled. "We had a guy that was helping out financially. It got fairly expensive after a while."

As Vaccaro explained, all the college coaches seemed to have their secret bagmen. AAU teams were no different with their "sponsorships." Vaccaro himself provided Adidas money to the Rines All-Stars, Rines recalled. "Sonny gave us money for the big stuff," he said. It was mainly help with funding costs to play in tournaments.

And, while the Bryants appeared to have resources, they, too, were seeking revenue. "Joe was always looking for money," Vaccaro explained.

At the very least, he declined to contribute to the AAU team's expenses. "Joe promised money but never delivered," Rines said.

Instead, a prominent local doctor stepped up to lead a small group in providing assistance for the family and the team, the coach explained. "We went to a lot of places that junior–senior year, and the older guys, they had some fun. Joe had fun with us."

The doctor apparently had no more interest than as a family friend of the Bryants' and as a fan eager to share in the moment. The shared experience laid the groundwork for Rines and the family to join forces that spring of 1996 in an effort to consider the offer Adidas was making to Kobe.

To the mainstream media, however, Sonny Vaccaro managed to keep his mission secret. Many at the NCAA and in the press assumed that Vaccaro's presence in New York meant that he was seeking to influence the college choice of troubled high school star Lamar Odom, who played for Gary Charles's AAU team.

"People were saying Sonny was trying to get to Lamar," Charles said with a laugh, "and meanwhile the bigger prize was a hundred miles south."

Indeed, as the months went on and Vaccaro learned more about Bryant, about just how unparalleled his work ethic was, the more eager Vaccaro became to close the deal.

"I was the middle guy," Charles explained. "It was Joe and I. And, another thing, we did not want Nike to smell what was going on."

Charles explained that he had carefully curried favor with Joe Bryant. "I felt that if I had any chance of getting Kobe I had to develop that relationship with Joe and keep it moving forward," he said. "By that spring, Joe and I had a great relationship that was unshakable at the time. I trusted and believed in him, and he believed in me."

Although Vaccaro and Charles knew that Pam and Kobe would be the ultimate decision makers in the deal, they took care to conduct all communications through the father.

"We never wanted Joe and Pam to think that we were overstepping our boundary," Charles explained.

Charles did check in with Kobe himself from time to time. "Kobe didn't show me any side of him that had doubt," the Long Island AAU coach said. But there was a point during Lower Merion's season when Bryant actually did experience considerable doubt about the decision to turn pro. It lasted for about a week as he lingered on thoughts of Duke and the Cameron Crazies, wondering what college life would be like. Bryant's competitive nature had really connected with the fiery Duke coach from the start. There were even whispers about Joe joining the Duke staff, but even if that was anything more than rumor, Krzyzewski never made an offer.

The social benefits of college that attracted other young players had no tremendous allure for Bryant. One of his high school teammates would later recall Kobe stopping by a party on occasion and seeming totally out of his element, uncomfortable and out of sorts. His attendance at any party that season was likely the teen's attempt to measure that social element, to gain a sense of what he might be missing.

Finally, Bryant addressed his doubt with his father one day in the family kitchen.

"When is the first time you ever doubted yourself?" Joe asked. "You never doubted yourself with high school. All those people who said you can't do this and you can't do that, you proved them wrong. Why start now? The only advice I can give you is, why start now?"

Bryant thought about what his father said and finally concluded that he was right.

"Kobe knew what was going on, but he wasn't part of the deal," Charles said. "I'd talk to the dad, and he would tell Kobe. And I'd say, 'Kobe good?' He'd say, 'Yeah, Kobe good.'"

In all their time building the relationship with the Bryants, Charles and Vaccaro had still not given the exact parameters of the deal, exactly how much money they would be offering, how much would be guaranteed. It remained the final element to be hashed out.

It only made sense to be cautious, Charles explained. "It was all brand-new. No one else was attempting these straight-to-the-NBA-from-high-school shoe deals back then."

They were breaking ground about how American professional basketball related to the amateur game. Their efforts with Felipe Lopez had been sort of a trial run. Now, Bryant presented a hard target.

"We also knew there had to be side money for Joe," Charles

recalled. "Without a doubt. That was the deal. Joe needed a job. That's why he coached at La Salle."

Vaccaro knew that if La Salle named Joe head coach, the Adidas deal was off. "Kobe wouldn't have gone pro," he said. "Joe told me that. He said that's the only thing. Now, I don't know if Kobe would have gone along, but that was Joe's plan."

"There was a lot of hope locally that Kobe would go to La Salle," Gregg Downer recalled.

Yet that spring, Joe Bryant was rapidly burning his bridges at his alma mater. The school then finally announced that Speedy Morris would keep his job. "The day Speedy Morris got the extension, everything changed," recalled Vontez Simpson, who was talking over the situation with Joe. "Joe was out of there."

The Philadelphia papers would later report that Jellybean had simply ceased going to work and would send one of his daughters to the school to pick up his paycheck. If Joe had retained any long-term goals of coaching in college, he had destroyed his opportunity, some of his friends thought. Morris would long remain bitter over how the situation was handled. The botched ending to Joe Bryant's tenure there meant that he couldn't exactly put the experience on his résumé and list Speedy Morris as a reference.

Perhaps what seemed oddest about Joe Bryant's actions was that a man who had found so much disappointment in the NBA would be such an advocate for having his son bypass college to begin work there immediately as a teen. Joe Bryant seemed perfectly willing to risk not just his son's future but his own as well.

"Joe knew he had a special talent on his hands," Charles explained.

Suddenly, there was even more pressure on the father to find revenue going forward. As the days rolled by, the circumstances made it even more imperative that any deal for Kobe include opportunity for the father as well.

"We knew that, and we told Joe that he would work for Adidas," Charles said. "So all of that played a part in what we were doing. There was no way Joe wanted to take that chance of his son going pro unless he had a guarantee."

The fact that Bryant needed cash flow was hardly unusual for former players. As Charles pointed out, former pros in just about all sports were having trouble holding on to the money they had made, especially players from the 1970s, when the pay was far below that of the overwhelming contracts that would be handed out later, after Michael Jordan made the sport more popular in the 1980s and 1990s and boosted the salary structure for stars into the tens of millions of dollars.

"Even Dr. J had to have a job," Charles said with a laugh. "When Joe played, how big could you really get?"

Clearly, however, Joe Bryant had correctly read certain key factors about the situation. One, the shoe industry and American pro basketball had evolved into a state where they were willing to pay millions on the speculation that a player might be great. The father also knew clearly that the sooner athletic talent could earn large amounts of money, the better. Professional athletic careers were far shorter than other careers. Time was precious. That was a no-brainer, and demand was just beginning to drive the marketplace for talent. Jerry Reinsdorf, chairman of the Chicago Bulls, had purchased the team for a few million in the early 1980s, then watched Jordan push the value of the franchise to beyond half a billion dollars in a few short years. In the wake of that, other men of wealth understandably wanted to capitalize on the money and fun that employing unique talent could bring them as owners of teams.

Beyond any of these circumstances, however, the largest factor in the equation that spring was Kobe's own will. He had little fear of pro basketball. It was the game he had grown up around in Italy, not college basketball. It was the game about which his father had talked incessantly. Bryant told himself he was ready to take a plunge that no guard had ever taken.

"There's no question," Sonny Vaccaro said, looking back in 2015. "He's the strongest-willed guy. He knew what he wanted from the start. He wanted to be better than all of them. Kevin Garnett wasn't sure about turning pro. He thought he had to because of his test scores. Jordan had played college ball. Kobe Bryant took the biggest step. Kobe had the biggest balls of all of them."

Troubles

No matter how ripe the circumstances were to produce a shoe contract for Bryant, it still almost didn't happen. As the days rolled on into late March, the Bryants grew edgier and wanted to know if Adidas was for real. The first trouble came in March, when Gary Charles got a call at work from Vaccaro's wife, Pam.

"Gary, the deal is off," she told him. "The deal is over. Sonny's upset and going crazy over here."

"Joe had come into New York for a meeting with Sonny with a lawyer," Charles recalled, "and one of the things that Sonny prided himself on was, it was just us. No one knew what was going on, just us. No lawyers. And here comes Joe with a lawyer. Now, Sonny never trusted anyone that was outside of our circle, and he didn't like it. He was upset. He said, 'I don't know what the hell is going on here.'"

Charles told Pam Vaccaro to try to calm her husband down.

"I wasn't that calm, either," Charles admitted.

He was so nervous, in fact, that he went and bought a Kit-Kat, his favorite treat, just to produce some calm. After all, he and Vaccaro had put a lot of effort into everything to get to this point. Once he was calm, Charles dropped some coins in a pay phone outside his Wall Street office and dialed Joe Bryant.

"Joe, what the hell?" Charles asked. "What happened? Sonny's pissed. Joe, why did you bring this guy? I'll tell you what you're going to do. You're going to grab Pam and you're going to get your ass back in your car and you're going to drive back to New York and we're going to close this deal today, by yourself."

That was just what the Bryants wanted to hear. Joe and Pam headed back up the turnpike to New York for an afternoon meeting.

Charles then went over to the hotel where Vaccaro was set to meet the Bryants. "I had to tell Sonny to be ready, calm his ass down," Charles recalled. "I said, 'Sonny, now listen, you don't have to go crazy. I went over the deal on the phone with Joe, the deal is done, just don't go crazy.' He said, 'OK, I'm sorry.'"

When Joe and Pam walked in, Vaccaro got up to embrace the father. "He gave Joe a peck on each side of the cheek, doing the hug thing," Charles said. The moment was classic Vaccaro. For years, the shoe executive had stirred suspicion that he was a mob-connected figure. When he first made a presentation to Nike officials in the late 1970s, they had immediately wondered about his past. Some of them even wanted to have the FBI run a background check on him. Rob Strasser had stopped that sort of thinking and had soon hired Vaccaro to launch the age of shoe payola for college coaches. Through his own checking account, Vaccaro had eventually distributed millions to college coaches to have their players wear Nike shoes.

Vaccaro over the years had actually enjoyed the speculation about his mob connections and even used the sense of power that came with it to his advantage. His kisses on the cheeks of players had left many of them wondering, "Who is this guy? What's going on here?"

Growing up near Pittsburgh, Vaccaro had been a high school running back of note in the 1950s (news stories from the era document he once scored four touchdowns in a game).

By age twenty-four, he had gained notoriety for founding the Dapper Dan Roundball Classic, a high school all-star tournament that quickly took off because it featured the country's top players and drew hundreds of college scouts.

"I knew the whole mob in Pittsburgh," he recalled in 2015 about the aura of organized crime connections he had. "I met the boss, knew the unders, but I never did anything with them. I was twenty-four when I started the Roundball Classic, but I never did anything with them. They let me be. They were proud of me."

The tournament made him a local celebrity, he said. "I knew everybody. I dined at the best restaurants. That's how I got to Vegas."

He began working the gambling junkets that took players from Pittsburgh to Vegas. His brother was already in Nevada, on his way to becoming one of the top sports oddsmakers in the entire gaming industry. Soon Vaccaro was spending part of the year in Pittsburgh with his tournament and another part in Vegas earning "commissions" placing bets for "clients" at the various sports books in the city. He watched the big-time poker players and soon enough took up that life himself, a dark period on his curriculum vitae that changed once Nike hired him to use his connections with major coaches to build its shoe business.

It worked famously, then led to his hunch about building an entire product line around Michael Jordan, which again boosted his stature in the business greater still, up until his mysterious firing by Nike.

He had used a joint friendship with Howie Garfinkel, guru of the New York Five-Star basketball camp, to contact Gary Charles and invite him to the Final Four in Minneapolis in 1992.

"I'll never forget it," Charles recalled. "I'd never seen anything like it in my whole life. Walked into the hotel, it was wall-to-wall college coaches. It was a meat market, all of them there. I called Sonny on the house phone. He said, 'Come up to my room.' Sonny opened up the door in a white robe. I remember seeing his wife, Pam, on the other side of him. I thought, 'Oh my God, how did this guy get this beautiful woman?'"

Vaccaro launched into his plan to invade AAU basketball and asked for Charles's help. "I really looked at him," Charles recalled. "I looked at Pam, I looked at him, I looked at Pam. And I said to myself, 'Any man who can get a woman that looks like that must know what he's doing.'"

By 1996, Vaccaro and Gary Charles presented quite a pair working for Adidas, hustling basketball deals. In those days, Charles was given to wearing black felt fedora hats and exotic sunglasses. And Vaccaro was Vaccaro, full of ideas and motivation to compete with Nike. And they were now on the verge of landing the big one.

Joe Bryant had known of Vaccaro as the guy who got the Air Jordan deal done. He was happy to have Vaccaro kissing him that day.

The Adidas men quickly laid out the deal, better than $1 million for Kobe guaranteed that first year as part of a deal that would be announced as a multiyear agreement worth $10 million. What wasn't announced was that Adidas would pay Joe a $150,000 kicker as an "employee." It was all of the budget that fledgling Adidas

America had, Vaccaro said, looking back. "Kobe was grateful that we were giving Joe money."

"So, are we good?" Charles recalled asking Joe that day in the hotel room. "Joe looks at me, I look back at Joe. I give him a nod, and he says, 'We're good.'"

Nothing would be officially signed until weeks later, but in that hotel room in late March, the deal had been laid out, the air cleared, intentions made known.

They all began hugging one another. "Man," Charles said, "what just happened here?"

Joe Bryant just broke into his Jellybean grin.

The Classic

By 1996, Vaccaro had packed up his Roundball Classic game in Pittsburgh and moved it to Detroit, where it was given a new name, Magic Johnson's Roundball Classic, complete with an array of yet more high school stars and a fine TV contract with Dick Vitale doing on-air commentary. It was a perfect opportunity for Adidas to subtly showcase their new star for the next generation of shoe marketing.

Bryant was clearly the elite player of his high school class. In the three seasons following his disastrous first year, he had led his high school to a 77–13 record. He had played all five positions on the floor. He had scored 1080 on his college boards, which meant there was no school in America that didn't want to showcase him on its basketball team. As a senior, he had averaged 30.8 points, 12 rebounds, 6.5 assists, 4 steals, and 3.8 blocked shots, to take Lower Merion to a 31–3 record. He had closed his career as southeastern Pennsylvania's all-time leading scorer at 2,883 points, better than both Wilt Chamberlain and Lionel Simmons.

In the wake of that performance, he was named the Naismith High School Player of the Year, the Gatorade National Boys Basketball Player of the Year, a McDonald's All American, and USA Today's All-USA Player of the Year.

For the airing of the Roundball Classic, Vitale, college basketball's premier broadcast personality, oohed and aahed over the "Diaper Dandies," his name for young basketball stars, and talked glowingly about Bryant's mature game and his fluent Italian. Vitale even offered his audience a tip that Bryant might be turning pro.

Vaccaro had Adidas chairman Peter Moore in Detroit that weekend for final approval of the deal, and Bryant didn't disappoint. "In some ways it was an audition," Vaccaro said. "He was brilliant. He was Kobe. He played really well during a scrimmage in practice. That all helped close it in Peter Moore's mind."

Vaccaro was struck by just how much Bryant was beginning to play the part of the next Jordan during a limo ride in Detroit the day before the game. His head was shaved. He talked like Jordan. Had adopted many of his mannerisms.

They were returning from a media session, where Bryant had performed with Jordan-like charm. In the car, Vaccaro mentioned Jordan in their conversation. Bryant leaned in to face the old, sad-eyed Italian man and remarked that he was going to be better than Jordan. "He told me," Vaccaro recalled, " 'I'm going to be better than he is.' " The comment gave Vaccaro reason for pause. That season, a renewed thirty-three-year-old Jordan had simply eviscerated the rest of the NBA while leading his Chicago Bulls to an all-time best 72–10 regular-season record.

In making the statement, Bryant was well aware of Vaccaro's history and success with Jordan. Although it seemed impossible, Vaccaro considered the thought that Bryant was even more confident than Jordan had been as a young player set to enter pro basketball.

Looking back two decades later, Vaccaro observed that the entire Adidas courtship had shaped the seventeen-year-old Bryant into thinking that he was the next Jordan. As one so supremely ambitious, Bryant had already locked in on Jordan's example and presence.

Michael Harris, a promoter who was working closely with Bryant that spring, recalled that Kobe had a closet at home filled with critical research. "It held all these VHS tapes of Michael's games," Harris said. "He'd pull them out and study them and do the moves."

"Look at what I added," Bryant would tell Harris, then do a move.

He was studying even harder for the role.

Now to have the men who had fostered the original Air Jordan trying to sign him to be next? "He had gotten the message subliminally and subconsciously," Vaccaro said. "And he enjoyed it."

The comparison would quickly become a burden for the young player in that the public came to see him as an upstart who had conjured up Jordan's greatness in his own mind. But far beyond any of his own adolescent hero fantasies, Bryant was launched by the industry, scouted and courted and groomed to play the role. That, of course, was only important in the public mind, in regards to Bryant's image.

The power of suggestion was shaping his path, certainly, but the power and might and endurance of his drive had little to do with such suggestion. The real essence was nothing that could be concocted or suggested or reproduced. That essence, Vaccaro said, was "the real Kobe," not his copying of Jordan that had been induced by the circumstances to feed his adolescent fantasies.

In the wake of Bryant passing the audition in Detroit, new trouble came with the debate over his selecting an agent. As April rolled along, the Bryants wanted to meet with Vaccaro in New Jersey to discuss their "Team Bryant" approach to managing their son's career.

"We set up this plan for Kobe," Sam Rines remembered. "We called it Team Bryant. It was a plan for the family and Kobe to all stay a part of what Kobe was doing, for his life and his lifestyle when he started making money. The plan was designed by a marketing director that worked at a casino."

Thus the Atlantic City setting for the meeting. "That was where things first started to change a little bit," said one source familiar with the situation. "When he was going to be drafted, they had put together this group of people to run things. At that time, a lot of players were putting together a team of people, including all their family members, to organize things. Pam was very nice and sweet, but she was definitely running the show. Kobe had started pulling into himself, and they started wrapping themselves around him."

"So we had this meeting down in Atlantic City," Sam Rines remembered, "and Sonny comes to the meeting."

"A lot of people tried to shoot me down once they knew he was going pro," Vaccaro remembered, adding that he was interrogated in the meeting by members of the group. "They wanted to do the marketing. Kobe's aunt was there. Nice, well dressed. But Pam was always the boss."

The meeting wasn't entirely unpleasant, but there was tension, because the group included a lawyer and wanted to choose Kobe's agent, Rines recalled, while Vaccaro already had plans to hire the agent himself. "Sonny sits there," Rines recalled, "and after about fifteen, twenty minutes, Sonny says, 'Kobe, I'm going to give you one ultimatum. If you don't sign this contract with our fellow, you're going to blow a million-dollar signing bonus with Adidas.' And that was it. Nothing else was entertained beyond that."

"They formed Team Bryant," Vaccaro recalled. "That's how they were all going to live forever on Team Bryant's 20 percent. I mean, seriously. I can't explain it any better. That was their plan."

"He strong-armed the whole thing," Rines said of Vaccaro. "He flew in and flew out. He wasn't there more than thirty minutes. No eating dinner, wasn't no hanging out. It was either, you sign with them, or the deal's off. We had it where we were looking at bringing in a different agent, a New York agent."

Actually, Vaccaro was hiring two agents for Bryant. One, Rick Bradley with William Morris, was hired because Bryant wanted to get into entertainment and music. William Morris handled the shoe deal, Vaccaro explained.

The second agent was Vaccaro's close friend, L.A.-based Arn Tellem, who would handle Bryant's less-lucrative rookie contract with an NBA team.

No one realized it at the time, but the hiring of Tellem would be absolutely critical to the career success of Kobe Bryant. Among his many attributes, Tellem had something critical that none of them understood in the moment—he was extremely close with Lakers executive Jerry West.

While Team Bryant left New Jersey frustrated that day, they didn't quite give up. A few days later, Gary Charles walked out of work, and there was Joe Bryant.

"I don't even think Sonny knows this," Charles said, "but Joe came to my job to pick me up in a limo. I was walking out of my job, and he was looking at me. Joe was in there with a couple of agents. Joe wanted me to sit in, and they took us to dinner and they gave their pitch."

Charles looked at Joe Bryant and said, "Tellem's the agent."

"OK," Joe said finally.

A short time later, Kobe and his family signed the agreement with Adidas and with the agents at Il Vagabondo, in New York. After the papers were signed, Kobe Bryant had perhaps a tinge of buyer's remorse and posed a question for the shoe man. "Mr. Vaccaro," he said, "what if I had gone to Duke—could I have gotten this shoe contract? Would Adidas have paid me this money?"

"No," Vaccaro remembered telling the teen. "We'd have to give the money and the contract to the school, to Duke and Coach K."

"Really?" Bryant replied. "Then I made the right decision, didn't I?"

Vaccaro remembered being struck by how little Kobe actually understood about the rules of amateur competition. "He never understood that until then," Vaccaro said. "We'd never had a discussion about how the coaches and the schools split the shoe money. But then, there was no reason for a high school kid to even think about a shoe contract in 1996. He was implying that if he could have gotten the money, maybe he would have gone to college."

As it was, Bryant had now signed on for a huge step, and he quickly turned to the many questions about his future.

Charles remembered taking a stroll with the young star down Broadway after he had made his decision.

"We were walking, and people were noticing it was Kobe," Charles recalled. "At some point he asked me a question: 'What pick do you think I'm going to get drafted?'"

Charles told him there were at least two players possibly ahead of him at his position.

"One of them is Antoine Walker," the AAU coach said.

"I'm better than Antoine Walker," Bryant replied, turning suddenly fierce in his demeanor. "What are you talking about?"

Charles remembered stopping and just looking at the teen and thinking to himself, "Yeah, that's why you're getting all these Lincolns. I guess we got the right guy."

"Antoine Walker just won the national championship in college basketball with Kentucky," Charles reminded him. "He's six eight."

"I'm still better than him," Bryant said, obviously annoyed.

"Yeah," Charles admitted, "you're right, but come on. Let's keep walking."

Charles told Bryant his other competition in the draft would be guard Kerry Kittles, out of Villanova.

"I could see them taking Kerry over me," Bryant replied, which again gave Charles yet another reason to pause and ponder how comprehensively the young player had already evaluated his competition on the landscape.

Later, after the draft had fallen gloriously in Bryant's favor, Charles would look back to that moment and laugh. "What I was watching," Charles observed, "was a very nice young man who was really obedient and respectful of his dad and his folks. He would hang on his dad's words, what his dad had to say. He was a sponge, he was taking everything in."

Brandy, You're a Fine Girl

"We need to make your prom huge," Big Mike told Kobe Bryant that spring.

Big Mike was Michael Harris, the owner of Best, a sports and entertainment promotional company that listed among its clients NFL players such as Ray Lewis and Simeon Rice, as well as the red-hot R&B group Boys II Men.

When Bryant first began driving as a teen, the vehicle was often his father's BMW. Mindful of the past, his mother had made sure he kept his driver's license and vehicle registration with him. He would be stopped because of the expensive vehicle, his skin color, and his age, she warned him. Sure enough, a short time later he was pulled over. When he got the SUV for his senior year, it was the same drill. But that spring, Bryant took to riding a bike everywhere, Michael Harris remembered. On the eve of cashing in his innocence, Bryant was perhaps indulging in a last embrace of childhood, the kind of youthful freedom he had almost never allowed himself over the years.

Harris lived quite a few miles away, but Bryant would pedal over to his house, hang out in the evening, then get back on the bike late at night and head out into the darkness.

Harris considered it dangerous, but Bryant thought nothing of it.

Harris had gotten to know Bryant quite well that late winter and spring, mostly through his associate, a former University of Virginia running back named Jerrod Washington, who was engaged to Sharia Bryant.

At first, Harris thought a date with R&B star Monica would be ideal for boosting the teen basketball star's celebrity profile.

"Man, I like Brandy," Bryant told him.

Harris knew that was true. He had been hanging out with Bryant often that spring, watching him go through grinding workouts, then rush home each afternoon to sit down with his sisters and catch *Moesha,* the new TV show that starred Brandy Norwood.

Bryant represented a chance for Harris to add basketball stars to his client list, so he hatched a plan.

First, Harris set up an opportunity for Bryant to meet the members of Boys II Men. The promoter called the members, who were set to appear at the Essence Festival in late April at Madison Square Garden.

"I'm gonna bring him up to Essence," he said. The R&B stars thought that would be cool, so in the jam-packed last week of April, as he was set to announce his decision about whether he'd go to college or turn pro, young Bryant took off for Manhattan and a room at the Four Seasons and a limo ride with the music group and the taping of the awards show, where he got to eyeball luminaries such as Halle Berry, Tyra Banks, Toni Braxton, and numerous others who would soon enough become his celebrity acquaintances. His head was spinning as if it were on a swivel that night, Bryant would say later.

Once they got back to the Four Seasons after the event, Harris phoned Bryant in his room and told him to come down to the suite of Boys II Men member Wanya Morris. Mike McCary, another member of the group, would be there, too, he said.

"I never let Kobe know anything about Brandy," Harris recalled.

Bryant walked into Wanya's room, and there was Brandy, his TV idol and heartthrob. He freaked out—it was one of the most nervous times in his life, Bryant would later confide.

"Oh, my God. Oh, my God," he said over and over, with everyone laughing at how excited he was. Actually, Harris thought he handled it well.

At the time, Wanya was essentially dating Brandy, and he wasn't real keen on Bryant taking her out, Harris recalled.

"This prom thing's big," Harris told him.

Wanya reluctantly agreed, and later that night, Bryant and Harris discussed the idea of Bryant asking Brandy to the prom. Yes, Bryant had his regular girlfriend, Jocelyn, Harris recalled, but she was young, studious, and innocent. Bryant needed a high-profile date to help create future opportunities.

"Like I was going to say no," Kobe said later. So Harris dialed Norwood up.

"Brandy, Brandy, Brandy," he said. "My man Kobe wants to ask you to his prom."

Just like that, the big idea was set in motion. It was agreed that Norwood's mother would reach out to Kobe's mother, a notion that absolutely delighted Pam Bryant.

The next night, in Philly, Boys II Men played in a celebrity basketball game and added Bryant as their ringer. He opened the show with a monster dunk and actually got to spend his first time alone with Brandy afterward.

No surprise, he was immediately smitten. She, too, had pursued her dreams, acting and singing, and to do so had given up much of her childhood and schooling to work privately with tutors. She was easy to talk to and nothing short of remarkable, Bryant decided.

The mothers connected and found everything to their liking, and the date was on. Bryant talked to his new friend almost every day. Brandy, who rarely answered calls, picked up for Bryant, Harris said.

In the coming weeks, Harris got a view of just how ambitious young Bryant was. He would stay out until 1 a.m., but no matter how late Bryant stayed out, he was up early and going through unbelievably demanding workouts each day.

Harris thought it strange, over-the-top, frankly.

Bryant's mind was always rushing to the NBA, with thoughts about how he would fare against pros.

He told Harris he could beat Mitch Richmond. "Dennis Rodman couldn't hold me," Bryant proclaimed.

" 'Are you crazy?' " Harris thought to himself. "He believed in himself far more than I or anybody else did."

Harris was far from convinced, but Kobe was a client. And, just as Harris had hoped, the Lower Merion prom, at Philly's Bellevue Hotel, was huge.

There had been noise among students and parents that Bryant and his flashy prom date were hijacking the event, yet many of those same people would line up for photos once the big night arrived.

People magazine was there, along with dozens of other reporters, even sports hacks. Bryant almost disappointed them. He and Jermaine Griffin were watching basketball videos — what else? — when time got away from them. They hustled into their tuxes. Griffin was taking John Lucas's daughter, a Lower Merion student, and Bryant had Brandy on his arm. Long-haired Matt Matkov, Bryant's good friend, was dumped by his date at the last minute, so all five piled into the limo. The celebrities spent their time cheering up Matkov for the big night.

Bryant and Brandy had actually enjoyed a test run the night before on their first date, a Barry White concert in Atlantic City, with Bryant's hotel room and expenses covered by the same doctor who had supported the AAU team, Rines explained. They strolled the boardwalk and saw fireworks. The day after the prom, the Bryants and Brandy and her mother returned to Atlantic City for yet more fun.

The Brandy prom weekend had added a huge touch of outrageousness to Kobe's profile, just as Harris had hoped. It would provide a paragraph in the many, many profiles written about him in the months and years ahead.

Bryant quickly developed a puppy love for his star date.

"That's just natural," Harris said. "He had his fantasies and his thoughts."

Just as it was natural that Wanya was bummed about Bryant's infatuation and Brandy's own warm feelings toward Bryant.

"Wanya got on me," Harris recalled with a laugh. "I tried to stay out of it. But Kobe was heading to newfound fame. He was getting a lot of attention, a lot of women.

"And she had considerable charm," Harris said of Brandy. "She was a very intelligent young woman. It was understandable that two very popular young men would get excited about her."

Amidst all the hoopla surrounding Bryant's leap to the NBA, a friend who worked at ESPN asked Harris in a televised interview, "You think he's that good?"

Harris said he decided to go for it. He figured if Kobe turned out to be as great as his ambitions, then everybody would remember Harris's comment. If Bryant flopped, no one would care what Harris had said in 1996.

"In the end, they'll compare Kobe to MJ," Harris told his friend from ESPN.

"I guess I kind of believed it," Harris said. "He was looked at as an introvert, but he had golden dreams. He was looking for people to support his dreams. He was different from the start, looked at things differently. He believed in himself far beyond what I or anybody else did."

Lost in the Bryant spotlight was another high schooler turning pro that year. Jermaine O'Neal was a big man, a seven footer, seen as less of a risk than Kobe, a guard. In the weeks before Bryant announced his decision, the debate had heightened over both players' choices. Chris Carrawell, who had played against Bryant and later signed to play at Duke, told reporters that Bryant was making "a bad decision. I understand the money. But it's better to go to school. At least for three years. I don't think they're ready, mentally or physically."

Rick Mahorn, on the other hand, who had witnessed Bryant operating in those summer showdowns with pro players, had no problem with the move. "He's ready if that's what he wants," Mahorn said. "There's no question about it."

Bryant admitted another, emotional reason for looking to the pro game. His old hero, Magic Johnson, had returned to the NBA in an attempt to reignite his competitive battles with Michael Jordan. The thought of going against both of them gave him another motivation for getting into the league as quickly as possible.

"I wanted to get in the league and play against those guys," he would later reveal.

On April 29, Jeremy Treatman helped the school set up the press conference in which the young star would announce his decision. Set in Lower Merion's gymnasium, the event attracted quite a range of regional and national media, including the *Washington Post*, ESPN, and the *New York Times*.

At the appointed moment, set up so that the stations could get the footage on the evening news, Bryant walked out, wearing his father's fine brown jacket, his pate cleanly shaved, sunglasses perched atop his head. It was his first true dress rehearsal for the role that Adidas was paying him to play. But, whereas a twenty-two-year-old Jordan had embraced his first big moments with his trademark serious demeanor, Bryant was filled with teen giggles and more than a trace of a smirk for the cameras.

His teammates were seated behind him, posing and enjoying the moment while facing the assembled media. They were in the gym where they had been through so many tough practices with Kobe Bryant, Robby Schwartz thought at the time. "I remember looking at him and was like, 'There are so many cameras here. There's, like, twenty-five microphones right there.' He had his sunglasses on his head, and he made the announcement, which was a funny, funny night, man. Who wears sunglasses on their head during a press conference? Who wears sunglasses inside?"

"There were a lot of people in that gym," Treatman recalled with a chuckle.

His shaved head glistening in the TV lights, Bryant stepped to the bank of microphones, paused as a smirk again spread across his face, and announced, "I have decided to skip college and take my talents to the NBA. I know I'll have to work extra hard, and I know this is a big step, but I can do it.

"It's the opportunity of a lifetime. It's time to seize it while I'm young. I don't know if I can reach the stars or the moon. If I fall off the cliff, so be it."

There would be a substantial negative reaction to the irreverence Bryant presented that night. His first big introduction to the world cast a negative image that would be replayed for two decades, any time a media organization wanted to prove his brashness.

The truth was more innocent, both Treatman and Schwartz said. He was simply young, aiming to enjoy his moment, but inexperienced and nervously trying to appear cool.

"I think he was hamming it up a little bit because he understood," Schwartz said. "See, I think he understood the gravity of the moment and what he was doing, and he wanted to have a little bit of fun with it. I kind of liked it.

"He sort of played it up, and he was trying to be entertaining," Schwartz added. "You know, it might have worked for some people and not worked for others. I think it all depended on your perception of him going into it. If your first view is of a high school student holding a press conference with sunglasses on his head, you might not love him right away."

The family had tried to prepare for the negative public reaction that had been building in advance of the announcement. But in the end, there was perhaps no way to anticipate the depth of disapproval the moment generated, Treatman said. "It was like the media took it personally. It didn't make any sense."

Columnist Mike DeCourcy in *The Sporting News* wrote, "I'm not sure why anyone cares if he's ready for such a life, because his folks apparently didn't."

On Philly's sports talk radio station, WIP, commentator Howard Eskin irritated Treatman with his criticism of the Bryants and the move. "He ripped Kobe, and he had never even seen Kobe play," the assistant coach said. "He came up with theory after theory as to why they were doing it. He thought [Joe] was behind it," Treatman said.

"They don't know me," Bryant told Treatman that week. "They don't know how bad I want it."

Joe and Pam Bryant, meanwhile, made an effort to explain things to reporters after the announcement.

"We were going to support him no matter what he chose to do," Pam said. "Whether it was college or going to the NBA, we're always going to support him. That's what we always do. This was Kobe's decision. He has goals, and we're always here to support him."

A reporter wondered if Joe Bryant wasn't allowing the move simply because he wanted to live vicariously through his son.

"If that were true, then Kobe would go to La Salle for two years, find a wife, have three kids, and raise a family," Mrs. Bryant said. "That was Joe's dream, and it's worked out pretty well for us. Joe played in the NBA. He doesn't have to live through anybody."

"I've been fortunate in the sense that I've been around and know the water he's about to tread," Joe told the media. "There are a lot of parents who would have no clue. I don't think you can fault me for having an understanding of what's going on. I've talked to all kinds of people, and I've touched a lot of bases. I think Kobe is lucky to have someone who's been there. Hey, I would like to have seen Kobe go to school for four years and go to Harvard. But is that reality? Would he have stayed in school for one or two years? This was Kobe's dream. This is his life, so it was his decision.... I don't have any doubt in my son. No doubt, just support and a lot of love."

Joe reminded reporters that his son had a unique maturity. "Living in Italy was the key," the father said. "The maturity and responsibility our kids learned over there. The people who have made negative comments really just don't know Kobe. He's a super kid, and he knows what he wants to do and can accomplish.

"My wife and I have been married for twenty-two years," he added. "We've been through ups and downs, but that's part of life. But the most important thing is that we wanted to raise our kids to be stronger and better people than we are."

"I think [the reaction] stunned Kobe," Treatman said. "I think the negative stuff out in L.A. later about the draft stunned him, too.

He was mature enough then to realize that the nature of publicity wasn't gonna change. He said he wasn't gonna care, that he would use it to motivate himself to work even harder."

The family had supporters as well, Treatman recalled. "The people that really mattered supported him. He had uncles, grandparents and parents, friends. The coaching staff at Lower Merion and his teammates supported him, too."

Pam Bryant acknowledged to reporters that she had concerns about the culture of pro sports, "concerns about drugs, alcohol, and fast women," but, she said, "Kids are exposed to that in high school. Kobe's a well-balanced young man. He's always stayed focused on what is important. I don't worry with Kobe or any of my children, because we have a good family foundation."

In retrospect, the moment was perhaps the crux of Kobe Bryant's career, despite the fact that it came so early in his life. Tex Winter—a coach who played a major role in Jordan's career and who eventually became Bryant's mentor—would often spend time contemplating the comparisons between the two players and the sources of their greatness. There were many differences, but the main difference, the coach concluded, was that Jordan spent three years in college, learning how to play a team game under highly structured coach Dean Smith. That background prepared Jordan to achieve his later greatness with the Chicago Bulls, Winter believed.

Winter developed tremendous affinity for Bryant and admired so much about his unflinching dedication, but he also came to believe that Bryant's lack of college experience was ultimately the thing that kept him from his goal of being the unquestioned greatest of all time.

Winter's point raises a question about that moment in the spring of 1996: what if Bryant's parents had displayed greater focus on college and on Bryant's personal growth? This question, of course, remains unanswerable. As it is, his career would still prove absolutely remarkable, the function of his unparalleled determination.

Certainly, young Bryant stepped boldly into the pro game and soon found himself caught up in events, but he also seized them as perhaps no one in the history of the game had ever done. For better or for worse, Kobe Bryant was setting his own course, marked by his guiding star, his sheer will to leave no stone unturned, no task undone, in his effort.

"When we gave him a million a year with money on the side for Joe, that showed my faith in him," Sonny Vaccaro said. "I gave him a fucking million dollars before he announced, before he was drafted. When I gave him all that money, it showed how much I loved him."

Now, with pieces of April all around, the only thing Vaccaro had to do was try to figure out how to get a seventeen-year-old kid selected in the first round of the NBA draft.

Chapter 17

OFF TO THE STARS

THE 1996 DRAFT developed with the usual whirlwind of mind games and high-stakes intrigue, made more dramatic than usual by the fact that time would show that the best player was a seventeen-year-old guard with no college experience. Only a few teams would come to see that at the time, specifically, the Los Angeles Lakers and the Philadelphia 76ers. Other teams were impressed with what they saw in scouting reports and workouts but were understandably reluctant to select a player like Kobe Bryant with a high draft pick.

Pro basketball had always considered itself a business for men, players with mature bodies and hard-won experience. Before 1996, in the league's four decades of existence, about a half dozen players, mostly big men, had gone directly from high school to the NBA, with mixed success.

The 1940s and World War II had opened the door for a few teenagers to enter the game, as pro basketball was morphing into the NBA. But in that era, most of the players were veterans in the true sense of the word. Many of them had served in World War II. They knew how to fight for a roster spot, which meant there wasn't much room for youngsters.

Connie Simmons and Joe Graboski were teens from that era who went on to long journeyman careers. For the most part, though, pro basketball didn't busy itself with young players.

The pros were a risky business back in the late 1940s and early 1950s. There were few fans, and there was hardly any press coverage, maybe a paragraph on the back pages of local newspaper sports sections. When the NBA started as the Basketball Association of America, in 1946, it had eleven teams, but that number soon dwindled to eight struggling clubs. In those days you played college basketball with the idea of earning a free education, plus a little pocket money from alums. Pro basketball players were paid little better than ditch diggers. Just about all of them had to have jobs on the side and in the off-season. They washed their own uniforms in hotel sinks — if they had hotel rooms.

Giving up an education to chase the limp dream of pro basketball was not some big-money play for the boys of that era; it seemed more like a stroll on the moon. Besides, the college game was the glamour game. It got all the media attention.

There were advantages for pro teams to protect college basketball as its proving ground. The NBA soon adopted a rule stipulating that if you left college early, you had to wait until your class graduated before you were eligible to play. Wilt Chamberlain, the master post weapon and physical specimen of his era, left the University of Kansas after two seasons, in 1958, and wasn't allowed to play in the NBA.

Instead he played for the Harlem Globetrotters until his class graduated and he was allowed to join the old Philadelphia Warriors. The NBA kept that attitude toward college players until the American Basketball Association jumped into business, in 1967, with no rules preventing players from bypassing college to join the pros.

Moses Malone, who went to the ABA out of high school, in 1974, then switched to the NBA, would become a hall-of-famer. Others, such as the Sixers' Darryl Dawkins — Joe's old teammate — arrived too early, struggled in the world of grown men, and never reached their potential.

By and large, pro teams shunned young players during the 1980s, especially those who wanted to go into the league directly from high school. But the National Collegiate Athletic Association decided to adopt tough new academic-eligibility rules in 1983 and then seemed to toughen those rules a little more each year, meaning that more and more athletes from disadvantaged backgrounds struggled to find a place in college hoops. Many of them wound up going to junior college, shoring up their grades and games, then moving on to Division I finishing school.

Those academic circumstances had forced the hand of six-foot-eleven Kevin Garnett, who went into the NBA straight out of high school, in 1995, which in turn had influenced Bryant to make his choice.

Though early entry was allowed, there was some resistance, not just from some NBA teams and the media but from NBA commissioner David Stern himself.

Tony DiLeo, the director of scouting for the Sixers at the time, recalled Stern making it known that he didn't want "NBA scouts in high school gyms" because their mere presence could induce young players to make bad decisions about their futures. He also wanted to protect the league itself from an influx of raw young talent unprepared for the life of a pro.

In the mid-2000s, Stern and the NBA's players association would agree to ban players from coming directly into the league and to bar NBA scouts from high school and AAU games.

But in 1996, the rules hadn't changed, and Joe Bryant already had an agreement from Adidas in his pocket. He decided to swing for the fences that spring. He knew that the Philadelphia 76ers had the number one pick. So he asked his old friend Tony DiLeo to put Kobe through informal workouts to prepare him for the formal workouts that other NBA teams would ask him to perform in their evaluations.

"Joe just wanted to have somebody else work with him a little bit, maybe a different voice," DiLeo remembered, "so Kobe would know what to expect."

DiLeo had never before fulfilled such a request, but he agreed. DiLeo had already seen Bryant go against pro players the summer before at St. Joseph's, and he had seen him play in high school, so he was interested to see how he would perform.

DiLeo also called in another of the team's longtime scouts, Joe's old coach, Gene Shue, to watch. The workouts didn't involve Bryant going against other players, just running through various drills. If you absolutely had to pick a weakness in Bryant's game at the time, it would probably be shooting, DiLeo said. "His shooting was good. You knew it was going to get much better because he had the mechanics and he had the work ethic. It was just a matter of time. So that was not a concern."

All the times that DiLeo had seen Bryant, all of the young player's ability came into sharp focus in those informal workouts, the scout recalled. "The more I worked with him, the more you could see this inner drive, this incredible inner drive to be great. You could just see it, the way he worked out, the way he just listened and took everything in and applied it."

Shue and DiLeo were both well aware of Joe's abilities. They saw those genes in the son's remarkable athleticism and his polished skills.

"You put that all together with this drive, it all adds up to be special," DiLeo said. "All of these great, great players, like Michael Jordan and Magic Johnson, they all had this incredible drive to be great. He had that. There are a lot of players out there with a lot of talent, and they just don't have that mental toughness, that mental drive, but the great ones do, and that was the thing that I saw when I was working Kobe out."

Shue was even more convinced of it. Both scouts were thinking that this teenager should be the top pick, as outrageous as the idea was at the time. "We thought he would be that good," DiLeo said.

Joe Bryant was beyond elated when DiLeo informed him of that.

Still, DiLeo and Shue both knew they faced hurdles because John Lucas, the old GM of the Sixers, had been fired and replaced by Brad Greenberg, who had previously worked for the Portland Trail Blazers.

Like many other experts, Greenberg considered Allen Iverson of Georgetown to be the top option in a very talented draft. In a 2015 interview, Greenberg pointed out that he had played against Joe Bryant in college, and he realized that Kobe had the markings of an excellent player, but he felt that he wasn't developed enough to be the number one overall pick. Greenberg also confirmed that DiLeo and Shue were adamant that they thought Bryant should be the top overall pick.

"Gene and I actually talked Brad into bringing this kid in for a draft workout," DiLeo recalled. "I said, 'Here's a kid who is really talented in our backyard. We have to bring him in for a workout.'"

So Greenberg agreed to allow Bryant to join the short list of players the team looked at for the number one pick. "We were just hoping we'd get him in and he'd be so impressive that maybe we would consider him for the number one pick or that we might try to make a trade for him," DiLeo recalled.

The scouts became even more sold on Bryant after Iverson went through a workout for the team. "It's funny," DiLeo recalled, "because Allen's first workout was really a terrible workout. We had to bring him back a second time, and then the second workout was much better."

Still, the team's two scouts saw nothing from Iverson that led them to change their minds. "I loved Allen Iverson as a player," Shue said in 2015. "The guy was just an incredible player, absolutely one of the toughest players we've had in the league, but I just happened to like Kobe better."

Bryant showed up for his official workout in a coat and tie, changed into his gear, and went to work again, wowing the Sixers' scouts.

The Sixers at that time had begun administering psychological tests to players they worked out, with a variety of questions for players to answer, plus a personal-interview session with a psychologist.

"It was very in-depth," DiLeo recalled.

The test was administered to Iverson, Stephon Marbury, Bryant, and a few others the Sixers worked out. Much later, there would be rumors that Bryant somehow produced red flags on his psychological tests at the time. That was not what the Sixers' test told them about Kobe Bryant, DiLeo recalled. "He was bright, very competitive. He had a personality to be a great player, very focused, maybe obsessive. It was a good profile."

Perhaps Bryant's obsessiveness turned up some questions with other teams, DiLeo said, adding that maybe it could be seen as a negative, but obsessiveness was the engine that drove the immense focus of the game's greatest players, such as Jordan, Magic Johnson, and Jerry West.

"We gave our opinion," Shue recalled, "but the organization had already made up their mind. They were going to take Allen Iverson."

Brad Greenberg was new to the situation, DiLeo said. "He didn't know everything we knew going back, way back, with Kobe. So it was a big risk. It was a big gamble. I thought the gamble of taking him number one was a big, big gamble," DiLeo admitted. "Brad had some reservations, and I can understand, taking a high school senior with the number one pick in the draft. Allen Iverson was there, Stephon Marbury. Marcus Camby was in that draft, so you know there were a lot of good players available."

At that point, DiLeo shifted his strategy and tried to talk Greenberg into trading former University of North Carolina star Jerry Stackhouse for another high pick to get Bryant. It seemed likely that Charlotte, picking thirteenth in the draft, would jump all over Stackhouse, who had just completed his rookie season in Philadelphia.

"That was my focus," DiLeo recalled. "Jerry had value to trade. He had a very good rookie sheet. Gene and I thought that Kobe would be better than Jerry, so that's why we were pushing for him."

At the time, it appeared that Iverson would be a perfect fit with Stackhouse as the Philly backcourt of the future. Stackhouse had shown that he was a good player. Kobe Bryant still remained very much a seventeen-year-old question mark, Greenberg recalled.

As it turned out, Iverson and Stackhouse would prove not to be good together, DiLeo said, looking back. "They weren't a perfect match. They were two young guys trying to prove themselves. They both needed the ball, and it didn't work out great between them."

For 76ers fans wondering what might have been, at first glance it seemed clear that Iverson and Bryant could well have had the same problems playing together. But DiLeo didn't think that would have been the case.

Truly great players like Bryant and Iverson find a way to work together, to help each other out, he said, adding that Sixers fans had never pondered what might have been because no one knew how badly the scouting staff wanted to get Bryant on the team.

"I know this is all crazy," Shue said, the disappointment still obvious in his voice twenty years later, "but the guy that we wanted in the draft was Kobe Bryant, and we made it known. If I would have been in charge, it would have been Kobe. He was unbelievable. He was a hell of a player. You never know how these things are going to turn out."

At the time, Larry Harris was scouting for the Milwaukee Bucks, who had the number five pick in the draft, and he scouted Bryant playing for Lower Merion that spring. It was the first time he had ever seen such a skilled high school player.

"I'd seen high school players before, but nobody like Kobe," Harris remembered. "Just his grace on the floor and how easy he played. He was clearly the best player on the floor, but he just made the game so easy for everyone else around him. I mean, he really was like a magician out there, really a great size. He had the long arms. I mean, he actually looked like a young Scottie Pippen out there, just the way he moved and how he looked and how long and athletic he was, and super highly skilled. His jump shot was good, good enough that you had to respect it, and he could get to the rim both right- and left-handed anytime he wanted to."

Harris didn't see Bryant as a ball hog, as many did at the time. "He wasn't one of those ball dominators, shot dominators," the scout said. "Even though he was the best player on the team, he did pass and make others around him better. He was ahead of his time."

But then Harris saw Bryant in the McDonald's All American Game that spring and began to have some questions.

"As good as Kobe was, he went to the McDonald's All American Game, and, not that a game defines who you are, but he did not stand out," Harris recalled. "He was good, but he wasn't dominant. He looked so skinny, and you wondered what kind of impact was he going to have in the NBA."

There was a bevy of top talent coming out of college in the draft, players with experience who were much more developed physically, Harris explained.

"When you're picking in the top five, top six, of the draft—not that Kobe wasn't worthy of that—you have doubt. Certainly today, you look at his career and can see it all, but at that time, just, with all the data that you had and everything you looked at, with what Ray Allen had done and what Steph Marbury had done in college, it was hard to say, 'Hey, we're going to take Kobe ahead of these guys.'"

And so, like a dozen teams in that NBA draft, the Milwaukee

Bucks decided against Kobe. They selected Marbury and swiftly traded him for Ray Allen.

Plus, there was one other factor hurting Bryant in Philadelphia, Harris said. The long shadow of his father as a hometown disappointment was one among many such examples that made NBA teams leery of taking a local player. "There's not, like, rules in the NBA against it," Harris observed, "but one of the things in general that people have to be careful about is drafting a local kid. You'd better make sure the player is as good as you think he is. It has to be without a doubt, almost like a no-brainer."

The local scene can quickly weigh on a local player, much as it would later on Derrick Rose in Chicago, Harris explained. "All the expectations and the tickets and the family, they're all there every day that you have to deal with. I mean, it can sometimes be a huge burden for a kid if they're not able to process and handle all that at such a young age."

It might well be that Brad Greenberg saved himself and the Sixers and Kobe Bryant from the crushing expectations and frustration that had engulfed his father just twenty years earlier.

A variety of teams worked Kobe out that spring. Many observers would offer up tales of his great performances in retrospect, years later, but the truth was, all of them ultimately made the same decision as the Sixers and the Bucks.

On the eve of the draft, Joe and Pam Bryant had dinner with the New Jersey Nets, and it seemed certain that the Nets were indeed going to take their son with the eighth overall pick, and the Bryants were delighted. He would be close to home but not too close. And there would be opportunity to play.

However, the NBA draft had long shown a knack for distending time. Doubt, it seemed, traveled at lightning speed, and a few hours could prove an eternity.

The Big Play

The great Jim Murray once observed that Jerry West "could spot talent through the window of a moving train." For years, West had focused his great passion and obsession on his playing career with the Lakers. He became the team's coach for an unhappy three years in the late 1970s, then moved into the front office and launched furiously into the mission of finding the best talent available for the franchise he loved so dearly. He kept the Showtime team around Magic Johnson stocked with fresh talent as the Lakers ran through five championships in the decade, until it all came to a halt, in November 1991, with Johnson's HIV announcement and retirement. The team fell on hard times as West searched continuously to find that next great player who could fulfill his vision for the Lakers the way Johnson had.

By 1996, he was lost in the mind-wrenching task of trying to find a way to land behemoth center Shaquille O'Neal, who had grown disenchanted with playing for the Orlando Magic after the team suffered a sweep in the play-offs for the second straight season.

Since he was so focused on O'Neal, West might never have thought about watching the workout of a young kid out of Philadelphia. Bryant was an afterthought, West would later explain.

But West was close friends with agent Arn Tellem. It would be Tellem who worked miracles that spring to make Bryant a Laker, Sonny Vaccaro pointed out. Bryant's going to Los Angeles and joining the Lakers, a franchise that prided itself on winning championships, would be the key factor in his greatness, Vaccaro said, pointing out that if Bryant had gone to the Nets or another team, he would have still likely become one of the all-time best at his position. But joining the Lakers allowed Bryant to win championships, which built up his aura as one of the absolute greatest guards in the history of the game, Vaccaro said.

All of which confirmed in Vaccaro's mind that he had been right to insist on Tellem as Bryant's agent. The New York agent proposed by Team Bryant could likely have landed him in the league with the Nets, but Tellem was the guy to get him a tryout with Jerry West. Bryant himself hadn't even considered the Lakers because they were picking twenty-fourth in the first round.

As it happened, Tellem's and West's families had vacationed together. It was only out of friendship with Tellem that West agreed to have Kobe Bryant conduct workouts for the Lakers.

He performed stupendously for West that day, going against former Lakers Michael Cooper and Larry Drew. The teen "marched over people," West would later confide.

A short time later, Bryant was set to return to Los Angeles to shoot an Adidas commercial. "I think you may be working out for the Lakers again," Joe told him one morning.

The tone of the second Lakers workout told Kobe that the team was quite serious about him. Before the workout, Bryant got his first opportunity to talk at length with Jerry West, who shared a few thoughts about competing in the NBA. It was the beginning of the mentoring relationship the team executive would share with the "kid," as fans in L.A. soon came to call him. "He knew so much about the game," Bryant said.

Also, this time he was working out before coach Del Harris, who hadn't seen the first workout, an indication of just how few expectations the team had heading into that first evaluation. The second workout was at a YMCA on an L.A. side street, and Bryant was mystified by the location of the out-of-the-way gym and the secretive nature of whole event. Bryant faced the highly regarded Dontae' Jones of Mississippi State, who had been the MVP of the NCAA tournament's Southeastern Regional that spring. First, the two players did shooting drills. Then Bryant played one-on-one against the hard-nosed college senior and beat him soundly, dunking on him.

The moment settled, in Bryant's mind, the issue of how he would have done in college. Bryant had been eager to attend the NBA's pre-draft camps in order to battle college players, but his agent and his father wouldn't allow it. Instead, he did individual workouts for teams from Phoenix (where he played a spirited game of one-on-one against big man Todd Fuller), New York, New Jersey (which he visited three different times and where he put on an impressive shooting display and formed a bond with coach John Calipari, who did every drill with him), and Boston.

According to Vaccaro, the Lakers stopped the second workout after just twenty minutes. West got up from his seat under one of the baskets and hurried to midcourt, where he grabbed Sonny Vaccaro by the arm and told him to shut it down.

"That's it," West whispered to Vaccaro. "I'm going to take him."

"It was one of the biggest moments of my life," Vaccaro said in 2015. "Here was Jerry West telling me that I had been right about this kid."

A few minutes later, West told Bryant the same: the franchise was going to do everything within its power to draft him.

Much later, word would leak out from the Lakers organization that West considered Bryant's workout to be the best he had ever seen. That's what he told legendary Lakers broadcaster Chick Hearn, who enjoyed telling the tale for years afterward. West had long held to the belief that as a scout, you could see what a player could do on the floor, but it was much harder, almost impossible, to read a player's heart, which was where real greatness lay. But Bryant's workout had been so impressive that for Jerry West, it had revealed his heart, just as it had earlier for Tony DiLeo. It was there in the skill set alone, in some ways, just the amount of work that a player would have to have done to possess such immaculate moves, the footwork and fakes and execution, the hours that must have been put into that kind of perfection.

When Bryant got back to his hotel room, he phoned Tellem, who asked nervously how it went. Bryant told him it went well.

"I love you, man," blurted an elated Tellem (on whom the HBO series *Arli$$* was partially based). The teen admonished his representative to "chill," but the moment had to have been exhilarating for them both.

Yet, even with West's glowing infatuation with Bryant, it was far from a done deal. First the Lakers would have to work out an agreement to trade up in the draft, high enough to select Bryant. Their research determined that the only team set to take him early was the Nets, with Calipari and executives John Nash and Willis Reed clearly impressed. The Nets had the eighth pick. After that, the next few teams were locked in on a different target, which meant that the Lakers could get him at the thirteenth overall pick by working out a deal with the Charlotte Hornets.

In order to keep the Nets from picking him, Tellem had to convince New Jersey that Bryant so disdained the Nets that he would refuse to play for them, that he would go instead to an Italian team and play if he had to. Jerry West also had to create the impression among the many eyes and ears around the league, including the Nets themselves, that he had absolutely no interest whatsoever in Kobe Bryant.

The Nets needed players, not a disgruntled teen on their hands. In his workouts for them, Nash and Calipari saw that Bryant was exceptional, but Tellem managed to convince the New Jersey team's ownership that the threat that Bryant would play overseas was serious. Bryant just loved Italy, Tellem said, and would rather play there than with a relatively poor NBA team. Tellem had created just enough doubt with ownership.

By the time it was their turn to pick, the Nets reluctantly backed off on draft day and selected Villanova guard Kerry Kittles instead.

The night of the draft, Vaccaro sat nervously with Bryant in the green room—the area where potential draftees waited—along with his parents, his two sisters, his uncle Chubby and cousin John, and Tellem. Shortly before the event started, Gary Charles informed Joe of the impending deal.

"Joe," Charles asked him. "Is Kobe OK? He's going to L.A."

"What?" he said.

"Yeah," Charles said. "We're working a deal. Just try to keep your mouth shut. Kobe's going to be OK."

"Shit," Joe said excitedly. "Hell, yeah, we'll be OK with that."

Joe and Arn Tellem then delivered the news to Bryant in the green room. Though Kobe was nervous about the moment, Lorenzen Wright, who would go to the Clippers, was seated next to Bryant's group, and the two players joked nervously and followed the proceedings with their own mock draft lists.

Once the Nets took Kittles, Bryant knew he was going to the Lakers.

Georgetown's Allen Iverson, Georgia Tech's Stephon Marbury, University of Massachusetts center Marcus Camby, University of California freshman Shareef Abdur-Rahim, and University of Connecticut guard Ray Allen all went ahead of him. He was finally selected with the thirteenth pick, by the Charlotte Hornets.

The Hornets had been one of the few teams that Bryant hadn't worked out for in the weeks before the selection. And less than an hour after his selection, trade rumors circulated throughout the media assembled at the draft.

Hornets GM Bob Bass confirmed that the team had reached an agreement with the Lakers before the draft to select an unknown player of the Lakers' choosing, with the intention of trading his rights for veteran center Vlade Divac. The Lakers had informed the Hornets that their pick would be Bryant just five minutes before the selection was due.

"We don't take high school kids," Hornets coach Dave Cowens would later tell reporters. "We never wanted him for ourselves. We don't think he can help us right away."

Regardless of Cowens's statement, word soon started circulating that Arn Tellem had forced the trade because Bryant wanted to be in a bigger market with more media opportunities.

Again the media were swift to attack and relay public anger over the apparently outrageous actions. That didn't stop sports radio in Philadelphia from questioning how a seventeen-year-old could dictate where he went in the draft.

"Apparently Cowens had not received a copy of the Kobe Bryant marketing plan," *The Sporting News* blasted. "That is the state of David Stern's NBA these days. The brats are running the day-care center. It isn't about basketball anymore. It's all about image."

Meanwhile, the Bryant family gathered to go out and celebrate the turn of events, all except for sister Sharia, who wasn't in the mood. Instead, as she later told Anthony Gilbert, she went back to her room and had a good cry.

South Street

The trade between Charlotte and the Lakers was delayed by Vlade Divac, who loved playing in Los Angeles. He threatened to retire rather than move, then changed his mind and agreed to the deal. Even then, the trade couldn't be finalized until July 10, due to a league moratorium on all deals until a new collective bargaining agreement for the players' union could be ratified. Once those things happened, Kobe Bryant became a Laker. Since the draftee was still seventeen, his parents had to cosign his contract with the team until August 23, when he turned eighteen.

Over the July Fourth weekend, while he was in limbo, Bryant ran into Donnie Carr on South Street in Philly. The old competitors had a long talk. Carr had gained a real appreciation for Bryant and had instantly regretted that his comment "If he's a pro, then I'm a pro," was overheard by a reporter. He would be kidded about it for the rest of his life. Always friendly with Carr, Bryant was animated that July day and launched into the amazing developments in his life. To Carr's astonishment, Bryant talked "about how Jerry West and those guys thought that he would be a starter for the Lakers in a year, how they were thinking about moving Nick Van Exel and Eddie Jones to make room for him."

The moment seemed almost surreal.

"He knew that then," Carr recalled. "He knew that. He told me that in the conversation on South Street right after he got drafted, that all the Lakers management was very high on him."

It was hard to fathom what was more astounding—the news itself, or that Bryant was throwing it right out there on the street in Philadelphia, where Lakers favorite Eddie Jones had played at Temple and where he spent time each off-season.

"He said that basically it was about to be him and Shaq's team," Carr said. "They wanted him and Shaq to be the one-two punch, and they were going to make room for him. I was shocked."

"For real?" Carr remembered asking Bryant.

"Yeah," Bryant replied.

"They about to open it up for me, man," Bryant said. "I'm gonna have to work it, man. They said the management is high for me, they going to create room for me, man."

This wasn't some college team he was talking about. This was the Lakers. "It was unbelievable," Carr said. "But everything he said eventually came to fruition. Every single thing he said came to fruition. He was confident how he was going to be an NBA star. He was telling me that he plugged in the work and he was looking forward to becoming a Lakers star soon."

At first, as they talked, Carr was buying everything that Bryant told him. The two of them enjoyed a bond as competitors. But as they continued to talk, a thought occurred to Carr.

"I remember, I just thought to myself, 'He's a little off his rocker. I don't know about this one.' Nick Van Exel was one of the better players in the NBA, Kobe was just fresh out of high school, Eddie Jones was a two-time All-Star. I'm like, 'What is he talking about?'"

Carr was struck by how Bryant's confidence was soaring that day, beyond anything he had ever seen from his friend. And he had seen a lot. The two players stood in contrast as perfect examples of the rapidly changing business of pro basketball.

"I was one of the top thirty players in the country," Carr recalled. He had been recruited by dozens of major schools, across the ACC, Big East, and other major conferences.

There had been ample public criticism of Joe Bryant as an assistant for La Salle, but he beat off major opposition to recruit Carr for coach Speedy Morris and the Explorers.

"He was always talkative, always friendly," Carr said of Joe. "He recruited me heavily to come to La Salle, and actually there was talk that me and Kobe might wind up being together. I was sold on going to La Salle because of the opportunity. I passed up a lot of prestigious schools."

As a mere freshman, Carr bolted out strong for the Explorers, putting in 30 points a game and leading the nation in scoring, becoming such a threat that he began drawing double teams in nearly every game he played. He finished the season averaging 23.9 points, sixth in all of Division I, and immediately confronted a moment of truth.

He could take his shot and risk turning pro right then when his stock was the highest. It was a gamble, but pro basketball teams in 1997 had leaped into an infatuation with youth, much like investors in futures markets. Teams were looking at the bargains, extra seasons, and potentially higher returns that youth offered.

Carr decided to do the traditional thing, to stay in school, where he scored and scored and scored to stack up more than 2,000 points to rank at the very top of La Salle's impressive roster of all-time scorers, which included Tom Gola and Lionel Simmons. But by the time four years had passed, NBA teams had begun to look at college seniors almost like items in a grocery store that were past their expiration date. Teenagers were drawing millions, while players in their twenties faced a rough go getting the attention of pro basketball. Carr wound up playing in Turkey, a strong league where he continued his pace as a top scorer. The basketball was excellent, the fans wildly enthusiastic, and Carr had two great years until he suffered a devastating knee injury. His playing career over, he would spend the ensuing seasons watching Bryant from afar, still running into his old friend from time to time.

"If I had known then what I know now, I would have gone," Carr said of that decision not to turn pro after his freshman season. "But I was foolish. I wound up coming back. I had an OK sophomore year. I pretty much had a really good career, but we were always one or two players away, so I didn't think I got my just due because we didn't win enough."

Carr would also look back on Jellybean's role in Kobe turning pro. "He gave his son the most valuable jewels," Carr said.

Summertime News

Shaquille O'Neal sent a jolt of joy through Southern California that summer when he agreed to a deal with the Lakers worth better than $120 million.

In many ways, the signing of O'Neal had been the end result of one continuous search since Magic Johnson's HIV announcement, five years earlier. For five long seasons, the circumstances had dragged on, with West torturing himself, looking for answers. Meanwhile, the Lakers had plodded through one unproductive campaign after another. Always a bundle of nervous energy during games, West grew into a picture of anxiety, often retreating to the Forum parking lot during games while the outcome was being settled. Otherwise he could be seen standing near section 26, peeking past the ushers at the action, his body twisted with tension.

Some observers were stunned that O'Neal would think of leaving Orlando and the opportunity to play with gifted young guard Anfernee "Penny" Hardaway. ESPN declared that there was no way O'Neal would be foolish enough to go because playing in Orlando presented him with the best opportunity to win championships.

Other observers, though, began to question the Magic's chemistry. There were whispers that Hardaway's immensely successful "Li'l Penny" marketing campaign had created a persona so large that it crimped even O'Neal's style. An even bigger factor was that Hardaway made the All-NBA First Team, while the presence of Hakeem Olajuwon and David Robinson blocked O'Neal's path to the honor.

Another factor was the team's losses in the 1995 and 1996 play-offs. In 1995, the Magic fell, 4–0, to Houston in the NBA Finals. In 1996, it was the Bulls who took them, 4–0, in the Eastern Conference championship series. The fun-loving O'Neal had wept after both of those series, the only times in his life he had cried over basketball other than after a loss in the state-championship game his junior year in high school, which had abruptly wiped out an unbeaten season. In Orlando, it was O'Neal, not Hardaway, the coaches, or his teammates, who bore the pressure for those losses.

O'Neal knew that the Lakers were a team with a history of taking special care of players. West, in particular, had been a superstar himself. He knew the pressures, the misunderstandings, the problems, that players of stature faced. It could be argued that no NBA executive went to the effort that West did to protect and nurture young stars.

Then there was the Lakers tradition. Their Hollywood affiliations, the aura in the Forum, were real attractions to O'Neal. Working in Los Angeles would mean he could take advantage of the Hollywood connections with his off-court interests, his rap music production and acting.

West and his staff saw that they had a shot at signing O'Neal but that it could cost them as much as $100 million, a figure large enough to frighten off most suitors. The situation left West struggling to find room under the salary cap to sign the big center. "If you have to give up your entire team for a cornerstone player such as Shaquille you'd consider it," he said at the time.

West figured he would have to come up with a $95-million offer to get his prize. But ultimately, that would prove to be many millions short of what was needed. To create more room under the salary cap over seven seasons, West practically gave away guard

Anthony Peeler and reserve forward George Lynch, sending them to Vancouver.

"The Lakers could have folded," said O'Neal's agent, Leonard Armato, himself a shoe representative, like Vaccaro, who had maneuvered his way into representing the center right out of Louisiana State University. "They may have been on the verge of it a few times. But Jerry West wouldn't do that. He was Mr. Clutch as a player and again in these dealings."

The Orlando counteroffer jumped to $115 million, then a little more. To push their offer to $123 million, the Lakers renounced seven players, including Magic Johnson and Sedale Threatt. Dumping their roster of players seemed to border on lunacy. If O'Neal stayed in Florida, the Lakers would have gutted their team for nothing.

The Magic could have paid more to sign their own free agent, but it became apparent that, as O'Neal claimed, money wasn't the key factor. The Orlando deal was front-loaded with as much as $20 million in cash the first year, but O'Neal looked west.

"They're a basketball organization," he would later say of the Lakers. "When I made my decision to move, it wasn't on money, it wasn't on movies, it wasn't on rap. I just wanted to feel appreciated, that's all. That's what it really comes down to. Not money. Who cares about money? Man, I mean, I got money."

By signing the twenty-four-year-old center, the Lakers had managed to snare the game's most physically dominating presence, something that had become a tradition with the team over the years, with signings of great centers from George Mikan to Wilt Chamberlain to Kareem Abdul-Jabbar, all of them the centerpieces of the franchise's dozen championships by 1996.

"To get this prize," West said at the time, "I think is something that when I look back on history and the time that I've spent with this team, this might be the single most important thing we've ever done."

In the midst of such wheeling and dealing, the drafting of Kobe Bryant seemed almost a carefully crafted afterthought.

Once his own contract was official, Bryant turned his focus to playing for the Lakers' developmental team in the Fila Summer

Pro League, one of several leagues that NBA teams used for summer work. "Nobody knew what to expect when he came in," recalled Larry Drew, the Lakers assistant who ran the team. "Everybody knew he was a talent."

Many observers suspected that Shaquille O'Neal's high-profile arrival in Los Angeles would help to obscure Bryant's introduction and take some of the public pressure off the young rookie. But hopes of that evaporated with his first appearance at the Pyramid, the five-thousand-seat arena in Long Beach where the summer league held games. Usually there were plenty of empty seats, but Bryant's first night brought an overflow crowd, and two thousand fans were turned away.

"I remember the first day he arrived," Drew recalled. "All the media and all the people that were there, chanting his name. It was a packed house. The first day he came, he didn't even get to dress to play, but there was a lot of electricity in the air about him being there."

Journalist Ric Bucher remembered catching sight of Bryant for the first time in the locker room during summer league. "He was a high school kid," Bucher recalled, "literally throwing his gym shorts and his shoes into a backpack, being interviewed by the media, and then, you know, walking out like, much like a guy who had just come out of high school."

Usually the Lakers used the league games to help prepare their rookies and young players for adjustment to the team, Drew said. "But there wasn't a lot done early the first few days he was there. We didn't get a chance to practice. In summer league, we normally get five or six days to practice and to get the players used to what we want to do. He came in right as the games were being played, so he was just kind of out there, kind of playing on instinct. He was like a little puppy let out of a cage. He was bouncing all over the place. Everybody could see that he was gonna be a special talent. You could see the swagger about his walk. He was a confident kid who didn't shy away, who had no fears about going against pro players."

Bryant showed that he had no qualms about stepping in and taking charge, even to the point of directing teammates on what to do, where to go on the floor. His rookie teammates were four and five years older than he, but if that gave him pause, he didn't show it.

"I just want to get out there and win," he told the *L.A. Times*. "If the coach needs me to be a leader, that's what I'll be. And no matter what, if I see something wrong, I'm going to give my input, just like Shaq would give his input. But it's important for me to stay within the concept of the team."

Most important, the star quality that West and Lakers owner Jerry Buss were desperate to see made itself known immediately. He scored 25 points in his first game, 36 in another, and averaged 24.5 points and about 5 rebounds over the four-game schedule.

Out on the West Coast with his AAU team, Gary Charles took Lamar Odom to see Bryant play toward the end of summer league. Bryant saw them standing at the upper level of the arena and waved them down.

"How are you doing?" Charles asked.

"Man," Bryant replied. "I'm killing them out here. You should see me. I am doing them up out here."

Charles started laughing and looked at him, dressed proudly in his Lakers gear.

"I'm like, 'Kobe, you're never gonna change,'" Charles remembered in 2015. "He was just happy to be a Laker."

Like West and Buss, Bryant, too, was looking for proof that he could star, and the summer league games provided him all the evidence he wanted. "I felt that I could always do what I did in high school, that it wasn't that hard," he explained later.

Gregg Downer hadn't really been consulted about Bryant's big move to the pro game. The coach had his concerns, not about Bryant's play, but about his adjustment as a teen in the busy city. He had heard that summer Bryant's talk in Philadelphia, "This is going to be my team"—that "alpha-type comment," as the coach described it. "I'm thinking to myself," Downer recalled, "like, he will not back down from Shaquille, like, he'll punch Shaquille in the face."

PART IV

CALIFORNIA STARS

Chapter 18

PACIFIC PALISADES

There were a number of story lines about the Lakers heading into Kobe Bryant's rookie year in the NBA. Rudy Garciduenas didn't see all of them, but he saw a lot. He had been the team's do-everything equipment manager for a dozen years and a volunteer even before that, so his roots with the franchise ran deep into the Showtime era, when Magic Johnson transformed the Lakers into a team that resembled an exotic sports car, speeding from end to end, making brilliant finishes routinely and stirring L.A.'s dormant basketball community into a nightly pep rally. Johnson's smile sent energy and enthusiasm coursing through L.A.'s car culture as nothing else ever had before.

With slick-haired Pat Riley always finding new ways to jack up the intensity, Magic, Kareem, Coop, Worthy, and all the other ballers made hearts jump everywhere they played. Those Lakers showed basketball what it was meant to be, with sharing, giving, loving, and smiles all around.

"It was a family," Garciduenas said wistfully of the Showtime era. "The players were just different then. Magic was the kind of player that didn't let his teammates get out of focus. It was all about the ultimate prize, and there were no exceptions. You either won the NBA championship or you did not. There was no second place back then."

When it all suddenly stopped, the loss of Showtime left a

tremendous longing among the millions of fans it had created. The good news was that West and owner Jerry Buss felt the same way as the fans, needing more. They all wanted that feeling of sleek dominance back in their lives in the worst sort of way.

Garciduenas's calm demeanor belied his own craving for the juice. He described himself as one of the "worker bees" in the Lakers organization, but he may have been the biggest junkie of them all. Nobody did anything for the Lakers like Rudy G, not even close. He had been there, home and away, on a daily basis with the biggest names in basketball, had seen them in their greatness and their smallness. He'd washed the jocks and socks and shorts and towels, made the myriad travel arrangements, rented all the gyms for road practices, and generally served as one of few sane anchors for Jerry Buss's Good Ship Lollipop. In many ways, Garciduenas and longtime team trainer Gary Vitti ran the entire day-to-day show right from the deck. How deep did it go? Later, when Phil Jackson wanted sage to burn in the locker room to drive away troublesome spirits, it was Rudy G. who went out and acquired the sage.

That fall of 1996, Rudy G. was just as he had always been: short, heavyset, goateed, poker-faced, judicious, and dedicated. He was the kind of low-key guy that the franchise depended on to whisk the team through its usual minimum of one hundred games, three hundred practices, and God knows how many flights—not to mention hours spent sitting in L.A. traffic—over the course of its eight-month seasons. He packed, unpacked, passed out, picked up, laundered, repacked, stacked, put away, hauled off, brought back, unloaded, and reloaded every single thing the Lakers did each day. Then he got up early the next morning and did it all over again. He knew the chintzy Lakers paid him substantially less than other teams paid their equipment guys, but he figured the team made up for it by giving him the opportunity to share in all its championships and big moments with the ever-changing cast of larger-than-life characters.

So it was understandable that Garciduenas, like all of Los Angeles, was curious to see what these two young stars and the host of new faces were going to bring to the court that fall.

Shaquille O'Neal didn't disappoint. His pockets stuffed with much of the $123 million the team owed him, O'Neal took one look at the beat-up vehicle Garciduenas used to pack up all that gear for team trips and went out and purchased him a brand-new ride. Twenty years later, Garciduenas still hadn't picked his jaw up off the floor. In his three decades around millionaires, no one had ever done such a thing for him, or would ever do such a thing for him again.

Bryant was an intense introvert, but he brought his own sort of charm to the table. He could speak Spanish and took to hanging out in Garciduenas's office to use the computer there. Surfing the Internet was a relatively new thing, and Bryant fell in love with it quickly. With all his extra individual workouts, he spent so much time around the Lakers offices that he needed a little space to hang out.

The equipment man figured out a lot about the two just by looking at their lockers. Bryant's was orderly, as he maintained close watch over his gear, making sure he had enough clean clothes for the many workouts he conducted each day. As for O'Neal's, you just never knew what you'd find in there, so Garciduenas took to giving him an extra hand in keeping it straight as the chaos necessitated.

The one thing that Bryant and O'Neal seemed to have in common, along with just about everybody else in the organization, was a penchant for impatience. Everybody wanted everything right now.

Garciduenas noticed how much pressure the rookie put on all the other, older Lakers with his intensity, his running and dunking in practice, his constant studying of videotape, his demeanor. The public didn't see it, nor did the media, but Bryant was a lone wolf and posed a threat to his older teammates. They eyed him, trying to figure him out. Bryant, meanwhile, kept to himself and gave them little to go on other than his game itself, which was overwhelming, with his energy and need to dominate.

Garciduenas was familiar with the personality type. Jerry West had infused the entire franchise for years with his intensity. There was no shortage of people shaking their heads and calling West crazy, and that included West himself.

He demanded perfection of himself and the team. Even the great Showtime clubs had distressed him, Garciduenas remembered.

The Lakers might be winning by 20 points, a comfortable enough lead for Garciduenas to slip down to the locker room to do some laundry in the fourth quarter. Soon enough West would join him, absolutely anguished over why they hadn't played better, damn the score.

The new teenager's attitude was a good match for that. "Kobe expected a lot of himself," Garciduenas recalled. "I mean, he challenged himself and everybody that was around him. He exhibited an enormous amount of just rare talent."

That talent, and the athletic way he practiced and sought to get to the rim on seemingly every play, posed an immensely welcome sight to the team's staff and management, but his youth generated a fair amount of disdain as well, Garciduenas explained.

"It was great to see somebody who had that incredible amount of talent, but, I mean, there's got to be a temperament that comes along with it. There's got to be a knowing how to use it and when to use it."

About that, Kobe Bryant had not a clue, and was in fact hindered by a blind spot the size of the sun. Bryant himself would eventually look back on the period and call himself an idiot.

That would be the teenager's burden for a long time.

King of the Hill

As jacked as they were over the talent, West and his staff engaged in a bit of fretting over the brand new concept: Just how would the organization deal with having an eighteen-year-old in the fold? With a new rookie-salary structure in place, he had signed a standard three-year, $3.5-million contract with the team. Having seen what the Hollywood life had done to a young Magic Johnson, the Lakers tried to think of ways to soften his adjustment.

Shortly after Kobe joined the Lakers, Joe and Pam Bryant packed up with younger daughter Shaya, who withdrew from La Salle, and moved to Los Angeles, where Kobe purchased a six-bedroom home in Pacific Palisades, high above the rest of the world around him.

Sonny Vaccaro also moved back across the country to assist

Adidas's bright, young star, even as the shoe man pursued the next major talent for the company. He saw significance in the fact that Bryant wanted the big, expensive house at the very top of the hill. Vaccaro had picked for Adidas a young man who wanted to reign over it all.

The shoe man and his wife, Pam, could look up and see it from the condo they moved into in the seaside community. The Bryant home also wasn't far down the street from that of Lakers coach Del Harris, a cozy arrangement indeed.

Sharia, Bryant's older sister, remained at Temple, where she was rapidly nearing the completion of her undergraduate degree in international business administration, the field of study that Bryant said he, too, would like to pursue someday.

Sometime later, Sharia would get her first view of her brother playing on television. "He's got more money and lives in California," she would tell *USA Today*. "But he's just Kobe to me."

Exactly who Kobe was remained open to debate in the Lakers locker room, but it was entirely clear at his home high on the hill. Bryant soon went on *The Tonight Show with Jay Leno* and quipped that he had put his parents on allowance.

Though Kobe was lord of the manor, it took Pam a while to get it. Joe would tell the story of Kobe coming home and trying to tell his mother of the big things he had done on the basketball court that day, only to hear her say, "That's good, honey. Now go take out the trash."

Pam set up the house as an Italian villa filled with art and expensive decor. It looked fantastic, representative of the life she had found in Europe, explained a friend. "All the time they talked about Italy and how she really grew to love cooking and making everything fresh. She made all these dishes. I mean, she cooked whatever he wanted. Everything was homemade, everything. I mean, she spent hours and hours. She adored him. They very much pampered him. It was very clear that Kobe could do what he wanted, and Pam allowed that to be. They were there to provide the support he needed in this adjustment to life in pro basketball."

Bryant had his own little world upstairs in the villa, with stunning views of both the city and the ocean, the friend said. "It was a very large room for Kobe upstairs, and it was its own sort of apartment. He had leather couches and big-screen TVs. Really, he didn't have to leave or do anything. He could have just stayed there."

There, in his retreat filled with stereo equipment, video-game gear, a computer, and video monitors, he could study basketball to his heart's content or even write poetry. If he tired of his virtual nightlife, he could get up and gaze out on the silvery Pacific or cast his thoughts to the sparkling lights of L.A. Even so, the entire situation seemed primed to offer a lesson in the fact that there was no hiding youth.

Step Back

Gary Charles had returned to L.A. in August and wound up hanging out with Bryant and a couple of veteran NBA players near the basketball courts at Venice Beach. Someone approached them about joining the pickup games there, and Bryant was set to jump in when one of the veterans told him he was crazy to do that. Bryant held off that day, but the idea had been planted.

A few weeks later, Charles heard the news. Bryant had been injured in early September while playing an outdoor pickup game at Venice Beach. "The first thing I heard about Kobe was that he had injured his wrist playing at Venice," recalled Derek Fisher, the Lakers' other first-round pick in 1996. "I just couldn't believe that a guy would be playing up at Venice Beach. That was my first experience with how excited and enthusiastic he was about just playing the game. He truly had a passion for playing. Regardless of where it was, what time of day, he was gonna play."

"I went up to tip-dunk the basketball," Bryant said. "The ball was bouncing on the rim and dropped in. I made the mistake of not holding on to the rim, grabbing the rim and coming down slowly. I just tried to back off in the air."

He tumbled to the pavement and banged his wrist. Immediately, three knots appeared, and he knew it was broken. The injury didn't require surgery, but it meant that he wouldn't be ready for the opening of training camp in October. For a rookie to miss training camp was a huge blow, especially as the Lakers adjusted to their new center. "This will set him back," Lakers executive Mitch Kupchak told reporters. "He's an eighteen-year-old player, and the first training camp is very important."

West didn't seem worried, though. "This guy will play in a Little League tournament," he said. "It doesn't bother me. He loves to play basketball. He's one of the more dedicated players I've ever seen."

Complicating the situation heading into the season was the fact that Bryant had no particular position but was viewed as a combination of a point guard, an off guard, and a small forward and would play at all three positions during parts of the next few seasons. His size and quickness were the core of a tremendous versatility, but missing training camp meant it would take him longer to find his place in the Lakers' rotation.

With all the new faces on the team, the camp brought an adjustment for rookies and veterans alike. "Everybody had to learn to play with Shaq, to face the basket and when to cut," recalled Travis Knight, another rookie that fall.

"That first day of training camp, Kobe was injured and everything," Fisher recalled, "but he still wanted to be out there, trying to do two-line layups and do everything that he possibly could to still be involved with practice and be a part of the group."

Establishing himself as part of the team was clearly important to Bryant, yet he maintained his distance from teammates off the court, answering questions about anything not related to basketball with one- or two-word replies. He seldom initiated any personal conversations at all, Fisher recalled.

The challenge of dealing with older, more accomplished players clearly pushed him far deeper within himself than he had ever been pushed at Lower Merion. The situation would factor heavily into the team's chemistry for the next three seasons and would vex players, coaches, and staff members alike.

"Kobe had a lot to learn about interacting with other people," Garciduenas observed. "He really hadn't been a student of human nature as much as he had been a student of basketball. So, you know, he didn't always do the right thing as far as his teammates.

He had that young and stubborn swagger about him. He was going to do what he thought was best, what he thought he should do, regardless of anybody else."

The rookie really didn't have a lot of people skills, but he did show a remarkable manner with the media. Some reporters would number among his strongest connections, and, like Jerry West, he wasn't as shy as most players about opening up to journalists. Scoop Jackson, then of *Slam* magazine, would be one of several who connected.

The two first met at a photo shoot for the hip-hop hoops magazine in Orlando, right before rookie orientation. "We had Kobe, Marcus Camby, Antoine Walker, Ray Allen. We put them all on the cover of the magazine. You look at it, Kobe's on the front of that cover, and his hand is tucked behind his back so he can't show the cast on his arm."

They were all billed as the next wave of young players coming into the league following Jordan.

"He was the youngest member of that group, and he wasn't necessarily the star," Jackson remembered. "Allen was a star. He had already been on our cover."

In private conversations, people had their doubts about Bryant, Jackson recalled. "What I remember is how comfortable he felt around all these cats that were supposed to be better than him. He wasn't arrogant. He was just comfortable, man. He was the one that was in a joking mood, he was the one that was playing around with the basketball, very, very loose, extremely loose. He was aware of his situation, he was extremely comfortable to be a kid. Not shy, not removed, he kept a basketball in his hand the whole time we were there."

It would be only later that Jackson would gain a fuller picture from Bryant's teammates. "They just started talking about what a different guy he was, just from a language standpoint, where he'd been and where he'd come from," Jackson said. "You're looking at a high school kid that's stuck in L.A. among superstars. Shaq is the center of that universe. You start hearing about Kobe, 'This cat talks seven languages. He didn't live through the same shit we did. He knows what to order when we go to a Chinese restaurant—like, he really knows.' Just a high level of intelligence that he had because of his world that they didn't necessarily have because of where they came from. They weren't dogging him or anything, it's just like, 'This cat is different.'"

Nonetheless, Bryant's teammates had plenty of hard-won experience that gave them advantages over him. He clearly recognized that. The Lakers brought longtime veteran Byron Scott back to the team to be a mentor. Scott took to Bryant because the rookie was different from so many young players passing through the league. Bryant was familiar with basketball history and wanted to soak up everything he could about Scott's days with Johnson and the Showtime Lakers. He also pushed for information and advice on training and pacing himself to be successful in the game.

Scott saw that many young players coming into the league had acquired such a veneer of cool that they would never have risked appearing so childlike by asking such questions. Bryant, however, never checked his curiosity.

Another high point was his friendship with Eddie Jones, then almost twenty-five, who was heading into his third season with the Lakers. He'd had a good start to his career, Garciduenas observed, but management was still trying to figure out if Jones's style fit the team.

Plus, Jones soon enough developed his own differences with O'Neal, who was sizing up his new teammates.

Bryant himself was no exception, and he soon accepted an invitation from the twenty-four-year-old O'Neal to go out to dinner. "It was good," Bryant said of his first sit-down with his teammate. "It was cool."

"There's clearly a looking-after-him attitude on this team," Kurt Rambis, a Lakers assistant that season, explained. "Not because he's a little baby and can't look out for himself, but because everybody has a real feel for what he's going through. We've all lived away from home for the first time. He's in this setting where almost every other person is a couple of years significantly older than him."

However, one longtime Lakers staff member relayed a harsher view of the rookie: "We weren't sure if Kobe was just quiet, or if he literally thought he was better than everybody else, if he thought he was this supreme athlete and everybody else was playing their roles just to make him better."

Given no evidence to the contrary, his teammates began to suspect that he was far more interested in his own personal accomplishments than he was in team goals, Derek Fisher said. "That's why people really misinterpreted him a lot of times as a guy who really thinks only of himself."

If training camp brought the initial difficulties of Bryant's pro career, it also brought the first comic relief, at least for his teammates. Veteran hazing of rookies had long been a staple of each new season, starting with the opening banquet of training camp. As called for by tradition, West would begin the proceedings after the meal with sparse comments about the road ahead. He reminded the players about league policies concerning gambling and fighting and how they should conduct themselves as Lakers. There was almost no talk of Lakers tradition. The players didn't need that. They could see that every time they walked in the Forum and looked up at all the championship banners hanging above.

Most of the rookie festivities in 1996's opening team dinner were saved for Bryant, whom the veterans made stand and sing one of Brandy's soulful ballads. "They didn't make everyone sing a song," Travis Knight recalled. "They made Kobe sing because of the Brandy thing. He did a good job, put a little effort into it. He knew most of the words. It was funny."

"They thought it was funny," he would confide later. "I didn't find it too funny. They made me sing 'I Wanna Be Down.' I knew most of the words 'cause I hear it all the time. The guys gave me a hard time about that."

Years before, West had long suffered in silence the fun that teammate Elgin Baylor often had at his expense, the nicknames mocking his hillbilly heritage and twang from West Virginia. That had long been the NBA way.

Slowly, Bryant managed to participate in training camp to some degree.

"He didn't play for a lot of training camp," Travis Knight recalled. "But he was running, doing a lot of sprinting drills, things like that. You could tell he was in good shape. He wasn't at all intimidated by the situation."

Bryant played his first NBA minutes on October 16, in a preseason game in Fresno, and put up 10 points and 5 rebounds. Two nights later, the Lakers played their first game of the preseason in the Forum against Bryant's hometown 76ers. Late in the game, he tried to force a dunk and collided with Philly reserve center Tim Kempton. The impact sent Bryant plummeting to the floor and left him with a badly strained hip flexor and yet more downtime.

In the aftermath, Eddie Jones advised him to stop trying to dunk so much.

After he healed Bryant worked on revising his dunking technique. From then on, he would seek to initiate contact with a defender to brace himself and protect against free falls and other crashes. Often the officials would give him the foul call, an added benefit. Sometimes, though, they would whistle him for the offensive foul for initiating the contact, annoying but still far better than more injuries.

With the hip flexor injury, he got no playing time in the regular-season home opener, a Lakers win over Phoenix. The next game, against Minnesota, he played briefly, had a shot blocked, and racked up a turnover. "I'm sure he would have liked to make a more auspicious debut," coach Del Harris told reporters. "It's OK. We already know he can play."

Sunset

Bryant had brought former St. Joe's trainer Joe Carbone with him to L.A. to conduct his daily workouts with him, away from the team. Although Vaccaro had thrown cold water on Team Bryant, the concept still fell into place as Bryant's personal entertainment company that eventually employed his sisters, an aunt, and his brother-in-law, among others. Another side deal was a book project with Jeremy Treatman, tentatively titled *My Freshman Year in the NBA*.

To write the book, Treatman made the trip to Los Angeles for that first game. The next night he headed out with Carbone to cruise Sunset Strip.

"A BMW pulled up next to us," Treatman recalled. "I hear, 'Joe! Treat!' And I'm like, 'I don't know anybody in L.A.!?!' I look up. It's Kobe! We looked over. And, even though I've known the kid since he was twelve, I was stargazing. I'm like, 'Holy shit! It's Kobe Bryant!' And he said, 'I've got to go. I'm meeting Tyra.' I'm like, 'Holy shit! Tyra Banks!'"

Though he was hanging out with Brandy, who lived just twenty minutes away from him, and now Banks, Bryant's personal life didn't gain much momentum. His early years in L.A., his mother would plan and host his birthday parties for him, an indication of the personal cocoon he inhabited, the growing frustration and loneliness he felt even away from the team. But the larger problem was that his basketball life hadn't immediately lived up to his immense expectations.

His first score didn't come until he hit a free throw in the third game, against the Knicks in Madison Square Garden. Reporter J. A. Adande came up from Washington to watch the contest and was surprised to see a pregame press conference staged for Bryant. "At the time, high school players coming to the NBA were still a novelty," Adande recalled. "There was a lot of interest in him. I remember him talking about taking college classes online. They asked him, how was he going to do it? and he said, 'Internet.' He was kind of smiling. It was a new phenomenon back then, the concept of studying online, but he was just so excited about everything. He was an excited young teenager, just happy to finally be in the league and bouncing with a lot of energy. The media were kind of excited to cover him. I don't think they were their usual, cynical selves. There was a lot of interest. Again, just the fact that they held a separate press conference for him in the room, I think, spoke to the level of interest in him. So back then it was, 'OK, who is this kid?' You know, the media hadn't seen or heard a whole lot about him. Really very few had actually seen him play."

There wasn't much opportunity for new fans to see him play. For the first time in his life, he was spending long stretches on the bench. His old Lower Merion crew hungrily watched each game on TV and found it odd to see Bryant sitting there. "I'm just taking it as a learning experience, sitting back and getting to watch the guys," he said. "You see so much sitting on the bench...Even though you're sweating and saying, 'Man, I want to be out there,' you just have to be patient and just learn."

His next road game was in Charlotte. Still sore over the draft, the crowd booed when he entered the game in the second period. He responded nervously, missing 4 of his first 5 shots, but at least he was able to quickly and easily get those shots. He notched his first NBA basket with a deep jumper. "It felt good," he said. "When I first took that three-point shot, I believed it was gonna go down. First it felt good, then it felt a little short. I kinda leaned back, eyein' it. When it went down, I was like, 'Shewww! My first three-pointer.'"

He also rang up three equally quick turnovers, including a play in which he stepped out of bounds in his eagerness to get to the basket and dunk.

"When I caught the ball in the corner," he admitted, "at first I said, 'I'm gonna shoot it. All right! I'm gonna stroke it.' But then I saw this big ol' lane under the hoop, and I started lickin' my chops. I said, 'Oh, man, I'm gonna finish this.' But I was overexcited. My back step was a little too long. That was just being overanxious getting to the hoop. I'm like, 'Man, if I can just get to that block, I can get this dunk! I'm there! I'm home. I'm free.' So that was a little overanxious right there."

Bryant's desire to dunk all the time brought his first nickname from O'Neal. He began calling Bryant "Showboat," which, at the time, despite Bryant's annoyance with the implied disrespect, didn't seem like a big deal. O'Neal was constantly joking about everything, but the nickname would soon enough prove a burr in their relationship.

As the team struggled to score that first month of the season, Bryant began thinking he could do more to help out. "I think of me stepping in there and being young and just having so much energy coming off the sideline; hopefully I can be a spark plug," he said.

He told Harris that he could beat any player in the league off the dribble one-on-one. He suggested the coaches consider having

O'Neal take a few steps out of the post at times to allow him room to attack the basket. The coach listened, then replied that that might be true. "But we're not going to move Shaq out of the post for you," Harris remembered telling Bryant. If he wanted to play more, Kobe would need to increase his efficiency by committing fewer turnovers and shooting a higher percentage, Harris explained.

The coach didn't tell Kobe this at the time, but what he disclosed in a 2015 interview was that the older players on the roster were watching like hawks "to make sure Bryant wasn't given anything."

The vets were certainly picking up on silent messages that Bryant was the anointed one. After all, he was outfitted in his Adidas shoes, which sent a statement every time he dressed out to play. The company was waiting to put out a signature shoe, not wanting to put too much pressure on his rookie season. Instead it simply issued the standard Adidas hoops shoe in Lakers colors and watched sales rise again and again as that first season rolled along.

Del Harris doubted, looking back in 2015, that anyone from the Lakers had told Bryant in July that Eddie Jones and Nick Van Exel would be traded to make room for him. Perhaps it was a figment of Bryant's young imagination, although Jerry West was known to talk a little too freely sometimes on such matters. But Bryant and all those around him had felt West's tremendous enthusiasm for the talent he had discovered, and the message had clearly crept into the team's view of Bryant.

Like most pro coaches, Harris took a wait-and-see approach with rookies. Bryant was no different except that Harris took even more caution because of the age factor. Besides, the coach had other problems. Stripping the roster to get O'Neal meant that the team had undergone the largest single turnover of players in franchise history. Of the sixteen athletes on the training-camp roster, only five—Jones, Van Exel, center Elden Campbell, forward Cedric Ceballos, and forward Corie Blount—had been a Laker the previous season.

As a result, Harris would spend most of the season searching for the right mix around O'Neal. Then, halfway through the schedule, Ceballos was traded away for Robert Horry. West also traded for forward George McCloud.

As Harris struggled to fit the new pieces of the Lakers together, he sometimes rubbed his team the wrong way. Few players cared for how Harris conducted practices.

West had lobbied hard to get Harris hired two years earlier. He was a veteran coach with an excellent reputation for Xs and Os and had produced solid teams. He was white-haired, devout, gentlemanly and kind, and he knew the game inside out.

He was a teacher of fundamentals, Rudy G. observed, but he could fall into the habit of droning on and on in practice.

It annoyed most of the players, but he clashed particularly with Van Exel, Garciduenas recalled. "Nick was anxious and so young at the time. I don't think he was well suited for Del's style of coaching. Del was a teacher. He loved to stand around and instruct and talk and have people listen, and Nick was the kind of guy that didn't have that much patience. He wanted to go out and do."

When Harris lectured, things dragged noticeably. Bryant, the practice monster, was shocked. "Practices were very structured at Lower Merion. Very intense," he would confide. "But a lot of times with Del, people just did what they wanted. Guys wouldn't even practice at all."

The other side to that argument was that the NBA was never meant to be a league for developing talent. With a schedule that called for three or four games a week, there wasn't time to have intense practices.

Even with their growing pains, the young Lakers moved forward with a sense of progress over the first five weeks of the 1996–97 season. After a win over Orlando on December 6, their record stood at 14–7. "We're gonna be fine," O'Neal said of the Lakers' start. "Even if we had gone 21–0 this month, we're not gonna win or lose anything the first month. As long as we satisfy ourselves. Our formula is to win about fifty or sixty games, get home-court advantage, and take it from there."

Even young Bryant knew it wasn't going to be that easy.

The New Edition

This new group of Lakers had begun calling themselves the Lake Show, a name that would come to signify the void left by Showtime.

Despite their inexperience together, they found a groove that December of 1996, winning seven of their first eight games. O'Neal presented trouble for opponents in the post. At the point, left-hander Van Exel displayed an unbridled bundle of moxie and quickness. Jones was a defensive terror on the wings. And Elden Campbell was a load at power forward or backup center. Expectations grew that December as they rolled past Detroit, Denver, Seattle, Orlando, Minnesota, Sacramento, Indiana, and Portland on their way to a midmonth meeting with Jordan and the Bulls. The Lakers had settled into a blitzing, open-court style, pressing and slamming opponents into submission. The approach suited Bryant's skills as a finisher, and the limited minutes he got were usually eventful as he made his first stops around the NBA map.

Obviously, the first visit to Chicago sent his hopes soaring. Here was Jordan the Magnificent, who could stand on the floor, hands on his hips, and level a gaze across the proceedings that sent a chill through everyone who saw it.

The Lakers promptly ran up a 22-point lead in the first half and held an 18-point edge at the end of the third quarter, only to see Jordan and his Bulls come charging back to win in overtime.

Bryant played a scant ten minutes against his idol and scored just 5 points. Jeremy Treatman was there, working on his book project. He witnessed a growing relationship between Shaq and Kobe. "At first he loved Shaq," Treatman recalled. In the team hotel after the game, Bryant told Treatman to come up to his room. But the former assistant coach had been there only a few minutes when Bryant said, "Let's go."

"I'm like, 'What? We're going somewhere?'" Treatman recalled.

He wasn't quite comfortable either in his new role or with Bryant's new identity. They got to the lobby, and soon O'Neal joined them.

"This is one of my high school coaches," Bryant said, introducing them.

Treatman couldn't believe that he was about to go out with Kobe and Shaq. His hopes rose when he walked with them to the limo out front, but just as he got near, Bryant suddenly turned and said, "See you later!"

"They went to see some jazz band," Treatman said. "For a second, I thought I was going."

In his talks with Bryant that first season, he heard of no trouble with O'Neal, Treatman said. "When people say they hated each other from the beginning, I say, no way. Joe and Kobe knew Shaq was signing. They wanted to play with Shaq. The animosity came later, over time, with the power struggle. From what I saw that first year in the league, they were pretty tight. They went out."

But where O'Neal enjoyed the L.A. club scene and nightlife, it was something that held little appeal for his workaholic younger teammate. "I just didn't like to go out that much," Bryant explained later when asked why he and O'Neal hadn't pursued an off-court friendship.

One other thing became clear. "Kobe didn't want to do a book and sit and be interviewed," Treatman recalled. "He hated it. He also knew that he couldn't complain about Del Harris and all these players to me. That was a big part of it. And I understood that. Joe would tell me, 'He's got fifteen years in this league. He's got to be with these guys every day. He can't go trash 'em when he's seventeen, eighteen years old.'"

His team answered the disappointment in Chicago by winning six of their next seven games, which included a five-game winning streak. The Lakers opened 1997 by winning a game in Sacramento, then beating the Kings again in the Forum on Friday night, January 3. From there, they slipped into Canada in the wee hours of Saturday. Less than eight hours later, they were dressed and ready to practice at General Motors Place, the Grizzlies' arena. With the hectic travel schedule, practice time had been negligible. Harris used the brief Saturday-morning session to focus his team on defending the high screen and roll, a reminder for the veterans and a key lesson for Bryant, who had struggled in adjusting to NBA defense at the two-guard position.

That night O'Neal dominated the Grizzlies inside, and Van Exel doled out 23 assists feeding him the ball, just one shy of Magic Johnson's team record. The game was Del Harris's perfect vision of the way things ought to be.

Van Exel admitted that the offense had sputtered during the

team's adjustment to playing with O'Neal. "I think at times we're too stagnant," the point guard said. "Everybody is standing around and watching when we throw the ball into the post. There's no movement. Everybody's watching to see what the big guy's gonna do. Then there are a lot of times when we're just careless with a lot of turnovers."

Sorting out all the Lakers' talent would bring headaches for Harris over the coming months. "You can see the pressure I'm under as a coach," Harris explained. "You got Kobe Bryant, who's got such a tremendous game, and yet ahead of him, at his normal position, are both Eddie Jones and Byron Scott. So I don't know where I'm going to get all the minutes for these guys. We've got some tremendous two and three players."

Like many little-used players, Bryant took to using pregame shoot-around time to make up for the lack of real practice time. He often worked with assistant coach Larry Drew, focusing on his crossover move and handling the ball in the half court. The coaches had settled on the idea of developing him as a backup point guard, which would allow him some extra minutes on the floor. Eager for opportunity, Bryant jumped at the idea.

And when he did get on the floor, good things tended to happen. Veteran Lakers beat writer Mitch Chortkoff remembered Bryant making a key play in a defeat of Sacramento during the stretch of wins. "Kobe stole the ball from Billy Owens, looked around, saw nobody was near him, so he did a 360 spin for a dunk," Chortkoff said with a smile. "That brought the crowd to its feet. That's an example of why Shaq made up the name Showboat. The night before, Kobe blocked a shot by Mitch Richmond at the end in a close game, and then, at the other end, the Lakers missed, but Kobe got the rebound with his back to the basket and put it back in over his head."

But Chortkoff also pointed out that Bryant had a bad turnover that cost the Lakers in a game against Portland, which made Harris anxious about playing him. Chortkoff had advised Harris that he would just have to live through those things as Bryant developed.

On the issue of his playing time, Bryant said, "I just sit there on the bench, trying to stay loose, and if he calls me I'm going to go out there and try to give it my all. It's nice to get in there and mix it up with the guys when it really counts. I'm starting to understand the flow of the game a little bit more. I'm starting to feel more comfortable out there on the floor. Now that we've had a little opportunity to practice I understand all of this a little more."

Part of his strategy for keeping his disappointment at bay was to focus on others who had faced far more difficult circumstances. "I read the autobiography of Jackie Robinson," Bryant said. "I was thinking about all the hard times I'd go through this year, and that it'd never compare to what he went through. That just kind of helped put things in perspective."

The Jump

In February, O'Neal would suffer the first of two knee injuries that caused him to miss a total of thirty games. First, he strained his right knee, causing him to miss the team's second game against the Bulls and the NBA All-Star Game. While O'Neal rested, his teammates managed a 106–90 whipping of the Bulls in the Forum. This time Bryant played just thirteen minutes and again scored 5 as the team rode 34 points inside from Elden Campbell. The loss broke an eight-game Chicago winning streak, with the 16-point margin matching the Bulls' worst defeat of the season. Chicago was 42–6 and had won seventeen of their previous eighteen games.

For Bryant, with his personal expectations so huge, it was hard to keep the negative thoughts at bay. "My rookie year I had no clue," he would say later. "I figured it would work out and I would realize my dream, but I didn't know how. I kept thinking about it all the time and wondering, 'How? How is it going to happen? How are the pieces going to fall in place?'"

He found the first big means of reaching the spotlight in snowy Cleveland, of all places. He, Travis Knight, and Derek Fisher had all been invited to play in the rookie game at the NBA's annual winter carnival, All-Star Weekend. In the past, the All-Star Weekend had featured an old-timers game, but a series of serious injuries had forced the league to drop that event. The need to promote its future stars prompted the NBA to replace the old-timers game with a rookie game, which pitted the best young players from the East and the West against each other.

Bryant eyed the event as a chance to show that, while he hadn't received playing time, he was better than all the other rookies. During the thirty-minute exhibition, Philadelphia's Allen Iverson used his quickness to score 19 and led the East team to victory. But Bryant led the charge from the West with 31 points, many of them delivered with his trademark flash.

About an hour after the rookie game, he was scheduled to participate in the slam dunk contest. First devised as an attraction during the last ABA All-Star Game, in 1976, the event had been revised by the NBA in 1984 and had been used to showcase some special high flying by Jordan, Dominique Wilkins, and a host of other players. By 1997, however, the event had been able to draw only hungry young players as participants, and memorable performances became rare.

As a result, the league had decided to phase it out after the 1997 event. For this supposed last event, the league selected an All-Star panel of judges: Julius Erving, Walt Frazier, and George Gervin. Bryant's sense of the game's history gave him more than a little extra buzz for a slam-dunk field that included Michael Finley of the Dallas Mavericks, Chris Carr of the Minnesota Timberwolves, Bob Sura of the Cleveland Cavaliers, and Darvin Ham of the Denver Nuggets.

His nervousness apparent, Kobe Bryant barely the made the final round of the event, but from there he trotted out a spectacular finish, good enough to claim the slam dunk trophy. From the left side, he attacked the basket, switched the ball between his legs, and whirled in to find the rim, a finish that ignited the building, with Brandy sitting a few rows up from courtside, pumping her fist in celebration. The finish brought Dr. J and the other judges to their feet. Spurred by the outburst, Bryant rushed to center court and flexed.

"The crowd got me real pumped up, and I just felt like flexing," he explained later. "I don't have much, but I flexed what I have."

Sonny Vaccaro and Joe Bryant had poor seats for the event, but the big moment left Vaccaro happy that shoe sales would be ringing away. "We were all the way up in the arena," he recalled. "Joe never sat long with us that day. He loved to get up and mingle when Kobe was doing well."

The many eyes on Bryant had gotten the first big indication that, like Kevin Garnett before him, Bryant was managing the challenge of going to pro basketball from high school. The road had been a little more troubled for Portland's Jermaine O'Neal, a seven-footer from South Carolina who had joined Bryant in the 1996 draft, with a smaller boost from Vaccaro and with Tellem as his agent. O'Neal's experiences in Portland had led him to have some midseason misgivings about bypassing college, which he later recanted. Fifty-one days younger than Bryant, Jermaine O'Neal said that he and the Lakers rookie spoke twice a month by phone.

"We've been friends," O'Neal said of Bryant. "But we've gotten even closer since we came into the league. We understand the situation we're in. We talk to each other and let each other know what's going on in each other's lives."

The young players were growing in their awareness that they were part of a high-dollar experiment. The NBA's owners received $125-million franchise fees every time they agreed to expand the league by adding a new team. The owners liked that money very much. They wanted to expand more, but NBA commissioner David Stern and others who cared about the game cautioned them about getting too greedy and expanding too quickly because it would stretch the talent base too thin, meaning that the quality of play in the league could decline dramatically.

Instead of adding teams more slowly, the owners looked to expand the talent base. One way to do that was to lure in European players. The other was to offer contracts to younger talent. Some owners saw that if more eighteen-year-olds could be brought into the league, then the owners might rake in more money.

Stern was already working on a way to stop that movement even before it really took hold. He knew that the league could face a big public backlash if it brought in young players who failed dramatically. Despite the adjustment of Bryant and others, the circumstances had led CBS college basketball broadcaster Billy Packer to declare that the NBA had become "the enemy" of basketball, a comment that angered league officials.

Packer, however, insisted that the NBA's grab for young players would eventually destroy the quality of the game in both college and the pros.

Utah Jazz president Frank Layden offered this perspective on the tension between pro sports owners and their greed. "They are short range," Layden said. "They're not concerned with quality. They are concerned with the effective making of money."

Fuel

O'Neal returned to action after All-Star Weekend in a road game in Minneapolis, only to injure a ligament in his left knee, causing him to miss twenty-eight more games, a huge blow to the young team's development.

Bryant's showing at the All-Star break had steeled his determination to make a bigger impact. To do that, however, he would need playing time, which would require that Harris have as much confidence in him as Bryant had in himself. Harris, however, concluded that the kid needed a more realistic view of the team and his role in it. "Del was a prophet," a Lakers staff member who worked closely with Harris would explain later. "Del saw this coming and tried a long time ago to get Kobe under control."

Harris would later explain to some Lakers staffers that the team's management had given him directives that Bryant had to receive playing time in order to learn. The staff members got the distinct impression that Harris would have preferred to have kept the eighteen-year-old on the bench.

West likely sympathized with Bryant's desire to get on the court because it resonated with his own career. He came to Los Angeles in 1960 and was joined by Fred Schaus, his college coach at West Virginia, who promptly kept him on the bench for a few weeks. West steamed the entire time and never forgave Schaus for keeping him out of the starting lineup, even though he played a lot.

West's dictum as an executive was that young players, especially good young players, have to play; there was simply no other way for them to get better.

"The main thing Kobe Bryant needs is experience," the Lakers executive would say during the season. "He doesn't need to work on anything. He just needs to play more."

O'Neal had an eye on Bryant's selfishness, but he followed West's lead with reporters. "He's gonna be fine," the center said, "once he gets a chance to go out there and shine and do his thing. He's gonna be fine."

"He's gonna be a good pro," Lakers assistant coach Larry Drew said of Bryant at the time. "But he has a lot to learn about the NBA game. He loves to play. He wants to be out there regardless. But he understands that this is a learning process and a slow process."

Bryant, though, saw the coaches as attempting to reshape his hopes and dreams. "I won't let them break me," he said again and again. "I'm in this for the long haul. I want to learn."

The anxiousness was contagious. Family friends recalled that Joe was a wreck, as if his own troubled time with the Sixers had come back to haunt him. The father had a small office in the family house at Pacific Palisades, where he was up early each morning, phoning back to the East Coast in pursuit of new deals for his son. "All he talked about was basketball," said one friend. "He was really struggling with Kobe's situation."

With Joe so emotional for much of the season, Sonny Vaccaro had stepped in as a voice of reason in the rookie's ear. After all, the shoe man had had a hand in getting Bryant into the situation. The Vaccaros would visit the Bryant house regularly for meals and consultations. Bryant wouldn't come down to greet him, or any guest for that matter, but Vaccaro would make his way upstairs and listen, encourage Kobe to stay positive and keep the perspective that the adjustment would have been easier on a weaker team. In the long run, he would be glad he was a Laker, Vaccaro kept telling him.

"He had put so much into basketball, he didn't have close friends," Vaccaro recalled. "I was his closest connection to reality in the sport of basketball. I was the one he trusted. What I did was listen to him, and then I would give my opinion. The things that I did for him had reinforced that I had belief in what he could do. I showed that every step of the way with him, and I think that's why our relationship was inseparable. I always talked to Kobe after the games, not every game, but a lot of times. I was his confidant. I'd call, and he'd talk."

Joe Bryant would echo Vaccaro's positive message in the wake of the All-Star Weekend. He counseled his son to find patience about playing time.

"My father tells me, 'Your time will come,'" Bryant said at the time.

He also then relied on the Catholicism in which he had been raised.

"I had that much trust in my father," he would explain later. "I had that much trust in the Lord in the special situation He had put me in."

Yet faith often seemed to wilt on the bench. As frustrating as the lack of minutes was their inconsistency, Bryant said. He never knew when the coach was suddenly going to decide to play him major minutes. He would play well, and just when it seemed as if he would get more time, Harris would hold back. "I felt like I was playing with one hand tied behind me," he said of the experience.

"One of the hardest things this year was not knowing whether you're going to play or how many minutes you're going to play," he would explain by the end of the season. "But at the same time that kind of helps you, because you just have to be ready every night."

Treatman recalled a growing anger with Harris from both Joe and Kobe, but they kept it to themselves. The coach said that Joe never once mentioned the situation to him or showed any anger. In fact, Harris recalled that Kobe Bryant thanked him for his handling of that rookie season years later one night in Dallas. Rudy G. and other staff members, however, could clearly see Joe Bryant's misery.

Bad Medicine

There were other adjustments for an eighteen-year-old in the land of big paychecks. One of the most challenging was Los Angeles itself.

Asked about off-court entanglements, he said, "Sure the group-ies come after you. Living in L.A., how could you not be approached by women like that? They tend to be older, but some are younger. You have to handle it in a professional manner.... I've learned all about that growing up."

Growing up was advisable considering the atmosphere of hyper-sexual behavior that had been a feature of the Lakers' team envi-ronment for decades, dating back to the early 1960s, when Jerry West and Elgin Baylor and then Wilt Chamberlain ruled the league. The period generated a lot of sex addicts in the NBA ranks, former Laker Lou Hudson once confided. It was work just keeping up with the demand.

"Even back in '68 and '69," recalled Doug Krikorian, a longtime L.A. sportswriter, "we'd get off the bus and go in the hotel lobby, and there'd be a bunch of women in there looking at Johnny Egan, who was a straight Catholic boy who would never play around on his wife, straight as a string. Even then these guys would be besieged with women."

For years, Lakers forward A. C. Green had managed to avoid that atmosphere by toting a Bible everywhere he went to fend off the throng of lusty females present in every city the Lakers visited. "The women were very aggressive, very aggressive," former Laker Ron Carter recalled of the team in the late '70s. "We were very pro-miscuous. That was the pre-AIDS era. The big thing then was her-pes.... Other than that, unprotected sex was very, very common. We were coming right off of the free love era.

"These women would come to the hotel," Carter added. "First of all, it always amazed me that they could figure out where we're staying. But they'd be there when we got there. They'd have the team roster. 'Can I speak to Magic Johnson?' 'I'm sorry, ma'am, that line is busy.' 'Can I speak to Kareem Abdul-Jabbar?' 'Sorry, that line is busy.' 'Can I speak to Jamaal Wilkes?' They're reading down the roster. They are there to get a Laker. I used to get down. I was the eleventh call. Every other guy would go in the room and take their phone off the hook, so it rings busy. I'd keep a phone on the hook. I'm waiting for the overflow. I know it's coming, espe-cially if we're in New York or Philadelphia."

For the long list of Lakers stars over the decades, scoring in the bedroom had seemed almost as important as scoring on the court. After all, they were Hollywood's team and had access to the world's casting couch. Movie stars? The porn industry? And basketball players? It had proved an intriguing combination for decades, with decidedly mixed results, evidenced by more than a bit of heartbreak.

There was Chamberlain's sad claim of making love to twenty thousand women. And Magic Johnson's stunning announcement that he was HIV positive followed by his admission that he had slept with three hundred to five hundred people per year. Team owner Jerry Buss, of course, had long been known for serially dating scores of beautiful young women (he was said to prefer eighteen-year-olds) and proudly keeping the photo collection of his conquests.

Opposing coaches were known to suggest that one reason the Lakers had become the NBA's dominant team over the years was the sexual frivolity. "That's why the best players wanted to play there, because of all the women," one coach said.

That certainly wasn't an allure for Bryant, though, at least in the early stages of his career. Asked if he phoned his parents often during road trips, he said, "Off and on, yeah, we've been talking. My mother calls me all the time."

Amid the issues, Bryant did recognize some of the sheer joy and wonder of his rookie experience. "It's fun," he tried telling himself. "I'm in the NBA."

The pace was a blur of hastily grabbed meals, of jetting from one section of the continent to the other on a weekly basis. Tuesday in Minneapolis, Thursday in Sacramento. Friday, back to L.A. for one of Pam Bryant's home-cooked meals. Then back out on the road again five days later. His loneliness grew. This team held no easy camaraderie, unlike the one at Lower Merion. His true consolation came only so long as room service could deliver the apple pie à la mode that he craved and the hotel TV offered TNT games. On buses and the team plane, he read or tuned the world out by stuffing his head between earphones.

"You can learn only so much by watching," Bryant told a reporter. "You have to get out there and make some mistakes to really grasp what you're trying to do."

"We brought him along a little slowly during the regular season—very slowly, actually—because we had a fifty-plus-win team, and he did not have training camp and was injured twice," Harris would explain later. "But his progress was gradual and obvious and definite."

Over the remainder of February and March, he had played sporadically. It seemed that Harris gave up on his plan to use him as a backup point guard. When Van Exel was injured in April, the replacement chores fell to rookie Derek Fisher. Harris clearly didn't trust Bryant's decision making with the ball or his defense.

Years later, the NBA would settle into the age of analytics, when teams began to develop more precise measures of a player's effectiveness that went beyond the traditional box-score stats. There was no such aid for him in 1997, but it was still clear that Bryant was accomplishing good things in the minutes he got. In the six games that he started at two guard as a rookie, the Lakers were 5–1, and with his ability to score, he clearly presented problems for opponents. Although he ranked eleventh on the team in minutes played, he was second on the team in offensive production on a per minute basis, ranking only behind O'Neal in points scored per minute played. In the games that Harris allowed him to play twenty minutes, he averaged 13 points, and if he was given twenty-five minutes or more, his scoring average jumped to better than 16 points, with a field goal percentage of .500. These were the kinds of numbers that West knew he could produce after watching him work out that day months earlier.

Whenever he went into the game, his ball-handling skills and scoring ability meant that he was going to draw a swarm of defenders. He just needed some work on the concept of giving up the ball. "It's a lot easier when you have guys like Eddie Jones and Byron and Elden and Shaq around you," Bryant acknowledged. "It makes the job a whole lot easier. You just go in there and try to create things, whether it's scoring opportunities for yourself or your teammates."

"I've seen the kid come a long way in a very short time," Byron Scott said. "He understands a lot of things that are going on out there now that he didn't at the beginning of the season."

Over the final weeks of the regular season, Harris upped his floor time, and Bryant responded by averaging 11 points per game. Still, it was too little, too late, in the eyes of his family and friends. Over the course of the season, he would play in seventy-one games and average a little better than fifteen minutes of playing time per game.

O'Neal returned from his knee injury on April 11 and immediately helped the Lakers to a win over Phoenix, bringing L.A.'s record to 53–25. Three days earlier, Bryant had come off the bench against Golden State and scored a career-high 24 points. The late-season playing time had brought a surge in his confidence. Asked to look back on his decision to turn professional, he told a reporter, "I definitely had a lot of fun," he said. "I wouldn't change it for the world."

Yet reports would emerge that he spent some time going to the nearby campus of UCLA, where he sat in his car, watching the students come and go in their lives and wondering what might have been.

With O'Neal's return, the Lakers won four straight games, bringing the regular season down to a final meeting with the Portland Trail Blazers. If the Lakers won, they would claim the Pacific Division title. O'Neal could have tied the game with 1.2 seconds to go but missed 2 free throws. With the loss, the Lakers finished at 56–26, their best record in seven seasons.

To prepare for the play-offs and their first-round matchup with Portland, the Lakers repaired to the College of the Desert for a minicamp. Asked if Bryant would be a factor in the series, Harris told reporters that the matchups would be difficult for the rookie. The Blazers featured the strong and wily Isaiah Rider at two guard and Cliff Robinson at small forward.

"We'll just have to see," the coach said, but added that Bryant had done "an amazing job" in his rookie season.

With O'Neal scoring 46 points in Game 1, the Lakers quickly took control of the series against Portland, then won Game 2 as well. Bryant played a total of six minutes over the two games, but his team held a 2–0 lead. In Game 3, with Portland's crowd shoving the Blazers back into contention, the Lakers could find no punch until Harris inserted Bryant. Immediately aggressive, he began driving to the basket and drawing fouls, creating offense for himself and his teammates. He would finish with 22 points, but that wasn't enough to bring the rest of the team alive. Portland won, 98–90, and closed the gap to 2–1 in the series.

Bryant's reward for the effort was hardly any playing time in Game 4. Nevertheless, the Blazers had no means of defending O'Neal and fell by the wayside, 3–1.

The next round brought the veteran Utah Jazz, routinely a tough matchup for the young Lakers, but in their late-season run, the Lakers had dispatched the Jazz 100–98, with 39 points from O'Neal. The outcome was enough to give Harris and his staff hope that they could keep the momentum going in the play-offs. The Jazz, though, took a 2–0 lead in the series at home. In Game 1, Bryant made just 1 of 7 shots, a three-pointer, in thirteen minutes of play. In Game 2, he played four minutes and scored a single basket. The Lakers managed to mix their post and perimeter games, with O'Neal scoring 25 and Robert Horry finding his range with 7 consecutive three-pointers. The effort earned the Lakers a shot to win it at the buzzer, but Karl Malone blocked Van Exel's shot, giving the Lakers a 103–101 loss and a 2–0 series deficit.

Game 3, in the Forum, brought a Laker blowout, 104–84, fueled by 17 fourth-quarter points from Bryant. In all, he would finish with 19 for the game, the team high. He made 13 of 14 free throws, an impressive display of poise down the stretch for an eighteen-year-old.

Unfortunately, the afterglow lasted only briefly. Malone answered furiously in Game 4, scoring 42 points to give his team a 3–1 series lead, with the next game returning to Utah. There, in Game 5, the Jazz jumped to an 11-point lead and seemed set to cruise. The Lakers lost Horry to a third-quarter ejection, weakening their defense. Still, they managed to roll the score back into reach and even held a 1-point lead with about nine minutes to play. From there, the lead shifted back and forth until O'Neal fouled out with just under two minutes to go. Then, with a minute left in regulation, Utah's John Stockton managed to blow past Bryant for a tying layup.

With the score knotted at 87–87, the teams went into a final flurry of fruitless possessions. Eddie Jones had a shot blocked, and

Malone missed a jumper. Then, with eleven seconds to go, Van Exel got a steal, which set up a last possession for Los Angeles. During the ensuing time-out, Harris decided that the ball and the shot should go to his little-used rookie. The plan? Spread the floor and let Bryant attack.

Questioned repeatedly about the decision later, the coach explained that Bryant's one-on-one skills made him the best choice to get off a solid shot. "I spent over half of the year being criticized for not playing Kobe," Harris said afterward. "Now I'm getting criticized for playing him."

According to plan, Bryant got the shot, a decent look at the basket from fourteen feet, with the defense in his face and the Delta Center crowd pounding down the noise. The building exploded when it fell—an air ball. Overtime would only extend his nightmare. With O'Neal out of the game, the Lakers found themselves putting the extra period in the rookie's hands. His three deep air balls goosed the home crowd into delight. Bryant raised his eyebrows, licked his lips, appeared almost, for a moment, to squeeze back a tear.

The loss sent the Jazz on their way to the conference championship and effectively ended phase one of Bryant's NBA education, somewhat brutally.

After the debacle, he sat quietly for a time, composed himself, then answered reporters' questions. Sure, it hurt, but he would keep the memory as motivation, he said. "You've got to put it behind you. But, yeah, you have to pull it out at the appropriate time. When it's summertime and you're a little tired, a little down, you're hurting and you don't feel like working out, you pull it out of your memory bank and remember the situation.

"Hopefully, that can give me a little boost."

"He's a young guy, and this is all new to him," Stockton told reporters. "He's played with a lot of confidence in this series, but he was asked to make some tough shots at the end, and he just didn't come up with them."

Asked what he planned to do with the off-season, Bryant explained that he would practice.

"I've still got a lot of energy left, man," he said.

Shortly after Bryant got back to Los Angeles, he was on the phone with Vaccaro.

"Kobe took three or four of the wildest goddamn three-pointers I've ever seen in my life," the shoe man recalled.

"How do you feel?" Vaccaro asked, right off the bat.

"I'm good, why?" Bryant asked suspiciously.

"Well," Vaccaro said hesitantly. "You missed the shots. I'm just saying. They're beating you up for those shots."

"Fuck 'em," Bryant replied quickly. "Nobody else wanted to shoot the ball."

Twenty years later, Vaccaro was still chuckling at the response.

"I'll never forget that as long as I live," he said.

Chapter 19

ON WITH THE FABLE

THE CLOSE OF the 1997 NBA season presented an existential crisis for Kobe Bryant. Basketball had long been a fable for his family. He had learned from watching his father that the court was this magical place where if you played well enough, you would be transported to other fantastical locations, such as Italy and the Swiss Alps and Vegas, like Dorothy clicking her heels together.

Two decades later, Vaccaro and Rines and Charles and many of the old crew who had been there for the early years would get upset with Bryant for stretching the truth in recalling moments of his career for the media. But in many ways he was like a boy sitting by a campfire, eyes wide with the glow and sparks flying all around. The stories expanded a bit in his mind and improved with the retelling. He was always the man-child who loved Disney and *Star Wars* and Jedi Knights and such stuff. When Tex Winter showed up to help coach the Lakers, Bryant immediately dubbed him his "Yoda."

"He had this very symbolic, metaphorical way of seeing things," observed George Mumford, the psychologist and competitive specialist who became one of Bryant's mentors. Bryant was a writer, too, a poet, so he viewed the world through the lens of fabulous narrative.

His favorite book as a senior in high school had been the sci-fi fantasy *Ender's Game,* about a protagonist trained from a young age to face increasingly difficult challenges in order to save the world.

Bryant's entire family had been swept away in Italy like the Swiss Family Robinson, as he imagined it, and they all had cried together, child Kobe and his sisters, even the parents, when the late-night call came announcing Magic Johnson's fall from grace. They supposedly wept in the car driving to the airport for their return to the United States. A deity in their make-believe world was threatened.

For the next six years young Bryant had lived his life as if on a mythical quest. The only way he could keep the whole dream going was to work harder and harder and harder, to spin his fantasies around and around until they wrapped him tight in a new reality. Visualization was immense for that. It drove his many hours of solitary practice time. In America, as in Italy, he took to playing entire games alone on the court in his own personal practice right before he played them for real in front of audiences.

"Perhaps no player has ever made more use of his imagination," *Sports Illustrated* once said of Bryant.

Then came that moment at the tail end of a hopeless play-off series in 1997, which threatened to shatter everything. The narrative was unraveling.

Where Michael Jordan's defining moment came early, at the end of his freshman season when he hit a late jump shot to drive his Tar Heels to the NCAA championship, Bryant's moment was the four air balls, likewise in what was his own equivalent of a freshman season.

Bryant and his father had spent that entire first year looking for the one big opportunity, Jeremy Treatman recalled. "Joe and Kobe were both telling me the same thing. He goes, 'Nobody can stop me one-on-one.' I'm like, 'Dude, you're eighteen. I agree with you, but your time is gonna come.' But they wanted it now. They wanted it right then."

Suddenly that moment they had wanted so badly was upon them, when they least expected it.

Del Harris would be criticized later for the move, but it wasn't as if the coach had many options when he gave the ball and the shot to the rookie. Robert Horry, aka Big Shot Bob, had been thrown out of the game in the third quarter. Byron Scott, the veteran guard, was out with an injury. Van Exel was limping. Shaq, who wasn't much of a late-game option because of his terrible free-throw shooting, had fouled out. Eddie Jones had just taken 2 shots and missed both.

"Kobe looked at me in the huddle and said, 'Coach, if you give me that ball, I'll drain it for you,'" Harris recalled immediately afterward. "I believed him. I'd go to Kobe again if we played the game over. He is the best one-on-one player we have. The team knows it."

"Believe." That was the sweetest word in the young pilgrim's vocabulary. He was always looking for people to believe in his fantasy, as Vaccaro, his biggest believer, explained.

His teammates weren't about to do that. Scoop Jackson recalled his conversations with those Lakers. "They knew how good he was, too," Jackson recalled. "They said he was too young for them to tell him that."

Harris had dutifully resisted until the moment was desperate.

"They killed our coach, Del Harris, for having him in there," West would say much later. "But I applaud Del Harris to this day for allowing this guy to get in there and play when no one else was playing or competing. I don't know if anyone on our team would have taken the shots that he took."

Back in Pennsylvania, Bryant's old crew was transfixed by the moment.

"That's the Kobe I know," Donnie Carr told himself as he watched the game on TV. "He misses ten straight shots, but he can't wait to take the next one. It was like he was never going to back down or be afraid of the challenge."

Robby Schwartz saw the game with his father. Like so many from Lower Merion, they followed Bryant's career as if it were their own. "Four of them, four air balls," Schwartz recalled. "We just couldn't believe that (a) he kept shooting, and (b) he kept not hitting anything."

"The score was tied," Harris said of his decision on the first shot, "and I was saying that the most important thing with six seconds to go was to get a shot. Now, if it goes in, he's gonna know that I believed in him when he was an eighteen-year-old kid. If it doesn't go in, he's still gonna know I believed in him, and we're gonna go to overtime and we'll see what happens. He got a shot. I've seen hundreds of times in that situation where a team doesn't even get it inbounds, much less get a good shot. He got a seventeen-foot open look off that right elbow. I can still see it. It just didn't go."

Harris was wrong that Bryant—or at least those on Team Bryant—would understand that the coach was in his corner. The Bryants had long come to believe the coach was against them. Those close to Bryant felt that it was strange that Harris chose the play-offs to shove the rookie into pressure situations, with the season on the line. Joe wondered to his friends if Harris was trying to sabotage Kobe's career.

Jeremy Treatman watched the situation unfold and was similarly dumbfounded. "It was almost like Del Harris was setting him up to fail," the writer said. "He hardly played him during the year, then put the ball in his hands with the season on the line."

"I'd give him that shot again, then, now, and forever," Harris said when asked about it a decade later.

To others close to Kobe, it wasn't the bad shots but Bryant's response to the failure that made the moment.

"Jumping from high school to the NBA is like a virgin sleeping with a forty-year-old woman with three kids," Toronto Raptors forward Walt Williams would observe that same year. "You better raise your game a lot or you'll be humiliated."

That evening after the loss Bryant went straight to a gym at a neighborhood school as soon as he got home to L.A.

"He went in the gym that night and shot until three or four in the morning," Scoop Jackson said. "There's no crying, there's no running to lay up with some woman he just met in a club. None of that shit. He went straight to the damn gym."

"There's not another teenager on the planet who could miss those shots, fail the Lakers, and recover from it," Vaccaro said, looking back.

Journalist Ric Bucher saw the moment and admired the young player. "I thought it was incredibly gutsy of him to do it," he recalled. "And I thought, 'You know what? At some point he's going to make those shots because he has the balls to take them even after he's missed.' We had a conversation about it, a private conversation about it, and I think he appreciated at that time that I wasn't like everybody else who was just ready to crush him for taking those shots, that I had a different view of it."

Where Jordan's sophomore year was spent as the young hero, basking in the unrestrained love of the basketball crazy Tar Heels fan base and riding the crest of confidence that came with a long-awaited national championship, Bryant, the sophomore, had to contend with a flood of doubt, not just his, but the doubt all around him. Bryant would ask himself again and again: What if he had gone to the rim on that last shot, torn it down with a jam or forced the Jazz to foul? What if? He asked that question in his mind over and over.

"It was an early turning point for me in being able to deal with adversity, deal with public scrutiny and self-doubt," he later recalled. "At eighteen years old, it was gut-check time."

"What if he didn't have that game?" Robby Schwartz asked in 2015. "What if he didn't have that moment? What if he made one of those shots? What if he made one of those shots to win the game? Would he have turned out to be as good or better? I think that that game was vital to how good he became. That level of embarrassment to happen to somebody like him? The next year he came out like a fucking maniac."

KB8

As if there weren't enough to keep Bryant busy as he worked and worked and worked before his nineteenth birthday, late that summer, Adidas moved forward with its plan to launch his signature shoe, the KB8.

Peter Moore, the designer and executive for Adidas, had first met with the Bryants in Philadelphia and was struck by how much the family believed in their son. "We left there thinking, 'This kid can sell shoes,'" Moore recalled of that first meeting. "He was the son, but he was treated like he was going to be the king. I got the impression that Kobe was a model child. He just didn't do many things wrong. And he was a smart kid, at least with me. He could articulate what he wanted, what he liked and what he didn't like."

Surprisingly and contrary to his image, Bryant had no desire to be Michael Jordan, Moore discovered. "I think Kobe thought Michael was a hell of a basketball player, but Kobe wanted to be his own icon. All of these guys are about themselves to some degree. Kobe wanted to be Kobe and wanted that to be what kids wanted."

Having been through his experience with Air Jordan, Moore believed that design was becoming more important than performance in the athletic-shoe business. So Adidas focused on Bryant's background in Italy. The designer would eventually base the young star's signature shoes on the Audi TT Roadster, but the first shoe was mostly straightforward.

Jordan had been the man who could fly, a magical concept that would sell shoes year after year, deep into the next century. That would not be Bryant's message.

"To me, Kobe was going to be the next great player, and I could make him the next great thing in basketball, which was style, to me," Moore explained. "I was going to make him 'style.' The intention of his shoe was, 'I got style. I play with style.' Totally different animal from Jordan. Two different deals appealing to two different kinds of kids. That becomes your core; after your core, the halo effect comes out, and you grow. He liked that idea because he thought it was kind of cool and all that, but in the end, he wanted to be the guy on the street."

From the start, Bryant wanted to be embraced by "street kids," Moore said. "When I met him, he was a cool kid, pretty good smile, very articulate. And when he talked about wanting to be this urban kid, I was like, 'They ain't gonna buy it. You don't have the language, they're not going to buy it. You're not an urban guy.'"

Still, many of the first Adidas ads showed Bryant in some version of a street game, pickup, beginning with a stylized romp in an ad set in Venice Beach. And, mimicking the way Jordan had been photographed in the iconic "Jumpman" shot across the Chicago skyline, the designer tried setting up Bryant in a similar shot in California, the only problem being that Los Angeles had no distinctive skyline, unlike Chicago.

Bryant's more immediate problem was appealing to his own teammates, which meant that all the shoe company's big plans posed yet another struggle for the teen. He risked disgusting his older teammates when they caught sight of him in his first signature shoes or had the sense that he was getting something far before his time.

Forward Rick Fox, a new free-agent addition to the Lakers, articulated the struggle that the veterans had with Bryant's shoe deal. "Whenever you're climbing the ladder at a rapid pace, the people at the top are wary," Fox observed, looking back six months later. "They have the grasp of power and the limelight, and they've climbed that ladder to get it. They don't want to give that up too easily. And they'll do whatever they can to knock you down. Even if you are a teammate."

Del Harris recalled that he was surprised to encounter huge ads for the KB8 in Barcelona that summer, near the site where the Olympic Games were conducted in 1992. "I already knew when he signed a multimillion-dollar deal with Adidas that they were going to use him. And Adidas is bigger in Europe than it is in the U.S. But thirty-foot posters and billboards were a bit of a surprise. I saw them just outside the Olympic facilities in Barcelona. You come right down the steps just below the fountain, and on one side they got one of Kobe's feet. And the other foot is on the other side. With Kobe wearing Adidas shoes thirty feet high."

For the white-haired, scholarly Harris, it was way over the top. "I thought it was inappropriate," the coach said months later of the buildup. "The NBA is in on it. Kobe is just gonna have to learn to deal with those things because he's a worldwide personality already. He's known literally worldwide.

"He's a good guy," Harris confided. "And he's bright. But everybody's trying to rush him into being something that no nineteen-year-old can ever be, including Michael himself. Michael was Michael Jordan from North Carolina at age nineteen, and he didn't become Michael until he was about twenty-seven. And he didn't become MJ until he was thirty. It didn't happen like that. Michael Jordan wasn't a media creation. He wasn't anything that everybody was hoping for at age nineteen. The guy got cut from his high school team at fifteen. He made it through on immense talent but also hard work over a period of time. And that's the way Kobe will have to make it."

The growing perception was that Bryant's advancement was being driven by forces other than the game itself. Reminded that Bulls coach Phil Jackson had put much time and effort into protecting Jordan from the pressures that shoved him in the wrong directions, Harris was asked if there were ways he could protect Bryant.

"It's out of my control," he replied.

The coaching staff directed Bryant to play again for the Lakers' team in the L.A. summer league, where he was told to develop as a team player, someone willing to pass out of double-teams instead of trying to beat them all the time. Larry Drew again coached the team, and Bryant again turned to his instincts, using his superior conditioning to blow past the competition. Drew and West weren't happy with what they saw. On one occasion the teen crossed words with Drew, who accused him of "playing like the old Kobe." He was still approaching the game in terms of himself, not the team, the assistant coach said.

West emphasized that the team's demands on Bryant were going to be greater with the upcoming season.

Outside of work with the team, Bryant also took a quick promotional trip to Europe and completed a summer-school course in Italian at UCLA, but beyond that, he spent his days and nights developing his game.

"I drive myself," Bryant confided, saying that work was more important than play. "I like to go out and have fun and have a good time. But I just don't feel right. While I'm out having a good time, I could be playing basketball or something, could be lifting weights. I could be working on something."

Despite the frustrations with his summer league play, the Lakers staff tried to keep his progress in perspective. "As a rookie, he had the chance to kind of grow up a little bit," Larry Drew said. "It was a tough year for him, but he handled it well. He's got that one year under his belt. There was a little bit of maturity that goes along with that. He got to see what the whole NBA life was about. He made a good adjustment. He's not surprised by many things anymore. And I try to stay in his ear as much as I can about things that happen out on the floor. He absorbs it, and he very much wants to learn. That's what makes this kid unique. He's always willing to learn."

Bryant faced other pressures that summer. His big step in 1996 had opened the door for a decade of talented high school players to enter the NBA directly. "What Kobe did made it possible for Tracy McGrady, and even LeBron James, several years later," Vaccaro said, looking back at the process. Vaccaro had identified another huge high school star, six-eight guard Tracy McGrady, and had given him a contract worth almost twice what Bryant had been able to command a year earlier. The McGrady contract had been made possible by Bryant's impact on Adidas shoe sales.

Nike's Phil Knight had been furious after Adidas signed Bryant, and he told a corporate gathering in Chicago shortly afterward that Nike would not lose another big star to the German company. Yet McGrady was another solid punch landed by Vaccaro, helping Adidas to gain more market share from the still-dominant Nike.

Vaccaro was absolutely delighted with the developments. That summer, the shoe man brought McGrady to Los Angeles and even set up a visit from the newest signee to the Bryant home. The two young players hit it off. "Kobe genuinely liked Tracy," Vaccaro said. "And Tracy genuinely liked Kobe. Tracy was deferential, but he still believed he was better."

That evening of the visit, as McGrady prepared to leave to return to his hotel, Pam Bryant agreed with her son's request that McGrady spend the night. He would stay about two weeks, with the two young stars working out and battling in one-on-one day after day.

It was a generous move by the watchful Bryant family, as they had made a point of holding many of their former friends at bay. After a Lakers game at the end of Bryant's rookie season, Gregg Downer and Jeremy Treatman were visiting with Bryant. "That was the height of his unhappiness," Treatman recalled. "And he goes, 'You guys want to come over later? I'll be home all day.'"

They dropped by, and the three of them soon ended up in the family hot tub, talking animatedly about basketball, when Pam Bryant stepped to a window and began speaking to her son in Italian. It quickly became clear she had ended their visit. "It was time for us to go," Treatman remembered. "It was basically our signal to leave."

The two coaches at least got closer than Sam Rines. He was in

Los Angeles with his AAU team and the generous donor who had paid for much of Bryant's elite experience, even the costs of his weekend with Brandy. Yet when Rines phoned about having the group drop by the house, he was told curtly by one of the sisters, "This isn't a shrine."

Though Bryant liked McGrady, his presence let the young Lakers star know that he was confronting not only the competition ahead of him in the league and in his own locker room, but also the threat of more top young talent coming in the draft.

It perhaps helped to ease Bryant's mind that with strong shoe sales, Adidas was already in the process of upgrading his contract. The second year of the first contract had brought what Vaccaro estimated was another $150,000 to Joe. It meant that the parents didn't have to depend entirely on their teen's income, even though they continued to spend, as some saw it, lavishly. Pam had continued to transform the massive home into an Italian villa stocked with all sorts of impressive African art. "It was really quite a nice collection," Peter Moore recalled.

Although the new deal itself was done quietly, some media outlets soon began reporting that Bryant's shoe contract as now worth an estimated $48 million. The one oversight by the shoe company, in retrospect, Vaccaro acknowledged two decades later, was that the upgraded deal would cut out the payments to Joe Bryant.

In the wake of the contract upgrade, deprived of his cash flow, Joe Bryant would begin to search the landscape for money. With that would come a tide of developments that unhinged them all.

The Fateful Season

When training camp opened, the Lakers boasted the youngest team in the league: Bryant was nineteen; Van Exel, Jones, and O'Neal were twenty-five; and Derek Fisher was twenty-three. It proved to be a gnarly mix of egos, playing styles, and experience levels, all pushed along by O'Neal's growing dissatisfaction.

Bryant arrived at camp sporting a retro seventies look, with a wispy goatee and his hair puffed into something of a mini-Afro.

Early that first week, he would have to view his air-balls sequence again. He laughed at it. The only thing that would have hurt, he later told a reporter, was if he had chickened out and passed the ball, if he had not taken that pressure on himself.

"I wanted those shots," Bryant would maintain at the time. "I just didn't make them. If I had it to do over again, put me in the same scenario, I'd take the shots again. I have no problem with that. Regardless of what anybody says."

His approach that fall left teammates and Lakers staff wide-eyed, as he revealed even harsher edges to his competitive nature. "This kid is really, really driven. I haven't seen it in a player in a long time, not to that extent," assistant coach Larry Drew said.

"Kobe's one of the most competitive guys that we've ever had on our team," agreed longtime Lakers trainer Gary Vitti, "to the point where when we practice and we scrimmage and his team loses, he's uncomfortable to be around. In simple practice pickup games he gets mad, you can't talk to him. He goes over and sits on the sideline, and he's mad. Really mad. That's his competitive nature. He just wants to win all the time. You need somebody like that to elevate your practices."

"It's always been there since I was four or five years old," Bryant said. "I can't explain it. You just don't feel right if you lose."

Slowly, word of his all-out approach began to emerge from the staff.

"It's unparalleled," Del Harris said of Bryant's work ethic. "He doesn't waste a minute. Before practice, after practice, during the summer, whenever. Kobe doesn't waste any motion."

Eddie Jones, who was playing the same position as Bryant, responded to the challenge and opened the season on a tear, good enough to be proclaimed the NBA Player of the Month for November. Prestigious league awards aside, what really mattered, however, was the team's audience of two, owner Jerry Buss and West, both of whom were completely sold on Bryant's overwhelming talent, despite his lack of understanding of team play. Insiders and speculators soon noticed that Jones's first-rate play only served to heighten his trade value.

The regular-season schedule had opened with the Lakers entertaining Utah and Bryant entertaining the crowd. He scored 23 points in a confidence-boosting win but didn't manage to meet Harris's standards for team play for the next two games. It wasn't until the fourth game, another win, that he broke out again with 25 points against Golden State. A late ankle sprain kept him out of action for a three-game road trip to Texas, where the Lakers racked up three more wins, bringing their start to seven straight victories. Bryant returned for a romp over Vancouver, then put the exclamation mark on the month in his team's first visit back to Utah since the play-off debacle. This time he blocked a three-point attempt by Utah's Bryon Russell in the closing seconds and sailed in for the clinching dunk.

"He's not a kid anymore," an ecstatic Harris had said after the Utah win.

With that, the Lakers were 9–0, and Bryant was the talk of NBA players and executives, a buzz that sizzled among the local media in every city the Lakers visited as November gave way to December.

"I don't want to sound blasphemous," Kings director of player personnel Jerry Reynolds told reporters, "but he really can be like Jordan."

The buzz only drove the glee of Lakers fans who wanted to see Harris play him more. So did NBA photographer Andrew Bernstein, who had spent the better part of two decades training his lens on the stardom of Magic Johnson and Michael Jordan.

"I was one of the guys who would have loved to see him in there more," Bernstein recalled. "When he was in there playing, it was like Michael was in there. It was amazing with Michael and Magic. You just put them in front of the camera, and that charisma comes out, that charm. Kobe has that, too. He's got that look, he's got that twinkle that Michael had, that Magic had. You can see it on film. And it's obvious how desperately Kobe wants to be like Michael. He's taken a lot of Michael's game and Michael's mannerisms and sort of adapted them to himself. You can see it when he comes in to the basket and he's up in the air and he does his little dipsy-doo. Sometimes he'll react like Michael did when he has a great dunk or he hits three threes in a row. He'll give you that Michael face."

With the surge, the Lakers found themselves leading the league in scoring, averaging 111.9 points per game, far ahead of the Phoenix Suns, who were second, at 103.6. Reporters began calling the Lakers the deepest team in the NBA. Six of them were averaging double figures in scoring, which allowed them to keep winning even as O'Neal, Bryant, forward/center Elden Campbell, and forward Robert Horry missed games due to various ailments. Bryant seemed to have accepted that his role that season was to come off the Lakers bench and provide scoring whenever it was needed. Almost all of his minutes would come spelling Eddie Jones at the two guard or as a backup for Fox at small forward.

Just when the team's groove seemed really good, O'Neal pulled an abdominal muscle against the Clippers, an injury so painful that it would keep him out for weeks. Suddenly the team needed Bryant's scoring even more, and he was happy to oblige, upping his average to better than 19 a game, a big number for a bench player. The Lakers, though, saw a dip in their fortunes as they adjusted to O'Neal's absence. Their 11–0 start soon sagged to 15–5. It was obvious that Bryant was too aggressive in looking for his own shot at the expense of team play. "I don't think he's aiming for triple-doubles yet," Rick Fox told reporters, in reference to Bryant's paucity of assists. "He definitely sees himself as a scorer. His mark on the court, as he sees it, is giving us 30 points in twenty minutes and then walking off with the win."

It was in O'Neal's absence that the first seed was planted. On December 12, Bryant scored 27 in a win over Houston, followed by 30 points, his career high, against Dallas two days later.

Looming on the coming road trip east was a stop in Chicago and a matchup with Jordan, which elevated the buzz about Bryant into a small-scale media moment. Suddenly reporters from virtually every magazine and news show knew they had to cover the game, all of them sensing some sort of coronation.

But Nick Van Exel saw that certain look in Jordan's eyes that suggested the contest would be decided early. True to their patented approach, the Bulls controlled the tempo, established a limited transition game that had the Lakers on ice by the end of the first quarter. The real measure of the defeat were the three fouls each that Bryant and Jones picked up in the first half, with Jones suffering through a miserable shooting night.

Bryant stalked off in the second period with his third foul just as Jordan was returning from a stretch on the bench. The teen sat dejectedly and watched Jordan score again, then flex his muscles in trademark fashion as he sauntered back down the floor.

In the third quarter of the blowout, Bryant would find the moment he was looking for, with Jordan guarding him. He cut from the left wing to the deep right frontcourt, where he received the ball and promptly executed Jordan's own trademark move on the master himself. With his back to Jordan, Bryant twitched a fake to his left as if going baseline, then pivoted hard right and elevated to stick a twenty-foot jumper right in the face of His Airness.

It was a moment to ignite both Bryant's confidence and the basketball public's perception that the game's next great player had arrived. Jordan went to the bench briefly, then returned to the game's extended garbage time for a playground-style duel with Bryant.

"Michael loves this stuff," Bulls guard Ron Harper observed afterward. "[Kobe] is a very young player who someday may take his throne, but I don't think Michael's ready to give up his throne yet. He came out to show everybody that he's Air Jordan still."

It became a night for sports-show highlight clips, with both players dancing in the post, draining jumpers from the perimeter, and weaving their way to handsome dunks. Jordan scored 36 points, and Bryant produced a career-high 33, all while wearing his new Adidas shoes.

"I had that same type of vibrancy when I was young," Jordan told reporters afterward. "It's exciting to match wits against physical skills, knowing that I've been around the game long enough that if I have to guard a Kobe Bryant...I can still hold my own."

The soon-to-be-thirty-five Jordan admitted to being a bit awed by the athleticism on display. "Did we used to jump like that? I don't remember that," he had said to teammate Scottie Pippen during a break.

"I think we did," replied Pippen, who sat out the game with an injury, "but it's so long ago I can't remember it."

"I felt like I was in the same shoes of some of the other players I've faced," Jordan said of guarding Bryant. "He certainly showed signs that he can be a force whenever he's in the game. He has a lot of different looks. As an offensive player, you want to give a lot of different looks, so that the defense is always guessing."

Jordan pointed out that, just like him, as a young, talented player, Bryant had to learn to make sure that his "taking over" didn't take away from the team effort.

"Man, that's the hardest part about ball," Bryant agreed, admitting that his urge to challenge Jordan individually had been gigantic. He said that the power to score was something he had to learn to control. "You have to just hold it back sometimes," he said. "It's so maddening. I just read how the defenses are playing me. Right now, they're playing me for the jump shot. They don't want me driving to the basket."

During a pause in play in the fourth period, Jordan was stunned to find Bryant brazenly asking advice on posting up.

"In the fourth quarter of that game, he asked me about my post-up move, in terms of, 'Do you keep your legs wide? Or do you keep your legs tight?' It was kind of shocking," Jordan said later. "I felt like an old guy when he asked me that. I told him on the offensive end you always try to feel and see where the defensive player is. In the post-up on my turnaround jump shot, I always use my legs to feel where the defense is playing so I can react to the defense. His biggest challenge will be harnessing what he knows and utilizing what he's got and implementing it on the floor. That's tough. That's experience. That's things that Larry Bird and Magic Johnson all taught me. There's no doubt that he has the skills to take over a basketball game."

The battle against Jordan generated a buzz that begat headlines and broadcast commentary, which in turn begat a bubbling pot of interest in Kobe Bryant. That, in turn, translated into All-Star votes.

Dennis Scott, of the Dallas Mavericks, soon told reporters that within a matter of a couple of years, Bryant "could be the man of this league."

Scottie Pippen agreed, saying, "The more you watch him and see some of the spectacular things he can do, you realize how great a player he is. You have to sit back and say, 'He's only a sophomore in college.' He's going to turn out to be a great pro."

All the praise and publicity came just as hundreds of thousands of fans were voting for the All-Star Game that December. Never mind that Bryant was a mere nineteen-year-old substitute, the fans voted him in as an All-Star starter, ahead of a whole range of established veterans, including Sacramento's Mitch Richmond, Utah's Jeff Hornacek, Portland's Isaiah Rider, Seattle's Hersey Hawkins, Houston's Clyde Drexler, Dallas's Michael Finley, and the player who started in front of Bryant on the Lakers, Eddie Jones. Before Bryant was voted in, the youngest All-Star starter in league history had been a twenty-year-old Magic Johnson.

It didn't hurt that the Lakers were playing well, even without O'Neal. In response to the Chicago loss, L.A. won four straight, and Bryant led the team twice in scoring, with 19 points. After a loss to the Celtics, the Lakers ripped through another streak of five wins against one loss. O'Neal returned just in time for the New Year, which dropped Bryant back down the Lakers' list of offensive priorities. Regardless, they rolled through January at a 9–4 pace, with O'Neal averaging 29 points a game and earning NBA Player of the Month honors. That momentum brought them right into a February visit from Jordan and his Bulls at the Forum.

This time the Lakers won despite Jordan scoring 31 to Bryant's 20. Bryant might have gotten caught up in the anticipation of the meeting, because his highlights from the contest were marred by poor shot selection.

"In the first half, I let my emotions dictate the tempo of my play," he admitted.

Rick Fox scored 25 to help drive a third-quarter Lakers surge that settled the contest.

It was up to the Western Conference coaches to select the All-Star substitutes, and the Lakers found themselves with four All-Star representatives as Van Exel, Jones, and O'Neal joined Bryant on the roster.

The location couldn't have been better for showcasing Bryant's new celebrity. "The All-Star Game could have been in Charlotte,"

Vaccaro recalled with a chuckle. "It was New York. Where else could you want it to be?"

Adidas hustled to get full-page Kobe ads in all the papers. The signature-shoe gamble was about to pay off. The light, twelve-ounce KB8 would remain a classic for years to come and bring the company an immediate bump in market share. Meanwhile, the NBA and its broadcast partners joined in the marketing frenzy with campaigns that juxtaposed Jordan, the game's giant, with Kobe, the upstart, a development that infuriated Karl Malone, the reigning league MVP.

The coronation began with the plastering of Bryant's image seemingly everywhere: In full-page newspaper ads promoting the All-Star Weekend and its broadcast events. On magazine covers and in international news feeds. On cable sports shows.

Each year the NBA All-Star Weekend featured a media session in which the players and coaches were brought into a huge hotel ballroom to sit at individual tables where hundreds of reporters and media crews would swarm them for questions and interviews. The forty-eighth All-Star Weekend opened with a similar publicity assault, and to no one's surprise, it was Bryant's table that immediately attracted a major throng of reporters, all squeezing in around him to videotape or record the comments of the next Jordan.

"Kobe has taken the league by storm," Orlando's Anfernee Hardaway said as he watched reporters crowding around the Bryant table.

"All this is incredible," Bryant said into the bank of microphones in his face. "My body's numb. My heart's racing. I don't know what to think. It's cool."

The dominant question, repeated often, was a request for Bryant to compare himself with Jordan. "There aren't any similarities," the teenager replied, "other than we're both six-six and we rely on athletic ability. I mean, he's Michael Jordan."

On Sunday morning, before the game, Bryant appeared on *Meet the Press* with NBA commissioner David Stern and other players. Later, when NBC broadcast a promotion for an upcoming Lakers–Rockets game, it was Bryant's image, not O'Neal's, that got top billing.

It was all enough to leave Detroit's Grant Hill shaking his head. "It makes you mature fast," he said. "It's good, but it's also a curse."

"I wanted eventually to be one of the best players in the league," Bryant would say, looking back two years later. "I just didn't know that other people would urge me to be that right away. Everybody was expecting me to be the next Michael. I thought I was going to sneak through the back door."

There was no back door for the Sunday night All-Star Game from New York, broadcast around the world. There was skinny Kobe Bryant in the starting lineup, matched up against Jordan. Sensing a show, Bryant dazzled with an array of first-quarter aerials that included a 360-degree slam and an alley-oop dunk on back-to-back possessions. Jordan was content to drop in a pair of fallaway jumpers, one of which caught Bryant in a fake and earned an added free throw.

"I came down being aggressive," Bryant told the assembly of reporters afterward. "He came back at me being aggressive. That's what it's all about. All I want to do is get a hand up, try to play him hard, try different tactics on him, see how he tries to get around me. I can use it for my knowledge in the future. He hit those two turnarounds. I was like, 'Cool, let's get it on.'"

Seattle coach George Karl, who was in charge of the West team, didn't think much of the Kobe Bryant Show, but the second half brought more of the same. With about four minutes to go in the third quarter, Bryant led a fast break and decided to finish on his own. He hid the ball behind his back with his left hand, then brought it out for a falling-down hook that dropped in as he tumbled to the baseline, with the crowd roaring as Karl frowned on the bench.

Getting the most attention was the screen that Karl Malone stepped up to set for Bryant, who waved him off.

"I got it," Bryant said.

Angered, the Utah star asked to be taken out of the contest.

Malone's comments and the ensuing media commentary later blindsided Bryant. "I probably waved him off, but I really don't remember the play," Bryant confessed.

With his team down by 15 in the third, Bryant had dropped in a three-pointer to pull the West within twelve points. At the end of the third quarter, Jordan had 17 points, 3 rebounds, and 4 assists in twenty-four minutes. Bryant's numbers were 18 points, 6 rebounds, and 1 assist in twenty-two minutes.

Coach Karl ended the Jordan versus Bryant affair by keeping the younger star on the bench for the fourth period. Jordan finished out the game and claimed All-Star Game MVP honors with 23 points, 6 rebounds, 8 assists, and 2 turnovers, all good enough to propel the East to a 135–114 victory.

"I didn't come out here to win the MVP, actually," Jordan, who had been battling a flu-like head cold, told the media. "I just wanted to make sure Kobe didn't dominate me. The hype was me against him. I knew I wasn't feeling 100 percent because I've been in bed for three days. He was just biting at the bit. I'm glad I was able to fight him off."

Later, some West veterans expressed surprise that Karl kept Bryant out of the final stage of the game, but Karl was known for using the All-Star setting to teach young players a lesson, as he did in 1994 by sending a swarming defense at Shaquille O'Neal.

Asked about Bryant, Karl said, "An All-Star Game is a mix of excitement, entertainment, and fundamentals. I thought we tried to be too entertaining."

Of the Bryant–Jordan matchup, Karl said, "I have trouble visualizing an individual challenge. It's a team game. Kobe made some great plays, but Michael and the East made better basketball decisions. Kobe will probably have the opportunity to come back here and add more 'simple' to what he's doing."

"It's tradition," Bryant told the media. "You let the veterans go in and do their thing. I was kind of happy. I just wanted to sit back, observe the whole thing, and soak it all up. This is the most fun I've ever had—Michael Jordan, my first All-Star Game in New York City. This might be his last All-Star Game. That made it incredible."

Waiting for Bryant back in Los Angeles after the event was a tough road, marked by the efforts of his coaches and teammates to "bring him back down" after the All-Star experience.

He returned to the team exhausted, but the Lakers' first game after the break was in Portland. Eddie Jones was out with the flu, meaning that Bryant would get his first and only start of the season, a Laker loss. Bryant finished with 17 points, but Harris was incensed at what he considered selfish play and poor defense against Portland's Isaiah Rider, who scored 24.

Jones was still out two nights later, back in Los Angeles, but Harris chose to start little-used Jon Barry rather than Bryant. Owner Jerry Buss appeared to be infuriated by the move and had heated words with Harris in front of reporters after the game, but the message got through clearly to Bryant.

Bryant downplayed his feelings publicly, but the circumstances only deepened his sense of alienation. "I don't start him," Harris said of his approach, "and I take him out when he doesn't play team ball. Everybody everywhere wants to see him play more. He will when he's more effective on a full-time basis. Everybody should be on the same standard. You have to play team basketball."

Bryant soon noticed that opposing defenses no longer paid him little mind. Now they sent extra defenders his way. "Early in the season, if I got by one guy, I was free," he would explain later. "But that changed."

The team lost its point guard right after the All-Star break. Van Exel went out with a knee injury that sent the Lakers as a whole spiraling into trouble. They lost seven out of the first dozen games on the schedule after the break.

It all contributed to a crisis of confidence in the "next Jordan." Bryant even suggested he was maybe "hitting the wall," the NBA term for young players reaching physical, mental, and emotional exhaustion. He made just 30 of 100 shots over one stretch, unleashing what *Sports Illustrated* would later describe as "the first rumblings of an anti-Kobe backlash."

The end of that February brought the Lakers on a road trip in which Bryant shot terribly, hitting 12 for 47 from the field through one four-game run.

"This is the toughest stretch I've ever gone through," he said at the time. "I'm hating it, but I'm loving it. It's part of the challenge, it's part of the fun. Am I pressing? Maybe. That's something I'll have to think about. I want to go through periods when I'm struggling, because that's when you learn, and the more you learn, the better you get."

Even his optimism irritated teammates, Bryant would later explain, adding that in the wake of the extensive media attention, his teammates thought he had become conceited. When writer Ian Thomsen was working on the magazine's first cover story about Bryant, he arrived in Los Angeles to begin interviews, and Eddie Jones refused to participate. Bryant was seemingly oblivious to how his teammates viewed him over much of his first two seasons, but it had become increasingly harder to ignore the volume and tenor of what was said in the locker room.

He had tried to maintain an even keel, he would say, looking back. Before the wash of attention, he had been playful and brash, talking the same trash to his teammates that they talked to him. But in the aftermath of the 1998 All-Star Game, it became increasingly clear that they interpreted his playfulness as an out-of-control ego.

"It seemed like they wanted to show me," he said.

Just weeks after the All-Star Game, *People* magazine named him to its list of the World's Most Beautiful People, generating another round of head shaking from teammates.

The result left him even more alienated. "I do my own thing," he explained when asked about off-court relationships.

"He said he was just being himself," Rick Fox observed, "but you know what? He's quickly becoming one of the main marketing tools of the NBA, which means that someone else isn't."

About the All-Star buildup, he would look back months later and remark, "I could have done without all that. That's something that the NBA wanted to do, that they felt like they needed to do. It was a growing process for me. It made me mature a lot faster, being under the microscope like that. I would have been happy to let my game speak for itself."

But, he added, "the league is always looking for something splashy, something spectacular. It's always a formula that they look for. They look for energy, they look for excitement."

O'Neal, in particular, continued to point out that he wanted to win a championship immediately and didn't have time to wait on Bryant to grow up. The Lakers season quickly fell into a finger-pointing session. Soon the L.A. papers were running stories that the players had met and voted 12–0 to ask that Harris be fired. The team downplayed those reports, but on their road trip, they had the look of a group about to come apart at the seams.

Bryant's shooting percentage had dropped to 34 percent, down from 45 percent before the outpouring of hype. With his decline in effectiveness, his playing time also fell, and his scoring average dropped to 14 points per game. Even so, Jordan's words remained strong in his mind, and he was determined to find a way to meet the demands of his coaches while pursuing his offensive ideal. "It's important to tone it down somewhat and stay within the team concept," he said. "But I'm aggressive. It's also important not to lose the aggressiveness."

When Bryant played poorly in a loss to Washington to end the road trip, his decline seemed to reach a low point.

"When I first came into the NBA," he told a reporter, "I was one of the first to come out of high school. I was seventeen years old — at the time the NBA was much more grown-up. It wasn't like now. I thought that you come into the NBA, you play basketball all day. The thing I was most excited about was coming to the NBA not having to, you know, not having to worry about writing a paper or doing homework. It was basketball all day, this is awesome."

The actual practice of playing in the NBA had been far more complicated than he realized, as had his means of dealing with it. He claimed that he hadn't even seen that he was acting withdrawn, he said. "The aloofness thing, honestly, I didn't really hear about it until later. A lot of it was just naïve, because I didn't read the papers. I didn't watch, like, the news. I had no clue what was going on, what people were saying about me. It sounds silly to say, but it's true. And I think because of that, a lot of people looked at it like, 'Woah, he must be arrogant.' But I didn't know what the hell was going on. I had a reporter one day come up to me and ask me about it, you know, 'People think you're arrogant, what's up with that?' And it absolutely just seemed to come out of left field. I was just like, 'What are you talking about?' And he was like, 'Haven't you read the papers?' From that day forward, I started reading the papers."

Cracks in the Foundation

Eddie Jones's reward for his hard work and good play that season had been the persistent rumor that he was about to be traded to the Sacramento Kings for guard Mitch Richmond. "I don't want to go to Sac," Jones told reporters.

Indeed, Jerry West had worked hard heading into the All-Star trade deadline to arrange the deal, the idea being that Richmond provided just the type of tough leadership and scoring that the young club needed. But Jerry Buss nixed the deal, pointing out that Richmond would soon be thirty-four and would soon need an expensive new contract.

The incident was a bitter for defeat for West, Del Harris said, looking back. And it marked the first major crack in his relationship with Buss. The owner had added a new level of legal approval for each move planned by West.

As the season wore on and the team threatened to unravel, West sat up nights, poring over every detail. He even went so far as to announce that he would step down as executive vice president by the end of the following season. As the play-offs approached, reporters speculated about his future, and West backed off a bit, saying he wouldn't make a decision until August. "I want to get myself calmed down," he told them, "where I don't have to worry about wins and losses, where I don't have to worry about injuries. Let somebody else worry about that."

The game was simple enough, but his young, talented roster was making it so complicated. Both he and the owner were losing faith in the players and in Harris.

"Talent and character win in this league; effort doesn't always win," he confided to *Los Angeles* magazine. "We win games sometimes when we're simply more talented. What I would like to see is for us to grow up more, become more professional in our approach to the game. And if there's some way you could give someone a pill to give them six or seven years of experience in the league..."

Wanting to tell them these things, he composed a letter to his young Lakers and delivered it to them soon after they returned from their trip east in the early days of March.

"Each of you are on the verge of letting this season slip right through your fingers," he wrote.

They responded by ringing up up twenty-two wins and just three losses over the last weeks of the regular season. Bryant hit a late three to seal a defeat of Utah in the last game of the regular season, after which Del Harris declared that it was his young charge's best performance of the year. Big, burly Antoine Carr of the Jazz appeared in the Lakers locker room afterward, looking for Bryant. Although he had Magic Johnson's old locker, the young guard dressed in an area separate from his teammates and often appeared for postgame interviews in a fine Italian suit. Spying Bryant, Carr presented a pair of shoes. "Sign these for my son?" he asked.

It seemed that good things might be ahead. After all, the Lakers had surpassed West's hopes of a sixty-win season with a 61–21 finish. Their record left them third best in the league, behind the sixty-two wins of Utah and Chicago. Across the NBA there was an increasingly loud chorus saying that the Lakers were poised to claim the league championship. They had been only the third team since the deployment of a shot clock in 1954 to lead the league in scoring while holding their opponents under 100 points.

All throughout this late-season surge, Harris had kept Bryant on a short tether, using him as a defensive pressure point with Eddie Jones but always yanking him back to the bench if his offensive efforts displayed a hint of the Jordanesque. Even so, he managed to finish the season with an impressive scoring average of 15.2 points per game.

Still, his public image had continued to take a beating. During the play-offs, an L.A. TV station ran a poll to see if fans thought the Lakers were better with or without Bryant. Fifty-five percent of the respondents said they were better without him. The poll would become a popular talking point about Bryant. Soon talk radio and newspaper columnists took up the subject. Even play-off opponents talked it up.

Bryant seemed to have his own answer, scoring 11 points down the stretch in the fourth quarter to forge a 104–102 victory in Game 1 of the Lakers' first-round series against Portland. He hardly played the next two games, then hit for 22 in a blowout that sealed the series for Los Angeles.

Up next were George Karl and Seattle, also winners of sixty-one games. Bryant played little in a blowout loss in Game 1. In Game 2, he sat out with the flu, and the Lakers won, which encouraged Harris to keep him on the bench for Game 3 as well. The Lakers again won, prompting Seattle's Sam Perkins to say that the Lakers didn't need Bryant, adding, "It seems like they're more at ease without him."

"What people didn't realize," Bryant would say later, "is that I could have played in those games. Del just didn't want me to play. You never knew what he was going to do."

In Game 4, Harris played Bryant just three minutes, and then eleven minutes in Game 5, as the Lakers closed out the series.

"More than anything it made me so anxious, made me so hungry just to play every aspect of the game," Bryant would say later. "I'd be sitting on the bench hearing the coaches say, 'Man, we've got to get some rebounds.' And it made me mad that I couldn't contribute. Besides seeing what the team was doing positively, it just made me hungry to go out there and help them any way I could."

"I know he felt he could have done more during those years if I had allowed him to do more," Harris recalled. "And he could have. It's just that we didn't need that at that time."

The Lakers advanced to the conference finals to once again face the Utah Jazz. Before the series, the coach warned Bryant that the team was playing well and he might not see much playing time.

The move to keep Bryant out of action through the early rounds had been approved by West, Harris said, looking back. "I never made a major move, even in a lineup, without going in and telling Jerry, 'Here's what I'm thinking. What do you think?' I always ran it past him first. The truth is, I mean, if Jerry had ever said, 'You know, you're really making a mistake—he needs to be in that lineup,' I would have done it. We had that kind of relationship."

The Jazz rolled out to a 40–15 lead in Game 1, and all the Lakers' play-off insecurities reappeared. On offense, the Jazz executed their screen-and-roll game to perfection. On defense, they weren't double-teaming O'Neal, which allowed them to keep focus on the Lakers perimeter. Van Exel shot 28 percent for the series, Fisher 34.8 percent, Bryant 36.7 percent, Elden Campbell 21.4 percent, Horry 36 percent, and Fox 40 percent.

"Harris kept expecting the guards to warm up, but it never happened," recalled Mitch Chortkoff, the veteran L.A. sportswriter.

Game 3 was perhaps the worst defeat, with the Lakers obviously clueless on their fabled home court, in the Great Western Forum, their fans offering their disapproval. Afterward, Bryant defiantly told reporters that the Lakers could still win the series. "Do you really believe that?" one media figure asked incredulously. "I guarantee you nobody else in this room thinks you can."

"Yeah, I do," Bryant replied.

The Lakers fell in four straight games.

Chapter 20

CHAOS THEORY

Despite all his sadness and frustration heading into his third season, Kobe Bryant still realized that there was much that he liked about his life. In fact, he was just like the Randy Newman song played at Lakers games, minus the irony—he loved L.A. He loved the entire vibe, loved the ocean, arching its silvery back every time he looked out his window, loved the stark, yellow hills when he took a spin up the Pacific Coast Highway. When he headed into town, he loved the tall palms silhouetted at night against the ever-present orange glow of the city, loved the rows of A-list celebrities hanging on his every move at his games, loved bringing juice to a sleepy crowd when he dunked, loved the laid-back Malibu beaches with the surfer dudes everywhere, loved hangin' in his pool, just doing nothing but letting the water do its work, loved just about all of it, right down to the BMW and the Escalade in his driveway.

And he loved his bank accounts, the sense of power, the whole psychological bump that accompanied the growing numbers. The truly fat cash came rolling in starting with the 1998 off-season. The Lakers rewarded him with a player contract worth $71 million, and his Adidas deal was upgraded to a reported $48 million; plus, he had an array of endorsement contracts with Sprite, Spalding, and other concerns, including his own Nintendo game. Sister Sharia, now pregnant, was both astounded and exasperated by the Nintendo TV ads that kept invading a show she was watching with her brother. "You're haunting me," she told him. "I'm so tired of seeing your face. Get away from me!"

Armed with her degree, Sharia had moved to L.A. with her husband to begin working for Bryant's marketing company, but soon enough she stopped going to malls with Kobe because of the growing number of autograph requests. "Sure, no problem," he would say while she waited. You stop to sign one, suddenly you're signing fifty.

NBA photographer Andrew Bernstein saw much the same when he traveled with the team. The autograph seekers were always there, whenever the Lakers' bus pulled up in front of hotels. Two years in, Bryant was still that most precious of commodities in L.A.'s entertainment industry: he was the next big thing. He had a greater store of naïveté to deplete before the cynicism set in. In some ways, that was what his older teammates resented most about him, that sway of brilliant youth he held over them, the sheer fucking audacity of it. They may have had their college, but he had a magic about him that they could never have.

Bernstein would watch him dutifully go out of his way to sign autographs for fans while his teammates headed up to their rooms. Nobody much wanted their scribble anyway, not really. If Bryant was in too big a rush, headed to practice, he always left the signature hounds with a promise to hang around; he'd catch them afterward. And he would. And they would always be there.

Agent Arn Tellem was beside himself with joy at the deals coming their way, with Bryant now raking in an estimated $5 million a year in off-the-court income. "The opportunities are incredible," Tellem remarked, his slightest trace of a double chin spreading as he grinned. "Most players have shoe deals and one or two others, but the opportunities Kobe has had are far greater than any other team athlete, aside from Jordan—and Kobe's have come quicker."

Despite a looming labor lockout for the NBA, Adidas made ready to release his second signature shoe, the KB8 II, which meant a full off-season calendar in the summer of 1998, including a month in Asia for Adidas, lighting up basketball camps from Korea to the Philippines to Australia to Japan. It was there that he learned how to handle the overwhelming, adoring crowds that glommed onto him on that side of the world. Pick a point. Keep your eye on it and keep walking. That became the routine.

He finally returned from Asia and took a brief rest, long enough to attend a quick benefit bowling event and to make a visit to Tellem's office, where he sat with his agent's children and wondered aloud if Jordan would really retire. Then he headed off to Europe for more Adidas camps, more crowds, more sheer awe at the world's response to him. He had a charm and enthusiasm for the kids in the camps unlike anything his Lakers teammates ever saw.

"When I went on the Europe tour and overseas in Asia, I was treated like a pop star," he said at the time, his voice reflecting a bit of wonder at the thousands of young kids screaming at him at the events. It was fun, but it was also an adjustment. From a young age, he had always known how to find his privacy, which now proved helpful in his avoiding a sense of being overwhelmed.

The financial windfall would bring some changes to the Bryant estate atop the mountain in Pacific Palisades.

"He was a kid," Del Harris recalled. "He lived with his mom and dad."

Every day was still his birthday around the house, just like when he was a kid, but it was starting to get really old. His mother made his breakfast to order each morning and tidied up his world. She even planned his birthday parties and other functions, which left them with a somewhat artificial and empty feel that only emphasized his real pain.

"He had no friends," Vaccaro explained. "No one to talk to. Not really."

His mom packed his travel bag and often tucked in one of his favorite videos, *Willy Wonka and the Chocolate Factory*, for all the reclusive hours he spent in hotel rooms. He had never been allowed to see the *Godfather* movies, but now he saw them and loved them—not for the violence, he said, but for the strong family bonds and because he loved everything Italian. Soon he would have a new niece and would become infatuated with her, spending his off hours on the road, shopping at Disney stores for gifts to shower her with. When Sharia and her husband soon began talking of moving out of the family home, Bryant couldn't understand. Why would Sharia want to distance herself from family?

But it wouldn't be long before Bryant himself had some of the same feelings. His mother's role in things had been valuable and natural, considering his age going into the league, but it was one destined for a painful transition as he matured.

After all, in addition to being a pro basketball player, Bryant was a rap artist, signed to a major studio recording deal and under pressure to deliver product for the entertainment industry. Anthony Bannister and other members of his music group were living in L.A., attempting to make progress with the huge challenge, all while Bryant was sorting out his complicated world with the Lakers. "I don't talk about guns and drugs and stuff," he said of his rap work. "That wouldn't make any sense."

Some songs would be about competition, some about himself. Much of it was obviously a search for nuance in a business and genre that had little time for that.

The situation also posed an increasingly uncomfortable issue with drug and alcohol use, particularly marijuana. So many musicians operated in a cloud of reefer that brought texture to their world of sound. Athletes were known to have their fun as well, except perhaps among those absolutely ruthless top competitors. But getting high was still a severe no-no with Kobe Bryant, as it was in high school. It just didn't seem possible to try to expand your mind and your game at the same time.

Coming to terms with such conflicts marked his transition into adulthood. Bryant, over the years, would make frequent use of the term "grown-assed man." He was attempting to become one of those as he turned twenty that August.

"He had brought out those kids in the singing group," recalled a family friend. "I remember that it just happened very quickly. He brought them out, put them in a house down the street from him."

The move wouldn't sit well with Pam, said the friend. "That was sort of, like, the first thing that he did without her blessing. But then there's this struggle that goes along with the question, what are you going to control and how are you going to control it? So she began picking and choosing her battles."

Pam Bryant was quite watchful of her son's income, and for good reason. From lottery winners to entertainment figures to sports stars, the pattern is well established. The injection of large sums of money into people's lives changes them, often dramatically, and not always for the better.

Sometimes the battles Mrs. Bryant chose seemed petty. "One thing really turned me off," explained the friend. "I was at the house and a kid brought a pizza to the house to deliver, a young kid. She didn't tip him. I was mortified. She gave him nothing. She wanted her exact change back. I mean, I was a waitress for a lot of my life. You would hear these things about players not tipping, but for her to do that at this ten-thousand-square-foot house was extraordinary."

One factor may have been the family's experience in Europe, where tipping was less of a custom than in the United States. Still, it struck the friend and others that money was beginning to change the Bryants.

Pam's parents visited fairly often and were delightful people, recalled the friend, but Big Joe was left behind, still on Willows Avenue, content to follow his grandson's wondrous new life on TV and with updates from Joe, which he would pass on to the family's adoring readers in the *Tribune*. Big Joe remained the Philadelphia connection for one of the city's greatest fairy tales.

Soon, some who visited the household observed an increasing level of anger in Kobe, apparently over the living arrangements. On one hand, he very much remained the loving son and brother, the kid who still hid in the bushes in a *Scream* mask and a long, black overcoat to frighten his sisters when they came up the walk. But on the other, it was awkward when he and Bannister brought girls back to the house he shared with his parents.

In an effort to get a little more distance from the family, Bryant purchased the home directly behind and down the slope from his Pacific Palisades manse for them to move into. That, in turn, required another huge decorating effort by his mother and sizable bills for more art and decor.

"They moved into the house down the hill," the friend recalled. "They were going to build this elaborate staircase down the hillside to their house. It was going to cost a ridiculous amount of money so they could climb up and down these steps."

No one apparently saw at the time that the whole arrangement was a great big metaphor for the parents' slipping grasp on control. Once finished, the staircase looked interesting, if only they could have maintained a reason to use it. Bryant clearly wanted the space to find his own independent adult life, but he admitted that his dedication to the game required so much, it was difficult to pursue relationships with either friends or lovers.

Despite such issues, things would have been quite good for young Mr. Bryant if not for the frustration in his professional life and the creeping awareness that he needed to find someone to be with. Considering his constant career focus, the harsh truth was that he was looking for a relationship to microwave, a deal that he could close without costing his competitive focus too much edge. He talked of retreating to Italy with a young wife, to raise a family far away from the fears of school violence in America.

Go, Fish

Heading into his third pro season, Bryant had continued furiously polishing his signature one-on-one move, often working on it alone in the grand old Forum, where the championship banners and the retired numbers of former great Lakers hung about the court, urging him on to glory. In fact, his summer workouts were conducted almost entirely with personal trainer Joe Carbone alone, even though Los Angeles was known for its high-test summer pickup basketball games among top pros. Bryant simply avoided all of that to grind away on improving his game, shooting more than 1,000 shots each and every day.

Though he continued to doggedly improve his game, Bryant had seen nothing in his two seasons to dent his belief that he could beat any player in the league off the dribble, if only Shaquille O'Neal would move his big ass out of the lane to give him room to attack.

Indeed, the move off the dribble would become the signature of his career in many ways. Bryant would work the ball, flexing his body and his focus, the ball moving rhythmically from fingertip to fingertip between his legs, his arms flaring to the sides like wings while his neck stiffened and his eyes grew still. He seemed to be looking nowhere and everywhere at the same time. Then he shifted left and assumed the same threatening pose. Who knew how many hours he'd spent working alone, perfecting this shifting setup for the crossover? Right. Left. Right. Left. Over and over again.

In the context of a game, the move was absolutely threatening, reptilian, like a cobra mesmerizing its target before the strike (several years later, Bryant would name himself Black Mamba as a testament to the approach). His neck would arch oddly as he prepared to flex his fake and locked in his peripheral vision, surveying the floor without giving up his intention. "I can still see the court," he explained. "Even if I have my head down sometimes, I can see it."

This instant created dread for opponents. Bryant may have been young, but he could embarrass people, driving right by them to the basket.

"It's the rhythm," he said proudly. "The defender can't do anything about it. He'll either back up, or close the gap even more. As for the eyes, it depends on who's guarding you. Some defenders like to look right here at your belt buckle. Other defenders like to look in your eyes. To see if they can follow the basketball."

So Bryant turned on the rhythmic dance. Flex right. Flex left. Explode. A quick fake, and he was off to the hole in his imaginary world in the empty Forum. In real games, he regularly displayed the reach, quickness, and leaping ability to knife his way through a defense to get to the rim. He often drew a foul, and because he shot hundreds of free throws a day, he was a high-percentage foul shooter. His penetration always meant trouble for opponents, unless, of course, it made trouble for Bryant himself and the Lakers.

"You can see when he goes into brain lock," observed one longtime Lakers staff member. "He'll dribble about fifteen times between his legs, and then he'll try to beat three defenders going to the basket. When he does that, a couple of things usually happen. He either gets in trouble and takes a bad shot, or he makes a bad pass."

Since he mostly worked out alone, his teammates rarely saw him developing his game. Between the obvious talent, the inexperience, and his reclusive nature, Bryant presented quite a mystery. Derek Fisher had come in as a rookie with Bryant, had played with him for two seasons, and still had absolutely no idea who the kid was.

The Lakers themselves had posed quite a mystery for the fans and for the media covering them until Fisher began to speak frankly in 1999 about Bryant and team chemistry. It was over the summer of 1998 that Fisher finally decided he needed to break through Bryant's isolation. "I had never just had a personal conversation with Kobe, or anything to get a better feel for who he is and what makes him tick as a person," the older guard explained.

Bryant's silence had left teammates with the impression that he considered himself above them. "He really is to himself," Fisher explained at the time, "so you don't know exactly how he feels. You don't know what makes him happy, what makes him sad. So it was hard for us early on to understand what he was going through, what he was trying to do, and that he was really trying to be a part of the team. But the way he played was just the way he knew how to play."

As a point guard, Fisher felt it incumbent upon himself to try to reach out, to improve the team's chemistry.

"I just kind of started thinking that we possibly could be the backcourt of the future for this organization," Fisher explained, "and that it was going to be really important for us to have some type of bond. We may not raise each other's kids and be godparents and do things like that for each other's families, but we had to have a working relationship. And that's when I kind of started. Even though he wasn't necessarily reaching out, I kind of started reaching out, trying to be more talkative, just trying to maybe spark conversation about anything just to get to know him a little better."

Over time, Fisher suspected that Bryant's silence might be a defense mechanism. As Bryant himself had told the media the previous season, he wasn't even aware of just how stark his manner appeared to teammates. It was almost as if Bryant feared that taking a more personal approach with the other Lakers might open him up to being swayed from his dreams and his goals. "From day one, he knew the things that he wanted to accomplish in his career," Fisher said. "Things that he's wanted to achieve, he already had that in mind. Because of his talent level, it's almost like a self-fulfilling prophecy for him. If he sees something, he can go and get it."

As a young, ambitious star, Bryant appeared to have a confidence and a power that other players didn't, Fisher explained. "When he entered the league, he had all of these things in mind, that he wanted to be an All-Star, that he wanted to be a starter, that he wanted to average 20 points a game. All of these things that eventually happened for him, he saw them. He wanted to come in and do those things, but he didn't want to come in talking about them. He has a certain confidence that other people don't have and can't carry.

"The more you experience time around him and get to see him in different situations, the more you understand that that's all it is, is confidence," Fisher explained. "It's not arrogance. It's not his personality. He's not a selfish person. He's not a guy that only thinks of himself. He's just a guy who has an immeasurable amount of confidence in his ability to play the game."

Fisher's off-season study of Kobe Bryant went longer than expected that late summer of 1998 because the NBA entered a lockout, a financial struggle between the league's owners and players. It was unknown how long the lockout would last, but it soon stretched into the new year as months of the season were lost to conflict. As negotiators tried to iron out the final details of a new labor agreement that January, players from each team got together for informal sessions to help prepare for when their teams could officially begin practice.

That was how Shaquille O'Neal, Derek Fisher, Corie Blount, and Bryant found themselves playing two-on-two in mid-January. The gathering was unique in that Bryant rarely played with teammates outside practice. It remained obvious that Bryant's struggles with his teammates from the previous season had cut deep into their relationships. His basic strategy for dealing with the other Lakers was to talk as little as possible.

"There are times you'll ask him a question, and he'll say yes or no. And that'll be it," Fisher observed at the time. "Other times he'll be a little more expressive. But Kobe does such a good job of never allowing people to know what's going on with him, how he's feeling or what he's thinking."

With his efforts the previous summer, Fisher had slowly begun to make progress in his efforts with Bryant. "I tried to find ways that we could just talk," he recalled. "Talk about things not even related to basketball, how his family was doing, things like that. I knew one of his sisters had gotten married and was pregnant. I'd ask how she was doing. He was fairly responsive."

Bryant was understandably suspicious of Fisher's efforts. The young guard had seen too many times when he was open on the wing in transition, the perfect situation for him to attack the basket, only to be disappointed by Fisher's failure to get him the ball. Sometimes, however, the two guards found themselves training in the same place at the same time that off-season. Bryant eyed how hard Fisher worked on his shooting and his conditioning. Work ethic was the one standard by which Bryant measured another player.

They had been friendly enough that Bryant agreed to play two-on-two with Fisher and Shaquille O'Neal and Blount in January 1999, a situation made dicey by the fact that Bryant approached any such game as all-out combat. That was how he had always done things, dating back to his days as a kid battling his father in one-on-one. They had always taken an extremely physical approach to their matchups, using elbows, hip checks, hard box-outs, and any other advantage available. After all, he and his father could battle furiously and then laugh about it.

That approach had long proved an irritant to Bryant's Lakers teammates. Only Eddie Jones seemed to relish the exchanges, which meant that he and Bryant would have furious battles in practice yet never feel the need to carry it beyond that. "I'm gonna bust your ass," Bryant would tell Jones during their little wars, which only drove the intensity higher.

For others, it was just another reason to dislike the teenager.

"That really was the way we all should have been competing," Fisher said later, looking back. "With Kobe's spirit."

That January pickup game would stand as a watershed moment in the Shaq–Kobe relationship. More than five weeks later, word that O'Neal had slapped Bryant during practice would leak into the L.A. newspapers. The reports didn't detail when the incident happened or what was involved, but it would be cited as a sign of their growing dislike for each other. Fisher remembered being amazed at those newspaper reports because they came so long after the incident and because there had been only four people in the gym at the time. Others, including Bryant, would later say no one got slapped that day.

"It had just been physical," Fisher recalled. "Both guys had gotten tired. Neither guy really started it. It started just from them both being physical."

According to reports, Bryant had supposedly ended up on the floor. "I think he really thought he could take Shaq," one Lakers player told a reporter. "I have to give him that: he has no fear of anything."

"Some true feelings came out," Fisher said. "They didn't really say all that much, but it was done in an extremely negative way. You could tell the guys had negative thoughts for each other."

The altercation would have repercussions, Fisher said. "It would always be remembered."

O'Neal had been wanting to make a point with Bryant, one Lakers staff member explained. "It sent a message, but Kobe didn't receive it."

Yet the process had still brought Fisher a new appreciation for his teammate, for his fire and desire for the game. He had this air, this confidence, that, frankly, Fisher envied. He wasn't yet sure that he liked Bryant, but he respected the hell out of him.

Capital

The 1999 NBA season looked like it just might not happen, but after months of the owner-imposed lockout, the players' association and the owners reached an agreement, shortly after Bryant and O'Neal's fateful two-on-two game. It came with a major blow for Bryant, because the new collective-bargaining agreement capped

Kobe Bryant celebrates winning the 2010 NBA championship over the Boston Celtics. This fifth title was his crowning achievement as an NBA player. (Nathaniel S. Butler/National Basketball Association/ Getty Images)

Joe Bryant began his NBA career with the Philadelphia 76ers. (Full Court Press)

Pam and Joe Bryant at one of Joe's legal hearings in 1976. (Bettmann/ Getty Images)

Kobe Bryant (*lower left*) on the 1996 Sonny Hill all-star team coached by Vontez Simpson. (Full Court Press)

With his Lower Merion teammates and coach Gregg Downer (*center-right*), who came together in 2012. (AP Photo/Douglas M. Bovitt)

Bryant famously announced he was bypassing college to enter the NBA draft in 1996. (AP Photo/Rusty Kennedy)

With Lakers team executive Jerry West (*left*) and coach Del Harris upon Bryant's trade from Charlotte to the Lakers in 1996. (Steve Grayson/WireImage/Getty Images)

Bryant was a huge hit as a seventeen-year-old rookie in the 1996 NBA summer league. (AP Photo/Michael Caulfield)

By his second NBA season, Bryant was beyond eager to match up with his idol, Michael Jordan. (Vincent Laforet/AFP/Getty Images)

With father Joe. (Andy Hayt/National Basketball Association/Getty Images)

Bryant and Shaquille O'Neal found championship chemistry in the
2000 playoffs. (Icon Sportswire via AP Images)

Author Roland Lazenby talking with Bryant and then-fiancée Vanessa
Laine during the locker room celebration of the Lakers' 2000 NBA
championship. (Jorge Ribeiro/Full Court Press)

With wife Vanessa at a news conference after sexual assault charges were filed against Bryant in July 2003. (AP Photo/Jerome T. Nakagawa)

Joe and Pam Bryant make a rare appearance at a Lakers game in 2004. (AP Photo/Jae C. Hong)

Elevating during his 81-point game against the Toronto Raptors in 2006. (AP Photo/Matt A. Brown)

Phil Jackson, Bryant, and Tex Winter (*left to right*) during the 2007 play-offs. (Andrew D. Bernstein/National Basketball Association/Getty Images)

Bryant celebrates Team USA's Olympic victory over Spain on the way to the gold medal in August 2008. (AP Photo/Eric Gay)

Bryant and his family celebrate his passing Michael Jordan on the NBA's all-time scoring list in 2015. (AP Photo/Mark J. Terrill)

During his final game in Philadelphia, Bryant greeted Philly hoops legend and old family friend Sonny Hill. (AP Photo/Matt Rourke)

After a tough 2015–16 season, Lakers fans were eager to celebrate Bryant's last game at Staples Center. (Lorna Tansey/Full Court Press)

Bryant's point total rose rapidly on the scoreboard during the fourth quarter of his last game at Staples Center, April 13, 2016. (Lorna Tansey/Full Court Press)

the size of the contract he could sign, trimming a deal that could have run well in excess of $100 million down to $71 million. In one fell swoop, he lost better than $30 million. His agent and his father had both pointed out that losing such money was no small thing. Bryant was one of only five players to vote against it.

"I felt good about what I did," Bryant said of his vote. "I can live with my decision. I hope everybody else can."

Despite his disappearance from the rotation during the 1998 play-offs, the Lakers seemed more focused than ever on his role as the future of the franchise.

"He's a twenty-year-old kid who has more energy than the whole team put together," Jerry West told a reporter. "When he looks at his game, all he needs to do is slow down, read situations, and not take the whole thing on himself. He's a big draw, and he's one of those guys you just sit back and say, 'Hmmm, I wonder what he's going to be like when he's twenty-five.'"

Howard Beck had begun covering the Lakers for the L.A. Daily News in that period and found Bryant surprisingly relaxed and genial, far different from how he was viewed by teammates.

"He did not carry himself like this young phenom," Beck recalled. "Much different, by the way, than what I later would see with LeBron James. You know, LeBron walked into the league feeling like he was the king, and acting like it. Kobe wasn't like that. Kobe didn't take on all the usual aspects of an NBA star, as we would think of them or the stereotype of them. He didn't have an entourage. He didn't wear jewelry. He didn't have tattoos back then. He didn't have a piercing.

"Kobe came in with a very squeaky-clean image, and he especially stood in contrast to his draft classmate Iverson, who came in as this brash hip-hop figure," Beck observed. "Everybody was so caught up in the idea of street cred back then, and Kobe somehow didn't have it because he was the wealthy suburban kid who grew up in Italy and then played in Lower Merion. He was mostly comfortable with who he was, but it bothered him that people would create these narratives of 'Well, Iverson is the genuine guy because of the way he looks, and Kobe's not genuine because of the way he looks and the way he speaks and where he was raised as a kid.'"

The inevitable comparisons with Philadelphia's star guard intrigued Bryant as much as anyone. In a private moment with a trusted reporter friend, he would ask if people thought Iverson was a better player. "AI's cool," Bryant said. "We talk."

On this and an array of questions, Bryant was relaxed and open with the media, Beck remembered. "I thought he was a really good dude. I enjoyed talking to him. There were no airs about him. He didn't hold himself at a distance. Those early years, it was rare to ever hear him curse. Like, he wasn't one to drop f-bombs in front of us. He wasn't one to talk tough. He was just an easygoing kid."

In some regards, Bryant was much like a child star, apart from the worldlier actors around him. He had no security guards keeping the world at bay in those days. Neither was he into self-promotion or the politicking with reporters that marked O'Neal's approach.

Announced on the cusp of training camp, his new six-year contract started at $9 million a season, with annual raises of no more than 12.5 percent. "It's quite a relief," Bryant said of the agreement. "So, we don't have to go through the whole season with people asking, 'Well, when is the deal? What's happening?'"

It was quite a raise from his previous contract, in which he was scheduled to earn $1.3 million for 1999. Although he professed not to be overly concerned by money, there was little way to inhabit the strange and rarefied atmosphere of the NBA and not be affected by it. Jordan himself viewed money as just another means of keeping score in his vast, personal competitive landscape.

Jordan, in fact, had made the league richer. With more money available, even West was caught in the throes of a financial standoff with Jerry Buss. Supposedly, the owner had promised the team's executive VP a $2 million bonus, then held off on delivering it. Faced with Buss reneging, West began hinting to reporters that he was thinking about leaving the Lakers to work for another team, which displeased O'Neal himself.

"If Jerry West would leave for health reasons that would be understandable," O'Neal told reporters. "If he would leave for any other reason I would be very, very upset. Jerry West is the reason I came to the Lakers."

In fact, West was the one lifeline between Bryant and O'Neal.

They both respected him immensely, and he, in turn, made his own efforts to get them working together better.

Eventually, the bonus was paid and West was given a fat, new contract, set to kick in at the start of the 1999–2000 season. At least part of Buss's reluctance to pay out extra money stemmed from the reshuffling of the team ownership structure to include Rupert Murdoch's Fox entertainment conglomerate as a minority partner, and plans to move the Lakers into Staples Center, a $300-million building under construction in downtown Los Angeles, for the 1999–2000 season.

The clearest sign of Buss's financial maneuverings was the team's decision not to renew Del Harris's contract before the 1999 season, despite the fact that he had just driven the team to sixty-one wins and the conference finals, that coming after he had bettered the team's win totals each season he had been on the job. The coach went into the schedule as a lame duck, and everyone involved sensed that the situation wouldn't fly very long.

Ol' 99

Although shortened, Bryant's third season was anticipated by fans and media alike to be the moment when he would assume a bigger role with the team. "We're hoping this is the year it all falls into place for Kobe," Del Harris told reporters. The only question was, where would he start? At two guard, Eddie Jones was an All-Star who had played well down the stretch of 1998, so the two of them presented management with something of a traffic jam. It was Rick Fox's foot injury and Robert Horry's heart issue that wound up solving the problem in the short term. Both players would miss time, which opened up a spot for Bryant at small forward, a move he solidified with his early-season performances, even though West considered him obviously more suited as a guard.

Among its other issues, the team had a void at power forward and badly needed someone to help O'Neal with the rebounding and defensive chores.

West had tried to trade for Tom Gugliotta or Charles Oakley but had no success, leaving both O'Neal and Jerry Buss pushing for the team to sign free agent Dennis Rodman. O'Neal told reporters that he needed a "thug" to play alongside him in the Lakers frontcourt. West, though, was wary of Rodman's age and unbridled nature.

The shortened schedule meant the deliberation was rushed. Because the labor lockout had cut more than three months out of the 1998–99 schedule, everything about the schedule was condensed. Usually training camp and eight or nine preseason games were scheduled across the month of October for each team, but the 1999 season didn't start until February, meaning that teams had just two weeks to prepare. And once the games did resume, the NBA was forced to reduce the season to fifty games and cram it into eighty-nine days—and three games into three nights, on some occasions.

Once the lockout was lifted, fans seemed reluctant to support the NBA the way they once had. Jordan, the most popular player in the history of the game, had retired. After the financial disputes, the league was just trying to get back to business as usual, but from the start of the season, attendance and television ratings drooped. So did scoring and shooting percentages. Across the league, fans, players, and coaches found themselves trying to cope with a strange season. "Our attendance is flat, maybe it's down a percent, our television rating, I'll call it flat," NBA commissioner David Stern told reporters. "To me, it doesn't matter. If we can somehow stay about average for the rest of the season, we would have achieved a great success, especially with cynics saying we were dead and buried."

Injuries sidelined a number of key players, leaving teams clearly feeling the ill effects of the rushed schedule. "Man, this is a dog year," the New York Knicks' Larry Johnson said. "A lot of guys are going to be out on the floor with some kind of hurt, but you just deal with it."

Teams weren't playing as well. Shots were missed. Scores were low. Turnovers were high. However, Bryant's extensive off-season conditioning work, a study of Scottie Pippen's defensive techniques, and his focus on offensive footwork meant that he charged out of the gate with a burst of energy that revealed just why the Lakers had committed so much money to a mere twenty-year-old.

"There's not a small forward in the league who can guard Kobe," Derek Harper — a veteran guard who was brought on at the beginning of the season — pointed out, adding that the only person stopping Bryant would be Bryant himself. "That's Kobe's biggest challenge," Harper said. "Knowing when to go, and knowing when to slow."

In the Lakers' season-opening win over the Houston Rockets, he snagged a career-high 10 rebounds, used his defense to frustrate the Rockets, and unveiled his new offensive skills to slash his way to 25 points.

The rebounding was immediately seized upon as a sign of his maturity. It was dirty work, but it was what his team needed. To prove that he was determined about it, he added another dozen boards in the Lakers' second game, a home loss to Utah.

The very next night, they traveled to San Antonio for a key road win, and Bryant fought his way to another 10 rebounds against the Spurs' large front line. Then, over the next two games, he kept it up, going for 10 rebounds a game, a threefold jump over the 3.1 boards he had averaged in 1998.

"I've added a lot of dimensions to my game," he said. "My mind-set coming into this season was to try to be a better rebounder, and be better defensively, try to cause some havoc on the defensive side.... Obviously I didn't know I was going to be a starter — so that gives me more chances to get rebounds."

It would have been interesting, perhaps, to see how things would have progressed with Del Harris, Eddie Jones, Elden Campbell, Van Exel, and the rest of the Lakers talent. But Jerry Buss was a man ready to deal. After the preseason and opening dozen games, Del Harris was fired, and assistant Kurt Rambis was promoted into the head job — on the same day that the team added free agent Dennis Rodman to the roster. After just eleven more games, the team decided to work a major trade, sending Eddie Jones and Elden Campbell to the Charlotte Hornets for what would essentially be Glen Rice and J. R. Reid. After a month of turmoil adjusting to that trade, the Lakers would abruptly release Rodman, after which the team would settle into a new and different round of internal conflict.

Each major change that season brought a blur of frustration, but there would always be one constant—O'Neal's and the rest of the team's issues with Bryant. The team would schedule a series of meetings to try to deal with chemistry problems, but the malignancy was never addressed frankly.

"It was all sort of beating around the bush," explained a longtime Lakers staff member. "The whole thing is about Kobe. The whole failure of the team is about him."

Asked about that opinion, Derek Fisher said, "That's the way I perceived it. That was the way that it was. There were a lot of people who felt that way. Nobody ever really came out and said that they felt Kobe's selfish play was our problem. But that's what everybody felt."

Bryant's friends and family would see the response as an intense case of envy, of his status and of the new contract and endorsement opportunities. The situation would grow so bad that some in his camp wondered if his teammates were intentionally failing to let him know when opponents were setting screens on his blind side.

In part, his defense mechanism for dealing with the matter was yet more alienation.

The trade of Jones meant the loss of one of Bryant's few allies on the roster. But when asked about the situation, Bryant acknowledged that he had no real relationship with any teammate. "All that matters is what we do on the court," he said.

The center, on the other hand, was gregarious and well liked in the locker room.

"For a guy whose structure is an intimidating figure just by his physical presence, he was incredibly unintimidating in every other way," Howard Beck observed of O'Neal. "He was easy to talk to. Whatever his faults, whether regarding Kobe or anything, Shaq was just a people person to the core. He just loves being around people. Shaq couldn't even hold grudges very well. One of the major differences between them is that Kobe did hold grudges and Kobe remembered everything, every slight, every sideways remark. Kobe wouldn't let go. I have always said this: it's very, very hard to gain his trust; it's very easy to lose it; and if you do, good luck getting it back."

Beck recalled having to write about Bryant and O'Neal's relationship in the wake of yet another incident between the two. "I'm asking him about whatever the latest dust-up with Kobe is, trying to do some reflective piece on the status of the relationship, and Shaq is like, 'Everything is cool, basically.' I'm thinking, 'How is everything cool? You guys talk all this shit about each other and all this other stuff.' He said something like, 'Look, bro, just because I'm mad at you on Monday, that doesn't mean we can't have lunch on Tuesday. We could have an argument on Wednesday, but then we could still go hang out on Thursday.' That was the Shaq view: 'I could rip the shit out of you on Monday, but Tuesday is a different day. We're all fine. We're good.' "

His approach with the media followed that same track. The center would get angry over something a reporter wrote, then let it pass.

"He can't help himself," Beck offered. "He doesn't have it within him to want to sustain that anger and resentment because he's too busy being like a party. He'd much rather be liked. He'd much rather have everybody laughing at his jokes. He just genuinely enjoys people, and I think that's one of Shaq's greatest virtues. He wouldn't carry it out for any length of time, especially if it was trivial stuff, and most of it was trivial stuff."

Bryant had played the unwilling straight man for three seasons. And, as Beck said, Bryant forgot none of it. In their first season in Los Angeles, O'Neal tried using humor to nudge Bryant toward being more of a team player. The center even composed a ditty, set to the tune of "The Greatest Love of All."

In the locker room, he would croon:

"I believe that Showboat is the future/Call the play and let that motherfucker shoot…"

He'd sing a verse, then come back with the next a little louder: "I believe that Showboat is the future…"

Bryant tried hard to feign amusement even as the moment fueled his furor.

"In Kobe's defense, he's a young guy, much younger than all these other guys," photographer Andrew Bernstein pointed out. "When he came in that first year, the Lakers had all these guys like

Byron Scott and Jerome Kersey, guys who could have been his father. Kobe seemed to feel that he had to create an image of himself that he was older than he was, more mature, grown-up, and above his years."

He often came off as humorless.

Of course, Bryant and O'Neal weren't alone in their differences. Basketball history is replete with stories of teammates who struggled to mesh their games and personalities. George Mikan and Jim Pollard both gained the Hall of Fame by leading the Minneapolis Lakers to six pro championships, but forty years after they last played together their conflicts as teammates remained fresh in their minds.

Larry Bird and Kevin McHale had their own détente on Boston Celtics teams that won three championships, as did Magic Johnson and Kareem Abdul-Jabbar, who won five NBA titles together. Abdul-Jabbar always felt that Johnson got the credit for their work together. "Because of Earvin's special charisma, the story was always written a different way," Abdul-Jabbar explained in 1993.

Harris had pleaded with Bryant to defer to O'Neal as Johnson had once deferred to Abdul-Jabbar. When Harris departed, Rambis took up the effort. West, too, had worked hard on the chemistry but would later remark that Bryant refused to defer to O'Neal in any way.

"He wouldn't defer to God Almighty," Vaccaro said with a laugh years later. "I'm just telling you. That's the truth. He had this ability just to shut people out, like, immediately. Like, on a phone call, he would just go, 'OK, it's over, that's it.' No, he's wired differently."

Shaq seemed a bit more willing to reach out to Bryant. When Bryant was heaving up the air balls in the 1997 play-offs, O'Neal had been the first person to his side, telling him not to worry, that redemption would soon be his. But that image seemed to fade with each passing day over the spring of 1999.

Just as rumors had persisted that O'Neal's envy of Penny Hardaway sparked his exit from Orlando, observers wondered if Bryant's marketing success in Los Angeles posed a similar threat. His number 8 Lakers jersey outsold O'Neal's in sporting-goods stores around Southern California, just one of many points of marketing competition between the two where Bryant had taken the upper hand. But his teammates were quick to shoot that idea down.

"People say Shaq is jealous. That's way far from the truth," Derek Fisher said. "All Shaq wants to do is win."

"I want him to get all those commercials and do all that stuff," O'Neal volunteered during an interview when asked about Bryant. "Because, with marketing, when they see Kobe, they see me. And when they see me, they see Kobe."

"Shaq really wanted to have this great relationship with this kid and [have] the two of them lead this team to a championship," offered one veteran Lakers employee. "He wasn't jealous of Kobe or anything like that. He still isn't. Shaq has tried to get him under control. The kid has this attitude, 'You may be Shaquille O'Neal, but I'm Kobe Bryant. I'm every bit the player you are, plus some.'"

There were times when Shaq's frustration would show. At one point during the 1999 season, O'Neal would point at Bryant across the Lakers locker room and announce, "There's the problem." Beyond that moment, though, the two would avoid direct confrontation, due in large part to the efforts of Rambis and the Lakers coaches to keep the rumblings from flaring into the kind of trouble that could never be repaired. "Shaq and I have never even talked about it," Bryant said when asked about their difficulties. "We communicate about it through the media, mostly."

Asked if he had tried to help Bryant through his growing pains, O'Neal replied, "I try not to help guys out too much. Experience is the best teacher. Kobe really didn't go to college. He went to high school, and he's different. Kobe's a great player, and he's gonna get a lot of press. He's a new, up-and-coming kid. Certain people understand that. Certain people don't. I understand that. I just try to stay out of his way and encourage him."

There were others who had a contentious relationship with Bryant. Ruben Patterson, the Lakers' twenty-three-year-old rookie from the University of Cincinnati, was a six-foot-five forward who possessed a strong defensive ability that stemmed from his emotional approach to the game and to life. He had played briefly overseas during the NBA lockout and then returned to the States to join the Lakers.

His personality clashed immediately with Bryant's, resulting in furious practice battles throughout the season between the two — again, not unlike Bryant's meetings with his own father.

"Between Ruben and Kobe something was always going on and escalating," Derek Fisher said. "Ruben wouldn't back down. It got out of line a couple of times, because of Ruben's nature. Kobe can get into a tussle and still not take it across the boundary. He can push and shove and fight for position and not react emotionally. On the other hand, Ruben is a rookie, a guy always trying to establish himself, and he wasn't gonna back down."

Bryant benefited from a double standard, a Lakers staff member alleged. "They would get competitive in practice. Kobe would bow him up, but Ruben couldn't do to Kobe what he wanted to do to him, because management would come down on him. Kobe was untouchable. Kobe could do what he wanted."

His teammates saw his efforts to dominate the ball as the height of selfishness. Harris had resisted West's insistence that Bryant had to play more because he was an exceptional talent who needed to play to develop, but once Harris was gone, Bryant started to dominate the team's rotations. And Rambis soon came to be viewed as skewing the team toward Bryant.

"As players, we had to deal with Kobe's success and the way the organization viewed Kobe," Fisher explained. "It was clear the organization was satisfied with how Kobe played, as was the coaching staff. It was clear they were not gonna hold him back or slow him down from [being] the player that he wanted to be."

The supposed preferential treatment meant that others on the team would have to sacrifice their development for Bryant's, Fisher added. "Shaq also benefited from the star system. That's the way the NBA works. But it can be demoralizing to a team, demoralizing to the players making the sacrifice."

Derek Harper tried to play a healing factor. It was obvious that the media buildup and expectations had had a dramatic effect on Bryant's development, Harper said. "Everybody has already pushed him to be the man, especially now that Michael has retired. Everybody is saying this is the guy who is going to carry the torch. And that's a lot of pressure for a young kid."

Still, Harper said he hadn't cautioned Bryant to ease off. "Because he won't," Harper said. "He really, really has this thing that he wants to be the best. There's no use in him taking it easy. He may as well go for it just the way that he's doing."

Harper did spend much of the season talking to his younger teammates about establishing unity and togetherness. His approach helped calm the passions to some degree. But as time went on, it became increasingly clear that it wasn't so much that his teammates didn't want to heal their differences; they just didn't seem to know how.

Bryant's heart plummeted with the weight of the negativity. In March, old teammate Rip Hamilton took off on a run with his University of Connecticut team on the way to the Final Four and then the NCAA championship. An envious and lonely Bryant followed along in phone calls with Hamilton. "I watched it and thought about how I would have done that play, and then I'd tell Richard about it," Bryant said at the time. "We do a lot of trash talking. I tell him if I'd been there I would have kicked his butt and he would have never made it to the Final Four."

The vicarious experience helped him deal with his frustrations. Inspired by his trash talking with Hamilton, he scored 38 points — with 3 rebounds, 4 assists, 2 steals, and a blocked shot, including 33 points in the second half — in Orlando against Penny Hardaway and the Magic, all while wearing his fancy Adidas KB8 IIs, which were still part of the company's "Feet You Wear" campaign. Despite the short season, Adidas had still gambled and released the high-top model, which wasn't exactly being embraced by the market. In Orlando, fellow Adidas endorser Peyton Manning was there to hang out in the Lakers locker room with him after the game, although the media hardly noticed Manning, who sat quietly nearby after the game as reporters crowded around Bryant.

"We got to know each other through Adidas," Manning explained quietly. "I'm here to hang out and support Kobe."

The translation was that Adidas was bringing out the big guns to try to salvage the shoe. But there wasn't much to salvage in and around the Lakers in the spring of 1999.

"It's been a season of many changes. Many changes," Bryant said wearily in April.

"If you really look at my numbers, they're pretty good. And no one is thinking about how I really just got into the game, that I'm still learning and I'm going to make mistakes," he said. "People don't know my game and what I need to do for myself to get better. Sometimes what they say may be true, but you get to a point where you hear and you don't hear."

It was best not to hear when your teammate was screaming at you in the locker room, threatening, "If you ever do that again, I'll kick your motherfucking ass."

"It's been a really difficult year for my son," Joe Bryant said to a reporter. "We can't do anything about it but give him hugs and kisses and lots of support when he gets home."

As the season wound to a close, Kobe expressed to a writer that he dreamed about playing for Tex Winter, the elderly Bulls assistant coach who had pioneered the triangle offense. Bryant had become infatuated with the system that had helped Jordan win six championships. The writer offered to set up a phone conversation between Bryant and Winter, who was still coaching for Chicago. They soon connected through long distance. It was Bryant's first contact with the man who would become his mentor and defender.

Bryant was likewise interested in a conversation with Jordan himself, to seek more advice, and the writer provided Jordan's number as well.

"What would you ask Michael?" the writer inquired.

Bryant thought a long while and replied, "I would ask him how to incorporate math into the game."

"I can tell him about that," Jordan said with a chuckle when informed of the question later. The two began talking, and Bryant told a reporter that getting advice from Jordan "is like getting advice from that Buddha that sits on the top of the mountain, who has everything figured out and passes on some of his knowledge to the next guy who's trying to climb that mountain."

The comparisons to Jordan had been yet another constant element that vexed teammates and staff alike. "No one was calling him the next Michael," recalled veteran sports journalist J. A.

Adande, "yet people were observing the way he patterned himself after Michael. It was a lot more pronounced at that time, but no one really thought he would ever warrant a serious comparison to Michael."

"He even runs like Michael Jordan," said the obviously frustrated Lakers staff member. "It's not good for him. The great basketball players try to take complicated things and find simple ways to do them. Kobe, with all his switching of the ball from hand to hand and faking, takes simple plays and tries to make them complicated."

Yet even this criticism connected him to the Bulls great. For more than a dozen years, Tex Winter had made the same complaint about Jordan. "He's more of a high-wire act, you know," Winter had observed in 1998, as Jordan was on his way to leading Chicago to a sixth league championship. "He's into degree of difficulty instead of just working, just trying to be real fundamentally sound."

Privately, Bryant indicated that he would need another three seasons to reach a dominance like the one Jordan had held over the league. "I just want to take over," he said. "I want to be the man."

The Lakers defeated Houston in the first round of the play-offs that season, then were swept by San Antonio in the next round. As things turned sour, Derek Harper was heard to murmur under his breath at the silly young stars around him, "Overrated motherfuckers."

San Antonio's fine coach, Gregg Popovich, was among those in the league who found it advantageous to foul O'Neal and face his sketchy free-throw shooting rather than allow him to dunk time after time. This strategy was on its way to becoming known as Hack-a-Shaq.

It pointed to the center's Achilles' heel. He couldn't consistently finish games as the primary option for the Lakers because he couldn't make free throws. Even Jordan had boldly declared it before the 1998 season.

The Lakers needed a finisher exactly like Bryant to play alongside him. It was obvious that the two stars needed each other, that they each prevented double teams from swarming the other. Everyone around them had tired of pointing it out.

Some in the media were observing a pattern about O'Neal's teams that long preceded Bryant. Each season, the center's teams ultimately collapsed and were swept by opponents.

"Remember," J. A. Adande recalled, "that at that time Shaq had been swept. He got swept his first play-off trip. The first series he got swept. Then he went to the NBA Finals the next year and got swept again, and the next year after that he got swept in the conference semifinals by the Bulls. He won one game in '97, then they got swept in '98, and he got swept again in '99 by the Spurs."

The pressure made the normally gregarious O'Neal sink into frustration.

"His frustration with losing grew, and the pressure to win grew," Rick Fox observed.

"What surprised me about Shaquille during his early days in Los Angeles was how frustrated he got," West said later. "He was not fun to be around. The shortcomings of our team and his teammates made him angry because he knew he was going to be judged on how much he won."

Given the media onslaught after the Lakers were swept out of the play-offs, along with the roller-coaster drama of the short season, Jerry Buss knew he needed an exceptional coach to make his collection of young talent work together. Phil Jackson, the man who had led the Chicago Bulls to six NBA titles, was a name that had frequently been discussed as the season played out. Getting the legendary coach to L.A. was something that both Kobe and Shaq could agree on.

A writer mentioned it to West one quiet afternoon in the Forum as the Lakers were getting swept by San Antonio.

"Fuck Phil Jackson," West had responded, flashing his anger over what he perceived as Jackson's criticism of the Lakers during the season.

Yet a month later, Jerry Buss and Shaq and Kobe got their wish, and it was Jerry West introducing the new coach at the press conference.

Chapter 21

CALIFORNIA STARS

He called it "getting ghost," his term for putting on that emotionless face and walking out of the locker room after a game, making a beeline for his black Mercedes coupe and disappearing. As he walked out of the Forum at the close of the profoundly discouraging 1999 season, he was asked what he would do for the summer. "Basketball," he replied tersely. "There is nothing else."

Ah, but there was much more on his agenda, and it would soon come at him like a train over the coming months.

On the surface, things seemed just fine for the Bryants by the fall of 1999. Their son was about to play for Phil Jackson, whose name and reputation alone were enough to create confidence that he could fix the Lakers' chemistry problems. After all, the great Jackson himself, the coach of those six Bulls championships, had said publicly that he saw their son as a "Jordanesque" player. What was not to like?

For three seasons, Joe Bryant had been constantly and obsessively fearful that the situation with the Lakers would fall apart. Now, their son's future at last seemed headed in the right direction. Joe's emotional state over his son's career had been an unrelenting factor in the family household, said the friend who gained a view of the family during the period. "He was very blinded with Kobe and how things should be with him, the coaches and what they should do. He needed to step back and give them some space, but then you'd say that to him, and he'd just step away. You can't be like that as a parent with a player on the team. You have all this pent-up frustration he had."

It was as if Joe, the nicest guy in the world, was incapable of listening on the issue, the friend said.

Whereas Kobe had moved on emotionally from so many people in their past, Joe still turned to them. He talked with Sam Rines and Gary Charles and Sonny Hill, the trusted souls who could chat when he was up early on the West Coast and it was 9 a.m. back east.

To some old friends, it was obvious that Joe was really bothered that his son didn't get along with Shaq. That was a huge problem, even bigger than Joe's problems at the Sixers, because a young Joe had been deferential to Julius Erving and the team's other veterans. But he had taught his son another way.

"You know what?" Charles would tell Joe when he would bring up Kobe and Shaq's issues. "That's what makes Kobe what he is, that's why he's where he's at. I call it confidence."

Just like Gregg Downer, Charles said he saw before Bryant even got to Los Angeles that his competitive nature was going to cause problems, "but that's what made him who he was."

Rines was likewise of the opinion that Bryant shouldn't have to defer to O'Neal. Listening to Joe, the AAU coach was amazed by the unfolding of events, both publicly and privately, in the young star's life. Always in need of revenue for his AAU team, Rines talked to Joe fairly often during the period. The coach had been promised support for his team going forward by both Adidas and the Bryants, and none of it had materialized.

In fact, Joe Bryant had another huge problem preying on his mind that fall. Yes, his son was rich, but Joe too needed money.

The situation highlighted a problem that hadn't really been articulated since his son had gone on *The Tonight Show* before the start of his rookie year and told Jay Leno that he had put his parents on allowance.

There remained the perception that the Bryants were not just running their son's life, they were running his money.

"They're living off him," Sam Rines said, looking back. "It's like, 'This is our money.'"

Kobe's updated Adidas contract had ended the father's payments. Sonny Vaccaro estimated that the shoe company had paid Joe about $300,000 over two years, but no more payments would be going directly to him.

Needing cash and a stable future for himself, Joe Bryant, then still just forty-five, supposedly settled upon two big ideas. First, he would talk his son into buying an Italian basketball team that Joe could run into his golden years, at which time Kobe would be ready to retire from the NBA and could then take over, either playing for or managing the club in Italy, or maybe both.

Second, Joe realized that working a shoe deal for his son had provided him great money on the side. But since Joe's run with Adidas had come to an end, even as his son was marching to heights with the European company, he started thinking about working on a deal behind the scenes for Kobe to eventually switch shoe brands. That would be the kind of play that could fix Joe's finances for years. Little did anyone suspect at the time that Joe's ideas would change the course of the athletic-shoe industry.

The shoe deal would take time and finesse, but the Italian team was something that could happen right away, that fall of 1999.

"Joe really wanted to do that," explained a family friend. "Kobe, you know, was like, that was crazy. Everyone thought it was a bad idea. But it was Joe in his mind that he could create that just from living in Italy. He thought he could absolutely do that, but nobody— nobody—thought it was a good idea."

Actually, there was part of Joe's plan that did appeal to his son. He had long romanticized his formative years growing up there and considered it a place he would like to live to raise his own family, far away from the dangers of America's gun culture.

"My kids could grow up without all this fear of shooting in the school and that type of madness," he had confided to a reporter. "I would like that type of happiness or peace."

So he agreed to his father's idea. Joe and Kobe posed for a press photo with Arn Tellem to announce that they had purchased the elite Olimpia Milano, the New York Yankees of Italian basketball, that fall. Bryant partnered with Wisconsin cheese manufacturer Pasquale Caputo, a native of Italy, to purchase the team, with each putting in an estimated $2 million to close the deal.

Joe would be in charge of the team, but, unfortunately, he had no real experience with any sort of business management.

"He tried to run it like an NBA team," explained a lawyer involved in the deal. "You couldn't do that."

The father apparently quickly received a harsh primer on cash flow. He paid too handsomely for players, and, combined with other issues, the company soon had serious money problems. Apparently, Kobe found himself putting more and more money into what appeared to be a bottomless pit, with team revenue far from matching expenses. It was hard to tell just how many millions Bryant put into the team before he pulled the plug, Sonny Vaccaro said. The Lakers star had just reached a new level of wealth, but in a few short months, it became clear that even he didn't have the kind of cash needed to bail out another team across the world.

"That was the whole falling-out, because Kobe didn't really have the money," Sam Rines remembered. "When I talked to Joe, I think Joe knew he messed up. He thought he could get out of it. He was just kind of saying Kobe didn't understand the whole picture."

"Maybe Kobe thought getting him the team in Italy would pull [Joe] away to do something else, but it was just the debacle," said the family friend. "He had no idea what he was doing. There was no telling him. You couldn't get involved. There's nothing anybody could do."

"I think there should have been a better line of communication," Sam Rines offered, "but I think people were taking Kobe and pulling him a certain way, because Kobe needed to become a man really quick. So I think what happens is, you're trying to become a man and there's money involved and people are trying to tell you things."

Early the next fall, in 2000, Bryant and Caputo allowed a group of Italian businessmen to take over the team just to keep it afloat. In less than a year, Italy's finest team was on the verge of bankruptcy, according to the lawyer associated with the deal. While the disaster was a small press item in America, it was well known in Italy, a place that mattered much to Kobe Bryant.

"They lost millions of dollars," Sonny Vaccaro recalled. "It was embarrassing."

The moment proved to be terrible, Vaccaro explained, because Bryant, who loved his father so dearly, who had idolized him, suffered a profound disappointment.

"He lost faith in his father," Vaccaro said, looking back, an assessment with which Rines agreed.

Bryant would say little about the disaster other than to attribute it to misunderstanding and a lack of communication.

The huge losses with the Italian team also cost Bryant's old AAU team. "We were promised money from Kobe and a couple of other things," Rines said in 2015, "but nothing ever materialized. And then Joe and Kobe had a little falling-out, and we knew that was it. I haven't talked to Joe in about four or five years. I talked to him before that pretty consistently for a while, and he was like, 'Just be patient, I have to build the relationship back up.'"

That might have been possible if not for the other great force that swept into Kobe Bryant's life that fall of 1999.

He was working with Anthony Bannister and the group of hip-hop artists from Philadelphia to finish up their album for release. At the same time, he was reportedly being encouraged by executives at Sony to make his own record, apart from the Philadelphia crew. The studio apparently reasoned that it had invested in the project for Kobe's presence. That was the selling point, the reason Sony had taken a half-million-dollar gamble.

Plus, Bryant's style appeared to be an increasingly awkward fit with Bannister's edge. It was obvious that Bryant had never seen the hard experiences Bannister wrote about, not even in films. Joe and Pam had made sure every media selection in their household throughout his upbringing was PG clean. "They had kept him from anything negative, violent, and overly sexual," Rebecca Tonahill, one of Bryant's friends during his early years in Los Angeles, would later tell Newsweek. "They thought they were doing him a favor, but they really weren't. He needed to know these things, if just for a reference point when hanging with the boys."

Or for laying down rap tracks.

Apparently Bryant's ego and confidence, as well as the influence of the studio, drove him toward his decision. He would finish the record alone. As the family friend recalled, the artists from Philadelphia soon packed up and headed home, and Pam Bryant was relieved to see them go.

Bryant and the studio, meanwhile, prepared the project for a grand release at the February 2000 All-Star Weekend with a performance by Bryant and Tyra Banks, who was on the list of celebrities, including Brandy and Destiny's Child members Kelly Rowland and Beyoncé Knowles, with whom Bryant formed brief relationships during the period. Venus Williams would make that list when Bryant sent her roses after she won her first Wimbledon championship.

At the time, the All-Star Weekend performance seemed like a good idea, complete with a megadose of star-power appeal, but the song and the appearance proved a disaster. Bryant rapped about finding true love, implying that he dated actresses because they were safer in not needing his fame and wealth.

Banks's accompaniment was to mouth the refrain:

> "K-O-B-E, I L-O-V-E you
> I believe you are very fine
> If you give me one chance, I promise to love you
> And be with you forever more."

The performance was panned by critics as laughable. He made a March appearance at the Soul Train Music Awards in L.A. to support the record. Asked about it by reporters, Bryant quizzically responded in Italian.

Humbling though the experience was, it had led him to the key relationship of his life. In the fall of 1999, as he was making a video for one of his songs, he met a pretty young dancer, Vanessa Urbieta Cornejo Laine, seventeen, who supposedly had been discovered by a music producer in a crowd at a hip-hop concert. She was at the studio, accompanied by her mother, to appear in a Snoop Dogg video as Bryant was working on his own shoot.

As Bryant explained later, it was love at first sight. Within days, he was flooding the offices of her Orange County high school with flowers to express his great love. And when he showed up at school to give her a ride home in his Mercedes, his presence created such chaos and disruption that it soon necessitated her being home-schooled to finish the year.

Though she was dancing in hip-hop videos, she was a good Catholic teen, sheltered by her family much as Bryant had been by his own family. Her mother was divorced and remarried, and she had taken the name of her stepfather. The *L.A. Times* would later report the family had money issues.

Like many young lovers, they had a plan, and that was to spend as much time together as possible. Pam, who had devastated her own father years before by falling in love with Jellybean, was now facing her own supreme disappointment. In time, the Bryants found themselves caught up in a conflict complicated by Kobe's millions, the evolving issue with the Italian team, and the fact that Vanessa Urbieta Cornejo Laine possessed a constitution every bit as tough as Pam's.

"And Pam was no joke," observed Gary Charles.

Indeed, the experience over the coming eighteen months would leave no one laughing.

"It's kind of one of those things that Kobe was wrapped up so hard, when he finally opened up he fell hard," Charles offered.

Both of these large events—his profound disappointment with his father and his sudden and deep infatuation with a raven-haired young beauty—brought dramatic upheaval in his life. Many of the people who had watched Bryant as a teen knew that change was coming.

"Over time these kids develop their own minds," Charles observed. "In the beginning when they're young, they listen to their moms and their dads and the confidants near them, but other people get in their ears and they start to develop their own minds and ideas of things that they want to do."

The Roadster

With Phil Jackson set to take over the Lakers in the fall of 1999, Adidas chairman Peter Moore struck out to complete his vision for Bryant's signature shoe, the Kobe, to be released for the upcoming season.

It was based on the Audi TT roadster, with a sleek, new-millennium design. "I saw a merger between sport, basketball, and style and fashion," Moore recalled. "I even hired the designers and the models that worked on the concept for Audi to design his shoe."

Moore considered the roadster a breakthrough in design and wanted to make a similar statement with Bryant.

"The first time I showed him this shoe and what we wanted to do with that shoe and the model, I could tell that he was excited, he lit up," Moore said. "That was fun. He got it, and he saw it was different. He thought it was pretty cool. They came in a yellow color— that was very cool."

Even Bryant's parents liked it, Moore said, which was a relief because "the whole family was a bit possessed and just a little off. But they loved the whole idea of the TT. They didn't understand it all, and I didn't explain it all."

Then came the key commercial to launch the concept. "The first thing you see is this guy in all-black leather with a helmet on," Moore explained, "and it shows him getting on a Ducati motorcycle. He fires it up and he drives it all through L.A. and drives it down into the arena."

Once there, the shot showed Bryant putting his foot down and showing the new shoe as he's taking his helmet off, then walking into brand-new Staples Center, a design feat in its own right. "He was fast and made a lot of turns and did all that stuff," Moore said. "It just fit with the style of his play. We thought, 'This will be the starting point for this kid.'"

The motorcycle was the perfect metaphor for Bryant's fearlessness. The rider, of course, was a stunt double. Industry standards, as well as insurance requirements and provisions in his Lakers contract, meant that he couldn't do the driving, though he would later buy a couple of the machines and spin around Southern California a bit.

"It was all about style, not about basketball at all," Moore said. The goal was to allow the young market to discover style all on its own through suggestion. "My bet was that kids were changing," Moore explained. "They were going to start buying more style than basketball."

Which was sort of where Moore had left off with Jordan and the

Jumpman logo, which had quickly moved beyond basketball itself. It was a different tack than Bryant's initial interest in trying to appeal directly to an inner-city audience, but Adidas hoped the new look would be a better fit. Still, Bryant was reluctant.

"He kind of bought what I was doing, but he really didn't believe it," Moore recalled. "He really didn't think it was that big of a deal, that important or exactly what he wanted it to be."

Only later would Moore realize that Bryant had reason to pause, no matter how great the design. After all, he would have to wear his fancy new shoes into locker rooms, to practice and games. The young star had been doing that for three seasons already, and he was starting to have his fill of being the hottest new thing.

Road Rules

As the record deal, the new shoe, and his new romance with Vanessa rolled through his life at the beginning of the 1999–2000 season, Bryant was getting to know his two new coaches, both of them stern realists in the business of basketball, not given to romantic notions of any form.

Tex Winter, the Lakers' new assistant coach and resident offensive genius, would take the kind of grandfatherly approach that Bryant had long responded to. Winter could be harsh in his assessments of players, but he stressed early on to Bryant that when he criticized— and he would criticize often—he was aiming his comments at the player's actions, not at the player himself. In truth, Winter was already quite taken with his new young charge, who studied the game so hard and practiced relentlessly, putting to use his fabulous talents to a degree that exceeded even that of the great Jordan. Winter had coached Jordan longer than any other coach, and to powerful results, yet had failed to connect with him on a personal level.

In Bryant, Winter saw greatness, flawed only by blind ambition and a critical lack of experience in the team game. Theirs would be the beginning of a beautiful relationship—Bryant soon dubbed him Yoda—of long hours studying and debating and discussing basketball, one the master of the team game, a purist unlike any other in the history of the very impure NBA, the other a young genius caught up in his own fable, pushed along at a furious pace by his demands and dreams.

As for the head coach, when Jackson was hired, Bryant had purchased his book *Sacred Hoops* and gone up to his hotel room in Los Angeles to greet him. Jackson had been intrigued at first, but the new head coach had a way of creating a void with his silence, with long pauses that left his players trying to figure him out. The coach had championships to win, and the young force of nature wearing number 8 clearly had the extra agenda of his own stardom. Bryant soon got the message that their relationship wasn't going to be all that chummy.

Jackson and Winter also brought with them the staff that had been a part of the magical dream of six titles with Jordan and his Bulls.

Chip Schaefer had been the team trainer for those Bulls and was now coming to the Lakers as a competition coordinator. Perhaps as much as any staff member, he had been closely involved in every aspect of Jordan's title reign. "Those teams were so close and so mature and adult and responsible," he recalled. "It was like bliss coaching and working with that group of people. It didn't get any better than that."

Now they all figured they'd be working with the glitz and glamour of Hollywood and the legendary Lakers. It didn't take long to figure out that the Lakers in the fall of 1999 didn't share the togetherness of Jackson's Bulls teams.

Though the group dynamics were off, Schaefer was surprised to find a Bryant whose "competitive drive and professional nature and his incredible dedication to being the best he could be were unparalleled in my career and completely genuine. It was very real."

Early in his tenure with the Lakers, the seventy-seven-year-old Winter, who had a half century of coaching under his belt, sat listening to the players unburden themselves about the team's deep problems and figured that there was almost no way they were going to win a championship that first year.

Just a season earlier, the Lakers had been a deeply talented team, but Buss had jettisoned much of that talent. The new coaches looked over the situation and concluded that they needed former Chicago star Scottie Pippen, who had gone to Houston when the Bulls broke up Jordan's championship team.

Jackson was vocal and insistent to both Jerry Buss and Jerry West that he absolutely needed the do-everything Pippen, who had in many ways been the heart of Chicago's title teams. Even though a deal could be had with Houston, West was flatly against it and was obviously filled with all sorts of emotion with the interloper Jackson taking over his team.

"He's got six weeks," West tersely told Jackson sidekick Charley Rosen as they sat together, looking down on the swarm of reporters around the team during media day, at the opening of training camp that fall. In retrospect, the remark was a huge blunder in that it ignited the vast gaseous store of resentment already gathered under the relationship between West and Jackson, even before the season started. Plus, the message was patently absurd, simply the kind of nervous anger that West had been venting for years around the franchise, but it meant that Jackson and his staff came to view West as someone intent on undermining them, especially with Bryant, as Rosen and several sources on the staff would admit later. Jackson privately left the impression that mastering the Lakers would be a test of wills not only with Bryant but with West, too.

Buss soon declared that he didn't have the money to go for the thirty-four-year-old Pippen, so the Lakers backed off, allowing the Portland Trail Blazers to snare him. Like that, the degree of difficulty increased dramatically for Jackson's Lakers. Pippen knew Winter's triangle offense inside and out, was a unique defender, and had the kind of presence that could have healed the Shaq–Kobe tussle quickly, Jackson's camp figured.

"He's perfect for the kind of system I like to run," Jackson said of Pippen, adding, "If I had a checkbook maybe like Paul Allen [Portland's owner], I could end it all."

The comment itself angered Buss, who was paying Jackson a whopping $8 million a season to coach the team.

Stuffing his disappointment, Jackson turned to his top task— setting the hierarchy of the team.

It was O'Neal who would take top priority in Jackson's plans from the very first day of training camp. The coach began by putting the onus squarely on the center's seven-foot-one, 330-pound frame. "This team should be looking to win sixty games," Jackson told the L.A. media as training camp opened. "That's a realistic goal."

He paused in the middle of that thought and looked at O'Neal, sitting nearby. "The ball is going into Shaq," Jackson said. "And he's going to have a responsibility to distribute the ball. It's going to be good for the team, and good for him."

The previous season, Kurt Rambis had attempted to install some plays that would have allowed new offensive weapon Glen Rice to shoot coming off screens. O'Neal tried them for a few weeks, then informed Rambis after a players' meeting that the plays would have to cease.

"If I'm on a team where we come down and call plays every time, then it's time for me to quit," O'Neal confided later. "Then I'm not gonna be an effective big man no more. If that's the case, then they're just using me as a token to set picks. I don't want to play like that. I want to run and get crazy and look at the fans and make faces. If I've got to come down and set picks and do all that, it's time for me to quit. Then I ain't got it anymore."

Jackson's six titles changed that mind-set immediately, Schaefer recalled. "I can remember even the first minutes of the first practice at UC–Santa Barbara in the fall of 1999, when Phil talked. It reminded me of the old E. F. Hutton commercials (when he talked, people listen). These guys were so excited to be coached and led. You could hear a pin drop. It was like, 'Man, sprinkle some of that fairy dust. Give it to me. Give me those pearls of wisdom.' So that group was incredibly coachable with him early on. They wanted everything and soaked up everything."

Even so, the thought of playing in Winter's triangle offense intimidated many of them. It required them to read the defense and make choices, as opposed to responding to simple play calls. Basically, the triangle required the wings on each side of the floor to play like football quarterbacks, reading the defense, then initiating a sequence of passes and cuts to counter what the opponent was doing.

After years of learning the system from Winter in Chicago, Jackson knew exactly what he had to do to move things in the right direction. In Chicago, Winter had watched in amazement as Jackson built a strong relationship with Jordan. "When you have a relationship that strong with the star player, the rest of the team just kind of falls in line," the older assistant explained. "Phil worked very hard at cultivating that relationship with Michael."

The first order for Jackson in Los Angeles was to build a similar relationship with O'Neal. Jackson knew that O'Neal was motivated by the opportunity to score lots of points, and the triangle offense was built for the post player to do that. So the coach fashioned a trade-off with the big center. If O'Neal would show the leadership Jackson wanted, then the system would provide him with the opportunity to score large numbers of points, Winter explained.

If O'Neal wasn't ready or didn't understand the triangle in training camp, Bryant was ready to volunteer as the volume scorer. Schaefer remembered the early sessions of practice that fall, with players not getting the offense.

"Kobe had a great line," Schaefer said. "He's like, 'Did any of you guys get TNT?' Because, you know, the Bulls were on TV so much. It's like he knew already, had completely mastered it. Before the first practice he knew. He certainly knew the right spots on the floor. He knew the right actions. He knew what he wanted to get out of it. It was amazing."

"How many Bulls games have you seen?" he asked his teammates. "Don't you pay attention? How could you not pay attention to this stuff?"

"He was extremely bright," Schaefer observed. "Obviously had he decided to go to college, he could have majored in anything, and I'm sure he would have been a 4.0 student in any endeavor he would have pursued."

O'Neal, though, was bright and picked up the offense quickly, Winter reported, then pointed out that post players usually do learn the system faster because they don't face the read challenge as the wings do.

Bryant was triangle ready in some ways but not in others. The offense required that the ball keep moving from player to player. Anyone who kept the ball too long, who resorted to one-on-one play instead of hitting the open man, was considered a "ball stopper."

For years to come, Bryant would be considered a foremost expert on the offense. Winter would often praise his knowledge. But Bryant was a frequent ball stopper, a frustrating if not totally unexpected development for Winter and Jackson. Still, Winter had long been familiar with the problem because Jordan himself had been a ball stopper. Winter considered it a full-time, nightly effort to persuade Jordan to share the ball with his teammates. Some nights would be better than others, and on those nights the offense would work better.

Winter realized that Bryant would be Jordan-like in that regard as well, only worse, because at least Jordan had played three years under Dean Smith, whose top assistant was Bill Guthridge, who had played in the triangle for Winter at Kansas State and then became Winter's assistant coach for several years.

Guthridge had brought many of the triangle's principles to North Carolina's disciplined system. Jordan had deferred to that system throughout college.

On the other end, the coaches, like Bryant's previous coaches, also disliked his tendency to be a "ball chaser" on defense. He would leave his man open to stalk the ball in hopes of getting steals, which then allowed him to execute spectacular dunks in the open court to finish breakaways. Jordan, too, could be a bit of a ball chaser at times, but Bryant's penchant for it particularly vexed his coaches and teammates because it made the team defense weaker, the big dunks notwithstanding.

The veterans on the team had been eager to see Jackson immediately begin disciplining Bryant, Derek Fisher recalled. But that didn't happen. "He still waited for a while before he started. He didn't just jump in. He really didn't," Fisher said. "He allowed Kobe to come in. I think Phil wanted to see firsthand how things were, how Kobe participated in the games and practice, how we felt about him, how he felt about us. Phil waited to see all that before he made any judgments about whether there needed to be adjustments. He didn't just come right in and tell Kobe he needed to curtail his game or his creativity. He really allowed things to develop, then here or there when it was pertinent, he would say something. It was never as if he was saying things to Kobe as if Kobe was the only guy on the team who needed to make adjustments, or to improve in certain areas."

Such patience was the coach's trademark. Jackson had once explained that he based much of his decision making on Carlos Castaneda's *The Teachings of Don Juan*: "Look at every path closely and deliberately. Try it as many times as you think necessary. Then ask yourself, and yourself alone, one question.... Does this path have a heart? If it does, the path is good. If it doesn't, it is of no use."

Another one of the things that Jackson initiated early was the use of psychologist George Mumford as a meditation expert, teaching the team mindfulness practices and how to breathe. For years now, O'Neal's teams had been folding in the play-offs. Jackson wanted them to know how to breathe when that trademark Shaq panic set in.

Early on, things seemed to go well, until Bryant broke his right hand in the first quarter of the first exhibition game, played in Kansas on October 13. Thinking that the injury wasn't serious, he returned to the game and finished with 18 points, 5 assists, 4 steals, and no turnovers in thirty minutes. X-rays later produced the diagnosis. He was to miss the first six weeks of the season, a total of fifteen games. The Lakers lost four of them.

"We won sixty-seven games that year," Schaefer observed. "It wouldn't be hard to imagine that with Kobe's presence, who knows, maybe we would have won close to seventy games that year. We certainly would have won a couple more. Who knows, we might have won sixty-eight, sixty-nine, seventy games."

Yet even a setback such as Bryant's broken right wrist proved to be a blessing. It allowed the coaches to mold the team identity.

Jackson's backup plan after not getting Pippen had been to sign free agent and former Bull Ron Harper, who would provide steadiness and leadership throughout the season, especially later, upon Bryant's return. Harper would be a steadying influence whenever the young guard's competitiveness raged out of control.

A big test for Bryant was sitting on the bench during a thunderous appearance by Vince Carter and the Toronto Raptors, a defeat that left Bryant antsy to play.

His return, however, wouldn't come until December 1, when he came off the bench to score 19 points in a win over Golden State.

"It was nice to have Kobe's energy," Jackson said. "He's just a wild, impulsive kid right now. He's still feeling his way."

"God, I had a headache, I was so excited," Bryant told reporters. "My head was literally throbbing. The first half, I felt like I was on speed or something. I couldn't calm down."

Bryant's frenetic energy was like some sort of super octane fuel for the Lakers that December. Immediately, the media began asking about the prospect of Bryant and O'Neal getting along, with Bryant's energy changing the Lakers' attack.

"I don't foresee any problems," Jackson said. "If there is, we'll rein him in."

The very next game, Bryant blocked a late Pippen shot to help get a win over Portland.

Chemistry

While integrating Bryant back into the rotation, Jackson once again focused on smoothing out the Lakers' chemistry issues. It was a process that had begun in training camp. "I'm going to stop some of the gossiping, stop some of the rumormongering among the personnel here," he had promised that first day.

The main strategy was to use the structured offense to keep the relationship between O'Neal and Bryant smoother on the court. Yet in their talks, the coaches found a lot of pent-up anger on the part of O'Neal and other veterans against Bryant.

At first, Jackson and his coaches hadn't realized the depth of the divide they faced. After the season, Winter would reveal that he was shocked by the level of animosity O'Neal expressed for Bryant when the coaches first arrived on the scene.

"There was a lot of hatred in his heart," Winter said.

O'Neal didn't hold back in team meetings. "He was saying really hateful things," Winter explained. "Kobe just took it and kept going."

The center's main message? The Lakers could not win a championship with Bryant, an opinion that he expressed often to management. During the off-season, former O'Neal teammate Penny Hardaway had contacted O'Neal about joining the team. The center jumped at the opportunity and phoned management. The implied message was that Bryant should be traded, but management declined that move.

Winter revealed that during the season, as the coaches worked to heal the rift between the players, it had been made clear that if the coaches' efforts didn't work, then "a move would have to be made, if they can't play together."

It seemed that the team wasn't about to trade the massive O'Neal, which meant that Bryant would have to go.

In 2015, Charley Rosen disclosed that indeed the team had a trade it could have made: swapping Bryant for Detroit's very talented Grant Hill.

"They made that offer," said Rosen. "Now, Grant Hill was, like, the super-teammate, intelligent, would have plugged into the triangle instantly, would have bought it. Great teammate, was at the top of his game. He still had, you know, injury questions, but Kobe that first year was really a problem for Phil. I said, 'Make that trade. Get that fucking kid out of here. He's driving you crazy. He's not executing, he's not relating to anybody. You could bring in this guy who is like a saint on the court, off the court.

" 'Do it, do it,' " Rosen recalled telling Jackson, then added, "Phil wouldn't do it. One reason was the age difference. Hill was five years older."

But there was another important reason why Jackson wouldn't go for the trade. "Kobe," the coach told Rosen, "has a competitive nature that is something that I can really relate to, something I can really appreciate."

In Chicago, Jackson and Jordan had been the most competitive people in the Bulls organization, Rosen said. In Los Angeles, in a very rough, very irritating form, Jackson had found that same type of competitive presence. Like Gregg Downer before him, the coach faced the challenge of "managing the personality."

Early on, it became clear that Jackson sided exclusively with O'Neal, and Winter took up the cause of Bryant.

"Kobe was frustrated," Ric Bucher recalled, "because he felt like Phil sided with Shaq, and Phil did because Phil knew that Shaq had the locker room. Shaq had a greater connection. Who did Phil respect more? I think Phil respected Kobe more overall, but Phil was playing the political game in that locker room. He needed to have Shaq. He needed Shaq more than he needed Kobe because Kobe was on an island anyway. Kobe just resented the hell out of that because he looked at Shaq and he went, 'This guy doesn't work as hard as I do. He is not in shape. He's a goofball. He's a clown, and I'm working my ass off, and I'm supposed to take a backseat to him?' You know, it's one of those things where I think at a more mature age, maybe he would have been able to deal with it in a different fashion, but maybe not. I think we all have a sense of justice. We all feel we want to be rewarded, and when we see that somebody who doesn't work as hard is given higher status, I think it rubs us all the wrong way. It's just a matter of how we deal with it."

Bryant's champion in this cause was Winter, who had been a star at Southern Cal in the 1940s as the teammate of Hall of Famer Bill Sharman. The elderly coach had quickly impressed the Lakers players with his ability with a medicine ball. He was every bit as fearless as Bryant and had been Jackson's "bad cop" in Chicago, the only coach on the staff who ever dared to directly challenge Jordan, which Winter had done with some frequency, fussing about his chest passes or any other infraction.

Rosen was sitting and watching the Lakers practice one day that first season when Winter suddenly jumped in front of a 330-pound O'Neal, running full speed, with the idea of taking a charge.

"Jesus, this guy is going to get himself killed," Rosen thought with a wince.

"He was willing to take it," Rosen recalled, "but Shaq pulled up at the last second, and Tex was right in front of him."

Winter was a nut about fundamental footwork, a factor that Jordan, Pippen, Bryant, all of his players came to prize, except perhaps O'Neal and Elvin Hayes, whom Winter coached years earlier with the Houston Rockets.

Hayes once called Winter "the Antichrist."

"There's all this stuff on the footwork," Schaefer recalled with a laugh. "Inside reverse pivot, outside reverse pivot, front turn, rear turn, whatever, and Kobe was fascinated by footwork. A lot of people that are that good of an athlete don't need that because they can get by somebody just out of pure athleticism, but I think Kobe realized, 'OK, if I'm quicker than my opponent and I have better footwork than my opponent, I'm really going to have something.'"

Schaefer recalled Winter and Bryant working on the details after practice one day that first season: "You know, people are sort of milling around, shooting free throws, getting ready to leave, and the two of them are just working in the half court. Tex, who probably was eighty or something at the time, was out there not just pointing it out but literally with a ball in his hand, demonstrating it. He'd show Kobe something, and Kobe would mimic it. Tex was coaching at that time maybe the best player in the world on what most people would consider rudimentary skill work, but Kobe ate that stuff up, loved it. Kobe was an indefatigable worker and just a passion for the practice court. You talk about some of the common things with Michael and Kobe, they both loved the practice, loved the work, loved the practice, loved the drill."

Winter, though, could be a pain on the bench during games. Once, during his extensive college coaching career, he had physically gone after a player in anger. In Chicago, he supposedly had to be restrained at times if center Luc Longley, a wonderful Australian gentleman, showed a bit too much passivity. He was almost that aggressive with Bryant at times.

"Tex had a way of just being in his ear during every time-out," Schaefer recalled, "and there was one moment where Kobe maybe kind of had had enough, because Tex doesn't really have kind of a governor over it. You know, he's going to be the most open person you're ever going to see. So he was telling him what he thought. You know, there's a time and a place to critique a player, and the minute he steps off the court, when he's trying to get a drink of Gatorade, isn't always the best time. But I think that's what Kobe loved about Tex. What's the old Greek saying? Was it Diogenes looking for one honest man? I think that's what Tex represented to a lot of people. Tex couldn't tell an untruth if his life depended on it. So I think that's what people like Michael and Kobe love about Tex. They welcome coaching. They welcome honest criticism."

Bryant finally had found someone he deferred to — a bit.

"I think he appreciated everything that Tex ever said to him," Schaefer said.

The Michael Effect

With Bryant back in the lineup, they ripped off sixteen straight wins, which would carry them well into January. Finally they lost a January 14 game at Indiana's Conseco Fieldhouse, and suddenly they found themselves in a 4–5 free fall over their next nine games, after which all the old panic came back.

The losses were relieved for one night by a home win versus Denver, with Jordan watching from the stands and Bryant hitting his first 8 shots and scoring 27 first-half points. "It just so happens that I have good games when he's here," Bryant said afterward. "He should show up more often."

The Lakers coaching staff hadn't been in Los Angeles long before they had begun comparing the two players. Obviously Jordan's hands were a little larger, Winter recalled, and Jordan was a little stronger holding position in the post. But the coaches couldn't help but marvel at the great will displayed by both men. As for the competitive nature, Bryant's eagerness to challenge Jordan that night pretty much summed it up. As alpha males, they stood alone at the top of that mountain.

Jackson recalled years later, for Fox Sports, that he got Jordan and Bryant together after that Denver game in a meeting room in Staples Center. The coach was hoping the former Bulls star could talk to Bryant about being patient, about "letting the game come to him."

Bryant was waiting in the room when Jackson brought Jordan in, the coach recalled. "The first thing Kobe says is, 'I could kick your ass one-on-one.' "

The next day's headlines accused Bryant of "showing off" for Jordan, and soon the Lakers were again pointing fingers and blaming their problems on Bryant's desire for stardom.

Winter, though, cited the team's poor defense. "We're getting broken down," the seventy-seven-year-old assistant coach confided. "We've been vulnerable to penetration all year long, the high screen and roll. Kobe has a real tough time with it. So does Derek Fisher. And the side screen and rolls. That's most everybody's offense this day and age, especially against us."

The coaches tread softly on the chemistry issue, which had elements that disturbed Winter. "Most coaches, Phil included, have always sort of had a whipping boy," Winter explained. "And I think he's very careful not to have that become Kobe, because he realizes that he's got a great young player here and he doesn't want to squelch him too much. And yet he wants to control him."

Before long Winter would conclude that, indeed, Jackson had made Bryant a whipping boy, a complaint that Winter would level over the next several seasons.

Where the players had at first seemed content with Jackson sitting back and letting Bryant learn from his mistakes, soon the team grew insistent that the coach rein in the young guard. Winter attributed it to O'Neal's influence on the rest of the roster, but the judgment of the team was widespread and profound.

"The coaches voiced to us that they weren't seeing the same things we were seeing when they watched film and when they watched what was going on," Derek Fisher explained. "They didn't see the same selfishness or one-on-one play that we saw. What I tried to tell some of the other guys is that this is our fourth year now, me, Shaq, Robert, Rick, Travis, so we still had issues that we had dealt with before this year.

"It was kind of similar to a relationship between a man and a woman, where you get upset with all of these things from the past that come up," Fisher explained. "That's really where a lot of this stuff stemmed from. The coaches saw that a lot of this stuff would come in due time. But we were so impatient because we had dealt with it before."

Winter contended that no matter what Bryant did, O'Neal and other teammates found fault with it, prompting the elderly assistant to finally put together a videotape to prove to O'Neal that Bryant was doing the right thing.

"I think Kobe's really leaning over backward to get the ball in to Shaq," Winter would confide as the season progressed. "If there's a problem there—and I think we'll work it out—it's that I don't think Shaq appreciates what Kobe is trying to do to help his game."

The issue would remain open and quite raw.

Jackson hadn't been shy about challenging Bryant as well as others, Rick Fox observed. "He is our leader now. In his interaction, he's gone as hard at guys as I've seen anybody go at someone. Maybe harder than they'd ever be on themselves. And that's a challenge. He's pushing buttons to make sure guys continually come to work, come to step their games up and get better."

Jackson also showed an early liking for zinging criticism of his players in the media. For example, he told *Sports Illustrated* that he doubted whether O'Neal could be a leader because his poor free-throw shooting meant that he couldn't deliver at the end of games.

"He's very open with his criticism," Fox said. "At the same time he's very open with his praise. You can live with somebody who when his mouth opens, you get the truth. Sometimes the truth hurts, and egos are bruised. But all he's doing is putting guys' egos in check. It's a fine line. He's obviously very good at what he does."

Jackson reminded O'Neal of his stepfather, a military man who was just as tough on Shaq as a child. "He's my white father," O'Neal said of the coach.

"Phil is all over Shaq, all the time," Lakers reserve John Salley said. "But Shaq can take it. It works for him."

Plus all the other Lakers saw that O'Neal was respectful of and obedient to Jackson's discipline. In short order, it was Jackson who had become the top dog in Los Angeles. As for O'Neal, Winter said, "My main concern is that I don't want him to be satisfied with where he is. I want him to realize what he's doing wrong, even on the free throws.... He's not easy to coach. He has kind of a resentment for anybody to tell him anything that he's doing wrong.

"I think Phil treads very softly on Shaq," Winter said. "I think he still is trying to read the situation as to what is the best way to motivate Shaq. I don't think he knows yet. And I certainly don't know."

Soon the All-Star Weekend loomed, the annual test of the team's envy over all the attention Bryant drew. The slam dunk contest had been revived for the first time since 1997, which meant Bryant was the defending champion and thinking about entering again, especially since Vince Carter was drawing raves as a high-flying young player. Jackson quietly urged Bryant to pass it by. Fisher said that the Lakers knew Bryant wanted to have a go at Carter, but he set that aside so that it wouldn't put a focus on individual accomplishments over team play. It proved to be a crucial factor in the team's growth, although O'Neal was clearly mimicking Bryant's crossover dribble during the All-Star warm-ups, then tossing the ball up into the stands to caricature the guard's turnovers. Such open hostility had to cease, Magic Johnson confided, concluding that Jackson would soon get it under control.

Another important moment at the All-Star Weekend came when Seattle's Gary Payton helped Bryant understand screen-and-roll defense as the two got together during a spare moment. "I don't think Gary knows how much he helped me," offered Bryant, who demonstrated such dramatic defensive improvement afterward that he would wind up being named to the league's All-Defensive First Team.

The humbling experience of his music performance also seemed to redirect the young star. Fisher even suggested that Bryant seemed to come out of All-Star Weekend a changed man with a greater focus on team play.

Not to be overlooked was the calming presence of Ron Harper in the backcourt, Chip Schaefer recalled. "That meant a lot to Kobe. Of all his teammates, I think he relished playing with Ron early in that first two years. He had built-in respect for Ron as a guy. At that point, Kobe hadn't won his first title yet, and Ron was coming off three of them with the Bulls. He looked at that as somebody that could help.

"It's not like he would take advice from just anybody," Schaefer remembered. "You had to earn your stripes as somebody that he would respect enough to listen to. It wasn't like he was going to listen to any person that's going to come in and try to give him advice."

Schaefer said that Bryant also seemed to enjoy Tyronn Lue, the team's diminutive second-year guard. "I can remember an episode where Tyronn had a turnover or two and came out of a game, and a fan behind the bench said something critical. I remember Kobe kind of barking at the fan in defense of Tyronn."

Bryant's taking up for a teammate was a small but important moment, Schaefer observed.

Despite making small strides with his teammates, Bryant still couldn't bridge the gulf with Jackson. Bryant had pointed out that he had yet to sit down for an in-depth conversation with the coach. Bryant kept expecting that conversation to occur. But it wouldn't happen for years, a situation that vexed Winter to no end.

"One of Phil's great talents is that he's a master of relationships and knowing what buttons to push with what people," Schaefer observed in 2015. "He didn't coach everybody the same way. He coached Shaquille in a way and pushed the buttons there, and he pushed buttons with Kobe and he pushed buttons with Robert Horry and he pushed buttons with Rick Fox, and on down the line.

"I always thought Phil batted pretty close to a thousand with all the buttons that he pushed with people over the years," Schaefer said, "but I know that obviously he ruffled Kobe's feathers."

Jackson took an unusual approach with Bryant, Scoop Jackson remembered. "Phil gives everybody books to read. Did you ever know what book he gave Kobe? Man, Kobe and I had an off-the-record conversation — I'll share it with you because it's true. The first book Phil gave him — and this is what fucked it up for him — Phil gave him the book *Black Like Me*."

The book, by journalist John Howard Griffin, was about a white man pretending to be black in the early 1960s.

"Kobe's like, 'What the fuck is this?'" Scoop Jackson remembered. "You can do a lot of mind tricks, but that crossed the line because of the racial issues. There was no context, no anything, just throw it at him. And if you know Phil, he did it in that Phil arrogance."

One of Jackson's staff members pointed out that Jackson routinely gave his players books aimed at expanding their view of themselves and the world around them.

"If you're going to play mind games, Kobe's very mature," Scoop Jackson observed. "He understands the mind games that Phil's going to play. That was a bad one. Kobe told me, 'What the fuck?' And I'm like, 'Hey, hey, I don't know.'"

"Kobe was a real contrast to the rest of his teammates, a real contrast to, let's face it, most of the guys in the NBA," Ric Bucher observed in 2015. "That's the other thing I appreciated about him. In some ways socially, he was less refined, certainly, in comparison to Jordan. He didn't have the opportunity to refine himself in the same way socially that Jordan did before he got to the NBA, but in other ways, you know, having lived in Italy and being overseas, he was sophisticated."

Whatever the coach did, it all added up to Jackson's very unique package, Bryant said of Jackson that season. "I think what has shaped this team, as far as his personality goes, is his sharpness as a person. He's very picky. He pays attention to detail. I think with this team that was something that we lacked in the past. We had a tendency to overlook things, just see the surface."

A late-February win over Portland sent the Lakers on another victory binge, this time nineteen straight games, highlighted by O'Neal scoring 61 points on his birthday. The streak finally ended in a mid-March loss in Washington. Afterward, new Wizards executive Michael Jordan enjoyed a cigar at his former coach's expense.

Immediately after losing to the Wizards, the Lakers ran off another eleven wins on their way to the 67–15 finish. April brought a pair of disappointing losses to San Antonio, including one to end the season, in which Spurs power forward Tim Duncan sat out and Jackson gave rookies and substitutes more playing time.

"It wasn't the most confident way to finish a sixty-seven-win season, losing two games, including one on the road," Fox admitted.

It was the second-best regular-season win total in the long and storied history of the franchise, behind only the 69–13 record compiled by the 1972 team led by West and Wilt Chamberlain.

Jackson's Lakers had already clinched home-court advantage for the play-offs, though, and the coach continued to take the long view.

Drums

Despite their gaudy record, the ghosts of play-offs past hovered over the Lakers that spring, to the point that it had become part of their personality. Jackson was ready with his zany remedies, such as burning sage in the locker room and beating a tom-tom before games to drive the intensity of his players. Mostly that just raised their eyebrows, although a few Lakers would admit the coach's banging on the tom-tom got their hearts beating faster.

George Mumford, who had been brought in to lead the Lakers in meditation and mindfulness training, just as he had for Jordan and the Bulls in Chicago, became one of the rare things that Bryant and O'Neal agreed upon. Bryant welcomed the mindfulness sessions because they offered specific mental training, much of it in the Zen mold, for reducing the stress of play-off competition, when the pressure hit the high side. "He's our secret weapon," O'Neal would say of Mumford.

Then there was Jackson's approach to scouting tapes. He interspersed game video with cuts from popular films, which proved to be another hit as these Lakers took on Jackson's new approach.

As he had done in Chicago, the coach took his players through a series of feature films to prepare them for the play-offs, splicing the entire feature in and around clips of the Lakers and their opponents' plays, using certain scenes to chide his players about their choices and actions. First was *American History X,* followed by *The Green Mile.* Jackson had a way of pausing the film at the most devilish, profane moment to emphasize one thing or another, often to the great hilarity of his players.

Derek Fisher pointed out that many of these video lessons seemed to highlight one or another of Bryant's transgressions. Even so, Bryant said that he didn't mind being singled out. "It's interesting," he said. "I like to try to figure what Phil was actually thinking when he put the clip in there. All the messages he has. It's good for you. I enjoy it. The team finds it funny. Some clips are funny. Some are made to be taken a little more seriously."

Jackson used *American History X* to emphasize the film's message about rejecting hatred.

Still, with O'Neal's frequent complaints that the team couldn't win a championship with Bryant, and the head coach not shy about piling on about his mistakes, a weaker personality could easily have crumbled under the pressure of the play-offs.

"The pressure is there, the pressure is there," Bryant acknowledged. "But it's how you deal with it. When you feel it, it's how you deal with it. You just give it your best. You prepare yourself as well as you can. You go out there and execute as well as you can. Then you sleep at night. That's all. Then you get up the next day and do the same thing. Keep it simple."

It sounded admirable, but behind the scenes in his private life, Bryant had immense fireworks of another nature, ignited by his giving Vanessa Laine a one hundred thousand dollar engagement ring that May. That, combined with Pam learning that her son had provided funds to Laine's family to deal with debts, set off intense family conflict.

In the midst of these difficulties, Bryant kept his own counsel, to the point that those who worked most closely with him would be surprised to learn much later of the dramatic set of events that unfolded away from public scrutiny.

With only a casual understanding of what was going on, Jackson and other figures with the team—not to mention Bryant's own agent—had cautioned him to take it slow in his plans for matrimony. There was perceived to be more than a bit of condescension in the head coach's take on the relationship.

Tex Winter, however, was soundly in Bryant's corner.

"Oh, good for you," the elderly assistant told him. "Now you can finally take your mind off of basketball a little bit. Now you can finally relax a little bit."

"Yeah, Tex," Bryant replied. "Maybe you're right."

"Just breathe." Mumford's message for the team also likely helped Bryant off the floor, although the adviser, who was becoming quite important to the young star, also knew nothing about his family issues.

Bryant instead was content to discuss the mental elements of competition with Mumford, as were teammates. "It was good because it gave people a chance to talk about things that might be on their mind, the hype, the pressure," Bryant explained. "I think it's good for them to talk about those things. It increased our performance a lot. It really has. I'm surprised other teams don't do that kind of stuff. Working with George helps us to get issues out of the way before they even start."

The pressures of performance, of the play-offs, could corrode a team's performance, Bryant explained. "Once it creeps into your team and your teammates, it can be destructive. Some people know how to handle it, some people don't. The pressure can get to you. You got to know how to suck it up."

Even with Mumford's work, the coaching staff had concerns about how the team would hold together under the play-off pressure. "The times that we've become frazzled and unraveled as a team, it's been around situations where we embarrass ourselves," Rick Fox noted.

Sure enough, they struggled to put away Sacramento and Phoenix in the first two rounds (Bryant hit a last-second shot to deliver a big win in Game 2 against Phoenix). Then the Lakers found themselves facing Pippen and Portland for the conference championship.

Jackson's team had gotten increasingly better over the season in the execution of the triangle, except when they played Portland because Pippen's vast experience with the offense allowed him to coach his teammates on how to counter it. With the Bulls, Winter and Jackson had regularly used the more sophisticated elements of the offense to surprise play-off opponents at key moments. Pippen wasn't going to allow many surprises in this huge showdown.

In Game 1, the Lakers survived an extreme "Hack-a-Shaq" fouling tactic by Portland coach Mike Dunleavy. Repeatedly squeezing, holding, and wrapping him up, the Blazers forced O'Neal to shoot 25 free throws in the fourth quarter alone. It did little more than delay the game to the point of irritation. The Lakers used the stopped play to set up their defense for each possession and won handily.

The Blazers then changed the tenor of the series by claiming Game 2 in a massive 106–77 win in Staples Center. The Lakers had, strangely, played without emotion and energy. The coaching staff left the building dumbfounded.

"We didn't expect a blowout," Jackson admitted.

The Blazers contained Bryant for most of the second half in the third game, in Portland, but he zipped an assist to Harper for the winning bucket in the game's final moments. Bryant also helped block a last-ditch shot by Portland center Arvydas Sabonis to preserve the victory, and also had a steal on the Blazers' previous possession.

"I had to take a chance. We've played all season long for this," said Bryant, who had been plagued by fouls for much of the second half. "I'm not going to let a guy get a clear look just because I have 5 fouls."

Sabonis wailed for a foul, but replays suggested that the block was clean.

"It was a surge for us," Bryant said. "Kind of a statement to Portland that we're not going to give up, that we're here to fight."

The 93–91 victory netted a 2–1 series lead. It was the first Lakers conference-finals road win in a decade.

With the Blazers fuming, the Lakers then got another win in Game 4, another contest marked by the Blazers' high energy at the opening of the game and by the Lakers' late surge to win.

Down 3–1, the Blazers returned to L.A. and took a game that reflected Pippen's great competitive nature. He used the occasion to break Jordan's all-time record for play-off steals.

Having fallen asleep in one close-out game, the Lakers promptly did it again in Game 6. Portland evened the series with more strong play from Pippen, while the Lakers again looked strangely passive. Only six other times had an NBA team come back from a 3–1 deficit to win a series, but the Blazers seemed quite capable of pulling it off.

The Blazers opened Game 7, back at Staples Center, by outplaying the Lakers again and taking a 16-point lead into the fourth quarter. They seemed poised to end any hopes Lakers fans had of a championship. Almost mysteriously, Jackson's team produced a miracle, the biggest Game 7 fourth-quarter comeback in NBA history.

Portland led, 75–60, with 10:28 left to play, but the Lakers stopped Portland ten consecutive times. It was Bryant's block of Bonzi Wells's shot that led to a Brian Shaw trey that cut the lead to 10 points with 9:38 remaining.

"You lose yourself in it," the Lakers' Glen Rice said of the comeback, a 25–4 run. "We were thinking, 'Keep going, keep applying the pressure, continue to keep going down on the offensive end, and keep getting good shots, and hopefully this team will fall in the end.' And they did."

Brian Shaw remembered the crucial stretch of the game: "We were down, like, 16 points going into the fourth quarter, at home, in Game 7. And Phil Jackson said we were concentrating too much on throwing the ball inside to Shaq, that we should take the shots when he kicked it out on double teams. That gave us the freedom, as perimeter guys, to go ahead and launch some threes and get back into the thing. I think I hit 3 or 4 threes in the fourth quarter. Rick Fox, Robert Horry started launching, too."

The Trail Blazers were forced to cease collapsing around O'Neal and come out to guard the perimeter, which in turn allowed the Lakers to again send the ball inside to O'Neal.

"It looked really glum for us at that time, being down 16 at home in Game 7," Shaw said. "I just remember thinking about playing with Shaq in Orlando, and we got swept when we got to the Finals. And I'm thinking, 'Man, are we going to go out again?' So we got the game back in a manageable position, and Kobe and Shaq pretty much took over down the stretch. I think that's where Kobe really grew up and came of age. And his greatness really started to show. It was do-or-die at that moment, and he made the plays. When you look back at it now, that has to be considered one of the greatest games played in Lakers play-off history, to get to the Finals with that group for the first time. Kobe just made some great plays. That Portland team was a very talented team, too. That's when Kobe grew up."

The Staples crowd fed their energy, which was highlighted by Bryant's alley-oop to O'Neal for a thunderous slam and an 85–79 lead. O'Neal offered up his seal of approval afterward: "Kobe's a great player.

"When he went to the hole, we caught eye contact and he just threw it up," O'Neal said. "I just went up... that was an opportunity for me to get an easy bucket."

"I thought I threw the ball too high," Bryant said. "Shaq went up and got it. I was like, 'Damn!'"

Afterward, the Blazers could only look on in glum, stunned silence as Los Angeles celebrated its first trip to the NBA Finals in nearly a decade.

"That was a daunting uphill battle that we had to face," Jackson said after his team had eclipsed a 15-point fourth-quarter deficit to win, 89–84. "We made it back."

In their hour of need, Bryant led the team in points (25), rebounds (11), and assists (7), to go with O'Neal's 18 points and 9 rebounds.

Witnesses could hardly believe what they were seeing—a bonding moment between the center and the guard—but the victory was proof. It was as if Bryant had refused to get discouraged, and that paid off by season's end. "I think they came to respect each other,"

Winter said, although the coaches could never be sure what the players were merely doing as a public gesture and what they truly felt. Scoop Jackson, for example, saw O'Neal running around at game's end, looking to celebrate with anyone but his foil.

Asked about O'Neal, Bryant shrugged. "We just do it our separate ways," he said. "That's all we did all season long. It just depended on what we needed in certain situations. So even though we go our separate ways, it all linked up in the end."

Indiana

With the start of the championship series, Ric Bucher had a keen eye for Bryant. "I'll never forget watching him when he first walked out on the NBA Finals court the first time," the journalist recalled. "You could see him gazing at the logo on the floor and the bunting up in the stands. I could tell that he was overwhelmed by where he was and what he was seeing, these little accoutrements of the NBA Finals and him being there.

"At times he'd have just this incredible killer mind-set, this willingness to stare down or battle men five, ten years older, then at the same time moments where you were reminded he was still very much a kid."

The Indiana Pacers roster was filled with such men, led by Reggie Miller and coached by Larry Bird. The Lakers coaches now turned their concerns to limiting such a great shooting team.

They didn't look like great shooters in Game 1. Reggie Miller made just 1 of 16 shots, and the Lakers won in a breeze, mainly by getting the ball to O'Neal and watching him work against an Indiana defense that for some strange reason failed to double-team. His 43 points and 19 rebounds produced a 104–87 victory.

"This offense is designed to go away from pressure," Derek Fisher observed. "We tried to attack the pressure against Portland. Indiana tried to single-cover Shaq. I'd be surprised if they don't play the next game differently."

For Game 2, the Pacers brought the double teams, but they didn't prevent L.A. from moving out to a 33–18 lead after the first quarter.

Bryant had injured his ankle early in the contest, which left him playing just nine minutes. The game finally narrowed to a 2-point Lakers margin in the third, but Bryant's scoring and O'Neal's overpowering presence were enough for the Lakers to seize a 2–0 series lead, 111–104.

With a ballooned ankle, Bryant sat out Game 3 on crutches— the only NBA Finals game he would miss in his long career. Indiana finally got a win, to pull within 2–1, all of which set up Game 4 as Bryant's big moment.

The ankle was stiff and sore, but he joined O'Neal in matching the Pacers bucket for bucket down the stretch in a game that headed to overtime, where O'Neal collected his sixth foul. Suddenly, the Lakers were Bryant's team to lead. He went over to the center and told him not to worry, that he would deliver.

Sitting nearby on press row, Ric Bucher was fascinated. "Kobe was playing on a bad ankle, and there was no way in hell that he was going to miss out with Shaq on the sideline and with Reggie Miller as the guy that he was battling," he recalled. "He was excited by the opportunity. The thought that the Lakers might be in jeopardy never occurred to him. The way Kobe thinks and the rest of the world thinks is so disparate. On media row everybody was like, 'Oh, they're in trouble.' Whatever. Kobe was like, 'Now I get to take over.' That he was not going to get the job done never occurred to him."

In the past, in Chicago, Jackson and Winter had spread the floor in such moments and allowed Jordan and his teammates to go to work with back cuts and other surprise elements. But with the Lakers, spreading the floor had never worked, Winter explained, because opposing teams would never leave O'Neal and kept the defense packed in. The spread floor might have worked if O'Neal had been willing to develop a ten- to fifteen-foot shot, allowing him to move away from the basket, but he never developed one.

Now, though, the behemoth was off the floor, and Jackson sent the Lakers into the wide look to confuse the defenders and give Bryant room to work. The sore ankle left him pulling up for midrange jumpers rather than trying to drive all the way to the hole.

In overtime, Bryant delivered the Lakers and offered irrefutable evidence that O'Neal had been wrong about the team not being able to win with him.

"The system worked out well for us," Bryant said. "In the fourth quarter, the triangle offense sometimes kind of goes out the window a little bit. The system in itself allows us to spread the floor toward the end of the game and penetrate. That works because with the triangle offense everybody is a threat throughout the ball game. So the defense is scared to leave off of guys to try to stop me. They're scared to leave off of Robert, and they're scared to leave Rick alone to try to stop me, because they know those guys will make shots.

"In Game 4 it worked really well," Bryant added. "We were able to spread the floor, and I hit a couple of jump shots for us and took us to the brink. During the season, I wanted to use the spread floor. I told him, 'Phil, man, why don't you open the court?' He said, 'We're not ready for that. We'll get to that.' I say open it up. That's when I can go to work. But I'm glad that we waited till the play-offs to use it."

Los Angeles had taken a 3–1 lead in the series, but Game 5 produced a loss, which sent the contest back to Staples Center, in Los Angeles. The city hadn't celebrated an NBA title won at home since Magic Johnson and Kareem Abdul-Jabbar led the Lakers to a win over the Detroit Pistons in the 1988 NBA championship series.

The morning of Game 6 found Jackson in the locker room beating his tom-tom, perhaps the most bizarre championship morning in the history of American pro basketball. "Everybody on the team seemed to perk up at the sound of it," Brian Shaw said.

Somehow the coach with all the wackiness and gizmos and burning sage had brought the divided team together for a splendid season, which they closed out that night.

Bryant went 8-for-27 from the floor for an ugly 26 points. He grabbed 10 rebounds and had 4 assists, 2 of them to O'Neal as the Lakers charged back in the fourth quarter to take the lead for the first time since the first period.

"In the fourth quarter, we found a place where they couldn't stop us," Jackson said afterward.

The job of making the key shots fell to Fox and Horry as the Lakers moved to a 101–94 lead, despite a stretch of missed O'Neal free throws. Then the Pacers began drawing fouls and making free throws, all of which set up a Jalen Rose trey to tie it, 103–103, with 5:08 left.

For a stretch the momentum then shifted back and forth between the two teams until the Pacers pulled again within 1 point, at 110–109, with 1:32 left. The Laker coaches called for screen-and-roll action out of their offense, a surprise, since the Lakers rarely used it.

O'Neal, who so hated setting screens, was now creating high monster picks for Bryant then rolling like thunder to the basket. The action worked, Bryant hit some late free throws, and the Lakers had a 116–111 victory and the franchise's first championship in a dozen seasons.

"We went back to the same thing that worked for us in Game 4, spreading the floor and penetrating, and then attacking them," Bryant said. "I was able to get to the free-throw line and knock down some free throws."

"I think we needed Phil to do it," O'Neal said. "Phil and his coaching staff was a staff that was going to bring this team over the hump. We always won fifty, sixty games. When we got into certain situations in the play-offs, we could never get over the hump. We had home-court advantage but we made a lot of mistakes in the play-offs. But Phil was able to keep his poise and have us watch film. When you look at a guy like Phil, if you're a leader, he's not worried. Why should you worry? He prepared us very well."

"I still think that if they hadn't made that comeback against Portland in 2000 in Game 7 that they wouldn't have won any championships," J. A. Adande offered in 2015, "because the strain of their relationship would have been so great and they wouldn't have had that championship together to fall back on. They would have had to break up. That fourth quarter against Portland, I really think, was the difference between three championships and zero championships."

The flimsiest of bonds between O'Neal and Bryant, with all the talented role players around them, had somehow been just enough to allow them to rise to the mountaintop, to glimpse the possibilities just long enough before the densest of fogs came rolling in yet again.

Chapter 22

WEDDING-BELL AND OTHER BLUES

Kobe Bryant had always been so good at Adidas camps. Though he was a private person, he was gifted with a natural charm, and his enthusiasm for the game meshed well with young campers. If they were old enough and had game, he would size them up to see if they were ready for his challenge. If they were younger, he was playful, teasing, ready to engage them in shooting games and fun.

By 2000, the German parent company of the American division of Adidas had deployed him all over the world for four years and was very pleased with the things he had helped accomplish in the battle for market share with Nike. The new title for the Los Angeles Lakers meant that his marketing power would surge even more. He had ascended to that elite level as a product endorser. It was understandable that the company anticipated it was headed to the promised land that chairman Peter Moore talked of, where cash registers would ring almost uncontrollably across the global marketplace. Adidas was poised to do very big things.

Vaccaro himself was feeling exceptionally good about his work for the company, with both Bryant and Tracy McGrady charging along in their NBA careers as the game's two most charismatic young figures. They weren't Michael Jordan. Nobody was. But they were "next," and his gamble had panned out so well that Vaccaro had been given a lifetime contract with Adidas.

The future looked very bright.

At least, it seemed that way until Vaccaro's ABCD Camp that summer of 2000 at Fairleigh Dickinson University, in New Jersey. That's when the serious trouble first emerged, at the same camp that had been Bryant's platform for a meteoric rise in the game.

"He was coming to camp to speak," recalled a family friend who was also associated with Adidas, "and we were very excited. Adidas is our sponsor, and the kids are out-of-their-minds excited for him to be there."

But Bryant, who was always punctual, was a no-show for his scheduled appearance. The Adidas staff knew that he was in the area because there had been a flap over his hotel when his new fiancée had refused the quarters arranged by Adidas.

"We always stayed in Hasbrouck Heights, at the Hilton, which was very convenient," explained the friend, "but she would not stay there. They had to stay in Manhattan, I believe at the Four Seasons. She refused to stay at the Hasbrouck Heights."

With the campers waiting eagerly on the great Kobe Bryant, the staff frantically tried to track him down, the friend recalled. "We're waiting and waiting and waiting. They're, like, twenty minutes late, thirty minutes, an hour, an hour and a half, two hours. They're not there. So we're trying to find out what the heck is going on. Well, they'd had a massive argument. Him and the girl. She doesn't want to go, and she doesn't want him to go. This is a big company that is paying you a lot of money, and you're supposed to be there. They don't show until very, very late."

The appearance might have been salvageable with just a touch of warmth, perhaps an apology. But when the couple did arrive, Vanessa Laine brought an eye-opening incivility to the event, the friend explained. "She shows up with him. I have never in my life met a young lady more rude to people than her to this day. I could not believe it. She would not shake anybody's hand. She wouldn't look at anybody. That's the only time I've been around her."

The Adidas representatives, including Vaccaro and the friend, had never met Bryant's fiancée, and they wouldn't that day. "I mean, she wouldn't talk to anybody," the friend said. "Wouldn't speak, not hello. I mean, not even hello. Sonny and I walked into the room, there was no 'Nice to meet you.' Not a word. It was unreal what happened that day. I just could not believe it. He was very nice and gracious. But when young people are around older people, whatever the situation is, it's somewhat expected that they will extend themselves even just a little bit. She had no problem ignoring everyone that walked in there. That is what she was, she was ignorant."

The friend remembered thinking, "This will never last. Kobe Bryant's surely not going to put up with such outrageous behavior."

Bryant's parents weren't present at the event. If they had been, they would have been extremely apologetic, the friend said. In retrospect, the friend would recognize that Adidas was dealing with an extremely spoiled teenager with a $100,000, seven-carat ring on her finger.

"She was very young," the friend said.

The friend had told Vaccaro much earlier that he should expect change from Bryant. "Kobe's young," she recalled telling Vaccaro, "but when he starts getting with the person that he's going to be with, he's going to become another person."

And that was what the friend saw in New Jersey that week. Kobe Bryant was becoming another person, shaped by this new relationship.

A similar review of Laine would soon be offered by the shop clerks and attendants of Southern California, by Bryant's teammates' spouses, by journalists and other independent observers. Kobe Bryant's betrothed was presented publicly as a harsh, abrasive, controlling personality. Later, she would come to be understood a little better. But in the early years, the press reports and personal accounts were not good.

For the friend, the New Jersey experience in July of 2000 also brought some insight into the reaction of Bryant's parents to the unfolding personal events behind the scenes, particularly Pam Bryant's strong reaction to her son's choice. With the announcement of their engagement that May, Laine had moved into the house on the top of the high hill in Pacific Palisades. She had made a transition from being a person from a family of limited income and in financial trouble to being a person with a lover with the means and desire to provide whatever she requested.

And all of it had developed virtually overnight.

Abruptly, the Bryants found themselves not only shut out of their son's life but living in the house down the hill. The expensive staircase Pam had insisted on was now virtually useless.

"Honestly, I could understand her getting upset, because it happened so fast," the friend said. "This girl came in and took everything over and started dictating to Kobe."

The whole Bryant family drama had made its way to this unwinding moment, from Joe first pushing his son toward pro basketball and the money available there, to Pam becoming withdrawn and obsessed with her son's finances.

Over the course of the whole crazy chain of events, Kobe Bryant had been "very, very loving, very open and nice. I mean, always," said the friend.

But there was no way the experience would not change him. His life was a virtual convergence of control freaks, including his new fiancée, his increasingly devious and brilliant coach, his mother, and right on down the line. That he could survive and battle his way to success would have seemed almost miraculous except that Bryant was a world-class control freak himself.

His means of control began with his prodigious effort. Confident in his talent, he had sought to out-work every single person on the NBA landscape, including the big-dog worker himself, Michael Jordan. Another element that provided him control was his great will.

His decision to turn pro and the public response would have been plenty to swamp most people, most families, the friend observed. "A lot of it was negative. They all said he should stay in school and were criticizing Sonny for signing him to a deal. You know there was just a lot of negative stuff that happened."

The negative publicity seemed to be the first thing that pushed Pam Bryant into overprotection mode. "It gets overwhelming, what they're going through, what's happening," the friend said. "Nothing has prepared them for it."

Another huge adjustment came with the immense flow of cash, tens of millions, that came into their lives with Bryant's second contract with the Lakers. The new level of money seemed to elevate the stakes in every phase, according to family friends and acquaintances.

Sadly, what happened, the situation with the Bryants being changed and divided by the money "is a very common tale, a sad story true of so many families of pro athletes and celebrities," observed Michael "Big Mike" Harris, the marketing and promotional consultant who had helped the Bryants early in the process.

The circumstances had obviously changed both Pam and Joe Bryant as well. Seeing their son, with whom they were so close, begin to shut them out was difficult, especially since their relationship with his new fiancée was so fraught with conflict.

Pam Bryant adored her son, the family friend said, and her sense of losing that relationship was very difficult.

There is often an inverse equation regarding families dealing with an upsurge in wealth, like the Bryants: The greater the wealth the greater the insecurity and fear. These feelings wound up in Pam Bryant like a spring, friends and family observed. By numerous accounts, she lashed out at her son and his fiancée that summer.

"Maybe that's why she acted out," the friend observed. "She might have been possessive in doing all this. I have seen that with families, that they're very protective of their sons, and rightfully so in a lot of ways. People bring ideas and deals to kids that if somebody isn't there watching the door, a lot of bad things can happen."

The sudden change in their son's life had caught the Bryants off guard, the friend said. "They could just never recover from this."

The changes in Bryant with his new love would eventually affect nearly all of his relationships, but clearly the ties with his parents and sisters were the biggest losses.

"That's the mystery," Sonny Vaccaro said in 2015. "That's the illogical substance of this story. How did this little girl take over his mind? How did she bring this sudden change in this strong-willed individual? He destroyed every relationship he had over this girl."

Howard Beck had met Bryant's sisters and his high school coach in his two years covering the Lakers. Beck would go on to work for years covering the NBA, and in 2015 he looked back over the decades and could think of no other NBA player who'd introduced him to their family members. It just wasn't done. But Bryant had been the sort of wholesome kid to do just that. And then he did the same with his fiancée, introducing Beck to Laine in the team's training room, in the din of the championship celebration. "Kobe just had this blitzed-out look on his face, this goofy look, holding the trophy, and Vanessa's sitting there, and he introduced her.

"That night they were still just boyfriend and girlfriend, just engaged," Beck recalled. "She was just a young Orange County girl."

One media person who saw her that night was struck by how dramatically her looks would change over the coming months. "The next time I saw her, a year later, she looked like Angelina Jolie," the media figure observed.

In the wake of the engagement, Bryant suddenly appeared with a pierced ear, a change made at Laine's bidding.

"At least he didn't get tattoos," said sister Sharia of her clean-cut brother's new look. Those, of course, would be coming. For the time being, the pierced ear sounded enough alarm.

"When we in the media asked about it, he was really annoyed," Howard Beck recalled. "It always bothered him that these little things, these life changes or little stylistic changes, would become news in any way. We were just asking because we were curious. He was sensitive to that, maybe because he had gone so far to culti-vate such a squeaky-clean image. It was like he felt it was necessary because the squeaky-clean image just didn't fit him anymore, because he was growing out of it, maybe because he didn't think it served him well, maybe because he didn't think that he was getting enough respect, and he'd be right on that one, by the way. Too many people got caught up in the imagery of Iverson back then, just the idea of Iverson. So at that point, whether intentionally or just per-sonal growth, personal evolution, Kobe did take on a tougher kind of tone, both on the court and with the media at certain points."

He took a tougher tone with his shoe company as well. He began bringing Laine to his design meetings with Peter Moore, who had pushed on into the Audi design concept for Bryant's next shoe to the point that it didn't just look like a car but seemed almost made like one, with panels that covered the laces. "She didn't like Adidas at all," Moore recalled. "She didn't think Adidas was cool. She didn't think Adidas was appealing to the urban kid. That was the deal."

Laine seemed focused on hip-hop as a cultural, design ideal, as did Bryant, who seemed preoccupied with Iverson's popularity at the time and still interested in appealing to inner-city kids.

It didn't help that from the start, Adidas encountered production problems while trying to manufacture the new shoe. "There were things in there that at that time were unheard of," Moore recalled. "There's no seams. There are these panels that are, like, welded together. It was stiff as a board."

Eventually, Adidas would figure out how to manufacture the shoe, but not in time for the selling season, and not in time for its young promotional figure. Bryant did try. He would spend much of the season trying to get comfortable in his new-age shoes, just as he tried to figure a way to pull his family life together.

Almost no one in or around the Lakers knew what he was going through, though in time he would come to be seen in the quietest whispers of even his closest allies as a guy stuck between two very difficult people, his mother and Vanessa Urbieta Cornejo Laine.

The Power Struggle

For years, Jerry West had been threatening to leave the Lakers. He was far too obsessed with them to actually do that, of course. Finally, after years of being underpaid, he had gotten his large deal from Jerry Buss. But as the Lakers had made their way through the 2000 play-offs, word again leaked out that the great Jerry West would leave the team. In all likelihood, West was feeling quite the squeeze because his big, new salary was incongruous with the millions Buss was paying Phil Jackson. The team simply wasn't built to hand out that kind of money to nonplayers.

Certainly, someone would have to go, and circumstances pointed to West, who had spent little time around the team with Jackson as coach. Jackson had made sure of that by quietly employing the same rule that he had tried to use in Chicago to keep team management away from the players. Namely, he decreed that only team members, not management, could ride the bus. This served to keep not only West at arm's length but also GM Mitch Kupchak and Jim Buss, the owner's son, who had begun working in management. Rudy Garciduenas noted that Kupchak, a former Lakers player, mostly ignored the rule and got on the bus whenever he felt like it.

Jackson's rule was viewed as divisive in Chicago and would be quietly but hugely divisive in L.A. as well. By the spring, West seemed thoroughly detached from the proceedings. He had made appearances at a few play-off games, but he stayed away from many others, trusting one friend or another to keep him abreast of the score with a call to his cell phone.

Nonetheless, West was still communicating with Bryant and O'Neal on occasion, which was seen by Jackson as an attempt to undermine his efforts, according to staff members.

"Phil always felt that West was rooting for the Lakers to lose when Phil was there," explained Charley Rosen, Jackson's longtime friend, confidant, coauthor, and one-time assistant coach. Rosen described West as a man unhappy that Jerry Buss had granted Magic Johnson a minority ownership in the team while never giving West any such reward for his decades of dedication to the team.

It's unclear what started the animosity between Jackson and West, but Rosen said that part of it was Jackson's belief that West undermined him in alliance with Bulls executive Jerry Krause, Jackson's sworn enemy, who happened to be friends with West.

"Do you remember that rumor that Kobe was going to retire or Kobe wanted a trade?" Rosen asked. "West started that rumor and fed it to Jerry Krause, and Krause is the one who came out with it."

The NBA was such a rumor mill, it seemed almost impossible to follow such a strand, but the men who competed there were known to continue settling scores long after events had transpired.

But their rivalry likely had even deeper roots than that. Walt Frazier, Jackson's teammate with the New York Knicks, had disclosed in 2000 that Jackson once accidentally broke West's nose after a game between the Knicks and Lakers in the early 1970s, as the teams were walking off the floor. One of Jackson's notoriously errant elbows had been the culprit, Frazier recalled with a chuckle.

The incident served as something of a symbol of the dislike the two men reserved for each other, which was born in the championship rivalry that the Knicks and Lakers shared in the early 1970s, when the teams met three times for the title.

"West was Mr. Clutch," Rosen explained. "Phil doesn't think that West was such a clutch player, mainly because Frazier could contain him whenever the Knicks played. So Phil kind of downgrades West as being Mr. Clutch."

Envy, of course, ran in both directions, perhaps. West was the NBA logo. He was revered around the NBA by players, coaches, and team officials. Bryant's and O'Neal's feelings were indicative of the respect that West had earned.

For all his rings, Jackson had never enjoyed any of that. "Phil had a tendency to rub it in," Tex Winter said at the time, explaining Jackson's lack of popularity.

"I don't want to say Phil is arrogant," Rosen said, looking back in 2015, "although a lot of people do perceive him as being arrogant. I just see him as confident."

Yet, Rosen said, it was hard not to acknowledge that Jackson had created another impression around the NBA — namely, that he was particularly rough on the team executives who had to work with him.

"Given Phil's makeup and the way he sees things and how deeply he looks at things," Rosen said, "what general manager or president or whatever could he have had a real harmonious relationship with?"

Rosen offered the opinion that Jackson and West couldn't have continued to work together with the Lakers because of their conflicts and because Jerry Buss wasn't going to pay big money to both of them.

Jackson had gotten an unheard-of $8 million per year in his first Lakers contract, from a team notoriously cheap in paying everybody but players, a team that counted every paper clip.

"It stemmed from that," Rosen said, alleging that West was also resentful "that Phil is going to come in with all his rings and he's going to save the franchise, when West was supposed to be the savior of the franchise. You add that to what went on before, while they were playing against each other and all that kind of stuff. He resented Phil's success. How many Finals did West play in before he finally won a championship?"

Many of the team's longtime employees considered Rosen's allegations against West patently absurd. Still, the conflict was fascinating because both men were supremely competitive and both unbending perfectionists.

West stayed away from the office the entire summer of 2000 and offered little input on the personnel decisions the team would have to make. It was actually Jackson who announced West's departure in a July interview with broadcaster Larry Burnett.

In early August West issued a brief written statement that thanked many but made no mention of Jackson, even though the coach had just directed West's beloved Lakers to a championship.

At the time, news reports out of Los Angeles indicated West had been unhappy that spring that Jackson, after the breakup of his marriage to his wife, June, had taken up with Jeanie Buss, the owner's daughter and a longtime team executive.

A story soon broke that Jackson had asked West to leave the Lakers locker room just after a game had ended in the Portland series. Jackson, who liked to speak privately with his players for a few moments without interruption, told West that the group was having a team meeting. Jackson's carefully crafted implication was that West was no longer part of the team. Speaking later, Winter confirmed Jackson knew that West's pride would be hurt by being asked to leave the locker room.

"Only someone with six rings could have done it," former Lakers coach Del Harris said of Jackson's move against West.

Not surprisingly, West didn't show up for the press conference announcing his departure. "Obviously, Jerry West is irreplaceable," Jerry Buss, who also failed to appear, said in a prepared statement. "What he has meant to the Lakers' franchise over the past forty years is immeasurable."

Jackson's dislodging of West from the organization would later prove to have far-reaching implications. It left both Buss and new team vice president Mitch Kupchak wary of Jackson, for one.

"I think Mitch Kupchak was a little intimidated by Phil," Winter observed privately. "I think Phil did it on purpose, with his persona and his style. He's very strong willed, very overpowering, very intelligent. All you have to do is look at Phil's record and look at the people he's gone over, at how Phil has just willed himself over people."

Jackson had used the force of his personality in an attempt to control the entire Chicago Bulls roster, including the substantial egos of Jordan and team general manager Jerry Krause. In Los Angeles, the coach was in the process of attempting a similar feat. His defenders would later explain that it had to be done with both teams to corral the many stray forces into a championship unit.

West's departure also meant that Jackson had more sway over the team's personnel decisions. The Lakers needed a power forward, a backup center to give O'Neal some help. Sure enough, later in the off-season, Kupchak engineered a trade that sent disgruntled Glen Rice to New York while bringing in Horace Grant, one of Jackson's former players, to fill the team's need at power forward. Jackson was able to add another of his former players without the opposition from West that had prevented him from acquiring Pippen a year earlier.

Ups and Downs

Sufficiently stocked with talent, the Lakers set out in search of another title. Instead, they quickly found trouble early in the 2000–2001 season. O'Neal came into training camp way out of shape, a development that deeply disappointed Jackson and his assistants, not to mention the workout freak Bryant. However, O'Neal wasn't alone. Jackson would determine that, beyond Bryant, only forward Rick Fox had come into camp in shape and ready to play, a common occurrence on teams that had just won titles.

Then point guard Derek Fisher suffered a foot injury and was lost to surgery and rehab that would cost him three-fourths of the season. As assistant coach Bill Bertka explained, Fisher was the only Lakers guard who could provide pressure on the opponent's ball handler. Ron Harper had once been a ball-pressure factor, but he was in his last season and was simply too old, his knees too creaky. Bryant could pressure the ball, but it also made him vulnerable to foul trouble. The lack of defensive intensity only worsened the chemistry problems. O'Neal's lack of conditioning had left him vulnerable to injury and poor play. He started the season by missing shots that he usually made, frequently shooting less than

50 percent during key stretches. His free throws plunged into the 20 percent range, which made him a laughingstock around the league.

In the vacuum of O'Neal's struggles, Bryant made it known that he was ready to take over the offense, a development that was predictably met with complaints from O'Neal about Bryant's selfishness.

"Shaq started pouting," Winter fussed. "In effect he was saying to us, 'If I'm not the primary option on offense, don't expect me to work hard on defense.'"

Although he played well, Bryant himself struggled to find consistency. He would make just 8 of 31 shots in a home loss to Milwaukee, then hit 20 of 26 to score 45 points in a win at Houston. After the Houston win, Jackson compared him to Jordan, but O'Neal fumed that Bryant was trying to hog all the glory.

"I'm just going to play within the flow of the game," Bryant said. "If people want to criticize that, they're going to criticize that."

As the New Year neared, Bryant was leading the league in scoring and had drawn some praise as the game's best all-around player. Even Jackson was among the observers who acknowledged the growth.

"He's got a level of commitment to his game and to wanting to be the best that few guys have," said Scott Skiles, then the coach in Phoenix.

As 2001 opened, the Lakers were a team sitting at 22–10 and operating with an uneasy truce. Bryant confided to Winter that, despite his individual success, he was miserable and even had doubts about his love for the game. "Kobe said that he'd spent a lot of time working on his game in the off-season, working on his shots, working on his moves, and improving his game so he would have a chance to be the best player that he could possibly be," Winter said. "Then to come back and have people fault the efforts he made through the summer to make himself what he was, that was very discouraging to him.

"My wife, Nancy, indicated to me that she thought Kobe's heart had been broken at that particular point," Winter added.

The guard was demoralized by what he saw as a double standard. It started with the fact that Jackson seemed willing to overlook O'Neal's laziness. Because of O'Neal's extreme sensitivity to criticism, his shortcomings brought only mild rebukes. All the while, Jackson maintained his aggressive criticism of Bryant.

"I just woke up one morning and decided I wasn't going to let it affect me anymore," Bryant later explained.

However, there would be no deserting the fray. Bryant had already vented his frustration to the national media in a story that would appear on the January cover of *ESPN: The Magazine*. Bryant warned his teammates before the article came out and even tried to back off his tough talk. But there it was in print. In the article, he revealed that Jackson had come to him in November and asked him to back off his aggressive approach. Instead of backing off his game, he needed to step it up more, Bryant replied.

Angered by the comments, O'Neal told reporters that Bryant's selfishness was the main reason the team wasn't playing well.

Bryant dove right back in, countering that O'Neal still wasn't in shape and still wasn't playing defense. Jackson likened the two to little children arguing in a sandbox. The Lakers dropped four of their next seven games, bringing their record to fifteen losses, as many as they had the entire previous season.

By February, there were rumors that the center was again pushing to have Bryant traded. Although Bryant and an injured O'Neal appeared to be buddies at the All-Star Game in Washington, that was just for show.

March brought more trouble, first with a series of injuries to Bryant's shoulders and ankles, and then with a deepening of the rift between Jackson and Bryant. This was followed at the end of the month by Jackson making incendiary allegations against Bryant in an interview with Rick Telander of the *Chicago Sun-Times*. The coach revealed the contents of a private conversation with his star guard, then brought up an old rumor about Bryant "sabotaging" his team's high school games to make himself a game savior.

The comments infuriated Winter and Bryant, and brought a strong rebuke from Gregg Downer, who told reporters that Jackson needed to apologize for spreading a story that wasn't true. Arn Tellem reportedly turned to Jerry West for counsel about dealing with Jackson and even contemplated a slander lawsuit against the coach.

Reporters wondered if Jackson wasn't panicking as his team fell apart. Later, the coach would be accused of leaking to his old friend Sam Smith of the *Chicago Tribune* a story that the Lakers were considering trading Bryant in the off-season. To longtime observers, the move — the use of media messages to influence events — was a Jackson trademark.

The coach certainly enjoyed the bully pulpit. He was quickly booked on NBC's *Tonight Show*, where host Jay Leno asked if he wanted to announce a trade of Bryant right on the air. With another organization, a coach of Jackson's power might have been able to force the trade. But Bryant enjoyed a strong relationship with Jerry Buss, while O'Neal openly admitted he and the owner were not close. The owner had also distanced himself from Jackson, even though daughter Jeanie Buss was quite unabashed in her love of the coach.

It was just the kind of drama that delighted the Hollywood fan base.

"Jerry Buss stayed out of the way, at least openly," Tex Winter observed. "The coaching staff rarely saw hide nor hair of him. It was strange, but he was inclined to have a number of people on his payroll that he listened to."

Among those confidants, minority owner Magic Johnson was quick to offer views about the team's state of mind. "He's not going to get traded," Johnson told reporters when asked about Bryant. "Just point blank. Enough said. I definitely think it has put a strain on the organization. You never want an organization or a team to seem like it's divided, or guys jumping on sides and things like that."

Yet, just as Phil Jackson's own anxiety was at its height, Bryant's approach abruptly changed that spring, almost miraculously. He began to attempt to do less on the court, and found more as a result.

Things began to calm a bit with the March 13 return of Derek Fisher. He came out making jump shots, leading the team, and running the offense. More important, his return meant that the Lakers could get more pressure on the ball, a key to keeping the rest of the defense active.

It was during this stretch, with team anxiety at its highest, that Bryant sat out ten games with an assortment of injuries. The team went 7–3 in his absence, capped by a sweep of a four-game road trip in early April.

He sat back and quietly helped make quick arrangements for his last-minute wedding, then returned to the lineup to help the team close out the regular season with an eight-game victory streak.

Nuptials

Behind the scenes, the mood in Bryant's family had remained anxious all season. "He was so torn by that situation, so upset about the directions he was being pulled," said a family friend.

At one point in the conflict, Del Harris and his wife had gained word of Bryant's troubles, and Mrs. Harris had phoned Scoop Jackson to see if he couldn't reach out to Bryant and talk to him. Jackson had been stunned by the call. For sure, he and Bryant had connected, but it was for talks here and there, certainly no truly close relationship. Jackson had phoned one of Bryant's sisters to find out some details, then phoned Bryant himself to tell him that if he needed to talk, Jackson was there. Mostly, the moment struck the journalist as revealing just how much Kobe Bryant was on an island, just how sadly he was bereft of friendship.

Others chimed in. Phil Jackson had talked of him holding off on the wedding for a few years. Even Jordan and other athletes cautioned him to slow down and think about a prenuptial agreement.

"He just said, 'I can make the money back,'" one player told a reporter. "He was like, 'She can have it, because I'm young and I don't see it ending like that way anyway.'"

His agent, Arn Tellem, made the strongest pleas for a prenup. That was his duty as a financial adviser, but it would backfire. "He had money," Gary Charles said of Bryant. "He was not trying to hear what people were trying to say."

The wedding was preceded by a shower held by Pam and the Bryant sisters at their house.

"I was invited to the wedding shower," said the friend. "I did not go. But I know that became a catastrophe that whole day."

Two people who worked with the Bryants phoned the friend after the event and expressed concern. "They said there was just such coldness in the room between Pam and the two girls and his fiancée and her mother," the friend said, "and it just escalated, from what I heard from a couple of girls that were there. They said Pam was trying to smooth everything over because she 'blown the girl up' to Kobe quite a few times and then she had realized there was nothing she could do. He was going to get married."

Shortly before the wedding, however, Bryant took some drastic action with respect to his family that left those around him bewildered. He apparently shuttered his entertainment company, putting his family members—Bryant's sisters, an aunt, and Sharia's husband—and other employees out of work. He also sold his parents' house down the hill, which necessitated they move quickly. Fortunately, Pam and Joe still owned their home back in the Philadelphia suburbs, the one that they'd purchased with Joe's first big NBA deal. "That was a shock, what Kobe did," said the family friend. "I'll never understand why he did that."

Sonny Vaccaro remembered Joe Bryant immediately afterward on the phone to him, desperately looking for work. Agent Arn Tellem would soon be shown the door as well, and would help find the father some coaching work, Vaccaro said.

In one fell swoop, in the days before the 2001 play-offs began, Bryant had simply removed his family from his life. Friends heard stories from family members about Bryant changing phone numbers and refusing to take their calls. All the friends that had witnessed the tightness of the family over the years were taken aback when Joe called them with the news afterward.

"The Bryant family was a great love affair—Pam, Joe, Kobe, the grandparents, the sisters," Vaccaro observed. "He was like the Russians with the Romanovs. He got rid of them all."

"When Joe called and told me this, I fell off my chair," Gary Charles recalled. "I thought, 'What the hell happened here?' I just couldn't believe what I was hearing."

"Pam never thought it would come to what it came to," the family friend said. "A lot of families go through difficult times when their sons get married. Moms have a difficult time, and, with their son having all this money, you want them to marry the right person. But this was not a normal circumstance."

Far from it. Pam Bryant returned to Philadelphia that week only to have her world slammed by yet another painful turn of events when she learned that her father had been diagnosed with stage-four cancer, with a very short time to live.

Alienated from their son, Pam and Joe went through a tough time. "They had nothing," Vaccaro said. "Everything was gone." Even so, Joe was still trying to find ways to make ends meet. Joe had phoned Gary Charles and discussed his wife's state of mind while proposing a business idea. A friend said she had received the distinct impression that in the wake of the disintegration of her family, Pam Bryant had suffered a profound heartbreak.

"Joe was trying to become an agent," Charles recalled, "and he had called me and said, 'Hey, man, let's create magic again.'"

Meanwhile, in Southern California, the twenty-two-year-old Bryant and his eighteen-year-old bride selected the secluded St. Edward the Confessor Catholic Church in Dana Point, an hour south of L.A., for their wedding, on April 18. There were a dozen guests, none of them teammates, and there were no members of his immediate family in attendance. He wore a black suit, while she was attired in a full-length Vera Wang dress and adorned with an estimated $500,000 worth of jewelry. They walked over rose petals and under a heart-shaped arch and traded platinum-and-diamond wedding bands to seal the deal. Vanessa's band was reported to be five carats and Bryant's fifteen.

"They are sweet together and very much in love," remarked the Santa Monica jeweler who made the rings. "Vanessa helped design Kobe's wedding band. He just loves that she did that for him. There wasn't really a perfect time to do it. But they wanted to have a private, intimate moment together, and they succeeded."

The next day at practice, Bryant informed his teammates that he was now hitched.

Word spread about the marriage, but Bryant kept the ugliness with his family private. Some who worked closely with Bryant never learned of it until many years later.

As word leaked to the few friends who found out about what

happened with the Bryant family, some thought it seemed unfair that he had treated his mother so harshly. If Bryant seemed heroic in his dogged professional pursuits, he now struck many as an ingrate. "I think it's a sin," said one of his coaches, looking back. Others saw the move as consistent, no matter how severe.

"There were moments," Ric Bucher observed, "where you have this guy who's a ninja and the ultimate warrior, somebody who's just hardened and tough, and then he could be affected by falling in love with a hot chick in a video? I don't mean to disparage Vanessa in that way, but that's kind of what it was. I'm sure that their relationship evolved beyond that, but he was smitten with the chick in the video with the dark eyes. Like, what guy hasn't had that happen? The difference is, Kobe's going to move mountains and drain oceans to make sure that he gets the girl. He's going to alienate his family and anybody that gets in the fucking way. 'No, no, no, you don't understand. I want her. I'm in love with her. Shut the fuck up. You don't know me.' Arn Tellem tried to talk a prenup to him. He was lovesick, man. He didn't want to hear any of that."

Vaccaro offered a simpler explanation for why Bryant did what he did, looking back. "He's insane."

Certainly the head-on collision between his burning new love and the emotional attachment to his family may have produced a temporary insanity of sorts, or at least a desperation.

George Mumford himself would dismiss such extreme notions, looking back. Bryant was a young man with a need to create the emotional space in which to live his very different life. He may have been brutally and desperately clumsy in angrily reacting to his mother. But it was hard for any outsider to see the pressures and expectations and disappointments that build up within family relationships. Just because Bryant was a high-profile figure didn't mean he wasn't prone to the same issues that bring similar ruptures to other families and relationships every day.

Whatever Bryant's motivations were for cutting his family off, it was clear that even when he was faced with two immovable personalities in his mother and his wife, his top priority remained his career.

After all, the play-offs were beckoning.

Chapter 23

BROKEN ANKLES, SHATTERED HEARTS

Somehow Kobe Bryant managed to turn all the pent-up emotion wrought by his family's hidden disintegration into an exceptional emergence in the 2001 NBA play-offs. What's more, he did it on a day's notice.

That had hardly seemed possible, based on both his team's and family's tremendous conflict and turmoil that season. But Bryant had quietly found strength from the practices of mindfulness and tai chi with George Mumford. A writer had first introduced Mumford to Bryant before a game in Houston late in his dismal third pro season. Bryant had been immediately suspicious and asked incredulously, "Phil Jackson actually uses precious practice time to have his players meditate?" Later, when Jackson brought Mumford to California with him to begin work with the Lakers, Bryant was at first resistant to any sort of "mind control."

Jackson called it "strengthening the muscle of the mind," and wanted his players to learn meditation with Mumford, so that they could breathe and deal with their collective panic in big games. The macho nature of many NBA players led them to deny there was any such thing as panic in the high-pressure circumstances, or even pressure at all.

Jordan, however, had talked of learning with Mumford how to

"be in the moment" during games, a key factor in the Chicago star's final three championships. That, in itself, prompted Bryant to begin taking Mumford seriously.

By the end of his second season with Jackson, Bryant had been practicing meditation and mindfulness for more than a year with Mumford and the team. That spring, as he executed a furious rupture in his personal life, all the while attempting to excel professionally, he turned tremendous focus to the task of "being in the moment."

That, he would reveal later, became part of his means of surviving, then thriving. He somehow, almost inconceivably, managed to block out everything, including the painful news about his grandfather Cox, a quietly precious figure in his life. The elder Cox stood as a man of tremendous accomplishment in a generation of black males who had been denied by American culture at every turn. Both his grandfathers possessed sharp, perceptive minds. But the elder Cox had been an athlete as well, and he absolutely adored his grandson, a relationship built long before Bryant became famous. The personality traits that Bryant shared with his mother, the intelligence and instinct, were likewise shared with John Cox II.

The discipline of the mindfulness had allowed him to cope.

"You're drained," Bryant explained later, "because you have so many emotions, a combination of hurt and pain that I refused to let myself feel, because I had to stay in the moment."

There were other factors in the mix. Bryant's new wife was quietly devout, just as his mother was, which helped bolster his own belief. In those early seasons, even before he met her, he had made occasional reference to his faith. He said he clearly found comfort and strength in Vanessa there as well.

Even if he could have forgotten the unsolvable condition of his personal life, the ever-present fundamental gap within the team remained another huge stone weighing on him. Still, Bryant's change in play after returning from his ankle injuries, and the winning streak on which the Lakers ended the season, did present some hope.

For years, various figures—Jerry West, Del Harris, Kurt Rambis, even Jackson with all his new-age devices—had sought a means of bringing the Lakers' two divided stars together. Even journalist J. A. Adande had tried his hand at it, first approaching O'Neal about joining him in a meeting with Bryant to put things on the table. The center said he would do it if Bryant would. Adande then approached Bryant, who promptly declined.

"See?" O'Neal told Adande.

That spring, a member of Jackson's staff had gone so far as to reach out to another journalist covering the team to warn, "You better talk to your boy to get him under control."

The journalist replied that he wouldn't even attempt such a thing. Bryant was young, but he was his own man, kept his own counsel. Yet, just as Phil Jackson's own anxiety was at its height, Bryant's approach abruptly changed that spring, almost miraculously. He began to attempt to do less on the court, and found more as a result.

Certainly his family situation played into it. But Chip Schaefer, the former Chicago Bulls trainer who was now a competitive coordinator with the Lakers and had begun to grow close with Bryant, saw a much simpler answer.

"He had, like, a chronic problem," Schaefer recalled. "He sprained both ankles in different episodes that spring, and he was getting frustrated until we kind of turned the corner with that and he was healthy again."

He became less of a ball stopper in the triangle, more concentrated on running the Shaq-focused offense, more patient and less insistent on his own agenda.

Schaefer had first noticed the change in a late regular-season contest at Milwaukee. With his ankle troubles, Bryant shot poorly but had 8 assists. The Lakers lost, but something had changed. "Sometimes for a guy that relies that much on athleticism, to have to pump the brakes a little bit is even a good thing," Schaefer said, looking back. "He did start playing well. I think he probably played differently because of the injuries."

The issue of Bryant's ankles, combined with much preaching and pleading from the assembled chorus, pulled Shaq and Kobe just close enough that May. At one point during the tumultuous spring, West had reportedly told O'Neal, "I played with two of the all-time greats, Wilt Chamberlain and Elgin Baylor. You don't think we had personal rivalries going on back then? You've got to stop being a baby. Put all this personal stuff aside and do what's important. Put the team's success first."

Bryant was also growing a bit in his ability to laugh at himself. For example, he had introduced Howard Beck to one of his high school coaches by saying, "This is the guy who taught me not to pass the ball."

"And then he laughs," Beck recalled. "Kobe could make fun of himself back then. Kobe could poke fun, and I always appreciated his self-deprecating aspect and his self-awareness. He knew the image that was being formed of him in the public eye, especially with some of Shaq's early shots and everything else."

O'Neal, too, played his role in the change and had actually begun easing off his hard line that spring. "In the last two or three days, I've heard Shaq say, 'I've rededicated myself.' To me, that's big," Magic Johnson told reporters as the tumult began to calm. "I've heard all the other stuff. But now, Shaq is saying, 'It's me. I'm the one who has to get into shape. I'm the one who has to be ready for the second-half run. I'm the one who has to close the middle down like I did last year. I'm the one who has to do it.' You see, now he's saying what he has to do. He's not blaming everybody else."

First, Mumford pointed out, things between Bryant and O'Neal weren't quite as bad as they had been perceived. Beyond his connection with Bryant, Mumford had a good relationship with O'Neal and worked quietly behind the scenes for months, patiently dealing with chemistry issues. The team's mind-set was about healing, even as tempers flared.

"We learned some things," Jackson said, "through some real hard lessons."

Another factor was the visual learning emphasized by the coach. With his arrival in Los Angeles, Jackson had directed that the locker room be expanded and outfitted with extensive video equipment, including a spacious viewing room for the team. Not only were teaching tapes viewed each morning before practice, players were encouraged to make individual use of the room to study, as Bryant had done so fervently on his own since coming to the NBA.

To prepare his team to face a slate of Western Conference teams with strong power forwards in the play-offs, Jackson spliced scenes of *Gladiator* in and around the scouting tapes he showed the team. Jackson was implying that at each turn, the team, like the gladiators thrown together in the film, would have to turn to the gate of the arena and face whatever challenge appeared next.

"The reality is, this is kind of a gladiator's life—here today, gone tomorrow," the coach explained. "And you've got to develop that teamwork and that team play, and that's really the challenge of coaches right now and of teams.

"We know what we are. We know what we're built on. We're built on the fact that Kobe and Shaq are the best one-two combination in the game, and the complementary players around them want to play as a team and want to figure in this."

O'Neal averaged 33.7 points over the final eleven games of the regular season. He was now in shape and playing defense as well as offense. It was enough to build confidence in Bryant.

"It's going to make things a lot easier," Bryant told reporters. "Then he and I can just run screen and roll. You're going to have to pick your poison."

Portland, Sacramento, and San Antonio all found themselves facing that choice. The Lakers swept all three on the way to an 11–0 run to the NBA Finals.

For Rudy Garciduenas, the Lakers equipment manager, the standard had always been the great Showtime teams. For much of the newer Lakers staff, including Schaefer, the standard had been their time in Chicago with Jordan's Bulls. But for Schaefer and Garciduenas, both pro-basketball lifers, the spring of 2001 provided an amazing experience as they watched the "Shaq-Kobe Lakers" come together in such dramatic fashion.

"We just caught fire late in that year," Schaefer recalled of the twenty-five straight games the club won throughout April and into the play-offs. "Even including Chicago, I've never seen a team play that well for that stretch where we didn't lose a game."

The success highlighted the role players who stocked the Lakers roster. Due to O'Neal's huge salary, Jerry Buss had been unwilling to pay for a third star, which meant that role players had to hit big, often wide-open shots, which they did.

"I mean, guys were just shooting lights-out," Schaefer said. "Brian Shaw hitting threes, Robert Horry hitting threes, Rick Fox hitting threes. They were in a rhythm that was just ridiculous. You wanted to bottle it. We just were so good."

Their success, in turn, prompted Bryant to work as a playmaker, then pick the right situation for exploding in big offensive games. His first such explosion came in Game 3 of the second round against Sacramento, a 103–81 Lakers win that saw him score a play-off career high of 36 points. The Kings were keying on O'Neal, who had scored 87 points in the first two games.

"Shaq came up to us and said, 'Don't worry about me, you guys just do whatever it takes,'" Bryant told reporters afterward. That proved to be all the green light he needed.

In Game 4, he set another career high, 48 points in forty-eight minutes on 15 of 29 from the floor, with a startling 16 rebounds and 3 assists. "He was possessed," Sacramento coach Rick Adelman said. "Even when he missed shots, he got them back."

Bryant was still aloof, but he had spoken to his teammates in the best way that he could that day. "His enthusiasm infuses this basketball club," Jackson observed. "That's a real important factor to remember, that he's got the energy, the drive, the moxie, and also a feel, an uncanny instinctual feel, for this basketball game that's really showing."

The staff had known the talent was there for such a performance. Still, to see it happen was a reward for Jackson and Winter, who had grown accustomed to Jordan making such showings almost seem routine in Chicago.

Bryant's momentum again surged in Game 1 of the Western Conference finals, a 104–90 Lakers blowout of the Spurs in San Antonio. Hitting 19 of 35 shots, Bryant had another 45, to go with O'Neal's 28.

"You're my idol," O'Neal said afterward. When the media questioned his sincerity, O'Neal insisted he was serious.

Despite their many efforts, the Lakers coaches had known that any real bonding between the two would have to come from their finding success in big games together. Such feelings were often transient but over time could create something better, a base of trust. That was always the best hope for team chemistry.

As Bryant and O'Neal played brilliantly, the Lakers pushed their way to another blowout, 111–82, and swept the series from Tim Duncan and San Antonio to play again for the title.

Lakers forward Rick Fox said, "It's very evident now that we all have learned to respect each other as players and to enjoy each other's company and understand how much we can make each other better."

In a darker take on the matter, a member of Jackson's staff credited the veteran role players more than the stars for the play-off wins. "One of the main reasons they won the titles was the surrounding cast. The team's two major talents were so eaten up with narcissism that it was the veteran leadership that made the difference at all the key moments. Harper was a leader on the floor, Horry was an intellectual leader, Fox stepped up and helped the team find its emotional level, and Shaw was a spiritual leader. Those guys should get a lot of the credit."

If the Lakers hadn't had to wait day after day following their sweeps of the Western Conference for a drawn-out, seven-game series between Philadelphia and Milwaukee, they might well have been able to keep that momentum to accomplish the first unbeaten slate in play-off history, Schaefer observed. Instead, they had to wait almost two weeks before the Finals began.

Their championship-series opponent was none other than Allen Iverson and the Sixers, who were making Philly's first trip to the NBA Finals since Moses Malone and Julius Erving had steamrolled their way to the league title in 1983.

Bryant's competitive urges soared out of control as Game 1 approached. In press comments, he acknowledged that Philly was his hometown but pointed out that the Sixers were now the enemy.

He had come out full of fire in Game 1 in Los Angeles and promptly tried to do too much, which left him absolutely furious with himself after Iverson scored 48 points and Philly claimed the first contest in overtime. Just like that, the great run had come to an end, and much of the blame was pointed at Bryant's competitive urges.

He recognized that and pulled himself back in line as the Lakers claimed Game 2. He got off to a quick start, scoring 8 of the Lakers' first 14 points. He finished with 12 in the first quarter, 16 at the half, and a game-high 31 total, along with 8 rebounds and 6 assists.

"I didn't want to come out and try to do too much to start the game and take us out of the rhythm of our offense," he said afterward, still smarting from his Game 1 mistakes.

The series then headed east for three more games. Before Game 3, the fans in First Union Center had chanted, "Ko-be...! Ko-be...!"

But any affection would soon disappear as the Lakers seized control. "Kobe made shots with guys' hands in his face," Iverson said. "When guys are hitting jump shots, there's not much you can do about it."

At one point, he and Iverson engaged in an animated conversation that drew Derek Fisher and the officials to break them apart. "He's doing whatever he has to do to inspire his team," Bryant said of Iverson. "But I don't care. We're here, we're the world champions. No matter how inspired your team may be, the championship has to come through the city of Los Angeles."

Bryant had invited his old nemesis Donnie Carr to that first game in Philly. Delighted, Carr watched Bryant in amazement and thought back to that first time when he saw the odd-looking kid from Italy in the Sonny Hill Future Stars League, with the big knee pads and the skinny legs.

"I remember he gave me some tickets and he gave me a backstage pass," Carr recalled. "I was backstage with him. He invited me back there. He was just like, 'Man, it's an unbelievable feeling playing for a team like this, we making history.' It was like he was at a different place, man. Everything was, like, you know, happening for him, so he was just like, 'Wow!'"

Carr also noticed that Bryant was all alone, that he was apparently paying a big price for this exalted view of the basketball landscape. "But at the end of the day, that was Kobe," Carr observed. "He always had a vision. I don't think he ever thought it would be that bad, like there wasn't nobody around with him. But he was determined to be at that place, man, to be the best. And I tell people all the time, I mean, for me, meeting him the first time to see him with two knee pads on, to seeing him as the best player in the world, I was just like, 'Wow, that's unbelievable, man.'"

Despite the moment with Carr, Bryant spent most of the week in Philadelphia sequestered in his hotel room, although he did take several calls from his favorite cousin, John Cox IV. "He basically stayed in his room," Cox told the *Tribune*'s Donald Hunt. "I think everybody knows Philly is a rough town. Plus he plays for the Lakers. I asked him if he was ready to deal with the fans. He said he expected things to be rough.

"It's been a long season for him," Cox said.

"I know he likes being a star and all," Robert Horry told reporters, "but sometimes, there is no way I would want to be Kobe Bryant."

In Game 4, O'Neal scored 34 points, and Bryant fell just shy of a triple-double with 19 points, 10 rebounds, and 9 assists as Los Angeles prevailed, 100–86.

"We're getting into a rhythm and starting to get our flow back, and no matter what kind of a run the Sixers throw at us we're going to bounce back," Bryant said.

The day before Game 5, in the media session, a reporter asked how he could still play for Jackson, with their issues. "Well, we just put it behind us…to the point where we actually joke about it," he said.

He cited a recent team scrimmage during which his team took a large lead and Jackson sat him down, which prompted Bryant to request that he be put back in so that he could "sabotage" things and make the score tight, so that he could again be a hero. His quip supposedly drew laughs from his teammates, but it all seemed a bit forced, considering that Jackson's comments about Kobe doing the same thing in high school were still fresh.

That same day, he made a passing remark to a fan in the arena that the Lakers were going to "cut the heart" out of the Sixers for Game 5. The remark was overheard by a veteran Philly sportswriter and reported, which served to inflame the city's sporting public.

For the final game, the fans reserved a special vitriol for Bryant, sending a chorus of boos to greet his every move. O'Neal powered his way to 29 points and 13 boards as the Lakers closed out the series in Game 5, 108–96. Bryant answered the boos with 26 points, 12 rebounds, and 6 assists, then exploded at the buzzer, jumping around and cradling the ball in one arm while shooting his other high in the air as a sign of dominance. It was an instant release in response to all those in his hometown who had demeaned him.

But NBA officials managing the event seemed concerned about the Lakers' celebrating on the floor in front of angry Philly fans and hustled the team quickly into the cramped, musty locker room, where Bryant's celebratory mood instantly dissolved. He retreated to the nearby handicapped stall as his teammates celebrated riotously.

"They're all in a big scrum, arms around each other in a circle and jumping up and down doing that," Howard Beck recalled, "and then they all started pouring champagne. Shaq had the championship hat on, head back, eyes closed, champagne spraying in his face, and that was the group.

"Kobe was sitting down by himself," Beck recalled. "I was the first one to walk over there. Like, he's just sitting there silent, looking down at the floor."

The moment he had fixated upon for days was now past, and the emotion of all the events came rolling in all at once, a great tide of recognition: his sadness over his grandfather, his joy at his marriage, his mixed feelings over his family, his happiness at how the team had played, his defiance against all those people in his hometown who had been against him from his earliest days.

Beck noticed that just about all the other media had surrounded the celebration scene with the team, and there was Bryant, alone.

"I walked over to him kind of cautiously, thinking, 'I don't want to interrupt some important reflective personal moment here,'" the writer recalled. "So I want to talk to him, I want to congratulate him. I want to see what's on his mind. I want to get some thoughts for my story. I'm trying not to intrude. I'm standing to the side of him, to his right, with my notepad out, waiting just for a moment for him where he's going to look up and acknowledge me and say it's cool to talk."

"I was too tired to come up with any conclusions," Bryant would say later, looking back. "I had a lot of things going on, man. It was a long season. I was drained. I was exhausted emotionally, physically, mentally."

It was then that Bryant's teammates tried to roust him out of an almost catatonic state. "Some of the players start coming over, spraying champagne," Beck recalled.

An NBA photographer would bring the trophy over and put it in Bryant's arms to stage a shot. Bryant almost seemed not to notice at first. His chest and shoulders quivered. He was releasing himself from the concentration and focus that allowed him to keep playing despite his personal trauma. "Oh, man," he told himself as he began to come back into focus. "I don't have to do that no more."

Later, when his uncle Chubby Cox and his aunt had quietly greeted him in the locker room, the full release came with his quiet sobbing.

"The hurt from the season was still there," he would say months later, looking back. "You're trained to stay in the moment and not think about that. You're always from one moment to the next, to the point where you can't enjoy the successes you've had. And you can't think of the pain that you went through before."

For days after Bryant returned to Los Angeles, his reception in his hometown continued to play on his mind, to the point that a week later he phoned a writer from the *Philadelphia Daily News* in an effort to make amends and explain himself. He knew he didn't want to stir up yet more anger and resentment. He said he considered all the booing of fans a Philly compliment, because that's how the city was.

"You can tell the Sixer fans they can boo me all they want," Bryant told the *Daily News*. "You know what, the whole thing is I can't help what people think about me. That's not what I'm trying to do. They can say whatever they want to say about me. But the fact of the matter is I come from Philadelphia. It's where I honed my basketball skills. You can take that however you want to take that. If you still think of me as a sellout, then think of me as a sellout. But I am always going to give props to where I honed my competitive skills, and that was in Philadelphia."

He said he had even encountered Sonny Hill at the arena and

was reminded of the old days and promised Hill's league an $8,000 donation, inspired by his own number 8 jersey.

"The Future League is what got me started, playing against the top players in Philadelphia," he said. "That league is all about the up-and-coming players in Philadelphia all competing against each other. We'd have games there all day long. It was West Philadelphia versus North Philadelphia and South Philadelphia. The Future League helped my career so much. I just wanted to give back to it."

Having made those concessions, he was hoping that would be enough, that he could have peace with his hometown.

In Los Angeles, as the city delighted in a new championship, it seemed that all was well with the Lakers, that their turbulence and infighting had settled down.

Yet on the eve of the league-championship series, Tim Brown of the *Los Angeles Times* had written a story about Jerry West working behind the scenes to help Bryant deal with the ugly situation that had unfolded over the spring.

The story reportedly infuriated Jackson and some of his associates because it seemed that West was claiming credit for the turnaround. Jackson wondered if West had leaked the story to the media.

Bryant himself offered a further dig at Jackson by showing up at the team's championship celebration wearing a number 44 West jersey. It seemed a small thing, but it was a powerful, emotional tribute to the Lakers great as well as a statement of defiance. "Oh man," Bryant told the media. "Jerry West was my mentor. And with everything that went on this season—he meant so much to me."

West, in an interview with T. J. Simers of the *Los Angeles Times*, was gracious in his comments, saying, "When basketball is played correctly with good players it is something great to see. It looks easy, but it's not. That's a tribute not only to the players, but to Phil Jackson and his staff, who got the players to buy into what they wanted. That's Phil's plan, having all the players touch the ball, and watching everyone contribute—that's how basketball should be played."

West said it because it was exactly true.

There was even cautious hope that the mood might be maintained. Bryant knew better. "We're happy," he said with a smirk, "until next January, when people start talking about trading one of us."

And Now

There was much wreckage to be addressed in the wake of triumph and tragedy. Bryant faced major adjustments at every turn, not the least of which was his long-term alienation from the family he had once held so dear. But first, he and Vanessa celebrated their marriage and the championship at a Southern California theme park. Having had no time for a honeymoon, they took in the cheap thrill of the rides as what they were, just two kids with their hair in the wind.

At first, his mother's and father's entreaties were met with only Bryant's silence. "He was capable of ignoring people," recalled the family friend, "and sometimes that's more of a torcher than anything else. When somebody ignores you, that's just as harmful as someone yelling at you."

Bryant began making plans to sell the home high above Pacific Palisades, with all its sad memories, to move south of Los Angeles to another grand home, and to buy yet another place, for his mother-in-law, nearby.

The many changes in his life would soon enough draw the attention of the *L.A. Times,* which eventually produced an unflattering profile of his young wife. The newspaper quoted extended family members on the record about the severity of her personality. There would be other conflicts in the couple's path, with various figures around his basketball life, including one that reportedly resulted in the dismissal of longtime personal trainer Joe Carbone, plus a lawsuit by a former housekeeper aimed at Vanessa's treatment of her.

"Nobody tells me anything positive about her from people that work in the Lakers arena," the family friend said in 2015. "There's just nothing. It's too bad. Everybody would say to me 'Oh, he doesn't realize what he's doing.' No, he definitely knows. He can't be an idiot about what's happened to his family. He definitely knows, and he's fine with it."

The relentless public scrutiny aside, time would prove Vanessa to be a loyal and stabilizing factor in Bryant's turbulent world. She could have walked away at several points with many tens of millions.

Instead, despite her youth and quick temper, she made her way as his wife and then as a mother.

Blaming her for the family breakup didn't address the fact that hard feelings had developed with the Bryants long before she entered his life. She had little to do with Kobe's disappointment with his father, Sam Rines pointed out. And friends had seen Bryant's slowly building anger with his mother long before Vanessa entered the picture. Bryant, in turn, had responded with his own anger. As one close adviser to Bryant pointed out, smothering maternal love can lead to alienation.

As for the entertainment company he shut down, it had become a burden that had served its purpose. Sharia's husband and Kobe's new brother-in-law, Jerrod Washington, was viewed by all as immaculate in his performance at the company. He had been especially good in managing all the many tasks and relationships involving the music industry as Bryant worked into the wee hours in 1999 to finish the recording, which had run way over budget.

Scoop Jackson had tried to warn him. The hip-hop hoops writer also covered music. There was so much bad product in the business, many people falsely assumed it was easy. "We talked about it briefly," Jackson recalled. "I remember telling him, 'Look, man, your shit better be tight.'"

The poor reception at All-Star Weekend had been a huge, unexpected blow. "He put it in perspective," Scoop Jackson offered. "You need to respect the ground that everybody else walks on. He didn't treat music the way he did basketball. It's a different investment. You can have supreme confidence, but you can't go in there thinking if you want to do this at a higher level, it takes less than what you put into basketball."

Bryant pulled the plug on the planned release of the recording, which in turn led to a host of expensive legal entanglements with Sony and various parties.

Though the cancellation of the record release was the entertainment company's main focus, there were other projects it had worked on before it was shuttered. To his credit, Joe had worked some deals for the company. And Bryant's sisters had more than earned their keep, managing Bryant's fan club and his coordination with the many endorsement partners and their needs. His aunt, likewise, had shown many strong skills in her efforts there. The business itself, Vaccaro and Rines explained, had been built from the early idea of Team Bryant.

True, Bryant had shut it all down, terminated it in anger, but his decision was far from a whim. The entire dynamic of his life had built to a crescendo of confusion and frustration and anger. Each of the factors had seemingly fed into his explosive decision to empty his life of his family.

Early that fall, his grandfather Cox passed away, bringing Bryant and his wife to Philadelphia for the service. Vanessa was eager to see his home place in the suburbs, which brought an awkward reengagement with his family and some healing, although Bryant's sisters remained angry with him for the caustic interruption of their lives. Bryant and his wife appeared at the service with their bodyguards in tow, which added to the friction, as did the appearance of his old girlfriend from Philadelphia.

But the funeral allowed him to make at least minimal reassurances with his family. He remained close to his grandmother Cox and comforted her with talk of his love and continued support.

He also arranged a modest payment to his sisters for their interrupted employment and trauma, but their business relationship had ended. Pam Bryant also negotiated her own modest settlement with her son and apparently got him to agree to purchase a property in Las Vegas for Joe and her to live in.

The relationship would never be the same, but at least it was better—for the time being. With his help, his family would settle in Las Vegas, where they would occupy a modest home and a modest life while Joe worked piecemeal coaching jobs, spending time in the WNBA with the Sparks as well as in Asia, from the Philippines to Japan, cobbling a living together with a mishmash of low-hanging options, some of them even aided by Arn Tellem. The sisters would both take employment in Las Vegas as well.

Around the same time, Joe Bryant had apparently still been working on one last grand plan for his son. Aware of his growing dissatisfaction with Adidas, Joe had begun pursuing another option, which, surprisingly, appealed to Kobe when he told him about it. Joe had reportedly made contacts to help him find a new shoe deal, a complicated process that would take some time.

After he dropped Arn Tellem in a move that produced yet more intense emotion and a sense of betrayal and anger, Bryant took up with Rob Pelinka, whom Vaccaro described as the lowest man on the totem pole in Tellem's office. Bryant was an immense prize for an agency to lose, an anchor for an array of businesses. That summer he would be identified as the top product endorser by none other than *SportsBusiness Daily* for his deals pitching Adidas, Sprite, and McDonald's burgers. His decision was a crushing blow to Tellem, and the agent's good friend Vaccaro would describe him as filled with bitterness about Bryant for years to come.

A young lawyer who had been a three-point specialist on Michigan's Fab Five teams, Pelinka was said to have insight into issues of the game itself. Bryant found it easier to connect with a younger agent willing to put into effect what he wanted without having to go around and around about it. Most of all, it was Pelinka's basic shrewdness that appealed to Bryant. The star likewise possessed the same sort of shrewd nature that had once allowed his grandfather to prosper in the intense vagaries of the Philadelphia Fire Department.

Pelinka would clear out the clutter of the many smaller, additional relationships in Bryant's life, since he had his young bride and they treasured their privacy. Sam Rines cited the immense challenge, after all the changes had been made, of even getting a pair of Lakers tickets when Rines's AAU team was on the West Coast. "When Rob Pelinka came in, he just blocked everybody," Rines remembered. "I just wanted tickets. I didn't need to talk to him. I didn't need to hang out with him. Two tickets, I would have been cool. But you know what? He was intimidating. God forbid Sam Rines talks to Kobe. Pelinka got you out of that loop, made it impossible for you to talk to him, made it impossible to hang out with him."

According to family friend Anthony Gilbert, in the aftermath of the changes, the only real glue holding the family together would prove to be older sister Sharia, who became something of a surrogate mother for Bryant, one satisfied with moving on with life with no real agenda other than her own family and keeping the lines of communication with her brother open.

"Sharia didn't like to talk about what had happened," Gilbert recalled. "She would just say that it was a really difficult time, that she was just torn, you know. Like she's sitting there left to pick up all the pieces."

The Changed World

The Lakers entered training camp with a different mood that fall of 2001. After the attacks on the World Trade Center in September and the subsequent calls for national unity, it hardly seemed appropriate for the world's best basketball team to engage in unrestrained pettiness and infighting. And so they didn't. It didn't hurt that there were two new championship banners that they could hang in Staples Center, proof that working together brought results. Scheduled to play a series of exhibition games in Japan, the Lakers saw those plans altered by travel concerns. Derek Fisher again injured his foot and required another surgery and another long recovery. O'Neal injured a toe, which required surgery and meant that he would miss training camp. Jackson himself missed much of training camp due to the death of his ninety-four-year-old mother, and Bryant had retreated to Philadelphia to bury his grandfather.

The circumstances only served to pull the team closer together, O'Neal told reporters. Even so — Jackson reminded his players, the fans, and media — that team would have to prove its chemistry all over again in 2002 if his players wanted to join the elite NBA teams that had won a third straight title.

If anything would prove a problem for the Lakers in 2002, it was the new zone defenses, which rule changes allowed for the first time in league history. Although he sat out with his toe injury, O'Neal watched with anger as teams began experimenting with new defensive schemes. He knew those zones would be used to corral him as soon as he returned from injury.

Indeed, the moment would be one of the milestones marking

the declining role of the big man in American professional basketball, as the game made its way toward pace and space.

On the personnel front, guard Ron Harper retired. His presence had helped Bryant and O'Neal resolve their differences. He would be sorely missed. The team replaced power forward Horace Grant, who left for Orlando in free agency, with Samaki Walker, a free agent from San Antonio. Also in camp as a free agent was Dickey Simpkins, who once played for Jackson with the Bulls. The coaches prized him, but the forward had a nonguaranteed contract. Buss wasn't about to cut a player with guaranteed money to keep a second-line forward, so he didn't make the final roster.

At guard, the Lakers brought in Lindsey Hunter from Milwaukee to help with shooting and point-guard play while Fisher recovered. Another key issue was the development of swing player Devean George, long considered a talent by the Lakers coaches. The same was true for power forward Slava Medvedenko, an intriguing offensive player limited by language barriers.

Mostly, the scoring load would fall to O'Neal and Bryant again, only this time they had a better view of things. "I'm not going to say he's turned 180 degrees," Jackson said of Bryant in December. "But there's certainly been a 90-degree swing of character, from his receptivity to his communication with his teammates and the working people in the organization."

With O'Neal suspended for a game on January 14, Bryant scored 56 points in just three quarters against Memphis in Staples Center, hitting 21 of 34 field goal attempts. "That was one of the most incredible things you'll probably ever see," Robert Horry said afterward. "Words can't describe what that cat did tonight. He was unreal."

The emotional moment of the season came at the All-Star Game, played in Philadelphia, of all places, where Bryant would score 31 points and earn most valuable player honors, only to be booed vigorously by the fans. The response seemed incongruous to the larger NBA television audience. Many observers would explain it as the residue of Bryant's battle with the Sixers in the NBA Finals, months earlier. But there was another hidden reason. The city's basketball community, with Sonny Hill as its mayor, was a tight group. Word of what Bryant had done to his family had spread through the grapevine as Joe unburdened himself to friends about the situation. Fans in the city didn't know all of the details of the breakup, but to them, it was just further evidence that Bryant was a monumentally spoiled jerk.

As he left the floor with the boos cascading down, he met Scoop Jackson. "I was the first person he saw when they booed him off the stage and he came back in the tunnel," Jackson recalled. "That's when he broke down and started crying. He couldn't understand it. He kind of pulled over to the corner."

Jackson stepped over and gave him a hug.

"It's going to be all right," the journalist told him.

"Scoop, I don't understand it," Bryant said through his tears.

"He was standing there literally with the trophy in his hand," Jackson recalled.

The journalist consoled him, telling him that it often takes the public a long time to understand an athlete. Look how long it took for Muhammad Ali to find understanding, Jackson pointed out.

"I was trying to console him," Jackson explained. "That's the first time I'd ever seen anything get to him. That got to him. We were literally standing there for five minutes, and he straightened the fuck up. I was, like, hitting him in the chest and saying, 'Fuck, man, they don't get it. They'll get it one day.'"

It was clear that Bryant in no way understood the antipathy of his hometown. It was as if the young star expected to be treated like family, Jackson said, adding, "We're all family."

Then again, that may have been what was happening. The angry crowd was treating Bryant like family.

Three-Peat

Though the Lakers struggled a bit through the regular season, it remained by far their most harmonious from a chemistry standpoint. They would manage fifty-eight wins entering the play-offs. They again swept Portland in the first round, then faced the Spurs in the conference semifinals for the second straight season. Again, Bryant delivered the key blows just as it seemed that the Spurs were about to force the issue. The Lakers took a 2–1 edge in the series, but San Antonio seized control in the second half of Game 4 in the Alamodome and had a 10-point lead with just under five minutes left.

Bryant answered by scoring 10 points in the final five minutes, his last 2 on a rebound and put-back with 5.1 seconds left, to push the Lakers to an 87–85 win and a 3–1 series lead.

It was the team's eleventh consecutive road win in the play-offs, dating back to their huge run in 2001.

On that day, Bryant had missed 16 of his first 23 shots when he launched the scoring outburst that included 2 three-pointers within 43 seconds of each other.

Though Jackson had largely been playing Bryant at guard instead of wing—putting him in the position Jordan had played so successfully in Chicago—for parts of the San Antonio series, Bryant moved back to the wing, where he was able to get behind the defense and find the open looks. It was hard for opponents to double-team either Bryant or Jordan in that position, a special feature of the triangle offense's spacing.

"The first thing about him is his talent is astounding," Spurs coach Gregg Popovich offered. "The second thing is his body exaggerates that talent with his height and his length. The third thing is he has the uncommon will to win. It's the same exact will to win as Michael Jordan."

Bryant's heroics propelled his team into the next round, where they struggled through a classic seven-game showdown with the testy Sacramento Kings. The presence of Jackson and his team in noisy Arco Arena always seemed to goose Sacramento's fans to new levels of rowdiness. The outcome of Game 4 of the series will gnaw at Kings fans as long as there is a Sacramento. The Lakers comeback itself was hard enough to take, but much later, disgraced official Tim Donaghy would imply that gamblers may have influenced the outcome in some way, although the allegation has never been supported by any sort of remotely conclusive evidence. Still, the game sits in history with an unofficial asterisk for Sacramento fans. The vision of their torment is Robert Horry whisking away their opportunity to take a 3–1 lead in the 2002 Western Conference finals.

In Game 4, the Lakers had to endure the booing of Staples Center regulars after they fell behind, 40–20, at the end of the first quarter. The Kings pushed that to 46–22 before the momentum began to turn. The omen for Sacramento came when Samaki Walker's three-point desperation heave was counted although it just missed the halftime buzzer. It was only the second three-pointer of Walker's career.

The Lakers tightened their defense and clamped down on the boards in the second half, and the Kings began losing their lead, which the Lakers kept whittling at down the stretch. At 1:39, Horry floated in a three-pointer that cut Sacramento's lead to 96–93. Then O'Neal canned 2 free throws to cut the lead to one with 26.9 seconds to play. Kings center Vlade Divac answered by making 1 of 2 free throws with 11.8 seconds to go. Their lead at two, the Kings stood for one final defensive effort.

Bryant drove the lane but missed, as did O'Neal on an offensive put-back. Divac batted the rebound outside, hoping to knock it out of play. Instead, it traveled right to Horry, waiting in three-point land.

"When it came rolling out, it was like, 'Oh, look what I got,'" he said afterward.

He floated in the winner as time expired. The strange turn of events was just the edge the Lakers needed. Instead of being down 3–1, they pulled even at 2–2.

Sacramento closed out the series with poor rebounding and a collapse at the free-throw line that saw them fall at home in the seventh game.

The Kings safely in their wake, the Lakers returned to the NBA Finals to meet the revamped New Jersey Nets, the team that had come so close to drafting Bryant, now led by Jason Kidd and coached by Bryant's rookie teammate and friend Byron Scott.

The Nets wouldn't be able to match up with Bryant and O'Neal. In fact, the two stars scored 71 of their team's 106 points in the pivotal Game 3. A key sequence came down to Bryant again living on the edge, losing his dribble under pressure by the Nets' Kidd and Kerry Kittles, then resecuring the ball and hitting a spinning jumper near the foul line to push the lead to 104–100 with nineteen seconds left. In the shot of the game, Bryant was pressured by Kidd.

"Big players make big plays," Kidd told reporters afterward.

That, of course, could serve as the Hollywood-style premise for the entire history of the team. To emphasize the point, Bryant celebrated the team's victory in Game 4 at Continental Airlines Arena by wearing a Michael Jordan jersey afterward.

The Lakers joined the Minneapolis Lakers, Bill Russell's Celtics, and Jackson's Chicago Bulls as the only teams ever to win three straight titles. Still, Magic Johnson told the Associated Press that Jackson's club wasn't as good as his Showtime teams, or Jordan's Chicago Bulls, or Larry Bird's Boston Celtics, for that matter. Johnson explained that the other teams featured stronger, deeper rosters, while Jackson's Lakers consisted of two stars and a host of role players.

It was Jackson's ninth NBA title, tying him with the Boston Celtics' legendary Red Auerbach for the most as a head coach. The play-off victory was also number 156 for Jackson, tying him with nemesis Pat Riley. The three Lakers titles also made for Jackson's third three-peat, and the Los Angeles Lakers finally had one of their own to celebrate. "The first one, it's a novelty, and it feels real good," Bryant observed, looking back over their run. "The first one will always be the best one. The second one, the adversity that we went through throughout the course of the year made that one special. We proved that we belonged. And this one, it's kind of making us step up as one the great teams. It feels great."

O'Neal congratulated Jackson "on bringing out the best in us," adding that the coach had given him a plan when they first met. Jackson had promised that if they stuck with the plan, they would be successful.

"I'm just glad that Jerry West was able to get him to sign up, because it was something I needed in my life," O'Neal said. "I was sort of a great player that didn't have any championships. Ever since I met Phil, now I have three."

For the second straight season, one of Jackson's two stars had subtly managed to credit Jerry West during the celebration of another championship.

For years Jackson had ruled his environment by seeking to keep both his staff assistants and his players slightly off balance. Entropy seemed to work just fine for the coach, until it didn't. In Chicago, it had played a role in both his success and in the franchise coming unhinged at the end of his tenure.

Three successful seasons of drama and chaos in Los Angeles had veteran Jackson observers wondering if the coach wasn't well on his way to similar alienation with the Lakers. His forming a relationship with the owner's daughter hadn't helped the situation any. Soon there were indications that Jackson was alienated from both Jerry Buss and his son Jim, who was slated to take over the team's basketball operations.

And GM Mitch Kupchak remained close with his old boss, Jerry West. "Phil and Kupchak, they never were really simpatico also," Charley Rosen said. "Phil had more veto power than he had, but who could have Phil gotten along with? When you come down to it, it's a dirty business where you've got to manipulate egomaniacs, and you've got to be one."

Jackson's rule of making the team bus a domain for players, coaches, and team staff wasn't making any friends either.

Thus, the coaching staff had the sneaking suspicion that three titles with this Lakers team might prove to be the limit. "The first championship that Phil won in L.A., I spoke to several of his assistant coaches," Rosen explained. "They felt that that team had the least, the lowest overall talent of any team that had won an NBA title that anybody could remember."

Which further suggested that time was now running out.

Jackson and his assistant coaches had come to that conclusion during their years in Chicago. It seemed the most they could squeeze out of any situation was three straight titles. Success had its boundaries, and that certainly seemed to be the maximum for the human element in the modern championship equation. The Lakers found themselves making strange, frustrating attempts to stretch that envelope over the next two campaigns. In the process, they would find out more about themselves than perhaps they wanted to know.

Winter and Jackson

Strangely, as if on a Hollywood cue, it became time for Jackson and Winter to hit a major rough spot in their long relationship. For a few observers, it was easy to see the cause of the growing conflict between the two coaching friends.

"Phil was a Shaq fan," explained Rosen, "and Tex was a Kobe fan. Phil would blame Kobe, Tex would blame Shaq. There was always a discussion about that, as much friction as there was between Phil and Tex."

The divide was nothing new, but even as the two players developed, each coach stayed set in his ways. This different view of the situation came from their different perspectives, Rosen pointed out. "When Tex was a basketball player, he was a guard. When Phil was a basketball player, he was a big man. So those big men relate better to big men. Guards relate better to guards."

Winter was animated, always saying what he thought, a guy who lived very much on the surface. Jackson, on the other hand, was sort of a slow boil. Dealing with him was like looking at the ocean. It was always what lay beneath the surface.

Bill Wennington, one of Jackson's players in Chicago, once observed that the coach was always operating three or four moves ahead of everybody else, which meant you had to stop, analyze what he was doing, and see where things were headed.

"People don't realize how difficult it is to coach an amazingly talented team," Rosen explained.

To make such teams winners, Jackson obviously felt he had to manipulate and control the circumstances and atmosphere around his teams. Just about all great coaches have shown themselves to be world-class control freaks. Jackson had fired another beloved Chicago mentor, Johnny Bach, in part because of Bach's undue influence on Michael Jordan.

The conflict of opinions between Winter and Jackson usually

played out behind closed doors, as Jackson employed such tactics as freezing out Bryant while being friendly with Shaq.

But, as usual, Jackson made use of the media to further his agenda. "I was writing for ESPN, *Page 2*, whatever it was," Rosen recalled. "I was out there covering the Lakers, and Tex had given me a lift back to my hotel after a game. Tex, you know, is a truth teller. Tex just says what's on his mind, no matter who's there or what's there, and he was really pissed off with Kobe. So Tex told me in the car going to the hotel that after a game, he went over to Kobe and said, 'I don't like the way you played tonight.' And Kobe said to Tex, 'I don't like the way you coached tonight.' So basically, you know, it was one of my first assignments for ESPN, and I was try-ing hard to make an impression. So I violated the confidential nature of the conversation, and I printed it. After I did, Phil said, 'Don't talk to Kobe. Kobe won't talk to you. He's pissed off at you. I don't know what he'll do.'"

Rosen certainly was trying to please ESPN, but he was also clearly trying to please Jackson. Longtime observers of Jackson's methods knew that the story was meant to drive a wedge between Winter and Bryant.

Some of Jackson's longtime staff began to believe that as his Lak-ers teams won championships, Jackson's ego, already substantial, seemed to surge. Winter's role in scouting preparation, planning and running practices, and masterminding the triangle offense had always been key to Jackson's teams. San Antonio's Tim Dun-can had watched the pair coach the All-Star team in 2000, had seen Winter's key role and teaching effort, and remarked, "It's obvi-ous who's the brains behind this operation."

However, in the wake of the 2002 title, Jackson wanted Winter to continue the parts of the relationship that involved the critical behind-the-scenes work but decided that he no longer wanted his assistant sitting beside him on the bench; instead, he had him sit behind him in a second row.

Jackson explained the move as being made out of consideration for Winter's age. But Winter wondered if Jackson hadn't become overly concerned with making sure he got the credit for the team's success. Another factor clearly was Winter's close relationship with

Bryant. Jackson's difficulties with Bryant had only served to empha-size Winter's role as Bryant's defender on the coaching staff.

Much as he had calculated that asking Jerry West to leave the locker room might induce the legend to leave the Lakers, Jackson may well have hoped that the move would send Winter a message. Indeed, Winter was so despondent about the move that he thought long and hard about retiring.

"You can't quit," Bryant told Winter. "If you do, I'll go crazy."

Some had already begun to wonder if he wasn't already there.

PART V

MAMBA

Chapter 24

ROCKY MOUNTAINS

Finally the shoe fell, so to speak. Kobe Bryant was already in the final stages of disengaging from Adidas. First he would have to display his full irritation and disinterest in the company that had bought his youthful services and made his dream of being a pro basketball player come alive right out of high school. During the 2002 championship series, Bryant had gotten rid of his awkward new shoes and gone back to the earlier Adidas model, the Kobe.

In making his exit, Bryant never bothered to phone Sonny Vaccaro and thank him for the experience, which had included money for his parents and guaranteed millions for Bryant before he ever played an NBA game. More than a dozen years later, Vaccaro still had never heard from Bryant and still seemed jilted by the departure, announced in the *Wall Street Journal* as a move by Bryant to spend an estimated $10 million to buy out his remaining contract.

It seemed outrageous that he would pay such a figure to make this exit.

"It was a devastating blow," Vaccaro recalled. "What he did with Adidas was horrible. They didn't do anything to deserve it. The money basically meant nothing, even the $10 million that Kobe spent. I felt hurt, but I think that was planned out. I think Nike was a willing co-conspirator. I think the deal was done before he went, personally. It was too calculated. Nike ended up paying it in some way, shape, or form. It wasn't Kobe doing it. I mean, we know that."

It had gotten ugly toward the end, with a chilly meeting in Germany between the superstar and officials of the parent company. "That was after he tried to wear this shoe," recalled Peter Moore, the designer and the chairman of Adidas America. "And then he went to Germany in the summer. What we were trying to do was paint the future for him, show him where we could take him."

Adidas gave an impressive presentation laying out Moore's vision for the Bryant product line, finally something to rival Jordan's Jumpman. "It was going to be not just playing shoes but [casual] shoes and clothes," Moore explained. "But it was going to be a while. It wasn't going to happen tomorrow morning."

The time was what Bryant didn't seem to have. He was angry over the failure of his latest signature shoe. Only in retrospect would Adidas come to understand that he furtively already had another deal in the works, one rumored to be initiated by Joe Bryant, who had seen his son's growing frustration. On the other hand, the Adidas contract was handsome, and the company's marketing of him had made Bryant a global star, just as Nike had shaped Jordan in the public mind. For the second straight year, Bryant had garnered the Teen Choice Award for the most admired athlete, an indication of the appeal he and Adidas had built in a few short seasons.

"I don't think the issue was ever financial," Moore said. "The issue was, did he believe that we could be what we said? And I think that he was not polite, let me put it that way, particularly to European Germans. They are formal, even though they try to be casual. They wanted him to go to dinner, and he didn't really want to go to dinner, so he just didn't go. To the Germans, it was a bit insulting."

"Hey, you're being a pain in the butt," Moore told him.

"I just want to do the business," Bryant replied testily. "I want to get down to the business of it."

"I said, 'OK,'" Moore recalled. "By this time he's got bodyguards. It's kind of weird. They're talking to their sleeves. And all of that was sort of the beginning of a different kind of guy, I guess, based on his fame. Jordan never had a bodyguard. He had his driver, who I'm sure carried a gun, but he didn't have, like, Secret Service guys running around, but Kobe did."

"He deliberately set out to piss them off," Vaccaro alleged of Bryant's approach in Germany. In the middle of the night, Bryant had supposedly checked out of the elite hotel provided by Adidas to move to another location, which was seen as another insult.

"He did everything possible to anger them," Vaccaro alleged. "It was rude."

Moore had seen it coming, with Bryant and his wife showing less and less interest over a series of meetings, the last of which came in Cleveland. "We had about three or four meetings with him and her," Moore remembered. "You can tell when you present to people whether they're digging it or not. She just didn't dig it. She didn't have much to say about it; she would go talk to him. That's all fine, that's part of the game. That's part of the work you have to do, but it was at a time when we were trying to do something very different and we needed him to really be involved. I don't think he was. I think he was beginning to think, 'I'll just go do something with Nike.'"

Adidas realized too late that Nike was using its endorsees to create doubt in Bryant, Moore suggested. "The shit that goes on in the locker rooms is pretty interesting. Nike's reps are always in there. They're not unopposed to saying, 'Why you wearing those funny shoes?' Shit like that works on those guys."

Moore had seen Jordan's growing frustration with Nike in 1987 when he tried to leave. Bryant now had that same mind-set. But there was one gigantic difference. From the very start of his relationship with Nike, Jordan had been given an unprecedented contract with a royalty that by 2015 — long after his playing days were over — was earning Jordan an estimated $100 million a year. Such a contract was too good to leave, Moore and Rob Strasser had told Jordan in 1987. Jordan's percentage played a major role in his becoming the first global athlete to reach $1 billion in wealth.

In 2002, Bryant had a nice contract with Adidas, but there was no royalty percentage in it. No one in all of basketball had such a royalty but Jordan. Bryant's camp made what was possibly a huge miscalculation by not pushing for one. Bryant was worth a royalty clause to Adidas. The company likely would have given him that to keep him as the endorsement anchor of its line.

"Kobe was worth far more to Adidas than to Nike," Sonny Vaccaro said. "Nike only wanted Kobe so that Adidas wouldn't have him."

Bryant might well have been granted a royalty by Adidas "if he had played hardball," Moore said in 2015. "At the time if he had said, 'I want 2 percent or 3 percent on each shoe,' he probably could have negotiated that."

But he was too petulant, too emotional on the issue, to conduct business. He had wanted to be clear of agent Arn Tellem, to have a comfort level in making his own decisions. Over time, he and Pelinka would make many astute decisions, but in hindsight it seems like they were too hasty in this case, basing their decision on emotion.

Did Bryant miss a major opportunity by switching shoe brands? The question sits there now in retrospect, much like the question about his decision to bypass college. What if he had remained with Adidas and negotiated a piece of the pie?

Bryant's rejection of Adidas would create interesting ripples throughout the shoe industry. While Bryant was trying to force his way out at Adidas, Vaccaro was also in the midst of trying to sign an Ohio teen named LeBron James. Vaccaro had grown quite close to James, according to Chris Dennis, James's mentor and financial manager at the time.

The bidding for James was expected to reach $100 million, but James would have gone with Adidas for less money because he was that close with Vaccaro, Chris Dennis explained.

Losing Kobe Bryant was such a blow to Adidas that the German parent company began backing off its aggressive plans in basketball, Vaccaro recalled. However, he had been assured, as the day approached for shoe companies to put in their bids for LeBron James, that Adidas would allow him to submit a viable proposal.

But at the last minute, Adidas backed out of the bidding, leaving Phil Knight and Nike to snare James as an endorser with an unprecedented $90-million deal for a high school player.

"You have to give Sonny credit," Dennis said in 2015 of Vaccaro. "He helped LeBron get his money."

The moment indicated just what a marketplace Kobe Bryant had created for young talent with his bold decision to turn pro in 1996.

"Kobe actually opened up a lot of doors financially," Vaccaro admitted, looking back. "His going pro allowed McGrady to get his money. And he was a factor in LeBron getting his."

"All those guys need to give Kobe a hug," Gary Charles said with a laugh. "And give me and Sonny a hug, too. I mean it. That was the impetus."

Vaccaro said he was so crushed by the company's last-second decision to pull out that he resigned the next day, giving up his lifetime contract with the company.

"When Kobe left and then when they backed off of LeBron, it was a fucking death deal for Adidas," Vaccaro offered. "But that was Kobe's personality. He can say 'fuck you' to anybody and not worry about it because, obviously, I was nobody to him by then. But that's what he's done. He just does things and like, 'It's over.' He can entirely shut you off. He had this ability just to shut people out, like, immediately, like on a phone call. He would just go, 'OK, it's over. That's it.' He's wired differently."

Adidas would make its way forward without Bryant, James, or Vaccaro. Moore, who had envisioned another Jumpman, was left to wonder what might have been in terms of their efforts to create something similar to Air Jordan for Bryant.

"We never really got into it," Moore said, looking back. Bryant had been too young, too wrapped up in other things, to see the future. "We kind of got a one-year or two-year blip," the designer-executive said. "We never really got to develop the story and develop the shoes, put it together with apparel with the right ad campaign behind it. I'm convinced to this day that we could have made him big. I don't know how big. We could have made him into something."

Bryant reached a buyout agreement that involved paying $10 million to Adidas. For Bryant to pay $10 million seemed a lot, but Vaccaro pointed out that Bryant wasn't paying it anyway. It and Bryant's new contract were well worth it to Nike to set their main competition back by years.

With the buyout agreement, Adidas was given a year to sell off its Bryant inventory. Regardless of the German company's suspicions that Nike had been involved in the deal, Bryant didn't sign with them immediately. Instead, he would spend a year as a shoe free agent, recalled Anthony Gilbert, the family friend and something of a "sneakerhead" who took a marketing job with Nike during the period.

"Kobe wasn't happy with Adidas because of two reasons," Gilbert observed. "The first reason is he felt they were doing too much for Tracy McGrady, and he came first. Kobe was like, 'Wait a minute. How come there's a Tracy McGrady billboard and I flip through *Slam* magazine and T-Mac is everywhere? What about me?' So that was the first strike. The second strike was like, 'You guys aren't marketing me nationally well enough and that's a problem.'

"Then it turned into, like, 'OK, I'm going to be a sneaker free agent for a year,' and that was a great year," Gilbert recalled. "That was legendary. For a year he wore whatever he wanted. He wore Converse Weapons that Magic used to wear. He wore Iversons. He'd wear Jordan. He wore whatever he wanted, and it was great. He was like, 'Hey, I don't endorse any shoe, and I'm going to wear every shoe,' and Nike loved it because they were feeding him well-known Jordan shoes, but in Laker colors."

Gilbert recalled of himself and other sneakerheads, "We're on the Internet, like, 'Oh, this is crazy. Did you see the Jordan Kobe? Are you kidding me?' He was wearing all the Nike shoes in Laker colors. He wore the Fab Five shoe in Laker colors."

With Adidas out of the picture, Bryant had cleaned the slate from his former life, erased family, agent, shoe company, purged his landscape of all the evidence of his Showboat days, all except the memories. In retrospect, it would be the first major effort in the remaking of his persona into that of a deadly snake, strangely enough.

Among his new beginnings would be a most precious thing. As the 2002 off-season unfolded, Bryant learned that he was going to be a father. "How about that," he said, truly delighted.

Big Fundamentals

The math that Bryant had so badly wanted Michael Jordan to teach him was suddenly upon them all for the 2002–03 season, although you couldn't tell it on opening night when he forced up 29 shots and made just 9 of them. He was absolutely furious with himself afterward. You could not force things. The basketball gods wouldn't allow it.

Like many of Phil Jackson's associates, George Mumford knew all about the basketball gods. He was something of a genius mystic. A reformed drug addict, he'd read everything, it seemed, not just read it, but processed it into a fascinating view of the world and how to clear away the detritus that collected on the soul. Years later Bryant would observe that he'd never forgotten a word Mumford had ever told him, and with Bryant's memory, Mumford believed it to be true.

Bryant was fascinated because among the many things the psychologist explored were those magical moments when an athlete entered "the zone."

To Mumford's amazement, during his time working with Jordan, Chicago's star almost seemed to have at his command an ability to jack himself almost routinely into that rare altered state of performance, far beyond what could be achieved by any other person Mumford had encountered (and Mumford had roomed with Julius Erving at the University of Massachusetts). Getting into the zone was such a special experience that those who possessed it struggled to understand it afterward. Yet they couldn't stop craving the wonder and mystery of the experience, much like the opiates that had once ensnared Mumford himself.

Tex Winter saw in Bryant a younger, less perfect Jordan, but a Jordan all the same, one clearly open to all the bountiful influence Winter had to offer.

For yet another season, Jackson simply refused to indulge any of Bryant's fantasies or romantic notions, even though he had done just the opposite with Jordan. The big difference seemed to be that Jordan was older when Jackson first began coaching him, and he was a realist, never espousing any sort of nonsense about dreams or self-belief. As he matured, Bryant had gotten better about talking less of those things as he went along, trying not to make it too obvious just how much he prized Jordan as a role model. But it was still obvious Bryant remained very wrapped in the embrace of his ambition, the one that Adidas had so powerfully reinforced in him.

Jackson, the son of two fundamentalist preachers, seemed to battle Bryant as if he were beating back Beelzebub himself, which quietly vexed Winter more and more as the experience unfolded.

Bryant was now just twenty-four and already heading into his seventh NBA season, yet Jackson still refused to have even a serious meeting with him, which presented a huge irony. Jackson, a man known for establishing strong relationships with his players, would willfully decline to form any sort of a deeper relationship with Bryant, whom he saw as self-indulgent beyond the pale. The coach had engaged in a lesser struggle with Jordan's immense will, but he had met with the Bulls star often and went to great lengths to nurture their mutual understanding.

His approach with Bryant continued a titanic, drawn-out battle between the game's most successful coach and the headstrong young player. At one point, even George Mumford had addressed the issue with Jackson. Apparently in response, the coach would de-emphasize Mumford and dramatically cut back his work with the team, despite the Lakers' three straight titles.

Having been raised by mystics himself, Jackson admired Mumford and his gift for getting players to see the competitive world with tremendous clarity, a clarity deeply based in the reality of human interaction. In the business of pro sports, where talk was cheap, it was not what people said, Mumford reasoned, but what they did. Players should not only examine the action of those around them but their own actions as well. But Jackson was so caught up in the struggle that he attempted to replace Mumford with a psychologist from the L.A. schools who specialized in the behavior of narcissists.

The die was already cast, however, at the beginning of the 2002–03 season. O'Neal had delayed getting surgery on his injured toe until late in the off-season, which meant that he would miss all of training camp and nearly the first two months of the season.

The door was open for Kobe Bryant, and he shoved through it, to Jackson's mix of relief and dismay.

There were serious questions, unarticulated as the season began, as to whether the dysfunction between Jackson and Bryant could be repaired. Later, Winter would privately cite the coach's mishandling of Bryant as a player as one of the primary factors in the eventual unraveling of the team.

"Very early in our time in Los Angeles, Phil made the decision to go with Shaq," Winter explained, "and he made it clear to Kobe and the press and everyone else that it was Shaq's team. He made it clear he was far more interested in accommodating Shaq than he was Kobe. Kobe seemed to accept this."

Looking back, Bryant tried to address the matter with understatement: "Phil was trying to figure me out a little bit. One of the things I told him is, 'There's nothing to figure out. I'm just trying to play the game and learn the game the best I can.' Once we got that established we started moving a little bit. But I didn't get into his mind games. I had so many other things to think about with this game. I didn't really have the time even to do that. I did notice Phil when he was trying to play mind games. It was funny. I found it funny."

"I was very much on Kobe, riding him and working with him very hard earlier in his career, and had to back off, basically, to a point where he felt better about our relationship—where I wasn't as restrictive with him," Jackson admitted to the *Los Angeles Times*. "He felt I was always on him, always on him. He did too much, he tried to do too many things. The more I let him have, the better he got as a basketball player. The more I restricted or got restrictive with him, the more adamantly he would go about doing the things I didn't want him to do."

"Kobe did not like to be controlled or be told what to do," equipment manager Rudy Garciduenas observed. "He wanted to express himself and have things his way."

Even as he acknowledged his approach, Jackson persisted in taking the harsh path with Bryant, while appearing to playfully coddle O'Neal. The discrepancy sometimes ate at Bryant as did Jackson's penchant for attacking him in the press.

"It's no secret," Chip Schaefer said, "that Kobe's work ethic and dedication was very different than Shaquille's, who would put in a good day's work too, but also enjoyed life. It's hard for a guy of that physical dimension. He's not going to get on a track at seven in the morning in July and do those things. It's just not who he is and who he was."

"Phil was dealing with two mighty big egos," Winter confided. "But in my mind I blamed Shaq more than Kobe. Kobe tried to sacrifice.

Kobe tried to please Shaq, because Kobe realized the team's effectiveness began with Shaq. But if you look at Shaq's quotes in the paper, it was always me, me, me. Give me the ball. It's my team, my city. Shaq is a wonderful person in a lot of ways. He's very compassionate, very generous. He has a great sense of humor. But he's moody; he's unpredictable. And he's very self-centered."

Without O'Neal, the team struggled through the first two months with nights where Jackson seemed to have little choice but to resort to Bryant's talents, and the young player happily emerged as a volume scorer in the raw mold of the man he had studied so intensely.

He wouldn't be able to carry the team every night. Early that season the Lakers stopped in Boston, and the Celtics coaching staff decided to focus their efforts on his teammates to let Bryant feast on single coverage, with the idea that one man wasn't going to beat them. He shot poorly in the first half, making 5 of 15 shots, and the Lakers fell behind, only to see Bryant come out firing in the second half, trying to drive a comeback. The Lakers managed to tie the game, only to lose in overtime. In the aftermath, the box score showed that Bryant had launched an amazing 47 field goal attempts and made just 17, for 41 points and a narrow loss. "I haven't seen anybody shoot 47 shots before. Ever. There's a limitation to what you can do," Jackson told reporters.

Three more times that first month of the season, he would strike for 45 points or better, along with a 44-point outing in December in Philadelphia, all signs that the efficiency of his high-volume approach was improving.

January brought the birth of his daughter, Natalia Diamante Bryant. "Beautiful, isn't it?" he had said in announcing the pregnancy earlier.

He celebrated on the floor with more fireworks, notching three games with better than 40 points, including an outing against Seattle in which he made an NBA record 12 three-pointers, followed by a February streak of nine straight games scoring better than 40 points, tying Michael Jordan's personal record (though still short of the record fourteen by Wilt Chamberlain). In previous seasons, such an outburst might have ruptured the peace, but it survived tenuously over the early weeks of 2003. Then again, Jackson had quietly nodded for his guard to be more aggressive.

Overall, Bryant went on a streak of thirteen games in which he scored 35 or more points. On February 6, Bryant rang up 46 points against the Knicks in Madison Square Garden, and he rolled through February 23 with 41 against Seattle in Staples Center. During the nine games in which he scored more than 40, the Lakers went 7–2.

"He's on a great run," Jordan, playing for the Washington Wizards, offered during the streak. "He's really finding a way to do it within the structure of the offense. I don't think it's any play that's outside of that. Once a player gets the kind of confidence that he has right now, it makes it very tough for the team to try to defend him."

Bryant would later thank his mentor by scoring 55, including 43 in the first half, against the Wizards in Jordan's last visit to Los Angeles, on March 28.

"The streak is a streak," Bryant had said after his display. "It's not going to win us any championships."

Indeed, nothing would that spring.

Jackson missed the first game of his coaching career with a kidney stone. Similarly, his team showed signs of wear, managing to win just fifty games in the regular season. Finally, in the play-offs, Robert Horry's threes stopped falling. And in the conference semifinals against San Antonio, the rest of the operation broke down. In the middle of the series, Jackson missed another weekend as doctors discovered his immediate need for an angioplasty procedure, following months of unexplained fatigue.

Despite his return to the bench, the Spurs eliminated the Lakers in six games, closing them out at Staples Center. The loss ended Jackson's record run of twenty-five consecutive play-off-series wins, and it kept him from moving past Red Auerbach for the most NBA titles won as a coach.

The Lakers themselves had won thirteen straight series, from the first round against Sacramento in 2000 to the first round against Minnesota in 2003.

"We are severely disappointed we couldn't make a run for the championship and get our opportunity to win a fourth," Jackson told reporters. "It tells us something about how difficult it is and how much dedication and discipline you have to have to win four years in a row."

"It's a foreign feeling," Bryant, who had averaged 32.1 points during the play-offs, told reporters. "I don't like the feeling. I don't think anybody else likes the feeling. I don't ever want to feel it again."

"Some things just sort of happen, like the pebble in a pond sets off ripples," Chip Schaefer said. "Shaquille delaying foot surgery one year leads to Robert Horry having to play maybe too many minutes too early in another year, which leads to him being worn out by the end of the year, which leads to us not winning it. We were going for a fourth straight title, which would have been ridiculous. Good luck ever having a team accomplish that. Maybe some people would see that as a failure, but if you're going to say a deep play-off run with a loss to the eventual champion and your fourth attempt at a title in the fourth year is some kind of failure, I'm going to disagree."

Ric Bucher's appreciation for Bryant had grown as he covered the Lakers' great run of championships. He had been amazed that the young star had never seemed to fall into self-satisfaction of any sort, always keeping his expectations well beyond his performance.

"Look at all that he achieved at a very young age," Bucher said. "Look at all the platitudes, look at all the money, to be honest with you, and it never detracted from his work ethic. It never dulled his desire to go out and prove to the next person or team or fan or whoever it was that he was the absolute best, that he was everything that he thought he was. It's human nature to have your appetite dulled by whatever it is that you've just achieved. There was something about Kobe where it only whetted his appetite more. Just setting the bar there and then keeping after it day after day after day in spite of the millions that come in, in spite of the trophies, in spite of all the things that could get you to relax a little bit and say, 'You know what, this is pretty good.' You see it all the time in pro sports. Guys win a single championship and they can never get back to that level again."

For the road ahead, such an unbending constitution would prove vital to Bryant, if for no other reason than survival itself.

In the County of Eagle

On July 4, 2003, a warrant for Byrant's arrest on charges of sexual assault was issued by the sheriff's department of Eagle County, Colorado. When he heard the news, Sonny Vaccaro was conducting his camp, the one that just eight years earlier had brought the emergence of Bryant after his junior year in high school. Vaccaro phoned Tracy McGrady and asked him, "Can you believe this shit?"

No one could. Kobe Bryant was the "golden child," the young phenom so caught up in his ambition that he hardly took time for a social life.

"He didn't even date," Jerry West had said.

Shelley Smith, a veteran ESPN reporter based in Los Angeles, had grown up in the immediate resort area around Vail, Colorado. One day early that July, Smith had gotten a call from her sister in Denver, who told her, "I know where you're going tomorrow."

"Where?" Smith asked.

"You're going to Eagle because Kobe's being arrested," her sister said.

"I thought it was a joke," Smith recalled. "And then I thought, 'There can't be anything to this. It has to be a farce.'"

She had met Bryant before he played his first NBA game, when Smith was in the process of coauthoring a book with NFL receiver Keyshawn Johnson. They were all in Bristol, Connecticut, at ESPN's studios, to do a humorous commercial with Bryant.

"I remember it was Stuart Scott trying to teach them to talk trash. It was, 'I'm the man.' 'No, I'm the man,'" Smith recalled. "And it was hilarious because the two of them ended up being the biggest trash talkers in their respective sports. It was sort of a parody. I remember meeting Kobe, and he was so young and so impressionable and thought he knew everything."

Johnson and Bryant later wound up in New York. "We put it in Keyshawn's book," she said, "because there was one night Kobe was calling Keyshawn to get him into the clubs. Keyshawn said, 'You're Kobe Bryant. Everyone knows you're only eighteen. I'm not getting you into the clubs.' I remember thinking how hilarious that was."

In her job with ESPN, Smith found herself covering the Lakers often. The team had its ups and downs, but she had formed a good relationship with Bryant.

"There's a video clip," she said, "where I'm interviewing someone else and he walks by and messes up my hair. We had a nice, friendly, professional relationship where he would give me a little extra stuff in the locker room if I needed it, an extra minute of his time. It just all seemed fun.

"He was available and cordial and a good kid to be around," she said. "It was a fun show, the Shaq and Kobe show."

Except when it wasn't.

"He was cold and hot," Smith recalled. "He would love you one day and then not talk to you the next. He had a love-hate relationship with the black reporters. He would sort of pick his favorites and talk to them. At one time Ric Bucher was his favorite. One day he'd be down with the black reporters, and then the next day he would shun them. He was very much hot and cold, and I don't know why. I don't know if he was confused about his identity or what. But with me he was always pretty much the same."

Talking to her sister that day, Smith realized she'd better contact her producers to explain that her family lived in the area and to see if they needed her to get on a plane.

"They at first said, 'No, let's wait,'" Smith recalled. "And then the very next morning, I got an early call saying, 'How fast can you get there?' It was like everyone was in denial. Like, 'This can't be.'

"You think you know athletes from the limited amount of time you spend with them," she observed, "just like they think they know us, and they don't."

At the end of June, Bryant had flown on a private jet to Colorado, where he was scheduled to undergo a surgical procedure on his troubled knee, something he hadn't informed the Lakers he was doing. That night, shortly after he checked into the exclusive Lodge and Spa at Cordillera resort, in the town of Edwards, in Eagle County, accompanied by three bodyguards and his personal trainer, the Lakers guard met a nineteen-year-old clerk at the front desk, who escorted him to his quarters.

The desk clerk later told police that upon arriving at work that day, she had learned that a special celebrity was scheduled to check in that night under the name Javier Rodriguez. She said she pushed the reservation clerk to disclose that "Rodriguez" was Bryant, and, although her shift was supposed to end at 7 p.m., she decided to stay on to meet the star upon his check-in, at 10:30 that night of June 30.

During the check-in, Bryant had invited her back to his room so that she could take him on a tour of the resort. Although his bodyguards were stationed in a hallway and would not allow even a bellman through to the area of Bryant's room, the clerk told police that she knew a back way to Bryant's quarters and used it to elude the bodyguards. Once she got there, Bryant joined her on a brief tour of the resort.

After the tour, both would later tell authorities, they returned to his room and engaged in "chitchat," then foreplay, then his removal of her black dress and panties, and what can only be described as crude, somewhat forlorn, sexual intercourse. Although she did not initially tell investigators that she performed oral sex on him afterward, she later admitted it and said that she did so out of fear. Bryant had initiated their mutual groping, the police report revealed, by asking for a hug.

She said Bryant raped her; he later told police the sex was consensual. Bryant admitted that he preferred rough sex and had grabbed her by the neck, apparently confirmed the next day by a red mark on her neck discovered in a medical exam related to the case.

Like many sexual assaults, the issue would quickly fall into a he-said, she-said situation between accuser and accused. Both parties lied or left out details in their initial interviews with police, which they later corrected.

Although the legal wrangling of the case would stretch out for months and would remain at the top of daily newscasts, the situation would eventually come down to a few key facts that were known to authorities relatively early in their investigation.

The accuser had engaged in sex with two other men that day, including the bellhop who had offered evidence supporting her version of events. According to the law, it wouldn't have mattered if the young woman had engaged in sex with thirty others that day. If she told Bryant no, and he used force and persisted, then he had committed rape. In theory, that seemed clear. In an actual court-room before a jury, it might prove to be another matter, but Eagle County district attorney Mark Hurlbert appeared quite confident in his case and was eager to move forward. The accuser, however, was facing Bryant's aggressive team of attorneys and entertaining growing second thoughts.

Smith and other reporters heard early on, even before he was formally charged, that Bryant's offers of an out-of-court settlement reached as high as $5 million.

Authorities surveilled Bryant recuperating at the Lodge the next day, then finally approached him in the wee hours of July 2 for questioning.

He provided authorities with his version of events—that the young woman was obviously eager to engage in sexual relations with him and initiated those relations, that she did not tell him no—which an investigator recorded with a microcassette. As they neared the end of the interrogation, the investigator shut off his recorder. At that point, almost as an aside, Bryant made a comment that he should have done as his teammate Shaquille O'Neal told Bryant he did and pay women off. Bryant relayed a tale in which O'Neal told him he'd paid a woman a million dollars. As Bryant later explained, when he made the comment he had no idea that it would become public. Indeed, officers reconstructed the comment from memory and later entered it in their report, which would be released to the public months later, after the case was over, causing Bryant and O'Neal himself substantial personal damage.

The incident seemed in such contrast to Bryant's image that reporters, fans, teammates and team employees expressed shock at the news that the twenty-four-year-old guard might be charged. Soon shock would give way to the incessant reality of tabloid head-lines, twenty-four-hour cable news coverage, and a story that threat-ened to swamp the team.

The 2003 season had revealed the Lakers needed depth and a talent upgrade. The Colorado news had broken just as the team prepared to announce the signings of future Hall of Famers Karl Malone and Gary Payton, both of whom took millions of dollars in pay cuts to join the team as free agents. Poised to harvest the media attention and speculation over just how great their club could be, the team's management instead found itself dealing with issues of a more serious nature.

"When everything comes clean, it will all be fine, you'll see," Bryant told the Los Angeles Times in a phone interview. "But you guys know me, I shouldn't have to say anything. You know I would never do something like that."

The accuser refused to settle, and Bryant was faced with charges that, under Colorado law, could land him in prison for decades. On July 18, Hurlbert, the district attorney, filed a formal charge of felony sexual assault against Bryant.

"I realized then that he was in big trouble," Smith recalled. "The sex assault laws in Colorado are really, really, really steep. We talked to lawyers who said if he was convicted, he would be labeled a sex offender the rest of his life and couldn't be within certain miles of schools. They would do things like show him pictures of animals and little kids to see if that aroused him. It was just unfair on how strict those laws are. Yet if you're on the other side of it as a victim, you understand. I'd be scared for anybody in that situation. Scared for him. Scared for the accuser.

"Then it became really real," Smith recalled, "because then the wheels were in motion."

With reporters came a throng of spectators, many of them wearing Lakers jerseys, sporting signs, and cheering for Bryant, who posted a $25,000 bond in regard to The People of the State of Colorado v. Kobe Bean Bryant, case number 03CR204.

It would later be revealed that Bryant had apparently informed Vanessa of the charges near midnight on July 3. Public records revealed that a 911 call was made from the couple's house shortly thereafter, and reporters secured confirmation from the Newport Beach Fire Department that paramedics treated a female at the residence at 1 a.m.

Vanessa Bryant subsequently appeared with her husband at the hastily assembled press conference discussing the case and later made other public appearances.

"I'm innocent," Bryant told reporters at the press conference. "You know, I didn't force her to do anything against her will. I'm innocent. You know, I sit here in front of you guys, furious at myself, disgusted at myself for making the mistake of adultery."

Soon there were press reports that Bryant had purchased his wife a $4 million diamond ring.

From that beginning would come a steady run of Bryant court appearances in Colorado, with hundreds of media representatives descending on the Colorado resort community. "It was just shocking for everybody involved," Smith recalled. "It set off this unbelievable year of going back and forth to Vail. I made seventeen trips to Vail, every hearing."

It was the first major sexual assault case involving such an elite athlete in the newly evolving age of cable news, and the sports network was suddenly faced with a crisis of nomenclature, Smith explained. "It was a tough thing for ESPN because we wanted to be fair to everyone. We had many discussions on whether she was an 'alleged victim' or 'accuser.' We decided on 'accuser,' and that has become standard since then because 'alleged victim' implies that she was victimized, even though you have 'alleged' there. 'Accuser,' we thought, was the most neutral, fair term for all parties involved. We also had conversations about the terminology. If you read the court transcripts, there's some pretty graphic terminology in there. We had conversations on whether we should use the word 'panties' or should we say 'underwear.' We decided on using 'underwear' because 'panties' was too provocative. We had people writing in to us, saying, 'My kids are watching *SportsCenter,* and they don't need to hear that.' I didn't want to sugarcoat things, but I also didn't want to offend people. How do you say he bent her over a chair and penetrated her vaginally? Because everybody thought it was anal, but it wasn't. That was a session we had long into the night, more than one night. How do you present the facts without sugarcoating them or offending people? It was fascinating in a weird sense because it was new ground. We'd never faced this before. I covered the O. J. Simpson trial, and it was not nearly as lurid as with Kobe."

Colorado also had a rape shield law to protect the accuser's identity. Watching Pamela Mackey, Bryant's attorney, attack the case was revelatory for Smith.

"We were very careful not to use the accuser's name," she recalled, "but his attorney used it all the time. And she'd go, 'Oh, excuse me.' She shredded the rape-shield law, which offended me horribly as a woman. But if that was me or my son being defended, I'd say, 'Go for it.' It was absolutely the lawyer you want to hire, and she got away with it."

Bryant's life became a battle fought on several fronts. There was the managing of a tense relationship at home in addition to the demands of his legal defense. Beyond that, he found himself scrambling to stop the disintegration of a carefully built portfolio of endorsement income. He had a lineup of contracts, including with Coca-Cola and McDonald's, that was the envy of the NBA, yet he would watch each of those relationships wither over the coming months, a development that cost him millions.

His "freelance" year without shoe endorsement duties allowed Nike to move cautiously in its relationship. The shoe manufacturer stood by Bryant, both Moore and Vaccaro observed.

For nearly two full years, the drama of Bryant's sexual assault case would drive the news cycle, playing out before a hungry public, and bring with it an intense examination of his life. Since it would take so long for the proceedings to resolve, Bryant and the Lakers moved ahead in their relationship regardless of the many questions.

Naturally, despite the fantastic turn of events, the team still harbored a number of strained relationships. It was true that O'Neal and Bryant had found a level of cooperation over the 2002 and 2003 campaigns. But the relationship between Bryant and Jackson still suffered, so much so that some of Jackson's assistants had urged him at the end of the 2003 season to "make peace with Kobe."

Jackson, however, declined that route and opted to take an even more aggressive strategy in dealing with the situation. The coach's relationship with Bryant was obviously deteriorating by the day, and it would not take long for O'Neal to pick up on those vibes. Not surprisingly, the tentative truce between the team's two stars quickly disappeared, and hostilities seemed ready to break out.

Somewhere in the process, O'Neal had learned that Bryant had made a comment to authorities about him paying off women, and that the comment had made it into the report. That information would not be disclosed publicly for more than a year, yet it fed the center's anger behind the scenes.

"I don't think there was any hiding their displeasure anymore," Rudy Garciduenas recalled.

Adding to the trouble was that Jackson, Bryant, and O'Neal were all nearing the end of their contracts. Looking back in 2015, Chip Schaefer observed that ideally, a franchise would not want its two biggest stars and its high-profile coach to be engaged in contract extensions all in the same year.

"They were two big personalities with a different perspective on the NBA and on basketball," Schaefer observed. "The fact that they were both free agents in '04—probably, that may have set up a him-or-me situation where if they weren't free the same year, that might not have come to that."

Such moments usually boil down to who gets the credit for a team's big success. In the minds of some, the bigger the check, the bigger the credit.

"It happened in Chicago, too, you know," Schaefer said of the breakup of Jordan's great teams. "Success, it's tough. Teams break apart for lack of success, and teams break apart that are successful, too, and both of those organizations were extraordinarily successful during that time. I'm not sure what happens, exactly."

It always seems to come down to the fact, Schaefer said, that intensely competitive people are trying to slice the same pie.

Having worked with Jordan and Jackson and Bryant and O'Neal over the heart of his professional career, Schaefer had made a study of competitive personalities. Whereas the public seemed infuriated by Jordan's emotional Hall of Fame speech in 2009, Schaefer deeply admired it. "I remember sitting there on my couch with my wife watching it," he said, "and I turned to her about halfway through and I said, 'This is the most real he's ever been with the cameras on before.' It was authentic. It was him. It was everything about him that I love personally. I thought it was great."

It was far from easy for such competitors to "be real," he said, adding that Jordan got crushed for doing so. "He is just this person who I think is unparalleled as the greatest player in the history of the game, telling us what he thought. It was a privilege for everyone to hear what he thought."

The truly great competitors have a switch that is always on, Schaefer said. "Ultracompetitive people, they don't seem to be able to switch it off and on. It's pretty much there all the time. It's woven into their nature, their personality. They find motivation where someone else might not even see the reason to be motivated."

During the 2003–04 season, the team's key figures would be motivated by their conflict and their contracts, and as the dysfunction gathered momentum, no one seemed to be able to find a solution, due to how the deals had been arranged by both circumstances and Lakers management. From the start, there was a sense that things were headed toward a huge confrontation.

O'Neal wanted a massive raise from Jerry Buss. Phil Jackson, meanwhile, wanted the team to trade Bryant. Bryant wanted to get away from Jackson and O'Neal. He had reached the point in his contract when he could opt out and entertain offers from other teams. The Lakers could ultimately offer more money than other teams to induce him to re-sign, but there was nothing stopping him from testing the market.

Opting out was a relatively routine process for NBA players, and Bryant, in limited interviews on the subject, had indicated that he would indeed test the marketplace, if for no other reason than that it offered him the opportunity to secure a raise from the Lakers.

Jackson, though, apparently sensed a growing conflict in which Bryant would have more power than ever in dealing with him, since both of their contracts would be up for negotiation. The coach opted to move forward against him with an aggressive public-relations strategy, a more comprehensive push than his usual tactic of needling his players through the media. His preseason comments, as training camp and the season neared in the fall of 2003, were aimed at suggesting that Bryant was being disloyal by planning to opt out of his contract during the summer of 2004. At the same time that Jackson was publicly expressing support for the young guard, the coach was also making his first moves in a months-long public-relations battle against him.

The big center had his own disputes with the team. After being named the MVP of three championship series, O'Neal knew that he deserved a contract extension. While he had nearly three years remaining at a whopping $30 million, he was hoping that the team would extend the deal with a pay raise. The team, on the other hand, hoped that O'Neal would take less money, in consideration of his age, his conditioning, and the number of injuries that had led him to miss games in recent seasons. O'Neal was not happy about the issue and openly pouted. At one point during a preseason game in Hawaii, he would yell at Jerry Buss, "Pay me!"

Some would say that the owner was privately infuriated by the scene, but J. A. Adande remembers the night a bit differently. "Shaq scores a jumper and he blocks a shot, both against Erick Dampier; then he looks over at Buss. We could never get exactly what he said, but it was something like, 'Now you're going to pay me,' or, 'Pay me!' He was rubbing his fingers together. It was just, like, a forty-second sequence in an exhibition game — against Erick Dampier, no less — and, like, now Shaq thinks he's supposed to be the highest-paid player."

Adande tracked down Buss as the owner was walking out that night.

"Shaq had a message for you," Adande said. "Did you see it?"

"Oh, yeah," Buss said. "I got the message."

"He was chuckling," Adande recalled. "You didn't see him deeply hurt or offended. Then Shaq kind of kept it going the next night. We were talking to Phil Jackson outside the locker room before the game, and Shaq just comes walking by, and he's still doing the same thing. He was rubbing his fingers together, you know, the money sign, and he was saying 'Pay me' as he walked down the aisle."

The Lakers could have gotten O'Neal's deal done before training camp, but, uncharacteristically, they hesitated, Adande said. "Jerry traditionally had kind of taken care of his guys and not let stuff linger on. So as it turned out, Shaq was right to be wary."

Bryant had spent the weeks leading up to training camp entertaining thoughts of not playing in the upcoming season, while he battled the charges against him. Faced with indecision, the guard missed the start of camp in Hawaii, where a host of camera crews and reporters waited to take in the spectacle of an accused rapist attempting to play basketball.

Before Bryant arrived in Hawaii, reporters asked O'Neal what it felt like to not have the whole team in camp.

"I can't answer that," O'Neal replied, "because the full team is here."

Jackson had long used Bryant's "outsider" status as a means of motivating and controlling the Lakers roster. But the comment from the team leader set the conflict at a new level.

The guard showed up in Hawaii the next day, and Winter noticed that his teammates seemed eager to pull him into the group and reassure him. But O'Neal's comment had relit the old fires that burned between the two.

Bryant told reporters that he'd rather be back in Los Angeles with his family. "You can't imagine what it's like going through what I've gone through, what I'm still going through," he said. "But I come out here to play, this is my job. I'm going to come out here, I'm going to do it well."

The charges had left him "terrified," Bryant admitted. "Not so much for myself," he said, "but just for what my family's been going through. They've got nothing to do with this. Just because their names have been dragged through the mud, I'm scared for them. I feel like I can deal with this. I have to deal with this. But my family, they're not to blame."

Bryant was true to his word: during the family blow-up over his marriage, and now with the legal trouble, Schaefer saw no evidence of Bryant allowing personal issues to interrupt his competitive effort.

"What's the old legend about the year Pete Rose hit over .400?" Schaefer recalled. "He was going through a lot of personal trouble. Kobe was like that. He did a great job with separating personal stuff, with his ability to compartmentalize those things. I never saw that manifest itself in any way, any different way at all, in his approach to work during any of his personal tribulations he ever had. I never saw him bring that to work."

Dream Team

The addition of Karl Malone and Gary Payton had created instant euphoria among Lakers fans. Recruited by O'Neal, the two had turned down substantial offers from other teams to sign with Los Angeles because it seemed an excellent opportunity to win a championship. The team had been repeatedly victimized by the screen and roll against San Antonio during the 2003 play-offs, and it was projected that Payton, an excellent defender, would help fix the team's defensive woes. Malone was just the power forward the team needed at both ends of the floor. Though he was nearing forty, Malone remained one of the best-conditioned athletes in the league.

Neither man, however, had any experience with Winter's complex triangle offense. As a rule of thumb, it took a player two years of work to become comfortable with the on-court reads and decisions the offense required. Payton and Malone were both known for their great skill in the running game, and both said they planned to run as much as possible to avoid the need for setting up in the offense. For years, the Lakers had been slowed by O'Neal's disdain for running the court. Now, though, Malone warned the center that he had "better be ready to get out and run."

That's exactly what the team did in its amazing jaunt through the first two months of the schedule. The Lakers zipped along on Malone's and Payton's energy, and in the process they managed to throw off much of the cloud of Bryant's uncertain legal status. As they pushed their record to 18–3, the Lakers invited accolades as one of the NBA's greatest teams ever.

"We had everybody for our first few games," O'Neal recalled, "and we looked pretty good."

The fairy tale ended quickly, however, when Malone sustained a knee injury, the first major injury of his long career. Malone was determined to return quickly, but his injury had been initially misdiagnosed, and his rehab efforts only damaged the knee further. It would keep him sidelined for most of three months, and as the team's performance sank, the tensions between O'Neal and Bryant and Jackson rose.

Particularly disruptive were Bryant's numerous trips to Colorado for the various pretrial hearings he faced, which interrupted the schedule of team practices and games. A week before Christmas, Bryant flew to Colorado at dawn for a hearing, then managed to make it back to Staples Center just before the second quarter of a game in which he would be accused of taking too many shots. Still, he settled the outcome with a last-second jumper that would begin a pattern of unique performances on days when he appeared both in court and on court.

Staples Center was scheduled to host the All-Star Weekend in February, with the idea that it would be an opportunity to celebrate the great history of basketball in Los Angeles. A statue of Magic Johnson outside Staples Center was to be unveiled during the week before the game itself, and an array of old Lakers agreed to help host the weekend events.

It just so happened that the days leading into the occasion also brought yet another round of public squabbles within the team. Sadly, questions about the team's chemistry dominated the All-Star event and overshadowed any planned celebration. Though the team had been winning, Jerry Buss was starting to complain about the triangle and the way the team was playing.

The big news came when the owner announced that the team was suspending its ongoing contract-extension talks with Jackson. The Lakers were playing in Houston, in their last game before the All-Star Weekend, when the news broke.

"The Lakers put out a press release that they were basically revoking their contract offer," Adande recalled. "That was wild. Before the game, we asked Kobe his reaction. He said, 'I don't care.' That's when we knew that there was a severe disconnect between Kobe and Phil. Shaq was asked the same question and said something like, 'It's very important for Phil to be here. If I'm going to be here, I want Phil to be here.' Kobe's reaction was just a very cold 'I don't care.' I knew I had to write about it. I just typed those three words on my computer screen, and I was staring at them for, like, an hour because I couldn't believe that he said that."

Bryant may not have had a relationship with Phil Jackson, but he had a nice one with the team owner. He and Buss weren't party pals, as Magic Johnson had been as a young player, hanging out in the clubs with Buss. But the owner and Bryant had quietly visited with each other numerous times since Bryant's first season in Los Angeles. As a man who watched his money, Buss appreciated the value that Bryant brought to the equation with his dedication, professionalism, and hard work, especially as such a young player. Earlier in the season, the owner told a reporter that he thought of Bryant as family. "I felt a lot of pain for him, [the way] a father experiences tremendous pain for the problems his son is having," Buss had said in November.

The Lakers' February announcement led to immediate speculation that Bryant, who had become vocal in his criticism of his coach, had managed to undermine Jackson's position with the team.

"Team insiders believe owner Jerry Buss suspended contract negotiations for O'Neal and Jackson as protection against future ultimatums brought by Bryant, who called out O'Neal, accusing him of being out of shape and lacking leadership skills, and revealed he held little respect for Jackson off the court," the *L.A. Times* told its readers.

Winter, however, confided that it was Jackson who had precipitated the halt in negotiations. "Before the All-Star break, Phil came into a meeting with us and made the comment that he couldn't coach Kobe anymore and he wouldn't come back next year if Kobe came back," Winter confided. "He apparently then told Mitch Kupchak the same thing. Mitch, being the general manager, relayed that information to Jerry Buss. It was really at that time that Jerry Buss made up his mind that he was going with Kobe and not Phil."

It didn't help that Jackson had asked for an increase in salary, from an estimated $8 million per season to $12 million. Jackson had had both a contract offer from the Lakers and a marriage offer from Jeanie Buss sitting on the table since the end of the 2003 season but had acted on neither proposal.

Despite the team turmoil and the sexual assault charge, fans had made Bryant the top vote-getter among Western Conference players for the All-Star Game. If there was still any doubt in Jackson's mind that Bryant's popularity remained strong, he heard solid proof most game nights in Staples Center when the team's fans chanted "MVP! MVP!"

With the turn of events, the media had descended upon the All-Star proceedings with questions about the Lakers breaking off of Jackson's negotiations and the team's drama.

"I think we would be a funny-looking organization if we didn't have drama," O'Neal said. "I've been here eight years, and we've had drama every year. I wouldn't want to come play for a bland organization in a bland city."

Jackson spoke openly with reporters about Bryant's belligerence and cited it as another example of the guard's disrespect for him, but the coach never hinted that he had precipitated the ending of negotiations himself.

Said another of Jackson's close associates: "It had crossed the line to where Phil just decided he couldn't work with the guy. That happens in relationships."

Not long after the All-Star Weekend, Adande and Brad Turner of the *L.A. Times* ran into Buss at an L.A. nightclub.

"Brad and I were at the Club Bliss," Adande recalled, "and Jerry Buss was there at a table. The Lakers had yanked Phil Jackson's contract off the table. Dr. Buss kind of gave hints that he wasn't a big fan of the triangle and Phil wasn't going to be long for the job. So Brad and I were both like, 'Holy shit.'"

Buss, meanwhile, remained publicly circumspect about his plans. To insiders, however, it was clear that Jackson had employed a high-stakes strategy to win control of the team from Bryant and had lost. Once the owner broke off negotiations, Jackson, ironically, began treating Bryant better.

"Phil started giving Kobe much more attention," Winter observed. "He started meeting with him individually. And Kobe's attitude toward Phil really changed. Their relationship got better, but it was too late. Buss had already made up his mind at that point. By that time, he had already told Phil he was not coming back. He had told Mitch Kupchak, too. Mitch seemed relieved that Buss had made a determination."

"I was getting the sense that Kobe was pushing to break up the team," Adande said, "and it was weird. In some ways, that was Kobe's most remarkable season. The way he was able to play with Colorado hanging over his head was incredible. On the other hand, he became more withdrawn from his teammates, from the media. It just became more driven for his agenda rather than the team agenda. He was very self-oriented then. I saw it for what it was. He was very noncommittal in terms of saying that 'I'm definitely going to be a Laker long-term.' He could have said, 'I'm not going anywhere.' He wouldn't say that. He kept all his options on the table. Everything that year was about his agenda, so I wrote it that way. That didn't set well with him. We pretty much didn't speak by the end of that season."

The turn of events had left both Malone and Payton dumbfounded. They had turned down big contracts thinking that they would find a championship chemistry in Los Angeles. The situation left some Lakers regulars trying to help their new teammates cope.

"I thought it was important," Derek Fisher recalled, "especially for the guys who hadn't been here before, that they see us stay steadfast and stay strong in our basic foundation, in our beliefs. When guys like Bryon Russell or Luke Walton or even Karl and Gary, guys who were in their first year on our team — it was important for them to see guys who have been here before really be able to keep a stern face and to keep focused and to continue to have a positive attitude and to have a certain work ethic when you come to practice because they're watching us. We were able to avoid the crisis mode. We'd been at the brink several times, but I think what Phil and his entire coaching staff brought was the ability to float around the brink of danger, to float around the brink of really maybe falling apart, and to still be able to figure out ways to stay composed and stay poised."

"Most of the time we found a way to get it together," O'Neal recalled later. "When it's all said and done, we knew how to get it done."

The Lakers somehow managed to do that after the All-Star break. It would help that Malone returned from his knee injury in March, and they regained a trace of their early chemistry.

Bryant's role, though, remained problematic, as did his shot selection. He averaged 27 points after the All-Star break, but his shooting percentages were down. In March, after some internal criticism, he took only 3 shots at home against Orlando and scored just 1 point in the first half, which left the Lakers trailing by 11. He went for 37 in the second half and tied a franchise record with 24 in the fourth period as Los Angeles won in overtime.

In April, against Sacramento, Bryant again turned in a strange first half, taking just 1 shot against stiff defense. The second half was little better, and he finished with 8 points, leading to speculation that he had tanked the game in response to criticism over his shots.

One anonymous teammate who thought Bryant intentionally blew the game told the *L.A. Times*, "I don't know how we can forgive him."

Furious over the comment, Bryant declined to speak with reporters for a week and a half, although he did go on an L.A. radio station to defend himself against the charge.

"That's another one of the reasons why it upsets me so much to hear people say I tanked a game," he said. "I fly all the way back here, show up for the game. I play hard, play my heart out, play hurt, and then they want to accuse me of tanking a game," he said.

The issue quieted after Jackson began urging him to be more aggressive offensively. In Portland on the last day of the regular season, he scored 37 points, including two spectacular late three-pointers, one to force overtime and another to win it in the second overtime. His performance made the Lakers the surprise champions of the Pacific Division.

The team's ongoing drama had continued to spike their TV ratings. Earlier in the season, Mavericks owner Mark Cuban had predicted that Bryant's charges would draw more interest in the league, a comment that was quickly discounted. Yet network executives weren't alone in seeing the Lakers as the league's main story line. League commissioner David Stern himself had made the mistake of quipping that the NBA's best option for the championship series would be "the Lakers against the Lakers."

Sadly, despite their hype as a legendarily great team, the Lakers never lived up to it, mainly because they had never jelled defensively, Winter observed later. "There were times when we played pretty good defense. Defense in pro ball is predicated on the support around the basket, the big man. Even though Shaq was a big presence, he was not a great shot blocker. And he didn't like to play the screen and roll, so he put his teammates in jeopardy. He didn't like to help. He liked to lay back off his man."

That situation would leave Payton open to criticism in the play-offs. The thirty-six-year-old guard fumed as he sat on the bench for lengthy stretches in the first round, against Houston, while Jackson played Fisher. The Lakers faced San Antonio in the second round, and the Spurs attacked Payton again and again with the screen and roll.

On the offensive end, Malone and Payton never found a comfort level in the triangle.

"It was late in both their careers," Winter said. "I think Karl could have learned the triangle in time. It was a struggle. That's not to say he didn't try. He was great to coach. It was just hard for him to find a comfort zone after spending so many years in that Utah offense. The really big thing is that he got hurt and missed so much of the season. That really killed us. And Payton had gotten older. He could have run the offense, but he wanted the ball. He was never a good shooter. He felt he worked better in another kind of offense."

The Lakers quickly fell behind the Spurs, 2–0, in the conference semifinals. It seemed that the series would end quickly, with the Spurs' Tony Parker and Tim Duncan running screen and roll after screen and roll. But, back in Los Angeles, the Lakers righted themselves and began one of the most improbable comebacks in franchise history.

Game 4 found Bryant again arriving by jet after a hearing in

Colorado. The Lakers trailed by 10 points late in the game, until Bryant drove them to the win.

"I think everybody is impressed with the way Kobe is able to compartmentalize," Spurs coach Gregg Popovich said afterward. "He's going through a tough time. You feel badly for him, for the young lady, for their families. The whole situation, it's just awful for everybody. You wish people didn't have to go through that, but that's the reality of the thing."

Popovich said the Lakers had suddenly begun to play as they had earlier in the season, when they launched their first run. Indeed, Malone struggled with his shot through much of the series, but his energy, his steadiness, his presence on defense, had again become major factors.

In Game 5 in San Antonio, the Lakers were clubbing the Spurs well into the second half, when they started to crumble and blow their 16-point lead. They lost the lead, regained it with a Bryant jumper with eleven seconds to go, then saw Tim Duncan launch an eighteen-foot prayer from the top of the key, with O'Neal squarely in his face. The shot fell with 0:00.4 left, and Spurs fans erupted in delirium.

The game seemed over, but Duncan's shot only served to set up the unbelievable. Payton, struggling to execute on the inbounds play, found Derek Fisher circling to the left of the lane. Fisher, a left-hander, had just enough time to catch and toss. The ball fell as the horn sounded. *Swish*.

"That's the cruelest loss I've ever been involved with," Popovich said.

Now leading the series 3–2, the Lakers headed back home, where they finished off San Antonio, causing media and fans alike to figure that the Lakers had just won their fourth title under Jackson, since the Spurs were viewed as their chief competition. That sense only deepened with their performance against the Minnesota Timberwolves and league MVP Kevin Garnett in the conference finals. The Wolves were a strong team with the addition of Latrell Sprewell and Sam Cassell, but none of that mattered against O'Neal and Bryant.

The Lakers moved on to the Finals, against the Detroit Pistons, meaning that Bryant was facing his old AAU teammate Rip Hamilton. Unfortunately, Karl Malone went down with a knee injury, so the Lakers had no answer at power forward against Ben Wallace.

After losing the first game at home, the Lakers managed an overtime win in Game 2 on yet more late-game heroics and a deep three from Bryant.

They were, however, strangely out of sync in Detroit, and their woes on the defensive boards deepened as they allowed the Pistons second shot opportunities time and again.

"Shaq defeated himself against Detroit," Winter said privately afterward. "He played way too passively. He had one big game. Outside of that, he didn't do much. His boxing out and rebounding in the championship series was awful. He had one assist in one of the Finals games. He's always been interested in being a scorer, but he hasn't had nearly enough concentration on defense and rebounding."

Adande, a friend of O'Neal's, saw it much as the center saw it: Bryant was playing selfishly and jacking up shots.

The undermanned Lakers lost all three games in Detroit and fell, 4–1. Buss left the building early during the second half of Game 5, a blowout. Word of the owner's dislike of the triangle offense soon began leaking out to the media at an increased rate. Winter, who had developed the triangle over years of coaching, said afterward that he didn't blame Buss for wanting to change. "The way we ran the offense was terrible," he said.

In the wake of the Finals debacle, the owner confirmed that Jackson would not be asked back as coach. In the days following the announcement, it became clear that the owner also had no desire to meet O'Neal's contract-extension demands and began making plans to trade the center.

The turn of events sparked speculation that Bryant, himself a free agent, was now running the team, that he had demanded the trading of O'Neal and the firing of Jackson.

Buss, Bryant, and even Lakers general manager Mitch Kupchak all said that the dismissal of Jackson and the trading of O'Neal were not done to placate Bryant. But suspicions only increased after

Buss, who had talked to reporters just once during the season, arranged a conference call in July while on vacation in Italy to explain the changes to reporters.

"The decision with Phil, the decision with Shaq, was made totally independent of Kobe," Buss said. "As a matter of fact, I thought maybe even Kobe would think that. So I went to Kobe, and I said, 'Kobe, I just want you to know, what I'm about to do has zero to do with you or your free agency.'"

Jackson himself countered with his own turn at influencing reporters as he drove from Los Angeles to his summer home in Montana. He dialed up columnists and radio talk shows to offer his version of events.

Jeanie Buss herself would weigh in later in an *L.A. Times* interview in which she explained that neither she nor the team could pin Jackson down on a commitment.

"It all really came down to the fact that Phil didn't want to make the commitment," Winter said. "And I don't blame him, because of his concerns about his health and the angioplasty. They wanted him to do it. It came down to Kobe or Phil, and Jerry Buss went with Kobe. Word got to Buss that Phil didn't want to coach Kobe. The irony is, by the end, they had worked things out to where they were working pretty good together by the end of the season. At least, I felt like they did."

With Jackson gone, the team moved quickly to trade O'Neal to Miami for forwards Lamar Odom, Brian Grant, and Caron Butler and a future first-round draft pick. Later, the team signed former Laker Vlade Divac, and Kupchak traded Payton to Boston for Chucky Atkins and backup center Chris Mihm.

That off-season also brought the departure of Derek Fisher to Golden State as a free agent, the trading of Rick Fox's rights to Boston, and the retirement of Horace Grant. There remained hope that Karl Malone might agree to come back to the team for one more season, but Malone wasn't sure of his knee and seemed intent on taking his time with his decision.

After considering offers from the Clippers and other teams, Bryant accepted a seven-year, $136-million contract with the Lakers. The guard showed up at his news conference at the team's training facility with Vanessa by his side, his daughter, Natalia, in his arms.

Bryant said he was bothered by speculation "that I had something to do with Phil and Shaquille leaving. That's something I didn't laugh at. That upsets me, it angers me, and it hurts me. They did what they had to do. They did what was best for them and their families. I enjoyed playing with them. I even said at the end of the season that I wouldn't mind playing with them for the rest of my career. But they each did what was best for their family. I let it be known that I'm comfortable playing with Shaq. We have our disagreements. We have our arguments. I said I'm comfortable playing with him and playing for Phil for the rest of my career. I told Phil that specifically. He asked me if him coming back made any impact on my decision coming back whatsoever. I said, 'No. I love playing for you.' We never really got along much as people. But as a coach, I thought he was absolutely excellent, and I learned so much from him."

No one seemed to believe him. The next day's papers were filled with columns lambasting his manipulation of the team.

"That's one of the things that frustrated me so much," Adande recalled in 2015. "In the early 2000s, we would report on the feud between Shaq and Kobe, and people would say, 'Aw, it's overblown. You guys are making too much out of this.' But, yes, it was a big deal. It led to the breakup of a franchise because the two couldn't coexist anymore. You really couldn't contain their two egos in the same locker room anymore. So I still think they left at least one championship on the table."

Only much later, after he had finally recognized his miscalculation, would that one lost ring come to rest in Bryant's craw, and, with it, his declaration, looking back: "I was an idiot."

Chapter 25

THE DAMAGE

The weight of his actions soon fell upon twenty-six-year-old Kobe Bryant in the heaviest of fashions. His jersey sales, just months earlier among the most popular in the NBA, plummeted out of the top fifty, and his presence in the sneaker industry disappeared. The MVP votes that had been steadily building over his career? By the end of the much-fraught 2004–05 season, he would earn not a one. Repeat, not a single vote for Most Valuable Player. It could all be measured in a new alienation that made his old isolation look like immense warmth in comparison.

Those things would seem like nothing against the personal losses to come.

Lakers equipment man Rudy Garciduenas recalled how painful it was just to watch Bryant struggle with the damage he had done to himself.

"The bottom fell out of everything," Garciduenas remembered.

Even so, Bryant was left with the slimmest threads of his good fortune. His wealth had purchased a lifeline to freedom. The criminal case against him unraveled swiftly and dramatically that August of 2004 with the disclosure in open court during a pretrial hearing that the accuser's underwear contained the DNA of three sexual partners.

It was a strange, unexpected conclusion to Shelley Smith's constant travel between games and hearings. She had been one of the few reporters to attempt to cover Kobe both on the court and in the courtroom.

"We went through every weather situation you can think of," she said of her days waiting outside the courthouse. "We'd watch him walk in, and we'd watch him walk out. I'd be in the courtroom and try to observe him. He was always the kind of guy who liked to make these faces and stuff. He really never did that during the trial. He was very emotionless. He let his attorneys go to work, and they really did cast a lot of doubt on this accuser as to her reputation and what her motives were, the fact that she'd had sex earlier in the day, the fact that semen had been found from a third person on her panties."

Smith likewise had watched the accuser and her family come and go throughout the ordeal. "They were very stoic as well," she said. "I reached out to them. We knew who they were and where they lived and tried every way to get them to talk. They wouldn't. Eagle's a very small town, and everyone knows each other. It's a working-class town right outside Vail. You work in Vail, you live in Eagle, that type of deal.

"I don't think I ever made eye contact with him that whole time in Eagle," Smith said. "He wasn't really talking much before games or after games. I didn't have much of a relationship with him, and then everything went to hell when the case was dropped."

The criminal trial was scheduled to start in September, but soon it was announced that the accuser would not testify and that she was filing a civil lawsuit against Bryant. The discussions apparently began with the demand that Bryant issue an immediate apology, which he did, saying that he was sorry for any harm she suffered due to his behavior.

Early that September, the criminal charges were dropped. "He dodged a big bullet," Scoop Jackson observed. "He dodged one of the largest situations I've seen in sports scandal history."

Looking back, Scoop Jackson suggested that the entire sad affair had been set in motion by Bryant's isolation. Perhaps just one good, true friend could have helped, could have told him, " 'Not the hotel clerk. Come on, man,' " Jackson offered. "There's not that guy there. He didn't have somebody saying, 'Man, you can't do this shit this way.' "

At the time, Jackson hadn't talked to Bryant, but soon thereafter he approached Kobe for a story about what it would be like to have basketball taken away from him.

"I'm fearful that's all you got," Jackson remembered telling him.

"I thought about that a lot," Bryant admitted.

"That's when I noticed him cutting people out of his life, especially from a media standpoint," Jackson recalled. "He was totally in another zone, a different dude."

Ric Bucher noticed the same. The journalist recalled dropping by Bryant's hotel room before games and just hanging out, watching hoops, chatting easily. Such moments were gone after Colorado, Bucher said. Before, Bryant had used a password to allow approved callers access to his hotel phone line. After Colorado, Bucher found that even Bryant's bodyguards now had aliases. He had to contact them first in hopes of trying to get through to Bryant.

"A guy had to walk me up to his room," Bucher recalled, adding that two security guards stood in Bryant's room the whole time they conversed. "We talked for, like, twenty minutes. He sat on the couch. I sat across from him, and it was, like, high tension. You just felt like he was on edge. I knew it didn't have anything to do with me personally, but it felt like he was that way with everybody. He put everybody at arm's length. It was hard to get a hold of him, it was hard to talk to him. It was hard to get his opinion or thought on anything. He was more guarded than he'd ever been."

Certainly some of that was understandable. The case had brought an unprecedented examination of his personal life. *Newsweek,* for example, had reported that months before the incident in Colorado, Bryant had contacted a divorce attorney, and that an ambulance answered an emergency call to the Bryant household the night Kobe confessed to his wife. The magazine confirmed through authorities that the ambulance crew treated a female during the call to the residence. Bryant would later deny contacting a lawyer, but he had denied numerous things that were later found to be true, which made it difficult to determine just what had happened.

His very unusual private world was now exposed, and his personal issues fed into the legal issues, which fed into the team issues.

* * *

As for his pointed denial that he had used his leverage to remove Phil Jackson as coach and to force O'Neal's trade, Bryant would admit to Ric Bucher years later that there was no way he was going to continue as a Laker if he had to keep working with the big center or the coach.

Bucher recalled that Bryant explained it this way: "There was no way that I was playing again with Shaq because I wanted to prove to all you motherfuckers that I didn't need him."

"That was at the real heart of it," Bucher said. "I kind of knew it was always there. He just never verbalized it. This was the first time he said it in quite these terms."

At the time that O'Neal and Jackson were sent packing, both Buss and Kupchak had insisted that Bryant was not the reason for the team's moves to let Jackson and O'Neal go. Time would reveal that they were clearly quibbling.

"It was made clear to me afterwards," J. A. Adande recalled, "that even if Kobe didn't necessarily say 'me or Shaq' or 'me or Phil,' that it was very obvious that that's the way he felt. So I think they gave themselves a little wiggle room that maybe Kobe didn't necessarily deliver an ultimatum, but Jerry Buss was very aware that Kobe felt that way, that he didn't want Phil to be around, and he didn't want Shaq to be around. Of course, everything they were doing that year was catering to Kobe because he was going to be a free agent and they didn't want to lose him."

According to Bucher, though, it wasn't necessarily the simple fact that he didn't get along with Shaq and Phil that made him resent them. The true answer was deeper and more complicated, tied in with Bryant's constant desire to be the best. "It's one of those things," Bucher said in 2015, looking back, "where I think at a more mature age maybe he would have been able to deal with it in a different fashion, but maybe not."

Bryant wanted to show that he didn't need O'Neal in order to be the kind of great player who could lead his team to championships, Bucher explained. "More than anything, it was, 'You're saying I need somebody else to get this done, and I'm going to prove that that's not true. I can get it done.'"

Even if O'Neal had been willing to defer to Bryant, the situation would not have worked, Bucher said, because "Kobe would have been concerned that people would still be looking at it as Shaq's success."

O'Neal himself seemed to understand that. "When you accomplish a mission, there are always some people who say, 'Hey, I can do this by myself,'" O'Neal had confided at the time. "That's what it was all about. Before we got our first championship, we were going real good. But as we got one, two, and three, people were thinking that they could do it by themselves. A lot of people tried to talk to him, but as the years went on, we weren't on the same page. I found out a long time ago that you can't do it by yourself. You have to do it with the team. Then Phil taught me the formula. The formula basically is that you have to lead the way and be consistent. Let's say that I would average 25 and he would average 20. You've got to do that every night. Now, every now and then, you can get spectacular, score 30, 40 points, but we always have to be consistent. Even if we have horrible games, they've got to be horrible 25s. And all these other guys, they just had to master their little roles. We had to master our big roles, and they had to master their little roles. When you put that together, you got something. When you look at all of our championship teams, we never had no super talent on those teams. By the time Phil got there, a lot of our talent was gone. Most of the big stuff was done by me or Kobe and, every now and then, Robert or Brian Shaw or Ron Harper. That's all you need. A lot of people want to harp on talent, talent, talent. But what's the last time a team won the championship in recent years that wasn't a true team? If you don't have a relationship with your guards or your shooters, then you won't go nowhere. Everybody has to be on the same page. But some people are very superficial and worry about individual things rather than the team."

Bryant would lose face further with the publication, late that fall of 2004, of Jackson's book *The Last Season*, in which the "Zen Master" described the young guard as "uncoachable." Jackson also confirmed for readers that he had requested that Bryant be traded. The book was also disparaging and somewhat dismissive of Jerry Buss himself, but Jackson identified Bryant as the true villain.

"He always had the scapegoat as long as management was there," Rudy Garciduenas observed. "People felt at that time that Kobe was trying to assert himself as being the top dog on the team. He wanted to express himself and, you know, have things his way. He didn't want to be in anyone's shadow any longer, and he wanted to make the team his own. He wanted to be the focal point, the guy."

Or, as Joe Bryant had taught him, he wanted to be "the man." As Charley Rosen explained, from the very first day that Phil Jackson and his staff came to Los Angeles, they had been wary of the influence that Jellybean was having on his son.

Jellybean, Rosen said, was long known to have the reputation that scoring lots of points was more important than winning.

Just as Bryant had once opted for an AAU team with less talent and a high school team with less talent to give himself room to play and grow, he now seemed intent on leading a Lakers team with less talent.

It meant that no longer would he have to stay out of the post due to O'Neal's lumbering presence. It meant, in retrospect, that, like his father many years earlier, he was on a highway to hell and blowing for a passing lane.

Trust

After months of investigation and hundreds of thousands of dollars in costs, authorities in Eagle County had been stopped from prosecuting Bryant. They couldn't have a trial, but they could still air the facts, some of which favored Bryant, some of which didn't. Just as training camp opened, authorities released the police report of the investigation, which corrected a few errors that the media had made in reporting the story. For instance, shortly after the incident hit the news, *Newsweek* had quoted an unnamed friend of the accuser in saying that Bryant had jumped on the young woman that night as soon as she entered his room. The police report would show clearly that that was not the case.

The police report also included Bryant's comments about O'Neal paying a million dollars to silence a woman.

Though O'Neal had long known about it, the revelation of Bryant's comment created a media firestorm that fall. Bryant was immediately painted as a traitor, as someone violating the "code" of an NBA locker room.

Shelley Smith was there at the team's media day to ask him about the situation. "I had been told privately by a number of players in the league that he broke the unwritten locker room code, that he ratted out Shaq to police," she recalled.

She wasn't the only ESPN reporter there that day to talk to Bryant. Jim Gray had been granted a sit-down with Bryant to discuss the upcoming season, but he didn't ask questions about the police report, Smith recalled. She, however, wasn't willing to ignore the importance of the story just because it was difficult to talk about. "My story," she said, "was what sources in the league had told me: 'Nobody's ever going to trust him again. He's going to walk on a bus and they're going to shut up. He's going to walk in a room and nobody's going to talk. He does not have the trust of anyone.' I went around to his teammates, and I said, 'Look, this has come out. Can you trust Kobe Bryant?' Everyone said, 'Yes, of course. He's the guy.' "

Smith had been taught as a journalist never to ask yes-or-no questions but to seek broader answers. However, she thought that in this case it was warranted. She approached Bryant and asked, "Do you believe you have the trust of your teammates?"

"Yeah," he said. "Why wouldn't I?"

"Well," Smith said, "because the police report came out yesterday, and in it, it said that you ratted out Shaq to the police. Some people around the league are saying that you broke what is an unwritten locker room code."

Bryant's face tightened.

"Whatever," he replied.

Smith admitted that she was "hoping he'd react the way he did."

That night, Gray's interview did not air on ESPN, but Smith's story did.

"I was told that Kobe and the Lakers were upset over that," she said.

She later covered the first game of the season and found Bryant in a scrum of reporters discussing the upcoming challenge. With a new coach, the Lakers would no longer be running the triangle, and Smith asked him how the offense would now work.

Bryant tersely brushed her off, and Smith thought at first that maybe she hadn't asked the question clearly. So she restated it: "Just for the layman at home, what's one thing they should look for? Where the ball's going to go?"

"That's it," Bryant said, and ended the session immediately.

Later, Smith recalled, a Lakers public-relations official told her producer, "Kobe says he'll never speak to Shelley ever again."

The Polarizer

Years later, numerous observers and media organizations would look back on the period and describe Bryant as the most polarizing athlete in America. Scoop Jackson, too, remembered a comment made by one of Bryant's teammates well before the Colorado incident. "You know," the teammate told the journalist, "we'd say he's easily the best player in the game right now if he wasn't such an asshole."

"He said it with a smile and laughed because they were teammates at the time," Jackson said, "but they were telling the truth. Like, 'We would honor him as the best player, we'd tell everybody he's the best player on the planet, if he wasn't such an asshole.'"

Only in an extremely competitive environment like the NBA would such a characteristic quietly be considered an attribute, one deemed absolutely necessary for a top player to have to drive his team to a championship. Over his years of working with alpha males such as Jordan and Bryant, George Mumford would expend much effort helping them to learn to relate to their less talented teammates. In time, Mumford would come to recognize that he was essentially helping them to gain a measure of compassion, the very human quality that can become obscured in some intensely competitive personalities.

As Chip Schaefer would observe, people such as Jordan and Bryant didn't have an on-off switch for their intense desire to compete. Fans obviously adored that instinct in Jordan or Bryant when it carried their favorite team to championships. Phil Jackson, however, once explained that it was the in days between games, in the times on the team bus, or at other moments when Jordan still had his competitive switch on and running that it could become hard to live with such a player.

It would become Mumford's goal to help supremely competitive players find a means of contending with what made them different, so that they would be able not just to compete at that highest level but also to find a means of channeling compassion into their everyday lives, despite their astronomical competitive instincts. That would become especially vital, Mumford reasoned, after their playing careers were over. But it was also essential to winning. Highly competitive personalities like Jordan and Bryant could absolutely kill a team atmosphere with displays of ruthlessness or selfishness.

In many ways, that would become Bryant's unarticulated mission in climbing out of the hole he found himself in during the fall of 2004. At the time, Bryant himself still felt that it was all about winning. But for those around him, there was hope that he was also on another path, one that would modify his extreme personality.

"I remember him still having to deal with the fallout from Colorado and all the sponsors that kind of dumped him," Rudy Garciduenas recalled. "He was still having issues with his marriage, which wasn't the easiest thing to repair. From the beginning, Kobe was not adept with social skills. I mean, he did not realize how to get through relationships and interactions with other people. He was a young guy, and it took the course of his career to figure out how to deal with people on a one-on-one basis and in a team atmosphere. You know, he was not the most socially gifted person to begin with."

Yet that fall, the very troubled Bryant was starting over with a new group of teammates, only now he had created a situation where he was supposed to be their leader.

"He wanted to stand out, and he wanted to have that claim to fame of having the team be his," Garciduenas recalled.

It proved problematic from the start, beginning with the release of the police report and the questions about trust.

"He alienated himself from the rest of his team," the longtime equipment manager observed. "That's not a good way to start, you know."

If you're aloof and don't explain yourself well, he added, "everybody can make assumptions about what you're doing or why you're doing it.... He'd always been off on his own. He wasn't the one to buy into the social circles that happened on all the different teams. He wasn't one to follow the group, so he created his own path. He kept himself at a distance, for sure, off the floor. And on the floor it took him some learning in trying to figure that out and how to get along with all of his teammates while he was fighting that persona at the same time."

Garciduenas saw similarities between Kobe and another great scorer, although one armed with a propensity for reflection that Bryant didn't seem to have at the time.

"Kareem was disconnected," Garciduenas said. "Kareem was just different. He sought pleasure from different things."

The great Abdul-Jabbar was bookish and mostly kept to himself, even though he was "The Cap"—the team captain. It worked for the Showtime teams through five Lakers championships because he was paired with the fierce and ebullient Magic Johnson.

"He was a very learned person, and again, he was another person who did not have the social graces," Garciduenas explained. "Some of the most difficult times for Kareem were interacting with other people, having to interact with fans and whatnot. He was totally uncomfortable, and he just did not have those gifts to start off with. He was standoffish to everyone he possibly could be, you know, and nobody understood it. I saw a different side of him in the locker room, things that people didn't normally see. He loosened up in that atmosphere."

Over time, especially after his career ended, Abdul-Jabbar learned to be quite gracious with people, Garciduenas explained. "Over age and over time, he learned a lot more."

If Bryant was learning the same way, he was doing so slowly. He had a public demeanor that often allowed him to mask the aloofness he displayed around teammates, but the alienation was deep.

Despite Bryant's reputation, the equipment manager found much that he liked and admired about the teenaged Kobe Bryant, who had walked into the Lakers' locker room in the Forum and assumed the locker that Magic Johnson once had. He had so much pluck and determination, such a forthright attitude about the game. He was just so serious.

And now, to Garciduenas, seeing all this damage Bryant had done to himself was profoundly sad.

Making the situation far worse was the departure of Derek Fisher in free agency, a major blow to Bryant's ability to relate to the team.

"Fish was his ally," Garciduenas explained. "Fish was probably the one who tried to stay the closest to him, and without Fish there, he lost a valuable person. Fish could always be the voice of reason."

If there was a presence that brought hope for a link between Bryant and the new teammates, it was Lamar Odom, who had gotten to know Bryant through their mutual connection with Vaccaro and Gary Charles, both of whom described Odom as looking up to Bryant.

"Lamar was the kind of person who wanted to be on good terms with everybody," Garciduenas recalled. "Kobe was one of those people that he thought it would be important to stay close with."

Odom seemed well aware of Bryant's aloofness and was in fact aloof himself in other ways. Gary Charles would recall Odom confiding that he and Bryant had their disagreements, that anger would flash between the two over that difficult first season and sometimes in the years ahead. But for the most part, they had that history together, and Bryant knew that Odom had an understanding of who he was.

Bryant would also make friends with Caron Butler, who was among the players to come from Miami in the O'Neal trade and who had survived a tough upbringing in Wisconsin to become a very effective NBA player. With that additional ally, Bryant would set out on his new road to find out.

Crash

To change the culture of the Lakers, Jerry Buss and Magic Johnson said that they were determined to build around Bryant's talents and again become a running team. They clearly had visions of bringing back the Showtime era, and why not? It had been a grand time for the franchise, but as they would again learn, there was simply no duplicating it, there was not even making a poor approximation.

To replace Phil Jackson, the Lakers first tried, at the request of Bryant, to lure Duke coach Mike Krzyzewski, who considered their offer but ultimately decided to remain in Durham.

After the departure of Jerry West and Jackson, Jerry Buss's son Jim was given an executive role with the team, and his first major move would be to bring in a new coach. Associates of Jeanie Buss would later complain that Jim essentially jumped in and offered the job to Rudy Tomjanovich without really consulting anyone about it, although it's likely that he consulted his father.

Jim Buss presented a hard figure for team employees to read. Unlike his enthusiastic and outgoing sister, who had worked for years as an administrator of her father's various sports teams, Jim Buss had gone to work in his father's real estate operations in Las Vegas. Early on, he seemed enamored with his father's playboy identity, recalled Ron Carter, a former Laker who worked for Buss. "Jimmy was more of a personality. I think he was really trying in many ways to emulate his father, but I think he got himself into a little trouble, with girls and gambling and whatnot. Basically, he had some maturing to do. Putting him in the Vegas office was probably not the best place for him to be."

After Jim's stint of trying to become a horse trainer, Jerry Buss had put his son in the Lakers' front office to learn how to run a basketball club. Team employees saw him as something of a reclusive figure who didn't even have an office in the team complex. "At that point, he was just a name on a phone list somewhere," Garciduenas explained.

He'd had no real background in basketball other than some instruction from West and Kupchak, whom his father had asked to teach him about the game. But it was obvious to team employees that he was eager to make good as the basketball boss of the team.

Tomjanovich had been the coach of the Houston Rockets for twelve seasons, taking them to two NBA championships, in 1994 and 1995, but he'd had to step down in May of 2003, two months after being diagnosed with bladder cancer.

By the summer of 2004, he had gotten clearance from his doctor to resume coaching. Rudy Garciduenas was an old friend. The equipment manager knew the personalities on the team well and was frankly concerned about Tomjanovich. At fifty-five, he was taking over a team that no longer featured the game's most dominant player, with Bryant trying to fill the void and to focus his efforts on making it his team. Garciduenas could see that the situation was going to generate an immense amount of pressure on all involved.

The 2004–05 Lakers season soon unfolded in a series of nasty turns that would leave the organization quickly spinning out of control. Lakers assistant GM Ronnie Lester had predicted before the season that it would take the Lakers two years to build the kind of depth they needed to be a solid running team. The addition of Odom, a versatile open-court player, was viewed as a big step in that direction.

Training camp each season always found Bryant with a freshly wound motor, Garciduenas recalled. "At the beginning of every season, you'd see it in Kobe. He'd be tremendously focused. He had spent the entire off-season getting himself into shape and working on things that he needed to work on. He tried to inspire others to do that, but he was definitely still learning his way around in a leadership role."

In 2003, Bryant's off-season had been lost to his troubles and surgeries. Instead of arriving with athletic upgrades, he had shown up in training camp with several tattoos in honor of his wife and family. For the 2004–05 season, he had redoubled his efforts by building a new, stronger physique and now weighed almost 230 pounds, bulk he figured he would need now that he was finally going to be able to work in the post with O'Neal out of the way.

In training camp, Bryant paused to look back on all that had happened and acknowledged that he had made mistakes. He said he wished he could go back and fix them, but he could not. Instead, he said, his only option was to push forward. Howard Beck, now covering the NBA for the *New York Times,* wrote that it was as close to a mea culpa from Bryant as the public was going to get.

Very soon, the memo about becoming a running team seemed to have been lost, as Tomjanovich took the team through training camp and into the early weeks of the season. Instead of a strong transition attack, the Lakers settled into an awkward identity as a drive-and-kick team that more often than not settled for a three-pointer. During the early part of the season, when the schedule was favorable, the Lakers prospered so long as their three-pointers were falling.

It was hoped that Karl Malone would return from knee surgery in time to give the team a major upgrade in talent and help on the defensive end. Little did the public know that behind the scenes, Malone and Bryant were feuding, which would erupt in a public spat over Malone's supposed inappropriate remarks to Vanessa Bryant.

"I'm not sure what was said," Rudy G. recalled. "From what I understand, it was a statement that could be construed in a couple of different ways. I'm not sure if the tension between Kobe and his wife wasn't also a factor in the whole thing. Once those kind of things start, they usually don't end up well."

Malone apologized publicly for the misunderstanding, but it was clear that his relationship with Bryant had been irreparably damaged. A few days later, Malone announced his retirement from the game, ending the coaching staff's hopes for his help over the second half of the season.

"Kobe was extremely hard on players who didn't live up to his expectations," Garciduenas offered. "If Kobe imagined one way for Karl to play, and Karl did not live up to that, then for Kobe, he was of no use after that."

Naturally, the fallout from the incident meant more damage to Bryant's public image and yet more conflict in his life.

The stress of coaching an angry and determined Bryant soon began to take a toll on Tomjanovich. Garciduenas had been worried that the strain of an NBA season would be too much for him too soon after going into remission. Garciduenas had lost his spouse to breast cancer after a long battle. "I was worried for Rudy's health," he recalled.

The Lakers muddled along to a 14–11 record on their way to a Christmas Day matchup with the Miami Heat and O'Neal. O'Neal's new team had charged out to the best record in the Eastern Conference. Jerry Buss commented to reporters that his former center had lost sixty pounds in preparing for the season, implying that if the center had lost sixty pounds earlier, the Lakers might have kept him. O'Neal later would dispute those reports, saying that Buss and the team had always used his weight against him.

"The number thing with the weight was, it was something they made up to make me look bad and feel bad, so that I would take less money," O'Neal said. "It didn't matter. If I was winning championships and taking them to the Finals, it didn't matter. Once Jerry West left the Lakers, there was no one in the front office I could trust. Jerry West always told the truth. After that, there wasn't anyone there. When it came to my leaving, [Kobe] could have spoken up. He could have said something. He didn't say anything."

The emotions left over from the breakup of the championship team would remain raw for years. O'Neal's Heat won the matchup on Christmas in overtime, despite Bryant's 42 points.

In January, Bryant suffered a severe ankle sprain while playing against Cleveland and LeBron James, and missed weeks of action as the direction of the team stalled and turned sour.

Under Tomjanovich's system, Bryant found himself in a situation a little like the one he'd experienced with Del Harris, with a casual practice attitude and much less structure on offense.

"I do think he realized why he missed Phil and Phil's offensive system," J. A. Adande recalled. "Rudy T. basically had Kobe with the ball right in the middle of the court, and it was very easy for opponents to send a double team to him. He realized, 'Wow!' He was really a lot better suited for the triangle because the triangle you get the ball on the wing, and you'd have a lot more space to operate one-on-one. It was a lot harder to send the double team. They were better off, for Kobe's purposes, using that offense than using Rudy's offense."

With Tomjanovich's offense often slipping toward inertia, Bryant soon began talking to the press about the team again employing parts of the old triangle to provide better spacing and ball movement. Tomjanovich assured reporters that he was fine with these ideas from Bryant, but his demeanor suggested otherwise.

Once again it was a situation that cast Bryant in an unfavorable light. Having been accused of engineering the ouster of Jackson and O'Neal, he now appeared intent on running the team.

Then, on February 2, came the stunning, abrupt resignation of Tomjanovich, due to mental and physical exhaustion. "Kobe's expectations of everybody put a lot of pressure on Rudy T.," Garciduenas recalled.

The sudden turn of events sent the team into a tailspin. Tomjanovich's resignation sparked immediate speculation about a Phil Jackson return, but the former coach made it clear that he wasn't going to join the club at midseason.

Under pressure from Jerry Buss to step in, longtime assistant Frank Hamblen took over, but the team's defense worsened, along with its effort. "When Frank Hamblen took over for Rudy midway through that season, he wound up, you know, installing some elements of the triangle," Adande recalled. "They didn't go full-fledged triangle, but they ran some triangle actions."

Behind the scenes of the coaching turmoil, Bryant's personal life was engaged in yet more crisis. More than a decade later, he would disclose that his wife suffered a miscarriage in early 2005, and he characterized it as being caused by the stress he had brought on his family with the Colorado incident.

He had just returned from the ankle injury in February when he learned that Big Joe, seventy-five, had died back in Philadelphia due to complications from his diabetes. His grandfather's death wouldn't become a media issue until the All-Star Weekend, when it was explained that Bryant would miss a Lakers practice to attend the funeral.

"He watched me play a lot of basketball games," Bryant told reporters when they asked about Big Joe. "He was a really private man. We're having a private ceremony and everything. He just had a big heart, a big, big heart. It's tough on all of us, but it was coming."

Jellybean had continued to phone his own father often to the very end, but it was Pam's side of the family that had been the far bigger priority of their lives for years.

Two years earlier, Bryant had talked briefly of the family rift with Bill Plaschke of the *Los Angeles Times*. "I want a father. I want my father," he had said then, without mentioning Pam, an indication of the direction of the rift. Bryant had kept at least occasional contact with his father.

Joe had talked to Kobe after Big Joe's passing. "My father, he's dealing with it pretty well," Bryant told reporters. "If he's all right, I'm all right."

The very next morning after Big Joe's death, Bryant and Vanessa woke up to find a major story in the *Los Angeles Times* by reporter Shawn Hubler detailing their relationship, Vanessa's caustic personality, her behavior toward shopping clerks, the growing power Bryant had assumed in her family with his money, and the breakup of her mother's second marriage as a result.

She was now viewed as the dark star, the hidden planet, in his life, what the *Times* described as "one of the few powerful influences on Los Angeles' most powerful professional athlete."

The story also highlighted the public's continued fascination with the purple "make-up" diamond that cost a supposed $4 million, a scenario so outrageous that *Saturday Night Live* had fashioned a skit out of it.

The article noted that the new vanity plate on her Mercedes was ICE QN. In many ways, the story brought clarity to the couple's image as the King and Queen of Ice. The story emphasized a quip by a *Sporting News* columnist: "Vanessa Bryant is the new Yoko."

The paper portrayed Vanessa as a very young woman dealing with a dramatic change of circumstances in her life, a crisis of having her sole identity be that of Mrs. Kobe Bryant, one created by moving in a matter of months from a family with parents out of work and on the brink of bankruptcy to the life of a young jet-set goddess with immense wealth at her command.

The newspaper captured the transformation in the recollections of one of her friends: "She'd bring pictures of Kobe to school, and we'd all be like 'Omygod!' I remember there was one of him playing with her puppies, and she would only let us look at it, we couldn't touch it. Even then, a lot of people didn't believe her. But then he gave her that massive engagement ring, and that shut everyone up."

Perhaps most troublesome of all was that the newspaper revived the critical issue of the lack of a prenuptial agreement, based on what the newspaper had learned from Stephen Laine, Vanessa's former stepfather. "We'd been going back and forth for months over a prenuptial agreement," Laine recalled, who explained that the prenup negotiations were settled right before their wedding, in 2001. "She just came home one day and said something to the effect that Kobe didn't want a prenup, that he loved her too much."

The Bitter End

The miscarriage, Big Joe's death, and the *L.A. Times* article all happened less than a week before the All-Star Game was scheduled to be played in Denver, where fans had taken to booing intensely every time Bryant touched the ball in games against the Nuggets, an intense, lingering reaction to the events in Eagle.

Denver proved an awkward place to be for such a drawn-out event as All-Star Weekend, especially with Bryant's lawyers still working behind the scenes to settle the civil suit with the accuser. But Bryant played well in the game, with 16 points, 7 assists, and 6 rebounds. He departed swiftly afterward for Big Joe's funeral, in Philadelphia, then jetted back to Los Angeles to resume the miserable season.

Two weeks later, as the Lakers made their way through a four-game losing streak, it was announced that the civil case between Bryant and his accuser had been settled, with the amount he paid undisclosed. The lawsuit had accused Bryant of holding the woman by the throat while raping her. Even before he had been charged, his offer had been rumored to be in the $5-million range, which left observers wondering how much the final tab, including legal bills for both sides, cost Kobe Bryant. Whatever it was, it was likely worth it, given that neither side wanted to provide depositions, which would have been necessary if the case had gone to trial.

The accuser, now married and pregnant, had no comment on the settlement. Neither did Bryant, except to apologize for the damage done to her.

From that point, things soon turned dismal, as the Lakers made their way through a 2–19 close to the season. In response to accusations of being an outsider, distant from his teammates, Bryant had announced before the season that he was going to have a more pronounced leadership role and, once training camp opened, had seemed to relish offering advice and guidance to his teammates. It didn't work.

Bryant's trademark stubbornness, combined with his attempt at leadership, would only serve to further damage his image, if that was possible. Teammate Chucky Atkins told the L.A. press in late March that Bryant was the team's general manager, a sarcastic confirmation of the fans' belief that Bryant had too much power over the Lakers.

Atkins later complained that reporters had tricked him into making the statement, but that didn't seem to be the case.

"Kobe had a tough time," Tex Winter confided. "I think his teammates really got down on him. He tried too hard to be a leader."

"Kobe was trying to be too vocal," Garciduenas recalled. "He didn't know how to lead the way his teammates wanted to be led. He was trying too hard. I mean, Kobe was really trying. He just wasn't sure how to go about it."

The situation produced yet another painful lesson. "Leaders are respected," Garciduenas observed, "and I don't think Kobe had earned that respect from a lot of people yet."

His difficulty in becoming a vocal leader came from the fact that he was exceedingly frank, which included his razor-sharp trash talk. "He always held them to high standards, along with himself," Garciduenas explained. "But he was never known to hold anything back when he was displeased. That was on the practice court and in the locker room.

"To me, Kobe was always a likable guy," the equipment manager added. "He was difficult to like, maybe, for his teammates because he was always in competition with them for being the marquee player, being the leader, and he wanted to be the scorer all the time. He wanted to be the responsible one, but that doesn't always fare well with your teammates. Socially he had gotten a lot better. He was a presence in the locker room, but at the same time, he was still learning that he didn't have to be the vocal one all the time."

Late in the season, a key injury to Odom was followed by an injury to center Chris Mihm and finally by a leg injury to Bryant himself. As the losses wore on, the atmosphere became increasingly difficult. Attendance began to drop, which only increased the pressure on the entire franchise. By the final weeks of the season, the circumstances for Bryant had become overwhelming, which deepened his anger and depression.

True, he had become the youngest player in NBA history to score 14,000 points. While he had rung up the league's second-highest scoring average (27.6 points per game, behind Allen Iverson's 30.7) for the 2004–05 season, Bryant made only 43.3 percent of his shots and had failed to make the NBA All-Defensive Team for the first time since 1999. His lack of a single vote for MVP emphasized the disdain in which he was held within the league as the season ended. His effort to force a remake of the Lakers had been an epic failure.

"I think Kobe has hit the wall," Winter said quietly that spring as criticism of Bryant rose to a chorus. "I'm worried about him. I don't know what it will take to get him revitalized. Expectations for the team have been so high because of the way things broke up."

The Lakers missed the play-offs, something they'd rarely done over their long history. It had been eleven years since the last time they'd missed. They would finish the 2005 season with a 34–48 record, behind their lowly crosstown rivals the Clippers.

"They'd had that losing streak," recalled a Jackson associate. "Frank didn't want to coach the fucking team to begin with. You know he's doing Dr. Jerry a favor. So after the last game, in the locker room, he goes through the usual bullshit. You know, 'You guys played hard,' blah, blah, blah, trying to be positive. 'I appreciate your effort,' you know. Kobe says, 'I've got to say something.' He stands up, points around the room, and says something like, 'You motherfuckers don't belong on the same court with me. You're all shit.' And he walked out of the locker room."

"It wasn't pretty," said another team source who witnessed the exchange. "But that's human nature when people deal with the frustrations of losing and things not going as they expect. It had to reach a point where it hit rock bottom."

There were obviously people in the locker room who said, "Who the hell does he think he is?" the source said. "But anyone who was on that team already knew who he was, what he thought of himself, what role he played. Everybody knew where Kobe was coming from, that he was always going to be the one to put the most pressure on himself and that that was definitely going to transfer to everyone else, too."

Besides, the NBA was a place where such emotion exploded onto the surface from time to time, the source explained. "There have been many situations on many teams where things come to a head. It's human nature."

The moment was just a reaction to the tremendous pressure that Bryant had brought to the season, to himself, to Tomjanovich, to his teammates, observed Rudy Garciduenas. "There were a lot of times Kobe didn't hide his feelings with his teammates. I mean, it wasn't something that was unexpected. He just couldn't deal with it anymore and said what he had on his mind."

Jackson's Return

Before he left on a late-winter trip to New Zealand, Jackson had told Tex Winter that he felt great and wanted to coach again in the NBA. Jackson even confided that it looked good for him to wind up coaching the Denver Nuggets the next season. Apparently Jackson had been talking behind the scenes with the Nuggets and thought he had the job in the bag. But while Jackson was off vacationing in the Pacific, the Nuggets hired George Karl as their coach.

Meanwhile, a groundswell movement had begun to bring him back to Los Angeles. It had started in late March and early April, when Jackson began showing up at Lakers offices and even attended a game with Jerry Buss. Winter figured that the Lakers were his choice over the many other teams that wanted him because of Jackson's affection for Jeanie Buss and the fact that he already had a home in Los Angeles. It didn't hurt, either, that the Lakers were a team that had some experience with the triangle offense, meaning that the learning curve for players there might be shorter. In fact, it could be argued that Bryant knew the triangle better than any other player in the league.

Jeanie Buss told the *New York Post* that she had no idea what Jackson would do, even though she remained his girlfriend.

Buss admitted to holding out hope that Jackson would return to her Lakers. "Kobe is not the reason Phil is not the Laker coach," she said. "The reason he's not the Laker coach is he had the opportunity to sign the extension and he waited. My father was coming to the conclusion he was going to trade Shaq. Kobe was a free agent and he had a coach who was noncommittal. He had to make a decision. Phil has always said Kobe is one of the best players, and any team with him can compete for a championship. I don't see it being a problem."

Some observers wondered if Bryant could get along with Jackson, especially after Jackson criticized the guard in his book. But Bryant obviously needed help turning the Lakers around. Winter, a mentor and confidant to both Jackson and Bryant, chuckled at the idea of Bryant and Jackson needing each other. It was the perfect irony of the high drama that had unfolded during Jackson's tenure in Los Angeles.

In a further note of irony, after his refusals to meet with his star for so many seasons, Jackson sought a meeting with Bryant as Jackson pondered renewing his relationship with the Lakers. The guard declined, saying he didn't want to be blamed if Jackson decided not to take the job.

Winter noted that even if Jackson did return, it wouldn't be easy for the Lakers in 2006. The team was already $20 million over the salary cap, and that didn't include the option for backup center Vlade Divac, another $5 million.

Jackson had to consider the situation. How would he react to a team that lost a lot of games? Would the stress send him into a tailspin, as it had Rudy Tomjanovich? Jackson had never been a good loser. He once threw two chairs onto the floor during a Continental Basketball Association game in Albany. Could he handle the stress this time around?

As May became June, Jackson turned sour on the idea, phoned his agent, and told him he didn't want to coach again. Then he changed his mind once more.

Finally, he and Bryant met, although it would take years for J. A.

Adande to get Jackson to admit what kind of agreement the two of them came to. In 2011, Jackson told Adande that he had promised Bryant not to attack him in the media.

"The amazing part to me is how they were able to have that second act when Phil came back," Adande said in 2015. "I'll never forget Kobe telling me one day, 'Everything I do, I do for Phil.' I wanted it on the record because I had long suspected that when he came back, he'd made an arrangement with Kobe that he wouldn't talk bad about him in the media."

Adande would go back and search news stories to confirm it. "Phil told me that they had an understanding that certain things wouldn't be said publicly when he came back," the journalist said. "It was clear that they had struck some type of deal because Phil wasn't afraid to call out anybody, as you know, but if you look back from 2005 to 2011, he never called out Kobe."

Jackson confidant Charley Rosen offered that the lovefest between Jackson and Bryant "was mainly for public consumption" and that the relationship still had its sparks and conflict over what would become another successful period in Lakers history.

Ultimately, on June 14, Jackson announced his decision to accept a three-year deal at a record $10 million per season.

"It wasn't about the money, but the intrigue of this situation," Jackson said in a press conference at Staples Center. "It's a tremendous story and a tremendous opportunity. It's a story of reconciliation, redemption, of reuniting—a lot of things in this make for a wonderful opportunity for the team, the Lakers, and myself."

Jackson wore a suit and sandals to the press conference and talked of the lessons he had learned. "More than anything, the lessons were about stress," he said, "in particular the stress that you get and how the release from that changes personalities. My kids, who have all weighed in on this, all wanted to talk about why I wanted to come back to this stressful job.

"I'm not the panacea for this basketball club," Jackson told the hastily assembled press conference. "It's not going to happen overnight. It's going to take some time. But we do think there is some hope, and we can make some changes that will really benefit this team and we can get back into the play-offs again."

Thought to have mixed feelings on Jackson taking over again, Buss was vacationing in Europe and said in a statement that he was "pleased to have Phil return to the Lakers," adding, "His record speaks for itself, and his success in this sport is unparalleled. Quite simply, Phil is the best coach in the business and probably the greatest coach of all time. We feel that he is the best person to lead this team and hope that he will be able to lead us back to the point of being a championship-caliber team."

For his part, though, Bryant, who was nearing his twenty-seventh birthday, had seemed less than enthusiastic when reporters had asked in May what he thought of Jackson's candidacy to return, and he now issued a prepared statement, saying, "When the Lakers began the search for a new head coach, I put my complete trust in Dr. Buss and Mitch Kupchak to select the person they thought was best for the Lakers organization. In Phil Jackson, they chose a proven winner. That is something I support."

Jackson made a point of telling reporters that Bryant had phoned his congratulations that morning. "You know, I think after we play a few games and get kind of a feel of working together, we'll really feel like we're ready to go," Jackson said. "I really encourage him to find a way to get his zest back for the game, not that he doesn't lose his competitive edge, but the whole game. He wants to come back and make some people eat some words."

An ESPN reporter tracked down O'Neal for his take on the news. It seemed obvious that the center was deeply troubled to see his old coach back with his declared enemy. O'Neal's Heat had just lost in Game 7 of the Eastern Conference finals to the Detroit Pistons. One of Jackson's staff commented privately that as much as the center disliked Bryant, he would have to admit that the Lakers guard could have helped him win that seventh game.

The other side of that, the staffer added, was that Bryant likewise needed O'Neal to lead the team into contention, and he remarked that it was unfortunate that the two never fully realized their value to each other.

The rupture itself, however, had created an exhaustion for such speculation. It was time to move on.

It seemed miracle enough that Bryant had somehow managed to

have his coach back. The reunion with Jackson also marked the first steps of Bryant's return to prominence as an endorser. The beginning of this business recovery came quietly, with Nike using a photo of Bryant in a *Sports Illustrated* ad that July, which was promptly protested by the Colorado Coalition Against Sexual Assault.

"Nike agrees with most NBA observers that Kobe Bryant is among the very best players in the game," said Nike spokesman Rodney Knox.

The stigma associated with his actions would be a long time in fading, but that, too, would begin soon enough. Directly ahead lay an explosion of another sort, the kind that replaced dread with wonder.

Chapter 26

RISE UP

It soon enough became clear that it wasn't just Allen Iverson's street cred that Kobe Bryant coveted. Perhaps more than anything he had wanted Iverson's freedom. For years, the Philadelphia guard had been in full attack mode, able to take on opponents whenever and however he saw fit. As a result, he had won NBA scoring titles in 1999, 2001, 2002, and 2005.

"Scoring is an individual goal," Iverson told *Sports Illustrated* during the 2005–06 season. Still, he sensed just how much his friend Bryant hungered to be the game's top scorer. "Honestly," Iverson said, "it would be good to see if Kobe could do it one time."

Lassoed and roped into the ambition of a good, then great, basketball team for eight of his NBA seasons, Bryant longed to flex his power at last that fall of 2005. Although it violated everything Phil Jackson believed about team basketball, the coach bit his tongue, twisted uncomfortably in his seat, and generally did everything possible to keep his agreement not to criticize Bryant publicly.

Bryant, for his part, feasted like a glutton, racing across the first three months of the season while taking an average of 27 shots per game, 10 more than his career average. That proved just a warm-up. From there, his scoring power surged down the stretch of the season.

Along the way, he created a masterpiece or two that would mark his place as one of the game's all-time volume scorers, the very heart of his legacy. Bryant would later explain that he saw himself as the sport's all-time best one-on-one player, and it was these explosive games that bolstered his argument.

At the same time, the process of that gluttony seemed over time to satiate somewhat his immense desire to dominate, to the point that he began to understand that, having put up big numbers, his real legacy lay with what Jackson had been trying to sell him on all along—the winning of championships.

He began to listen to his coach as well as his own inner urge to win above all else, which in turn would bring him a bit closer to Jackson. In the interim, Bryant presented quite a spectacle from the fall of 2005 right through the spring of 2007. He was clearly a man in search of his limits.

The young Lakers gained momentum that fall of 2005, as Bryant put up huge scoring nights frequently. Still, there remained certain obstacles to his happiness, as he was reminded when he returned to Philadelphia in November to face Iverson. Bryant, who had averaged 34.8 points over the season's first two weeks, shot a miserable 7 for 27, for 17 points in his hometown. The Lakers lost before a Sixers crowd that again booed lustily every time Bryant touched the ball.

"I love it," he said, his voice growing more comfortable with the lie each time he said it. "I love it. I love it. I mean, I love it. This is where it all began for me."

What else could he say? He loved it perhaps only in that it fed his competitive anger and determination.

The scoring surge didn't belong to just Bryant. The 2005–06 season brought the quiet unleashing of an array of top scorers, mostly because the NBA had changed the interpretation of its rules to prevent defensive players from impeding any wing or backcourt player. No longer would defenders be able to subject a player to the immensely physical play that Jordan had faced from muscular defenders on his rise to the top.

The results of the change were evident when four players— Bryant, Iverson, LeBron James, and Gilbert Arenas—all jumped out of the gate to average 30 points a game or better, the first time that had been done in almost fifty years. Wilt Chamberlain, Jerry

West, Oscar Robertson, Bob Pettit, and Walt Bellamy did it in the epic 1962 season in that age before zone defenses or even much double-teaming was deployed in the NBA.

New Jersey Nets executive Rod Thorn, a longtime expert on NBA rules, acknowledged in 2006 that the shift was dramatic. Perimeter defenders were no longer allowed to use their hands, a barred arm, or any sort of physical contact to impede or block the movement of either a cutter or a ball handler.

Thorn explained that the NBA had changed the rule to give an advantage to the offensive player. "It's more difficult now to guard the quick wing player who can handle the ball," Thorn said of the change. "I think it helps skilled players over someone who just has strength or toughness. What the NBA is trying to do is promote unimpeded movement for dribblers or cutters.

"My opinion is that the game had gone too much toward favoring strong players over skilled players," Thorn said at the time. "The NBA felt there was too much body, too much hand-checking, being used by defenders to the detriment of the game. There was a feeling that there was too much advantage for a defensive player who could merely use his strength to control the offensive player."

The new interpretations of the rules attempted to address that issue, Thorn said. "If the refs perceive that a defender is bumping the cutter, or bumping a ball handler, then they'll blow their whistles."

Unhindered by the physical challenge of defenders, offensive players found many more opportunities to attack the basket—and draw fouls.

"The good wing players—LeBron, Kobe, Arenas, [Dwyane] Wade, Carter—shot a lot of free throws with the way the game is now called," Thorn said.

The results were immediate and pleasing to the league's front office.

Offensive players were freed as never before, and fans were thrilled by higher-scoring games. Television ratings jumped with the excitement, and reporters began filing more stories, signaling an NBA revival not seen since the days when Jordan played for the Bulls.

The league had made an obvious move to try to pick up scoring averages that had been in gradual decline since the late 1980s. And it seemed to be working.

Not everyone was enthused about the changes. Tex Winter, now eighty-three and the veteran of more than a half century of coaching, had serious misgivings about what the league had done.

Winter acknowledged that the outgrowth of the new interpretation of the rules was the rise of the superdominant offensive player, led by Bryant, with his string of 40-, 50-, even 60-point games.

"It's brought all these 40-point scorers," Winter said. "They can't score 40 points unless they get 15 to 20 free throws."

"They should be protected, but not that much," Winter said. "I don't think that just touching a player should be a foul."

Ironically, this attempt to pick up scoring also slowed the pace of NBA games because numerous foul calls meant a parade of free throws on many game nights that first season, Winter said. "The fans are not going to like that whistle blowing all the time. It's slowed down the pace of the game."

Winter's other complaint with the new officiating was that the game still allowed the same old physical play in the post while turning the perimeter and wing into a no-touch zone.

"That doesn't make sense to me," Winter said. "If you can do all that tough stuff inside, why can't you do it outside?"

"Defense has basically stayed the same in the low post. Out on the court there's no doubt that the interpretation has changed," Thorn conceded.

Over time, the change could be seen as one more factor that de-emphasized the role of big men in the game.

But for talented wing scorers, the rule changes were a dream, and they would help promote the emergence of a new generation of offensive stars, including LeBron James, Gilbert Arenas, Dwyane Wade, and several others.

Bryant, of course, had proved his abilities long before the NBA began changing its approach. He was a player ready to step out and seize opportunity in any rules format, and he did that decisively in the 2005–06 season.

Boogie Nights

Bryant shook off the Philadelphia experience and went on to turn in three more big games that November, all in Staples Center, with 42 points in a win over the Knicks, 43 in a loss to Chicago, and 46 in a loss to the New Jersey Nets. Considering the angry close to the previous season, it was fair game for observers to wonder if his massive scoring numbers meant that the Lakers star might have substantial trust issues.

In fact, Bryant's teammates began the season sensing that he didn't trust them much at all, Lakers forward Brian Cook quietly confided later that season. Then came a game at Toronto on December 7 when Bryant took just a dozen shots, passed out 11 assists, scored just 11 points, and the Lakers won.

"I don't think he shot but two or three shots in the first half," Cook would recall two months after the event. "He just distributed the ball and had, like, 11 assists. Now we've gotten the sense from him that he sees we're gonna help him out. We know Kobe's capable of doing anything. We just gotta help him out and be in the right spots and run our offense, and I think everything will be fine."

Lakers forward Devean George had played with Bryant for a half dozen seasons, but that season he, too, began seeing a subtle change even as Bryant plowed his way through a series of big scoring nights. That change wouldn't be dramatic, and it wouldn't materialize every night—far from it—but it formed the basis of something that could become team play.

Bryant's leadership was also improving, gradually. "I see him really, really focused," George confided at the time. "Really, really outspoken and getting his point across verbally now. He used to just lead by example. Now he's doing a whole lot more talking, letting guys know. 'Get here. Move there. Move the ball. Step up.' Whatever. He's trying to take younger guys under his wing and let them know. I think that's the biggest difference. He's definitely taking a different route in trying to pick everybody up, pick everybody's game up, get everybody on the same page, get the team rolling. I think that's the difference this year in what he's doing."

Of course, there was still the big scoring agenda, and with his talent and the new rules, it meant that on many nights, when his teammates struggled, the opportunity and necessity came at Bryant hand in hand.

He scored 42 points at Dallas and 41 against Washington in Staples Center in December, both wins. Then came a home loss against Houston that infuriated him. He had taken just 13 shots and tried to coax more from his teammates, who didn't deliver.

The Mavericks came to Staples Center two days later, and during the morning shoot-around before the game, Bryant supposedly mumbled about taking care of business himself.

He scored 62 points in just three quarters, making 18 of 31 shots and, better yet, 22 of 25 free throws, to build such a big lead that he could afford to sit out the entire fourth quarter. In fact, for three quarters he had outscored Dallas by himself.

During the fourth, Phil Jackson sent assistant coach Brian Shaw down the bench to ask Bryant if he wanted to return to the game. It was one of those pivotal moments in Bryant's life, and if there was anyone who understood that, it was Brian Shaw.

"I first met Kobe in Italy in 1989," Shaw recalled in 2015. He had played as a rookie with the Boston Celtics, then surprisingly signed with an Italian team for his second pro season. "I went over and played in Italy and played against his father, and Kobe was maybe nine, ten, years old at the time. He was just a typical kid of a player or coach, always on the floor, challenging the pro guys who were trying to warm up. He had a nice, pleasant personality. I got to know him and his family a little bit then."

Ever the fabulist, Bryant would later tell people that Shaw was one of the pro players he defeated in one-on-one as a child. "If you let him tell the story, he did," Shaw said with a laugh, looking back. "You didn't take him seriously. He was just a little kid who was running in and out of the layup line and things of that nature. Now he tells a story that has grown over the years that he challenged me. It started out as a game of H-O-R-S-E and that he was ten and I was twenty-two or twenty-three and that he beat me. By the time I was a teammate with him in our first Finals in 2000, it grew to being that he beat me in a one-on-one game. As years went on, the legend grew and the story changed."

Pressed for the truth of long ago, Shaw said, "In his recollection, he beat me. It would be hard for me to believe that, at twenty-three, I lost to a ten-year-old. But . . . if that is the case, I can say I had something to do with his greatness because I helped build his confidence at an early age."

Besides, Shaw added, laughing, Bryant beat him plenty of times after practice once they became teammates on the Lakers.

In fact, Shaw's presence on the Lakers coaching staff for Jackson's second tenure with the team marked an important but unarticulated change in how Bryant was seen.

As Charley Rosen had explained, Jackson and his assistants had viewed a young Kobe with suspicion in 1999 because they were dubious of his father. Joe Bryant, Rosen said, was seen as an NBA cynic who supposedly had once proclaimed that scoring lots of points was more important than winning.

Now Shaw was an assistant on a team on which Kobe was scoring lots of points, and the team was struggling to win. Longtime Jackson observers might consider it no coincidence that Jackson chose Shaw to deliver the message about going back in the game. Tex Winter confided at the time that Shaw had unique value in that he was an assistant coach unafraid to challenge the psychologically intimidating Jackson. Shaw was also not shy about expressing his admiration for Bryant's unequaled work ethic.

"I walked over to Kobe," Shaw recalled, "and I said, 'Coach wants to know if you want to stay in and get 8 more points and get 70 and then he'll pull you out.' Kobe looked up at the scoreboard and saw we were up by 30 or whatever, and he said, 'Nah, I'll get it another time.'"

Shaw recalled being stunned and angered by the response.

"There's not many guys who can say they got 70 points in a game," he told Bryant. "You better go back into the game."

"No. No," Bryant replied. "Don't worry about it. We don't need that now."

"I just shook my head," Shaw recalled.

Asked later how many points he might have scored had he played the fourth, Bryant did the quick math and said, "Maybe 80."

On December 28, he scored 45 points in an overtime loss to Memphis but got into a scuffle running down the court with Mike Miller of the Grizzlies and threw an elbow into his throat, which drew a two-game suspension from the league that cost him the first two games of 2006. Bryant returned on January 6 and scored 48 against Philadelphia in Staples Center, including 7 three-point field goals without a miss. The next night he scored 50 against the Clippers, including 40 in the second half.

He then chalked up his fourth straight game of at least 45 points, with 45 points and 10 rebounds against Indiana. No one had accomplished that feat since Chamberlain in November of 1964. Bryant, Wilt, and Elgin Baylor were the only three players ever to achieve such a feat.

Over the seven games between January 11 and January 22, Bryant made a franchise record 62 consecutive free throws.

Monday, January 16, was Martin Luther King Jr. Day, with Shaq's Miami Heat visiting the Lakers. Just days earlier, former Boston great Bill Russell had told O'Neal of his own effort to make peace with Wilt Chamberlain after a falling-out during their playing days. Russell encouraged O'Neal to make peace with Bryant, and there was simply no better time or place or opportunity than MLK Day. Bryant was stretching before the game when O'Neal approached him with an extended hand. Bryant was stunned. The center offered congratulations on the birth of Bryant's first daughter and on the pregnancy of Vanessa with their soon-to-be-born second daughter.

Before tip-off, they hugged again as the fans cheered happily.

"It made me feel good," Bryant remarked. "We've been through so many wars together."

It was good to be able to move on, he added, good for the city of Los Angeles, good for its youth.

"The great Bill Russell ordered me to do it," O'Neal explained. Bryant celebrated the "peace" with 37 points, including a dozen over the last eight minutes, to earn the Lakers a win.

A few nights later, he scored 51 points at Sacramento, which further juiced his already high confidence.

Homage

If the scoring displays showed anything, they revealed that Bryant was clearly a man in search of his limits. His ability to perform at this high level was solidly based on his years of extreme personal practice.

It began with his immaculate footwork—an array of pivots, reverse pivots, jab steps, and feints that allowed him to create the room to rise up in a tight space, often pinned in against the sideline; to elevate over the defender and make seemingly impossible shots under impossible circumstances. This unique skill was the perfectly formed product of his study of untold hours of videotape of every single one of the game's great scorers. It also involved conversations and more film study with Tex Winter about footwork, and time spent with Jerry West talking about a million important details, such as the angle of his elbow in relation to his forehead for the perfect shot.

Even throughout his troubled years, despite the constant noise from his conflict with O'Neal, Bryant had already established his greatness in the minds of many key opponents, so his effort to rebuild his team and his reputation proved quite compelling to many of the people he encountered on a nightly basis around the NBA, so much so that even as he struggled so publicly, Bryant was building respect among his peers. "Every time we played them and the game was tight, we guarded him well," said San Antonio Spurs coach Gregg Popovich, looking back. "But he'd still pull up or fade away and shoot from the right quadrant or the baseline and jump over everybody and still knock down the shot. And then he would smile after he did it."

The thing lost to many observers because of his offensive explosion was the tremendous effort he expended defensively many nights.

"At some point in the game, he would decide to guard someone else, someone who was hurting his team," Popovich explained. "And he would just lock that player up. He never gets credit for that, but he's done it a lot."

For admirers such as Popovich, who had a full understanding of what allowed a singular player like Bryant to stand far above so many others, the essence "was his mental toughness and a willingness and an ability to accept responsibility on a night-after-night basis.

"That's what really separates the great players like Kobe from the rest," Popovich observed. "There are a lot of good players in the NBA, but they're spotty. They'll produce, like, every third night. But it takes a special mental toughness and a feeling of responsibility to your group to want to do it night after night after night. And that's what separates Kobe."

Tim Duncan, Popovich's partner in so many great battles against Bryant, identified the same quality. "It's his competitive nature, the way he can bring it every night," he explained. "He wants to be the best every single night."

As Rudy Garciduenas had seen in his years working for the Lakers, there were the rare few who simply cared far more about the game than everyone else. Jerry West was clearly one of those. Magic Johnson, too. And Bryant was another. Of all the great players that had worn a Lakers uniform, the list of those who cared at that elevated level was very short.

Chip Schaefer certainly saw it. For years, he had been one of Phil Jackson's most trusted and dedicated aides doing so many critical things at the heart of first Jackson's Bulls and then his Lakers. A thoughtful, reflective man, Schaefer had a deep admiration for Winter, an intense loyalty to Jackson. And over time, he had become Bryant's go-to aide as far as workouts, which meant that Schaefer was on call around the clock. In so many ways, like Garciduenas, he was a critical glue factor in both of the teams he served.

It didn't hurt that Schaefer had an endless supply of Jordan stories to share when Bryant wanted to take a break in his workouts.

"We certainly had our conversations about Michael," Schaefer recalled, "and he would ask me specific questions about how he would handle situations. Kobe was often curious about how, not just basketball specific stuff, but even some of the peripheral things like if a team was going through something, how would Michael react toward a teammate? He was interested in what kind of leadership and management Michael would have."

Schaefer could also see the happiness that Bryant felt at having Jackson and his staff back and the triangle offense back. "He loved playing in that system," Schaefer said.

Bryant preferred getting his practices out of the way in the early morning, even in the offseason.

"So I'd be in my car at five in the morning, both of us coming in from Orange County to get his workouts in before dawn in the summertime," Schaefer recalled. "To find an NBA player that disciplined these days, good luck with that."

Schaefer would usually create an optimum program in terms of diet, strength training, conditioning, and recovery with the hopes that a player might follow 50 percent of it. Nobody could achieve 100 percent on such programs, Schaefer offered, but Bryant was the one athlete who actually got close, both during the season and off.

"It was amazing," Schaefer explained. "A game could end, and we would fly to the next city. We'd get in, it would be three in the morning, and he would want me to come do a stretch with him or something. Instead of just going to bed or whatever, he couldn't switch it off."

Meanwhile, Brian Shaw pointed out that on the flight, while his teammates were sleeping, Bryant would watch the game he just played to review his and the team's performance, then watch scouting video of his next opponent, all usually before allowing himself rest.

No other NBA player had anything close to such a commitment, Shaw said.

Bryant always chose to do the most optimum thing. "Even people on my end might at some point say, 'Enough, I want to go to bed,'" Schaefer explained, "but his level of dedication just never switched off."

Instead of slowing as he aged, Bryant increased his intensity.

"The most dedicated athlete I've ever worked with by far," Schaefer said, adding that Jordan had a similar discipline to Bryant, but no one came close in terms of the daily grind that Bryant chose.

If Jordan had a couple of poor shooting games in a row, when Schaefer arrived for work at the Bulls facilities in the morning, he could hear the star in the gym putting up shots.

Jordan would do extra work when he needed to, Schaefer said. "Kobe was always going. His dedication to being the best basketball player, to me, was unparalleled."

Not surprisingly, because Schaefer spent so much time with Bryant, he hardly considered him aloof. Schaefer on occasion would be dining with his family at the same restaurant as Bryant, and the star would take the time to come over to say hello to Schaefer's family.

Bryant likewise could show a personal touch with an array of opponents around the league, as he once had with Donnie Carr. Vin Baker recalled running into Bryant on a flight and afterward Bryant stopping to see if he needed a lift from the airport.

David West, a young forward with the New Orleans Hornets, recalled a similar connection.

"One time in L.A., after the game, I was leaving Staples Center," West remembered in 2015, "and he came by and tapped me on the shoulder and said, 'Man, you're getting better.' And, man, that meant a lot to me. That was a big deal for me.

"I was about twenty-four and still trying to find my way in the league. That was the first time he had ever spoken to me. And I'll be honest, I was shocked that he even knew who I was, and then to acknowledge me and compliment me....A couple of years later, we were on an All-Star team together, and I was able to see him up close. I was able to listen to him about basketball. That was pretty neat."

The league's young players had watched him play on TV for the past decade. His fierceness and approach had inspired so many of them, including players such as Damian Lillard of Portland and Paul George of Indiana, who would come into pro basketball over the ensuing years. There was no question that Bryant still had his conflicts, but his manner and graciousness meant that despite all the public tribulation and negativity of his life, he was building a base of growing admiration in and around the game.

Much of that would come from his many competitive exchanges in games. "I was guarding him in a game in L.A.," recalled Luc Mbah a Moute, a veteran journeyman who took tremendous pride in his defensive play. "There was only a couple of seconds left on the clock at the end of the third quarter. I usually don't talk to guys

I guard, but I was talking to him this time. I was pretty much telling him, 'I know what you're going to do. You're not going to get a shot off.' And he says, 'Oh, yes, I am.'

"And then I told him, 'I know exactly what you're going to do. You're going to pull up [for a jumper].' Then, with two seconds left, he acts like he's going to go to the basket. But he took just one dribble and stopped on a dime—I thought he was going to take a second dribble—and as soon as he stopped, before he even takes the shot, he says, 'Got you.'

"He then shoots the ball, it goes in, and he turns around, looks at me, and starts laughing. He probably laughed about it during the whole time-out and, even when he came back onto the court, he was still laughing. I was so mad. I was so mad he could score on me even when I knew what he was going to do."

The Feast

Sunday, January 22, brought Toronto to Staples Center. Bryant would reveal much later that it was the birthday of his grandfather Cox, now departed almost five years, and his grandmother Cox was in L.A. to see him play. Reportedly, his granny had never seen him play live as a Laker. Three days before had been his daughter Natalia's third birthday, so there was plenty of family-related emotion working in his mojo.

Other than that, the moment came with no great foreshadowing. He had gulped pepperoni pizza and grape soda the night before, and he stayed with that theme the next day for the pregame by eating a hamburger and fries. Mostly, his knees ached. Really ached, he recalled.

His goal in the first quarter was to try to loosen up the knees a bit, but the Raptors came out in a loose zone, which provided him with the opportunity to score some easy baskets early with dribble penetration.

That proved all the taste he needed. Bryant turned on his usual bountiful energy, but his teammates dragged along in a stupor, as if they'd all been doing tequila shots at sunrise. Their jumpers, when they got them, clanged and banged and whiffed, and the Lakers fell behind noticeably.

Sensing yet again that he needed to be aggressive, Bryant steadily brought the attack, utilizing a variety of shots, including what teammate Devean George called a "flat-footed jumper." It was a surprise shot that Bryant had perfected "by grabbing a teammate after practice to make him guard him a hundred times" until he had it just right, George would later recall.

With a three-pointer early in the second quarter, Bryant was off at a brisk pace, with 17 points in thirteen minutes of playing time. It was clear that he could get just about any shot he wanted, anytime he wanted, against the Raptors, but his team was still losing. When Toronto's Mike James knocked down a floater off the glass late in the second period, the Raptors led 52–37. With 1:27 left in the quarter, Bryant stole the ball, was fouled by Jalen Rose, and made the first free throw. When he missed the second, it ended his streak at 62 straight.

At the half, he had 26 points on 10 of 18 shooting. His teammates had just 23 altogether and had made just 10 of their 32 shots.

Toronto opened again in a zone for the second half, and Mike James quickly knocked down a three to push the Raptors' lead to 66–49. Bryant, meanwhile, launched headfirst into a second half that gave Granny quite the thrill. As the blood started flowing in the third, Phil Jackson stood up from the bench, pushed his glasses up on his nose, folded his arms, and then, with a strange look of pain and concern, nodded and pointed at Bryant. Behind the scenes all season, the coach had been urging his star guard to throw the ball inside to Kwame Brown, who had terrible hands, or to Chris Mihm, who struggled with inconsistency. The effort to make them scorers remained a work in progress.

Bryant had dutifully sent the ball inside to Brown, but the center kept fumbling it, leading Jackson at one point to call a time-out in frustration. "Jesus Christ, Kwame!" Devean George remembered the coach fussing. "I hope the wife doesn't let you hold the baby!"

Finally, with about six minutes to go in the third, Lamar Odom made 1 of 2 free throws, his first point of the day, ending a run of 19 straight points Bryant had scored for the Lakers.

Not that Bryant was thinking about putting on the brakes, but as the momentum gathered, Odom was in his ear, telling him to keep pushing. Seconds later, Bryant hit another three to lift his total to 41, and Toronto coach Sam Mitchell called time to discuss trying to cool him down a bit. Bryant, meanwhile, made a beeline for the Lakers bench and sat there, monklike, seemingly in a daze. He had scored 15 points in the first six minutes of the period and went right back to work after the time-out, motoring to the right corner, giving a pump fake to draw the foul from Morris Peterson, then making the jumper.

Moments later, he bent over, took a jab step, then rose up to hit a deep three, to cut Toronto's lead to 78–73.

Over the remainder of the period, Bryant pushed the agenda, first eclipsing the Raptors, then taking a 91–85 lead for the Lakers.

He had made 11 of 15 shots in the third, and his Lakers had closed the quarter on a 12–0 run, which had set cell phones to buzzing around the insular world of the NBA, just as they had for his 62 in three quarters against Dallas in December. In Philadelphia, Allen Iverson told callers he was going to sit back, have a little popcorn, and enjoy the show.

As for the coaches watching the game on TV, they couldn't understand why the Raptors weren't double-teaming Bryant more. When the Celtics allowed Jordan to score 63 points against them in a 1986 play-off game, they had likewise declined to double-team him. It was the old philosophy: let the big dog score and focus on shutting down his teammates, acknowledged George Karl, coaching Denver at the time, who also watched Bryant's game on TV. Karl kept waiting for more double teams, and some eventually came. But not many.

As the third ended, Bryant walked toward the bench, squeezing the ball with both hands, absently soaking in its feel, as if the ball were the moment itself and he wanted even more out of it. He again took a seat alone at the end of the bench, not wanting anyone or anything to shake his rising mojo. His teammates had been giddy for two quarters now but tried not to let that intrude on whatever he was feeling. He had 53 points, and the building coursed with energy. At the other end of the floor, the Raptors were trying to fend off a sense of panic.

Early in the fourth, Bryant took off on a spinning drive into the lane and was poked in the eye. Knocked to his hands and knees in the lane, he yelled at the refs for the no-call and drew a technical foul.

By the nine-minute mark of the fourth period, Toronto as a team had scored 25 in the second half, while Bryant himself was at 35 and counting.

Three minutes later, his total for the game jumped to 61 after he scored on a drive from the right, to bring the Lakers' lead to 9. Then he hit 3 free throws to eclipse his personal best of 62 points against Dallas.

On the bench, all Brian Shaw could think of was his refusal to keep playing that other night, how he had said, "I'll get it another time." Now that time appeared to be coming at them headlong.

At 4:28, Odom sent him the ball on the left sideline, where he crouched in the basic triple-threat position, the ball tucked on his right hip, then ripped it through to the other side and took off to the left, into the frontcourt, to pull up and elevate for yet another two-pointer, bringing his total to 72, passing Elgin Baylor for the Lakers' all-time single-game record.

Bryant turned and jogged back up the floor, a deep scowl on his face as he glanced at the clock, as "MVP" flashed across the scoreboard. With the Lakers now holding a 17-point lead, speculation mounted along press row as to when Jackson might put him on the bench, now that the record was broken. The Zen Master, however, seemed content to extend the moment a little longer, to see where Bryant might take this thing.

The Raptors were now throwing furious double teams at him, and Bryant coolly split them to draw fouls and keep piling up points at the line. With six seconds to go and the crowd approaching delirium, Jackson called down the bench for rookie Devin Green, who entered the game for his first-ever NBA playing time. Green hugged Kobe Bryant, sending him toward the bench and the awaiting gauntlet of high fives and hugs. He had scored 81 points, the second-highest single-game total in NBA history, behind Wilt Chamberlain's 100-point game in Hershey, Pennsylvania, in 1962.

The Lakers had been down by as many as 18 in the third period when Bryant locked in. They won by 18, 122–104. Kobe had made

28 of his 46 shots, including 7 three-pointers, and had gone 18 for 20 on free throws. The Lakers' next leading scorer was Smush Parker, who finished with 13.

Afterward, the noisy locker room quieted when Jackson entered. Often a man of few words around his teams, content to have his gaze do the work, he now let it roll over the happy group, Devean George remembered.

"Hey, Kobe," the coach said finally. "I think that shoulder's gonna need some ice."

Brian Shaw could only smile. "The game was still in the balance," he emphasized in 2015. "We were losing most of that game, so we needed all 81 of those points. And he gave it to them in a variety of ways: three-pointers, free throws, post-ups, drives to the basket. Just every way you could get it, he got it."

Shaw had come into the league as the teammate of Larry Bird and Kevin McHale. As a tall guard, he had battled against Jordan and Magic and Clyde Drexler, the entire array of old-school greats and even the earlier versions of Bryant himself.

"That, in my time," Shaw said, "was the best performance I've ever seen."

In Chicago, the phone of former Bulls great Scottie Pippen rang at 3 a.m. with a call about Bryant's big game. He spent the rest of the night tossing and turning over the mere thought of it. Defensive minds everywhere were likewise vexed. Jordan, meanwhile, issued not a word about basketball's big event.

Others, however, had plenty to say, and much of it wasn't positive. The *San Diego Union-Tribune* declared that Bryant had scored his points in a "meaningless game."

Greg Couch with the *Chicago Sun-Times* called Bryant a "zero as a hero."

Vince Carter, Bryant's sometime AAU teammate, suggested the performance sent a bad message to kids, who might be too easily impressed. In Miami, Shaquille O'Neal was reported to have sneered when his teammates brought up the subject and told them, "Give me 50 shots and see how many I score."

"If somebody gets 81 on me, I'm going to clothesline him," Miami's Antoine Walker told reporters.

Other observers balked at the negative reaction and saw Bryant's 81 as possibly better than Chamberlain's 100. Kareem Abdul-Jabbar weighed in, implying that, at least stylistically, Bryant's game was better than Wilt's. "Yes, it was," Abdul-Jabbar, a special assistant coach for the Lakers, told L.A. reporters. "That's because of the wide variety of shots that he used, driving, pulling up, behind the three-point line, it was an incredible feat of versatility."

Even Phil Jackson, who had spent much of his time in Los Angeles finding ways to curb Bryant's excesses, seemed appalled by the negative reaction to the big game. The coach seemed on the defensive because Bryant's performance had left old-timers muttering about the decline in team play.

"I think people didn't see the game and just lost context of what the game is about," Jackson said, pointing out that many appeared to have seen no more than a few highlights on ESPN, if that.

So, what did Bryant's 81-point game really mean? Certainly it meant that people were going to be talking about him for a long time. It was a performance for the record book. And in the aftermath, the Lakers coaching staff would do yet more head scratching, trying to figure out how to merge Bryant's exceptional skill and talent with a young, inconsistent roster that seemed ready to soar some nights and ready to fold many others.

"I honestly do not know why I scored that many points," Bryant himself would say later. "I just came out like any other game and tried to do what I could to help my team win. I must admit, once the point total got up, people started telling me about it. But Wilt's record was never in jeopardy. The fact of the matter is I've been in the league long enough to understand that the individual things don't mean anything. It's how you perform as a team that will be one's lasting impact."

In the wake of the event, Tex Winter offered, "The problem here is that the other players have to learn to step up. The problem is not Kobe."

The team around Jordan was much stronger than the team around Bryant, as former Jordan teammate Steve Kerr, a broadcast analyst at the time, pointed out.

Bryant was told how Jordan had once learned to trust his teammates and was rewarded for it by Kerr and guard John Paxson both hitting big shots to win championships. "It's a process," Bryant observed. "With us, it's inconsistent. Some nights the trust is there. Some nights it's not. It's a process. Over the course of a year, when you find yourselves in big-time pressure situations, that's when the trust becomes cemented. I'm sure with Paxson his play in big-time critical situations showed that he could step up. And that's when the trust became cemented. And that's how it works with us."

Winter, who coached Jordan for better than a decade, said he had never seen the Chicago star go off on such a scoring spree. "Kobe has an incredible sense of when to push for and look for his own shot," the coach said.

His critics would return again and again to what they perceived as Bryant's personal agenda. "He's told me he wants to be the best to ever play the game," Winter confided the week after his big game. "I hope that's just out of his reach, yet not out of sight."

Winter had been pushing the team concept at Bryant for years. "He knows what it takes," the elderly coach emphasized, "and he wants it to be as a team. But it's really a matter of our other players learning how to step up."

Winter said that Bryant's big night obviously both pleased and disturbed Jackson, who also constantly preached team play. Likewise, Bryant's teammates seemed happy to celebrate the moment but were also bothered "that they were mostly spectators," Winter said.

Winter had long observed that both Jordan and Bryant, because of their incredible ability and ruthless, competitive natures, were not entirely popular with teammates. "Michael, though, was a lot harder on his teammates than Kobe," Winter offered. "Michael could come down really hard on them at times."

The basketball public had long obviously adored Jordan's competitiveness, yet at the same time they seemed to begrudge a similar trait in Bryant, as if for years now he had been trespassing on Jordan's domain. Bryant's answer to that was simply that he didn't care. "I'm going to let my play do the talking," he said quietly several weeks after the big night on his grandfather's birthday.

* * *

Later that season, the Lakers would sign veteran Jim Jackson after an injury to Slava Medvedenko. Jim Jackson had first met Bryant as a rookie, when he had joined him for dinner one night in Los Angeles. "You could tell that, with his competitive drive, he was not afraid of the moment," Jackson recalled of the rookie. "He was not afraid to step on people's toes as a young player, even if it wasn't popular."

Now, almost a decade later, as his new teammate, Jim Jackson was struck by how Bryant had changed. He still possessed the ungodly focus, but Bryant had learned to bring a precision to it. "That included his workouts, his eating habits, how he approached the game itself," Jim Jackson recalled. "It wasn't that he was just a better athlete. By the time I was his teammate, he was saying, 'I'm a better basketball player, mentally and physically.' He knew it all, all the things around the court, all the things his teammates were supposed to do in their assignments, plus all the things that came with his growth."

Jim Jackson observed that Bryant still remained basically aloof and spoke to his teammates in the only language he knew. "The way he fit in was playing basketball," Jackson explained. "He was always on the outside looking in."

Jackson also sensed that Bryant talked little because he remained so wary of revealing weaknesses, even though he didn't have many on the court. Jackson had played for years against Bryant, who by then was quite familiar to everyone around the league. "You scouted him and knew that maybe you wanted to push him a little more to the left than right, but that didn't mean you would be able to stop him."

It was much harder to defend him when he was playing in the triangle, Jim Jackson added. "With the triangle, he didn't have to work as hard in that system because of the floor spacing and the freedom of movement of the ball. It put him in position fifteen to eighteen feet from the basket, where he could be very productive."

It was also very obvious, Jim Jackson said, that Phil Jackson didn't allow Bryant a lot of time in the triangle's weak side sweet spots that Jordan had once found to be so productive. It was an issue that Tex Winter often complained about.

"Phil didn't trust him," Jim Jackson said. "I don't think he trusted him as much as Michael, in regards to being able to make plays for his teammates, not just for himself."

That was the subtle beauty of Phil Jackson's dynamic coaching, Jim Jackson added, looking back on his time with the Lakers. "It's about how to get to these dynamic personalities, to make them understand what the objective is. Phil's approach with Kobe seemed to be a lot different from his approach with Michael. That's the beauty of coaching."

Phil Jackson was in the process of shaping Bryant's great will that season, Jim Jackson observed. "It was different. Kobe had to figure out how to influence his teammates so that he could trust them and so that they could trust him. Kobe's thing was, 'I expect you to play at a certain level all the time.'"

He now had a younger roster around him, one that he could make far more demands upon than he could of the veterans who were around him earlier in his career, Jim Jackson observed. "He had Luke Walton, Kwame Brown, Lamar Odom, Smush Parker, and those guys. It was a tough crew for Kobe to adjust to. But it came at a time when I think he needed it."

Bryant had obviously wearied of being the "kid" among older players and was now trying to step up to a new stature within the team. Having younger players around him was a critical part of that shift.

There had to be some subtle growth on these trust issues before the team could really start winning again, Jim Jackson suggested. And, as Rudy Garciduenas had said, it was obvious to Jim Jackson that, for all his growth, Bryant had still suffered quite a bit of damage from the issues he had brought upon himself.

In reality, the recovery itself revealed extraordinary character, Jim Jackson explained. "To have the ability to still be able to focus? I don't think people still understand just how big that was. For him to go through all that turmoil and still be able to come out and play at a high level?"

Jackson had merely caught the last months of a bleak, bleak time in Bryant's life. "His refuge was to be able to get out on the court and let it go," Jackson said.

With the team in position to make the play-offs, Tex Winter was around even more as a consultant that spring. Jackson saw that the old coach could be somewhat brusque at times in coaching Bryant and that Bryant didn't seem bothered by it, that in fact he was quite receptive to the coaching.

"That's how he was supposed to be," Jim Jackson said. "Tough on him."

All in all, Bryant regained much lost ground in 2005–06. He returned to the All-NBA First Team and the All-Defensive First Team. He won his first league scoring title by averaging 35.4 points per game, then the eighth-highest all-time scoring average and the highest scoring average in nineteen seasons, since Jordan had averaged 37.1 points per game in the 1986–87 season. Bryant also averaged 5.3 rebounds, 4.5 assists, and 1.84 steals in eighty games and led his team in scoring for seventy-five of those games. He set a franchise record for points in a quarter—30—and tied another Lakers record with 23 free throws in a game.

At the start of the season, the Lakers were thought to have only a slim chance of making the play-offs, but Bryant and Phil Jackson were able to nudge them into the postseason. During the first-round play-off series, versus Phoenix, Bryant's scoring average dropped to 27.9 points per game, but he shot better from the field, grabbed more rebounds, and passed for more assists than he had in the regular season.

The Lakers, surprisingly, took a 3-1 lead over the Suns and seemed poised for a major upset, only to stumble and fold embarrassingly with three straight losses, including a blowout defeat in Game 7. After spending much effort letting his teammates work, Bryant had attempted to settle the issue in Game 6 and scored 50 in an overtime loss, but he couldn't hold off the favored Suns from regaining control. The outcome left both Jackson and Bryant aching, a pain made all the worse by O'Neal's claiming another championship in June 2006 with the Miami Heat. The circumstances served to create a sense of urgency for the Lakers and a growing frustration in Bryant himself.

USA, USA!

In January 2006, as he was gaining fame for his 81-point game, Bryant had gotten a call from Jerry Colangelo, the new managing director of Team USA, who was in the process of rebuilding the American Olympic basketball program.

Bryant agreed to Colangelo's request for a meeting and immediately went to his office in Phoenix to discuss the prospect of playing on Team USA.

"He had wanted to participate in USA basketball a number of times," Colangelo recalled, "but it had never happened, for whatever reason."

There had always been a surgery or his personal life getting in the way, but the timing seemed good now.

"Kobe," Colangelo said as they sat down, "what if I said to you that on this team I want you to be a distributor, not a scorer?"

"I was pulling his chain a little bit," Colangelo admitted.

"I'll be whatever it takes," Bryant said immediately.

"He just wanted to be a part of it," Colangelo said. "To me, that was a heck of a statement on his part."

Colangelo's choice to head up the program was Duke's Mike Krzyzewski, whom Bryant had admired for so long. The coach likewise admired Bryant for his approach to the game and for all his hard work.

Their mutual respect would come to be another key factor in Bryant's rebuilding of his life and reputation. "There's a great relationship between Kobe and Coach K," Colangelo said in 2015, looking back. "Once you're around and in the presence of people you respect, it all just builds. That was the reason I selected him as coach."

The process of preparation for the 2008 Olympics began that summer of 2006. Bryant would get to discover what Shaquille O'Neal had been enjoying—being Dwyane Wade's teammate—just as he would discover what it meant to play alongside LeBron James.

As a fellow two guard, Wade would also relish the chance to play with Kobe. Nearly four years younger than Bryant, Wade was the product of four years of college play at Marquette. Despite their relatively close ages, Bryant already had a decade of seasoning as a pro.

"When I came into the NBA, he was twenty-four and I was twenty-one," Wade recalled. "He was the best two guard in the game. To me, he was the measuring stick to where I wanted to be someday, not only individually, but as a winner."

It didn't take long before Wade found himself facing Bryant in a game. "It was, like, the tenth game of my rookie year," he recalled. "We played them in L.A. They had Gary Payton, Karl Malone, Shaq, and Kobe. My eyes were buck-wide-open. They had four Hall of Famers. And they kicked our butt."

Mainly, Wade recalled the terror — "I was scared as shit." And nervous, even though his team, the Heat, didn't have him as the primary defender on Bryant, Wade remembered. "But I'll always remember one play: I got a steal on Kobe; I ripped Kobe Bryant. I was so excited to do that. That was a real highlight for me. So every time I got a chance to compete against him, I tried my best. Some days, he got the better of me. Sometimes, I got the better of him. But I just had a great time competing against him. We had a long period of time where we had some classic battles."

The three of them would headline the new and improved edition of Team USA, commonly known as the Dream Team, once the most feared name in international basketball, before a tough few years that led them to lose the gold at the 2004 Olympics.

O'Neal declined to join them, but all three of them made the three-year commitments that Colangelo required to play for Team USA, with the goal of reclaiming the gold at the 2008 Olympics, in China.

Before they could do that, James, Wade, and Bryant had to make a strong showing at the 2006 FIBA World Championship, in Japan.

"We've got a lot of work to do," said Bryant, who had sat at home in June and watched O'Neal and Wade lead the Miami Heat to the NBA championship. "It's a lot of work, but it's also going to be a lot of fun. I'm looking forward to competing with my new teammates and representing the United States."

It was all new territory for the U.S. basketball program. "In the past, Team USA would just kind of throw things together in the weeks before the Olympics," Tex Winter confided. "Now Jerry Colangelo has put together a program that will really focus on the gold, on making the Dream Team the best again.

"Kobe and LeBron and Dwyane have agreed to be teammates for the next three years," Winter pointed out. "There's never been anything quite like that before."

"I'm going to be a busy little guy, but it's exciting," Krzyzewski said that June as he prepared for the opening of the Dream Team's tryout camp, in July. "This has been the busiest year of my life, by far."

Krzyzewski had to select a team of twelve to fifteen from the twenty-three players invited to tryouts in Las Vegas, Nevada. That list included other NBA stars, such as Shawn Marion of the Phoenix Suns, Paul Pierce of the Boston Celtics, Elton Brand of the Los Angeles Clippers, and Carmelo Anthony of the Denver Nuggets.

The players invited for tryouts also included a list of specialists and role players such as defensive whiz Bruce Bowen of the San Antonio Spurs and sweet-passing big man Brad Miller of the Sacramento Kings.

Filling out the list with role players came at the expense of Allen Iverson, who wanted to play but was not invited to tryouts, a move that angered many American basketball fans. Other stars, such as O'Neal and San Antonio's Tim Duncan, declined to play because of conflicts and the lengthy commitment Colangelo wanted from the players.

The twenty-three finalists that headed into July tryouts included a great list of blossoming talent, such as Orlando Magic center Dwight Howard and Toronto power forward Chris Bosh.

"I don't envy Mike Krzyzewski," Tex Winter said. "He has some difficult decisions to make in cutting that team down to a dozen or so. There could be some big names who wind up not making it."

"I think it's smart to add balance and solid role players," observed Scottie Pippen, who played on the original Dream Team that won the gold in 1992, in Barcelona. "They want superstars who will agree to play defense and good team basketball. And they need some people who will sacrifice and do the dirty work. But it's hard to leave an Allen Iverson off that roster."

The frontcourt, with Howard and Bosh, would feature mostly speed and quickness, Winter said. "It's an indication of just how much talent is available in American basketball. My gosh. The incredible thing is that Jerry Colangelo has been able to get them all to commit to a three-year team effort. That was the thing that always hurt USA basketball. It was always thrown together as an afterthought. This is no afterthought. This is well planned. And I think it will bring the desired results."

"This is the first standing USA Men's Senior National Team, and the twenty-three players selected will give us everything we need to form a great USA team," said Colangelo. "We feel we have versatility, shooters, size, quickness, role players, and defensive stoppers. In making the player selections we took into consideration the style of play anticipated to be used by the coaching staff."

Overconfidence had become the flaw in American basketball. Recent losses had created an awareness that the days of USA dominance were gone.

"I don't think it's going to be any cakewalk, even with the team Colangelo's assembled," Winter said. "You can say that there's an incredible amount of basketball talent in America. But that's also true of the international scene. You look at the talent worldwide, and it's just amazing. It's never been like this before. There are so many players in so many countries. It will turn your head around just trying to keep track of them all."

Pippen agreed. "Basketball worldwide has definitely grown," the former Bull said. "But that can't be used as an excuse. America really needed to clean up their act and do a better job of competing. This is really a step in the right direction. It's up to this young generation of stars to step up and compete, to bring the gold back home to the United States."

"I just feel so blessed to be able to play on this team at this time in my life," Bryant said. "It's a huge honor, one I've dreamed about. I take this very seriously. The commitment is big. It's a lot with

NBA players who have families and a long season. But this is very important. It's something we want."

Now fans would get to see what it would be like to have Bryant, James, and Wade all on the floor at the same time. That in itself became a tremendous draw, not just for the fans but for the game's insiders.

Bryant's impact on the team would be felt from the first moment of the team's first practice in Las Vegas. LeBron James had come down from his room in the team hotel and was headed for the team bus to go to practice when he saw a thoroughly drenched Bryant emerging from the weight room. He had been working for hours before practice.

James thought, "So that's what he's all about," according Chris Dennis, a James adviser earlier in his career.

"Kobe in his first practice was diving on the floor," Colangelo recalled. "That set the tone."

Bryant's Olympic experience would allow him to heavily influence a generation of players, Colangelo said. "In the weight room, he set the tone for a lot of players. They saw him doing it. They started going in and doing the extra work. There's no doubt about the fact that he made a major contribution to USA Basketball.

"It was good for him," Colangelo offered. "Good for his soul."

More

That summer of 2006, Winter began poring over tapes of the Lakers' summer-league games. Jackson had sent him the tapes so that Winter could evaluate the progress of the younger players on the roster, several of whom would be critical to the team's chances for the upcoming season.

Winter wasn't enthusiastic about the talent he saw, which suggested that Jackson and the Lakers were facing a stiff dose of reality—life without Shaquille O'Neal would take a long time to recover from.

Jackson was concerned about the situation, Winter confided. "Phil's got the attitude that he's gonna do the best he possibly can do with the players available. He's back to the point of knowing that he's not putting an NBA championship team on the floor but of having the best team he can have with the talent available.

"I think Phil is pretty realistic about things. He's not a dreamer."

What made this reality so problematic was the aura and tradition of the Lakers, Winter said. "The expectations are always so high. They won't go away. That's part of the franchise."

The dearth of talent was headed for a collision that soon threatened to derail Bryant's career in Los Angeles. The situation left the guard sensing that he was watching the best years of his career slip away.

"His patience might be wearing a little thin," Winter said of Bryant. "On the other hand, he seems OK with things. I think he likes the idea of it being his team. That's what he wanted, and that's what he's got. He's like Phil. He's a realist."

"I think it was just part of a journey for us," Bryant said publicly. "We still have some more strides to take to get to our ultimate destination. I'm happy with the fact that we took steps forward and didn't take a step back. We're moving in the right direction."

In one season, the player and head coach who were once so antagonistic toward each other had found a remarkable working relationship. They shared intensely competitive natures. That would be their primary asset for the road ahead.

Still, without more talent, they would remain on a middling path.

"To say that we're going to be a championship-contending team [this] year, I'm not prepared to say that," general manager Mitch Kupchak said, "although I think it's a possibility."

"We don't believe that we have to have a superstar come in here to be able to advance," Jackson said. "We know we have enough physical talent and size to be able to compete in the Western Conference."

Surgery on his right knee over the summer had stopped Bryant from continuing his efforts with Team USA, which meant that the eight to twelve weeks of recovery kept him from his usual summer workouts.

As part of his transformation from his Showboat era, Bryant had started calling himself Black Mamba, based on his infatuation with a Quentin Tarantino film. To complete the makeover, he also switched jersey numbers, going from number 8 to number 24, saying he did it because it was a new chapter in his career.

As for his new best friend, Phil Jackson, Bryant said, "I think our relationship is just different because the dynamics of the team are different. He and I have an open relationship. It feels really, really great to be a part of it."

Around Bryant, the team added veterans Vladimir Radmanović and Maurice Evans to bolster depth and perimeter scoring. The new faces moved Luke Walton out of the starting lineup and back to more of a sixth-man role.

The Lakers desperately needed to cut back on the 41 minutes per game that Bryant had played during the previous season, the fourth most in the NBA.

But that didn't happen. He averaged 40.8 minutes, good enough for 31.6 points a game with 5.7 rebounds and 5.4 assists.

He had a steadier year with a little more talent around him. Kwame Brown showed progress. Lamar Odom learned how to run the offense and where to find his spots to score. And Bryant again led the league in scoring. But the Lakers were far from ready to compete for the prize.

The fireworks started as March opened with a seven-game losing streak, and Bryant struggled. On March 16, he came out of it with 65 points in Staples Center against Portland, while hitting 23 of 39 shots from the field and 8 of 12 from three-point range, with 11 of 12 from the line.

Two nights later, he hit Minnesota for 50, this time going 17 for 35, for a second win. Then the Lakers headed out on the road to Memphis, where Bryant drove a third straight win, with 60, again with efficiency, making 20 of 37 shots. The Lakers then boarded their plane for a quick flight in the wee hours down to New Orleans, where for the second time in twenty-four hours and for the fourth game night in a row, he rang up another huge game, with 50 points in a win over the Hornets. "I always knew he was a fierce competitor," David West, then with New Orleans said, looking back. "But I got to see how fierce up close when he had that 50-point game streak going on. He came into New Orleans and gave us one of those 50-point games. I saw just how difficult it was to guard him. It takes the whole team to guard him; you can't leave the guy who is guarding him to guard him by himself.

"What really makes him special is that he always believes that the next shot is going in, and it usually does."

Indeed, Bryant tapered off the string of four 50-plus games — exceeded only by the great Wilt Chamberlain — by scoring 43 against Golden State two nights later, back in Staples Center, for a fifth straight win.

His output dipped for a game, then popped back as he scored 53 in a loss at Staples Center in which he took 44 shots and made 19. He scored 46 and then 50 twice more down the stretch that spring as it became clearer and clearer that the whole thing was driven by a surging new anger. He began showing Jerry Buss a new side to their relationship: defiance. The owner, long possessed of a low-key sort of menace, had never brooked anything of the sort from any of his players.

Buss would soon find himself just about done with Kobe Bryant.

Chapter 27

LEGACY

The good stuff almost didn't happen, not with Bryant's aggressive instincts driving everything. After he scored 60 in a road win over the Memphis Grizzlies that spring of 2007, Jackson had remarked, "At one point, we got the offensive rebound and [had] a whole new twenty-four-second [shot clock] left. Lamar gave the ball right back to him, and Kobe went right back at them. He just smells blood in the water and he's going to go after you."

He had no thoughts of anything but attack. Jackson could never quite get used to it, even though Jordan had been much the same way at the same age, with Bulls assistant coach Johnny Bach in his ear, quoting Admiral Halsey, telling him, "Attack! Attack! Attack!" Jackson alternately loved and loathed the recklessness of both players.

Bryant was twenty-eight that spring, which was near enough to twenty-nine, which was near enough to thirty, to set his basketball biological clock ticking loudly.

Donnie Carr had seen him at a game in New Orleans during that period, and Bryant was limping afterward. Even so, Bryant was always happy to see Carr, called him "D.C.," considered him a true connection to the fabulous past.

"What you limping for?" Carr asked with a smile.

Bryant smirked, then chuckled. "I'm not a young 'un no more, D.C.," he replied. "I got to pace myself, you know what I mean? I'm limping because of all the wear and tear of all these NBA seasons, man."

Carr walked with Bryant toward the Lakers' bus, and before they parted, they took a photo together. Bryant's loneliness seemed obvious, Carr said, looking back. "It was the price he paid for that greatness."

The alienation was just like all the other hurts, whether it was knees or ankles or a shoulder—he just absorbed them all and kept going at that furious pace.

Bryant was starting to recognize that he could score all the points he wanted, but he was getting nowhere. Another player might have felt relieved that the Lakers had stuck with him through all his troubles, that he was well on his way to recovering from the damage. But even as he had his run of big games that spring, Bryant was brimming with anger at the team's lack of talent. He kept talking of it in the press.

That postseason of 2007, the Lakers lost to Phoenix once again. Then, early in the off-season, Bryant encountered a group of fans armed with a camera phone in a shopping center parking lot. They asked a question about the state of the team, and the moment was almost like the one years earlier when he had run into Carr on South Street in Philly and candidly spilled his thoughts about his bright future. He was immediately chummy with the fans and launched into a marked criticism of the front office and young center Andrew Bynum, who had come into the league with plenty of talent but a suspect work ethic. Bryant threatened to seek a trade if things didn't improve. The video the fans shot that day soon went viral. It certainly wasn't the first time he'd complained about the team, but Bryant had unleashed his anger. Jerry Buss was furious. He had stood by Bryant through it all, and now this was his way of saying thanks?

The owner had long shown that he was not a man quick to anger. But there was no doubt that Buss always made sure to get his way. As he aged, Buss had turned mysteriously aloof, a beloved figure in Los Angeles as team owner. He was the man who brought championship players to the Lakers, and as such was the object of immense respect with a many-splendored aura of power among the people he held sway over.

Buss's numerous qualities, his vast intelligence, and his vision for his team were bolstered by his narrative as a young man who emerged from an impoverished childhood by virtue of his mental power to gain his doctoral degree at the University of Southern California, which in turn allowed him to build relationships and wealth, to become a regal figure lording over the Lakers. In that role, he displayed an uncommon love for his players and an eye for athletic and executive talent, and ultimately that quality had allowed him to be the driving force of a great franchise.

Former Laker Ron Carter pointed out that while he worked for Buss, the owner made his money quite brilliantly and quite legally, that the team and the Forum Club were actually a honeypot that allowed Buss to attract celebrities and wealthy players to invest in his real estate syndication deals.

Basically, Buss was creating entities to invest in real estate syndication with the idea that he would accelerate the tax deductions and mortgage payments on properties held by his limited partnerships, Carter explained.

When the deductions had been maxed out on the trust, Buss would create another limited partnership to sell it to, basically selling the real estate back and forth between the entities he controlled while legally maximizing write-offs and other benefits, as Carter said.

The former player would learn much from Buss, and the owner even paid for Carter's master's degree at nearby Pepperdine University. After he purchased the franchise and his Showtime teams began winning championships, the owner's box at Lakers games soon became a great place to entertain prospective real estate investors.

"We were doing syndication deals," Carter explained. "Jerry would hold investment meetings at the Forum. He would invite all the limited partners of those specific partnerships to dinner. We'd hold an investment meeting at the Forum in the Forum Club, and we would explain to them how we were going to sell the real estate or trade the real estate to a new partnership, and the new partnership was going to have some special people in it, like Magic Johnson and Kareem Abdul-Jabbar and whoever else he could convince.

Back at that time Magic, Mark McGwire, Lawrence Taylor, Carl Banks—these are some of the people who put money into the partnerships. We then used that influx of cash plus the real estate to buy new buildings, and we bought some beautiful properties in Brentwood and Beverly Hills, multiunit apartment buildings."

Because Buss held a PhD in chemistry, he named his partnerships after chemical compounds, Carter recalled. "He was making so much money with these real estate syndications that his lawyers said, 'Look, Jerry, cut us in. Can we get a little piece of the action?'"

Buss's company—Mariani, Buss and Associates—was run out of a Southern California strip mall, and for a time it essentially operated two NBA teams, the Lakers and the Indiana Pacers, which was owned by Buss friend and longtime business partner Frank Mariani, an engineer.

Buss later moved into pay-per-view cable TV to monetize the regional broadcast rights to the Lakers. Not only was the team a honeypot for attracting real estate deals, but it was a powerful entertainment property that would soon enough snare mega TV deals worth more than a billion.

That, in turn, allowed Buss to play a major role in the building of Staples Center in 2000. Buss didn't even realize how big of a boon it would be to build the stadium, Jerry West explained in a 2008 interview. "That became a license to print money."

Buss had experienced some cash-flow problems in the eighties, and he was indicted for fraud in Arizona during that period over the taxes he failed to pay on huge bundles of houses he bought there. Buss simply paid the back taxes, and the charges went away, Carter recalled.

Few people had ever rebuked Jerry Buss in public the way Bryant had. The star had crossed the line, and inside observers around the team figured that Bryant's time as a Laker might be coming to an end. As an owner, Buss had never hesitated to move big properties when they had outlived their usefulness. O'Neal made noise in the 2003–04 season, and Buss promptly shipped him out of town. Jackson had alienated the front office and the team's star that same season, and he was sent away for a year, too.

Early in their relationship, Buss had supposedly promised Bryant that he would be a Laker for life. The owner knew better than anyone that Hollywood was the place of stars. For the Lakers to work, they had to offer the game's shiniest star, and Bryant had been that—and more. "I just think he was mesmerized by, you know, Kobe's flash and flair," journalist J. A. Adande, a Southern California native, said of Buss. "And, you know, for everything that Jerry Buss's team had done, he still could be dazzled, and I think Kobe dazzled him. Jerry also recognized what would sell in L.A., and Kobe's always been the guy in L.A., because he's the flash, and the flash works out here. You need to be exciting and dazzling, and that's one of the reasons that he was more popular than Shaq. But the second reason is the work ethic. L.A. is a hardworking town. People don't think of it that way because they don't see smokestacks and factories and conveyor lines. People think that all those things constitute hard work. Well, even the movie industry, as glamorous as it might be on the top end, requires a lot of hard work and diligence on the lower end. It requires a lot of work to break through; plus, the practice of making movies— these guys are at the set at three thirty, four thirty, in the morning, setting up the set, the lighting; the caterers, the sound people, all those people, work long days, you know, driving long distances to commute to work, so that's the industry of the town, the entertainment industry, but that industry is a very hardworking industry. So that's the Laker fan base. It's a hardworking fan base, and they respect hard work."

It wasn't just other players that Bryant inspired with his insane work schedule and effort. Management noticed, too.

"That's why he was so popular with Jerry Buss," Adande offered, "and I'm sure, to a degree, his popularity with the fans made him more beloved by Jerry Buss because again it increased the assets of his franchise, the value of his franchise."

But now Bryant genuinely seemed to want out, and it appeared that he had no qualms about embarrassing the owner. The situation quickly grew tense during the 2007 off-season, as Buss ordered the team's front office to begin searching for trade options for Kobe Bryant. Throughout the summer and fall, the situation remained strained and immensely complicated. Bryant's frustration and venting of anger over the team's roster had also led to new damage to his relationships with his teammates and with the fans. You didn't have to do much more than mention Bryant's name that summer, and you'd find yourself listening to a tirade about how Bryant was a spoiled brat, ball hog, and crybaby.

The one voice quietly offering support remained Tex Winter. Winter agreed that Bryant was probably too emotional in making his case, but the longtime coach pointed out that Bryant had put his heart and soul into the franchise for eleven seasons, working hard every single day, rarely taking even a moment off. In so doing, Bryant had earned a right that other players didn't have, Winter said.

Winter argued that the team needed to be pushed into getting better, and since Bryant was the team leader, it was his job to do it. "He's the only one who has that power," Winter said. "Who else has the clout to speak up?"

As for the many comments that Bryant was merely a whining ball hog whose career was waning, Winter offered his opinion there, as well.

"Actually, we study the game tapes," Winter said. "For the most part, he's not forcing up a lot of bad shots. He gets hot and does take a lot of questionable shots, but a lot of them go in. He'll take shots that not many other players are going to be able to hit, and he hits them."

What Winter shook his head at was Bryant's frequent selection as a member of the NBA's All-Defensive Team. "I'd like to see him play better defense," Winter said. "He feels like there's a certain way he's got to play the game, and it doesn't involve a lot of basically sound defense. He's doing a lot of switching and zoning up, trying to come up with interceptions and steals. He's basically playing a lot of one-man zone."

Winter said he wanted to see Bryant exhibit more defensive focus and more reliance on his teammates.

Bryant would turn twenty-nine that August and was already entering his twelfth NBA season with a pressing awareness that the time to win was now. Winter, who was eighty-five, knew all about time. "Kobe has a sense of urgency about his career," the elderly coach said. "He wants to win. Isn't that how he's supposed to think?"

Bryant himself answered many of his critics with his play during workouts with Team USA that summer. There were critics who had predicted that Bryant's selfishness would sink Team USA that summer. Instead, Bryant had responded by unleashing his full love for the game in a bundle of surprisingly youthful defensive energy for international competition.

His international play left Winter eager to see how Bryant would respond if a better Lakers team could be built around him. A team with better talent would take off the immense pressure on Bryant to focus on scoring, Winter reasoned. Yet as fall approached, the pressure remained very high, if for no other reason than his giant expectations for himself. It was what had fascinated so many about him since he entered the NBA at age seventeen, determined to do whatever it took to be successful. By 2007, that apparently meant rattling cages and yelling in frustration at very rich men, inviting public ridicule. His public demands were simply a new wrinkle on his old approach of going to great lengths to reach his goals.

In the public mind, Bryant had always been seen as flying way too high for his own good, with no safety net below, a balls-out-and-gunning approach. It was why, despite his troubles, he remained perhaps the most compelling story in American professional sports. No one else had ever seemed willing to risk so much. For Bryant, there had always seemed so much at stake that, for all his youthful charm, his story seemed headed for some sort of disgusting splat, the harshest of endings for his cautionary tale.

In the fall of 2007, his youth was escaping, but the questions remained. Deals with both Chicago and Detroit had been arranged and were on the table. So the questions fell to Bryant. What would it be, Mr. Bryant? What was the answer that he had always insisted on pushing so hard, so insanely for? Would he stay or would he go? Where did he stand with Jerry Buss's Lakers? For better? Or for worse?

Resolution

It was the kind of situation that would have to be worked out between the two men, as J. A. Adande would come to understand.

"You know," Adande recalled, "I thought Dr. Buss was wrong to get rid of Phil and Shaq, so I thought he had a bad run in the middle of the 2000s. I thought he was wrong to kind of give Kobe that much power and basically turn the franchise over to him. But he rectified it. He brought Phil back. He put Kobe in his place a little bit."

It wouldn't be until Jerry Buss's funeral, in 2013, that Lakers fans heard Bryant's take on the issue, Adande recalled. "It was interesting to hear Kobe tell the story after Jerry Buss died about how Buss really convinced him there was no better place for him to be than the Lakers. Kobe wanted to leave, and he met with Buss, and Buss said, 'Look: (a) I can't trade you. I can't devalue my team like that. And (b) it will be worse off for you to leave here.' So it really dawned on Kobe, like, 'OK, I'm here. I can't just force my way out by trade. It's not going to happen.'"

"Kobe was going to try and challenge the way things were happening," Rudy Garciduenas explained, "and sometimes they don't always work out the way you want them to, you know. He learned that Dr. Buss was not someone to challenge. If that's what the ultimatum was, Dr. Buss was going to take him up on it. Dr. Buss was an accomplished owner and businessman. You can't, you know, try and hold something over his head and not expect him to do anything about it."

They both had gained a renewed sense of purpose from the exchange.

More good news for the new season was that Derek Fisher was back with the club after a strong 2007 play-off season in Utah that indicated he still had plenty to offer upon entering his twelfth season. He brought strong professionalism and an ability to stand up to Bryant while remaining his close ally. That in itself brought a surge of team chemistry and the ever-scarce "trust." It didn't hurt that he could still provide a bit of ball pressure and could knock down the open shots when needed.

Fisher would always have trouble defending the screen and roll and was now more prone than ever to getting broken down by quick young guards, but he eased the load on Bryant.

"A lot of responsibility that Kobe had put on himself could now be shared with Fish," Rudy Garciduenas observed. "Fish was the captain. So they could share that now, and he could rely on Fish to have a lot more interaction with the other teammates."

Fisher had his tricks for heading off Bryant's alienation from teammates. "He knew Kobe couldn't do that to the teammates, that it only created more problems," Garciduenas explained.

The equipment manager had gotten the sense that Fisher had been watching the team intensely from afar the previous two seasons.

With Fisher helping with off-the-court issues, Tex Winter went to work to help Bryant adapt his game so that he could remain effective without relying so heavily on his waning athleticism. A big part of that was working on his post game.

Bryant himself came into the NBA with amazingly good post skills, but there had never been room for him to play in the post with O'Neal occupying the lane during their years together with the Lakers.

In his experience with Jordan, though, Winter felt that Jordan managed to become the premier post weapon of his time, even though he wasn't playing the traditional big-man role. In a lot of ways, Bryant was Jordan's equal as a post player, Winter said, except for one critical element. "What's happened to Kobe and his post play—and he is a great post player—is that he's catching the ball just out of the lane, and the defenders are forcing him out toward the wing.

"It's hard for him to get a deep post position," Winter explained. "Michael had a knack for holding his ground a little better than Kobe. Those strong defenders force Kobe out of there. When that happens, we need to go away from Kobe instead of challenging the defense there. You don't want him to start on the post and end up out on the wing."

The situation led some to wonder if Bryant's difficulties in the post didn't push him sometimes toward an overreliance on the three-pointer. "I like to see him take threes when he's got 'em," Winter said. "He's an excellent three-point shooter. I like to see him take them when the floor is spaced and the defense is not closing out fast enough. If the ball is moved quickly, then he has a chance at a good look. Plus, defenders foul him on the close-out, and he gets a chance at a four-point play. He would get more four-point plays if officials called it when defenders fouled him on the three."

After studying tape intensely, Winter decided that Bryant also found advantage when he charged up in transition and the defense reacted slowly. "If they back up on him, he'll move right to that three-point line and hit it," Winter said.

Winter acknowledged that Bryant had once again begun doing much of his scoring while "not really running the triangle sequence options" that defined the offense. "But he is running out of the triangle format and making use of the offense's spacing and ball movement," Winter offered.

When the team did run the offense, Bryant found most of his success at small forward, which allowed him to work "behind the defense," as Winter had often explained. "He gets the ball in position where he's isolated and can attack the basket a little better. He gets more isolation that way. The triangle creates opportunity for him, and he knows that."

Even after all these years and all of Bryant's offensive success, he still tended to be a ball stopper in the offense, often because his teammates deferred so much to his dominant game and personality.

In their eighth season together, the coach considered Bryant a receptive student, up to a point. "You know Kobe," Winter confided with a chuckle. "He has his game plan. I think he hears me. But he feels there's a certain way he's got to play the game. But it doesn't involve a lot of basically sound defense.

"The way Kobe plays defensively affects the team," Winter added. "Anybody that doesn't play consistently good defense hurts the team. That's not only Kobe. Our other guards tend to gamble and get beat. Another problem is that the screen and roll is not played correctly."

Despite the dispute with Buss, Bryant had come into training camp with a positive attitude and found himself developing some chemistry with Andrew Bynum in the post. Bryant's relationships with his teammates also showed improvement, Rudy Garciduenas recalled, in part because Jackson had "seen that it was no longer beneficial to be adversarial with Kobe." Over their two seasons back together, Jackson and Bryant had grown much closer, were able to discuss differences rather than act them out in silly drama, Garciduenas said. "With Phil's guidance, Kobe learned a lot about himself and learned about what it takes to motivate teammates. Kobe learned a lot of those subtleties through Phil and was maturing through that whole episode."

Garciduenas also sensed that Jackson now wanted to be more of a factor in Bryant's life, more of an influence. That clearly worked for both of them.

"I think Phil is appreciative of what Kobe is and what he can do for a team," Winter explained. "He's given him a lot more green light recently than he would ordinarily."

Asked if Bryant now had the same kind of green light to attack that Jordan once enjoyed, Winter replied: "Pretty much."

Bryant's four-game streak of 50-point games the previous spring still played on the mind of the elderly coach. He said Bryant's performance had been more impressive than Wilt Chamberlain's seven-game streak in 1961–62.

"Wilt's streak was more about gimmickry that season," Winter recalled. "Kobe's gotten these points against tough competition, which is something else Wilt didn't face, not consistently."

NBA teams of Chamberlain's era were not overly aggressive defensively, Winter explained. He felt compelled to mention that his own Kansas State team in 1958 had ended Chamberlain's career early at the University of Kansas. Winter's State team also beat Chamberlain and the Jayhawks on their own floor.

"When Kansas got Wilt as a recruit, everyone just assumed they'd win three straight championships," he recalled.

After losing to UNC in triple overtime in the 1957 NCAA championship game as a sophomore, Wilt's team lost to Winter's Kansas State team in the play-offs his junior year. Frustrated, Chamberlain left college ball to tour with the Harlem Globetrotters during his senior season and joined the NBA a year later, in 1960.

Other than Bill Russell, there weren't many quality big men in an NBA that featured fewer than a dozen teams, Winter offered. "He just out-manned most of the centers in those days. Kobe is not a seven-foot-one giant. He's a normal-sized two or three man. For him to go off on the kind of scoring tear that he did is remarkable.

It was necessary for this team to win five straight games. Without it, I doubt seriously if we could have won."

The Change

The Lakers seemed on their way to finding some rhythm in January until Bynum injured his knee, suddenly casting the season in doubt. But then an early-February trade brought center Pau Gasol from Memphis, in exchange for Kwame Brown and the rights to Pau's brother, Marc Gasol, who was still playing in Spain. Memphis executive Jerry West struck the deal with his old team, which sent up howls of complaint from Grizzlies fans that West was gifting the Lakers with an All-Star while receiving little in return. But over the years, Marc Gasol would prove quite a prize for Memphis, making the trade look more and more like a solid deal for the Grizzlies, who wanted to trade long-term success for a quality player at the peak of his prime.

That's not to say that the trade wasn't fantastic for the Lakers. Pau Gasol's presence changed the arc of Bryant's life almost instantly. He had tremendous hands for catching the ball in the post. Bryant saw it immediately and would later recall that he told Phil Jackson, "We're going to the Finals."

Only Bryant and Fisher remained from Jackson's championship teams earlier in the decade. The two guards shared a rock-ribbed competitive nature that made them a perfect combination with Gasol, who in turn pulled the talents of Odom, Walton, and others more into play. The seven-foot Spaniard was known for his versatility, which gave yet another huge boost to team chemistry. "He was just such a nice guy," Garciduenas recalled, adding that it didn't hurt to have someone else in the locker room fluent in Spanish.

Gasol's highlight footage ran from the routinely ridiculously good (Gasol in his face-up game, breaking down defenses) to the sublime (Gasol late in a blowout play-off win, going behind his back on the dribble at midcourt to complete a sizzling assist). The center's skills arguably made him the ultimate jewel of Winter's triangle offense, whether he was playing in the post, on the wing, or in the pinch post (at the elbow of the lane).

Gasol had a dependable face-up shot, and his spin moves in the post, right and left, brought to mind Boston legend Kevin McHale, except McHale never dreamed of Gasol's mobility. Or his court vision, for that matter. No-look passes and over-the-shoulder surprises dotted the Spaniard's résumé.

Most important for Gasol was his timing. He came to Los Angeles just when Bryant and his teammates needed him the most. In a little more than three years, Gasol would take his rightful place among the pantheon of Lakers big men, in rare company with Kareem Abdul-Jabbar, George Mikan, Wilt Chamberlain, and Shaquille O'Neal.

At the same time, Gasol also managed to save the reputation of European basketball. There was a time when NBA insiders could hear the whispers around the league, complaints that European players were soft. Gasol himself had been accused of that on occasion, but his overall play with the Lakers was so strong, it erased any doubts.

Gasol's post play immediately helped the team rocket off on a ten-game winning streak. The team was just 31–17 for the season when Gasol was added to the roster, but the club finished on a 26–8 run that thoroughly convinced voters that Bryant was the league MVP.

The irony of Bryant's league MVP honor was that he gained it as his scoring average had dipped in line with great team play. During the season, he averaged 28.3 points, 6.3 rebounds, 5.4 assists, and 1.84 steals while playing in all eighty-two games. He had scored more than 40 points just seven times. Much to Winter's chagrin, he was also once again named to the All-Defensive First Team. Over the season, he had reached the milestones of 21,000 points and 4,000 career assists.

Bryant scored 49 points in the second play-off game that season, a win over Denver, but largely stayed within the team format as the Lakers rolled through Denver, Utah, and San Antonio on their way to the NBA championship series. In the process, Bryant's Lakers became favored to win the league title.

Among those who figured the Lakers would take it all was Michael Jordan. During the league's pre-draft camp in Orlando late that May, Jordan sat and talked quietly about how hard Bryant had worked to be great. He and Bryant were obviously close, and Jordan spoke up to defend Bryant against critics that claimed he was merely copying Jordan.

Jordan said he didn't see what all the big fuss was about. After all, human behavior was mimetic. That's how humans learned. They copied and aped another. Jordan acknowledged that Bryant was the best of a generation of players who had sought to Be Like Mike. "But how many people lighted the path for me?" Jordan asked. "That's the evolution of basketball. There's no way I could have played the way I played if I didn't watch David Thompson and guys prior to me. There's no way Kobe could have played the way he's played without watching me play. So, you know, that's the evolution of basketball. You cannot change that."

Bryant was the one who had "done the work" in the face of the example he presented, Jordan said.

Jordan admitted to being more than a casual observer of Bryant's career. In fact, he was fascinated by it, even able to relive some of his own experience by watching Bryant play. After all, he too played for Jackson in Winter's same triangle offense. Their careers had found them occupying the same locations on the floor, attacking defenses in similar fashion, driving their teams as an offensive force, yet rarely slacking on defense.

Soon enough Jordan was sitting back and watching Bryant and his Lakers take on an old nemesis, the Boston Celtics, the first time the two teams had met in the championship series in twenty-one years. Even so, the meeting harkened back to another age in the NBA a half century earlier.

In those days, the sensation of the league was high-flying Lakers forward Elgin Baylor, the man with the original hang time who had come in as a rookie in 1958 and terrorized the league with huge games. The Lakers were a very bad team in Minneapolis then that had once ruled the league with George Mikan and Jim Pollard. Even though they had a losing record in the 1959 regular season, Baylor's high-wire act led them to the championship series where they met the Celtics for the first time.

Boston quickly swept them, the first sweep in league history, and that jump-started the karma. The Lakers moved to Los Angeles in 1960, and soon Jerry West and Baylor teamed up together to become pro basketball's dynamic duo. Hollywood demanded star power, and the two young players provided it. Both showed the ability to average better than 30 points a game.

But come championship time every year, their Lakers faced Boston's confounding center, Bill Russell. Six times in the '60s the Lakers challenged the Celtics for the title. Six times West, Baylor, and the Lakers lost. Each time they watched as Celtics boss Red Auerbach lit up his victory cigar and hooted.

"There were an awful lot of times I wanted to shove that cigar down his throat," Lakers coach Fred Schaus once explained.

As the losses to the green-clad Celtics piled up, West got to where he could not stand the sight of green, would not wear anything green, did not want anything green around him.

"It got to the point that it controlled my life," West explained.

For the first five times that his Lakers lost, the Celtics were favored. But in 1969, the Lakers had home-court advantage, they had the giant Wilt Chamberlain at center, they had every reason to believe it was finally their time. But they lost Game 7 in Los Angeles to Russell and company. West had played brilliantly and was named the Most Valuable Player of the series, the only time in league history that the MVP came from the losing team.

In those days, *Sport* magazine awarded a fancy car to the Finals MVP. Already inconsolable over the loss, West recoiled at the sight of the auto.

It was green.

Which summed up the Lakers' inferiority complex up through when the Showtime team took on Larry Bird and the Celtics in the 1984 championship series and lost yet again. The next season, though, Magic Johnson and his teammates finally broke through and beat the Celtics in Boston Garden, which left Jerry Buss celebrating deliriously. The Showtime teams would get another championship win over Boston in 1987, but there remained plenty of demons in the minds of longtime Lakers fans as the series renewed again in early June 2008.

Although the Lakers were considered slight favorites, Tex Winter was deeply worried about Boston's rugged frontcourt, featuring Kevin Garnett and Kendrick Perkins. They were just too tough for the Lakers, Winter predicted. To go with them, the Celtics had put together a tough veteran roster, including Paul Pierce, Ray Allen, and Rajon Rondo, to create a superteam in Boston.

Game 1, played on June 5, 2008, at the TD Banknorth Garden, featured Paul Pierce hitting the big shots that drove a 98–88 Celtics victory. Just as Winter had feared, Boston had outrebounded the Lakers, 46–33, and Bryant had pushed up 26 shots and made just 9. Another win over the Lakers in Game 2 jacked Boston's home record during the play-offs to 12–1. The Lakers had played better, rebounded better, shot better, but were done in by Boston's strong bench. Los Angeles pulled the series to 2–1 with an 87–81 Game 3 victory at Staples Center as Bryant scored 36. But Game 4 brought an L.A. nightmare as the Celtics sprinted from 20 points down with five minutes to go in the third period to take a commanding 3–1 lead with a 97–91 victory.

After the outcome, Jackson said his players had had their "hearts cut out."

Facing elimination on their home floor, the Lakers got out to a big lead in the first half of Game 5, then again toyed with yet another big collapse before finding the footing to survive and send the series back to Boston, 103–98. "To have done anything less would have been humiliation," Winter said afterward.

The humiliation arrived in Game 6 back in Boston, where the Celtics drilled the Lakers 131–92, serving up one of the worst whippings in championship history, to claim the series 4–2 and win Boston's seventeenth title. Surely, it was the ugliest ending to a championship series in the league's history and rivaled the 129–96 close-out whipping the Celtics put on the Lakers in 1965 when they were left undermanned by Elgin Baylor's knee injury and Jerry West had to take on Boston almost by himself.

The 2008 debacle was a night of such deep humiliation that it breathed life into the Lakers' chip on their shoulder from the past. Suddenly, Bryant and Gasol understood that the Boston–L.A. rivalry was all about those long-held personal demons and curses, many of them emanating from the tortured persona of West himself. The loss to the Celtics so badly humiliated Bryant's Lakers that it virtually wiped out any good feelings about Bryant's winning his first league-MVP award.

Not long after the series ended, in the summer of 2008, Shaquille O'Neal celebrated Bryant's loss by taking the stage at a New York nightclub and unleashing his famous free-style rap: "You know how I be, last week Kobe couldn't do without me," O'Neal told the delighted crowd, which began chanting after him. He made reference to Bryant's comment to Colorado police.

"Kobe ratted me out, that's why I'm getting divorced," O'Neal offered, shaking his rear end as he rapped. "He said Shaq gave a bitch a mil—I don't do that, 'cause my name's Shaquille. I love 'em but don't leave 'em. I got a vasectomy, now I can't breed 'em. Kobe, how my ass taste?"

It was the last, taunting question that the crowd particularly loved, as did the Internet audience. The moment and the championship embarrassment completed a perfectly sour close to one of his finest seasons.

Given the Finger

Soon after the disaster of the Finals, it was time for Bryant to fulfill his three-year obligation to USA Basketball in the 2008 Summer Olympics. The Olympic experience and the opportunity to play for Mike Krzyzewski were already immensely important for Bryant, but in the wake of the Lakers' profoundly embarrassing NBA Finals loss, the Games took on even greater significance.

Playing in the Olympics would come at the cost of a medical procedure that Bryant likely would have needed that off-season. The previous January, Bryant had torn a ligament in his pinkie finger while trying to steal the ball from James during a Lakers win over Cleveland. After getting treatment on the sidelines, Bryant finished the game with 20 points but afterward told the *L.A. Times* that his pain was "probably the most I'd ever played with."

Some critics had always questioned the drama factor with Bryant's injuries and raised the issue that he used injury as an excuse, which seemed ludicrous to the people working up close with him, beginning with Chip Schaefer and Lakers trainer Gary Vitti. Jackson, who challenged Bryant on a number of fronts, clearly admired his ability to play through pain.

"These are things that you just don't want to do anything with that hand, let alone play basketball or pound the ball or dribble it or shoot it," Jackson told reporters, in terms of the finger. "It's a lot of difficulty, but it's a trademark of who Kobe is."

He was advised to have surgery, but the season was going too well to back off, Bryant would later explain. That, of course, meant that he would also not be able to have surgery after the season because of the Olympics, in Beijing in August.

Pinkie aside, as he prepared for Bryant's needs in advance of the Team USA experience, equipment manager Rudy Garciduenas recalled seeing Bryant brimming with enthusiasm for the competition. It would not take long for him to impress his teammates yet again with his trademark dedication.

"Probably the best memory I have of him was playing with him in the Olympics," Dwyane Wade said in 2015, recalling a story similar to Lebron James's from the first summer the team worked together. "I remember one day we got into a city very early, and everybody wanted to go get some sleep before we had practice the next day. I remember getting up the next day and going there and Kobe was sitting down, iced down, drenched."

"What were you doing?" Wade asked.

"I'm on my second workout already," Bryant said.

"He was on his second workout before anyone else had even showed up," Wade recalled. "That's when I knew he was a different beast. It told me about his work ethic and his will to be great."

The example inspired him and others on the team, Wade said. "I had always been a hard worker myself—I never slacked in that category—but you understand why a guy is that great when you see things like that."

It was Bryant's own sort of mind game, too, a challenge thrown down and on display for his teammates. It violated the idea of "cool" that often enveloped the sport, even at its highest levels, and stuffed the notion, "Never let them see you sweat."

Bryant was the antithesis of that. He put his sweat on display for his Olympic teammates, though he avoided the fellowship in the dining hall. Off the floor, Bryant was seen by some as an icy sphinx. There were none of the all-night card games that Jordan had thrown on his Olympic teammates, leaving them to shake their heads and tell their friends and families in amazement, "He doesn't sleep."

One member of the Olympic coaching staff would later privately complain that Bryant's aloofness during the experience kept him apart from the team's camaraderie—which was likely true, as it had long been his modus operandi—and was inexcusable. Despite Bryant's aloofness, there were bonds formed on Team USA, but they were mostly on the floor, made amid their success together.

Bryant's lack of concern about being cool extended right onto the floor. Playing for Krzyzewski, Bryant looked at times remarkably like a Duke freshman, squatting low, slapping the floor as an announcement of his defensive intentions. For two years, his energy had helped drive Team USA forward. As Colangelo had asked, Bryant focused on being a ball distributor and the kind of defender that Krzyzewski demanded.

As Winter had long pointed out, in the fire of competition, it was difficult for great talents to remain disciplined, to hold back the urge to take over, but Kobe managed it. As his bad ankles had once helped Bryant tone down his game to help the Lakers come together in 2001, as Chip Schaefer had pointed out, his injured finger likely played a role in Bryant not attempting to do too much that August of 2008 in China, when he showed the profile of a consummate team player.

Team USA brimmed with talent and rolled through eight Olympic contests by wide margins, with Bryant averaging 15 points, 2.8 rebounds, 2.1 assists, and 1.1 steals per game.

He had 25 to break open a closer game with Australia in the quarterfinals, then a dozen against Argentina in the semis. Throughout the Games, Bryant used his dribble drive to break down opponents, then kicked the ball to teammates for open shots. His playmaking was a driving force in the American success. In an earlier game against Spain, he'd initiated physical contact with Lakers teammate Pau Gasol, playing for his home country. When they met again in the gold-medal game, Gasol and his Spanish teammates were fired up to take down the Americans. The result was the biggest challenge of all for Bryant and his teammates, and they managed a 118–107 victory to close their quest.

He returned to the sideline in the waning moments, and Krzyzewski sought him out for an embrace. As they hugged, Bryant poured bottled water over the coach's head. Surprised, Krzyzewski blinked, then finally laughed and bent over to find a towel, which allowed Bryant to wind up and smack him quite hard on the rump.

The moment served as his answer to O'Neal's crude rap earlier in the summer. If he knew how anything tasted, it was Olympic victory, an accomplishment that Bryant would later evaluate as greater than even his NBA titles because it was won in representation of his country.

The aftermath might have seemed the time to deal with his injured finger, but Bryant was leery of delaying his start to the new NBA season. He had a completely torn ligament in his pinkie finger, an avulsion fracture, which meant that when the ligament tore, it pulled away pieces of bone from the finger. He decided he would again have to tape it up and keep playing. He had concluded that the failure against the Celtics was his as a leader. He came to realize that he had eased up on his teammates, thinking that they had all come together after Gasol's arrival. It had been a gross miscalculation of just how much he needed to drive the roster.

As Scoop Jackson observed, Garnett and his Celtics had been "tremendous assholes" during the championship series and had intimidated the Lakers. "Kobe knew he was dealing with two of the biggest assholes in the game that he had to go up against," Scoop Jackson offered. "That's Paul Pierce and Kevin Garnett. And you can't beat two assholes without being an asshole. You've got to be able to elevate to that level, and Kevin was the centerpiece to that team at the time, even though it was Paul's team. But Kevin was the lead asshole."

Besides providing unequaled energy, Garnett spared no one, Scoop Jackson recalled. "Kevin was getting in his teammates' ass, being the player that every teammate on that Boston Celtics team hated because of how he treated them, how he got at them all the time. That's love/hate—they hated him because he was such an asshole."

Bryant knew it was time to draw a bit upon his mother's dark side, a concept he would eventually articulate as "embracing the villain" within himself in order to vanquish opponents.

"He did it willfully," Scoop Jackson recalled. "He was like, 'OK, I've got to take this asshole thing to a whole other level because now the asshole is not just about me. I got to be the asshole universally in order to get us where we need to be. And Kobe knew that. He was like, 'I got to be an asshole.'"

There was some concern over Bryant's decision not to repair the pinkie. Jerry West had watched the Olympics closely and afterward ran into Tex Winter and told him that the Lakers better start keeping a close watch over Bryant's playing time because he looked as if he was starting to wear down. Being unwise could end his career before its time, West warned. Winter, as well as others, had sensed the same for a while. Bryant's ever-intense workout approach itself was cited as a culprit as well.

Obviously a sign of the toll was his mounting injuries. He had had so many over the years. He would soon strain his back operating a vacuum cleaner, of all things. But Bryant himself professed not to have time for injuries. There was a championship to be won, a legacy at stake.

Aiding in their quest for revenge would be Bryant's old friend Winter. For three years, Winter had been racked with pain from shingles, and it had cost him time with the team over the seasons. Finally he decided that the best way to keep his mind off the pain was to come back to the team and engage the mystery and contradictions of Kobe Bryant.

Winter saw early on that the 2008–09 Lakers were going to have defensive promise. Coming out of the Olympics, Bryant showed encouraging flashes of inspired defensive play, which coursed through the roster in Los Angeles.

More important, the team and its coach seemed to be on the same page now. The pain of the Celtics loss had united them all and added new purpose, and the humiliation had pulled Jackson out of the Zen cool with which he approached everything. "It's motivated him to the point that he wants to get with it," Winter observed. "And he is getting with it. He's controlling things a lot more than he did in the past."

Finally, Winter explained, the club had the sort of depth Jackson had hoped for, with Trevor Ariza back from injury. Andrew Bynum had hesitated on his surgery and would miss part of the season as a result. But the roster had matured, and the know-how was there and growing.

Winter also pointed out that the Olympic experience had helped Bryant settle into a team role even further, and his healthy play didn't disappear once he returned from China.

He also pushed for Bryant to find even more confidence in his perimeter game to cut down on his sorties to the basket, which always seemed to contribute to the potential for more injury.

"Kobe's gotta hit shots," Winter said, apprising the situation. "He's gotta take those outside shots. They're important to the team. He can't go to the basket all the time."

It was always a question of balance for Bryant, Winter lamented. The coach reminded him constantly that he needed to keep a steady mix of shooting and driving. That sounded simple, but it was never easy to measure balance over the course of a game. "Kobe just can't rely on one thing or the other too much," Winter said. "Kobe wants to involve everybody else, and that's good. But sometimes it's maybe too much so. With players like Kobe and Jordan, it's always a question of balance."

The biggest issue remained Bryant's minutes. As the season began, Jackson announced that his star's playing time would be trimmed back. Clearly, the process of hauling the Lakers around during their four-year rebuilding process had weighed heavily on him.

As Bryant himself had often said, it wasn't the age but the mileage that mattered in a playing career. At age thirty-one, his odometer was beginning to measure the wear and tear.

The delight of November was that the Lakers put forth a good starting lineup and a deep, energetic bench that allowed Jackson to keep Bryant in his seat for longer stretches. He didn't need to score all the points, with the reserves taking apart opponents.

Though Lamar Odom became something of a poster child for the lack of consistency and mental toughness that hurt the Lakers against the Celtics, he gave the Lakers roster flexibility that they needed. Bynum's return from injury moved Pau Gasol back to power forward. Gasol at power forward would mean moving Odom to small forward, although Odom often played guard on offense in the triangle with Bryant on the wing, much as Pippen had for the Bulls. Odom also easily switched to power forward when the Lakers found matchups preventing them from playing Gasol and Bynum together.

But then the bench mysteriously declined in December as Bryant's teammates suddenly found themselves struggling with the mental part of the game.

"I think some of the players' makeup is that they're not real confident in their abilities. And I think it does show through," Winter said, the irritation obvious in his voice, adding that the situation left Bryant and Pau Gasol carrying the team. "It gets to the point where Kobe feels like he has to take over. It gets pretty discouraging when your teammates don't come through like we'd all want them to."

When his teammates struggled and Bryant moved to shoulder more of the load, that only served to send the team into its familiar destructive spiral of the past.

"There's no support then," Winter said. "The other players just aren't involved when he does that."

In the past Jackson had employed psychologists to strengthen the competitive minds of his players. Winter, though, didn't see that as the answer this time around.

"They have to work it out on their own," he said. "As professionals they should have a strong enough competitive nature to do that."

Not surprisingly, the answer involved a familiar theme. "A lot depends on Kobe, on whether he can keep the right attitude and play the right way," Winter said. "If he becomes discouraged with his teammates, as he has been at times, and starts to take over all by himself, that wouldn't be good. But that's always the difficulty with a player of his abilities."

It was perhaps where Bryant was most similar to Michael Jordan, Winter said, then added that it was also where he was similar to other greats such as West and Oscar Robertson.

"One thing about those rare players like Kobe and Michael and West and Oscar," Winter said, "they want to be the best, and they are never satisfied with anything less. That's what makes them what they are. They're all very complex."

Despite his concerns, Winter held to optimism, mainly because Jackson remained in charge. "Phil holds up really well," Winter said. "He's never too high and never too down. That's a great characteristic as a coach."

It was a characteristic that had allowed Jackson to weather many a storm over the years. But as the 2008–09 season unfolded, Jackson began talking about stepping down after the following year.

For veteran Jackson watchers, that claim was business as usual, him doing his part to step up the urgency for his team, which would hopefully help fortify a talented young group that had had its mental fragility exposed just six months earlier against the Celtics.

The Lakers' Christmas Day game against Boston gave them a chance to exorcise some demons. They took the advantage in the middle of a six-game winning streak and entered the New Year with a 25–5 record.

They would move to 37–9 by the end of January, an improvement that marked Bryant's growth as a leader, Brian Shaw quietly observed at the time. Most people didn't understand the huge challenge of Bryant's task following the team's devastating loss to Boston, Shaw said. It began with the constant effort to make himself better first, with all the focus Bryant put into playing at a high level, the assistant coach explained. "He still has all that discipline, all that attention to detail."

But over the past year, Bryant had turned a similar effort toward building his team and teammates, Shaw explained. "The area he has grown in the most has been his leadership and his trust of the other players on the team now. He has complete trust. He's more open with them than he's been with any group that we've had here in Los Angeles to this point.

"He manned up," Shaw said of Bryant. "He said at the end of the

Boston series last year that they were the better team. They were tougher. They were more physical."

Bryant told his teammates that they all—including himself—needed to become physically and mentally stronger.

"Kobe said, 'We can't make guys tough that aren't tough. But they can physically prepare themselves, and we can cover for each other's weaknesses.' And that's what we focused on. That's something he made a point of saying," Shaw explained.

"He's done a good job all year of gauging things when our team comes out in a game and we're a little sluggish," Shaw said. "He's more aggressive then to get us into a game. If guys are up to the task right at the beginning, then he defers. He'll set guys up and play more of a facilitator role. Then we always know that we can go to him in the fourth quarter and get what we need."

Bryant's leadership continued to mesh with Gasol's own stepped-up performance, with his rebounding, toughness, and smarts. In their first full season together, the Spaniard and Bryant made remarkable strides.

The Lakers finished the season strong and had just started into the play-offs with a great deal of momentum when news came that Tex Winter had suffered a stroke at an event in Kansas for one of his old teams. The sudden absence of his mentor jolted Jackson, but Bryant gamely predicted that Winter would battle back.

He would not. His ability to communicate was permanently damaged, along with other functions. Winter would slowly recover while watching his Lakers on TV, but he would never coach again.

Bryant slowly came to realize that he would have Winter's nagging presence with him no longer. His mind kept returning to an odd, throwaway moment with Winter just before the Lakers headed to the parade to celebrate their 2000 title. Totally ignoring the occasion, the old coach began fussing at the Lakers about chest passes and how none of them could throw one correctly. Bryant had to chuckle every time he thought of it. Here the Lakers were, going out to celebrate the huge accomplishment, with Winter's ill-timed criticism ringing in their ears. His "Yoda" was totally, completely obsessed with perfection, much like Bryant himself. That, as much as anything, rested at the heart of their kinship.

Lakers assistant Craig Hodges, who had played for Winter at Long Beach State and with the Chicago Bulls, kept in close touch with Winter's family in the wake of the stroke. He expressed confidence that Winter was following the team closely on TV back in his Oregon home.

Aware that Winter's eyes were still on him, Bryant honored his coach with measured performances that spring as the Lakers first pushed Utah aside, then engaged the Houston Rockets and Ron Artest in a seven-game battle. Then they beat Denver in six games, sending the Lakers to the championship series against Dwight Howard and the Orlando Magic.

The series against Denver was the moment when something special began clicking with the Lakers after years of effort. Their work in the triangle offense would approach a state of being that Winter called "the automatics," meaning that the coaches didn't have to call plays because the players were so well versed in the triangle offense, they could simply read the defense and make the cuts and passes to counteract it. As Luke Walton—another of Tex Winter's protégés on the Lakers—would explain, the players themselves realized it in Game 6 of the Western Conference finals, when they soared to a different level and destroyed the Denver Nuggets.

Still, even though the team had played extremely well in the Western Conference finals against the Nuggets, the Lakers players knew that Winter wouldn't have allowed himself to be very pleased.

"He would have found something to yell at us about," Walton said with a smile.

As they worked to win Jackson's tenth title, the Lakers were quite mindful of Winter. That factored in to their determination to reach that special level with the automatics. As Walton explained, they didn't have to articulate such notions. They were better left unsaid.

Jackson had been hurt deeply by Winter's condition, according to close associates. It was not something the coach addressed publicly, and even with the team, he approached it only subtly. "He's constantly teaching us and telling us things his teacher has told him," Walton said of Jackson. "We're all thinking about Tex, and we miss him."

In Game 1 of the Finals, against Orlando, the same great tide lifted the Lakers again and carried them off to that special place. Naturally, a big factor was the play of Bryant, who scored 40 points. But it was also much more than that. It was how Bryant and his Lakers accomplished the win. He scored largely within the context of the triangle offense. The Lakers went to their "automatics" and simply took what the defense gave them, which had always been Winter's main directive. From the 25-point final margin, it was easy to deduce that Orlando was quite charitable. Afterward, the Magic players and coaches had the same hangdog look that Bulls opponents used to wear in the late 1990s.

As veteran Magic assistant Brendan Malone suggested before Game 1, Orlando would counter the triangle by slowing the flow of Lakers cutting to the basket. "We have to keep a body on the cutters," he explained. It might have worked against a young team that couldn't use all the "automatics" of the triangle offense, like the Lakers had been in previous years. But, as Walton explained, this Lakers team had grown in its relationship with the offense, and now they were able to read and react to the Orlando defense.

"It's been a constant change," Walton explained, "but toward the end of that Denver series, that's when we really took a step to the next level."

The players, Walton said, had come "to know that pretty much every time, if we make the right reads, we're gonna get a good shot."

Being on the floor in those Zen moments made for a rare and wonderful level of basketball, Walton observed. "If you have the ball, you're looking around and seeing people move and cut. It's a great way to play basketball."

It was a beautiful tribute to Winter.

In addition to seeing the offense he created being played at such a high level, the old coach would have surely loved to see Kobe Bryant prove that finally, he was a full-fledged leader. Like Jordan before him, Bryant was not exactly loved by his teammates. But he had earned their immense respect.

In Game 3, the Magic opened with torrid shooting, and because Bryant was so determined to close out the championship, he answered with his own scoring outburst in the first half, which kept the Lakers in the game.

However, he appeared to have worn himself down, which helped explain his struggles and the key late turnover that cost the Lakers in the fourth quarter. Bryant had also shown signs of extreme fatigue in the Lakers' conference-finals battle with Denver.

Bryant's loss of energy in Game 3 seemed to confirm West's concern that he needed to play less each game. The coaching staff had been vigilant about the issue that season, Shaw said, but he added that it remained difficult because of Bryant's competitive nature. In Game 3, Jackson had left Bryant on the bench for a stretch of the fourth quarter in hopes he could recuperate. "He always wants to stay in the game," Shaw said. "As a coach, you have to give him rests. You have to protect him from himself. There are times when he's really pleading on the sideline, 'Leave me in. Leave me in.' We do that, but for the most part you have to fight that and give him rests."

Managing Bryant's minutes and trying to pace that overwhelmingly competitive nature would prove a giant factor over the remainder of his career.

But in the short term, Bryant and the Lakers would bounce back easily. After the loss in Game 3, they disassembled the Magic in two straight games to win the championship series, 4–1, and Bryant was named Finals MVP for the first time.

J. A. Adande recalled that O'Neal tweeted immediately after the title was won,"I'm sure Kobe's going to say 'Shaq, tell me how my ass tastes.' Congratulations, Kobe."

Adande went back into the arena in Orlando and showed the tweet to a still-celebrating Bryant.

"I held up my phone," Adande recalled, "and I said, 'Kobe, look what Shaq said.' Kobe was as happy as I've ever seen him. He was in such a good mood. He wasn't even going to let Shaq ruin it. He just said, 'Shaq's a fool.' Like, he said it in an endearing way."

Déjà Vu

Jerry West had raised hackles and eyebrows during the play-offs when he announced that LeBron James had supplanted Bryant as the best player in the NBA. On one level, West was simply doing something he'd been paid to do for the past thirty years—honestly evaluating the talent he saw in the league. James was simply bigger and stronger and more powerful than Bryant and, as a result, could do more things on the court than Bryant.

West was quite familiar with the circumstances. He himself had spent his entire career being compared with the bigger, stronger presence of Oscar Robertson. In fact, West was more than a little obsessed with these comparisons and used them to drive and motivate himself. But West had long known that such debates were never truly resolved, that they were the lifeblood of an NBA career, that they drove fan interest and player performance. Larry Bird and Magic Johnson were a perfect example of two players who spent their careers locked in a competition that drove both to the heights of the game.

So was James better than Bryant?

West also made this observation: you can see what a player can do on the floor, his physical abilities, but it is almost impossible to read a player's heart.

In the wake of the Finals that year, this much was clear about Bryant: At age thirty-one, he was determined to make the full effort, leaving nothing undone. Heart was not an issue.

For Bryant, the answer to any comparisons to other players was clear. It was about championships. That was how they would be judged by time.

Bryant had fractured his right index finger in January of 2009, another painful finger injury that affected his shot. Heading into the 2009–10 season, there again was no time for surgery. There was only time to prepare for the season, which featured a fundamental change. Trevor Ariza was signed by Houston, and Houston forward Ron Artest was signed by the Lakers. Without Ariza's shooting, if the Lakers were going to win a title in 2010, it would not be with the elevated execution of the triangle that they had come to know in 2009. It would be with the added toughness and grit of Ron Artest.

Like many older players who had come up in the game by the strength of their instincts, Artest found the triangle absolutely befuddling, which meant that the team's execution would be in danger of regression.

But Artest, a strong personality, was hungry to win an NBA title, and the energy and intimidation he brought to the game infused the Lakers for a repeat.

Going into the season, Jerry Buss announced that he was stepping back and turning the franchise over to his son Jim, which only goosed the internal power struggle between Jim and his sister Jeanie Buss and Jackson, her longtime boyfriend.

Jackson was also vague about his future in coaching. He told reporters that whether the Lakers were repeat NBA champions would be a big factor—but not the only one—in determining whether he returned as coach the following season.

The *Los Angeles Times* reported the Lakers and Pau Gasol (who earned $16.5 million in 2010 and $17.8 million in 2011) had agreed in principle to a three-year extension that would carry Gasol through the 2013–14 season.

The *Times* also suggested that Bryant, who had the right to opt out of his contract at the conclusion of 2010 to become an unrestricted free agent, would soon sign a new deal.

The team was furthermore reported to have asked Jackson, the NBA's highest-paid coach, with a $12-million annual salary, and its biggest winner, with ten championships under his belt, to take a pay cut to help defray the huge costs of keeping the team together. When reporters asked Jackson if he would take a pay cut, he ended the session by saying, "Why would you?"

Although the Lakers got off to a strong start despite early injuries, Lamar Odom paused after a January road game to acknowledge that the team missed Winter's unique perspective. There was little doubt, he added, what the coach would be telling the club.

"He would be telling Kobe to move the ball," Odom said with a laugh. "But he was always telling Kobe to move the ball, even when Kobe was moving the ball. He would tell us to ping the ball. He would say we should be passing a lot better, having a lot more assists."

And if the team had defensive breakdowns, Winter would still blame the troubles on improper offensive execution, Odom said.

That was because the triangle, a team offense, was predicated on floor balance that always left players in position to get back on defense to prevent easy fast-break baskets.

It was a system, often derided by critics, that had been good enough to win ten of the previous twenty NBA championships. Was it good enough to win one more? Pro basketball had long been viewed as a freelancing domain until it came to be ruled by Winter's disciplined approach to team play.

"People don't realize it's mostly a zone offense," Odom explained. "You overload one side, and you always have people in rebounding position. You just kind of pick your spots. It's a pass-first offense. You just pass the ball to the open man and see what develops from there."

Odom said he could still hear Winter right there in his ear, telling him how to adjust his play. "Experience is the best teacher in the world," Odom explained, with more than a bit of tenderness in his voice. "He'd been around the block. And Tex always had stories for me. I miss his presence. We all miss Tex. A lot."

Though adjusting to life without Winter's team involvement meant a change for the Lakers, one thing stayed the same—Bryant's approach to the game.

"We know what he wants to do," Odom said with a laugh. "He's gonna come out and be offensively aggressive at all times. But he earns that. He earns that."

Now in his second full season with Bryant, Gasol had pointed out in January that he had to keep working the offensive boards because he was getting only about 5 shots a game in the offense.

Some observers took that as criticism of Bryant, but both Gasol and Odom said that wasn't the case.

It was more a testament to Gasol's effectiveness and the efforts of opposing defenses. "Pau's always prepared. You see him catch the ball and just go with that pretty left hook. He has an awesome array of moves and shots. We try to get him the ball as much as possible," Odom said of Gasol's role. "When Kobe gets going, you got to understand that he's going to stay aggressive, he's gonna stay in the attack mode. Pau's so versatile, so underrated as a rebounder. There are so many ways he can hurt a team. His passing. He hits me down low with passes all the time. He's always around 4 or 5 or 6 assists a night."

The put-back buckets of Gasol and his teammates after missed shots had come to be jokingly called "Kobe assists" by opponents and fans, meaning that teammates were more likely to rebound one of his misses than to have the ball passed to them.

Despite the fact that Gasol was not running many plays for Bryant, roster instability and injuries had only heightened the team's appreciation of Gasol.

The seven-footer had missed the start of the 2010 season with a hamstring injury, but upon returning to the lineup and regaining some strength and flexibility, he settled in to average 18.3 points and 11.3 rebounds, the perfect complement to Bryant's 27 points, 5.4 rebounds, and 5 assists per game.

Bryant's big year highlighted the other measure of Gasol's impact—the double teams he drew virtually every time he caught the ball in the post. "Teams double Pau a lot," Odom said. "A lot."

Those double teams created space for Bryant to move and attack. "My favorite player, to be honest with you, is Pau Gasol," Bryant would tell campers at his basketball academy. "His versatility is unmatched. He's a great example for a lot of kids. He can use his left hand as well as he can use his right. He's a big guy who can put the ball on the floor, post, shoot, rebound. He does everything fundamentally."

Gasol's alliance with Bryant resulted in an absolutely deadly screen-and-roll combo, one that gave the demanding Bryant reason to share a rare smile. His satisfaction with their alliance only increased throughout the 2010 play-offs.

Over the season, Bryant had hit six game-winning field goals, more than any NBA player in a decade, and he became the youngest player in NBA history to score 25,000 career points. In a January game versus Toronto, he posted his career high in rebounds, with 16.

He scored better than 40 points eight times, and he racked up his hundredth 40-point game during the season.

And at Memphis on February 1, he scored 44 (how fitting, Jerry West's number), to move past West as the storied franchise's all-time leading scorer.

Though he continued to play at a high level on offense, Bryant's season was marred by injuries. A strained tendon near Bryant's left ankle ended his streak of three-plus years without missing a game, benching him for two weeks in February.

His injuries didn't always mean losses for his team, though. One of the highlights of the season was Bryant easing through a February loss in Dallas while racked with back spasms, to go with his finger problem, scoring 10 points and orchestrating things while his teammates stepped up with the other 86.

Still, Artest's struggles with the triangle offense meant that Jackson relied on the structured approach less and less. That and the injuries meant they won only fifty-seven games in 2010, still good enough to win the Pacific Division.

Though the Lakers posted a good record that season, it seemed obvious that Bryant, who had recently signed a three-year contract extension with the Lakers for almost $30 million per season, was now beginning to face the challenges that all great players face as they age. He'd become worn down by the grueling march to the last two NBA Finals and by his role on Team USA in winning the 2008 Olympic gold medal. The index-finger injury had required a major adjustment, one that had allowed him to keep playing but with a lower shooting percentage.

He now found himself in a growing reality that he couldn't escape, just as other greats had. Larry Bird had spent his later years in the NBA battling heel spurs and a bad back, the price he paid for the all-out way he played. For Magic Johnson, the end had come with an embarrassing loss to Jordan and the Bulls in the 1991 NBA Finals, followed a few months later by the stunning revelation that he was HIV positive. His later attempts at a comeback were hard to watch.

Jerry West had fought through an array of injuries to finally help his Los Angeles Lakers to a championship in 1972, after the team had failed in seven previous trips to the NBA Finals. Two seasons later, West found himself tangled in a contract dispute with Lakers owner Jack Kent Cooke, so he played one final, furious exhibition game and retired in a bitter huff. He then filed a lawsuit against the team for which he had played his entire career.

Michael Jordan was thought to be the one who would finally leave the game on his own terms. He defeated the Utah Jazz with a killer shot in the 1998 NBA Finals to win a sixth championship for the Chicago Bulls. It all seemed so perfect until he gave in and attempted a comeback with the Washington Wizards three years later, which produced two miserably lost seasons. That failed effort had been rewarded by an ugly scene in which Jordan was fired as an executive by Washington owner Abe Pollin.

Pro basketball's select few—its greatest competitors—had all reached the heights of fame and glory only to find themselves staring at a harsh reality: their youth was gone, having been spent in a seemingly endless, dizzying cycle of games and practices, a blur of physically challenging seasons punctuated by summers that were far too brief and much too busy. They all spent the last few years of their careers trying to cheat time until finally realizing that their hour had come round at last. Now Bryant, in the midst of the Herculean task of trying to claim a back-to-back title, was getting the first glimpse of that reality. Lakers fans presented an imposing Greek chorus in Los Angeles, and the nervous twitter about the slipping quality of Bryant's play had begun to grow.

Bryant himself, set to turn thirty-two that August, had acknowledged it. Likewise, Jackson hadn't hesitated to address the fact that Bryant could no longer make some of the miracle plays that he once made seem so routine.

As West had warned, Bryant needed more "recovery" time.

Unfortunately, circumstances with the Lakers had allowed little room for moderation of his minutes. Such was the way with superstars. They had to be on the floor. By that first-round series with Oklahoma City, in his fourteenth season, Bryant had already played better than 44,400 minutes of regular-season and play-off basketball. By the end of the play-offs, that number would rise to nearly 45,000 minutes.

Jordan, long considered the standard because he drove the Bulls to a championship as a thirty-five-year-old NBA guard, played a total of 48,485 minutes over his fifteen-year career, the final 5,000 of which were frustration-filled in Washington.

Jackson had long considered it a marvel that Jordan was able to play at such a high level at age thirty-five while winning a sixth title, yet Jordan had taken off nearly two seasons earlier in his career to play baseball.

With this in mind, Bryant had explained his goal for the end-game of his career: "Keep playing until the wheels fall off."

The wheels hadn't fallen off by the 2010 play-offs, but a lug nut had begun to roll around in the hubcap.

The age disparity was obvious as the Lakers took on a talented young Oklahoma City Thunder in the first round of the 2010 play-offs. Bryant scored 39 points and Gasol 25 in Game 2 to put the Lakers up 2–0. Yet Games 3 and 4 in the series only served to revive the noise about Bryant's aging. Kevin Durant, Oklahoma City's brilliant young star, had established himself as a top offensive player that season, but there were questions about his defense. In the second half of Game 3, Durant answered that when he asked to cover Bryant. It was obvious that the unexpected switch and Durant's length created trouble for Bryant, whose missed shots in the fourth quarter created an opportunity for the Thunder to get a confidence-building win.

In Game 4, Bryant clearly backed off his own game to respond to Jackson's entreaties to use the Lakers' size against the Thunder. With a less-aggressive Bryant making passes, taking only 10 shots and scoring only a dozen points, Oklahoma City pushed to a blow-out win.

With the series tied, 2–2, the teams returned to Los Angeles for Game 5. A younger Bryant might have tried to take over the game on his own, but instead he kept faith in his teammates and again played a team game, taking just 9 shots as his Lakers blew out the Thunder and went on to claim the series.

Coming out of the Thunder series, the Lakers ditched the Utah Jazz in four quick second-round games and defeated the fast-moving Phoenix Suns in six in the conference finals, including an epic Game 5 in which Bryant tallied 30 points, 11 rebounds, and 9 assists.

Waiting as a reward in the Finals were the Boston Celtics, providing the Lakers with a chance to foreclose on old demons.

When well-known stats analyst John Hollinger picked the Lakers to beat the Celtics, it set off nervous tweets among L.A. fans everywhere. It was an omen, they said.

That very silly mind-set summed up the long history between the NBA's two most successful teams. The 2008 triumph had renewed the Celtics' ownership of the Lakers.

According to stereotype, it was why Boston fans fell to loud and rowdy morning drinking during the play-offs and why Lakers fans quickly dialed for extra appointments with their therapists.

It was Hollywood versus Beantown again. Star power versus Celtic mystique. The two teams had met eleven times for the championship, and history had confirmed that after it was over, Hollywood just about always ended up on the couch.

In Game 1, Bryant had 6 assists and scored 30 for the tenth time in the previous eleven play-off games, while Gasol secured 14 boards as Los Angeles whipped Boston, 102–89, at Staples Center. In Game 2, however, the Celtics quickly wiped out L.A.'s home-court advantage, 103–94, behind Ray Allen's 11 three-pointers, an NBA Finals record.

Tied at a game apiece, the series moved to Boston for Game 3 on June 8, where Bryant scored 29 points, while Bynum and Gasol had 10 rebounds each. The third game, though, belonged to Fisher, who scored 11 points on 5-of-7 shooting in the final quarter, to finish with 16 to stun the Celtics. Boston then struck back to claim Game 4, 96–89, despite 33 from Bryant and 21 from Gasol. Working on that momentum, the Celtics overcame 38 points by Bryant to take a 3–2 series lead with a 92–86 win in Game 5, the last game in Boston.

Could the Lakers win two at home to claim the title? They answered resoundingly with a 89–67 blowout in Game 6 back in Staples Center on June 15, with Bryant scoring 26 and Gasol passing brilliantly out of the post for 9 assists, to go with his 13 rebounds. The Boston collapse had been driven by a first-quarter knee injury to center Kendrick Perkins.

Next up was Game 7, Celtics versus Lakers, one of those rare moments in championship history, and Bryant needed to be ready with his full villain, what his critics saw as the true nature of the man whom Scoop Jackson affectionately called "the greatest asshole in the history of the game."

Some observers were surprised by how much the pressure of the final game seemed to get to Bryant. Scoop Jackson wondered if the pressure was caused by the game itself or by "the outside conversation surrounding that game"—in other words, the fact that a good portion of Bryant's legacy would hinge on the outcome. Bryant was the guy who had always invited history, even as a kid. He was going to be the greatest, and suddenly this game was the full culmination of all his ambition.

"That was the moment he'd been waiting for his whole life," Jackson said. "It wasn't just a culmination of him getting another ring and closer to Jordan's six championship rings. Kobe's play in that game was going to dictate the legitimacy of him being in the conversation with Jordan."

Bryant himself called it "being at the table" with Jordan and the other greats of the game. He was playing for his seat at that table. And if the Lakers lost that game, the outcome would have weighed on him like a great stone, taking him to the bottom of the abyss. "That would have killed him," Scoop Jackson said. "The other players on that Lakers team knew how important that game was to Kobe, too. Not just for them and the organization. But for Kobe."

The circumstances elevated everything. "I think players recognize that," Scoop Jackson offered. "They recognize greatness when they're around it. The players on that Lakers team recognized just how great Kobe was. They also knew that he was going to have to live with this far more than they were if he had lost. Their losing that game in Game 7 was not going to have the same impact on their careers as it was on Kobe's legacy. And they understood that. They saw it every day. They're like, 'This dude is in a situation that nobody in the room is in. This is Kobe's entire legacy on the line right now.'"

The game didn't start well. It was an ugly, low-scoring affair, and Bryant struggled mightily from the floor as the Celtics surged to a 40–34 halftime lead. Gasol's rebounding (he would finish with 18), Fisher's heady play, and Artest's defense and big shots all led to a Lakers revival in the fourth quarter that allowed them to tie the score at 64–64 with six minutes to go.

It was fitting that Bryant, for all his greatness, finally had to trust his teammates completely, especially his old ally Fisher, whom so many Lakers fans had derided as too old to play.

Bryant made just 6 of 24 shots from the field, with 11 free throws, to finish with 23 points, 15 rebounds, and 2 assists. Artest, who would soon change his name to Metta World Peace, scored 20, Gasol 19, and Fisher 10.

Tired and desperate, the Celtics began fouling as the Lakers inched to an 83–79 win that ignited delirium and cemented the 2010 Lakers' reputation as one of the greatest clubs of all time, as well as Bryant's own claim to a "place at the table." He had made 8 of 9 free throws under immense pressure in the fourth period to deliver the win.

He was again named the Finals MVP. His feats now included a whopping twelve All-Star appearances and three All-Star MVP awards (2002, 2007, and 2009). He had been named twelve times to the All-NBA Team and ten times to the All-Defensive Team. In 2009, *The Sporting News* would name him the NBA Athlete of the Decade, and TNT would name him the NBA Player of the Decade.

As impressive as these honors were, none of the accolades quite compared to the intangible reward of Los Angeles beating Boston in a magnificent seven-game championship series in 2010.

Back in Philadelphia, his high school coaches and teammates had sat transfixed, watching the full moment of his redemption. He had sought to climb these heights and along the way had done himself tremendous damage, suffered so publicly, then had battled to regain his way and had arrived at the celebratory moment with a complete and profound exhaustion.

J. A. Adande recalled that Bryant had been in a terrible mood heading into the series, refusing to admit so much as that the series against the Celtics had any sort of special meaning. Just the opposite was obvious, Adande recalled. "It was all very nostalgic, and in 2010 that was about those two teams, that particular set of teams, Kobe and Pau and Derek Fisher, Lamar Odom, going up against Kevin Garnett and Paul Pierce and Ray Allen and Doc Rivers. You know that was a rivalry between those two teams, and Kobe was horrendous in that Game 7. It really was just a poorly played game all around, one of the sloppiest Game 7s I ever seen by both teams, but the tension in that arena was at the highest level. That might be the most tense game I've ever covered, Game 7 of that NBA Finals between those two franchises. These two teams really wanted to beat each other. The tension of it got to Kobe, and he admitted afterwards that it got to him. He was just missing shot after shot at the beginning, and I could not believe it. I couldn't believe what a horrendous performance it was. People were talking like, 'This is going to take him down and undo his legacy.'"

If he had lost, Bryant would have been just 4–3 in championship series. But the Lakers had prevailed, and his legacy was intact.

"Immediately afterwards," Adande recalled, "the first thing on his mind: 'OK, what does it mean that you've got five championships now?' He said, 'It means that I've got one more than Shaq.' He couldn't wait to get that out there."

Chapter 28

THE MAN

Aʟʟ ʜɪs ʟɪfe, as far back as he could remember, Kobe Bryant had longed to be "the man," to dominate the game to such a degree that he could bask in the glow and recognition that came with it, with the entire basketball universe having to bow down before him and acknowledge his dominance.

Now he was there, in that moment. It was his team—no one else's, certainly not Shaquille O'Neal's—that had made the run to the league-championship series three straight years and come away with two titles. During the run, he had stood in the warm media spotlight, a place he inhabited quite ably, with his well-spoken presence and passion.

Journalist David McMenamin had started covering the Lakers beat during the period and found himself trying to fit in with a group of Los Angeles reporters who had long covered Bryant and the team. That in itself was a challenge, but one of McMenamin's advantages was that he had seen Bryant play in high school. McMenamin had gone to a school that rivaled Lower Merion in suburban Philadelphia; it was such a rivalry that when McMenamin informed the star of his background, Bryant looked at him with a frown and asked, "Then what are you talking to me for?"

It was McMenamin's first time covering Phil Jackson, but he had read *The Last Season* and was amazed that the coach and Bryant could work together after its publication. "Phil had a major bridge to repair, you know," McMenamin observed. "It's pretty scathing, the stuff that's in that book. I thought it was remarkable that Phil always bit his tongue when it came to criticizing Kobe."

Instead, Jackson had taken to turning his criticism on other players and used them to discipline the team. "Pau Gasol was his whipping boy, and Lamar Odom was his whipping boy," McMenamin recalled. "Both of those guys he would tweak constantly in the press, but even if Kobe did whatever, you know, like, a typical Kobe Bryant poor night where he shoots too much and doesn't pass enough, and it was pretty obvious to everyone watching, Phil would find a way to couch that and not make a direct criticism of Kobe. It didn't stop us as a press corps from continuing to ask the questions that needed to be asked when Kobe had a poor night. But we kind of came to the expectation that we weren't going to get anything going down that road."

Those nights, of course, were juxtaposed with Bryant's nights of full genius, the nights when, as McMenamin described it, "he was putting moves together on the court that always struck me. He could combine a jab step with a pump fake, throw it off the backboard to himself, and finish with the reverse layup, and it was all preordained, premeditated, and executed perfectly, all while a defense was completely designed to try to stop him."

No matter what those defenses did, Bryant's competitive spirit could usually find some masterful combination of things to overcome them. It had allowed him to vanquish the top opponents three years running. Because of that obvious genius, Bryant seemed to expect the media and the public they represented merely to accept him now as he was on the surface, without looking too closely, McMenamin observed. "Looking back at my six seasons covering him, I still kind of wonder how much I picked up about him personally, and how much any of us did. You could tell his intelligence from speaking to him. You knew that he knew his league. He knew the history of the league. He knew the world around him. He knew when a guy from the media walked into the room, he could size him up pretty quickly in terms of what they're getting at."

It seemed that Bryant wasn't just trying to control the narrative about his life by limiting what Phil Jackson had to say, but also by limiting all the media as well. That included filmmaker Spike Lee, who had negotiated to film a documentary of Bryant, shot with thirty cameras during an April 13, 2008, game against San Antonio. The film, titled *Kobe Doin' Work,* covered a day in Bryant's life, focusing on his extraordinary work and dedication. Microphones were placed on Bryant and Jackson with, amazingly, full access to both while the Lakers were trying to close out a hotly contested regular season. Bryant was to provide voice-over commentary at a later date, in February 2009, after a Lakers game versus the Knicks in Madison Square Garden. In the interim, there were press reports that Bryant and Lee, the noted filmmaker and Knicks fan, were struggling over creative control of the project. Such struggles over Bryant's creative projects harkened back to his ill-fated rap recording and would crop up again later with another documentary, *Kobe Bryant's Muse,* for Showtime. It was reported that Lee, in an effort to fend off Bryant's move for control, had threatened to shift the focus of the film to San Antonio forward Tim Duncan, but Lee denied these reports.

At some point, Bryant apparently obtained the measure of control he wanted, and the film went forward, with the voice-over work scheduled for that February of 2009. To emphasize his dominance, the day before the voice-over session, Bryant went at the Knicks for a brutally efficient 61 points, which broke the Garden scoring record, eclipsing Jordan's record of 55 by an opponent and even Bernard King's record of 60 by a Knick. Carmelo Anthony would score 62 in 2014 to reclaim the building's scoring record for the Knicks, but Bryant's big night remained the all-time high by an opponent. It was quite a performance, accomplished without a single garbage bucket because Bryant had no rebounds at all in nearly thirty-seven minutes' playing time. He made 19 of 31 shots from the field, 3 of 6 three-pointers, and all 20 of his free-throw attempts, all while allowing teammate Pau Gasol the room to score 31 himself in the 126–117 Lakers victory.

Bryant commented afterward that he had been motivated by the desire to not have to listen to Lee talk trash in the voice-over session the next day. The eighty-eight-minute film aired commercial-free on May 16, 2009, and would stand, in retrospect, as a classic example of Bryant's great desire to control his narrative. His efforts weren't unlike those of the NBA itself, which had evolved from being a casual and friendly press environment, in the 1980s and

1990s, to being a business tightly controlled by its media-relations departments in the new century.

Bryant's command of the media was another gift he shared with Jordan. As with their play itself, Jordan was the master in this regard, Bryant an understudy close on his heels. Both men had a special presence that allowed them to inhabit and master a media scrum much as a prince might master his court. Bryant became quite comfortable in that role during his championship seasons.

"This helped you sometimes when you're trying to write a story," McMenamin offered, "and I guess the line of questioning was something that he could see helping him, so he's going to give you a more robust answer, usually something thoughtful, including some punchy quotes. But it could also hurt you because he could kind of get to that next step before you get there, and if it's not something he really wants to entertain, then he'll try to shut you down on that line of questioning. That for me made it a challenge, but a welcome challenge, in dealing with him."

As he gained the success he had so hungered for, Bryant got to the point that when the press corps circled round him, "he became way more open," McMenamin recalled. "I think he didn't care as much. He thought that, you know, everything's already been said, everything's already been written. It was like, 'I'm Teflon. I have five rings. I'm unassailable when it comes to my legacy, so let's just make this exercise more fun for the next ten minutes. I'll let it all hang out there if you guys let it all hang there, and, you know, let's have this process be entertaining.'"

A select few reporters wouldn't go along, however. Although years had passed, Bryant had kept ESPN's Shelley Smith on the outside, as if she were a reminder, a symbol, of his Colorado troubles. Perhaps it had something to do with the fact that she was a female reporter. Perhaps not. There were other women routinely covering the beat. But if a group of reporters had gathered round him in a scrum and she walked up to join the interview, he would quickly end the session and walk off.

Realizing that her presence was ruining opportunities for her media colleagues to talk to the star, she began sending someone else over with a microphone to record his comments.

At the NBA Finals each year, just about all the interviews were done in large, formal media sessions that were aired on TV. Smith admitted that she and some colleagues got a laugh out of watching Bryant when she asked a question in the press conferences. He had no choice but to respond in that setting.

"I would ask a question, and everyone would love to see what his reaction was," she recalled. "He'd screw up his face and give some perfunctory answer. So it went on like that."

After Tiger Woods "hit the tree," as Smith summed up the moment when the golfer's life came apart after the wreck that led to revelations of his widespread sexual activities, her boss at ESPN sent reporters out across the world of sports to explore the issue. Smith was tasked with asking Bryant about it. She chose to approach a media scrum without a camera crew that night. Things had thawed oh-so-slightly with Bryant, to the point that "he wasn't running away when I came up," Smith recalled.

She mentioned Woods's troubles and asked, "What did you think of Tiger's statement?"

"That's when he ended it," she recalled.

Bryant immediately grew furious and departed the session, walking past Smith, only to stop, turn, point his finger like a pistol at the back of her head, and pretend as though he was squeezing the trigger.

Smith, who had her back turned, did not see the gesture, but several others did, although no one ever reported it in a story.

"It was just one more thing for him to be mad at me about," Smith recalled.

Her boss later apologized for forgetting about her relationship with Kobe.

"I don't have a relationship with Kobe," she replied. "I haven't had one since the trial got dropped. So I was in no jeopardy. It was a fair question."

Bryant's personal life had been generating its own share of press alongside the rise of his professional success. Beyond a good amount of Hollywood gossip, there seemed to be a stream of Internet reports and speculation about Bryant and a variety of females, a group that would come to include a *Playboy* model and one of the Laker Girls, among other figures.

In all fairness to Bryant, this sort of alleged activity was far from exclusive to him. For decades, it had quietly been a defining element of all American professional sports—from baseball and hockey, to football and basketball—just as it had been for rock and rap stars and other music and entertainment-industry figures in a culture that worshipped celebrity. Jordan himself had been identified in many such reports, although it was his good fortune to have completed much of his career before the Internet got cranked up, feeding on rumors, sexual innuendo, and gossip.

The Lakers, of course, had long inhabited a hypersexual environment in Los Angeles. The team's history and character weren't an excuse for Bryant's alleged actions but merely an explanation of the culture and tradition he had come to rule. The sexual assault charge had jolted him out of his experimentation with the role, but the atmosphere around the team had remained an unrelenting temptation.

In the era before Bryant, the team's facilities at the Forum itself became the lair where Magic Johnson would have sex with one or more women in the team's training rooms or sauna just moments after a game. Then, according to routine, he would put on a robe and step out to hold postgame interviews for waiting reporters. "It's difficult to imagine," Garciduenas once admitted, "but Earvin was used to doing anything he wanted. And people loved Earvin so much that nothing he did was wrong. It was never really hidden from anybody, what Earvin did. He was always pretty up-front with it. That was part of him. You had to learn to accept it."

"You would go to the end of the tunnel," recalled the late Joe McDonnell, a longtime reporter covering the team, "and the women would be handing their phone numbers to the ball boy, or Magic would have seen somebody that he liked. 'Bring her in, and bring her in.' Everybody knew what was going on back in the weight room and everything else. The women were just ridiculous. Not only the ones with Buss, but the ones who came to hang around just to try to be part of the scene. We knew. Magic would always help me out in a way. I always knew he was going to be the last guy out of the shower, or wherever he was coming from. He was 99 percent of the time always the last guy to come out and get dressed.

The weight room was used, the sauna room was used. You'd better have been friends with somebody or know somebody if you were gonna try and walk back there because the security there was as great as anywhere else in the country. The way I always looked at it was that was their business. I didn't care. I wished it was me."

"When I first started with the team, it was astounding," Garciduenas remembered. "But it was an existence, a way of life with Earvin. I came to understand Earvin and the way he did things, his love for women. When you're a person of that stature, it's almost expected. All the movie stars get the same attention. It's part of the business."

Ron Carter recalled coming to the team in 1978 and being stunned by the veterans' attitudes and sexual habits. "All the old school guys—these guys were like sex addicts. They were crazy with it. It was there and it was available. Actually, it was a part of the mentality that the veteran players would teach you how to manage the women. Kobe could have used some of that."

As a teen living with his family in Los Angeles, Bryant had been wary of the supposed climate, but like all the other elements of his responsibilities as the leader of the franchise, he had apparently grown used to it. Part of the trouble came with the wives and girl-friends of other Lakers who didn't particularly care for Vanessa Bryant, who was seen as distant and lacking warmth, to the point that one of them admitted to journalist Allison Samuels that she rather enjoyed informing Bryant's wife about his alleged dalliances.

The Last Mind Bender

Bryant celebrated the 2010 championship by taking in soccer's World Cup, in South Africa that summer. In the six seasons since his legal troubles, he had managed to reclaim his role in global sports marketing, measured in part by his jersey sales worldwide. The NBA itself now proudly proclaimed its global reach, citing the fact that 30 percent of all its merchandise sales came from the international market. In Europe, his jersey was the leading seller for the third straight season, demonstrating that he had been able to reclaim the base that Adidas had once built there for him. And in the massive Chinese market, he was also tops, ahead of LeBron James and Dwyane Wade.

After Bryant's flirtation with the soccer crowds that summer, he returned to L.A. to figure out what to do about his splintered index finger and to prepare for another campaign. The upcoming season was imperiled briefly by the request from Jerry and Jim Buss that Phil Jackson take a pay cut in signing a new contract, in the wake of the team's success. It seemed an odd request, but the NBA was steeling itself for another labor lockout in the summer of 2011, and the Lakers seemed insistent on cutting their costs in preparation.

It would later become clear that both the Busses and Bryant had come to believe that the league's other owners were forcing the lockout, in part to counter the large market success of the Lakers. The league's owners wanted a new labor agreement that would supposedly allow the smaller-market teams a better chance to compete against the glitz, glamour, and marketing power of the Lakers. Several years later, Bryant would confirm that this was the team's mind-set in an interview with journalist Chuck Klosterman for *GQ*. "There is only one team like the Lakers," Bryant offered. "Everything that was done with that lockout was to restrict the Lakers' ability to get players and to create a sense of parity, for the San Antonios of the world and the Sacramentos of the world."

Even as the team was asking Jackson for a pay cut from his annual salary of $12 million and preparing a plan for the layoff of many employees during the lockout, the Lakers were in the process of closing what *Forbes* described as "the richest local television rights deal in the NBA," a twenty-year contract with Time Warner Cable that averaged $200 million a year, worth as much as $5 billion over the life of the contract. The deal included the launch of two new regional sports networks, one in English, the other in Spanish.

Jackson consulted with his doctors and pondered the new contract for a few days after the team won the title. With Jerry Buss having given his son Jim the upper hand in the sibling rivalry with Jeanie, it appeared that the only way for Jackson to keep open the possibility of coaching would be to win it all again, if indeed he wanted to keep at it with his health issues and the wear and tear of

NBA travel. He agreed to a new one-year contract and announced that the upcoming season would be his "last stand."

"This year, there's no maybe," he said.

The challenge of pursuing a third straight title was as much mental as physical. Three straight had always been the standard for Jackson's teams. His Bulls had won three straight, then rebuilt to win three more. His Lakers had won three with O'Neal, then fell apart. His fourth iteration of championship-level teams with Bryant had made three straight runs at a title. Could they do the trick once more and earn a third title? Jackson himself was worn down, having suffered through heart, hip, knee, and back ailments and surgeries. "To watch anybody go through physical issues is not easy," Rudy Garciduenas said of Jackson. "You'd see Phil walk in every morning.... He had undergone some physical hardships, and you watched him do it every day."

To accommodate Jackson's pain, the staff had arranged for him to sit in a special elevated chair during games, which had become a symbol of both the gradual breakdown of his body and the royal, distant demeanor opponents around the league attributed to him.

Though Jackson agreed to come back, his relationship with Jerry and Jim Buss remained strained. The summer before his stroke, Tex Winter revealed that Jim Buss had advised Andrew Bynum, who was viewed as Buss's pet of a draft pick, to seek outside coaching because Jackson and his staff weren't viewed as good coaches for big men. Winter viewed the comment as ludicrous and disrespectful, but it increased Bynum's alienation within the team and the view that he was somehow beyond the coaching staff.

"We just always were aware that there was tension," Garciduenas explained.

Beyond the internal issues of the team, Bryant himself faced increasingly difficult challenges with his degenerating knees and began quietly looking around for medical help. The Lakers' fortunes were made more precipitous by the struggles of Metta World Peace in his second season in Los Angeles. He struggled much of the year to find any sort of consistency. Despite his continued knee and shoulder and finger issues, Bryant did his part, appearing in all eighty-two games, making the All-NBA First Team again, as well as the

All-Defensive Team, and once more filling out the stat sheet while averaging 25.3 points, 5.1 rebounds, 4.7 assists, and 1.21 steals.

With Jackson trimming his playing time to 33.9 minutes a game, Bryant's efficiency grew as well, and he still produced the big games he so dearly loved. Twenty-three times during the season he scored better than 30 points, including three games in which he scored better than 40 points. In another sign that his troubled past had receded in the wake of the Lakers' championships, fans worldwide responded by making him the leading vote getter in the All-Star balloting for the second time in his career, and the first time since his Colorado troubles. He rewarded them by gaining his fourth All-Star MVP award with 37 points, 14 rebounds, 3 assists, and 3 steals in the midseason event, held in Los Angeles, before an adoring crowd.

That season, for the seventeenth time in his career, he also recorded a triple-double. In November, he became the youngest player in league history to rack up 26,000 points. By January, he was moving past the 27,000-point milestone, again as the youngest ever to do so, and chugging on up the short list of the game's all-time leading scorers.

The big embarrassment came in April, when he was called for an offensive foul against the Spurs and lashed out by calling official Bennie Adams a "faggot," which resulted in a swift $100,000 fine from the NBA for using homophobic language. Bryant was contrite, but, although he could afford the fine, he appealed it. *Forbes* magazine placed him sixth on its list of top-earning athletes that June, with an annual income of $34.8 million, including $10 million in endorsement earnings and a $24.8-million salary from the Lakers. LeBron James was the other top NBA earner on the list, at nearly $10 million better than Bryant and in third place behind golfers Phil Mickelson and Tiger Woods.

As for the team's fortunes, assistant coach Chuck Person was given the freedom to restructure the Lakers' defense around center Andrew Bynum, even though the club was the reigning two-time NBA champion and seemed to have a defense that already worked quite well. After all, it had last been seen stuffing the Boston Celtics in the second half of Game 7 of the 2010 NBA Finals.

The idea of the new defense, though, was to keep Bynum closer to the basket and to require less mobility from him, perhaps to help him avoid more injury to the knees that had troubled him.

"Everything we do now revolves around him," Person said that spring of the team's defensive approach. "He's the boss." The new defense looked strong enough during stretches late in the regular season as the Lakers closed out another Pacific Division title with a 57–25 record, but it would be exposed at key points during the play-offs.

Facing top-notch point guard Chris Paul and the New Orleans Hornets in the first round, a team the Lakers had beaten four times during the season, Bryant and his teammates lost Game 1 at home for the first time in fifteen years, despite Bryant's 34 points on 13-for-26 shooting. Gasol had struggled, prompting Bryant to chide him, saying, "He's not naturally aggressive."

Bryant insisted on guarding Chris Paul for Game 2, and the Lakers won with balanced scoring and only 11 points from Bryant. The Lakers then won Game 3 in New Orleans, with Bryant scoring 30 and Gasol breaking out of a slump. But Bryant went scoreless in the first half of Game 4 as Chris Paul chugged and juked his way to a triple-double to tie the series. Worse, Bryant sprained his ankle late in the fourth quarter and left the arena on crutches. He reportedly declined either an X-ray or an MRI before Game 5 and helped lead the Lakers to the key win back home. They closed out the series with a good team win in Game 6, in New Orleans, then turned to face the surging Dallas Mavericks. They promptly lost the first two games of the series in Staples Center. In the first game, Bryant and his teammates blew a 16-point lead. In the second, they suffered a tremendous mental breakdown, beginning with the so-named Metta World Peace hitting diminutive Dallas guard J. J. Barea in the closing minutes, which would result in a one-game suspension.

Afterward, Bynum told reporters the Lakers had "trust issues," which served as the prelude to their coming meltdown.

In Game 3, in Dallas, without Metta World Peace, the Lakers played close but lost. In the gap between Games 3 and 4, the team's on-court struggles would be overshadowed by the way the team's front office thoughtlessly notified key long-term employees, including Rudy Garciduenas and Chip Schaefer, that they were being laid off.

Garciduenas said the news came in a letter about insurance issues, a simple notification with no mention of his twenty-seven years of service to the team.

"That's when everything blew up," Schaefer recalled. "It was really rough. I'm not talking anything out of school. It was well documented that they'd made the decision. They didn't want to pay anybody during the lockout. That's what we were told. So the second round of the play-offs between Games 3 and 4 in New Orleans, we were all—the entire coaching staff, the entire sports-medicine staff, was told that when our contracts expired, that we weren't going to get a contract, that during the lockout we weren't going to be paid. That was unorthodox. Virtually every other team in the league paid their employees during the lockout, at least half salaries or something. So we were all kind of terminated."

Some team employees would later be rehired, but neither Garciduenas nor Schaefer nor much of the team's scouting staff would work for the Lakers again.

"To this day no one has ever said this is why that happened," Schaefer said in 2015. "But there's sort of this unspoken knowledge that Jim Buss wanted all vestiges of anybody attached to Phil to be let go. And nobody had more attachment to Phil than me, so that was it for me."

The losses included longtime associate GM Ronnie Lester, a Jerry West protégé who had worked his way up through the scouting ranks of the team. The loss of key employees, whether high ranking or low, would later be viewed as the severing of a crucial tendon of the franchise, eliminating those who connected its past with the present. It would be offered as part of the explanation for its coming decline.

Even after the earthshaking news within the franchise, there was still another game to be played. The 2009 championship had lifted Jackson past the great Red Auerbach for the number of championships won by an NBA coach, and Jackson's children had shown up to celebrate the moment. In 2011, his children showed up after Game 3, for a very different reason.

"They know the end is near," McMenamin recalled. "This is it."

Game 4 would be a blowout, a humbling 122–86 Lakers loss in

which Kobe Bryant would score 17 points on 7 for 18 from the field and 0 for 5 on three-pointers.

"Phil doesn't even walk out of the stadium in Dallas," McMenamin recalled. "I mean, he's carted off, but that's the point where he was. His health was in bad shape."

Bryant, however, had maintained going into that final game that winning the series was still possible—had claimed that he really, truly believed it—which had left McMenamin asking, "Do I really know this guy?

"Maybe he really did," McMenamin said, looking back. "Maybe he really believed that."

Spinning Blood

After the drubbing at the hands of the Mavericks, it would come to light that in Phil Jackson's last season, Bryant, the great practice monster of the NBA, had quietly ceased practicing because his knees were so bad. Months later, Bryant acknowledged the difficulty of the situation. "Kobe did say that he regretted that final season with Phil because he wasn't able to give him his all physically," David McMenamin recalled.

Bryant had been such a force for the Lakers for so long that his absence from practice helped contribute to a strange lack of rhythm on the team.

It was obvious in the play-offs when they struggled with lowly New Orleans. Reporters covering the series began giving each other quizzical looks. Dave McMenamin still kept up hope, thinking that if they had kept pushing in one of those early games in Los Angeles, the Lakers might have somehow forced their way past Dallas and, with their confidence restored, might have then gotten to the championship series. Fans then would have been rewarded with a series between Bryant's Lakers and LeBron James's Miami Heat.

Instead, it had come down to a sad display, one in sharp contrast to the two previous seasons.

The Lakers would move quickly to trade Derek Fisher in the

aftermath of the 2011 failure. Fisher had been a buoy to the team, McMenamin recalled. "Derek was one of the players you'd see on the court when something was going poorly, where he would put his arm around Kobe and gather the other guys at the foul line and be that vocal leader and certainly have Kobe's ear."

Fisher's departure would cut another strand connecting the team to the Jackson era, but it also cut away a key element that allowed Bryant to function in a team. Though the two weren't great friends off the court—Fisher would later reveal that in all his years as Bryant's teammate, he had never even so much as visited Bryant's house—they had a close competitive relationship. At the end of the 2009 season, in the tiny locker room in the old Orlando Arena, Fisher and Bryant had sat together against a wall, somewhat apart from the rest of the team, basking in the championship glow.

As Bryant faced losing his head coach and a teammate who was an important anchor to the Lakers, his career was about to devolve into an array of intriguing and unanswerable questions. Unlike his former coach, however, Bryant had salvaged his relationship with Buss. The two championships Bryant gained after his challenge of Buss had renewed his faith in the aging owner. If the man wanted to leave his team in the hands of questionable son Jim and executive Mitch Kupchak, Bryant saw that as his best path forward, under the circumstances. "They had had their run-in when he demanded a trade before," McMenamin recalled, "but at that point, everything was reverent. All you ever heard from Kobe was 'Dr. Buss'; it was never 'Jerry Buss,' never 'the owner.' It was always 'Dr. Buss.'"

One thing was clear: if he was going to keep playing at a high level, he had to do something about his degenerating knees. With the labor lockout, enforced soon after the close of the 2011 season, Bryant turned to what would become an annual pilgrimage to Germany for an experimental treatment that brought relief. There, under Dr. Hans-Wilhelm Müller-Wohlfahrt, he would undergo Orthokine treatment.

Orthokine, which had yet to be approved in the United States, is a procedure that bears some similarity to Regenokine, a platelet-rich plasma. Orthokine takes blood from a patient's arm, warms it, then spins it to separate the platelets. Those healing platelets were then to be reinjected into the knee. An American health clinic would draw the blood from Bryant and ship it overseas for the process, which took several weeks, at which time Bryant would make a quick fall trip to Germany to be treated.

Orthokine is not illegal; nor does the treatment involve steroids, human growth hormones, or other banned substances. Public figures such as Pope John Paul II and Willie Nelson reportedly have undergone Orthokine.

The treatments had three effects for Bryant. Most important, they apparently resulted in a quick improvement. Second, word of the treatment meant that Bryant would face renewed questions about the effects of the aging process on his game. Third, they cemented his image as a person who would try anything to keep competing. Bryant desperately wanted to win a sixth championship to tie Michael Jordan's number of titles and, if possible, win at least another if not more beyond that.

He returned to the United States to set about the business of playing for new Lakers coach Mike Brown, who had been hired by Jim Buss reportedly because he had worked with Tim Duncan in San Antonio as an assistant coach and with LeBron James in Cleveland as the head coach. Brown had coached James into the NBA Finals in 2007, when the Cavaliers were swept by San Antonio.

Suddenly a ray of light appeared, on the eve of the official ending of the league's five-month labor lockout, as Kupchak and Jim Buss concluded an amazing blockbuster, a three-team trade to bring in point guard Chris Paul, who had advised the New Orleans Hornets that he was going to leave the team the following summer in free agency.

The proposed trade would have sent Paul to the Lakers and Pau Gasol to the Houston Rockets. The Hornets, a team in financial straits, whose operations had been taken over by the NBA itself, were set to receive a substantial lode of talent in return, including Lamar Odom, from the Lakers, and two other very good veteran NBA players, Kevin Martin and Luis Scola, plus exciting young guard Goran Dragić and a 2012 first-round pick that Houston had acquired from the New York Knicks. It was the kind of infusion of talent that certainly could have served New Orleans well going forward.

Chris Paul's presence on the Lakers likewise would have opened vistas for Bryant's final seasons of competition. Paul's ability to both score and distribute the ball might well have altered the career arc of center Andrew Bynum and new coach Mike Brown. It could have made the Lakers quite attractive as a free-agent location. It might even have allowed Bryant a more graceful presence in the game as an aging player and kept the window open for the possibility of another title. It might have altered the image of Jim Buss as an executive going forward.

But none of those things happened because the trade did not happen. Since the league essentially owned the Hornets, NBA commissioner David Stern stepped in within hours of the agreement and nixed the trade in an unprecedented move, amid reports that other NBA owners were furious that the Lakers, a perennial power long considered to have an unfair advantage, were now poised to gain yet another edge. The owners were all gathered in New York for a league board of governors meeting to ratify the new labor agreement. An NBA spokesman quickly denied that the owners themselves had even discussed the Paul deal.

Yet several media outlets were able to obtain an email to Stern from Cleveland Cavaliers owner Dan Gilbert that called the Paul deal "a travesty" and requested that Stern put the deal to a vote of "the 29 owners of the Hornets," which made reference to the league's other owners' essentially also owning the New Orleans franchise.

Rather than do that, Stern simply killed the deal, which had been the result of long hours of work by the executives of the three teams involved.

Would Stern have made such a move if the great and powerful Jerry Buss were not advanced in years and in declining health? That thought merely joined the list of unanswerable questions.

For years to come, Lakers fans would remain furious at the commissioner's unprecedented move and were angered even further when Chris Paul was later dealt to the rival Clippers. Odom, devastated by the idea of leaving the Lakers, was later traded to Dallas. Gasol, who had long been the subject of numerous trade rumors, some of them idiotic, was likewise deeply affected by the turn of events, as were the entire roster and organization of the Lakers.

Perhaps no one, however, was as embittered by Stern's actions as Bryant. He would remain that way for years. "The Lakers pulled off a trade that immediately set us up for a championship, a run of championships later, *and* which saved money," Bryant would tell journalist Chuck Klosterman in 2015. "Now, the NBA vetoed that trade. But the Lakers pulled that shit off, and no one would have thought it was even possible. The trade got vetoed, because they'd just staged the whole lockout to restrict the Lakers."

Meanwhile, the labor deal, designed to foster competitive balance and prevent small-market teams from losing their stars to large-market teams such as the Lakers, was ratified, and the NBA soon reopened for business.

It was hoped that Mike Brown might be able to get through to Andrew Bynum, who had long said that he wanted to be more of a priority on offense. Though Brown was considered a good defensive coach, if somewhat disorganized offensively, in the hiring process, he had touted his experience as an assistant coach with San Antonio's big-guns team, which featured Tim Duncan on offense.

Bryant said little publicly after Brown's hiring, but he did make it clear that he and Pau Gasol would remain the first two options in the Lakers offense.

Bynum "will have to fall in line," Bryant was quoted as saying.

In the midst of this whirlwind of events, as the shortened season was beginning, family conflict again boiled up ferociously, first that December, when Vanessa filed for divorce, citing irreconcilable differences. News reports pointed to her years of suffering the humiliation of gossip about and allegations of his philandering. Due to her insistence that they not arrange a prenup before their wedding, Vanessa now held many of the cards as they separated and began divorce negotiations through their attorneys.

After a number of years of marriage, California law afforded a spouse maximum protection in the courts, and Bryant soon realized he faced quite a heavy sanction as the sole provider in the relationship.

According to one attorney, under state law, Vanessa would be entitled to half the property the two acquired since their marriage; in addition, Bryant would have to pay approximately $365,000 per month in child support for his two daughters and as much as $1 million a month in support for Vanessa. The settlement was going to cost Bryant tens of millions of dollars, perhaps more than $100 million before everything was said and done. After all, in and around 2006, he had founded a series of successful businesses, including an advertising company and a documentary film unit, among others, that could have been counted as part of Vanessa's share.

For some who saw them from the inside, the divorce filing was a profoundly sad moment. "As far as Vanessa goes," McMenamin offered, "I just saw a very loyal wife, someone many years into his career still coming to the games, sitting outside the locker room, waiting for him to finish and get dressed so they could go home together."

For all the Hollywood trappings and all the ups and downs and drama, in many ways their marriage had the markings of a very conservative relationship. She had seemed quite involved in his life, quite supportive and dutiful, despite the fiery elements of her nature.

Bryant's growing realization of his losses, both personal and financial, would mark a sobering year away from his marriage, marked by more rumors of questionable behavior.

Bryant's marital issues were set against a backdrop of a struggling Lakers team with a new coach searching for a new way to play. Mike Brown's answer was to up Bryant's playing time by almost five minutes a game, which was alarming to those who sensed that the situation was rapidly diminishing what was left of his store of competitive moments.

Bryant's path was made even more difficult right from the start. With a season shortened by the lockout, teams played just two exhibition games, and in one of those games, Bryant was going for a rebound.

"He landed very awkwardly," recalled Mark Medina, who covered the Lakers for the *Los Angeles Daily News*, "took a nasty fall and landed on his right wrist, and basically they determined that he fractured it. He had a torn ligament in his wrist, and he didn't have surgery on that, either."

Bryant wore a brace or a cast of Kinesio tape between games, Medina recalled, which added to the array of remedies he employed to get through the short, jam-packed schedule. From a calf-stretch block he used for added protection against knee and ankle injuries, to the tubs of ice water after each game, to the huge ice packs on his knees, to the postgame ice wrap for his right wrist, to efforts to allay the pain in his right index finger, which was now plagued by arthritis, Bryant approached competition as a veritable MASH unit, complete with a numbing injection for the wrist before games. He was able to keep playing with the broken wrist because doctors determined that the bones were not out of alignment.

"It's fair to wonder where all this will take Bryant," wrote Kevin Ding of the *Orange County Register.*

The season had started on Christmas Day, followed by five games in a rush, culminating on New Year's Day, with Bryant shooting 6 for 28 in a loss at Denver, a day that also saw him become the youngest player to reach the 28,000-point milestone.

His playing with a fractured wrist was bound to have some impact on his scoring, Mark Medina recalled. "There were some games where he was not shooting well. Mike Brown was pretty defensive of Kobe's approach, saying that, 'One, he's being aggressive, and for Kobe's standards those are good shots that he would normally make, but he's having this wrist issue.'"

Bryant came out of those shooting issues headlong into a run of strong games. Then, on January 10, he scored 48 to lead a win over Phoenix on 18 of 31 from the floor and followed it up with three more 40-point games in a row, helping to drive his team to six wins in seven contests.

"Against Phoenix he had 48 points on basically a fractured wrist," Medina recalled. "Now obviously, I think the pain and all that was subsiding, but again—a fractured wrist and a torn ligament. And all he did was basically get injections for it."

Early on, Bryant expressed support for Mike Brown, but problems soon arose.

"Everyone said he's a great guy, well prepared," Dave McMenamin recalled of Brown's tenure. "I don't think he read the room very well."

Whereas Phil Jackson had spent good effort trying to preserve Bryant, Brown grew to rely on him more and more. "It was just a stark difference," McMenamin recalled. "Phil was the type where it was a less-is-more approach. They're not having long shoot-arounds. In fact, they're never practicing after a back-to-back. You know, as the season wore on, Phil wouldn't keep them on the court for more than forty-five minutes. Mike wasn't that way. Mike would run, you know, two-and-a-half-hour practices. I think right there he lost the team pretty early on."

The players seemed to turn more to the assistant coaches, and Bryant turned back to the triangle in practices late in the season.

"It wasn't what Mike wanted to run," McMenamin recalled, "probably in part just to distance himself from Phil, because he was in a tough situation, being the guy to take over for Phil."

The team's veterans, especially Gasol, were comfortable with the triangle. They went 8–4 over the last dozen games heading into the play-offs. Bryant had crammed much into a short schedule. He was again named a player on the All-NBA First Team as well as a starter in the All-Star Game. He averaged 27.9 points (second in the league), 5.4 rebounds, 4.6 assists, 1.19 steals, and 0.31 blocks in an eye-popping 38.5 minutes a game. In twenty-four games he scored better than 30 points, including five games with better than 40. He had become the franchise all-time leader in field goals and free throws made, and by March had reached the 29,000-point milestone. It was on a trip back home to Philadelphia in February that he moved into fifth place on the league's all-time scoring list.

He finally missed seven games in April, with tenosynovitis of the left shin. For the play-offs, he would up his playing time to 39.7 minutes a game and his scoring to 30 points a game as the Lakers took on Denver in the first round, a seven-game series that included his 43-point effort when the Lakers lost Game 5. He helped lead them to a Game 7 win to advance to the second round, where they exited for the second year in a row, this time against Oklahoma City. They lost in five games, despite his 42 points on 18 of 33 from the field in the close-out game.

"I'm not fading into the shadows, if that's what you're asking," Bryant replied after the game, to a question about the Lakers' future. "I'm not going anywhere. We're not going anywhere."

Endgame

Putting another disappointing season behind him, Bryant threw his effort again into Team USA, this time for the 2012 Olympics, in London. His role was different this time around, and he deferred the scoring load to teammates LeBron James, Carmelo Anthony, and Kevin Durant. In the first five games, Bryant averaged just 9.4 points on 38.9 percent shooting.

He punctuated that with an outburst, scoring 20 second-half points in a win over Australia, hitting 4 three-pointers in a sixty-six-second flurry. In Team USA's semifinal win against Argentina, he scored 13, and in the tight gold-medal victory over Spain, he contributed 17.

"He was still on the team," J. A. Adande recalled, "but you could start to see the signs that he wasn't the best player anymore. In 2008, you could still make a strong case that he was the best player, even better than LeBron. In the gold-medal game, who was the guy that they went to? They went to Kobe Bryant. In 2012, LeBron was better than him, Durant was better than him, Carmelo was playing better than him. You know, he wasn't the guy anymore."

Instead, he became the designated trash talker, fueling a running debate over which Team USA edition was better, the 2012 team or the original Dream Team in 1992, led by Jordan, Magic Johnson, and Charles Barkley.

"He was the guy when the raging Dream Team debate was going on," Adande recalled. "I don't even know how it got started, because it was a stupid question to ask, but as it raged along, Kobe was the guy talking back and speaking up on his team's behalf. I asked him about it at an Olympic team event in Las Vegas. He was unafraid to go back at Michael. Michael had called him out, and he went back at him. I thought, 'Man, you're not afraid.'

"He said, 'Michael knows I'm a bad motherfucker.'"

Bryant mostly treated his second Olympic appearance as a farewell tour. Afterward, he gave Pau Gasol, who was again playing for the Spaniards, a big hug and had more of the same for coach Mike Krzyzewski. Then he confirmed for NBC Sports' Craig Sager that this would be his last Olympics.

He was surprisingly optimistic upon his return to Los Angeles, despite the fact that his Lakers had spent the past two seasons making early play-off exits. The reason for much of that optimism was the team's off-season acquisitions of center Dwight Howard and former league MVP Steve Nash. The fan base was quite excited as well, although both players had serious back issues and Nash was thirty-eight.

Bryant began thinking that he might be able to knock down another championship or two with the upgrade. Even so, in a quiet moment, he would concede that he had given thought to retiring after his two-year, $58-million contract expired, following the 2013–14 season.

In addition to bringing the new talent on board, early in the 2012–13 season, the Lakers fired Mike Brown. Jim Buss and GM Mitch Kupchak then engaged Jackson about returning once more to the franchise, leading Lakers fans and the media to believe that Jackson was about to become coach again.

"That was such a bizarre night because I had gone to the game," J. A. Adande recalled. "It was a Sunday night. I wrote my column on Phil Jackson, what a great fit he was going to be, because all signs were pointing toward Phil. Like, the last conversation I had had with somebody from Phil's camp on my way to the game was that, 'Yeah, we're just waiting for a few details. It's looking good.' Kobe was talking after the game. He was very confident that Phil was going to be the coach. I mean, he was already talking like it was a done deal. I wrote my column, I sent it in. I get home. I checked Twitter, and I had a Twitter from Mike Bresnahan of the *L.A. Times* that Mike D'Antoni is the new Lakers coach, not Phil. I called and I got confirmation, and lo and behold, Mike D'Antoni was the coach."

Apparently, while Jackson was contemplating their offer, the Lakers abruptly hired former Phoenix Suns and New York Knicks coach Mike D'Antoni, informing Jackson about the switch in a late-night phone call. It was a strange, hasty move. At the time, D'Antoni was coming out of knee-replacement surgery and was so debilitated that he couldn't even make it to Los Angeles until several days after his hiring.

"The thing is, what was the rush to do it when he couldn't even come out for the press conference?" J. A. Adande said, looking back. "They had to wait, like, three days for the press conference because he was laid up in New York, where he'd just had his knee replaced. Like, why hire a coach who couldn't even have a press conference and who couldn't even coach the first three games because he was coming back from knee surgery? What was the rush? Who was going to scoop him up before you got to him? It just showed lack of foresight on the franchise's part."

The timing made it seem as if Jim Buss and Kupchak had purposely pulled the rug on Jackson and, by extension, Buss's sister Jeanie. Perhaps they were simply clumsy. Either way, it was a terrible way to handle a sensitive, important matter.

With Jerry Buss terminally ill, Jim Buss later suggested that he made the decision based on the wishes of his dying father.

Predictably, Jeanie Buss was so angry over the move that when D'Antoni finally got to Los Angeles, Mitch Kupchak told him he wouldn't even bother to take him down to the team president's office for an introduction. In Jeanie's defense, she was struggling with her father's illness. As she spent as much time with him as possible, she was already filled with the anger and exhaustion from that experience.

During the two seasons he coached the Lakers, D'Antoni never met Jeanie Buss—not beyond once sort of trying to acknowledge her with a wave in a restaurant.

D'Antoni faced many obstacles with the Lakers when he was hired, but he got a hint of the one element that would hold the entire enterprise together. That December, Bryant became only the fifth and the youngest player in NBA history to rack up 30,000 points. Later that month, on December 11, he scored 42 points in a loss at Cleveland on 16 of 28 shooting from the floor. The Lakers next had to go to Madison Square Garden, the scene of D'Antoni's long frustration with another damaged franchise, the Knicks. Bryant was in tremendous pain. "He had a bad back," D'Antoni recalled. "He couldn't even walk. I've had bad backs, and they're not fun. God, he couldn't walk and he's in the locker room and he's trying, he's got his legs up. I'm thinking, 'No way he can play this game,' and then he comes out playing. I couldn't even hardly take him out that game."

"Kobe, you've got to come out," the team's new coach told him.

"I can't," Bryant replied, "because if I come out, my back will stiffen up, and then I really can't play."

D'Antoni then began using the only response that seemed to work with Bryant. "OK," the coach said.

"He played through it," the coach recalled of Bryant's forty-four minutes in a 9-point loss, as the team's early record teetered between success and failure. Bryant was obviously aware of Jerry Buss's condition, aware that the owner might somehow be watching. But the moment was really no deviation from his approach over the years.

"Unbelievable," D'Antoni said of getting to know his new star up close. "I mean, I'm looking at him and saying, 'How does he do this?'"

The period proved a dizzying time for both the team and Bryant. The night before the Knicks loss, on that December road trip, Bryant and Vanessa were seen together at the 12-12-12 Hurricane Sandy relief concert at Madison Square Garden. On New Year's Eve, they were together again. In January, they conceded the obvious: they'd put aside their divorce. "We are pleased to announce that we have reconciled. Our divorce action will be dismissed," Vanessa posted on her Instagram page. "We are looking forward to our future together."

The message was signed, "Kobe & Vanessa."

Bryant confirmed the news on his Facebook page.

The Hollywood-media take on the decision to end the divorce was that both were incurable loners who had found a level of comfort with each other. After all, they were both good Catholic kids when they got married, and divorce was problematic in their faith. The financial settlement for Vanessa looked great to outsiders, but what she seemed to want most was to continue to be Mrs. Kobe Bryant. In one satisfying sense for many observers, Bryant was finally called to task for his own insistence on refusing a prenup. But the moment and the relationship were far too complicated for any one simple answer. The star himself was going through so many things with his team and in his life, he apparently longed for companionship from the woman he called "Mamacita" around the house.

Chip Schaefer had long maintained from his experience working with Bryant that, despite all his ambition and drive, the basketball star found nothing more important than his two daughters. The children were the priority for which he would skip a workout, Schaefer recalled. "Those girls meant everything to him."

Whatever the motivation for the reconciliation, Bryant had long encountered self-destruction in life, and by age thirty-four, he had learned to back away and move toward centering his approach. In a life filled with focus on competitive titles and glory, he was perhaps learning once more that there were other important things to be won.

That February of 2013 brought the loss of Jerry Buss, consumed after months of battling cancer. Bryant spoke at the memorial service at the Nokia Theater along with several others, including Jerry West, Phil Jackson, Kareem Abdul-Jabbar, and Magic Johnson.

Bryant told the throng that winning had been the driving force between the two of them. "He explained that he learned to trust from Jerry Buss," Mark Medina recalled. "And he talked specifically of when the team wanted to hire Phil back in 2005 and he was skeptical of that. Jerry just kept telling him to trust him."

Bryant spoke as well of his conflict with Buss in 2007 and said that he also learned to trust the owner then. "What he learned," Medina recalled, "is that when you trust in Jerry Buss, things tend to work out."

Bryant observed that the trust was based on the inescapable fact that Buss knew what he was doing, Medina explained. "So the key was to have trust in the organization because of the foundation he had laid it on."

The moment helped to explain much about Bryant's approach over the final seasons of his career. His ambition and desire to win were still burning, and some observers had expected that as the Lakers' fortunes turned worse and his yearning for another championship surged, he might attempt to move to a team more suited to compete for a title. But Bryant began asserting through it all that he was a Laker for life.

Despite much fan consternation and their own sibling rivalry, the Buss children would return that loyalty to Bryant, as difficult as the process would be at times over the coming seasons. In an era largely absent of such loyalty, their mutual exchange proved remarkable, despite the team's struggles and public-relations nightmare they would bring.

In his comments at the memorial service, Bryant also seemed to be directing a message at his coaches and teammates. They had all gotten off to a rough start together. Mike D'Antoni was portrayed in the media as having an excellent relationship with Bryant, due to the fact that the coach had been a star for years in the Italian league, but the two men hardly knew each other and rarely spoke.

Basketball-wise, D'Antoni's hiring had been flawed from the start. D'Antoni, known for his Steve Nash–led Seven Seconds or Less offensive philosophy, was a genuinely good guy and a brilliant basketball mind but mostly an avant-garde, up-tempo offensive scientist, one whose theories would have substantial influence on the emergence of the great Golden State Warriors team, led by Stephen Curry, that emerged in 2015 and ignited a long-brewing small ball basketball revolution.

An early proponent of the pace-and-space craze that soon took the NBA by storm, D'Antoni had been a pioneer of the logic of greater use of the three-pointer, especially as shooting success neared 40 percent. He was admittedly not all that interested in post play—and that didn't seem to mesh at the time with the Lakers, a team built around a strong post player in Gasol. Likewise, D'Antoni was not seen as a strong defensive mind.

Soon a dynamic would develop among D'Antoni's Lakers. Bryant would pass the coach in the hallway and not speak, a silence that went beyond his normal aloof manner. Gasol had struggled mightily in D'Antoni's system, and Bryant appeared angry over how his championship teammate was being treated. "The perspective with that was that Mike had come in with that reputation that he doesn't believe in post play, he doesn't devote enough attention to defense," Mark Medina explained.

Even worse was Bryant's relationship with Dwight Howard, long known around the league as a physical specimen and a strong rebounder but also a goofball and something of a prima donna. D'Antoni liked Howard, perhaps because he had little post game but could be a monster setting screens and could score rolling to the basket, which provided him a head start on a dunk.

But few of D'Antoni's ideas had an early impact. Nash was mostly injured, and Howard was struggling to deal with his bad back while working his way into form. It was obvious that his effort and approach displeased the ever-impatient Bryant.

Feeling the disrespect, Howard in turn clearly took to mocking Bryant on occasion—not a wise choice, given the star's history with a similar approach from O'Neal. With all the key stars working through the limitations imposed by their injuries while dealing with the big expectations of the fan base, D'Antoni soon found himself confronted with foul team chemistry.

The word was that D'Antoni had been hired based on Dr. Buss's articulated wish to see the revival of a Showtime-style running game. Like many fans, Magic Johnson had been infuriated by the switcheroo that seemed to disrespect Phil Jackson, and when the coach mentioned Showtime in his early comments, the Lakers legend pounced on the very idea, totally dismissing it.

"They didn't want any part of it," Mike D'Antoni said in 2015. "I didn't realize it. I don't know why, but, yeah, I think they wanted a Laker guy, and I wasn't a Laker guy. I don't think it was me, personally. I don't think it was anybody other than they kind of wanted that in there. It was tough from the beginning."

D'Antoni offered that the difference in philosophy might have been overcome with one good, healthy point guard. Nash had been a great point guard but was rarely healthy with the Lakers, at his advanced age. Backup Steve Blake likewise struggled with injuries as the new coaching regime tried to get things together at midseason, and it didn't help that D'Antoni was fighting through his own recovery from his knee-replacement surgery.

"Both Steve Blake and Steve Nash weren't available for about a month," the coach explained. "That was huge. That's huge in a way that my teams have always been kind of point-guard dominant, and you know they have to run the show, and we were really void on it. We tried different things until we eventually got Blake. When we did get Steve Blake healthy, you know, finally, that's when things turned around. If we could have gotten Nash healthy, I think we would have made a good run for it."

Actually, they did, despite the circumstances. "It had a lot to do with Kobe's individual will," D'Antoni explained, "because I don't think we ever came together as a team and never really flowed easily. There was a lot of talent and Kobe's insistence of just playing every minute and playing hard as hell. I mean, he got us in the play-offs, and, you know, you would have to tip your hat to him. It wasn't fun for anybody because it was a struggle. Every game was a struggle. Every practice was a struggle. Every chemistry issue was a struggle."

Once the season—and in many ways the viability of Bryant's competitive career—came to a close, D'Antoni fell under criticism for not managing his star better, but there was little way to hold Bryant back from the challenge, the coach explained. "He was adamant. I talked to him. Mitch talked to him. You know Kobe is tops. He's just got that spirit. He just thought that's what the team had to have. Maybe they did have to have that. I don't know, but there was no holding him back. After every game you keep asking Kobe, 'You can't do this. How do you feel?' He feels great. You go to the next game. 'Kobe, we've got to do things different.'"

During games, D'Antoni would ask, "You going to come out?"

"No, coach, I'm not coming out," Bryant would reply.

Faced with the roster issues, D'Antoni wouldn't argue.

"I'd say, 'OK,'" the coach recalled. "That's Kobe. He was hell-bent and determined to get us to the play-offs and showing everybody what he could do, and his body was broke down."

In the process, the team mysteriously came alive, despite lacking chemistry and health and even much in the way of conversation. D'Antoni said it was all due to Kobe Bryant's vast, unbreakable will. The turnaround seemed to be fueled by a team meeting after a loss in Memphis on January 23, although emotional factors, such as the death of Jerry Buss, added some impetus.

The Lakers rolled through a 28–12 finish that spring that took them right into the play-off mix. As usual, Bryant had big moments sprinkled across the season. He fueled the resurgence with 14 points, 9 rebounds, and a season-high 14 assists in late January against Utah. Then he did it again two nights later against Oklahoma City, with another 14 assists, 21 points, and 9 rebounds. He settled into a less-is-more stretch as the Lakers won seven of nine games, then erupted a month later for 40 points on 14-of-23 shooting in a win over Portland on February 22. Sensing that the team needed more, he upped his scoring; then, as February became March, he scored 34 points with a game-winning layup against Atlanta; then, a few nights later, he scored 42 points with 12 assists and 7 rebounds in a win at New Orleans, with another 41 two nights later.

Despite missing two games in mid-March with a badly sprained ankle, he pressed on to the end of the month, when he had another 14 assists with 9 rebounds while scoring 19 points in a win at Sacramento. That night, he passed the great Wilt Chamberlain, who had scored 31,419 points over his NBA career. Bryant was now fourth on the league's all-time scoring list, with Jordan himself ahead in the distance.

He then recorded his nineteenth career triple-double, with 23 points, 11 rebounds, and 11 assists, on April 2 against Dallas and followed it up eight days later with a season-high 47 points. He made 14 of 27 from the floor and all 18 of his free throws, with 8 rebounds, 5 assists, 3 steals, and 4 blocked shots in a win at Portland. He played all forty-eight minutes that night to get the win, and during the previous five games, as he drove the team to four wins against a loss, he had played forty-seven, forty-seven, forty-two, forty-seven, and forty-one, a brutal display of determination.

Two nights later, while getting a win over Golden State in Staples Center, he had already run up forty-four minutes and fifty-four seconds of play when it all came to an end at the elbow of the lane. As he pushed off to the left against the Warriors' Harrison Barnes, the Achilles snapped and Bryant drew the foul.

Pau Gasol said he had seen many things out of his teammate over the years but nothing like what happened next, as Bryant, racked with pain and agony, insisted on taking the free throws, then walked off the floor under his own power.

As much as D'Antoni and Bryant failed to connect, the coach

had been transfixed down the stretch of the season and never more so than when witnessing what in essence could be seen as the end of Bryant's career. "The fact that he went back out on that floor with a torn Achilles and walked...walked up there and sank two foul shots and walked off," D'Antoni said in 2015, "I mean, most people would have to be carted away in an ambulance, but, you know, he walked up there and made the two foul shots. I mean, the guy was unbelievable."

In the season, he had appeared in seventy-eight games and finished third in the league in scoring at 27.3 points, with 5.6 rebounds, 6 assists, and 1.36 steals, all in 38.6 minutes a game. He had compiled 2 triple-doubles and 16 double-doubles over his determined drive to put his team in the play-offs. Thirty-five times he had better than 30 points, in eight games topping 40 points. The fans had rewarded this effort by making him tops in All-Star votes for the third time in his career. He had passed Magic Johnson as the team's all-time leader in steals.

On the night he tore his Achilles, he shed tears while talking to reporters in the locker room and vowed to return from the devastating injury for the next season.

The Lakers won the final two regular-season games without him, and, as Mark Medina pointed out, there was a sense that Bryant's absence provided the opportunity for Dwight Howard to show what he could become for the franchise.

ESPN broadcaster Stephen A. Smith would later tell a story that Shaquille O'Neal was at a Lakers game when Bryant summoned him to the locker room during the game to confess that it wasn't until he played with other centers that he came to realize he had failed to recognize O'Neal's greatness, that he regretted his failure had cost them the opportunity to win more championships.

"Shaq came to a game," J. A. Adande recalled, "and he and Kobe kind of shared a moment. I think they both realized it. You would hear it from Kobe. Kobe got mad at me for writing a column in which all I did was mention Andrew Bynum in the same paragraph as Shaq. Kobe kind of took it to the extreme. He was like, 'Don't you ever mention Bynum in the same sentence as him.' I went back and reread it. I said, 'It wasn't in the same sentence. It was the same paragraph.' Kobe was like, 'Even the same paragraph. You can't compare those two.' So Kobe started having more complimentary things to say about Shaq, and Shaq started to be a little more conciliatory toward Kobe."

Adande, who had been far closer with O'Neal than Bryant, had first noticed a change in the relationship in 2011, at O'Neal's retirement press conference, held at his home in Orlando. The NBA Finals were being played in Miami that year, and Adande drove up from South Florida to hear what O'Neal had to say.

"When I asked Shaq the question, I think he had a sense of where I was going," Adande recalled, "but he still kind of took it unprompted and started talking about how he wished he and Kobe could have been on better terms, that that was kind of one of the regrets of his career. He said a lot of it was marketing. He said they kind of played it up, or at least he played it up because he knew it garnered interest and people loved talking about the Laker drama with Kobe and Shaq."

Drama and conflict were always high on the media's list of news values, but it had been especially so with Bryant and O'Neal. Now Bryant was in conflict with yet another center, even as he hobbled around with injury.

The Lakers faced the San Antonio Spurs in the first round that spring. Howard did not play well, and soon the Lakers were on their way to getting swept. Howard was ejected in the third quarter of Game 4.

"There was a real strong feeling of, this could be Dwight's last game as a Laker," Mark Medina recalled. "The fans were booing him when he got ejected. His teammates were supporting him publicly, but there was a feeling that he kind of left them out to dry by getting ejected so early in the second half. He had shared some words with Mitch Kupchak on his way to the players' tunnel. I don't know what he said, but they didn't seem to be very friendly. Then the symbolism could not have been greater. I don't know for a fact that this was intentional or a mere coincidence, but after Dwight was ejected, a few moments after that, Kobe comes out on the floor at Staples Center on crutches to sit behind the bench. The entire arena goes wild, giving him a standing ovation. He's hugging Pau and lending moral support. The symbolism spoke for itself where

here's Dwight not being able to handle the adversity of that game and gets ejected, and then Kobe comes out as the long-loved Laker to show that he's still fighting for them, even on the sideline, on crutches."

With the season over, and facing a difficult rehabilitation after surgery, Bryant would soon turn his attention to another personal matter—his mother had released his cherished personal memorabilia to a New Jersey auction house for sale to the highest bidders. The Bryants had earned a reported half million dollars from the sale, and family friends said they held the sale only because Bryant had provided them little support over the years. Parents and son had reconciled off and on over the years, when Bryant's father coached for the Los Angeles Sparks WNBA team and especially during Kobe's later championships. After that, however, Joe was again taking obscure coaching jobs in Asia while Pam kept a base in their modest home in Las Vegas. Bryant's two sisters also maintained their separate lives in Nevada. In the legal fight over the memorabilia, his grandmother Cox came quickly to Pam's aid and verified her account that Kobe had given his parents the memorabilia. His sister Sharia, however, took her brother's side in the debate, and soon enough Bryant won back his cherished jerseys and medals and whatnot.

Old friends from Philadelphia had been aghast at Bryant attacking his mother on Twitter and at the ugliness of the battle.

"From what I hear, I'm afraid the relationship is irreparably broken," said Gregg Downer, Bryant's old coach.

Rupture had become a constant refrain in Kobe Bryant's life, which meant that mending was, too. And rehab. And recovery. He embraced them all.

Epilogue

That summer after the ruptured Achilles and subsequent surgery, his life became all about the romance tale of the scar on his heel. To Bryant, it seemed almost a metaphor for all the things he had faced in his life and for all his determination and work to overcome them.

And the horrific grind of coming back from such an injury, all the rehab and rebuilding of his game? Just another part of the romance.

He had always been happy to let you know that he reveled in the work. It had always been his particular mind game, that he was going to outwork you and there was nothing you could do about it because you couldn't possibly outwork him. Now he turned that mind game on himself. Where doubt would have consumed most elite athletes at his age, his belief ballooned. That had always been his behemoth—belief. Now it expanded to dirigible size, blocking out the light as he healed and lost himself in the gym.

Dwight Howard, meanwhile, was in free agency, and re-signing him was a priority for a desperate Lakers franchise clearly hemmed in by the NBA's new collective bargaining agreement and Stern's nixing of the Paul trade. Overnight, it seemed, things had changed for the franchise considered too cool for school, a team that— bolstered by Jerry Buss's presence and sense of trust with players, along with the Hollywood climate and the women—had always been a virtual magnet for free agents. As Ron Carter once explained, when you became a Laker, you became handsomer, you were paraded about before Hollywood's stars every game night. Suddenly that atmosphere had evaporated. The Busses and Kupchak were rightfully concerned about losing Howard because talent would now be much harder for the team to come by—they were so concerned that the Lakers put up billboards around Los Angeles that seemed to be pleading for Dwight Howard to stay. The Lakers could pay him millions more than any other team, but the billboards illustrated a sense of panic that prevailed within the NBA's once-haughty franchise.

Meanwhile, Bryant's attitude toward Howard seemed to be, "Fuck him. I ain't kissing his goofy ass. Let him go."

Go he did, sacrificing millions to leave the Lakers for the Houston Rockets. It only added fuel to the fire that Bryant's game, his demands on his teammates for excellence, and his attitude were all repellents for free agents.

Jordan had been every bit as demanding of his teammates and, as Tex Winter once explained, far harsher than Bryant had ever been, and that had never deterred Chicago from finding the players it needed to fit around him. But the league had changed, the game had changed, the money had changed. And it was certainly true that in the years after his last run of championship basketball, Bryant had become absolutely synonymous with the franchise. In many ways, J. A. Adande observed, Kobe Bryant was the last Laker. He would tell Bryant that eventually. All the iconic figures had departed. Magic Johnson had sold his minority share of ownership, Jerry West had left in 2000, and broadcaster Chick Hearn had died, in 2002, followed by Buss, in 2013.

Bryant was the last, left to fight furiously against age and injury, in a new era, when the league seemed to be suddenly populated with very young players. It was an era he had ushered in, one in which teams were eager to embrace younger, rawer, cheaper talent. In many ways, the NBA had become a constant process of speculation on youth. Now Bryant and Kevin Garnett were ancient figureheads of the movement, still fighting to stay in the game.

Bryant vowed to be back in six months, by the start of training camp. Team officials, including Jeanie Buss, wanted him to take a full year to recover. He would have none of it. He didn't make it back for training camp. That would have been absurd. No one could have recovered from an Achilles tear in that time. Still, he managed to make his debut on December 8, 2013, against Toronto. He finished with 9 points, 8 rebounds, 4 assists, and 2 steals, playing point guard in D'Antoni's system. His return lasted six games, until he fractured his knee on December 20. Sisyphus had pushed the huge stone to the top of the hill, only to watch it quickly roll back down again.

It was a new injury, a new rehab schedule to embrace, to be attacked with Bryant's same old determination. Out of respect for his astonishing body of work, fans across the world voted him into the All-Star Game as a starter that February, the kind of respect that fanned his flame. Bryant knew he had supporters out there, everywhere. They had erected a statue of him in China. Over the many years, he still had so many detractors, legions of people who sneered at the mere mention of his name, but there were millions upon millions who had locked in on his great passion. He knew the faithful were there. They spoke to him at every turn.

As did Jordan's presence ahead in the distance, well within reach on the all-time scoring list, his idol, right there to pass, just as he was that last night they had played against each other in the spring of 2003 in Los Angeles, when Bryant had run around scoring points like Road Runner and the great Jordan could only watch. So Bryant fell again into the romance of the rehab.

He returned from the knee injury the following season, on opening night, October 28, 2014, against Houston. Just by stepping onto the floor, he tied a record belonging to another of his old nemeses, Utah's John Stockton, for the most seasons by an NBA player with one team.

D'Antoni was gone, having walked away in the off-season, and Bryant's old friend Byron Scott was the coach. Bolstered by his experience with Bryant and the star's mounting injury record, Scott stood up a little better to Bryant's insistence on playing. Though he averaged only 34.5 minutes per game, he had some impressive moments in his brief time on the court. Bryant made a statement against Golden State, the team that had seen him go down with the Achilles, scoring 44 against them on November 16, making him just one of four players to score 44 or more points in a game after age thirty-six.

On November 30, against Toronto, he had run up 31 points, 11 rebounds, and 12 assists, to reach 6,000 assists in his career—he was now the only player in NBA history to compile better than 30,000 points and 6,000 assists. He seemed to have gained a new liking for that notion and in mid-January passed out a career-high 17 assists against Cleveland.

The highest scoring average by a player in his nineteenth season had been Kareem's 14.6 points per game, and Bryant easily eclipsed that mark, averaging 22.3 points, 5.7 rebounds, 5.6 assists, and 1.34 steals at age thirty-six, a time when most guards had long gone home to bed.

The most important target on his list fell away at Minnesota on December, 14, 2014, at the 5:24 mark of the second quarter. Bryant hit a free throw for the 32,293rd point of his career, which meant that he had finally eclipsed MJ, to move into third place on the NBA's all-time career scoring list. Vanessa and the girls were there with a huge spray of balloons. Yes, the points were gigantic, but having his family together and there to share in the accomplishment, despite all the mistakes he had made, seemed most remarkable.

The moment brought to mind Bryant's statement upon their reconciliation. "I am happy to say that Vanessa and I are moving on with our lives together as a family," he wrote. "When the show ends and the music stops, the journey is made beautiful by having that someone to share it with. Thank you all for your support and prayers!"

The glory of passing Jordan was the last important moment on the court that season, as Bryant suffered a rotator cuff tear on January 21. The rotator cuff surgery meant that he had once more shoved the great stone to the top of the mountain, only to see it roll away again. His old friend rehab was back, and he embraced it as he had before, with the goal of being there for the start of the 2015–16 season, his twentieth in the NBA.

Recovery

ESPN's Shelley Smith faced her own battles at the time, with the announcement in the fall of 2014 that she had breast cancer, which brought its harsh treatments and the usual loss of hair. She had bravely gone to work, showing that bald was truly beautiful. As she had explained, her relationship with Bryant had "just continued to fester" over the years after the disastrous Tiger Woods question.

In a recent season, she had covered the All-Star Game for ESPN Radio, and the broadcast giant switched her to cover the East locker room rather than the West, where she might have had to deal with Bryant. No one wanted the embarrassment that that might have caused in a key on-air moment.

Still, she had to do interviews, and Tim Frank, one of the NBA's most capable and personable media-relations veterans, went to Bryant and asked him to do an interview with Smith.

"He refused to do it," she recalled.

In another circumstance during the play-offs, she had needed a quick interview afterward for game coverage. Footage from the moment showed longtime Lakers PR man John Black going to Bryant and asking him to do the interview.

"You can see it on tape," Smith recalled, "John Black going over to Kobe and saying, 'I need you to do ESPN with Shelley,' and you can hear him say, 'Aw, hell, no!'"

"That was the last time we tried," she said, "and I was not going to apologize. I didn't do anything wrong."

She had spoken to her bosses about the Tiger Woods question. They had reviewed it and agreed that she had done nothing wrong in asking an obvious question. Although Smith never discussed it, in many ways the Woods comparison with Bryant was fascinating. Both were athletes at the top of their game who suffered a massive falling-out of fan support over a sex scandal. But, while the golfer's issues had brought him down both in the public eye and in competition, Bryant managed to survive and then regain his status within his sport. It was another testament to Bryant's ability to will himself through his problems.

Bryant and Smith had spent more than a decade in a cold standoff. "I hoped that things would have gotten better and moved on," she said, "but I never apologized, he never apologized."

After missing time with her illness, she had returned to work in April of 2015, as Bryant was working hard to rehab his shoulder. That fall, upon his return, ESPN asked her to make yet another attempt to interview Bryant, almost as if someone at the network was fascinated by the standoff, as if someone wanted to chip through Bryant's carefully crafted exterior to see how he would respond.

"I didn't want to do the interview," she admitted, "because I didn't want to risk the fact of not getting him. The viewers had a right to hear from him, and if he wasn't going to talk to me, then we'd have somebody else do it."

"I think the time is now," Shari Greenberg, one of her producers, told Smith. "I think he's mellowed, you being sick."

"I just don't want to risk it," Smith replied.

"It wasn't that I was afraid," Smith recalled. After all she had been through fighting cancer, she simply didn't need the rejection yet again.

"I really want you to do this," Greenberg told her.

Finally Smith relented and agreed to approach Bryant off camera first. Smith made the interview request through Alison Bogli, another of the Lakers' media-relations employees. Bogli came out of the Lakers locker room and said Bryant had agreed to do the interview.

"With me?" Smith asked. "Does he recognize me? Does he know? My hair's really short now. Does he think it's someone else?"

Bogli assured her that Bryant knew.

He emerged from the locker room and offered Smith his hand.

"You'll do this with me?" she asked. "Come here," he said, breaking into a smile, "and give me a hug."

"I couldn't have been more shocked," Smith recalled. "Honestly, I didn't think I'd see that in my lifetime."

Smith hugged Bryant and said, "I've missed talking to you. I'm glad we're mending this fence."

Bryant replied quietly that there were a lot more important things in their lives than their feud.

They sat then for the interview.

"I'm glad you're healthy," Bryant told her.

"I'm glad you're healthy," Smith answered.

"Your hair looks great," he said of the strawberry-blond growth emerging in the wake of the cancer treatments.

Smith then inquired about his girls.

"It was like we were catching up over ten years," she said. "It was kind of surreal—like, ten years had gone by, and nothing had happened between us. He gave me a great interview. One of the best I've ever had from him. People from ESPN were emailing me, saying how comfortable he was."

She had asked him what he had learned most about himself over the ten years, saying that it had been a long time. By then, the emotion of the moment had almost overcome Smith.

"I was almost in tears," she said, "not for anything other than I was glad it was over. It was awkward having to avoid him. I didn't want to be the story.

"I think he became not so protective but just really scared," Smith said of the Colorado incident. "He didn't trust anybody. He had a reason to be scared."

Bryant himself would look back on the rape charges and admit that he was frightened, absolutely terrified of going to prison for decades. It was an important moment for Bryant, the man whose supreme confidence had made him one of the most decorated professional athletes of all time. He was *scared*. It suggested that somewhere underneath the aloof exterior and the seemingly limitless determination to achieve greatness at any cost, there resided a very real human being.

So Bryant yet again returned to the NBA after all his injuries. He did so with his five championship rings in tow, as well as a tractor-trailer load of questions about his ability to pull off remaining a credible NBA player at age thirty-seven, with years of wear and tear on his wheels.

Charley Rosen offered that all the years of extreme workouts had taken their toll on Bryant, and, combined with the Achilles tear, that would reveal a star bereft of his tremendous athleticism and his ability to rise up and clear his way for the remarkable shots that had defined his attack.

Charles Barkley, the TV analyst, suggested that Bryant and the Lakers wouldn't even make the play-offs in 2015–16.

The doubts about his ability to remain effective, of course, belonged to outsiders. Bryant wouldn't entertain any himself, at least not publicly. He plunged forward with the diamond-hard confidence fully intact. He wasn't about to let a bad shoulder and a bum knee and a traumatic Achilles injury defeat him.

Such confidence had led often to charges of arrogance and narcissism. For both Bryant and Jordan.

"You have to be somewhat narcissistic to be as good as those guys are," George Mumford said frankly.

Bryant's intense desire to dominate presented almost a mirror image to Jordan's own immense will and drive. But there was one big difference, and it evidenced itself in their very different relationships with Jackson.

"Michael was more respectful," Mumford offered.

Over the years, Bryant had remained Jordan-like in his approach except for one key facet. Tim Cone, a triangle offense guru, had spent countless thousands of hours studying videotape of Jordan and Bryant as Cone coached his teams in the Philippines to eighteen professional titles. Jordan was able to bring great discipline to his movements as a player, Cone said.

The irony for Bryant was that while he displayed incomparable discipline in his preparation to play games, in his film study and conditioning, he was never able to achieve that supreme discipline on the court in his movements as a player.

Sonny Vaccaro observed that the Lakers star had never been accorded the status as the league's leading figure as Jordan had enjoyed.

The reason for that was rooted in Bryant's "outsider" status, being raised largely in Europe and being largely a different, singular creature on the NBA landscape.

"He is so effin' bright," Vaccaro said of the circumstances. "I think his intelligence influenced his acceptance by the other players in the league and by the public."

The public disdain could be found everywhere perhaps but Los Angeles, where he had been immediately worshipped as "The Kid," the flashy prize in the eyes of Jerry Buss.

He never fell from his place in the owner's heart, and in recognition of that, the Buss children had chosen in 2013 to give Bryant a two-year contract extension worth better than $40 million. It was what their father would have done, just as Dr. Buss gave Magic Johnson a large deal even as his career ended. The $25 million Bryant would be paid for the 2015–16 season would make him the league's highest-paid player.

Those who were skeptical of Bryant's ability to regain his star status also pointed out that even if he managed to be a useful player on the court, there was no way he would live up to his astronomical salary. The move left many Lakers partisans howling that it weighed down the franchise's salary-cap room and its ability to make moves for the future. There seemed no doubt that the deal cut into Bryant's appreciation among the team's fans over his final two seasons, and it was widely derided by basketball insiders, who understood that careful management of the salary cap was one of the most important factors to a successful team in the modern NBA.

Undeterred, Bryant had moved on now into his final Jordan

irony. Bryant's last two years with the Lakers had some remarkable parallels with Jordan's return to basketball, more than a decade before. After walking away from the Bulls after the 1998 championship, His Royal Airness returned to play for the Washington Wizards in 2001 for two final seasons, limited by bad knees and a weak roster around him. His old friends were amazed that Jordan would take on such a burden when he knew in advance that he had absolutely no chance of winning.

Jordan insisted that he would serve as a teacher for his younger teammates. He, too, brought in an old friend—his former coach in Chicago, Doug Collins—to serve as coach. Jordan did indeed spend many nights trying to serve as an instructor to his teammates. But his old competitiveness and his legendary harshness also got in the way. Jordan made tens of millions of dollars for the Washington franchise, but the experience ended in the ugliest fashion, with Jordan being fired after alienating many of his teammates and owner Abe Pollin.

Bryant was now heading into an upcoming season with a roster that wouldn't compete for a championship but had lots of raw talent, including young players such as Julius Randle, D'Angelo Russell, and Jordan Clarkson, who were figured to be the future of the Lakers franchise. He faced perhaps his greatest challenge in seeking to reestablish his game while being a good mentor to the younger players. Every game would bring appraisals of the confidence and all that ego and drive he would carry to the floor and to the locker room. Many observers saw that same mix of factors that had led to a clouding of Jordan's judgment in his final two seasons.

Would Bryant be able to learn from Jordan's example and dial back his own vibe? His climb to the top of the mountain had been a lonely path for Bryant. He'd never known any other way. Could he manage to leave a legacy not just for himself but also for the players who would wear Forum blue and gold for years to come?

The legendary confidence led him to purse his lips and say yes with trademark defiance. Some observers thought that he should give Jordan a call to talk about it. Confidence, after all, had long been a tricky thing for both of them. Sometimes it was just the devil whispering in your ear.

That certainly seemed the case as the 2015–16 season began and he turned in absolutely unwatchable performances. The profound decline of his game was saddening to most NBA observers, even to those who had criticized Bryant over the years. Many observers were shocked to see him having staggeringly bad shooting nights nearly every single game. In the months of November and December, he had nine games in which he averaged less than 30 percent from the field but took more than 10 shots, including a night when he shot just 1 for 14. It was just confirmation to the coterie of Jackson and Rosen, who knew the Achilles and the insane wear and tear he put himself through over the seasons would be his undoing.

For the first time in his life, Kobe Bryant was absolutely and completely exposed on the basketball court, a place that had always been his ultimate refuge. To make matters worse, he was still averaging around thirty minutes per game, cutting into the minutes that should have been earmarked for his younger teammates.

With criticism about his play building, Bryant made a sudden December announcement that he planned to retire at season's end. It served as an odd, awkward acknowledgment of the obvious: he no longer had the physical ability to play the game at anything remotely near a high level.

His retirement was announced in a love letter he wrote to the game, citing his obsessive passion for the sport. He promised to be done by season's end, likely in April, since the Lakers were terrible and off to a 3–13 start. Many, including Charles Barkley, wondered why he didn't just retire, effective immediately. To many of those who knew him, Bryant sounded like an addict, still very much intoxicated, postponing the inevitable for as long as possible.

The circumstances pitted his one-time greatness against his current pathos. Bryant had promised several years before to play "till the wheels fall off" and to never engage in the sad act of traveling from one NBA city to another, seeking and receiving kudos and retirement gifts. But after his retirement announcement, that's exactly what his final season became. The crowds showed up in droves to see Bryant chuck up bricks, and he received a hero's welcome in every opposing arena as the Lakers piled up losses.

He returned for the annual trip to Philadelphia in December, where he was greeted by Sonny Hill and cheered and toasted by his hometown crowd, with old coaches and friends eager to scrounge one of the scarce tickets to greet him. Bryant finally basked in a love that had largely been denied him for two decades.

And he began playing better—he wasn't great, but he was no longer terrible. His adoring public continued to show up from around the globe and one more time made him the leading vote getter for the All-Star Game in frigid Toronto; he earned more votes than even the brilliant and immensely popular Stephen Curry, who was leading his Warriors on an all-time run to the play-offs.

Rather than arrive in Toronto with his trademark fire, Bryant showed up with something different, a quiet, almost laid-back appreciation of the moment as the event became the apex of his extended farewell tour.

Over time, he had begun to reveal that he had accepted that his time was past, that he could look forward to a future after the game, for which he had been quietly preparing.

"The challenge," he had told the *New Yorker* during a revealing interview, "also has to shift to doing something that a majority of people think that us athletes can't do, which is retire and be great at something else. Giorgio Armani didn't start Armani until he was forty. Forty! There's such a life ahead."

He would later reveal that his big idea was to deploy branding as narrative, which could be argued was something he had attempted his entire career, since Adidas had signed him as a teen. There was little doubt that he had much to offer, much life yet to live, along with a hope that perhaps he could dispense with his great branding idea.

After all, he had already made $328.23 million in NBA salary over the years, second only to the $335.87 million earned by Kevin Garnett. With cash like that, there seemed no need for him to continue to control his narrative. His record as a competitor was fully in the books, indisputable.

Yet, known to few, Bryant was plotting an extraordinary exit. His last game would be in mid-April at Staples Center against the Utah Jazz. With the sentimentality over this final season growing by the day, he began licensing an array of high-priced memorabilia, a limited number of hats and jackets to be sold for thousands of dollars each. After all, Bryant knew well his market, the Hollywood stars and millionaires who had been seated courtside at his games for two decades.

Bryant had set up his final moment months earlier in his poem "Dear Basketball": "My heart can take the pounding. My mind can handle the grind. But my body knows it's time to say goodbye."

Bryant also worked to prepare one last surprise for his big game. He didn't want to have his final game marked by a poor performance, rendering it a sad, pointless affair. After all, his narrative was brand. So he trained and prepared to put on one final show, never mind the limits of age that had held him back all season. He figured he could lay it all on the line one final time and come up with a respectably memorable outing. Who knew? He might even muster 30 or 40 points if he got hot in his last game, the 1,346th regular season game of his career.

It made sense. Years earlier he had sought from Jordan the wisdom of numbers, the science of volume scoring. That had long been his touchstone. His final season could not be numbered in victories, but if he could recapture a bit of the magic for one final game, that would allow him another sort of victory over the major foe that faced all athletes—time.

"I can't believe this actually happened, to be honest with you," he would explain later.

Neither could the Jazz.

"A lot of us were in shock," Utah's Gordon Hayward said afterward.

In his last pregame speech to his young teammates, Bryant had one request.

"Y'all need to play hard," he said. "That's what I want."

What he got was something entirely different, a sequence from a dreamscape. The Lakers trailed throughout the contest until the fourth period, when they found themselves down by 14. By then, Bryant had come very alive on his way to an unthinkable 60-point game. At age thirty-seven. Best of all, his final descent into the "zone" drove the Lakers to a 101–96 comeback win that had fans standing, laughing, cheering, crying, reaching to the sky for joy.

The numbers themselves say a lot about the bizarre nature of the outcome.

Bryant outscored the Jazz in the fourth quarter 23–21 all by himself.

He scored 17 consecutive points to drive the comeback.

Despite a season of high point totals, no other NBA player had scored 60 points in a game in 2015–16.

As journalist Howard Beck pointed out, there had been only thirty-one 60-point games in the NBA since 1963. The total had been achieved just eight times in the previous eleven seasons, and Bryant owned five of those.

In 1969, at age thirty-two, Wilt Chamberlain had achieved the distinction of being the oldest player to score 60 (he had 66 actually), until the big close to Bryant's career when he achieved the feat, at thirty-seven.

To get his big night, Bryant took a career-high 50 shots and made 22 of them. He took 21 three-pointers and made 6. He was fully aware how odd things were that night. "My teammates were just continuing to encourage me, continuing to say, 'Shoot, shoot, shoot, shoot,'" he said afterward. "It's like reversed. You go from being the villain to now being some type of a hero, and then go from everybody saying 'Pass the ball' to 'Shoot the ball.' It's really strange."

That same night in Oakland, the Golden State Warriors were completing an historic season by winning 73 games, the most ever in a season, greater than Jordan's 72-win 1996 Chicago Bulls. But somehow Bryant had managed to upstage them with his stupendous exit.

In the process, he had taken one final opportunity to remind Lakers fans in Los Angeles why they had loved him lo the many years. Yet that was nothing compared with China, where his finale attracted more than 110 million viewers of the man they consider an Elvis-like figure.

"I can't believe how fast twenty years went by," he said in thanking the Staples Center crowd after the game.

Ever the fabulist, he was the boy who had lived his dream. With his announced plans to become a writer now that his playing days were over, Bryant had authored a near-perfect ending.

"You can't write something better than this," he said.

Then he closed his comments with his arm raised and pointed in tribute to the crowd. "Mamba out," he said.

Moments later, a T-shirt with that phrase was available for sale on his website. As he had ached to be for his entire career, he was finally, completely, the man—the figure in total control. It seemed he had found an answer for everything, except perhaps the most important item. Joe and Pam Bryant were absent from his final game, their differences largely unresolved.

Sadly, Joe Bryant reported to a friend over the summer of 2016 that wife Pam had been diagnosed with a brain tumor. The diagnosis was followed by surgery, and Joe then reported that Pam had returned home afterward and was making progress in her recovery. Such a family trauma seemed likely to increase the chances of a reconciliation and the hope for tighter bonds between Bryant and his parents.

That July, apparently during or after his mother's illness, Bryant had penned "A Letter to My Younger Self" for the *Players' Tribune*, seemingly an attempt to explain in part his termination years earlier of financial support for his parents.

If there could be an important scene conjured up for the Bryants, it would be the one that Roberto Maltinti envisioned—that somehow they could gather for another Christmas, high up in the mountains in the little Tuscan village of Ciriglio, where Pam had always decorated their home so beautifully for the holidays. If they could only get back to that place, Maltinti said wistfully, their conflicts would melt away and they could once again find the love that had made them such an endearing family.

That would be it, then, a wrap on this story, with the family all together again in the soft candlelight, spouses and grandchildren too, all warm and happy in the holiday glow, with Joe and Kobe out in the driveway, both too old for one-on-one, but maybe a little H-O-R-S-E would do just fine.

And, oh my, just imagine the trash talk...

ACKNOWLEDGMENTS

Thanks to the many people who have granted interviews and offered their insights on Kobe Bryant and his family. In addition, so vital to this effort over the years has been the work of an array of journalists in Philadelphia and Los Angeles and across the NBA.

Many thanks to Jeremy Treatman, who assisted me in identifying key people to be interviewed and discussed his own Kobe experiences. Gery Woelfel contributed numerous interviews of NBA players and coaches about their memories of Bryant. Donald Hunt offered keen insight and research help for this project.

Larry Burnett also helped with interviews and background research.

Pat and Sue Flynn aided tremendously my research in Italy as did Alessandro Conti.

A variety of people—Patricia Wells, Karen Lazenby, Morgan Thumas, Mike Hollowell—helped transcribe the four hundred hours' worth of interviews for this project.

Mike Hollowell contributed research in Philadelphia, and Morgan Thumas also aided me in research.

In addition to friendship, Jorge Ribeiro contributed a great photograph of me interviewing Kobe in 2000. And Lorna Tansey likewise contributed photos of Bryant's last game in Staples.

I also must thank my longtime agent, Matthew Carnicelli, for his belief in my work and his many efforts to bring it to a larger audience.

Likewise, John Parsley, an immensely dedicated and gifted editor at Little, Brown, has played a huge role in my growth as a writer.

In so many ways, the entire staff at Little, Brown has also played a role in that growth, including editor Malin von Euler-Hogan. I would like to thank freelance editor William Boggess, as well as

Ben Allen—who heads up a great production team—and copyeditor Katharine Cooper. Proofreader Scott Bryan Wilson did a great job, as did indexer Heather Laskey and jacket designer Neil Alexander Heacox. From Little, Brown's production and manufacturing staff there's also production coordinator Melissa Mathlin and printer coordinator Lisa Ferris to thank.

Critical contributions were also made by legal counsel Chris Nolan.

Elizabeth Garriga and Maggie Southard formed an outstanding publicity team for the project.

And, finally, I want to thank Gabriella Mongelli and Jeff Fraler for their special efforts in editing *Showboat*'s paperback edition.

NOTES AND SOURCES

Interviews

I would like to thank the following for granting interviews for this book and for other projects of mine over the years that provided insight for this work. They include, in no particular order: Gary Charles, Mo Howard, Vontez Simpson, Gilbert Saunders, Jerry Colangelo, Gene Shue, Paul Westhead, Leon Douglas, Rudy Garciduenas, Mike D'Antoni, Chip Schaefer, Sonny Hill, Pat Williams, Peter Moore, Sonny Vaccaro, Pam Vaccaro, Sam Rines, Mike Harris, George Mumford, Anthony Gilbert, Jeremy Treatman, Gregg Downer, Jermaine Griffin, Donald Hunt, John Smallwood, Robbie Schwartz, Donnie Carr, Evan Monsky, Del Harris, Larry Harris, Tony DiLeo, Shaun Powell, Brad Greenberg, Brian Shaw, Gregg Popovich, Tim Duncan, Tony Parker, Greg Foster, David West, Paul George, Dwyane Wade, Raja Bell, Shawn Marion, Pau Gasol, Luc Mbah a Moute, Anfernee "Penny" Hardaway, Oscar Robertson, Spencer Haywood, Roberto Maltinti, Michella Rotella, Lorenzo Vivarelli, Alessandro Conti, Jacomo Vittori, Dick Weiss, Robert "Scoop" Jackson, J. A. Adande, Howard Beck, Ric Bucher, Dave McMenamin, Mark Medina, Hugh Delehanty, Jorge Ribeiro, Hal Wissel, Scott Wissel, Kelly Carter, Derek Fisher, Michael Jordan, Tex Winter, Tim Cone, Chick Hearn, Tyronn Lue, Luke Walton, Mike Wise, Kwame Brown, Jon Barry, Steve Kerr, Jim Jackson, Lamar Odom, Shaquille O'Neal, Robert Horry, Phil Jackson, Gary Vitti, Eddie Jones, Ron Harper, Nick Van Exel, Dennis Rodman, Jack Haley, Dr. Jack Ramsay, Jim Cleamons, Jerry West, Earvin "Magic" Johnson, Jerry Buss, Joe Dumars, James Edwards, David Aldridge, Scottie Pippen, Matt Guokas, Mitch Lawrence, Johnny Bach, Marques Johnson, Brendan Malone, and Billy Packer, among others.

Although Kobe Bryant did not participate in this effort, I have interviewed him many times over the years. I want to thank Gery Woelfel, Jeremy Treatman, Morgan Thumas, and Larry Burnett for their help in research and in gaining interviews for this text.

Magazines, Newspapers, and Websites

For my research, I am indebted to the following publications and websites: the *Philadelphia Tribune*, *Philadelphia Daily News*, the *Philadelphia Inquirer*, Philly.com, *Bleacher Report*, *Grantland*, *The New Yorker*, *GQ*, *Philadelphia* magazine, the *Delaware County Times*, the *Chicago Defender*, the *Chicago Tribune*, the *Chicago Sun-Times*, the *Daily Southtown*, the *Detroit News*, the *Detroit Free Press*, the *Daily Herald*, *ESPN The Magazine*, *Hoop* magazine, the *Houston Post*, the *Houston Chronicle*, *Inside Sports*, *Sport* magazine, the *Los Angeles Times*, *The National*, the *New York Daily News*, the *New York Times*, the *New York Post*, the *Charlotte Observer*, the *Roanoke Times*, *USA Today*, *The Oregonian*, the *San Antonio Express-News*, *Sports*

Illustrated, Lindy's Sports Pro Basketball annual magazine, *Basketball Times*, the *Boston Globe*, the *Sporting News, Street & Smith's Pro Basketball Yearbook*, the *Washington Post*, ESPN.com, the *Basketball Jones* (blog), *Deadspin* (blog), *HoopsHype* (blog), NBA.com, and Lakers.com, among others.

Books

Abrams, Jonathan. *Boys Among Men*. New York: Crown Archetype, 2016.

Bird, Larry, Earvin Johnson, and Jackie MacMullan. *When the Game Was Ours*. Boston: Houghton Mifflin Harcourt, 2009.

Boyd, Todd. *Young, Black, Rich, and Famous: The Rise of the NBA, the Hip Hop Invasion, and the Transformation of American Culture*. New York: Doubleday, 2003.

Bradley, Robert D. *The Basketball Draft Fact Book*. Plymouth, UK: Scarecrow Press, 2013.

Buss, Jeanie, and Steve Springer. *Laker Girl*. Chicago: Triumph Books, 2010.

Christgau, John. *Tricksters in the Madhouse: Lakers vs. Globetrotters, 1948*. Lincoln: University of Nebraska, 2004.

Christopher, Matt. *On the Court with... Kobe Bryant*. New York: Little, Brown and Company, 2001.

George, Nelson. *Elevating the Game: The History and Aesthetics of Black Men in Basketball*. New York: Simon & Schuster, 1993.

Halberstam, David. *Playing for Keeps: Michael Jordan and the World He Made*. New York: Random House, 1999.

Heisler, Mark. *Madmen's Ball: The Continuing Saga of Kobe, Phil, and the Los Angeles Lakers*. Chicago: Triumph Books, 2004.

Hollander, Zander. *The Modern Encyclopedia of Basketball*. New York: Four Winds, 1969.

Hollander, Zander, and Alex Sachare. *The Official NBA Basketball Encyclopedia*. New York: Villard, 1989.

Hunt, Donald. *The Philadelphia Big 5: Great Moments in Philadelphia's Storied College Basketball History*. Champaign, IL: Sagamore, 1996.

Indovino, Shaina. *Kobe Bryant*. Broomall, PA: Mason Crest, 2015.

Jackson, Phil, and Michael Arkush. *The Last Season: A Team in Search of Its Soul*. New York: Penguin, 2004.

Jackson, Phil, and Hugh Delehanty. *Eleven Rings: The Soul of Success*. New York: Penguin, 2013.

———. *Sacred Hoops: Spiritual Lessons of a Hardwood Warrior*. New York: Hyperion, 1995.

Jackson, Phil, and Charles Rosen. *More than a Game*. New York: Seven Stories, 2001.

Jones, Gordon, and Eric Stark. *100 Things 76ers Fans Should Know and Do Before They Die*. Chicago: Triumph Books, 2014.

Jordan, Michael, and Mark Vancil. *For the Love of the Game: My Story*. New York: Crown, 1998.

Jordan, Michael, and Pat Williams. *Quotable Michael Jordan*. Hendersonville, TN: TowleHouse, 2004.

Kalb, Elliott. *Who's Better, Who's Best in Basketball?: Mr. Stats Sets the Record Straight on the Top 50 NBA Players of All Time*. Chicago: Contemporary, 2004.

Krugel, Mitchell. *One Last Shot: The Story of Michael Jordan's Comeback*. New York: St. Martin's, 2003.

LaFeber, Walter. *Michael Jordan and the New Global Capitalism*. New York: W.W. Norton, 1999.

Lavner, Fred. *BOOM!: Comic Confessions of a Boomer Corner Boy*. Philadelphia: Lulu Books, 2015.

Limardi, Claudio. *Dr. Kobe & Mr. Bryant: The Story*. Bologna, Italy: Libri di Sport, 2004.

McCallum, Jack. *Dream Team: How Michael, Magic, Larry, Charles, and the Greatest Team of All Time Conquered the World and Changed the Game of Basketball Forever*. New York: Ballantine, 2012.

Mulligan, Stephen. *Were You There?: Over 300 Wonderful, Weird, and Wacky Moments from the Pittsburgh Civic/Mellon Arena*. Pittsburgh: RoseDog Books, 2011.

Mumford, George. *The Mindful Athlete: Secrets to Pure Performance*. Berkeley: Parallax, 2015.

O'Neal, Shaquille. *Shaq Talks Back*. New York: St. Martin's, 2001.

O'Neal, Shaquille, and Jackie MacMullan. *Shaq Uncut: My Story*. New York: Grand Central, 2011.

Pearlman, Jeff. *Showtime: Magic, Kareem, Riley, and the Los Angeles Lakers Dynasty of the 1980s*. New York: Gotham, 2014.

Robinson, Rob. *Oregon Sports Stories: History, Highlights, and Reflections*. Charleston, SC: The History Press, 2013.

Sachare, Alex, and Dave Sloan. *The Sporting News Official NBA Guide: 1990–91 Edition*. St. Louis: Sporting News, 1991.

Savage, Jim. *The Encyclopedia of the NCAA Basketball Tournament: The Complete Independent Guide to College Basketball's Championship Event*. New York: Dell, 1990.

Schnakenberg, Robert. *Kobe Bryant*. New York: Chelsea House, 2013.

Strasser, J. B., and Laurie Becklund. *Swoosh: The Unauthorized Story of Nike, and the Men Who Played There*. New York: HarperBusiness, 1993.

Wetzel, Dan, and Donald Yaeger. *Sole Influence: Basketball, Corporate Greed, and the Corruption of America's Youth*. New York: Warner Books, 2000.

Williams, Gail. *Oh How the Mighty Fall*. Charleston, SC: CreateSpace Independent Publishing, 2013.

Williams, Pat, and Bill Lyon. *We Owed You One!: The Uphill Struggle of the Philadelphia 76ers*. Wilmington, DE: TriMark, 1983.

Newspaper, Magazine, and Online Articles

Abrams, Jonathan. "Paul Silas, NBA Lifer." *Grantland* (online). November 12, 2014. Accessed March 3, 2016. http://grantland.com/features/paul-silas-nba-career-boston-celtics-st-louis-atlanta-hawks-phoenix-suns-denver-nuggets-seattle-supersonics-charlotte-bobcats-lenny-wilkens-dave-cowens-bill-russell/.

Advertising Age (online). "Nike Inc." September 15, 2003. Accessed February 28, 2016. http://adage.com/article/adage-encyclopedia/nike/98797/.

Ahmed, Shahan. "Lakers Underachieve, Leave Summer League Friday" *NBC Southern California* (online). July 9, 2015. Accessed February 27, 2016. http://

www.nbclosangeles.com/news/sports/Lakers-disappoint-in-2015-Summer
-League-316246851.html

Amick, Sam. "After Adjustment Period, Jeanie Buss Ushering in 'Different Generation' for Lakers." *USA Today*. June 28, 2015.

———. "Kobe Bryant Rehabbed But Rusty in Return to Lakers." *USA Today*. October 5, 2015.

Araton, Harvey. "Kobe Bryant Hopes to Finish with a Flourish That Isn't Orchestrated." *New York Times*. November 7, 2015.

Ark TV (online). "The E! True Hollywood Story—Kobe Bryant." N.d. Accessed February 29, 2016. http://tv.ark.com/transcript/the_e!_true_hollywood_story-%28kobe_bryant%29/6834/EP/Wednesday_April_21_2010/268221/.

Armour, Terry. "Ain't Over Till...: Bulls 129, Lakers 123." *Chicago Tribune*. December 18, 1996.

Associated Press. "Joe Bryant Elevated to Head Coach of the Sparks." *Los Angeles Sentinel*. July 14, 2011.

———. "Kobe Bryant in Upcoming NBA TV Interview: 'I Can't Say It Is the End.'" *Score* (online). February 15, 2015. Accessed March 2, 2016. http://www.thescore.com/nba/news/701531.

———. "Kobe Bryant's Hometown Heartsick after Sexual Assault Charge Filed." *Fox News* (online). July 24, 2003. Accessed March 1, 2016. http://www.foxnews.com/story/2003/07/24/kobe-bryant-hometown-heartsick-after-sexual-assault-charge-filed.html.

———. "Under-Table Money, Steroid Use Are Alleged in Book About Nike." *Los Angeles Times*. January 16, 1992.

Astramskas, David. "The Origin of Nike's Jumpman Logo Aka The $5.2 Billion Michael Jordan Image." *BallIsLife* (online). August 8, 2013. Accessed February 28, 2016. http://ballislife.com/origin-of-jumpan-jordan-logo/.

AudiWorld (online). "The Kobe: Adidas & Audi Collaborate." November 27, 2000. Accessed February 28, 2016. http://www.audiworld.com/news/00/kobe/content.shtml.

Automotive Intelligence News (online). "'The Kobe': Adidas—Audi—Design Story." November 7, 2000. Accessed February 28, 2016. http://www.autointell.com/news-2000/November-2000/November-07-00-p9.htm.

Badenhausen, Kurt. "The Business of Michael Jordan Is Booming." *Forbes*. September 22, 2011.

———. "Kobe, LeBron Lead NBA's Highest-Paid Players 2014." *Forbes*. January 22, 2014.

———. "LeBron James Is NBA's Top Shoe Salesman with $340 Million for Nike." *Forbes*. March 18, 2015.

Baler, Bill. "Former New Orleans Hornets GM Bob Bass Lives with the Decision of Trading Kobe Bryant for Vlade Divac." *Times-Picayune*. March 28, 2009.

Ballard, Chris. "Where Does Greatness Come From?" *Sports Illustrated*. May 14, 2014.

Banks, Alec. "Kobe Bryant: Greatest Career Moments." *Highsnobiety* (online). December 3, 2015. Accessed February 29, 2016. http://www.highsnobiety.com/2015/12/03/kobe-bryant-career-highlights/.

Barker, Barbara. "Hard for Jerry West to See Kobe Fade Away." *Newsday*. December 4, 2015.

Barocci, Andrea. "Kobe Bryant, orgoglio italiano." *NBA Italia* (online). June 10, 2015. Accessed March 2, 2016. http://www.nbaitalianews.it/2015/06/kobe-bryant-orgoglio-italiano/.

———. "Se sceglie l'Italia, Kobe va alla Reggiana." *NBA Italia* (online). June 14, 2015. Accessed March 1, 2016. http://www.nbaitalianews.it/2015/06/barocci-se-sceglie-litalia-kobe-va-alla-reggiana/#more-14946.

Barron, David. "All-Star MVPs Becoming Norm for Kobe in Odd-Numbered Years." *Houston Chronicle*. December 20, 2012.

Basketball- Reference (online). "Buffalo Braves at Philadelphia 76ers, Box Score, April 18, 1976." N.d. Accessed February 27, 2016. http://www.basketball-reference.com/boxscores/197604180PHI.html.

———. "Los Angeles Lakers at San Diego Clippers, Box Score, March 12, 1981." N.d. Accessed March 3, 2016. http://www.basketball-reference.com/boxscores/198103120SDC.html.

———. "1975-76 Philadelphia 76ers Roster and Stats." N.d. Accessed February 27, 2016. http://www.basketball-reference.com/teams/PHI/1976.html.

Basketbawful (online). "Kobe Bryant Is Ready for [Insert Subject Here]." September 26, 2006. Accessed March 3, 2016. http://basketbawful.blogspot.com/2006_08_27_basketbawful_archive.html.

Basketreggio (online). "Kobe si ritira. Evviva Kobe (da the Players Tribune)." April 13, 2016. http://www.basketreggio.it/kobe-si-ritira-evviva-kobe-da-the-players-tribune/.

Basket USA (online). "[Happy Birthday] Kobe Bryant et l'Italie, una storia importante." August 23, 2015. Accessed February 29, 2016. http://www.basketusa.com/news/88685/kobe-bryant-italie/.

Battat, Michael. "Nike: The Formula for $50 Billion in Sales in 2020." *Seeking Alpha* (online). November 10, 2015. Accessed February 29, 2016. http://seekingalpha.com/article/3673106-nike-formula-50-billion-sales-2020.

Beck, Howard. "KG, the Oral History, Part 2: Glory in Boston, Quirky Traits and Returning Home." *Bleacher Report* (online). May 18, 2015. Accessed March 2, 2016. http://bleacherreport.com/articles/2445357-kg-the-oral-history-part-2-glory-in-boston-quirky-traits-and-returning-home?utm_source=newsletter&utm_medium=newsletter&utm_campaign=nba.

———. "A Man in Full: An Oral History of Kevin Garnett, the Player Who Changed the NBA." *Bleacher Report* (online). May 18, 2015. Accessed March 1, 2016. http://bleacherreport.com/articles/2421236-a-man-in-full-the-many-sides-of-kevin-garnett-the-player-who-changed-the-nba?utm_source=newsletter&utm_medium=newsletter&utm_campaign=nba.

———. "Amid the Points and Applause, One Single Shot Ignited Love Story of Kobe, NYC." *Bleacher Report* (online). November 9, 2015. Accessed February 29, 2016. http://bleacherreport.com/articles/2587406-amid-the-points-and-applause-one-single-shot-ignited-love-story-of-kobe-nyc?utm_source=newsletter&utm_medium=newsletter&utm_campaign=new-york-knicks.

Benbow, Dana Hunsinger. "The Unlikely Bond of Kobe Bryant and Tamika Catchings." *USA Today*. March 1, 2015.

Bernucca, Chris. "Darryl Dawkins Was the Coolest Guy on Earth—or Any Other Planet." *Sheridan Hoops* (online). August 28, 2015. Accessed February 28, 2016.

http://www.sheridanhoops.com/2015/08/28/bernucca-darryl-dawkins-was-the
-coolest-guy-on-earth-or-any-other-planet/.

Bethea, Charles. "Q&A with Atlanta's Kent Bazemore: On Playing with Kobe, Pranking with Whoopee Cushions, and Nailing a Bench Celebration." *Grantland* (online). March 18, 2015. Accessed March 3, 2016. http://grantland.com/the-triangle/nba-atlanta-hawks-interview-kent-bazemore/.

Bieler, Des. "Kobe Bryant and Jimmy Fallon Reminisced about a 1996 Beer Run." *Washington Post*. February 5, 2015.

Binole, Gina. "Three Stripes and You're In." *Portland Business Journal*. May 31, 1998.

Biuzzi, David, and Alessandro Marmuggi. "Indovina chi viene a cena? A tavola c'è Kobe Bryant." *Tirreno*. April 18, 2015.

Black Like Moi (online). "Kobe's Father, Mother and Grandmother Are Calling He and His Wife Liars." May 14, 2013. Accessed March 3, 2016. http://black likemoi.com/2013/05/kobes-father-mother-and-grandmother-are-calling-he -and-his-wife-liars/.

Blauer, Charlotte. "Rob Strasser's Vision." Charlotte Blauer Consulting (online). April 15, 2013. Accessed February 27, 2016. http://charlotteblauer.com/blog/2013/4/15/rob-strassers-vision.

Bleacher Report (online). "Spurs Give Touching Video Tribute to Kobe." February 7, 2016. Accessed February 29, 2016. http://bleacherreport.com/articles/track/10091492-spurs-give-touching-video-tribute-to-kobe.

Blinebury, Fran. "Philly Hoops Scene Wouldn't Be What It Is without Hill." NBA.com (online). February 18, 2015. Accessed March 1, 2016. http://www.nba.com/2015/news/features/fran_blinebury/02/18/barrier-breakers -sonny-hill/.

Block, Justin, and Gus Turner. "The 24 Best Kobe Bryant References in Rap History: 'I Had Dreams of the League, One Day I'd Play Kobe/Or Walk up to Puff and He Would Really Know Me'—Kanye West." *Complex* (online). August 22, 2014. Accessed February 29, 2016. http://www.complex.com/sports/2014/08/the-24-best-kobe-bryant-references-in-rap-history/kanye-west-kobe-bryant -ego-remix.

Bohlin, Michael. "Horace Grant Calls Kobe Bryant a Close Second to Michael Jordan." *247Sports* (online). July 24, 2015. Accessed February 27, 2016. http://lakers.247sports.com/Bolt/Horace-Grant-calls-Kobe-Bryant-a-close -second-to-Michael-Jordan-38373203/.

Boivin, Paola. "Remembering Kobe Bryant's Damage on Phoenix Suns (Look Out, Steve Nash)." *Azcentral* (online). May 24, 2015. Accessed March 1, 2016. http://www.azcentral.com/story/sports/heat-index/2015/05/23/kobe-bryant -lakers-suns-nash-jackson-trade-nba-dunk-playoffs/27842847/.

Bondy, Stefan. "Kobe Bryant Talks Derek Fisher's Firing, Jordan Comparisons." *New York Daily News*. February 14, 2016.

Bonsignore, Vincent. "Lakers Coach Mike D'Antoni's Mantra: 'No Problems, Only Solutions.'" *Los Angeles Daily News*. November 19, 2012.

BoSox Tavern (online). "San Diego Clippers: Doomed from the Beginning." November 17, 2010. Accessed March 3, 2016. http://bosox-tavern.blogspot.com/2010/11/san-diego-clippers-doomed-from.html.

Braxton, Greg. "Kobe Bryant Calls the Shots on His Showtime Documentary 'Muse.'" *Los Angeles Times*. February 28, 2015.

Bresnahan, Mike. "Jeanie Buss Explains Kobe Bryant's Contract, Phil Jackson Situation." *Los Angeles Times*. March 19, 2014.

———. "Kobe Bryant Holds Court, Briefly, in Lakers' Exhibition Opener." *Los Angeles Times*. October 4, 2015.

———. "Kobe Bryant Says Post-Playing Career Will Be Different from Magic Johnson's." *Los Angeles Times*. December 4, 2015.

———. "Kobe Bryant's Biggest Regret Might Be 2004 Finals." *Los Angeles Times*. December 5, 2015.

———. "Shaquille O'Neal on Kobe Bryant: 'Hopefully He's Happy.'" *Los Angeles Times*. December 7, 2015.

———. "Who Was 'That Guy' at the Jerry Buss Memorial? Family Friend Greg Tomlinson Tells His Story." *Forbes*. March 15, 2013.

———. "With More Pain and Less Game, Lakers' Kobe Bryant Decides He'll Retire after Season." *Los Angeles Times*. November 30, 2015.

Brown, Jerry. "D'Antoni's Career Blossomed in Europe." *East Valley Tribune*. October 6, 2006.

Brown, Tim. "After a Year When He Feuded with Shaq, Got Married, Won a Title and Lost His Grandfather, Kobe Bryant Is Clearly..." *Los Angeles Times*. December 25, 2001.

———. "Bryant Is Back in Camp." *Los Angeles Times*. October 5, 2001.

———. "Kobe Fires, But Lakers Fall Back." *Los Angeles Times*. November 8, 2002.

BR Studios. "The Last Night Kobe Was King." *Bleacher Report* (online). February 10, 2016. Accessed February 29, 2016. http://bleacherreport.com/articles/2615307-the-last-night-kobe-was-king?utm_source=newsletter&utm_medium=newsletter&utm_campaign=nba.

Bryant, Kobe. "Dear Basketball." *Players Tribune* (online). N.d. Accessed February 29, 2016. http://www.theplayerstribune.com/dear-basketball/?utm_medium=email&utm_campaign=November%2B29th%2B-%2BFinal&utm_content=November%2B29th%2B-%2BFinal%2BCID_fa0458043810ae4e7e84dcd733801b17&utm_source=newsletter&utm_term=READ+MY+LETTER.

———. "Uncle John." *Genius* (online). N.d. Accessed February 28, 2016. http://genius.com/4570745.

———. "Zero." *Players Tribune* (online). N.d. Accessed March 2, 2016. http://www.theplayerstribune.com/kobe-passes-jordan/.

Bucher, Ric. "Kobe Bryant Helped Team USA Basketball Regain Its Dominance with Single Game." *Bleacher Report* (online). September 15, 2015. Accessed February 28, 2016. http://bleacherreport.com/articles/2199457-kobe-bryant-helped-team-usa-basketball-regain-its-dominance-with-single-game.

———. "Lakers Owners Jeanie and Jim Buss on Power Sharing and the Future of Their Family Franchise." *Hollywood Reporter*. August 23, 2013.

Buha, Jovan. "Michael Jordan and Kobe Bryant Trash-Talk Each Other at 2003 All-Star Game." *Fox Sports* (online). January 28, 2008. Accessed February 29, 2016. http://www.foxsports.com/nba/story/michael-jordan-kobe-bryant-los-angeles-lakers-tbt-2003-all-star-game-trash-talk-012816.

Bulls.com (online). "Phil Jackson and Sam Smith's Relationship Dates Back to Coach's Early CBA Days." January 17, 2013. Accessed March 4, 2016. http://

www.nba.com/bulls/history/phil-jackson-and-sam-smiths-relationship-dates
-back-coachs-early-cba-days.html.

Burneko, Albert. "Michael Jordan's Ghost Is Retiring, at Fucking Last." *Deadspin*
(online). November 30, 2015. Accessed February 29, 2016. http://deadspin
.com/michael-jordans-ghost-is-retiring-at-fucking-last-1745260048.

Burns, Greg. "Cheese Baron, NBA Star to Hoop It Up in Milan." *Chicago Tribune*.
December 15, 1999.

———. "Cheese Whiz Melts Milan's Hoops Heart." *Chicago Tribune*. September
23, 1999.

Cacciola, Scott. "In Philadelphia, a Feel-Good Moment for Kobe Bryant, If a Brief
One." *New York Times*. December 1, 2015.

———. "Kobe Bryant's Long Goodbye." *New York Times*. December 16, 2015.

Cahill, Dan. "Kobe Bryant Poem Resembles Michael Jordan Retirement Letter."
Chicago Sun-Times. November 30, 2015.

Campbell, Marc. "'The Jungle': Philadelphia's Mean Streets." *DangerousMinds*
(online). December 4, 2010. Accessed February 28, 2016. http://dangerous
minds.net/comments/the_jungle_philadelphias_mean_streets.

Caparella, Kitty. "Gang of Writers: How a Teen Paper Documented Life in the
'Hood.'" Philly.com (online). November 11, 2008. Accessed February 28, 2016.
http://articles.philly.com/2008-11-11/news/24992528_1_gang-members
-street-gangs-gang-life.

Carapella, Jake. "The Last Mohican." *SLAMonline* (online). March 26, 2015.
Accessed February 29, 2016. http://www.slamonline.com/nba/kobe-bryant
-the-last-mohican/#f142gYjXl3MowAYE.97.

Cardboard Connection (online). "Complete History and Visual Guide to Kobe Bryant Shoes." N.d. Accessed February 28, 2016. http://www.cardboardconnection
.com/kobe-bryant-shoes-guide-history.

Carmichael, Emma. "Kobe Bryant's Wife Has Reportedly Filed for Divorce."
Deadspin (online). December 16, 2011. Accessed February 29, 2016. http://
deadspin.com/5868948/kobe-bryants-wife-has-reportedly-filed-for-divorce.

Carter, Kelly E. "Hobnobbing with Kobe Bryant, Margrit Mondavi and Marchese
Piero Antinori." Kelley E. Carter Blog (online). July 8, 2015. Accessed February 28, 2016. http://kellyecarter.com/hobnobbing-with-kobe-bryant-margrit
-mondavi-and-marchese-piero-antinori/.

CBS News (online). "Bryant's Ownership in Italy Short Lived." October 18, 2000.
Accessed March 3, 2016. http://www.cbsnews.com/news/bryants-ownership-in
-italy-short-lived/.

———. "Kobe Buys Pop's Former Team." December 14, 1999. Accessed March 1,
2016. http://www.cbsnews.com/news/kobe-buys-pops-former-team/.

Charry, Rob. "Coach Bryant? Akiba Once Led by Kobe's Dad." *Forward*. February
27, 2004.

Chiari, Mike. "LeBron James, Kobe Bryant Reportedly Were at Center of 2007
Trade Talks." *Bleacher Report* (online). February 10, 2016. Accessed February 29, 2016. http://bleacherreport.com/articles/2615568-lebron-james
-kobe-bryant-reportedly-were-at-center-of-2007-trade-talks?utm
_source=newsletter&utm_medium=newsletter&utm_campaign=
cleveland-cavaliers.

Chicago Sun-Times. (online). "Kobe Bryant Told Michael Jordan He'd Kick His Ass—Phil Jackson." January 23, 2014. Accessed February 28, 2016. http://chicagobeta.suntimes.wordpress-prod-wp.aggrego.com/news/7/71/790634/kobe-bryant-told-michael-jordan-hed-kick-his-ass-phil-jackson.

Chicago Tribune. "Kobe Bryant's Wife Vanessa Files for Divorce." December 16, 2011.

Chopra, Gotham. "The Tao of Kobe Bryant: How I Learned to Stop Hating the Laker Legend." *Daily Beast* (online). February 27, 2015. Accessed March 3, 2016. http://www.thedailybeast.com/articles/2015/02/27/the-tao-of-kobe-bryant-how-i-learned-to-stop-hating-the-laker-legend.html.

Club Valiants (online). "The History of the Valiants." N.d. Accessed February 29, 2016. http://www.clubvaliantsinc.com/our-history/.

CNN (online). "Kobe Bryant Fast Facts." November 29, 2015. Accessed February 27, 2016. http://www.cnn.com/2013/04/29/us/kobe-bryant-fast-facts/.

———. "Larry King Live: Panel Discusses Kobe Bryant Case." July 21, 2003. Accessed February 28, 2016. http://www.cnn.com/TRANSCRIPTS/0307/21/lkl.00.html.

Colapinto, John. "Looking Good." *The New Yorker.* March 26, 2012.

Collen, Jess. "Kobe Bryant Has Also Lost a Step When It Comes to Trademark Registration." *Forbes.* December 3, 2015.

Complex (online). "50 Things You Didn't Know About Adidas: 32: Peter Moore, the Man Who Designed the Air Jordan 1, Also Designed Something for Adidas." N.d. Accessed February 28, 2016. http://www.complex.com/sneakers/2014/08/50-things-you-didnt-know-about-adidas/peter-moore.

———. "Switching Sides: When Athletes Change Sneaker Endorsements." July 17, 2009. Accessed February 28, 2016. http://www.complex.com/sneakers/2009/07/switching-sides-when-athletes-change-sneaker-endorsements.

Concepcion, Jason. "An Annotated Journey through Shaq and Kobe's Supposed Beef-Squashing Podcast." *Grantland* (online). September 3, 2015. Accessed February 28, 2016. http://grantland.com/the-triangle/nba-shaquille-oneal-kobe-bryant-podcast-annotation/.

Contactmusic.com (online). "Ex-Pal Reveals Kobe's Accuser Plotted to Lure Eminem into Bed." September 8, 2004. Accessed February 29, 2016. http://www.contactmusic.com/kobe-bryant/news/ex.pal-reveals-kobe.s-accuser-plotted-to-lure-eminem-into-bed.

Conway, Tyler. "Mike Krzyzewski Announces 2016 Olympic Games Will Be His Last as USA Coach." *Bleacher Report* (online). October 19, 2015. Accessed February 28, 2016. http://bleacherreport.com/articles/2580581-mike-krzyzewski-announces-2016-olympic-games-will-be-his-last-as-usa-coach.

Cook, Bonnie L. "1970s Also Were Deadly for City's Police Officers." Philly.com (online). September 25, 2008. Accessed February 28, 2016. http://articles.philly.com/2008-09-25/news/25247110_1_police-officers-officer-down-memorial-page-shot-at-point-blank-range.

Cook, Scott. "Kobe Bryant: The NBA's Most Hated Man." *Daily Caller* (online). March 17, 2015. Accessed February 29, 2016. http://dailycaller.com/2015/03/17/kobe-bryant-the-nbas-most-hated-man-video/2/.

Cornbread the Legend (online). "1965–1967: Philadelphia Gang Wars." N.d. Accessed February 28, 2016. http://cornbreadthelegend.com/pages/1965-1967-philadelphia-gang-wars.

Corriere Fiorentino (online). "Kobe Bryant torna a Cireglio, dove cominciò a gio-care." July 26, 2013. Accessed February 29, 2016. http://corrierefiorentino .corriere.it/firenze/notizie/sport/2013/25-luglio-2013/kobe-bryant-torna -cireglio-2222340722964.shtml?refresh_ce-cp.

Corrigan, Drew. "Former Lakers Player Andrew Goudelock Talks about the Time Kobe Bryant Took His Teammates to Las Vegas and Let Them 'Ball Out.'" *Complex* (online). May 25, 2015. Accessed March 1, 2016. http://www.complex .com/sports/2015/05/andrew-goudelock-talks-about-time-kobe-bryant-took -teammates-las-vegas.

Crawford, Kirkland. "Kobe Confirms He Called Off Trade to Pistons in 2007." *Detroit Free Press.* February 23, 2015.

Crecente, Brian. "Bryan Accuser, Tabloid Settle Suit. Faber to Receive Undis-closed Amount from *Globe* publisher." *Rocky Mountain* (online). January 28, 2005. Accessed February 29, 2016. https://la.utexas.edu/users/ jmciver/357L/P4/RMN_Bryant%20accuser%20tabloid%20settle%20s uit_012805.htm.

Crothers, Tim. "A Tough Question: When Tracy McGrady of Toronto Is Asked If He's Happy That He Skipped College, the Reply Is Yes, But..." *Sports Illus-trated.* December 29, 1997.

Crowley, Michael. "Muhammad Ali Was a Rebel. Michael Jordan Is a Brand Name." *Nieman Reports* (online). September 15, 1999. http://niemanreports .org/articles/muhammad-ali-was-a-rebel-michael-jordan-is-a-brand -name/.

Cyphers, Luke. "There's No Escape from Nike World." *New York Daily News.* November 12, 1995.

Daulerio, A.J. "This Dirty Kobe Bryant Business." *Deadspin* (online). May 28, 2008. Accessed February 28, 2016. http://deadspin.com/5011467/this-dirty -kobe-bryant-business.

Davis, Ken. "Making The Proper Pitch." *Hartford Courant.* November 9, 2000.

Dawidoff, Nicholas. "The Obtuse Triangle." *New York Times.* June 27, 2015.

Degheri, Travis. "The San Diego Clippers: A Dream Ends." *Journal of San Diego His-tory* (online). https://www.sandiegohistory.org/journal/v55-3/pdf/v55-3degheri .pdf.

DeMarzo, John. "Kobe Bryant: Phil Jackson's Mind Games Drove Me to the Brink." *New York Post.* February 17, 2015.

Ding, Kevin. "Bryant's Genes, Work Led Him Here." *Orange County Register.* August 21, 2011.

———. "Kobe Didn't Find a Win, But He May Have Rediscovered His Passion in NBA Return." *Bleacher Report* (online). October 29, 2015. Accessed Febru-ary 29, 2016. http://bleacherreport.com/articles/2583939-kobe-didnt-find-a -win-but-he-may-have-rediscovered-his-passion-in-nba-return.

———. "Lakers, Byron Scott Allowing Kobe Bryant to Be His Own Worst Enemy." *Bleacher Report* (online). November 2, 2015. Accessed February 29, 2016. http://bleacherreport.com/articles/2585175-lakers-byron-scott-allowing -kobe-bryant-to-be-his-own-worst-enemy?utm_source=newsletter&utm _medium=newsletter&utm_campaign=nba.

———. "Jim Buss in 2005: 'Eventually, My Dad Retires.'" *Orange County Regis-ter.* May 26, 2011.

Draper, Kevin. "Kobe Bryant Finally Did Byron Scott's Job for Him." *Deadspin* (online). December 10, 2015. Accessed February 29, 2016. http://deadspin .com/kobe-bryant-finally-did-byron-scotts-job-for-him-1747253325.

Drury, Flora. "Kobe Bryant Reveals His Wife Miscarried Because of the Stress of His Rape Case in Colorado and Says He Blames Himself." *Daily Mail* (online). March 3, 2015. Accessed February 29, 2016. http://www.dailymail.co.uk/ news/article-2977293/Kobe-Bryant-s-wife-miscarried-stress-Colorado-rape -case-LA-Lakers-star-believes.html.

Duangdao, Dan. "Lakers News: Kobe Returns to Italy for First Time, Wants to Own Team." *Lakers Nation* (online). August 3, 2013. Accessed February 29, 2016. http://www.lakersnation.com/lakers-news-kobe-returns-to-italy-for-first -time-wants-to-own-team/2013/08/03/.

Dubasik, Zac. "The History of Kobe Bryant's Signature Sneakers." *Solecollector* (online). August 19, 2014. Accessed February 28, 2016. http://solecollector .com/news/2014/08/the-history-of-kobe-bryant-s-signature-sneakers1.

Dubin, Jared. "Kobe Bryant No Longer Great—But That's O.K." *Sports Illustrated: The Cauldron* (online). October 16, 2015. Accessed February 28, 2016. http:// www.si.com/thecauldron/2015/10/13/kobe-bryant-los-angeles-lakers-health -decline.

Duncan, Apryl. "Kobe Bryant's Endorsement Deals." *About Money* (online). Updated December 15, 2014. Accessed February 28, 2016. http://advertising .about.com/od/kobebryant/a/bryantsendorse.htm.

Dwyer, Kelly. "An Underage Kobe Bryant Used His Laker Status to Buy Beer with Jimmy Fallon." *Yahoo!* (online). February 5, 2015. Accessed March 2, 2016. http://sports.yahoo.com/blogs/nba-ball-dont-lie/an-underage-kobe-bryant -used-his-laker-status-to-buy-beer-with-jimmy-fallon-ideo-205833061.html.

ECAC Sports (online). "Top Moments in ECAC History: ECAC Awards Automatic Qualifier to Division I Men's Basketball Regional Champions." January 10, 2014. Accessed February 29, 2016. http://ecacsports.com/archives/general _news/2013-14/top_moments_ecac_division_i_mens_basketball_aq.

Eggert-Crowe, Madison, and Scott Gabriel Knowles. "Bicentennial (1976)." *Encyclopedia of Greater Philadelphia* (online). N.d. Accessed March 1, 2016. http:// philadelphiaencyclopedia.org/archive/bicentennial-1976/.

Eisenberg, Jeff. "Magic Johnson on Kobe: 'Closest Thing We've Seen to Michael Jordan.'" *Yahoo!* (online). November 29, 2015. Accessed February 29, 2016. http://sports.yahoo.com/blogs/nba-ball-dont-lie/magic-johnson-on-kobe ---closest-thing-we-ve-seen-to-michael-jordan-043851861.html?soc _src=mediacontentstory&soc_trk=fb.

Ellis, C. Y. "Kobe Bryant: A Career in Kicks." *Hoopsvibe* (online). December 22, 2007. Accessed February 28, 2016. http://www.hoopsvibe.com/features/48049 -kobe-bryant-a-career-in-kicks-2.

Engvall, Nick. "Remembering Kobe Bryant's Sneaker Free Agency." *Solecollector* (online). December 5, 2015. Accessed February 27, 2016. http://solecollector .com/news/2015/12/kobe-bryant-sneaker-free-agency.

Esparza, Raf. "Jerry West Knew Kobe and Shaq Would Clash." *1stSlice* (online). May 6, 2015. Accessed March 1, 2016. http://www.1stslice.com/jerry-west -knew-kobe-and-shaq-would-clash/.

ESPN (online). "Bryant Passes Jordan, Has Shot to Be No. 1." December 14, 2014. Accessed February 28, 2016. http://espn.go.com/blog/statsinfo/post/_/id/100032/bryant-passes-jordan-has-shot-to-be-no-1.

————. "Kobe Bryant 4-for-6 from Long Range in Preseason Rout; 'His Timing Looks Great.'" October 12, 2015. Accessed February 28, 2016. http://scores.espn.go.com/nba/recap?gameId=400830089.

————. "Lakers' Kobe Bryant Purchases Italian Basketball Team." December 14, 1999. Accessed March 1, 2016. http://espn.go.com/gen/newswire/1999/991214/00233085.html.

————. "Trial Date Set for Kobe Bryant Case." May 13, 2013. Accessed February 28, 2016. http://espn.go.com/los-angeles/nba/story/_/id/9274335/june-17-trial-date-set-kobe-bryant-auction-case.

Evans, Bradford. "Kobe Bryant Is Headed into a Battle with an Undefeated Foe." *Sports Journal* (online). May 26, 2015. Accessed March 2, 2016. http://www.h4-entertainment.com/2015/05/kobe-bryant-is-headed-into-a-battle-with-an-undefeated-foe/.

Examiner (online). "Katelyn Faber's Name Resurfaces after Kobe Bryant Divorce Made Public." December 1, 2011. Accessed February 29, 2016. http://www.examiner.com/article/katelyn-faber-s-name-resurfaces-after-kobe-bryant-divorce-made-public.

————. "Kobe Bryant's Wife Vanessa Has 'Had Enough' of Cheating, Files for Divorce." December 16, 2016. Accessed February 29, 2016. http://www.examiner.com/article/kobe-bryant-s-wife-vanessa-has-had-enough-of-cheating-files-for-divorce.

Faigen, Harrison. "Jordan Hill Says 'A Lot of People Can't Handle' Kobe Bryant's Jawing." *SB Nation* (online). July 14, 2015. Accessed February 27, 2016. http://www.silverscreenandroll.com/2015/7/14/8967039/kobe-bryant-la-lakers-free-agency-jordan-hill.

————. "What Kobe Bryant Can Learn from the Way Michael Jordan Ended His Career." *SB Nation* (online). August 1, 2015. Accessed February 27, 2016. http://www.silverscreenandroll.com/2015/8/1/9084381/la-lakers-kobe-bryant-mchael-jordan.

Farraj, Julieann Sayegh. "Why Did Vanessa Wait 10 Years to Divorce Kobe Bryant?" Lawyers.com (online). December 27, 2011. Accessed February 27, 27, 2016. http://family-law.lawyers.com/blogs/archives/18120-why-did-vanessa-wait-10-years-to-divorce-kobe-bryant.html.

Farrell, Perry A. "Rip Hamilton: Pistons Should Have Won '3 or 4' Titles." *Detroit Free Press*. February 27, 2015.

Feldman, Dan. "Kobe Bryant Wanted to Be Traded from Lakers to Bulls in 2007." *NBC Sports* (online). February 23, 2015. Accessed March 3, 2016. http://nba.nbcsports.com/2015/02/23/kobe-bryant-wanted-to-be-traded-from-lakers-to-bulls-in-2007/.

Ferrari, Glauco. "Basketball in Italy." *Life in Italy* (online). June 1, 2012. Accessed March 3, 2016. http://www.lifeinitaly.com/sport/basketball.

Fields-Meyer, Thomas. "Fe-Fi-Fo-Fum!" *People* (online). June 5, 2000. Accessed February 29, 2016. http://www.people.com/people/article/0,,20131438,00.html.

Finish Line (online). "OG Ad: The Adidas KB 8 II." September 11, 2014. Accessed February 29, 2016. http://blog.finishline.com/2014/09/11/og-ad-the-adidas-kb-8-ii/.

Fitzpatrick, Frank. "Frank's Place: Warriors' Departure from Philly Still Hurts." Philly.com (online). June 15, 2015. Accessed February 29, 2016. http://articles.philly.com/2015-06-15/sports/63415068_1_nba-finals-eastern-conference-50-points.

Fluck, Adam. "Tex Winter and the Pursuit of Perfection." Bulls.com (online). January 16, 2013. Accessed March 3, 2016. http://www.nba.com/bulls/history/winter_pippenpaxson_110812.html.

Follorou, Jacques. "L'énigme de la mort, en 2009, du mafieux corse Francis Mariani en passe d'être résolue." *Le Monde.* June 24, 2013.

Foss, Mike. "Kobe Bryant's Swan Song Is Going to Last Another 81 Games and No One Can Stop It." *USA Today* (online). October 29, 2015. Accessed February 29, 2016. http://ftw.usatoday.com/2015/10/kobe-bryants-swan-song-is-going-to-last-another-81-games-and-no-one-can-stop-it.

Foster, D.J. "The 10 Most Revealing Quotes from Kobe Bryant's 'Muse.'" *Fox Sports* (online). March 4, 2015. Accessed March 3, 2016. http://www.foxsports.com/nba/story/los-angeles-lakers-kobe-bryant-muse-documentary-quotes-moments-030315.

Fox News (online). "Kobe Accuser Identifies Herself in Civil Suit." October 15, 2004. Accessed February 29, 2016. http://www.foxnews.com/story/2004/10/15/kobe-accuser-identifies-herself-in-civil-suit.html.

———. "Kobe Bryant Cheated on Latina Wife with Multiple Women, Reports Say." December 19, 2011. Accessed February 28, 2016. http://latino.foxnews.com/latino/entertainment/2011/12/19/kobe-bryants-latina-wife-knew-about-multiple-women/.

———. "Kobe Bryant Smiling But Vanessa Still Wants Divorce." April 17, 2012. Accessed March 3, 2016. http://latino.foxnews.com/latino/entertainment/2012/04/17/kobe-bryant-smiling-but-vanessa-still-wants-divorce/.

———. "Naming Kobe Bryant's Accuser." October 20, 2004. Accessed February 29, 2016. http://www.foxnews.com/story/2004/10/20/naming-kobe-bryant-accuser.html.

Fox Sports (online). "Trial Date Set for Kobe Bryant's Case against Auction House." May 15, 2014. Accessed March 3, 2016. http://www.foxsports.com/nba/story/los-angeles-lakers-kobe-bryant-trial-date-set-goldin-auctions-pamela-bryant-051413.

Frammolino, Ralph, and Tim Brown. "Reebok Won't Foot the Bill for Bryant's Shoe Endorsement." *Los Angeles Times.* February 15, 2003.

Franklin, Drew. "Calipari Passed on Kobe Bryant for Kerry Kittles." *Kentucky Sports Radio* (online). April 17, 2015. Accessed March 2, 2016. http://kentuckysportsradio.com/basketball-2/calipari-passed-on-kobe-bryant-for-kerry-kittles/.

Fredrick, Scott. "Adidas Kobe III Unreleased Sample Black/Purple 2001/2002." *DeFY. New York* (online). May 14, 2011. Accessed February 28, 2016. http://www.defynewyork.com/2011/05/15/adidas-kobe-iii-unreleased-sample-blackpurple-20012002/.

Free Library (online). "Surprise! Kid Kobe May Debut Tonight." November 1, 1996. Accessed March 3, 2016. http://www.thefreelibrary.com/SURPRISE! +KID+KOBE+MAY+DEBUT+TONIGHT.-a084001344.

Friedman, David. "Bryant Joins Erving and Jordan in Elite 30,000 Point Club." *20 Second Timeout* (online). December 6, 2012. Accessed March 1, 2016. http://20secondtimeout.blogspot.com/2012/12/bryant-joins-erving-and -jordan-in-elite.html.

———. "Julius Erving Ignored as Kobe Bryant Joins Exclusive 25,000/ 5000/5000 Club." *20 Second Timeout* (online). February 4, 2011. Accessed March 1, 2016. http://20secondtimeout.blogspot.com/2011/02/julius-erving- ignored-as-kobe-bryant.html.

———. "Maestro Bryant Orchestrates Lakers' Championship, Wins Finals MVP." *20 Second Timeout* (online). June 15, 2009. Accessed February 28, 2016. http://20secondtimeout.blogspot.com/2009/06/maestro-bryant-orchestrates -lakers.html.

———. "Ralph Wiley Understood Kobe Bryant's Genius." *20 Second Timeout* (online). July 6, 2012. Accessed March 1, 2016. http://20secondtimeout .blogspot.com/2012/07/ralph-wiley-understood-kobe-bryants.html.

From the Left (online). "Lakers Star Kobe Bryant Fined $100,000 for Homophobic Slur." April 13, 2011. Accessed February 28, 2016. https://fromtheleft.wordpress. com/2011/04/13/lakers-star-kobe-bryant-fined-100000-for-homophobic-slur/.

Gabriel, Kerith. "He Must Be from Philly." Philly.com (online). July 12, 2011. Accessed February 28, 2016. http://articles.philly.com/2011-07-12/sports/ 29764986_1_gibraltar-entertainment-joe-bryant-tupac.

Gaines, Cork. "Kobe Bryant Once Made a Young Teammate Cry by Saying He Needed to Rethink His 'Life Purpose.'" *Business Insider* (online). July 11, 2015. Accessed February 27, 2016. http://www.businessinsider.com/kobe-bryant -made-a-teammate-cry-2015-7.

Garrison, Drew. "Byron Scott Says Kobe Bryant Has the 'Privilege' to Shoot All the Dang Time, Sets Ugly Double Standard." *Silver Screen & Roll* (online). November 23, 2015. Accessed February 29, 2016. http://www.silverscreenandroll.com /2015/11/23/9788168/la-lakers-byron-scott-kobe-bryant-shots.

———. "Kobe Bryant Once Took His Helicopter to Las Vegas, Spoiled His Lakers Teammates." *Silver Screen & Roll* (online). May 28, 2015. Accessed February 28, 2016. http://www.silverscreenandroll.com/2015/5/28/8679051/la-lakers- kobe-bryant-helicopter-story.

Gavin, Mike. "Bird Remembers When Michael Jordan Took On Kobe." *Newsday*. February 8, 2015.

Ginsburg, Steve. "West Says It's 'Painful' to Watch Retiring NBA Star Bryant Play." *Reuters* (online). November 30, 2015. Accessed February 29, 2016. http://www. reuters.com/article/us-nba-kobe-west-idUSKBN0TJ2TI20151130.

Gloster, Rob. "Jerry Buss, Lakers' Owner for 10 NBA Championships, Dies at 80." *Bloomberg* (online). February 19, 2013. Accessed February 29, 2016. http://www.bloomberg.com/news/articles/2013-02-18/jerry-buss-los -angeles-lakers-owner-during-dynasty-dies-at-79.

Golianopoulos, Thomas. "The Secret History of Kobe Bryant's Rap Career." *Grantland* (online). April 12, 2013. Accessed February 27, 2016. http://www

.grantland.com/Features/the-secret-history-kobe-bryant-failed-attempt-rap
-carees/

Golliver, Ben. "Kobe Bryant Inspires Hate, Awe in Vintage Game against Timberwolves." *Sports Illustrated* (online). February 3, 2016. Accessed February
29, 2016. http://www.si.com/nba/2016/02/03/kobe-bryant-andrew-wiggins
-lakers-timberwolves-vintage-performance.

Goudreau, Jenna. "LA Lakers' Jeanie Buss Doesn't Play by the Rules." *Forbes.*
June 24, 2011.

Graham, Kristen. "A Documentary: The Story of Catholic Philadelphia." Saint
Joseph's University (online). N.d. Accessed February 29, 2016. https://www
.sju.edu/news-events/magazines/sju-magazine/sju-magazine-summer
-2015/documentary-story-catholic-philadelphia.

Grautski, Amara. "Kobe Says He Was 'an Idiot' While Reflecting on Shaq Feud."
New York Daily News. August 27, 2015.

Greenberg, Mel. "In His New Job, Bryant to Face His Old Coach." Philly.com
(online). May 19, 2006. Accessed March 3, 2016. http://articles.philly.com/
2006-05-19/sports/25400963_1_lakers-star-kobe-bryant-joe-jelly-bean
-bryant-wnba.

Gregory, Sean. "Expect Big Things Out of Kobe's Bryant's Retirement." *Time.*
November 30, 2015.

Gupta, Rapti. "Kobe's Wife Vanessa Bryant Sells Newport Beach Mansion."
Realty Today (online). January 10, 2013. Accessed February 29, 2016. http://
www.realtytoday.com/articles/3254/20130110/kobe-s-wife-vanessa-bryant
-sells-newport.htm.

Hansford, Corey. "Kobe Bryant Discusses Giorgio Armani's Impact on His
Post-Basketball Life." *Lakers Nation* (online). February 28, 2015. Accessed
March 3, 2016. http://www.lakersnation.com/kobe-bryant-discusses-giorgio
-armanis-impact-on-his-post-basketball-life/2015/02/28/.

———. "Kobe Bryant's High School Teammates Speak on His Recovery." *Lakers
Nation* (online). February 13, 2014. Accessed March 1, 2016. http://www.lakers
nation.com/kobe-bryants-high-school-teammates-speak-on-his-recovery/
2014/02/13/.

Hardwood Paroxysm (online). "Kobe Bryant Memories." March 18, 2015. Accessed
March 3, 2016. http://fansided.com/2015/03/18/kobe-byrant-memories/.

Hazell, Ricardo A. "The Incredible Life and Trying Basketball Times of Kobe
Bryant (Pt. 1)." *Shadow League* (online). December 23, 2013. Accessed March
2, 2016. http://www.theshadowleague.com/articles/the-incredible-life-and
-trying-basketball-times-of-kobe-bryant-pt-1.

Heisler, Mark. "Kobe or Not Kobe: The Answer's Finally in the Affirmative."
Sheridan Hoops (online). April 19, 2012. Accessed March 3, 2016. http://
www.sheridanhoops.com/2012/04/19/kobe-or-not-kobe-the-answers
-finally-in-the-affirmative/.

Herbert, James. "Colangelo Says Kobe Could Play for Team USA: 'Would Be a
Great Story.'" *CBS Sports* (online). August 11, 2015. Accessed February 28,
2016. http://www.cbssports.com/nba/eye-on-basketball/25266919/colangelo
-says-kobe-bryant-could-play-for-team-usa-would-be-a-great-story.

———. "Joe 'Jellybean' Bryant: There Won't Be Another Kobe or Michael." *CBS
Sports* (online). December 14, 2015. Accessed February 29, 2016. http://www

.cbssports.com/nba/eye-on-basketball/25413286/joe-bryant-discusses-son-ko
bes-retirement-michael-jordan-comparisons.

Heumann, Ina. "Remembering Rob Strasser—Larger Than Life." Adidas Group
Blog (online). October 30, 2013. Accessed February 27, 2016. http://blog
.adidas-group.com/2013/10/remembering-rob-strasser---larger-than-
life/.

Highkin, Sean. "Jeanie Buss Says Next Season Will Be a 'Celebration' of Kobe Bryant's Career." *NBC Sports* (online). April 26, 2015. Accessed March 1, 2016.
http://nba.nbcsports.com/2015/04/26/jeanie-buss-says-next-season-will
-be-a-celebration-of-kobe-bryants-career/.

Hingston, Sandy. "Is Kobe Bryant the Worst Person in the World?" *Philadelphia*
(online). December 15, 2014. Accessed February 29, 2016. http://www
.phillymag.com/news/2014/12/15/kobe-bryant-worst-person-world/.

Holloway, Shakeem. "Lakers Panel: Our Favorite Kobe Bryant Moments." *Lake
Show Life* (online). August 24, 2015. Accessed February 28, 2016. http://
lakeshowlife.com/2015/08/24/lakers-panel-our-favorite-kobe-bryant
-moments/.

Holmes, Baxter. "Kobe Bryant on First Game in Nearly 9 Months: It Was 'Good to
Get Out There.'" *ESPN* (online). October 5, 2015. Accessed February 28, 2016.
http://espn.go.com/losangeles/nba/story/_/id/13812221/kobe-bryant
-losangeles-lakers-returns-court-utah-jazz-preseason-opener.

———. "Kobe Bryant Reflects on 2004 Finals Loss to Pistons, Content with Five
Rings." *ESPN* (online). December 5, 2015. Accessed February 29, 2016.
http://espn.go.com/blog/los-angeles/lakers/post/_/id/42306/kobe
-reflects-on-2004-finals-loss-to-pistons-says-hes-content-with-just-five
-rings.

———. "Kobe Bryant Says It's Fine If He's Not Voted into 2016 All-Star Game."
ESPN (online). December 16, 2015. Accessed February 29, 2016. http://espn
.go.com/nba/story/_/id/14383590/los-angeles-lakers-kobe-bryant-says-fine
-not-voted-2016-all-star-game.

———. "Kobe Bryant Sets NBA Record for Seasons Played with One Franchise."
ESPN (online). October 29, 2015. Accessed February 29, 2016. http://espn
.go.com/nba/story/_/id/13995859/kobe-bryant-losangeles-lakers-sets-nba
-record-seasons-played-one-franchise.

———. "Kobe Bryant, Shaquille O'Neal Clear the Air in Wide-Ranging Podcast."
ESPN (online). August 31, 2015. Accessed February 28, 2016. http://espn
.go.com/blog/los-angeles/lakers/post/_/id/41768/kobe-bryant-shaquille-oneal
-clear-the-air?utm_source=newsletter&utm_medium=newsletter&utm
_campaign=nba.

———. "Kobe Bryant: 'Shocked Doesn't Do It Justice' over All-Star Voting Lead."
ESPN (online). December 26, 2015. Accessed February 27, 2016.

———. "Kobe on Pulling Back, Not Taking Over: 'It Has to Be Done.'" *ESPN*
(online). October 31, 2015. Accessed February 29, 2016. http://espn.go.com/
nba/story/_/id/14015006/kobe-bryant-losangeles-lakers-says-done-trying
-take-games.

———. "Lakers from the Outside: The Kobe Issue." *ESPN* (online). October 7,
2015. Accessed February 28, 2016. http://espn.go.com/nba/story/_/id/
13815620/losangeles-lakers-the-kobe-bryant-issue.

HoopsVibe (online). "Kobe Bryant Settlement with Katelyn Faber—How Much?" March 1, 2005. Accessed February 29, 2016. http://www.hoopsvibe.com/gossip/52439-kobe-bryant-settlement-with-katelyn-faber-how-much.

Howard, Greg. "Skip Bayless Claims Rape Charges Helped Kobe Bryant Sell Sneakers." *Deadspin* (online). October 21, 2014. Accessed February 28, 2016. http://deadspin.com/skip-bayless-claims-rape-charges-helped-kobe-bryant-sel-1648935985.

Hubert, James. "Kobe Bryant 'Crazy' to Still Be Playing, Says Lakers Can Make Playoffs." *CBS Sports* (online). August 4, 2015. Accessed February 27, 2016. http://www.cbssports.com/nba/eye-on-basketball/25259462/kobe-bryant-crazy-to-still-be-playing-says-lakers-can-make-playoffs.

Hubler, Shawn. "Vanessa Laine Was Just Another Sheltered Orange County Teen—Then She Fell in Love with a Phenomenon." *Daily Press.* March 5, 2005.

Hughes, Grant. "Envisioning the Perfect, Uncompromising End to Kobe's Career." *Bleacher Report* (online). November 11, 2015. Accessed February 29, 2016. http://bleacherreport.com/articles/2587639-envisioning-the-perfect-uncompromising-end-to-kobe-bryants-career?utm_source=newsletter&utm_medium=newsletter&utm_campaign=nba.

———. "Million-Dollar Men: How the NBA's Richest Earners Made Their on-Court Cash." *Bleacher Report* (online). July 14, 2015. Accessed February 27, 2016. http://bleacherreport.com/articles/2522709-million-dollar-men-how-the-nbas-biggest-earners-made-their-on-court-cash.

Hunt, Donald. "Sonny Hill League a Must Stop over Years." *Philadelphia Tribune.* July 16, 2012.

Iandorio, Iacopo. "Italian Graffiti." *Gazzetta dello Sport.* November 4, 2000. Accessed February 29, 2016. http://archiviostorico.gazzetta.it/2000/novem bre/04/italian_graffiti_sw_0_0011041203.shtml.

James, Sue Ellen. "Whether It's the L.A. Lakers or a Lovely Woman, Jerry Buss Is Interested in Champions." *People.* February 11, 1980.

Jenkins, Lee. "Kobe's Final Challenge." *Sports Illustrated.* June 7, 2010.

———. "Year 20." *Time Warner Cable* (online). October 28, 2015. Accessed February 29, 2016. http://www.twcsportsnet.com/videos/2015/10/28/lee-jenkins-essay-on-kobe-bryant-year-20.

Jensen, Mike. "Bryant Crashes the Boardrooms. At 21, He Has Mastered NBA Fame. Now He Is Going Global." Philly.com (online). June 16, 2000. Accessed February 28, 2016. http://articles.philly.com/2000-06-16/news/25601431_1_olimpia-milano-kobe-bryant-lakers.

———. "Hoop Schemes: Basketball's Sneaker War for Aggressive Manufacturers, School-Age Recruits Are Getting Younger and Younger." Philly.com (online). October 26, 1997. Accessed March 3, 2016. http://articles.philly.com/1997-10-26/sports/25537293_1_fila-adidas-shoe.

———. "New Front Is Opened in the Sneaker Wars; Nike and Adidas Each Want the Best Players." Philly.com (online). July 21, 1995. Accessed February 27, 2016.

Jerardi, Dick. "Who at Lower Merion Knew Bryant Would Be NBA Star So Soon?" Knight Ridder/Tribune News Service (online). June 21, 2000. Accessed March 1. 2016. https://www.highbeam.com/doc/1G1-62865941.html.

Johnson, K.C. "As Kobe Bryant's Chicago Finale Approaches Sunday, What If…" *Chicago Tribune*. February 20, 2016.

Johnson, William Oscar. "Jerry Is Never behind the Eight Ball." *Sports Illustrated*. June 18, 1979. Accessed February 29, 2016.

Joseph, Adi. "Kobe Bryant Leads Moving Lakers Tribute to Jerry Buss." *USA Today*. February 21, 2013.

Julian, Claude. "Current Affairs: Is Kobe a Cheater?" *Stunnerbaby* (online). Stunnerbaby.com. December 1, 2011. Accessed February 28, 2016. http://stunner babymag.com/2.0/2011/12/01/current-affairs-is-a-kobe-cheater/.

Kamer, Foster. "101 Masterpieces: The Air Jordan III." *Mental Floss* (online). N.d. Accessed February 27, 2016. http://mentalfloss.com/article/57721/101 -masterpieces-air-jordan-iii.

Katz, Donald. "Triumph of the Swoosh." *Sports Illustrated*. April 16, 1993.

Kawakami, Tim. "Bryant Gets to Make and Call the Shots." *Los Angeles Times*. December 14, 1999.

Kaye, Elizabeth. "Lakers: The Dream Team." *Los Angeles*. April 2004.

KB8fan'sHomepages (online). "The Players in the Kobe Bryant Case." N.d. Accessed February 29, 2016. http://www.geocities.ws/imakb8fan/NamesFaces.html.

Kersey, Stephen. "Kobe Bryant's Sister Comes to His Defense Against Parents." *EveryJoe* (online). May 13, 2013. Accessed March 3, 2016. http://www .everyjoe.com/2013/05/13/sports/sharia-washington-photos-kobe-bryant-sister/.

Kirkpatrick, Curry. "The Old Soft Shoe." *Sports Illustrated*. November 25, 1992.

Kish, Matthew. "Can Adidas Group North America's New President Make Nike Sweat?" *Portland Business Journal*. July 18, 2014.

———. "ESPN Documentary Examines How Nike and Adidas Pitchman Sonny Vaccaro Helped Birth NCAA Sneaker Deals." *Portland Business Journal*. April 6, 2015.

———. "The *PBJ* Interview: Sonny Vaccaro on Building Nike Hoops and Possibly Upending the NCAA." *Portland Business Journal*. April 10, 2015.

———. "Sonny Vaccaro on Why There Will Never Be Another Michael Jordan." *Portland Business Journal*. April 9, 2015.

Klosterman, Chuck. "GQ&A: Kobe Bryant." *GQ*. February 17, 2015.

Knoblauch, Austin. "Kobe Bryant." *Los Angeles Times* (online). August 24, 2014. Accessed February 29, 2016. http://projects.latimes.com/lakers/player/kobe -bryant/.

———. "Shaquille O'Neal, Scottie Pippen Talk Epic Smack in Lakers vs. Bulls Battle." *Los Angeles Times* (online). July 21, 2015. Accessed February 29, 2016. http://www.latimes.com/sports/sportsnow/la-sp-sn-shaquille-oneal-scottie-pi ppen-lakers-bulls-20150721-htmlstory.html.

Kobe Bryant Universe. "Welcome to Kobe Bryant Universe!!!" N.d. Accessed February 28, 2016. http://www.kobebryantuniverse.com/.

Krulikowski, Anne E. "Southwest Philadelphia." *Encyclopedia of Greater Philadelphia* (online). N.d. Accessed February 29, 2016. http://philadelphiaency clopedia.org/archive/southwest-philadelphia-essay/.

Laird, Sam. "Kobe Bryant or Michael Jordan? YouTube Mashup Shows Uncanny Symmetry." *Mashable* (online). August 29, 2015. Accessed February 29, 2016. http://mashable.com/2012/08/28/kobe-bryant-michael-jordan-youtube/.

Lalli. "Elimination Day?" *Philly Sports History* (online). April 24, 2011. Accessed March 3, 2016. http://phillysportshistory.com/2011/04/24/elimination-day/.

Lambroschini, Charles. "The Corsican Connection." *New York Times*. May 18, 2012.

Larkin, Mike. "How Kobe Bryant's Wife 'Almost Filed for Divorce Four Years Ago.'" *Daily Mail* (online). December 20, 2011. Accessed February 28, 2016. http://www.dailymail.co.uk/tvshowbiz/article-2076419/Kobe-Bryant -divorce-Wife-Vanessa-filed-divorce-4-years-ago.html.

Lashinsky, Adam. "Fortune's Businessperson of the Year: Nike's Master Crafts-man." *Fortune*. November 12, 2015. Accessed February 29, 2016. http://fortune .com/2015/11/12/nike-ceo-mark-parker/.

Legends Clothing Company Blog (online). "10 Best AAU Basketball Teams Ever." June 13, 2014. Accessed March 3, 2016. https://www.legendssf.com/blogs/ legends-blog/14491885-10-best-aau-basketball-teams-ever.

Lewis, Brian. "Karl Malone: I'll Fight Kobe If He's Still Mad I Flirted with Wife." *New York Post*. February 12, 2015.

Ley, Tom. "Kobe Bryant Doesn't Have Any Friends." *Deadspin* (online). February 17, 2015. Accessed March 3, 2016. http://deadspin.com/kobe-bryant-doesnt -have-any-friends-1686269981.

Lidz, Franz. "She's Got Balls. Will Jeanie Buss, Daughter of Lakers Owner Jerry Buss, Be the Next to Rule Her Father's Sports Kingdom, or Will One of Her Brothers Rise to Power? A Fractured Family Fable." *Sports Illustrated*. Novem-ber 2, 1998.

Littlefield, Bill. "Meet Kobe Bryant's 'Muse': His High School English Teacher." *Only a Game* (online). WBUR. December 12, 2015. Accessed December 2016. http://onlyagame.wbur.org/2015/12/12/kobe-bryant-poem-jeanne -mastriano.

Livingston, Bill. "Covering Dr. J — 5 Years of Love, Playoffs and Music in the Air at the Woodstock of the NBA." Cleveland *Plain Dealer*. June 14, 2013.

Loving, James. "NBA Beat Part 2 — The Bryants, Father (Jellybean) & Son (Kobe)." *National Radio* (online). February 8, 2012. http://www.national radio.com/NBA_BEAT_FEB_12_Part_2.shtml.

MacMullan, Jackie. "Kobe Bryant: Imitating Greatness." *ESPN* (online). June 4, 2010. Accessed February 29, 2016. http://espn.go.com/nba/playoffs/2010/ columns/story?columnist=macmullan_jackie&page=kobefilmstudy -100604.

————. "Lakers to Van Exel: Get with the Program. Indiana Jones for Mullin? Jackson May Sit Rather Than Split." *Sports Illustrated*. May 26, 1997.

Mahoney, Brian. "Kobe's Wish: Treat Visits like He Did Jordan's Last All-Star." *Asso-ciated Press* (online). November 9, 2015. Accessed February 29, 2016. http:// www.apnewsarchive.com/2015/Kobe%27s_wish%3A_Treat_visits_like_he _did_Jordan%27s_last_All-Star/id-03ac95f622b144938fa72f53d4520e51.

Manfred, Tony. "Phil Jackson Says Kobe Bryant Trains Harder Than Michael Jor-dan Did." *Business Insider* (online). September 24, 2014. Accessed February 29, 2016. http://www.businessinsider.com/jackson-kobe-trains-michael-jordan -2014-9.

Manfred, Tony. "Where Are They Now? The Players from Kobe Bryant's Legend-ary 1996 NBA Draft." *Business Insider* (online). February 15, 2015. Accessed

March 3, 2016. http://www.businessinsider.com/where-are-they-now-1996 -nba-draft-2015-2.

Markazi, Arash. "Kobe Bryant Goes off on Teammates." *ESPN* (online). December 12, 2014. Accessed February 28, 2016. http://espn.go.com/nba/story/_/ id/12016979/los-angeles-lakers-star-kobe-bryant-critical-teammates-heated -scrimmage.

Martin, Brian. "Kobe's Top 10 Scoring Performances." NBA.com (online). N.d. Accessed February 29, 2016. http://stats.nba.com/featured/kobe_top_10 _scoring_performances_2014_12_14.html.

Martin, Josh. "Kobe Bryant's 'Gay Slur' and the 10 Stupidest Moments of His Career." *Bleacher Report* (online). April 25, 2011. Accessed February 29, 2016. http://bleacherreport.com/articles/676445-kobe-bryants-gay-slur-and-the-10 -stupidest-moments-of-his-career.

Martinez, Juan. "#MambaDay: The Kobe Bryant Adidas and Nike Signature Shoe Rankings." *Kicks on Fire* (online). April 12, 2016. http://www.kickson fire.com/kobe-bryant-nike-adidas-signature-shoe-rankings/.

Mather, Victor. "Kobe Bryant's Decline Puts Lakers on Wrong Side of History." *New York Times*. November 27, 2015.

Matthews, Laura. "Vanessa Bryant Gets $75 Million, 3 Mansions from Kobe Bryant Divorce." *International Business Times* (online). January 20, 2012. Accessed February 29, 2016. http://www.ibtimes.com/vanessa-bryant-gets-75-million -3-mansions-kobe-bryant-divorce-report-398520.

McCallum, Jack. "Cirque de L.A. Kobe Bryant Couldn't Persuade Mike Krzyzewski to Join the Lakers, Who Showed They'll Jump through Hoops to Keep Their Star Happy." *Sports Illustrated*. July 12, 2004.

McCauley, Janie. "John Cox Following in Father's Footsteps." *CBS College Sports* (online). February 10, 2005. Accessed February 28, 2016. http://www.cstv .com/sports/m-baskbl/stories/021105acb.html.

McGraw, Mike. "Hamilton Ready to Renew Long-term Rivalry with Bryant." *Daily Herald* (online). December 23, 2011. Accessed March 3, 2016. http:// www.dailyherald.com/article/20111223/sports/712239675/.

McMenamin, Dave. "Colangelo: Kobe 'Would Love to Ride Off into Sunset' with Gold Medal." *ESPN* (online). August 14, 2015. Accessed February 28, 2016. http://espn.go.com/nba/story/_/id/13435153/jerry-colangelo-ruled-kobe -bryant-2016-rio-olympics.

Medina, Mark. "Byron Scott: Lakers' Kobe Bryant Showed 'No Fear' Even during Rookie Season." *Los Angeles Daily News* (online). March 19, 2015. Accessed March 3, 2016. http://www.dailynews.com/sports/20150319/byron-scott-lakers -kobe-bryant-showed-no-fear-even-during-rookie-season.

———. "Kobe Bryant's 'Airball Game' in 1997 Was a Defining Moment in His Career." *Los Angeles Daily News* (online). January 15, 2016. Accessed February 29, 2016. http://www.dailynews.com/sports/20160115/kobe-bryants-airball -game-in-1997-was-as-defining-moment-in-his-career.

———. "Kobe Bryant's Parents Say He Lied about Memorabilia." *Inside the Lakers* (online). May 13, 2013. Accessed March 3, 2016. http://www.insidesocal.com/ lakers/2013/05/13/kobe-bryants-parents-say-he-lied-about-memorabilia/.

———. "Kobe Bryant's Storied Legacy, Both Good and Bad, Thrives in Philadelphia." *Los Angeles Daily News* (online). June 2, 2014. Accessed March 1, 2016.

http://www.dailynews.com/sports/20140206/kobe-bryants-storied-legacy
-both-good-and-bad-thrives-in-philadelphia.

———. "Timberwolves Almost Drafted Kobe Bryant in 1996 NBA Draft."
Press-Telegram (online). March 25, 2015. Accessed February 29, 2016. http://
www.presstelegram.com/sports/20150325/timberwolves-almost-drafted
-kobe-bryant-in-1996-nba-draft/1.

Metropolis (online). "Philadelphia Street Gangs: Philadelphia Metropolis." N.d.
Accessed February 28, 2016. http://www.phlmetropolis.com/tag/philadel
phia+street+gangs.

Milburn, Karen. "Footloose and for Real—Nike's Success Exposed in 'Swoosh.'"
Seattle Times. February 6, 1992.

Milligan, Chuck, and Rev. Ron Ballew. "History of Black Firefighters." Legeros
.com (online). N.d. Accessed March 1, 2016. http://www.legeros.com/
history/ebf/national.shtml#Philadelphia.

Missanelli, M. G. "Mr. Basketball a Hero for His Work with Teens, Sonny Hill Is
Not without Critics." Philly.com (online). July 12, 1987. Accessed March 1, 2016.
http://articles.philly.com/1987-07-12/sports/26201611_1_sonny-hill-summer
-leagues-religious-leaders.

Molinet, Jason. "Kobe Bryant Carries Guilt over Wife's Miscarriage." *New York
Daily News* (online). March 3, 2015. Accessed March 3, 2016. http://www
.nydailynews.com/sports/basketball/kobe-bryant-carries-guilt-wife
-miscarriage-article-1.2135283.

Moore, Matt. "Ex-Laker Jordan Hill on Kobe Bryant: All You Hear Is His Mouth."
CBS Sports (online). July 17, 2015. Accessed February 27, 2016.

Moran, Robert. "Gang Turf Wars Plague Phila. Neighborhoods; Violent Street
'Crews' Contribute to City Mayhem." Philly.com (online). November 6, 2006.
Accessed February 28, 2016. http://articles.philly.com/2006-11-06/news/
25407744_1_gang-problem-neighborhood-gangs-bloods.

Morkides, Chris. "Bryant Follows in Father's All-Star Footsteps." Philly.com (online).
April 1, 1996. Accessed March 2, 2016. http://articles.philly.com/1996-04-01/
sports/25659508_1_dunk-competition-mcdonald-s-all-american-slam.

———. "Kobe, Team Approach the Crossroads." *HoopsHype* (online). December 23,
2008. Accessed March 1, 2016. http://hoopshype.com/2008/12/23/kobe-team-
approach-the-crossroads/.

MSN (online). "Phil Jackson's Impact on Kobe." November 30, 2015. Accessed
February 29, 2016. http://www.msn.com/en-us/video/watch/phil-jacksons
-impact-on-kobe/vi-AAfPsMJ.

Mulligan, Thomas S. "Adidas to Put U.S. Market in Hands of Ex-Nike Whiz." *Los
Angeles Times*. February 5, 1993.

Murdock, Logan. "Lakers Head Coaches Rode Kobe Bryant into the Ground."
Lake Show Life (online). September 9, 2015. Accessed February 28, 2016.
https://lakeshowlife.com/2015/09/09/lakers-head-coaches-rode-kobe
-bryant-into-the-ground/.

Murphy, David. "Remembering Jerry Buss One Year After His Passing." *Bleacher
Report* (online). February 18, 2014. Accessed February 29, 2016. http://
bleacherreport.com/articles/1963309-remembering-jerry-buss-one-year
-after-his-passing.

Mutoni, Marcel. "Jerry West on Kobe and Shaq: 'Those Two Different Personalities Had to Clash.'" *SLAMonline* (online). May 7, 2015. Accessed March 1, 2016. http://www.slamonline.com/media/slam-tv/jerry-west-on-kobe-and-shaq -those-two-different-personalities-had-to-clash/#YhqglbI8wygFsYDv.97.

———. "Kobe Bryant Shooting for the First Time Since Shoulder Surgery." *SLAMonline* (online). August 24, 2015. Accessed February 28, 2016. http:// www.slamonline.com/nba/kobe-bryant-shooting-for-the-first-time-since -shoulder-surgery/#18qR3bqZASoUriAE.97.

———. "Kobe Bryant Tells Critics to Count His Five Rings." *SLAMonline* (online). June 8, 2015. Accessed March 2, 2016. http://www.slamonline.com/ nba/kobe-bryant-tells-critics-to-count-his-five-rings/#KL62ckWBgQrvs qUa.97.

Nathan, Alec. "The Most Egotistical Things Kobe Bryant Has Ever Said." *Bleacher Report* (online). February 22, 2013. Accessed February 29, 2016. http:// bleacherreport.com/articles/1536728-the-most-egotistical-things-kobe -bryant-has-ever-said.

NBA.com (online). "Mitch Kupchak Exit Interview 2014-15." April 16, 2015. http://www.nba.com/lakers/news/1415_exitInterview_kupchak.

NBA Italia News (online). "Kobe Bryant, Orgoglio Italiano." June 10, 2015. Accessed March 2, 2016. http://www.nbaitalianews.it/2015/06/kobe-bryant -orgoglio-italiano/.

Neuharth-Keusch, AJ. "Kobe Bryant's NBA Career by the Numbers." *USA Today*. December 1, 2015.

Newcomb, Tim. "History of Kobe Bryant's Signature Shoes." *Sports Illustrated* (online). N.d. Accessed February 29, 2016. http://www.si.com/nba/photos/ 2014/12/11/kobe-bryant-signature-shoes-nike-adidas.

New York Post (online). "Kobe Bryant Says He's Basically Falling Apart." November 16, 2015. Accessed February 29, 2016. http://nypost.com/2015/11/16/ kobe-bryant-says-hes-basically-falling-apart/.

New York Times. "Rob Strasser, 46, Dies; Ex-Executive for Nike." November 1, 1993.

New York Times. "A Stunning Verdict from L.A.: Lakers Beat Bulls." February 5, 1997.

Next Level (online). "When AAU Comes before ABC's." N.d. Accessed March 2, 2016. http://www.nextlevelcaac.com/aau_before_abcs.htm.

Nuok (online). "Quando Kobe Bryant giocava a Pistoia..." May 26, 2012. Accessed February 29, 2016. http://www.nuok.it/pistojah/quando-kobe-bryant-giocava -a-pistoia/.

Odeven, Ed. "Fukuoka Triumphs in First Game under New Coach Joe Bryant." *Japan Times* (online). January 18, 2015. Accessed March 2, 2016. http://www .japantimes.co.jp/sports/2015/01/18/basketball/bj-league/fukuoka-triumphs -first-game-new-coach-joe-bryant/#.VNJVWmR4qXo.

O'Donnell, Jake. "Stephen A. Smith Calls Out Jim Buss for Wasting the Last Years of Kobe's Career." *SportsGrid* (online). November 30, 2015. Accessed February 29, 2016. http://www.sportsgrid.com/nba/stephen-a-smith-calls -out-jim-buss-for-wasting-the-last-years-of-kobes-career/.

Ogden, Rob. "Tracy McGrady: Kobe Was Obsessed with Emulating Jordan." *Chicago Sun-Times*. February 22, 2016.

Oram, Bill. "Kobe Bryant's Visit an 'Unexpected Gift' for Visiting Pau Gasol." *Orange County Register.* January 29, 2015.

Our Sports Central (online). "Frenzy Come Up Short in Jellybean's Debut." January 27, 2005. Accessed February 28, 2016. http://www.oursportscentral.com/services/releases/frenzy-come-up-short-in-jellybeans-debut/n-3114604.

Owens, Kevin. "Why Does Philadelphia Really Hate Kobe Bryant?" *SB Nation* (online). September 22, 2011. Accessed February 29, 2016. http://philly.sb nation.com/philadelphia-76ers/2011/9/22/2442077/why-does-philadelphia -really-hate-kobe-bryant.

Pacini, Elisa. "Kobe Bryant a sorpresa tra i vecchi amici di Cireglio." *Tirreno.* July 26, 2013.

Palmer, Chris. "Lakers' Infusion of Young Talent to Test Kobe's Ability to Take Needed Step Back." *Bleacher Report* (online). July 15, 2015. Accessed February 27, 2016. http://bleacherreport.com/articles/2512893-lakers-infusion-of-young -talent-to-test-kobes-ability-to-take-needed-step-back?utm _source=newsletter&utm_medium=newsletter&utm_campaign=nba.

Pandian, Ananth. "Kobe Bryant Receives His Lowest Player Rating Ever in NBA 2016." *CBS Sports* (online). August 29, 2015. Accessed February 28, 2016. http://www.cbssports.com/nba/eye-on-basketball/25284135/kobe-bryant -gets-his-lowest-ever-player-rating-in-nba-2k16.

Papanek, Johnny. "Trouble? Call the Bomb Squad." *Sports Illustrated.* December 19, 1977.

Parnell, David J. "Filmmaker Gotham Chopra, on Kobe Bryant's Muse and Success through Storytelling." *Forbes* (online). March 16, 2015. Accessed March 3, 2016. http://www.forbes.com/sites/davidparnell/2015/03/16/filmmaker-gotham -chopra-on-kobe-bryants-muse-and-success-through-storytelling/3/#71b8531 c3bd1.

Patton, Phil. "If the Car Fits, Wear It: Audi Leaves Its Footprint on Footwear." *New York Times.* March 24, 2001.

PBS: Frontline (online). "Interview Sonny Vaccaro." January 16, 2013. Accessed March 4, 2016. http://www.pbs.org/wgbh/pages/frontline/money-and-march -madness/interviews/sonny-vaccaro.html.

People (online). "Smooth Move." May 7, 2001. Accessed February 29, 2016. http://www.people.com/people/archive/article/0,,20134313,00.html.

Petchesky, Barry. "Kobe Understands Kobe Better Than Anyone Else." *Deadspin* (online). December 15, 2015. Accessed February 29, 2016. http://deadspin .com/kobe-understands-kobe-better-than-anyone-else-1748383485.

Peters, Micah. "Kobe Bryant on Past Feud with Shaq: 'I Was an Idiot When I Was a Kid.'" *USA Today* (online). August 26, 2015. Accessed February 28, 2016. http://ftw.usatoday.com/2015/08/kobe-bryant-on-past-feud-with-shaq-i-was -an-idiot-when-i-was-a-kid.

Peterson, Hayley. "4 Mistakes That Led to Adidas' Downfall." *Business Insider* (online). March 23, 2015. Accessed March 3, 2016. http://www.business insider.com/heres-where-adidas-went-wrong-2015-3.

Petkac, Luke. "The Sneaker Evolution of Kobe Bryant." *Bleacher Report* (online). February 1, 2013. Accessed February 28, 2016. http://bleacherreport.com/articles/1509138-the-sneaker-evolution-of-kobe-bryant.

Pickering, Ross. "Kobe Bryant Talked Trash to Rodney Hood, Here's What He Said." *Lakerholicz* (online). October 10, 2015. Accessed February 28, 2016. http://lakerholicz.com/kobe-bryant-talked-trash-to-rodney-hood-heres -what-he-said/2015/10/10.

Pincus, Eric, and Broderick Turner. "Kobe Bryant to Retire after This Season: 'My Body Knows It's Time to Say Goodbye.'" *Los Angeles Times*. November 29, 2015.

Pincus, Eric. "Kobe Bryant Gives Lakers a Vintage Performance in 111-107 Win over Nuggets." *Los Angeles Times*. December 22, 2015.

———. "Kobe Bryant on Lakers Beating Warriors: 'I've Seen Stranger Things Happen.'" *Los Angeles Times*. November 24, 2015.

Plaschke, Bill. "Kobe Bryant Finally Surrenders to His Basketball Mortality." *Los Angeles Times*. November 29, 2015.

Players Tribune (online). "The Chirp: Athletes React to Kobe's Retirement." November 30, 2015. Accessed February 29, 2016. http://www.theplayers tribune.com/kobe-bryant-retirement-reaction/?utm_medium=email&utm _campaign=November%2B30th&utm_content=November%2B30th%2BCI D_591e6f0bcf3b6750474aa1105c02aed9&utm_source=newsletter&utm _term=READ+THEIR+REACTIONS.

———. "On the Line: Pau Gasol." December 3, 2015. Accessed February 29, 2016. http://www.theplayerstribune.com/pau-gasol-kobe-lakers-radio/?utm _medium=email&utm_campaign=December%2B3rd%2B-%2BFinal&utm _content=December%2B3rd%2B-%2BFinal%2BCID_24ceb9cf916e66aaa07f c97581d65787&utm_source=newsletter&utm_term=LISTEN+TO+PAU.

Portland Business Journal (online). "Former Nike Guru Retires from Adidas." May 28, 1998. Accessed February 28, 2016. http://www.bizjournals.com/ portland/stories/1998/05/25/daily6.html.

Pucin, Diane. "76ers Put End to All the Talk." *Los Angeles Times*. June 7, 2001.

Rapp, Timothy. "Kobe Bryant, Shaquille O'Neal's Top Quotes from the Latest 'Big Podcast.'" *Bleacher Report* (online). August 31, 2015. Accessed February 28, 2016. http://bleacherreport.com/articles/2558537-kobe-bryant-shaquille-oneals -top-quotes-from-the-latest-big-podcast?utm_source=newsletter&utm _medium=newsletter&utm_campaign=nba.

RealGM (online). "Analyzing Kobe Bryant's NBA Finals Stats...Not So Impres- sive." May 22, 2010. Accessed February 29, 2016. http://forums.realgm.com/ boards/viewtopic.php?t=1013948.

Reilly, Rick. "Life of Reilly." *ESPN* (com). April 20, 2009. Accessed February 29, 2016. http://espn.go.com/espnmag/story?id=4068270.

Richcreek, Katie. "Kobe Bryant Names Top 5 Players He's Faced, Includes Michael Jordan and LeBron." *Bleacher Report* (online). December 21, 2015. Accessed February 27, 2016. http://bleacherreport.com/articles/2601415 -kobe-bryant-names-top-5-players-hes-faced-includes-michael-jordan-lebron.

Rickman, Martin. "Behind the Mask: Rip Hamilton on Beating Duke, Getting Advice from Kobe and MJ, and His Facial Fashion Statement." *UPROXX* (online). March 23, 2015. Accessed March 3, 2016. http://uproxx.com/sports/ rip-hamilton-detroit-pistons-uconn-huskies/.

Rodgers, Joe. "Kobe Bryant on Michael Jordan Comparisons: 'My 37 Isn't MJ's 37.'" *Sporting News* (online). October 7, 2015. Accessed February 28, 2016.

http://www.sportingnews.com/nba-news/4657405-kobe-bryant-michael
-jordan-comparisions-age-seasons-nba-games.

Rojadirecta (online). "Lakers @ Clippers 12/10/79 (Magic Johnson Debut)." December 19, 1979. Accessed March 3, 2016. http://forum.rojadirecta.es/showthread .php?44138-NBA-Lakers-Clippers-12-10-79-%28Magic-Johnson-Debut%29.

Rosen, Charley. "How Phil Became Phil." *Today's FastBreak* (online). October 2, 2015. Accessed February 28, 2016. http://www.todaysfastbreak.com/from -the-courts/rosen-how-phil-became-phil/.

———. "The Phil Files: Everybody's a Critic." *ESPN* (online). July 27, 2015. Accessed February 27, 2016. http://espn.go.com/nba/story/_/id/13307527/the -phil-files-part-5-kobe-bryant-jerry-krause-criticisms.

———. "Why Kobe Bryant Is Breaking Down." *Today's FastBreak* (online). September 3, 2015. Accessed February 28, 2016. http://www.todaysfastbreak. com/nba-west/pacific/los-angeles-lakers/rosen-why-kobe-bryant-is -breaking-down/.

Rothstein, Matthew. "What Pau Gasol Once Did That Caused Kobe to Tell Phil Jackson, 'We're Going to the Finals!'" *UPROXX* (online). January 26, 2016. Accessed February 29, 2016. http://uproxx.com/dimemag/kobe-bryant-pau -gasol-championships/.

Rovell, Darren. "Kobe Is a Free Agent—on the Shoe Market." *ESPN* (online). N.d. Accessed February 28, 2016. http://assets.espn.go.com/nba/news/2002/ 0715/1405908.html.

Rowland, Mark. "Prince of the City." *Los Angeles.* January 1999.

Sager, Mike. "Kobe Bryant Doesn't Want Your Love." *Esquire.* November 30, 2015.

Samuels, Allison. "Kobe Bryant Marital Breakup Reveals the Ugly Side of NBA Marriages." *Daily Beast* (online). December 21, 2011. Accessed February 28, 2016. http://www.thedailybeast.com/articles/2011/12/21/kobe-bryant-marital -breakup-reveals-the-ugly-side-of-nba-marriages.html.

———. "Kobe Bryant's Wife Vanessa Files for Divorce." *Chicago Tribune* (online). December 16, 2011. Accessed February 28, 2016. http://articles.chicagotri- bune.com/2011-12-16/sports/chi-kobe-bryants-wife-files-for-divorce -20111216_1_vanessa-bryant-wife-files-kobe-bryant.

———. "Kobe off the Court." *Newsweek.* October 12, 2003.

Samuels, Ebenezer. "Gary Charles, L.I. Panthers Director, Vows to Keep Grass-roots Basketball of America Going." *New York Daily News* (online). August 10, 2010. Accessed March 2, 2016. http://www.nydailynews.com/sports/high -school/gary-charles-panthers-director-vows-grassroots-basketball -america-article-1.201703.

Sander, Libby. "The Gospel According to Sonny." *Chronicle of Higher Education* (online). July 25, 2010. Accessed March 3, 2016. http://chronicle.com/article/ The-Gospel-According-to-Sonny/123672/.

Schlemmer, Zach. "Meet the Newest Member of Kobe Bryant's Footwear Legacy." *Sneaker News* (online). March 27, 2015. Accessed February 29, 2016. http://sneakernews.com/2015/03/27/meet-the-newest-member-of-kobe -bryants-footwear-legacy/.

Schneider, Eric C. "Crime." *Encyclopedia of Greater Philadelphia* (online). N.d. Accessed February 28, 2016. http://philadelphiaencyclopedia.org/archive/crime/.

"Selfie sotto la torre di Pisa per Kobe Bryant e moglie." *Tirreno*. April 20, 2015.

Sherman, Rodger. "A Brief History of Kobe Bryant Helping People Decide They Don't Want to Play for the Lakers." *SBNation* (online). July 1, 2015. Accessed February 27, 2016. http://www.sbnation.com/2015/7/1/8880543/kobe-bryant -lakers-nba-free-agency-lamarcus-aldridge-dwight-howard.

Showtime (online). "Kobe Bryant's Muse: Highlights from the Red Carpet." February 2015. Accessed March 3, 2016. http://www.sho.com/sho/video/titles/35057/ kobe-bryants-muse-highlights-from-the-red-carpet.

Shultz, Alex. "Lakers Media Day: Kobe Bryant Coy about This Being His Last Season." *Los Angeles Times*. September 28, 2015.

Sieczkowski, Cavan. "Kobe Bryant Divorce: Alleged Mistresses from Carla DiBello to Katelyn Faber." *International Business Times* (online). December 20, 2011. Accessed February 28, 2016. http://www.ibtimes.com/kobe-bryant -divorce-alleged-mistresses-carla-dibello-katelyn-faber-photos-553621.

Siemers, Erik. "Adidas' Drive to the Hoop." *Portland Business Journal*. December 21, 2012.

———. "Peter Moore: Basketball Was Adidas America's Launching Point." *Portland Business Journal: Threads and Laces* (online). December 21, 2012. Accessed February 28, 2016. http://www.bizjournals.com/portland/blog/ threads_and_laces/2012/12/peter-moore-basketball-was-adidas.html.

Silary, Ted. "Kobe's Kin Makes Name for Himself." Philly.com (online). December 19, 1997. Accessed February 29, 2016. http://articles.philly.com/1997-12 -19/sports/25555918_1_cox-displays-grandfather-john-cox-kobe-bryant.

———. "Spirit of St. Tommy Burke's Second Straight CL Title in 1972 Was Memorable Trip." Philly.com (online). April 3, 1992. Accessed February 28, 2016. http://articles.philly.com/1992-04-03/sports/26006357_1_black-kids-cl-title -catholic-league.

Slade, Jacques. " 'Muse' Documentary About Kobe Bryant Is Good But Leaves Us Wanting More." *PostGame* (online). March 2, 2015. Accessed March 3, 2016. http://www.thepostgame.com/blog/daily-take/201503/muse-kobe-bryant -documentary-showtime-lakers-basketball.

SLAMonline (online). "Manchild in the Promised Land." January 13, 2014. Accessed February 29, 2016. http://www.slamonline.com/the-magazine/ features/kobe-bryant-slam-magazine-feature/#zcVUdEfEUitLJTqr.97.

Smallwood, John. "The Greatest? Kobe Bryant's Complex Legacy." Philly.com (online). March 27, 2015. Accessed February 29, 2016. http://www.philly .com/philly/sports/sixers/Kobe_Bryants_legacy.html.

Smiley, Brett. "Mamba Memories: 17 Great Moments in Kobe." *Fox Sports @ The Buzzer* (online). February 17, 2015. Accessed February 27, 2016. http://www .foxsports.com/buzzer/story/los-angeles-lakers-kobe-bryant-mamba -memories-021715.

Smith, Chris. "Battle of Soles." *New York Magazine*. March 3, 1997.

Smith, Marcia C., Heather Lourie, Bill Rams, and Kevin Dingg. "Scrutiny Intensifies for Private Bryant." *Baltimore Sun*. August 5, 2003.

Smith, Sam. "Pau Gasol Reflects on an All-Star Career and Life." NBA.com (online). February 14, 2016. Accessed February 29, 2016. http://www.nba .com/bulls/news/samsmith/allstar/pau-gasol-reflects-all-star-career-and-life.

Smith, Stephen A. "Kobe Bryant Set to Sign 'Big' Endorsement Deal with Adidas." Philly.com (online). May 17, 1996. Accessed February 28, 2016. http://articles.philly.com/1996-05-17/sports/25624618_1_adidas-bryant-family-college-basketball.

Soriano, Darius. "Coming Full Circle with Kobe Bryant." *ESPN: Forum Blue & Gold* (online). October 9, 2015. Accessed February 28, 2016. http://www.forumblueandgold.com/2015/10/09/coming-full-circle-with-kobe-bryant/.

SoundCloud (online). "The One and Only Shaquille O'Neal Going Off the Dribble on His Relationship w/ Kobe Bryant in L.A." N.d. Accessed February 28, 2016. https://soundcloud.com/siriusxmnba/the-one-and-only-shaquille-oneal-going-off-the-dribble-on-his-relationship-with-kobe-bryant-in-la?utm_source=newsletter&utm_medium=newsletter&utm_campaign=new-york-knicks.

Spangler, Todd. "Kobe Bryant Dunks into China with Alibaba Pact." *Boston Herald*. August 3, 2015.

Spears, Mark J. "Jerry Colangelo Talks Team USA, LeBron and Post-Coach K Era." *Yahoo!* (online). July 30, 2015. Accessed February 28, 2016. http://sports.yahoo.com/news/jerry-colangelo-talks-team-usa--lebron-and-post-coach-k-era-161049175.html.

SportsBusiness Daily (online). "Kobe Bryant Signs Multi-Year Extension with Nike." June 5, 2007. Accessed February 28, 2016. http://www.sportsbusinessdaily.com/Daily/Issues/2007/06/Issue-174/Sponsorships-Advertising-Marketing/Kobe-Bryant-Signs-Multi-Year-Extension-With-Nike.aspx.

Sports Business News (online). "Dr. Jerry Buss, a Sports Icon, a Sports Industry Titan." February 18, 2013. Accessed February 29, 2016. http://sportsbusinessnews.com/content/dr-jerry-buss-sports-icon-sports-industry-titan.

Sports Illustrated: Extra Mustard (online). "Kobe Bryant Randomly Emailed Anna Wintour to Talk about Leadership." February 26, 2015. Accessed March 3, 2016. http://www.si.com/extra-mustard/2015/02/26/lakers-kobe-bryant-anna-wintour-email?xid=aol_home.

Sports Illustrated: Wire (online). "Ex-Laker Samaki Walker Says Kobe Bryant Punched Him over $100." Updated January 27, 2016. http://www.si.com/nba/2016/01/26/samaki-walker-kobe-bryant-punched-over-100-dollars.

———. "Kobe Bryant to Lakers' Byron Scott: 'Coach, This Might Be My Last Year.'" November 9, 2015. Accessed February 29, 2016. http://www.si.com/nba/2015/11/09/loa-angeles-lakers-kobe-bryant-coach-byron-scott-retirement.

———. "Lakers' Kobe Bryant Disses Himself, Says He's 200th Best Player in NBA." November 2, 2015. Accessed February 29, 2016. http://www.si.com/nba/2015/11/02/kobe-bryant-los-angeles-lakers-struggles-200th-best-player-i-freaking-suck?xid=aol_home.

Sports Media (online). "History and Memorable Cases in Sports Law." April 2, 2013. Accessed February 29, 2016. http://www.sportsmedia101.com/sportslaw/history/.

SportsTwo (online). "Joe Bryant Wants Kobe in Phoenix." February 24, 1994. Accessed March 3, 2016. http://www.sportstwo.com/threads/joe-bryant-wants-kobe-in-phoenix.55268/.

Springer, Steve. "Buss, Mariani Settle Tax Bill, Pay $1 Million." *Los Angeles Times*. May 11, 1985.

————. "Buss—The Next Generation." *Los Angeles Times*. November 24, 2002.

————. "From Bread Line to Lakers Owner, Jerry Buss Left a Lasting Impact on the NBA." *Yahoo!* (online). February 18, 2013. Accessed February 29, 2016. http://sports.yahoo.com/news/nba--from-bread-line-to-lakers-owner--jerry-buss -left-a-lasting-impact-on-the-nba-161337054.html.

Stanford Daily. "Gilbert Returns Charges of *LA Times* Reporters." February 3, 1982.

Starner, Tom. "In a League of His Own: Sonny Hill Has Helped a Horde of Philadelphia Kids Find Direction on—and off—the Basketball Court." *Sports Illustrated*. July 29, 1991.

Stein, Mark, and Annie Marie Cruz. "Drill Kobe's Quest." *ESPN* (online). July 10, 2012. Accessed March 1, 2016. http://espn.go.com/espn/magazine/archives/ news/story?page=magazine-20021111-article33.

Stevenson, Seth. "Heir Jordan: Will Nike's $90 Million Gamble Pay Off?" *Slate* (online). May 22, 2003. Accessed February 28, 2016. http://www.slate.com/ articles/business/moneybox/2003/05/heir_jordan.html.

Strahler, Steven R. "When Michael Jordan Wore Really Short Shorts." *Crain's Chicago Business* (online). December 10, 2015. Accessed February 29, 2016. http://www.chicagobusiness.com/article/20151210/NEWS07/151209754/ -tbt-when-michael-jordan-wore-really-short-shorts.

Strasser, J. B., and Laurie Becklund. "Flying High with Air Jordan: Nike: Company's Products Line Takes Off, But Reebok Becomes No. 1. Sonny Vaccaro Is Told That He Is Quitting." *Los Angeles Times*. February 18, 1992.

————. "Vaccaro: The Dean of Shoes: Nike: He Sells Company on Paying College Coaches and Providing Shoes for Their Camps and Teams." *Los Angeles Times*. February 15, 1992.

Taylor, Phil. "While the Spotlight Shines Mostly on Kobe and Shaq, It's Eddie Jones Who's Been Lighting It Up for the Lakers." *Sports Illustrated*. December 1, 1997.

Team Stream Now. "Jerry West: It Doesn't Seem Possible to Replicate Kobe's 20 Years with Lakers." *Bleacher Report* (online). November 2, 2015. Accessed February 29, 2016. http://bleacherreport.com/articles/2585300-jerry-west-it-doesnt -seem-possible-to-replicate-kobes-20-years-with-lakers.

Temkin, Barry. "Exposure Camps: Battleground, with Kids in Line of Fire." *Chicago Tribune*. April 28, 1996.

Terry, Mike. "Bryant Not Just Kobe's Dad, He's Working-Class." *Black Athlete* (online). June 25, 2006. Accessed February 28, 2016. http://blackathlete .net/2006/06/bryant-not-just-kobes-dad-hes-working-class/.

————. "Sparks Hope Different Makes a Difference." *Los Angeles Times*. April 26, 2006.

Thomas, Dexter. "Forget Coaching, Kobe Bryant: The Rap Game Needs You." *Los Angeles Times*. December 1, 2015.

Thompson, Jack. "Broken Hand Sidelines Bryant." *Chicago Tribune*. October 15, 1999.

Thomsen, Ian. "After Years of Achievement, Bryant Still Striving for Next Peak." *Sports Illustrated* (online). July 9, 2012. Accessed February 28, 2016. http:// www.si.com/more-sports/2012/07/09/kobe-bryant-team-usa.

————. "Show Time!" *Sports Illustrated*. April 27, 1998.

TMZ (online). "Kobe Bryant and Wife Hit Vegas—Looking Happy?" August 29, 2007. Accessed February 28, 2016. http://www.tmz.com/2007/08/29/kobe -bryant-and-wife-hit-vegas-looking-happy/.

———. "Kobe Bryant's Dad Sued—Sparks Are Flying." January 17, 2010. Accessed February 28, 2016. http://www.tmz.com/2010/01/17/kobe-bryant -dad-joe-jellybean-sparks-lawsuit/.

———. "Vanessa Bryant's Ex-Step Dad: She's Just like Her Gold-Digging Mother." December 20, 2011. Accessed February 29, 2016. http://www.tmz .com/2011/12/20/vanessa-bryant-kobe-divorce-step-dad/#.TvCQDlaGCuk.

Treatman, Jeremy. "Injuries and Departures Will Take Toll on Aces." Philly.com (online). December 7, 1992. Accessed February 29, 2016. http://articles .philly.com/1992-12-07/sports/25994435_1_aces-gregg-downer-guard.

Trebay, Guy. "Measuring Up." *New York Times*, June 6, 2005.

Tsai, Michael. "Kobe's Return Boosts Lakers' Intensity Level." *Honolulu Advertiser.* October 5, 2005.

Tsuji, Alysha. "Kobe Bryant Receives Offer from Italian Basketball Team That His Dad Played for." *USA Today* (online). December 7, 2015. Accessed February 29, 2016. http://ftw.usatoday.com/2015/12/kobe-bryant-receives-offer-from-italian -basketball-team-that-his-dad-played-for.

Turner, Broderick. "Kobe Bryant Plans to Keep Emotions in Check during Farewell Tour with Lakers." *Los Angeles Times.* November 30, 2015.

———. "Kobe Bryant's Latest Injury Is Not a Cause for Concern for Lakers." *Los Angeles Times.* October 16, 2015.

Verne, Jean-Michel. "Corse: Exécuté en plein jour." *ParisMatch.* August 19, 2012.

Viola, Mitja. "In Italy, Holding Out Hope for Bryant's Return." *New York Times* (online). March 16, 2011. Accessed March 3, 2016. http://offthedribble.blogs .nytimes.com/2011/03/16/in-italy-holding-out-hope-for-bryants-return/?_r=1.

Voreacos, David. "Kobe Bryant Memorabilia Case Ends with Parents' Apology." *Las Vegas Review-Journal.* June 12, 2013.

Wallace, Charles P. "Adidas: Back in the Game, the Venerable German Shoemaker Has Pulled Its Financial Socks Up. Now It's Scoring Some Points in the U.S. Market." *Fortune,* August 18 1997.

Wall Street Journal (online). "Nike Signs Kobe Bryant to $40 Million Contract." June 25, 2003. Accessed February 28, 2016. http://www.wsj.com/articles/ SB105649507860753000.

Walter, Brad. "Cool as Kobe: The Inside Story of the Lakers' Legendary Star." *Sydney Morning Herald.* September 29, 2010.

Ward, Ryan. "Kobe Bryant Wants to Be Remembered as 'Overachiever.'" *Lakers Nation* (online). November 8, 2015. Accessed February 29, 2016. http://www .lakersnation.com/kobe-bryant-wants-to-be-remembered-as-a-talented-overac hiever/2015/11/08/.

———. "Rare Footage and Interview of Kobe Bryant in High School." *Lakers Nation* (online). August 17, 2014. Accessed March 2, 2016. http://www.lakers nation.com/rare-footage-and-interview-of-kobe-bryant-in-high -school/2014/08/17/.

Welty, Matt. "50 Things You Probably Didn't Know about Adidas." *Business Insider* (online). August 20, 2014. Accessed February 28, 2016. http://www

.businessinsider.com/50-things-you-didnt-know-about-adidas -2014-8?pundits_only=0&get_all_comments=1&no_reply_filter=1# comment-53f60127eab8eabc764be8e3.

Wen, Grace. "Kobe's in the House." *Honolulu Star-Bulletin*. October 5, 2001.

Wetzel, Daniel. "For Nike, Jordan Delivered the Goods and More." *Yahoo!* (online). September 8, 2008. Accessed February 28, 2016. http://sports .yahoo.com/nba/news?slug=dw-jordannike090709.

Wharton, David. "Real Estate Savvy Helped Seal Deal." *Los Angeles Times*. March 3, 2013.

Whicker, Mark. "Kobe Bryant and Tiger Woods Are Riding Off into the Sunset." *Los Angeles Daily News*. September 28, 2015.

Wilder, Chris. "Kobe Bryant and Parents: Not Quite Settled." *Ebony*. June 17, 2013.

Wiley, Ralph. "Kobe's Pulling All the Strings." *ESPN* (online). N.d. Accessed March 1, 2016. http://espn.go.com/page2/s/wiley/030218.html.

———. "MJ vs. Kobe @ 22." *ESPN* (online). N.d. Accessed March 1, 2016. http:// espn.go.com/page2/s/wiley/010524.html.

———. "The Seven Voyages of Kobe." *ESPN* (online). N.d. Accessed March 1, 2016. http://espn.go.com/page2/s/wiley/020516.html.

Williams, Cody. "Kobe Bryant Was Voted 'Most Likely to Succeed' in High School." *Fansided* (online). May 29, 2015. Accessed March 1, 2016. http://fan sided.com/2015/05/29/kobe-bryant-voted-most-likely-to-succeed-high -school/.

Wilson, Charles. "The Subway-Accessible, Surf-Ready, Urban Beach Paradise." *New York Times Magazine*. March 15, 2012.

Winters, Serena. "Kobe Bryant Reflects on Who Challenged Him to Be a Great Leader." *Lakers Nation* (online). April 21, 2015. Accessed March 1, 2016. http://www.lakersnation.com/kobe-bryant-reflects-on-who-challenged -him-to-be-a-great-leader/2015/04/21/.

———. "Video: Derek Fisher Talks Lakers, Relationship with Kobe Bryant." *Lakers Nation* (online). February 1, 2015. Accessed March 2, 2016. http://www .lakersnation.com/video-derek-fisher-talks-lakers-relationship-with -kobe-bryant/2015/02/01/.

Wolf, Morgan. "Catching up with…Felipe Lopez." *Sports Illustrated*. August 14, 2014.

Woollard, Deidre. "Kobe Bryant Memorabilia Heads to Auction." *Pursuitist* (online). May 1, 2013. Accessed February 28, 2016. http://pursuitist.com/ kobe-bryant-memorabilia-heads-to-auction/.

Yannacone, Jamie. "NBA Finals: Main Liners Rooting for Kobe to Shine, Sixers to Win." *Mainline Media News* (online). June 8, 2001. Accessed March 1, 2016. http://www.mainlinemedianews.com/articles/2001/06/06/main_line _suburban_life/sports/1920928.txt.

Yeung, Kevin. "The Quick-Read: Nemanja Bjelica and T. J. McConnell Rise, Kobe Bryant Falls." *Hardwood Paroxysm* (online). November 9, 2015. Accessed February 29, 2016. http://hardwoodparoxysm.com/2015/11/09/the-quick-read -nemanja-bjelica-and-t-j-mcconnell-kobe-bryant/.

Yuscavage, Chris. "Kobe Bryant Talks About Playing Against Michael Jordan for the First Time." *Complex* (online). February 15, 2015. Accessed March 2, 2016.

http://www.complex.com/sports/2015/02/kobe-bryant-talks-about-playing-michael-jordan-for-first-time.

Zengerle, Jason. "Empty Garden." *New Republic.* April 15, 2009.

Zucker, Joseph. "Kobe Bryant Injury: Updates on Lakers Star's Recovery from Shoulder Surgery." *Bleacher Report* (online). Accessed February 28, 2016. http://bleacherreport.com/articles/2553361-kobe-bryant-injury-updates-on-lakers-stars-recovery-from-shoulder-surgery.

Multimedia

"2001/06/15, PHI vs LAL (NBA Finals Game 5)" YouTube video, 9:55, from original NBC television broadcast. Posted May 26, 2010. Accessed February 29, 2016. https://www.youtube.com/watch?v=8jQ2gIt5BFE.

"8Teen | Kobe Bryant's Muse" YouTube video, 0:30, preview of Showtime television documentary *Kobe Bryant's Muse.* Posted February 15, 2015. Accessed March 3, 2016. https://www.youtube.com/watch?v=7sRtg5GPlM4.

"Championship Celebration of the Los Angeles Lakers." YouTube video, 4:33, from NBA.com highlight reel. Posted June 22, 2009. Accessed February 29, 2016. https://www.youtube.com/watch?v=zkRc9RBmapg.

"ESPN SportsCentury—Kobe Bryant." YouTube video, 40:30, from original ESPN SportsCentury television documentary. Posted March 10, 2013. Accessed February 28, 2016. https://www.youtube.com/watch?v=PCBOKu22yiM.

"Grantland Basketball Hour w/ Guest Host Kobe Bryant (Full Episode)." YouTube video, 46:01, from original ESPN *Grantland Basketball Hour* television program. Posted February 23, 2015. Accessed March 03, 2016. https://www.youtube.com/watch?v=qzFYt3K1sqg.

"ILuvBBall Interviews Gary Charles at 2014 AABClassic." YouTube video, 2:01, interview from iLuvBBall.com. Posted November 22, 2014. Accessed March 2, 2016. https://www.youtube.com/watch?v=ZNUfWrdqF7I.

"Jeremy Lin Post Game Interview—Calling out Kobe? Lakers vs Warriors." YouTube video, 2:13, from original Time Warner Sportsnet television broadcast. Posted November 16, 2014. Accessed February 27, 2016. https://www.youtube.com/watch?v=aFa1A9Tzd_w.

"Joe Bryant at Jazz Game 3." YouTube video, 0:20. Posted May 12, 2010. Accessed March 2, 2016. https://www.youtube.com/watch?v=ZMCv95cmIkk.

"Kobe Adidas Italy Commercial." YouTube video, 0:31, from Italian Adidas television commercial. Posted July 15, 2006. Accessed February 28, 2016. https://www.youtube.com/watch?v=a12wsaadrjo.

"Kobe Bryant—1997 NBA Slam Dunk Contest (Champion)." YouTube video, 6:56, from original TNT television broadcast. Posted June 29, 2013. Accessed February 29, 2016. https://www.youtube.com/watch?v=UqVibdD3UqA.

"Kobe Bryant Adidas Commercial 1998." YouTube video, 0:30, from Adidas television commercial. Posted September 14, 1998. Accessed February 29, 2016. https://www.youtube.com/watch?v=8rrQJUUeQmw.

"Kobe Bryant (Age 25) Publicly Apologizes to Shaq with Stephen A. Smith (2004)." YouTube video, 2:18, from original ESPN television broadcast. Posted May 30, 2015. Accessed February 27, 2016. https://www.youtube.com/watch?v=N_rRScSLnGY.

"Kobe Bryant Calls Dwight Howard 'Soft' and a 'Bitch Ass Nigga'! Uncut." YouTube video, 5:48, from original TNT television broadcast. Posted October 30, 2014. Accessed February 27, 2016. https://www.youtube.com/watch?v=qaZkZQmyJT8.

"Kobe Bryant Calls Dwight Howard 'Soft as a Motherf***er' and a 'Bi**h A** Ni*ga' *Court Side*." YouTube video, 0:08. Posted October 29, 2014. Accessed February 27, 2016. https://www.youtube.com/watch?v=h2XhTpUiZEM.

"Kobe Bryant Divorce Meltdown." *Funny or Die* online video, 3:32. December 21, 2011. Accessed March 2, 2016. http://club937.com/funny-or-die-kobe-bryant -divorce-meltdown-video/.

"Kobe Bryant Fight Scottie Pippen." YouTube video, 0:52, from original TNT television broadcast. Posted June 20, 2014. Accessed February 27, 2016. https://www.youtube.com/watch?v=khfVk1cNWsI.

"Kobe Bryant Full Highlights vs Spurs 2008 WCF GM5—39 Pts, 4th Qtr Take-over" YouTube video, 10:34, from original TNT television broadcast. Posted August 1, 2014. Accessed February 28, 2016. https://www.youtube.com/watch?v=5aXVxcLm2qQ.

"Kobe Bryant in 1995 High School Slam Dunk Contest." YouTube video, 5:37, from unknown source. Posted October 17, 2008. Accessed March 2, 2016. https://www.youtube.com/watch?v=KPw7MCAXHBk.

"Kobe Bryant Never Did Catch Up to Michael Jordan." *FiveThirtyEight* podcast, 45:21. December 1, 2015. Accessed February 29, 2016. http://fivethirtyeight .com/features/kobe-bryant-never-did-catch-up-to-michael-jordan/.

"Kobe Bryant on Reclaiming Olympic Basketball Glory at Beijing 2008." You-Tube video, 8:31, official video provided by the International Olympic Committee. Posted March 28, 2015. Accessed February 29, 2016. https://www .youtube.com/watch?v=ztUZnHfvWR8.

"Kobe Bryant Rare Vid of Rapping." YouTube video 0:23, clip from Jordan McKnight "Hold Me" music video. Posted August 29, 2013. Accessed February 27, 2016. https://www.youtube.com/watch?v=u5BcaFX1Rjs.

"Kobe Bryant's Rape Victim Katelynn Faber Does a Freestyle Rap about the Incident Horrible!" YouTube video, 2:23, from unknown source. Posted July 26, 2013. Accessed February 29, 2016. https://www.youtube.com/watch?v =3m2d7QAIX8Q.

"Kobe Bryant's Top 50 Dunks of His Career." YouTube video, 14:11, compilation from various television broadcasts. Posted July 26, 2015. Accessed February 29, 2016. https://www.youtube.com/watch?v=YtfZe0FUoJo.

"Kobe Bryant Talks about Michael Jackson." YouTube video, 1:40, from AOL Fan-House online video. Posted July 6, 2009. Accessed March 2, 2016. https:// www.youtube.com/watch?v=xMgDhlJjWpc.

"Kobe Bryant TimeLine." YouTube video, 0:52. Posted April 16, 2015. Accessed March 2, 2016. https://www.youtube.com/watch?v=7bFAAkqPqLU.

"Kobe Bryant Versus Charles Barkley on TNT." YouTube video, 8:03, from original TNT television broadcast. Posted May 18, 2006. Accessed March 2, 2016. https://www.youtube.com/watch?v=hjTm2Dl1bTo.

"Kobe Bryant Vows Lakers Will Be 'Much Better' Next Season." YouTube video, 0:35, Lakers Nation (blog) video of Toberman Center Charity Auction. Posted April 6, 2015. Accessed February 29, 2016. https://www.youtube.com/watch?v=4-HNyNscFBw.

"Kobe Bryant vs LeBron James—Epic Rivalry." YouTube video, 6:53, compilation from various television broadcasts. Posted February 10, 2015. Accessed February 29, 2016. https://www.youtube.com/watch?v=eSJTmkQv1aw.

"Kobe Bryant vs Metta World Peace Full Highlights 2009 WCSF G2—65 Pts Combined! Intense Duel!" YouTube video, 9:44, from original TNT television broadcast. Posted February 20, 2015. Accessed February 27, 2016. https://www.youtube.com/watch?v=Izuuvca3jF4.

"Kobe Bryant vs Shaquille O'Neal Full Duel Highlights 2009.03.01—82 Pts Combined, Must Watch!" YouTube video, 9:35, from original ESPN television broadcast. Posted March 9, 2015. Accessed March 3, 2016. https://www.you tube.com/watch?v=viXdSc2XJQM.

"Lakers vs. Portland!! A Must Watch Kobe Crazy Shot in 2OT." YouTube video, 4:13, from original ESPN broadcast. Posted February 18, 2006. Accessed February 29, 2016. https://www.youtube.com/watch?v=k56E-3SfoFg.

"L.A. Lakers NBA Champions 2001." YouTube video, 6:23, compilation from various television broadcasts. Posted June 25, 2011. Accessed February 29, 2016. https://www.youtube.com/watch?v=hgUVyfeiZlU.

"Norristown vs Lower Merion 1995 'Kobe Bryant High School Game against Big Star'" YouTube video, 12:54, from Big Star and Raw Sports Films. Posted August 16, 2014. Accessed March 2, 2016. https://www.youtube.com/watch?v=jcqsP_5q9pE.

"Reggie Miller and Kobe Bryant Fight 2002." YouTube video, 3:11, from original television broadcast. Posted October 2, 2014. Accessed February 27, 2016.

"Shots Fired at Shaq Kobe Bryant after Winning the 2010 NBA Championship!" YouTube video, 1:37, from original NBA TV television broadcast. Posted June 18, 2010. Accessed February 27, 2016.

"Throwback: Kobe Bryant vs Tracy McGrady Full Duel Highlights 2001.11.11 Lakers vs Magic—Sick!" YouTube video, 7:49, from original Fox Sports Net television broadcast. Posted August 11, 2014. Accessed February 28, 2016. https://www.youtube.com/watch?v=zgoAXIAtJSo.

"VIDEO: Kobe Would Always Look Jordan in the Eyes." CBS Sports video, 0:56, from Showtime television documentary Kobe Bryant's Muse. Posted February 27, 2015. Accessed March 3, 2016. http://www.cbssports.com/nba/eye-on -basketball/25083588/video-kobe-would-always-look-jordan-in-the-eyes.

INDEX

AAU (Amateur Athletic Union) basketball, 122, 124–25
ABCD Camp, 144–46, 147, 155–56, 356
Abdul-Jabbar, Kareem, x, 60, 234, 502, 563
    1979–80 season of, 75
    at Buss's memorial service, 553
    Garciduenas on, 444
    on Johnson, 314
    on Kobe's 81-point game, 477
Abdur-Rahim, Shareef, 228
Abrams, Jonathan, 77
Adams, Alvan, 56
Adams, Bennie, 538
Adams, Patch, 66
Adande, J. A., 527–28, 549
    on Bryant-O'Neal relationship, 354, 375, 434, 517, 558–59
    on Jackson, 425–26, 427, 438, 457, 550–51
    on Jerry Buss, 494
    on Jordan, 318–19
    on Kobe, 318–19, 428, 432, 438, 562
    on Lakers, 449, 450
    on O'Neal, 320, 422–23, 438, 497
Adelman, Rick, 378
Adidas America, 133, 141, 144–45, 404
    contracts with Kobe: Kobe's buy out of, 401, 403–4, 405–6; original, 201–2, 206, 216; upgraded, 279, 296, 322–23
    Kobe's line of signature shoes for, 274–76, 286, 297–98, 317, 328–29, 360–61
Air Jordan, 133, 134–35, 138–39
Allen, Paul, 331
Allen, Ray, 153, 224, 228, 246, 505, 525, 527
Amateur Athletic Union (AAU) basketball, 122, 124–25
American Basketball Association, 49, 218
American History X, 346
Anthony, Carmelo, 484, 531, 549
Arenas, Gilbert, 461, 462, 463

Ariza, Trevor, 511, 518
Arizin, Paul, 54
Armato, Leonard, 234
Artest, Ron (Metta World Peace), 91, 515, 518–19, 522, 526, 527, 537, 539
Atkins, Chucky, 433, 453
Atlanta Hawks, 56, 557
Attles, Al, 47, 49
Auerbach, Red, 394, 411, 504, 540

Bach, Johnny, 396, 490
Baker, Jimmie, 30
Baker League, 24–25, 26, 65, 79, 89, 169
Banks, Tyra, 208, 250, 326
Bannister, Anthony, 114–15, 117, 118, 229, 325
Barea, J. J., 539
Barkley, Charles, 72, 549, 567, 570
Barnes, Harrison, 557
Barry, Jon, 289
Bass, Bob, 229
Battle, John, 88
Baylor, Elgin, 248, 263, 375, 467, 475, 503, 504, 505
Becciani, Piero, 89
Beck, Howard
    on Bryant-O'Neal relationship, 312–13
    on Kobe, 307, 308, 375, 382, 383, 447, 573
    on meeting Vanessa, 359–60
Bellamy, Walt, 462
Bernstein, Andrew, 281, 297, 313–14
Bertka, Bill, 365
Bibby, Mike, 159, 178
Bird, Larry, 75, 87, 284, 314, 351, 476, 518, 522
Black, John, 565
Black Like Me (Griffin), 344
Blake, Steve, 555–56
Blount, Corie, 252, 304, 305
Boerwinkle, Tom, 49
Bogli, Alison, 566

Bomb Squad, 51, 69, 71, 72

Bosh, Chris, 484, 485

Boston Celtics, 285, 394, 410, 504–6, 509–10, 513, 524–28

Boys II Men, 208, 209

Bradley, Bill, 24, 25

Bradley, Rick, 205

Bresnahan, Mike, 550

Bridges, Larry, 139

Brown, Kwame, 473, 480, 486, 501

Brown, Mike, 543, 544, 545, 546, 547–48, 550

Brown, Tim, 384

Brunson, Rick, 103–4

Bryant, Ann (grandmother), 21

Bryant, "Big" Joe (grandfather), 18–19, 21, 33, 44
    death of, 450
    Edward Howard and, 27–28
    focus on family, 19–20, 21, 23, 28, 34–35, 49, 77
    Kobe and, 76, 113

Bryant, Joe (great-grandfather), 21

Bryant, Joe "Jellybean" (father), 9, 12, 33, 83, 96, 121, 440
    with 76ers, 51–54, 55, 56–58, 70, 72
    ABCD Camp and, 145–46
    as Akiba girls' varsity team coach, 113–14
    anxiety about Kobe's Lakers' career, 261, 262, 321–22
    arrest and trial of, 13–17, 58–61
    Baker League and, 65, 79, 89, 169
    as car salesman, 79, 80
    early life of, 18, 21–24, 25, 27, 29–36
    Gary Charles and, 162, 163, 195–97, 205–6, 322, 370, 371
    Houston Rockets and, 78
    in Italy, xii, 4, 81–90, 92–93, 95, 97
    Kobe's AAU team and, 123
    at Kobe's NBA draft, 228
    as La Salle coaching staff, 159, 160, 197, 231
    as La Salle player, 37–40, 51–54
    as Los Angeles Sparks coach, 560
    as Lower Merion coaching staff, 104, 105, 107
    in NBA draft, 40, 47, 48–49
    nickname of, 11–12
    Olimpia Milano and, 323–25, 386
    Powell and, 173
    pro seasons in Europe, 82–86, 88–90, 92, 95, 97–98
    push out of NBA, 78–79
    relationship with Kobe, 68; during adolescence, 6, 100, 101–2, 105, 125, 127, 130–31, 132; after move to L.A., 300–301, 358–59, 370–72, 386; financial, 194–95, 197–200, 279, 322–25, 358–59, 370–72, 386; reduced contact, 6, 451, 574
    relationship with Pam, 14, 41, 42, 45, 46–47, 86, 94, 97, 545
    Rines and, 124
    role in Adidas's contract with Kobe, 162, 163, 195, 196–98, 205–6
    role in turning Kobe pro, 177, 214, 219, 232
    San Diego Clippers and, 72–73, 74–75, 77
    as showboat in NBA, 56
    signing with 76ers, 13, 14
    stoking of Kobe's confidence, xi, 4, 83, 84–85, 96, 121

Bryant, Kobe Bean
    1996–97 season of, 241–60, 264–68, 271–74
    1997–98 season of, 279–85, 288–91, 293–95
    1999 season of, 296, 307–11, 317, 319
    1999–2000 season of, 329–30, 333–43, 345–54
    2000–2001 season of, 3–4, 365–69, 373–83
    2001–02 season of, 389, 390–94
    2002–03 season of, 406, 407–8, 410–12
    2003–04 season of, 423, 425, 427, 429, 430–32
    2004–05 season of, 435, 447–50, 453–54
    2005–06 season of, 460–62, 463, 464–67, 472–76, 479–81
    2006–07 season of, 488–90
    2007–08 season of, 497–500, 501, 502, 505–6, 509
    2008–09 season of, 511–17
    2009–10 season of, 518, 519, 520–22, 523, 524–28, 531
    2010–11 season of, 537–38, 539, 541
    2011–12 season of, 546–48
    2012–13 season of, 551–52, 554–60
    2013–14 season of, 562
    2014–15 season of, 563
    2015–16 season of, xiii, 567, 569, 570–74
    ABCD Camp and, 145–46, 155–56, 356
    Adidas contracts with: Kobe's buy out of, 401, 403–4, 405–6; original, 201–2, 206, 216; upgraded, 279, 296, 322–23
    agents of, 204–6, 388

alienation of, x, 250, 264, 303–14, 491, 498, 508
alleged extramarital dalliances of, 533–34, 535
arrogance of, 290, 291
birth of, 65–66
Brandy and, 179, 208–11, 248, 250
Buss and, 368, 426, 432–33, 438, 489, 491, 493–94, 497, 542, 553
competitive drive of, 81–82, 84, 92–93, 121, 279, 528
confidence of, xi, 4, 83, 84–85, 96, 121, 230–31
contract negotiations with Lakers, 421–22, 433–34, 438, 522, 568
damage from injuries, 522–23, 537, 541, 542–43, 551–52, 557–58, 559–60
early life of, 4, 76, 77, 95–96, 99–100, 102–4, 147
endorsement earnings of, 296, 388, 419, 459, 538
Fisher and, 303–4, 305
girlfriends of, 179, 193–94, 208–11
goals of, ix, x, 5–7, 75, 95–96, 324, 380–81, 529
in high school: on AAU teams, 122–28, 129, 147–49, 156–57; decision to turn pro, 195–96, 206, 211–15; as a freshman, 104–8; as a junior, 150–55; Osgood-Schlatter disease during, 102–3; as a senior, 158–61, 172–90, 202–3; as a sophomore, 109–18, 121–24, 122, 128, 129, 190; summer workouts with 76ers, 165–69
homophobic language used by, 538
in Italy, 5, 81–84, 86–88, 90–93, 95, 98
Jackson and. See Jackson, Phil: Kobe and
Jordan and, 318, 502–3, 549
media and, 246, 270, 308–9, 414, 441–42, 530–33, 564–67
NBA draft and, 215, 219–24, 225–29
on NBA lockout in 2011, 536, 545
nicknames of, xi–xii, 251, 302, 488
O'Neal and. See O'Neal, Shaquille: relationship with Kobe
perfectionism of, 68–69, 241–42, 358
rap music and, 115–18, 129, 190, 299, 325–26
reaction to Johnson's HIV announcement, x, 97, 271
relationship with father, 68; during adolescence, 6, 100, 101–2, 105, 125, 127, 130–31, 132; after move to L.A.,
300–301, 358–59, 370–72, 386; financial, 194–95, 197–200, 279, 322–25, 358–59, 370–72, 386; reduced contact, 6, 451, 574
relationship with mother, 4, 67, 243; during adolescence, 112, 127, 132, 192, 209; after move to L.A., 243, 250, 278–79, 298–301, 357–59; financial, 199–200, 204–5, 279, 300, 358–59, 370–72, 386, 560; reduced contact, 6, 371, 574
relationship with Sharia, 132, 179, 204, 297, 298–99, 370, 386–87, 388–89, 560
relationship with Shaya, 179, 204, 370, 386–87
relationship with Vanessa, 356–57, 360–61, 385–86, 546, 563–64; divorce filing, 545–46, 552; engagement, 346–47; Hubler's story on, 451–52; meeting and dating, 326–27; reconciliation, 552–53, 564; sexual assault case and, 417–18, 437; wedding of, 369, 371
religion and, 262
retirement of, x, 550, 570
selfishness of, 81–82, 127–28, 312, 341, 366, 367, 428, 432
sexual assault case against, 413–19; criminal charges dropped in, 436; informing Vanessa of charges in, 417, 437; Kobe on fears after, 566–67; legal defense of, 419, 425, 435; media coverage of, 413, 414, 416, 417, 418–19, 435–36, 441–42; reactions to, 413, 416, 429–30, 435; release of police report investigation in, 440–41; settlement in civil case, 452
similarities between mother and, 41–42, 68, 82, 93–94, 182
on Team USA, 482–86, 487, 496, 506–9, 522, 549–50
temper of, 68, 125, 129, 182–84, 279
West and, 226–28, 277, 362
Winter and. See Winter, Tex
work ethic of, 41–42, 280, 470, 471, 507
Bryant, Natalia Diamante, 410
Bryant, Pam Cox (mother), 43, 57, 68, 182
auctioning of Kobe's personal memorabilia, 560
family background of, 42–44, 45–46, 67
in Italy, 86, 87, 93, 97, 98
at Joe's trial, 61

Bryant, Pam Cox (mother) *(cont.)*
  at Kobe's NBA draft, 228
  as overly protective of Kobe, 178–79, 358
  perfectionism of, 66–67, 68–69
  reaction to Joe's arrest, 58
  relationship with Joe, 14, 41, 42, 45,
    46–47, 86, 94, 97, 129
  relationship with Kobe: during
    adolescence, 112, 127, 132, 192, 209;
    after move to L.A., 243, 250, 278–79,
    298–301, 357–59; doting on Kobe, 4,
    67, 243; financial, 199–200, 204–5,
    279, 300, 358–59, 370–72, 386;
    reduced contact, 6, 371, 574
  similarities between Kobe and, 41–42, 68,
    82, 93–94, 182
  struggles as NBA wife, 76, 78, 80
  Vanessa and, 327, 347, 357–58, 370–71, 386
Bryant, Sharia, 192, 208, 228, 229, 243
  birth of, 57, 65
  early life of, 61, 83, 86, 94, 104
  on Kobe, 81–82, 194, 296–97
  relationship with Kobe: 132, 179, 204, 297,
    298–99, 370, 386–87, 388–89, 560
  Vanessa and, 370–71
Bryant, Shaya, 83, 86, 104, 192, 228, 242
  birth of, 65
  relationship with Kobe, 179, 204, 370,
    386–87
  Vanessa and, 370–71
Bryant, Vanessa (wife). *See* Laine, Vanessa
  Urbieta Cornejo
Bucher, Ric, 372, 414, 437, 438
  on Jackson, 337–38
  on Kobe, 235, 273–74, 344, 351, 352, 412
Buffalo Braves, 57
Burnett, Larry, 364
Burton, Willie, 168
Buss, Jeanie
  D'Antoni and, 551
  Jackson and, 364, 395, 427, 433, 455, 456
  Jim Buss and, 446, 519, 536
  Kobe and, 562
Buss, Jerry, x, 264, 292, 492
  1997–98 season and, 280, 289, 294
  2000–2001 season and, 377
  2003–04 season and, 425, 432
  2004–05 season and, 446, 450
  contract negotiations and, 421, 422–23,
    427, 428, 432–33, 438, 493
  death of, 551, 552, 562
  fraud charges against, 493
  funeral of, 497

Jackson and, 320, 427, 428, 432, 458,
  493, 537
Jim Buss and, 519, 536
Johnson and, 362
Kobe and, 368, 426, 432–33, 438, 489,
  491, 493–94, 497, 542, 553
on O'Neal, 449
on Pippen, 331
Rodman and, 310
syndication deals of, 492–93
terminal illness of, 551, 552
on West, 364
West's financial standoff with, 308–9
Buss, Jim, 446, 542, 543
  Jackson and, 361–62, 395, 536, 537, 540,
    550–51
  Jeanie and, 446, 519, 536
Butler, Caron, 433, 445
Bynum, Andrew, 491, 499, 501, 511–12,
  537, 538–39, 544

Caldwell, Joe, 56
Calipari, John, 226, 227, 228
Camby, Marcus, 222, 228, 246
Campbell, Elden, 252, 254, 257, 282, 295, 311
Capone, Eugenio, 92
Caputo, Pasquale, 323, 324
Carbone, Joe, 249, 250, 301, 385
Carr, Antoine, 293
Carr, Chris, 258
Carr, Donnie, 102–3, 104, 145, 155, 231–32
  high school rivalry with Kobe, 103,
    153–55, 156, 175–76
  on Joe Bryant, 231
  on Kobe, 150, 165–66, 170, 186, 230–31,
    272, 380, 490–91
Carrawell, Chris, 211
Carter, Ron, 60, 263, 446, 492–93, 536, 561
Carter, Vince, 148, 149, 335, 476
Cartwright, Bill, 58
Casey, Don, 38
Cassell, Sam, 431
Castaneda, Carlos, 334–35
Ceballos, Cedric, 252
Chamberlain, Wilt, 47, 54, 202, 234, 502
  76ers trade of, 55
  on Baker League, 24–25
  with Boston Celtics, 504
  Harlem Globetrotters and, 218, 500
  on number of sexual encounters, 264
  records held by, 345, 410, 462–63, 467,
    475, 477, 489, 557, 573
  West on rivalry with, 375

Chaney, John, 33
Charles, Gary, 198, 201, 236
  Joe Bryant and, 162, 163, 195–97, 205–6, 322, 370, 371
  on Kobe, 6, 207, 228, 327, 369
  on Lopez, 162
  on Pam Cox Bryant, 327
  role in Kobe's Adidas contract, 160–61, 162–63, 195–97, 199–200, 201–2
Charlotte Hornets, 228–29
Cheeks, Maurice "Mo," 72, 166–67, 200
CHEIZAW, 118
Chicago Bulls, 49, 198, 254, 257, 282–84, 285, 394, 464
Chortkoff, Mitch, 256, 295
Clarkson, Jordan, 569
Clement, Kristen "Ace," 193–94
Cleveland Cavaliers, 449, 563
Colangelo, Jerry, 482, 483, 484, 485, 486, 508
Collier, Jason, 180
Collins, Doug, 70, 569
Commonwealth v. Joseph Washington Bryant III, 61
Cone, Tim, 567–68
Conti, Alessandro, 90, 91, 95, 98
Cook, Brian, 464
Cooke, Jack Kent, 522
Cooper, Michael, 226
Couch, Greg, 476
Cowens, Dave, 75, 229
Cox, John, II, 41, 43, 44, 46, 371, 374, 387
Cox, John, IV, 132, 228, 381
Cox, John, Sr., 42–43
Cox, John Arthur "Chubby," III, 41, 43, 58, 66
  family background of, 42–44, 45–46, 67
  felony charges against, 58
  Kobe and, 6, 96, 228, 383
Cox, Mildred Williams, 43, 46, 387, 472, 560
Cox, Pam. *See* Bryant, Pam Cox (mother)
Cuban, Mark, 429
Cunningham, Billy, 51, 56, 71, 72, 77
Curry, Stephen, 554, 571

Dabney, Emory, 166, 176, 189
Dallas Mavericks, 465, 539–41
Daly, Chuck, 38, 71
Dampier, Erick, 422
D'Antoni, Mike, 92, 550–52, 554–56, 558, 562, 563
Dapper Dan Roundball Classic, 34, 35, 200, 202
Davis, Arthur, 153

Davis, Virgil, 47
Dawkins, Darryl "Chocolate Thunder," 49, 51, 52, 53–54, 70–71
DeCourcy, Mike, 213
Delaware County Times, 56, 61
Dennis, Chris, 142–43, 404, 486
Denver Nuggets, 455, 502, 515, 517, 548
Detroit Pistons, 353, 432
DiLeo, Tony, 167–68, 219–20, 221, 222
Ding, Kevin, 547
Divac, Vlade, 229, 393, 433, 456
Dixon, F. Eugene, 71
Donaghy, Tim, 392
Douglas, Leon, 67, 84, 89–90, 91, 92, 93, 95
Downer, Gregg, 105, 180–81, 182, 187, 188
  on Bryant family relationship, 560
  on challenge of managing Kobe, 337
  concerns about Kobe, 104, 122, 236
  first impression of Kobe, 101–2
  on hopes Kobe would go to La Salle, 197
  on Jackson's comments about Kobe, 367
  on Jermaine Griffin, 109
  on Kobe: at ABCD Camp, 156; at Beach Ball Classic, 179, 180; beating Joe at basketball, 130; as a freshman, 104–8; as a junior, 151–52, 153; during senior year, 152–53, 158, 185–86; in state championship play-offs, 189
  on "seat-belt rule" for coaches, 107
  visit to Kobe in L.A., 278
Dragić, Goran, 543
Drew, Larry, 226, 235, 256, 261, 277, 280
Drexler, Clyde, 285, 476
Driesell, Lefty, 25, 36
Duncan, Tim, 345, 397, 430, 431, 469, 531, 543, 545
Dunleavy, Mike, 348
Dunne, Raymond, 16
Durant, Kevin, 524, 549
Durrett, Kenny, 22, 35

Earl, Lester, 155, 156, 178, 180
Eberz, Eric, 159
Egan, Johnny, 263
Erving, Julius "Dr. J," 70, 94, 121, 198, 258, 379, 407
Eskin, Howard, 213
ESPN, 212, 232, 418–19
Evans, Maurice, 488

Falk, David, 134
Farrell, Jack, 30–32

Festus, Eugene, 61
FIBA World Championship in 2006, 483–84
Finley, Michael, 258, 285
Fisher, Derek, 257, 316, 433, 445
    1996–97 season of, 265
    1997–98 season of, 279, 295
    1999–2000 season of, 340, 341, 343, 351
    2000–2001 season of, 365, 368, 380
    2001–02 season of, 389
    2003–04 season of, 428, 430, 431
    2007–08 season of, 497–98, 501
    2009–2010 season of, 526–27
    on Jackson, 334, 346
    on Kobe, 244, 245, 248, 304, 312, 316
    Kobe and, 303–4, 305, 497–98
    Lakers' trade of, 541–42
    on Shaq-Kobe relationship, 306, 315
Fitzpatrick, Frank, 54
Forbes, 536, 538
Fox, Rick, 309, 320, 344, 433
    1997–98 season of, 282, 285
    1999–2000 season of, 345, 347–48, 349, 353
    2000–2001 season of, 378, 379
    on Jackson, 341, 342
    on Kobe, 276.290
Frank, Tim, 564
Frazier, Walt, 24–25, 258, 362–63
Free, Lloyd (World B. Free), 49, 51, 52, 53–54, 69–70, 71–72
Freeman, Kevin, 148
Fulks, "Jumpin'" Joe, 54
Fuller, Todd, 226

Gallagher, Jack, 31
Garciduenas, Rudy, 239, 240, 377, 447, 448, 450
    on Abdul-Jabbar, 444
    on Buss, 497
    on Fisher, 479–98
    on Gasol, 501
    on Harris, 253
    on Jackson, 362, 499–500, 537
    on Johnson, 534, 535
    on Jones, 247
    on Kobe, 242–42, 245–46, 409, 435, 440, 443–45, 455, 469
    on layoffs before 2011 lockout, 539–40
    on O'Neal, 240–41, 420
Garfinkel, Howie, 201
Garnett, Kevin, 159, 177, 259, 571
    2003–04 season of, 431
    2007–08 season of, 505, 509–10

2009–10 season of, 527
    going pro out of high school, 159, 160, 161, 198, 219, 259
Gasol, Marc, 501
Gasol, Pau, 519, 530, 543, 545
    2007–08 season of, 501–2, 505–6
    2008–09 season of, 512, 514
    2009–10 season of, 520–21, 524, 525–27, 531
    2010–11 season of, 539
    2011–12 season of, 548
    2012–13 season of, 554, 557, 559–60
    in Summer Olympics, 509, 550
George, Carmela, 109–10
George, Devean, 390, 464, 473, 476
Gervin, George, 258
Gibbons, Bob, 155
Gilbert, Anthony, 7, 192, 194, 229, 388–89, 405–6
Gilbert, Dan, 544
Gola, Tom, 35, 54, 231
Golden State Warriors, 47, 49, 433
    1996–97 season of, 266
    1997–98 season of, 281
    1999–2000 season of, 335
    2006–07 season of, 489
    2012–13 season of, 557
    2014–15 season of, 37, 563
    2015–16 season of, 571, 573
Golianopoulos, Thomas, 115
Gottlieb, Eddie, 54
Graboski, Joe, 217
Granik, Russ, 137
Grant, Brian, 433
Grant, Horace, 365, 390, 433
Gray, Jim, 441
Green, A. C., 263
Green, Devin, 475
Green, Draymond, 37
Greenberg, Brad, 220–22, 224
Greenberg, Shari, 565
Greer, Hal, 25
Griffin, Jermaine, 109–12, 114–18, 130–32, 172, 181, 187, 190, 210
Griffin, John Howard, 344
groupies, 263–64, 533–35
Guerin, Richie, 56
Gugliotta, Tom, 309
Guthridge, Bill, 334

Ham, Darvin, 258
Hamblen, Frank, 450

Hamilton, Richard "Rip," 148, 151, 156, 157, 187, 317, 432
Hardaway, Anfernee "Penny," 232–33, 286, 314, 317, 336
Harlem Globetrotters, 55, 56, 218, 500
Harper, Derek, 311, 316, 319
Harper, Ron, 283, 335, 343, 348, 365, 379, 390
Harris, Del, 78, 276, 292, 369
    on Kobe, 249, 277, 280, 298
    as Lakers coach, 226, 311, 314; during 1996–97 season, 251–53, 255, 256, 260, 262, 265–68, 271–73; during 1997–98 season, 281, 289, 291–95; during 1999 season, 309, 311
    West and, 253, 260–61, 272, 316
Harris, Larry, 223–24
Harris, Michael "Big Mike," 162, 203, 207–11, 359
Hatfield, Tinker, 138
Hawkins, Hersey, 285
Hayes, Elvin, 338
Hearn, Chick, 227, 562
Hewitt, Paul, 159
Hill, Grant, 287, 337
Hill, Sonny, 383, 391
    Baker League founded by, 24–25, 26, 65, 79, 89, 169
    on Chubby Cox, 45
    on Joe Bryant, 75
    Joe Bryant and, 60, 79–80, 322
    Kobe and, 571
    Nike and, 145
    See also Sonny Hill League
Hodges, Craig, 515
Hollinger, John, 524
Holloway, Shaheen, 126
Hornacek, Jeff, 285
Horry, Robert "Big Shot Bob," 252, 344, 381
    1996–97 season of, 267, 271
    1997–98 season of, 282, 295
    1999 season of, 309
    1999–2000 season of, 349, 353
    2000–2001 season of, 379
    2001–02 season of, 390, 393
    2002–03 season of, 411
Houston Rockets, 78, 311, 319, 430, 465, 515, 518, 561, 563
Howard, Dwight, 484, 485, 515, 550, 555, 558–60, 561
Howard, Edward, 27–28, 34
Howard, Mo, 7, 25, 27, 34, 35, 36

on Big Joe, 21, 27–28
on Chubby Cox, 45, 67
on Coxes, 46
on Joe Bryant, 57; with 76ers, 50, 52, 53, 69, 70, 72, 73; attractions of material success to, 46; conversation about Kobe going pro, 168; at La Salle, 38; lack of NBA's respect for, 79; nickname of, 11–12; in Public League, 31, 32; style of playing basketball, 30
on John Cox II, 44
on Kobe, 100–101, 166–67
on Pam Cox Bryant, 42, 67
Hubler, Shawn, 451
Hudson, Lou, 59, 263
Hunt, Donald, 381
Hunter, Lindsey, 390
Hurlbert, Mark, 416, 417

Indiana Pacers, 351–54, 493
Iverson, Allen, 4, 246, 258, 361, 454, 460, 474
    2000–2001 season of, 379, 380
    2005–06 season of, 461
    Beck on, 307
    Kobe on, 308
    NBA draft and, 220, 221–22, 228
    Team USA and, 484, 485

Jackson, Jim, 479–81
Jackson, Phil, 180, 347, 369
    coaching style of, 240, 334–35, 341–42, 345–46, 373, 396–97
    contract negotiations with Lakers, 421–22, 425–28, 432, 433, 434, 439, 493, 536–37
    health of, 433, 536–37, 541
    Jeanie Buss and, 364, 395, 427, 433, 455, 456
    Jim Buss and, 519, 536, 537, 550–51
    Jordan and, 277, 332–33, 337, 365, 407, 443, 490
    Kobe and, 456–57, 458; contract negotiations and, 421–22, 425–26, 434; first meeting between, 330; during Jackson's time with Lakers, 479–80, 487, 488, 499–500, 507, 530; during sexual assault charges, 427–28; use of media, 366–68, 381, 384, 457; void and clashes between, 341–45, 407–9, 419, 423, 439

Jackson, Phil (cont.)
Kupchak and, 361–2, 364, 395
as Lakers' coach, 320, 363, 455–58; during
1999–2000 season, 331–32, 334–37,
341–42, 345–46, 348–50, 352–54;
during 2000–2001 season, 366,
367–68, 376–77, 378, 381; during
2001–02 season, 389, 390, 392, 394;
during 2002–03 season, 407–8,
411–12; during 2003–04 season,
421–22, 425, 429, 430, 431; during
2005–06 season, 465–66, 473, 475,
477, 478–81; during 2006–07
season, 490; during 2007–08
season, 499–500, 501, 505; during
2008–09 season, 510–11, 512, 513,
514, 515, 517; during 2009–10
season, 519, 522; during 2010–11
season, 536–37, 538, 540–41
The Last Season, 439, 529–30
O'Neal and, 331–33, 337–38, 342–44,
366–67, 396, 408–9
West and, 320, 331, 361–65, 384, 398
Winter and, 396–98, 455, 515
Jackson, Scoop, 246–47, 272, 273, 351, 442
on 2010 NBA Finals, 526
on Garnett and Pierce, 509–10
on Jackson, 344
on Kobe cutting people out of his life, 437
on Kobe's entertainment company, 386
on Kobe's lack of friends, 369
on sexual assault charges against Kobe, 436
Jackson, Stephen, 159
James, LeBron, 142, 278, 307, 404, 543
2004–05 season of, 449
2005–06 season of, 461
endorsement earnings of, 404, 538
on Team USA, 482–84, 486, 549
West on, 517–18
James, Mike, 473
John Paul II, 543
Johnson, Earvin "Magic," 220, 221, 314,
469, 553
1979–80 season of, 75
in 1985 championship series, 504
announcement of HIV, ix, 97, 225, 264,
271, 522
competition with Bird, 518
on hiring of D'Antoni, 555
on Jackson's Lakers, 394
Joe as fan of, 77–78
Jordan on, 284
Kobe as a fan of, 87, 88, 94

Lakers' renouncement of, 234
minority ownership in Lakers, 362, 368,
562
on O'Neal, 342
return to NBA, 212, 522
sex with women after games, 534
style/skill of playing basketball, 37
transformation of Lakers, 239
Johnson, Keyshawn, 413–14
Johnson, Larry, 310
Johnston, Neil, 54
Jones, Bobby, 72
Jones, Caldwell, 69
Jones, Dontae', 226
Jones, Eddie, 104, 167, 168, 249, 290
1996–97 season of, 254, 267–68
1997–98 season of, 279–80, 282, 283,
288, 292, 293
1999 season of, 309
on Kobe, 103, 169
Kobe on trade of, 230, 231, 252
Kobe's friendship with, 247, 305, 312
Lakers' trading of, 311, 312
Jones, Wali, 25
Jordan, Deloris, 135, 144
Jordan, James, 143
Jordan, Michael, 88, 198, 276, 410, 481
1996–97 season of, 254
1997–98 season of, 282–84, 285,
286–88, 522–23
advice to Kobe on prenuptial agreement,
369
comeback attempt of, 523, 569
defense of Kobe, 502–3
discussions with Kobe, 318, 549
drive to be great, 220
as driving fashion, 137–38
fascination with Kobe's career, 503
Hall of Fame speech in 2009, 420–21
Jackson and, 277, 332–33, 337, 365, 407,
443, 490
Knight and, 140–41
Kobe on initial reaction to, 80
Kobe's research of games of, 203
learning to trust teammates, 477–78
media and, 532
Mumford and, 373–74, 407, 442
Nike and, 134–37, 139–41, 164, 201, 403
obsessiveness of, 221
on O'Neal, 319
Pollin's firing of, 523
retirement from NBA, 144, 310
Schaefer on, 470–71

self-consciousness of, 138
Washington Wizards and, 345, 411
Winter on, 68–69, 334, 340, 498, 513, 562

Karl, George, 287, 288, 294, 455, 474
KB8 (Kobe's signature shoe), 274–76, 286, 317
KB8 II (Kobe's second signature shoe), 297–98
Kempton, Tim, 249
Kerr, Steve, 477–78
Kersey, Jerome, 314
Ketner, Lari, 159, 160
Kidd, Jason, 393, 394
Kieserman, Jimmy, 104
King, Bernard, 531
Kittles, Kerry, 159, 207, 228, 394
Klosterman, Chuck, 536, 545
Knight, Phil, 133–34, 140, 141–42, 143, 144, 278, 404
Knight, Travis, 245, 248–49, 257
Knowles, Beyoncé, 326
Knox, Rodney, 459
Kobe Bryant's Muse, 188, 531
Kobe Doin' Work, 531
Kosloff, Irv, 48, 61
Krause, Jerry, 362, 365
Krikorian, Doug, 263
Krzyzewski, Mike, 446
    attempt to recruit Kobe, 158–59, 196
    as Team USA coach, 482, 484, 506, 508, 509, 550
Kupchak, Mitch, 361, 365, 433, 478, 559
    contract negotiations and, 438
    Jackson and, 362, 364, 395, 427, 428, 550–51
    on Kobe's wrist injury, 245

L.A. Times. See Los Angeles Times
La Salle Explorers, 37, 38–40, 231
Laine, Stephen, 452
Laine, Vanessa Urbieta Cornejo, 385, 387, 448, 450, 467
    Bryant family and, 327, 347, 357–58, 370–71, 386
    financial issues of, 327, 347, 357
    perceptions of, 356–57, 360–61, 535
    relationship with Kobe, 356–57, 360–61, 385–86, 546, 563–64; engagement, 346–47; filing for divorce, 545–46, 552; Hubler's story on, 451–52; meeting and dating, 326–27; reconciliation, 552–53, 564; sexual

assault case and, 417–18, 437; wedding of, 369, 371
    religion and, 327, 374
Last Season, The (Jackson), 439, 529–30
Layden, Frank, 260
Lee, Spike, 139, 530–31
Leno, Jay, 243, 322, 368
Lester, Ronnie, 447, 540
Levin, Irv, 74
Lewis, Reginald S., 23
Linehan, John, 187, 188, 189
Lipton, Harold, 74
Lombardi, Robert, 17
Longley, Luc, 339
Lopez, Felipe, 143, 162, 196
Los Angeles Clippers, 454, 467
Los Angeles Lakers, 239–40, 503–4
    1979–80 season of, 74–75
    1996 NBA draft and, 225–29
    1996–97 season of, 248–57, 260, 265–68, 271–73, 288–89
    1997–98 season of, 279–89, 291, 292–95
    1999 season of, 309, 311, 317, 319–20, 332
    1999–2000 season of, 329–30, 333–34, 335–41, 342–46, 347–54
    2000–2001 season of, 3–4, 365–69, 373, 375–80, 381–82
    2001–02 season of, 389–90, 391–94
    2002–03 season of, 406, 407–8, 410–12
    2003–04 season of, 421–23, 424–25, 429–32
    2004–05 season of, 447–50, 453–54
    2005–06 season of, 460–62, 464–67, 472–78, 479–81
    2006–07 season of, 488–90
    2007–08 season of, 497–500, 501–3, 504–6, 509
    2008–09 season of, 510–17
    2009–10 season of, 518–22, 523, 524–28, 531
    2010–11 season of, 537–41
    2011–12 season of, 546–48
    2012–13 season of, 550–52, 554–60
    2013–14 season of, 562
    2014–15 season of, 563–64
    2015–16 season of, xiii, 567, 569, 570–74
    groupies and sexual activities of, 263–64, 533–35
    layoff of employees of, 539–40
Los Angeles Sparks, 560
Los Angeles Times, 327, 385, 426, 451–52, 519

Lower Merion Aces
  1992–93 season of, 105, 108
  1993–94 season of, 122
  1994–95 season of, 150–52
  1995–96 season of, 175–76, 178, 180–81,
    185–90, 202
Lucas, John, 166, 168, 169, 210, 220
Lucas, Maurice, 70
Lue, Tyronn, 343
Lynch, George, 234

Mackey, Pamela, 419
Magic Johnson's Roundball Classic, 202–3
Mahorn, Rick, 165, 166, 173, 175, 211–12
Malone, Brendan, 516
Malone, Karl, x, 286, 417, 448, 483
  1996–97 season of, 267, 268
  1997–98 season of, 286, 287
  2003–04 season of, 424–25, 428, 430,
    432, 433
Malone, Moses, 52, 78, 218, 379
Maltinti, Roberto, 91, 93–94, 95, 574
Manning, Peyton, 317
Maravich, "Pistol" Pete, 56
Marbury, Stephon, 146, 221, 222, 224, 228
Mariani, Frank, 493
Martin, Kevin, 543
Massimino, Rollie, 38
Mastriano, Jeanne, 112
Matkov, Matt, 210
Maxwell, Vern, 168
Mbah a Moute, Luc, 471
McCarter, Andre, 27
McCary, Mike, 209
McCloud, George, 252
McDonnell, Joe, 534–35
McGinnis, George, 51, 70, 72
McGrady, Tracy, 278, 279, 355, 404, 406, 413
McHale, Kevin, 314, 476, 502
McKie, Aaron, 103, 488
McKinney, Jack, 38
McMahon, Jack, 48, 71
McMenamin, David, 529–30, 532, 540–42,
    546, 548
Medina, Mark, 546–47, 553, 554, 558, 559
Medvedenko, Slava, 390, 479
Memphis Grizzlies, 467, 490, 501
Mercury, Freddie, 99
Miami Heat, 448–49, 458, 467, 481
Mickelson, Phil, 538
Mieuli, Franklin, 48
Mihm, Chris, 433, 454, 473
Mikan, George, 234, 314, 502, 503

Miller, Mike, 467
Miller, Reggie, 351, 352
Milwaukee Bucks, 56, 223–24
Minneapolis Lakers, 22, 394, 503–4
Minnesota Timberwolves, 431
Mitchell, Sam, 474
Mix, Steve, 51, 69
Monroe, Earl "the Pearl," 22, 24, 25
Monsky, Evan, 106, 111
Moore, Peter, 133, 134, 141, 203, 355
  on banning of Nike Air Ships, 136
  on Bryant family, 275, 328
  on commercial for Nike Air Ships, 137
  departure from Nike, 140
  on design of the Kobe, 328–29
  Jordan and, 135, 137–38, 141, 403
  on Knight, 144
  on Kobe's departure from Adidas, 402–3,
    404, 405
  launch of KB8, 275
  on Spike Lee ads, 139
  Vaccaro and, 142, 164
  on Vanessa, 360–61, 403
Morris, Speedy, 159–60, 197, 231
Morris, Wayna, 209, 211
Müller-Wohlfahrt, Hans-Wilhelm, 542
Mumford, George, 347, 376
  Jordan and, 373–74, 407, 442, 567
  on Kobe, xi, 270, 372, 567
  Lakers' use of, 335, 345–46, 373–74, 408
  on supremely competitive players, 442,
    443
Murdoch, Rupert, 309
Murray, Jim, 224

Narberth League, 25–26
Nash, John, 227, 228
Nash, Steve, xii, 550, 554–55
National Basketball Association (NBA), 55,
    217–18, 531–32
  change in interpretation of rules, 461–63
  lockout in 2011, 536, 540, 543, 545
  lockout in 1998–99, 304, 306, 310
National Collegiate Athletic Association
    (NCAA), 36, 142, 164, 218–19
New Jersey Nets, 224, 227–28, 393–94,
    464
New Orleans Hornets, 539, 541, 543, 544
New York Knicks, 48, 411, 531, 551–52
New York Times, 109–10, 212
Newell, Pete, 59, 60
Newsday, 173–74, 176
Newsweek, 437, 440

Nike, 140, 144–45
    Air Jordan and, 133, 134–35, 138–39
    Jordan and, 134–37, 139–41, 164, 201
    Kobe and, 155, 401, 402, 405, 419
    LeBron James and, 404
    Spike Lee's ads for, 139
    Vaccaro and, 134, 164, 200, 201
Nike Air Ships, 136–37
Norwood, Brandy, 179, 208–11, 248, 250, 326

Oakley, Charles, 309
Odom, Lamar, 155, 178, 433, 543, 544
    2004–05 season of, 454
    2005–06 season of, 473–74, 475, 480
    2006–07 season of, 488, 490
    2007–08 season of, 501
    2008–09 season of, 512
    2009–10 season of, 519, 527
    Charles and, 236
    on Gasol, 520, 521
    Jackson and, 530
    Kobe and, 445
    Vaccaro and, 195
    on Winter's triangle offense, 519–20
Oklahoma City Thunder, 524, 548, 557
Olajuwon, Hakeem, 233
Olimpia Milano, 323–24
Olimpia Pistoia, 89, 90
Olympics, 482–86, 487, 496, 506–9, 522,
        549–50
O'Neal, Jermaine, 155, 156, 178, 211, 259
O'Neal, Shaquille, 312, 409–10, 502
    1994–95 season of, 233
    1995–96 season of, 233
    1996–97 season of, 253–57, 260, 265,
        266–67, 268, 271–72
    1997–98 season of, 279, 282, 285, 295
    1999 season of, 309, 319–20, 332
    1999–2000 season of, 331–32, 336–38,
        341, 345–46, 348, 349–54
    2000–2001 season of, 365–66, 375–79,
        381–82
    2001–02 season of, 389–90, 393, 394
    2002–03 season of, 408, 410
    2003–04 season of, 424, 430, 431–32
    2004–05 season of, 448–49, 458
    2005–06 season of, 467, 481
    2008 Olympics and, 483
    contract negotiations and, 421, 422–23,
        432, 434, 438, 493
    Garciduenas and, 240–41
    Jackson and, 331–33, 337–38, 342–44,
        366–67, 396, 408–9

on Kobe's 81-point game, 476
    Lakers' deal with, 232–33, 252
    Lakers' trading of, 433, 445
    nickname for Kobe, xi–xii, 251
    relationship with Kobe, xi, 528; during
        1999–2000 season, 336, 341, 342,
        350–51; during 2000–2001 season,
        366, 367, 375, 376, 378–79; during
        2003–4 season, 419–21, 423, 438–39;
        after Kobe's comments about during
        sexual assault investigation, 416,
        420, 440–41, 506; development of
        animosity in, 255, 304–6; ego and
        selfishness as straining, 261, 290,
        314–15, 366, 367; O'Neal's crude rap
        about Kobe, 506; steps toward peace,
        467, 517, 558–59; Winter on, 336,
        341, 366, 409–10
    West and, 225, 232–34, 252, 362, 394, 449
Orlando Magic, 225, 232–34, 317, 427,
        515–17
Orthokine treatment, 542–43
Osgood-Schlatter disease, 102–3
Owens, Billy, 256

Packer, Billy, 134, 260
Pangrazio, Dan, 181
Parker, Smush, 476, 480
Parker, Tony, 430
Patterson, Ruben, 315
Paul, Chris, 539, 543–44, 561
Paxson, John, 477–78
Payton, Gary, 343, 417, 424, 428, 430, 431,
        433, 483
Peeler, Anthony, 234
Pelinka, Rob, 388, 404
People, 210, 290
Perkins, Kendrick, 505, 525
Perkins, Sam, 294
Perry, Scott, 159
Person, Chuck, 538–39
Peterson, Morris, 474
Pettit, Bob, 462
Pettit, Brendan, 181
Philadelphia
    basketball leagues in, 23–27, 30–32, 33–34
    gangs in, 23, 26
    migration of African Americans to, 20–21
    police violence in, 14–15, 17
Philadelphia 76ers, 54–55
    1967 NBA title win of, 55
    1975–76 season of, 51–54, 55, 56–58
    1976–77 season of, 70–71

Philadelphia 76ers (cont.)
  1977–78 season of, 65, 71
  1996 NBA draft and, 220–22, 224
  2000–2001 season of, 4, 379–80, 381–82
  2005–06 season of, 461, 467
  Bomb Squad of, 51, 69, 71, 72
  hiring of Cunningham, 71
  Kobe's summer workouts with, 165–69
  signing of Joe Bryant, 48–49
Philadelphia Daily News, 23, 383
Philadelphia Tribune
  Big Joe and, 19, 33
  Coxes and, 42, 43, 47
  Joe Bryant and, 14, 52, 55, 57, 86, 97
  on Kobe, 76
  on Pam Cox Bryant, 57
Philadelphia Warriors, 54, 218
Phillips, Richie, 47, 48–49, 58–59,
  60–61, 71
Phoenix Suns, 282, 348, 481, 524, 547
Pierce, Paul, 484, 505, 509, 527
Pippen, Scottie, 138, 311, 476, 512
  1999–2000 season with Blazers, 336,
    348, 349
  Jackson and, 330–31
  on Kobe, 283, 284–85
  on Team USA, 484–85
Pitino, Rick, 158
Plaschke, Bill, 451
Pollard, Jim, 55–56, 314, 503
Pollin, Abe, 523, 569
Popovich, Gregg, 319, 392, 431, 468–69
Portland Trail Blazers, 331
  1976–77 season of, 70
  1996–97 season of, 266–67
  1997–98 season of, 288–89, 294
  1999–2000 season of, 336, 345, 348–50
  2000–2001 season of, 377
  2001–02 season of, 392
  2006–07 season of, 488
  2012–13 season of, 557
Powell, Shaun, 165, 173–75, 176
Pride, Joe "Mad Dog," 33

Radmanović, Vladimir, 488
Rambis, Kurt, 247, 311, 314, 316, 332, 374
Reed, Willis, 227
Reggio Calabria, 89
Reggio Emilia, 95
Reid, J. R., 311
Reinsdorf, Jerry, 198
Rentmeester, Jacobus, 138
Reynolds, Jerry, 281

Rice, Glen, 311, 332, 349, 365
Richmond, Mitch, 210, 256, 285, 292
Rider, Isaiah, 266, 285, 289
Riley, Pat, 239, 394
Rines, Sam, 122–28, 322, 325
  on Bryants after moving to L.A., 279
  on Carr vs. Kobe, 176
  on Clement and Kobe, 193–94
  on games during Kobe's junior year, 151
  on Hamilton, 148
  on Joe Bryant, 124, 170, 194–95, 322,
    324–25
  on Kobe, 128, 168, 185; athleticism of,
    169; as a freshman, 108, 125; during
    national tournament in Las Vegas,
    156–57; over-thinking issues, 127;
    penchant for tall tales, 148, 270;
    selfishness of, 126, 128, 149;
    as a showman, xii; as a sophomore,
    128; temper of, 125
  Pam Cox Bryant and, 192, 193
  on Pelinka, 388
  Vaccaro and, 146–47, 194, 204–5
  on Vanessa, 386
Riswold, Jim, 139
Rivers, Doc, 527
Rizzo, Frank, 26
Robertson, Oscar, 462, 513, 518
Robinson, Cliff, 266
Robinson, David, 233
Rodman, Dennis, 210, 310, 311
Rodriguez, Javier, 415
Rogul, Herm L., 76, 77
Rondo, Rajon, 505
Rose, Derrick, 224
Rosen, Charley
  on animosity between Jackson and West,
    362–63
  on Jackson, 337, 395, 396, 397, 457
  on Joe's influence on Kobe, 440, 466
  on Kobe's injuries and extreme
    workouts, 567
  on Winter, 338
Rotella, Michella, 81
Rowland, Kelly, 326
Russell, Bill, 467, 500, 504
Russell, Bryon, 281, 428
Russell, Cazzie, 25
Ryan, Bob, 79

Sabonis, Arvydas, 348
Sacramento Kings, 255, 348, 377–78,
  392–93, 429

Sager, Craig, 550
Salley, John, 342
Salmon, Jimmy, 147
Salter, Linda, 14, 16
Sam Rines All-Stars, 122–26, 148–49,
    156–57, 194
Sampson, Ralph, 78
Samuels, Allison, 535
San Antonio Spurs, 311, 345, 377–79, 392,
    411, 430–31, 502, 538, 559
San Diego Clippers, 72–73, 74–75, 77
Sanchez, Kevin "Sandman," 115
Saunders, Edmund, 148, 149
Saunders, Gilbert
    in Dapper Dan Roundball Classic, 35
    on family's acceptance of Joe Bryant, 13
    on Farrell, 31
    on Joe Bryant, 23, 30, 45, 46–47, 60,
        68
    on John Cox II, 46
    on Sonny Hill, 24
    on Westhead, 38
Schaefer, Chip, 330, 332, 333, 335, 375, 377,
    378, 379
    on 2008 Summer Olympics, 508
    on Jackson's coaching style, 343–44
    on Jordan, 420–21, 442, 470–71
    on Kobe, 333, 423–24, 442, 469, 470,
        471, 507, 553
    on Lakers' 2002–03 season, 412
    on layoffs before 2011 lockout, 539–40
    on O'Neal, 409
    on Winter, 337–38
Schaus, Fred, 260, 504
Schwartz, Robby, 100, 171–72
    on Aces' bus rides, 190
    on Chester in state semifinals, 187
    on Clement and Kobe, 193
    on Downer, 182
    on Kobe, 158, 172–73, 180, 182–85, 189,
        272, 274
    on Kobe turning pro, 212, 213
    on Leo Stacy, 187–88
    on team dynamics with Kobe, 181–82
Scola, Luis, 543
Scott, Byron, 265, 271, 274, 314, 393,
    563
Scott, Dennis, 284
Scott, Stuart, 413
Seddon, Dennis, 176
Sharman, Bill, 76, 338
Shaw, Brian, 349–50, 378, 465–66, 475,
    476, 513–14, 517

She's Gotta Have It (Lee), 139
Shields, Tee, 95
showboating, xi, 55–56
Shue, Gene, 45, 48, 51–56, 71–74, 219–20,
    222
    on Iverson, 221
    on Joe Bryant vs. Magic Johnson, 75
    on police beating Joe Bryant, 17
Silas, Paul, 75, 77
Simers, T. J., 384
Simmons, Connie, 217
Simmons, J. Earl, 61
Simmons, Lionel, 202, 231
Simpkins, Dickey, 390
Simpson, Vontez
    on Big Joe, 19
    on Farrell, 31
    on Joe Bryant, 13, 29, 34, 47, 70
    on Pam Cox Bryant, 42, 45
    on Public League, 22
Skiles, Scott, 366
Sloan, Jerry, 49
Smallwood, John, 41
Smith, Dean, 334
Smith, Elmore, 56
Smith, Sam, 368
Smith, Shelley, 413–14, 416–19, 435–36,
    441–42, 532–33, 564–67
Smith, Stephen A., 558
Sojourner, Mike, 33, 35
Sonny Hill All-Stars, 147, 156
Sonny Hill League, 25–27
    founding of, 25, 26
    Joe Bryant and, 24, 25, 27, 30, 49,
        80, 89
    Kobe and, 95–96, 102–4, 147, 384
Sony Music, 118, 325
Sporting News, The, 229, 527
Sports Illustrated, 289
Sports Incorporated, 140
Sprewell, Latrell, 431
Stackhouse, Jerry, 166, 167–68,
    222
Stacy, Leo, 187–88
Sterling, Donald, 77
Stern, David, 134, 136, 219, 259, 286, 310,
    430, 544, 561
Stockton, John, 267, 268, 563
Strasser, Rob, 133, 134, 135–37, 140–41,
    200, 403
Summitt, Pat, 193
Sura, Bob, 258
Syracuse Nationals, 54–55

Tarkanian, Jerry, 142
Taylor, Bill, 39
Teachings of Don Juan, The (Castaneda), 334–35
Team USA, 482–86, 487, 496, 506–9, 522, 549–50
Telander, Rick, 367
Tellem, Arn, 205, 227–28, 229, 297, 323
  advice on prenuptial agreement, 369, 372
  Joe Bryant and, 387
  Kobe's dismissal of, 370, 388, 404
  West and, 205, 225, 368
Thomas, Charlie, 79
Thomas, Tim, 147, 148, 149, 155, 156, 159
Thompson, David, 503
Thompson, Julius, 19, 20–22, 23, 24, 26, 31, 32–33, 37
Thomsen, Ian, 290
Thorn, Rod, 462
Threatt, Sedale, 234
Time Warner Cable, 536
Tomjanovich, Rudy, 446–48, 449–50, 455, 456
Tonahill, Rebecca, 325
Toronto Raptors, 335, 473–75, 562, 563
Treatman, Jeremy, 176, 178, 181, 250–51, 255, 262
  on Joe Bryant, 113–14, 169, 262
  on Kobe in high school; decision to turn pro, 169, 212, 213, 214–15; as a freshman, 108; as a junior, 151, 152; as a senior, 177, 178–79, 180, 186, 187, 188, 189
  on Kobe's rookie season with Lakers, 271, 272
  on Kobe's sisters and female cousins, 179
  on Kobe's temper, 182–84
  on Pam Cox Bryant, 132, 178–79, 278
Turner, Brad, 427

Utah Jazz
  1996–97 season of, 267–68
  1997–98 season of, 281, 293, 294–95, 523
  2007–08 season of, 502
  2008–09 season of, 515
  2009–2010 season of, 524
  2012–13 season of, 557
  2015–16 season of, xiii, 571–72

Vaccaro, Pam, 199, 201, 243
Vaccaro, Sonny, 133, 146, 200–201, 228, 355–56
  ABCD Camp and, 144–46, 155–56, 356
  on Bryant-O'Neal relationship, 314
  on Bryants' financial situation, 279, 323, 324–25, 370, 371
  on drug use in the NBA in the seventies, 59
  on fines for banned Nike Air Ships, 136
  Knight's dismissal of, 142, 164
  on Kobe, 568; after 1997 play-off series game, 269, 273; alienation of family, 6, 370, 372; ending relationship with Adidas, 401, 403, 405; lack of close friends in L.A., 261–62, 298; Lakers' draft workouts, 225, 226–27; penchant for tall tales, 148, 270; strong will of, 198; transformation of, 5, 203
  LeBron James and, 404
  McGrady and, 278
  move back to Los Angeles, 242–43
  NCAA and, 142, 164
  Nike's hiring of, 134, 200, 201
  on Pelinka, 388
  resignation from Adidas, 405
  Rines and, 146–47, 194, 204–5
  role in Air Jordan, 134, 163, 201
  role in Kobe's Adidas contract, 142, 143, 206, 216; focus on Kobe for contract, 146–47, 156, 157, 161; negotiations with Bryants, 199–200, 201–2; secret planning for negotiations, 160–65, 195, 196
  Roundball Classic and, 34, 200, 202–3
  on sexual assault charges against Kobe, 413, 419
  on Strasser's memorial service, 144
  on Tellem as Kobe's agent, 205, 225
  on Vanessa, 359
Van Exel, Nick, 230, 252, 253
  1996–97 season of, 254, 255–56, 265, 267, 268, 271
  1997–98 season of, 279, 282, 289, 295
Vertlieb, Dick, 48, 49
Vitale, Dick, 202–3
Vitti, Gary, 240, 280, 507
Vittori, Jacomo, 81, 82, 84, 90, 91, 94

Wade, Dwyane, 463, 482–84, 486, 507, 536
Walker, Antoine, 206–7, 246, 496
Walker, Samaki, 390, 393
Wall Street Journal, 401
Wallace, Ben, 432

Walton, Bill, 74, 75, 78
Walton, Luke, 428, 480, 488, 501, 515, 516
Washington, Jerrod, 208, 370, 386
Washington Post, 212
Washington Wizards, 345, 411
Weiss, Dick
  on 76ers, 55, 69–70
  on Baker League games, 24
  on Big Joe, 19
  on drug use in the NBA, 60
  on Erving, 70
  on Hill League, 25, 26–27
  on Joe Bryant, 29, 33, 35, 50
  on La Salle's reputation, 35
  on Pam Cox Bryant, 41
  on Philadelphia Warriors, 54
  on Philly Public League, 22
  on racial tensions, 26
Wells, Bonzi, 349
Wennington, Bill, 396
West, David, 471, 488
West, Jerry, 76, 225–26, 241–42, 469
  1996–97 season training camp and,
    248
  1997–98 season and, 280, 292–93,
    294
  basketball career of, 4, 345, 463, 504,
    505, 522
  on Bryant-O'Neal relationship, 314
  on building of Staples Center, 493
  at Buss's memorial service, 553
  childhood of, 88
  departure from Lakers, 364, 365
  financial standoff with Buss, 308–9
  Harris and, 253, 260–61, 272, 316
  Jackson and, 320, 331, 361–64, 384,
    398
  on Joe Bryant, 78
  on Kobe, 245, 413, 510, 517, 523
  Kobe and, 226–28, 277, 362
  on LeBron James, 517–18
  O'Neal and, 225, 232–34, 252, 362, 394,
    449
  on Rodman trade, 309–10
  Tellem and, 205, 225
Westhead, Paul, 35, 36, 37, 38, 74–75
  on Big Joe, 19
  on Farrell, 31
  on Joe Bryant, 9, 29, 35–36, 37, 39–40,
    78–79
  on Kobe's gene pool, 66
  on Pam Cox Bryant, 42

Wilkens, Lenny, 56, 258
Wilkins, Dominique, 87
Williams, Gail, 44
Williams, Pat
  on contract negotiations, 48
  on Dawkins, 70–71
  on Joe Bryant, 48, 49, 51, 58, 60, 61, 69,
    72–73
  on Kobe, 68
  on Lloyd Free, 72
  on Pam Cox Bryant, 76
  on Shue, 52, 71
Williams, Venus, 326
Williams, Walt, 273
Winter, Nancy, 366
Winter, Tex, 318, 481, 510–11, 512
  1999–2000 season and, 329–30, 333–34,
    336, 337–41, 350–51, 352
  2000–2001 season and, 366, 368, 378
  2003–04 season and, 430, 432
  2007–08 season and, 498–99, 502,
    504–5
  on Bryant-O'Neal relationship, 336, 341,
    366, 409–10
  on Chamberlain, 500
  comparisons between Jordan and Kobe,
    68–69, 215, 407
  criticism of Jordan, 319
  on Jackson, 332–33, 364, 408–9, 426,
    428–29, 433
  Jackson and, 396–98, 455, 515
  on Jim Buss, 537
  on Kobe's 81-point game, 477, 478
  on NBA's change in interpretation of
    rules, 463
  pain from shingles, 510
  relationship with Kobe, 347; as Kobe's
    defender, 337–39, 341, 396, 398, 453,
    495–96; as Kobe's mentor, 270,
    329–30, 514
  on Shaw, 466
  stroke suffered by, 514–15
  on Team USA, 484, 485, 508
  triangle offense of, 332, 333, 424, 515, 516,
    519–20
Wise, Charlie, 39
Woods, Loren, 155
Woods, Tiger, 533, 538, 565
World B. Free, 49, 51, 52, 53–54, 69–70,
    71–72
World Peace, Metta. *See* Artest, Ron
Wright, Lorenzen, 228

ABOUT THE AUTHOR

ROLAND LAZENBY is the author of the bestselling and definitive biographies *Michael Jordan: The Life* and *Jerry West: The Life and Legend of a Basketball Icon,* among other books. He has spent the past three decades interviewing NBA players, coaches, staff members, and other figures while writing about the league. He lives in Salem, Virginia.

Also by Roland Lazenby

Michael Jordan: The Life

Jerry West: The Life and Legend of a Basketball Icon

les